A HARMONY OF THE BOOKS

OF

SAMUEL, KINGS, AND CHRONICLES

The Books of the Kings of Judah and Israel

BY

WILLIAM DAY CROCKETT

BAKER BOOK HOUSE
Grand Rapids, Michigan 49506

Reprinted 1985 by
Baker Book House Company

Paperback Edition
ISBN: 0-8010-2511-7

Library of Congress Catalog Card
Number: A53-9880

Fourth printing, July 1989

Printed in the United States of America

PREFACE

MANY and many a time during the latter years of my College course, as I had taken up my Bible for the daily chapter, had I thought of the time in the near future of my Seminary days, when the Book of Books itself would be my constant study. But the ideal was never realized ; for there were ever a hundred other volumes claiming one's attention : Greek and Hebrew, and Theology and History, and Homiletics and Church Polity, and a score of allied subjects besides. And while the Bible was back of them all, while the Bible inspired them all, there was not in my own life the deep, earnest study of God's Word for which I had longed for years. Without doubt, it was all my own fault ; at any rate, the Bible study was not there.

It was at this juncture that the idea came for a Harmony of the Books of Samuel, Kings, and Chronicles. I had begun, for my own private Bible study, a Harmony of the Four Gospels. A long walk succeeded the first two hours' work on the Gospel narratives; and with it came the thought : A thousand men have done this work before ; why not accept some of the work that they have done—at least for a while—and try your skill in unplowed fields ? The result of that thought was the conception of the present volume.

Until the completion of the first draft of the manuscript, I was not aware that such a work had ever been undertaken before. Since then I have learned that there are certain works, out of date and out of print, that have embodied the conception, more or less fully. But so far as it has been possible to learn, the present work is the only one of its kind.

The volume as it stands to-day is the outgrowth of its first conception, in its general outline. The six books of the Old Testament that have been used as material, have been subjected to the most careful analysis ; and the result is a " Harmony," divided into five books, under the general name of " The Books of the Kings of Judah and Israel "—which, by the way, happens to be the title, with the exception of the addition of one letter, of one of the thirty and more Books of Old Testament times now lost to the world—which Books, in their turn, have been, more or less, the original material from which the six books under consideration have been compiled. The question of the compilation or the editing of the said books, however, does not fall within the province of this work.

The result of our study is something more than simply a Harmony of the Books

of First and Second Samuel, First and Second Kings, and First and Second Chronicles; it embodies a careful analytical outline, the value of which, it is thought, will
be as great as those sections displaying the Harmony idea—an outline, toward the
perfection of which every verse of the six books in question has contributed its share—
an outline, in which books, parts, divisions, sections, subsections, and even the sub-
divisions of the subsections, all have their own individual *raison d'être.*

From the very nature of the case, the Harmony involves a study of the chronology.
Such study, while it has been one of the most fascinating features of the whole work,
has likewise been the most difficult. In the matter of Biblical chronology, the basal
law seems to be, "Every man for himself, and the critic take the hindermost." In
conformity with the workings of this law, the author of the present work does not
profess to agree with any one among the many different authorities on Bible chronology—that is, in detail; though it would be here proper to state that all the material
available for chronological study has been used, and where traditional views and
interpretations have been departed from, it has been only after the maturest consideration and the most careful weighing of evidence.

It would simply be an impossibility, in a volume of this size, to give all the
reasons for adopting the particular order in the disputed cases; for those reasons are
oftentimes purely internal. A full discussion of the reasons for the particular order
of events in Elisha's life, for example, would occupy many pages. The same may be
said of the interpretation of the life and history of David; but where it has been
feasible, attention has been called to such reasons in the footnotes.

For the merits of the chronology, my especial thanks are due to Dr. Willis J.
Beecher, Professor of the Hebrew Language and Literature in the Auburn Theological
Seminary, whose study and system of chronology have not only been of inestimable
value in the preparation of this work, but whose personal suggestions have always
been most helpful.

The text is that of the Revised Version of 1884, which, for purposes of historical
study, is confessedly the best English version to be had. The footnotes are, to a
great extent, the marginal readings of the Revised Version; though from the natural
requirements of the Harmony, several hundred of these have been omitted as needless,
and a few others for other reasons. Many have been slightly changed, or added to,
for the convenience of the student. The remaining notes are inserted for chronological or other explanatory reasons.

The Four Gospels, as the original material for the study of the life of Christ, must
ever be the ground of absorbing and supremest interest to the Bible student. What
those four books are to the New Testament, as the field for historical study, the six
books of Samuel, Kings, and Chronicles are to the Old: they are the principal sources

of Old Testament history and chronology, and are the books most under discussion to-day. A Harmony of the Gospels has already become the indispensable aid to every student of the life of Christ, or even of the literature of the New Testament. It is hoped that this work will meet a long-felt want for some such study of the principal historical books of the Older Revelation.

A "Harmony," the volume has been called, though, as already stated above, it is much more than a mere Harmony. On the other hand, it is to be remembered that much that is arranged in parallel columns in it is not harmonious—cannot be made harmonious. And yet, in this very connection, it is also to be remembered, that the parallel passages are valuable, not so much for their perfect correspondences as for their many differences; for God's Word and we are the richer far for every such difference. It is hoped that the careful study of these pages will help to reconcile some of these divergencies. Many will probably never be solved until we come to stand before the Great White Throne. But if this volume will aid in any way to a clearer knowledge of some of the many knowable things, and by that knowledge, aid—though but indirectly—in the fulfilling of the loving Master's greatest prayer, that the Kingdom may come, it will accomplish that whereunto it is sent.

WILLIAM D. CROCKETT.

FIRST PRESBYTERIAN MANSE
Canton, Pennsylvania

INTRODUCTION

By Professor WILLIS J. BEECHER, D.D.,

I GLADLY accept the invitation to write a few words of introduction to the volume which my friend Mr. Crockett has prepared. Not many words are needed. The plan of the book speaks for itself.

In Old Testament study, at present, the thing that most demands investigation is the Old Testament itself. This fact is so obvious as to be accepted by all and understood by only a very few. By studying the Old Testament itself, some mean the looking up of points therein for illustrating current religious doctrine and experience. Others mean the repeating of the interpretations of the history, as these have been handed down to us from the time of Josephus. Others mean the examination of the new knowledge concerning the Bible derived from travels and surveys and explorations. Yet others understand the mental unraveling of the literary work done by the men who wrote the books of the Old Testament, the analyzing of these into certain real or supposed original documents, with conjectures as to the authorship of the original documents, and the processes by which they were combined until they assumed the form in which we now have them.

All these ways of study have their value, but none of them is, properly speaking, the study of the Old Testament as it now exists. The first is the study of certain matters in the Old Testament, and not of the Old Testament itself. One might pursue it for a lifetime without acquiring anything like a connected idea as to either the books or their contents. The second, except indirectly, is not a study of the Old Testament at all. From babyhood we have been familiar with the current superficial understanding of the events recorded; it is time that we turn from this and ask what the Old Testament actually says concerning these events. The third is indissolubly connected with the second. If through our traditional mistakes we misinterpret the statements made in the Scriptures, this will lead us equally to misinterpret what the monuments have to say on the same subjects. And the fourth form of study above mentioned is not a study of the Old Testament, but of the real or supposed sources of the Old Testament. As far as it is based upon an inadequate understanding of the Old Testament as it stands, so far is it necessarily crude and misleading.

What we need is something different from these four forms of study, something that is presupposed by each of the four, something that is demanded as the basis of each of the four, namely, the study of the contents and the form of the books of the Old Testament as they stand. When we thoroughly understand the things which the existing Old Testament says, and the literary form in which it says them, we shall be better prepared to analyze our existing Scriptures into their primary component parts, and to understand those parts ; and we shall be qualified to perceive the true bearing of the information gained by recent discoveries, to estimate traditional interpretations rightly, to appreciate more fully the religious teachings.

It is a thing especially commendable in the work of my friend Mr. Crockett that he has labored in this part of the field, here where labor is needed. He has set himself to understand, and to help others understand, a portion of the contents of the Old Testament itself.

In large sections of the volume he has done nothing more than print parallel accounts in parallel columns for ready reference. So far the value is merely mechanical—a mere bit of convenient machinery. This by itself was worth the doing, but he has done far more than this. He has himself attained to a firm grasp upon the history as a whole, and has attempted, by a careful analysis, to show others how to take the same grasp. In traversing three fourths of the path this was relatively simple. It was the remaining fourth, lying in separate sections at half a dozen different points, that taxed his skill and industry and patience. The larger half of the value of his work is that which appears, in comparatively small bulk, in these difficult sections.

Of course, not all his results will at once be accepted as final. Every scholar will think him correct to the extent to which he agrees with him, and no further. It is for these best parts of Mr. Crockett's work that fault is most likely to be found with him. The reader will occasionally miss the confusing but familiar landmarks of the Josephan interpretation of the history, and will be ready at once to exclaim that Mr. Crockett has lost his way. In such instances, however, he will do well to take the trouble to understand the offered interpretation before absolutely rejecting it.

I have enough confidence in the intelligence and industry of the present generation of students of the Bible to lead me to expect that this volume will have wide acceptance and usefulness.

AUBURN, New York

CONTENTS.

THE BOOKS OF THE KINGS OF JUDAH AND ISRAEL.

BOOK I.—UNTIL THE FOUNDING OF THE MONARCHY.

BOOK II.—THE REIGN OF SAUL.

BOOK III.—THE REIGN OF DAVID.

BOOK IV.—THE REIGN OF SOLOMON.

BOOK V.—THE KINGDOMS OF JUDAH AND ISRAEL.

Analytical Outline of the Books of Samuel, Kings, and Chronicles.

BOOK FIRST.
Until the Founding of the Monarchy.

PART I.
GENEALOGICAL TABLES, WITH BRIEF HISTORICAL STATEMENTS.

I. Genealogies of the Patriarchs.

1. The Genealogy from Adam to Noah.

   1 Chronicles 1 : 1–4.

2. The Descendants of Noah's Sons.

   1 Chronicles 1 : 5–23.

3. From Shem to Abraham.

   1 Chronicles 1 : 24–27.

4. The Descendants of Abraham.

   1 Chronicles 1 : 28–42.

5. The Kings and Dukes of Edom.

   1 Chronicles 1 : 43–54.

6. The twelve Sons of Israel.

   1 Chronicles 2 : 1, 2.

II. Genealogies of the Tribes of Israel.

7. The Tribe of Judah.
   (1) General Genealogies of the Tribe.

   1 Chronicles 2 : 3–17, 21–41.   1 Chronicles 4 : 1–23.

3

(2) Three Accounts of the Descendants of Caleb.

    1 Chronicles 2 : 18-20.   1 Chronicles 2 : 42–49.   1 Chronicles 2 : 50–55.

(3) The Family of David.

       1 Chronicles 3 : 1–9.

(4) The Line of David, through Solomon.

       1 Chronicles 3 : 10–24.

8. The Tribe of Levi.

  (1) The Line of Aaron.

               1 Chronicles 6 : 1–15.   1 Chronicles 6 : 49–53.

  (2) The Descendants of Gershom, Kohath, and Merari.

       1 Chronicles 6 : 16–30.

  (3) The Ancestors of the Songmasters, Heman, Asaph, and Ethan.

       1 Chronicles 6 : 31–48.

  (4) The Cities of the Levites.

       1 Chronicles 6 : 54–81.

9. The Tribe of Reuben.

       1 Chronicles 5 : 1–10.

10. The Tribe of Gad.

       1 Chronicles 5 : 11–17.

11. The Half-Tribe of Manasseh (east of Jordan).

       1 Chronicles 5 : 23, 24.

12. The Tribe of Simeon.

       1 Chronicles 4 : 24–43.

13. The Tribe of Issachar.

       1 Chronicles 7 : 1–5.

14. The Tribe of Naphtali.

       1 Chronicles 7 : 13.

15. The Half-Tribe of Manasseh (west of Jordan).

       1 Chronicles 7 : 14–19.

16. The Tribe of Ephraim.

       1 Chronicles 7 : 20–29.

17. The Tribe of Asher.

       1 Chronicles 7 : 30–40.

18. The Tribe of Benjamin.

  (1) General Genealogies of the Tribe.

               1 Chronicles 7 : 6–12.   1 Chronicles 8 : 1–28.

  (2) The House of Saul.

     [1 Samuel 14 : 49–51.]   1 Chronicles 8 : 29–40.   1 Chronicles 9 : 35–44.

19. Appendix : Additional Historical Statements.

  (1) War of the three Transjordanic Tribes with Arab Nations.

       1 Chronicles 5 : 18–22.

  (2) The Inhabitants of Jerusalem.

       1 Chronicles 9 : 2–34, 1a.

PART II.

THE CLOSE OF THE THEOCRACY.

I. The Early Life of Samuel.

20. Samuel's Birth and Infancy.
    (1) Samuel's Birth in Answer to Prayer.
        I Samuel 1 : 1-20.
    (2) Samuel's Consecration to the Lord.
        I Samuel 1 : 21-28.
    (3) Hannah's Song of Thanksgiving.
        I Samuel 2 : 1-10.
21. Samuel at Shiloh.
    (1) The faithless Priests.
        I Samuel 2 : 12-17.
    (2) Eli's Expostulation with his Sons.
        I Samuel 2 : 22-25.
    (3) Samuel's Ministry before the Lord.
        I Samuel 2 : 11, 26. I Samuel 2 : 18-21.
    (4) The Fall of Eli's House foretold.
        I Samuel 2 : 27-36.
    (5) Samuel's Call.
        I Samuel 3 : 1-18.
    (6) Samuel established as a Prophet.
        I Samuel 3 : 19-4 : 1a.

II. The Period of National Disaster.

22. Israel's Defeat and Loss of the Ark.
    I Samuel 4 : 1b-11a.
23. The Fall of the House of Eli.
    I Samuel 4 : 11b-22.
24. The Ark of God.
    (1) The Chastisement of the Philistines for the Removal of the Ark.
        I Samuel 5 : 1-12.
    (2) The Restoration of the Ark with expiatory Gifts.
        I Samuel 6 : 1-11.
    (3) The Reception and Settlement of the Ark in Israel.
        I Samuel 6 : 12-7 : 1.
25. The twenty Years of Waiting.
    I Samuel 7 : 2.

III. Samuel, the Last of the Judges.

26. National Repentance through Samuel's Labors.
    1 Samuel 7 : 3–6.
27. Israel's Victory over the Philistines.
    1 Samuel 7 : 7–12.
28. Summary Statement of Samuel's Work as Judge.
    1 Samuel 7 : 13–17.

BOOK SECOND.
The Reign of Saul.

PART I.

ESTABLISHMENT BY SAMUEL OF SAUL AS FIRST KING OF ISRAEL.

29. The persistent Demand of the People for a King.
    1 Samuel 8 : 1–22.
30. Samuel meets Saul, who is destined by Jehovah to be King over Israel.
    1 Samuel 9: 1–25.
31. Saul is privately anointed by Samuel.
    1 Samuel 9 : 26–10: 1.
32. The Signs of the Divine Confirmation.
    1 Samuel 10 : 2–16.
33. The Choice of Saul by Lot at Mizpeh.
    1 Samuel 10: 17–21.
34. The Installation of Saul as King.
    1 Samuel 10 : 22–25.
35. Saul's brief Retirement to private Life.
    1 Samuel 10 : 26, 27.

PART II.

SAUL'S REIGN UNTIL HIS REJECTION.

36. A generic Account of the Whole of Saul's Reign.
    1 Samuel 14 : 47–52.
37. Confirmation and general Recognition of Saul as King.
    (1) Saul's Victory over the Ammonites.
        1 Samuel 11 : 1–11.
    (2) Confirmation of Saul as King at Gilgal.
        1 Samuel 11 : 12–15.

(3) Samuel's last Transaction with the People at Gilgal.
1 Samuel 12 : 1-25.

38. The Beginnings of Royalty.
1 Samuel 13 : 1, 2.

39. The War against the Philistines.

(1) Jonathan's Exploit in Gibeah.
1 Samuel 13 . 3*a*.

(2) Saul summons Israel to Gilgal.
1 Samuel 13 : 3*b*, 4.

(3) The Philistines encamp in Michmash.
1 Samuel 13 : 5.

(4) The Distress of Israel.
1 Samuel 13 : 6, 7, 19-23.

(5) Saul wrongly offers Sacrifice.
1 Samuel 13 : 8, 9.

(6) Samuel's Prophecy of Retribution.
1 Samuel 13 : 10-14.

(7) Saul moves his Headquarters to Gibeah.
1 Samuel 13 : 15, 16.

(8) The three marauding Bands of the Philistines.
1 Samuel 13 : 17, 18.

(9) Jonathan's bold Attack on the Philistines.
1 Samuel 14 : 1-16.

(10) Flight and Overthrow of the Philistines.
1 Samuel 14 : 17-23.

(11) Saul's rash Curse and its Consequences.
1 Samuel 14 : 24-46.

40. Jehovah's Rejection of Saul.

(1) The Commission to destroy Amalek.
1 Samuel 15 : 1-3.

(2) Saul's Disobedience.
1 Samuel 15 : 4-9.

(3) The Penalty of Disobedience.
1 Samuel 15 : 10-31.

(4) The Fate of Agag.
1 Samuel 15 : 32, 33.

(5) Samuel and Saul part.
1 Samuel 15 : 34, 35.

PART III.
THE DECLINE OF SAUL AND THE RISE OF DAVID.

I. The Early History of David.

41. David chosen and anointed as Saul's Successor by Samuel.
    1 Samuel 16: 1-13.
42. David's Introduction to the Court of Saul.
    1 Samuel 16: 14-23.

II. David's Advancement and Saul's growing Jealousy.

43. The Story of David and Goliath.
    (1) The Invasion of the Philistines.
        1 Samuel 17: 1-3.
    (2) The Challenge of Goliath.
        1 Samuel 17: 4-11.
    (3) David is sent by his Father to his Brethren in the Army.
        1 Samuel 17: 12-22.
    (4) David accepts Goliath's Challenge
        1 Samuel 17: 23-37.
    (5) David's Contest with Goliath.
        1 Samuel 17: 38-51.
    (6) David once more in the royal Presence.
        1 Samuel 17: 55-58.
    (7) The Deed of Shammah.
        [2 Samuel 23: 11*b*, 12.]   [1 Chronicles 11: 13, 14.]
    (8) The Rout of the Philistines.
        1 Samuel 17: 52-54.
44. David at the Court of Saul.
    (1) Saul attaches David to his Suit.
        1 Samuel 18: 2.
    (2) Jonathan's Friendship for David.
        1 Samuel 18: 1, 3, 4.
    (3) David's Popularity.
        1 Samuel 18: 5.
    (4) Saul's Hatred toward David.
        1 Samuel 18: 6-16.
    (5) Saul's artful Attempt against David's Life.
        1 Samuel 18: 17-29.
    (6) David's increasing Popularity.
        1 Samuel 18: 30.

(7) Jonathan proves his Friendship for David.
    1 Samuel 19:1-7.
45. David is forced to leave Court.
  (1) David escapes by Michal's Help.
    1 Samuel 19:8-17.
  (2) David's Flight to Ramah and Saul's Pursuit.
    1 Samuel 19:18-24.
  (3) The Conference between David and Jonathan.
    1 Samuel 20:1-23.
  (4) Jonathan learns his Father's Intentions towards David.
    1 Samuel 20:24-34.
  (5) The Parting between David and Jonathan.
    1 Samuel 20:35-42.

III. David's Outlaw Life.

46. David's Flight.
  (1) To Nob, to Ahimelech, the High Priest.
    1 Samuel 21:1-9.
  (2) To Achish, King of Gath.
    1 Samuel 21:10-15.
  (3) To the Cave of Adullam.
    1 Samuel 22:1, 2.   1 Chronicles 12:16-18.
  (4) To Mizpeh of Moab, where he finds Asylum for his Parents.
    1 Samuel 22:3, 4.
  (5) To the Forest of Hereth, in Judah.
    1 Samuel 22:5.
47. Saul's Vengeance on the Priests of Nob.
    1 Samuel 22:6-20.
48. David in Keilah.
  (1) David rescues Keilah.
    1 Samuel 23:1-5.
  (2) Abiathar joins David.
    1 Samuel 22:21-23; 23:6.
  (3) David escapes from Keilah.
    1 Samuel 23:7-13.
49. David's last Meeting with Jonathan.
    1 Samuel 23:14-18.
50. David's Betrayal by the Ziphites.
    1 Samuel 23:19-24a.
51. David's Escape from Saul in the Wilderness of Maon.
    1 Samuel 23:24b-28.

52. David in the Wilderness of En-gedi : He spares Saul in the Cave.
     1 Samuel 23 : 29–24 : 22.
53. The Death of Samuel.
     1 Samuel 25 : 1a.
54. David in the Wilderness of Paran : the History of Nabal and Abigail.
     1 Samuel 25 : 1b–38.
55. David's matrimonial Relations.
     1 Samuel 25 : 39–44.
56. David, betrayed again by the Ziphites, spares Saul the second Time.
     1 Samuel 26 : 1–25.
57. David again in the Land of the Philistines.
     (1) David once more flees to Achish, King of Gath.
          1 Samuel 27 : 1–4.
     (2) Achish grants Ziklag to David.
          1 Samuel 27 : 5, 6.
     (3) David's Operations while at Ziklag.
          1 Samuel 27 : 7–12.
     (4) List of the Men who came to David at Ziklag.
                                        1 Chronicles 12 : 1–7.

IV. Saul's Downfall in War with the Philistines.

58. The Philistines prepare for a Campaign against Israel.
     1 Samuel 28 : 1a.
59. David and the Philistine Invasion of Israel.
     (1) Achish places Confidence in David.
          1 Samuel 28 : 1b, 2.
     (2) David encamps with the Philistines in Aphek : the Israelites pitch in Jezreel.
          1 Samuel 29 : 1, 2.
     (3) David, dismissed from the Philistine Army, starts for Ziklag.
          1 Samuel 29 : 3–11a.
     (4) The Philistines march toward Jezreel.
          1 Samuel 29 : 11b.
     (5) List of the Men who joined David on his Way to Ziklag.
                                        1 Chronicles 12 : 19–22.
60. David's Victory over the Amalekites who had destroyed Ziklag.
     1 Samuel 30 : 1–31.
61. The Philistines pitch in Shunem : the Israelites in Gilboa.
     1 Samuel 28 : 4.
62. Saul's Visit to the Witch of Endor.
     1 Samuel 28 : 3, 5–25.

63. The Fall of the House of Saul.
    (1) The Battle of Mount Gilboa.
       1 Samuel 31: 1-13.   1 Chronicles 10 : 1-14.
    (2) The Accident to Mephibosheth.
       2 Samuel 4:4.

BOOK THIRD.
The Reign of David.

PART I.

THE SEVEN AND A HALF YEARS IN HEBRON.
I. David's Behavior on Hearing of Saul's Death.

64. The News of Saul's Death is brought to David.
    2 Samuel 1 : 1-16.
65. David's Lamentation for Saul and Jonathan.
    2 Samuel 1 : 17-27.

II. The Rival Kingdoms.

66. David is anointed King over Judah.
    2 Samuel 2 : 1-4a.
67. David's Message to the Men of Jabesh-gilead.
    2 Samuel 2 : 4b-7.
68. Ish-bosheth is made King of Israel.
    2 Samuel 2 : 8-11.
69. The Civil War.
    2 Samuel 2 : 12-3 : 1.
70. David's Family in Hebron.
    2 Samuel 3 · 2-5.

III. Events leading to David's Elevation to the Throne of Israel.

71. Abner's Quarrel with Ish-bosheth.
    2 Samuel 3 : 6-11.
72. Abner's Desertion to David: Michal restored to David.
    2 Samuel 3 : 12-21.
73. Joab's Murder of Abner: David's Lamentation.
    2 Samuel 3 : 22-39.
74. The Murder of Ish-bosheth.
    2 Samuel 4 : 1-3, 5-7.
75. David punishes the Murderers of Ish-bosheth.
    2 Samuel 4 : 8-12.

PART II.
THE PERIOD OF DAVID'S WARS.

76. David is made King over Israel.
     2 Samuel 5:1-3.   1 Chronicles 11:1-3.
77. Data concerning the Number of Warriors who made David King.
                                                         1 Chronicles 12:23-40.
78. Jerusalem captured and made the Capital.
     2 Samuel 5:6-10.   1 Chronicles 11:4-9.
79. Defensive Wars against the Philistines.
     (1) The first Campaign.
         A. David goes "down to the Hold."
             2 Samuel 5:17.   1 Chronicles 14:8.
         B. The Gadites who "separated themselves unto David."
                                                         1 Chronicles 12:8-15.
         C. The Deed of "the three mighty Men."
             2 Samuel 5:18. 2 Sam. 23:13-17. 1 Chron. 11:15-19. 1 Chronicles 14:9.
         D. David's Victory at Baal-perazim.
             2 Samuel 5:19-21.   1 Chronicles 14:10-12.
     (2) The second Campaign.
         2 Samuel 5:22-25.   1 Chronicles 14:13-17.
80. David's Alliance with Hiram of Tyre.
     2 Samuel 5:11, 12.   1 Chronicles 14:1, 2.
81. Offensive Wars against the Philistines.
     (1) A Summary of these Wars.
         2 Samuel 8:1.   1 Chronicles 18:1.
     (2) The first Campaign.
         2 Samuel 21:15-17a.
     (3) Withdrawal of David from active military Service.
         2 Samuel 21:17b.
     (4) The second Campaign.
         2 Samuel 21:18.   1 Chronicles 20:4.
     (5) The third Campaign.
         2 Samuel 21:19.   1 Chronicles 20:5.
     (6) The fourth Campaign.
         2 Samuel 21:20-22.   1 Chronicles 20:6-8.
82. The Ammonite-Syrian Campaign.
     (1) David's Ambassadors insulted by the Ammonites.
         2 Samuel 10:1-5.   1 Chronicles 19:1-5.

(2) The Israelitish Victory under the Leadership of Joab.
   2 Samuel 10:6–14.   1 Chronicles 19:6–15.
83. The Syrian Campaign.
   2 Samuel 10:15–19.   1 Chronicles 19:16–19,
84. The second Ammonite Campaign.
   (1) Joab lays Siege to Rabbah.
   2 Samuel 11:1.   1 Chronicles 20:1a.
   (2) David's Fall.
   2 Samuel 11:2–27.
   (3) David's Repentance.
   2 Samuel 12:1–24a.
   (4) The Capture of Rabbah.
   2 Samuel 12:26–31.   1 Chronicles 20:1b–3.
85. The Campaign against Moab.
   (1) The Conquest by David.
   2 Samuel 8:2.   1 Chronicles 18:2.
   (2) The Exploit of Benaiah.
   2 Samuel 23:20a.   1 Chronicles 11:22a.
86. Decisive Campaign against Hadadezer.
   2 Samuel 8:3, 4, 7, 8.   1 Kings 11:[23b], 24a.   1 Chronicles 18:3, 4, 7, 8.
                             1 Kings 11:24b—Footnote.
87. Subjugation of Damascus.
   2 Samuel 8:5, 6.   1 Chronicles 18:5, 6.
88. Submission of Hamath.
   2 Samuel 8:9–11.   1 Chronicles 18:9–11a.
89. Subjugation of Edom.
   2 Samuel 8:13, 14a.   1 Kings 11:15–17, [14b], 18.   1 Chronicles 18:12, 13a.
                          1 Kings 11:19, 20—Footnote.
90. Summary of David's Wars : the Nations conquered.
   2 Samuel 8:[11d], 12, [11b], 14b.   1 Chronicles 18:11c,11b,13b.
91. List of David's Heroes.
   (1) The " first " three.
      A. Jashobeam.
      2 Samuel 23:8.   1 Chronicles 11:10, 11.
      B. Eleazar.
      2 Samuel 23:9, 10.   1 Chronicles 11:12.
      C. Shammah.
      2 Samuel 23:11, 12.   1 Chronicles 11:13, 14.
   (2) The "three mighty Men."
      A. Their Exploit at Bethlehem.
      [2 Samuel 23:13-17.]   [1 Chronicles 11:15-19.]

      B. Abishai.
        2 Samuel 23 : 18, 19.   1 Chronicles 11 : 20, 21.
      C. Benaiah.
        2 Samuel 23 : [20*a*], 20*b*–23.   1 Chronicles 11 : [22*a*], 22*b*–25.
    (3) The remaining Heroes.
        2 Samuel 23 : 24–39.   1 Chronicles 11 : 26–47.

92. The Administration and Officers of the Kingdom during this Period.
        2 Samuel 8 : 15–18.   1 Chronicles 18 : 14–17.

93. David's Song of Thanksgiving.
        2 Samuel 22 : 1–51.

PART III.

THE PERIOD OF REST.

94. Removal of the Ark from Kirjath-jearim.

    (1) To the House of Obed-edom.
        2 Samuel 6: 1–11.   1 Chronicles 13:1–14.

    (2) To Jerusalem.
        2 Samuel 6 : 12–19*a*.   1 Chronicles 15 : 1–16 : 3.

    (3) David's Hymn of Praise.
                             1 Chronicles 16 : 4–36.

    (4) Concluding Statements.
        2 Samuel 6 : 19*b*–23.   1 Chronicles 16 : 37–43.

95. The Promise of eternal Dominion to the House of David.

    (1) David's Purpose to build a Temple to Jehovah.
        2 Samuel 7 : 1–3.   1 Chronicles 17 : 1, 2.

    (2) The Lord's Answer through Nathan.
        2 Samuel 7 :4–17.   1 Chronicles 17 : 3-15.

    (3) David's Prayer and Thanksgiving.
        2 Samuel 7 : 18–29.   1 Chronicles 17 : 16–27.

96. David's Kindness towards Jonathan's Son, Mephibosheth.
        2 Samuel 9: 1–13.

97. The Birth of Solomon.
        2 Samuel 12 : 24*b*, 25.

98. David's Family in Jerusalem.
        2 Samuel 5 : 13–16.   1 Chronicles 3 : 5–9.   1 Chronicles 14 : 3-7.

PART IV.
THE PERIOD OF INTERNAL DISSENSIONS.
I. Family Troubles.

99. Amnon's Crime.
    2 Samuel 13:1-22.
100. Absalom's Vengeance.
    2 Samuel 13:23-36.
101. Absalom's Flight and Sojourn in Geshur.
    2 Samuel 13:37-39.
102. The Recall of Absalom.
    (1) Joab's Stratagem.
        2 Samuel 14:1-20.
    (2) Absalom's Return.
        2 Samuel 14:21-24.
    (3) Absalom and his Family.
        2 Samuel 14:25-27.
    (4) Absalom's Waiting in Jerusalem.
        2 Samuel 14:28.
    (5) Absalom's Readmission to Court.
        2 Samuel 14:29-33.
103. Absalom stealing the Hearts of the Men of Israel.
    2 Samuel 15:1-6.

II. National Calamities.

104. The three Years' Famine.
    (1) The Execution of Saul's Grandsons.
        2 Samuel 21:1-10.
    (2) The Burial of Saul and his Sons.
        2 Samuel 21:11-14.
105. The three Days' Pestilence.
    (1) David's Sin in numbering the People.
        2 Samuel 24:1-9.   1 Chronicles 21:1-6.
    (2) The Choice of Punishments.
        2 Samuel 24:10-14.   1 Chronicles 21:7-13.
    (3) The Pestilence.
        2 Samuel 24:15-17.   1 Chronicles 21:14-17.
    (4) David purchases Araunah's Threshing-floor and erects an Altar.
        2 Samuel 24:18-25.   1 Chronicles 21:18-30.

III. David's Final Arrangements.

106. Preparations for the Building of the Temple.

    (1) The Temple Site chosen.

                                  1 Chronicles 22 : 1.

    (2) David's Plans and Foresight.

                                  1 Chronicles 22 : 2-5.

    (3) David's Charge to Solomon.

                                  1 Chronicles 22 :6–16.

    (4) David's Charge to the Princes.

                                  1 Chronicles 22 : 17–19.

107. The National Convention.

    (1) The Convention summoned.

                                  1 Chronicles 23 : 1a, 2.

    (2) Data concerning the Officials " gathered."

        A. The Number and Distribution of the Levites.

                                  1 Chronicles 23 : 3–5.

        B. The twenty-four Houses of the Levites.

                1 Chronicles 23 : 6–23.   1 Chronicles 24 : 20–30a.

        C. The Duties of the Levites.

                1 Chronicles 23 : 24–32.   1 Chronicles 24 : 30b, 31.

        D. The twenty-four Courses of Priests.

                                  1 Chronicles 24 : 1–19.

        E. The twenty-four Classes of Singers.

                                  1 Chronicles 25 : 1–31.

        F. The Courses of the Doorkeepers.

                                  1 Chronicles 26 : 1–19.

        G. The Officers of the Treasuries of " the House of God."

                                  1 Chronicles 26 : 20–28.

        H. The Officers and Judges " for the outward Business."

                                  1 Chronicles 26 : 29–32.

        I. The twelve Captains of the Army.

                                  1 Chronicles 27 : 1–15.

        J. The Chiefs of the twelve Tribes.

                                  1 Chronicles 27 : 16–24.

        K. The Overseers of the King's Treasuries and Possessions.

                                  1 Chronicles 27 : 25–31.

        L. The Officers of State.

                                  1 Chronicles 27 : 32–34.

(3) The Convening into an Assembly of the secular Officials "gathered."

1 Chronicles 28 : 1.

(4) The public Acts in National Convention.

    A. David causes Solomon to be made King (first Time).

1 Chronicles 23 : 1*b*.

    B. David's Address.

1 Chronicles 28 : 2–8.

    C. David directs Solomon concerning the Building of the Temple.

1 Chronicles 28 : 9–21.

    D. Contributions of David and the Officials for the Building of the Temple.

1 Chronicles 29 : 1–9.

    E. David's Thanksgiving and Prayer.

1 Chronicles 29 : 10–19.

(5) Close of the Convention.

1 Chronicles 29 : 20–22*a*.

IV. Absalom's Rebellion.

108. The Outbreak of the Rebellion.
    2 Samuel 15 : 7–12.
109. David's Flight.
    (1) He hastily leaves Jerusalem.
        2 Samuel 15 : 13–18.
    (2) Ittai's Fidelity.
        2 Samuel 15 : 19–23.
    (3) The Priests and the Ark.
        2 Samuel 15 : 24–29.
    (4) Hushai is sent back to the City.
        2 Samuel 15 : 30–37*a*.
    (5) The lying Ziba and his Present.
        2 Samuel 16 : 1–4.
    (6) The Cursing of Shimei.
        2 Samuel 16 : 5–14.
110. Absalom in Jerusalem.
    (1) His Entrance into the City.
        2 Samuel 15 : 37*b*.   2 Samuel 16 : 15.
    (2) Hushai meets Absalom.
        2 Samuel 16 : 16–19.
    (3) The Counsels of Ahithophel.
        2 Samuel 16 : 20–17 : 4.

(4) Ahithophel's Counsel is thwarted by Hushai.
  2 Samuel 17 : 5-14.
(5) Hushai's Message to David.
  2 Samuel 17 : 15-22.
(6) Ahithophel's Suicide.
  2 Samuel 17 : 23.
III. The Civil War.
  (1) Absalom's Pursuit.
    2 Samuel 17 : 24-26.
  (2) The Reception of David at Mahanaim.
    2 Samuel 17 : 27-29.
  (3) The Battle of Mount Ephraim.
    2 Samuel 18 : 1-8.
  (4) Absalom is murdered by Joab.
    2 Samuel 18 : 9-18.
  (5) The Tidings brought to David : his Grief for Absalom.
    2 Samuel 18 : 19-33.

V. The Restoration of David's Authority.

112. Joab's Reproval of David's unworthy Grief.
  2 Samuel 19 : 1-8a.
113. Negotiations for David's Recall.
  2 Samuel 19 : 8b-14.
114. David's Return.
  (1) The homeward March begins.
    2 Samuel 19 : 15.
  (2) Shimei is pardoned.
    2 Samuel 19 : 16-23.
  (3) The Meeting with Mephibosheth.
    2 Samuel 19 : 24-30.
  (4) Barzillai's Farewell.
    2 Samuel 19 : 31-40a.
  (5) The Strife between Judah and Israel.
    2 Samuel 19 : 40b-43.
115. Sheba's Insurrection.
  (1) The Outbreak of the Revolt.
    2 Samuel 20 : 1, 2.
  (2) David re-enters Jerusalem.
    2 Samuel 20 : 3.

(3) Joab, after murdering Amasa, pursues Sheba.
2 Samuel 20 : 4-14.
(4) Siege of Abel of Beth-maacah, Death of Sheba, and End of the Rebellion.
2 Samuel 20 : 15-22.

116. The Officers of State after the Restoration.
2 Samuel 20 : 23-26.

VI.   The Closing Days of David's Life.

117. David's failing Health : Abishag the Shunammite.
1 Kings 1 : 1-4.
118. Solomon is made King " the second Time."
(1) Adonijah attempts to seize the Kingdom.
1 Kings 1 : 5-10.
(2) Nathan and Bath-sheba's counter *Coup d' état.*
1 Kings 1 : 11-37.
(3) Solomon's second Anointing.
1 Kings 1 : 38-40.   1 Chronicles 29:22*b.*
(4) Adonijah's Alarm and Submission.
1 Kings 1 : 41-53.
119. David's last prophetic Words.
2 Samuel 23 : 1-7.
120. David's last Words to Solomon.
1 Kings 2 : 1-9.
121. The Death of David.
2 Samuel 5 : 4, 5.   1 Kings 2 : 11, 10.   1 Ch. 3 : 4*b.*   1 Ch. 29 : 26–30.

BOOK FOURTH.

The Reign of Solomon.

PART I.

THE BEGINNING OF SOLOMON'S REIGN.

122. Solomon's Accession to the Throne.
1 Kings 2 : 12.   1 Ch. 29 : 23-25.   2 Ch. 1 : 1.
123. Solomon's Removal of his Adversaries.
(1) Adonijah, asking Abishag to Wife, is put to Death.
1 Kings 2 : 13-25.
(2) Abiathar is degraded from the Priesthood.
1 Kings 2 : 26, 27.
(3) Joab's Flight and Death.
1 Kings 2 : 28-34.

(4) The Elevation of Benaiah and Zadok.
        1 Kings 2 : 35.

(5) Shimei meets with his Deserts.
        1 Kings 2 : 36–46.

124. Solomon marries Pharaoh's Daughter.
        1 Kings 3 : 1.

125. Spiritual Condition of Solomon and his Kingdom.
        1 Kings 3 : 2, 3.

126. Solomon's Sacrifice at Gibeon.
        1 Kings 3 : 4.   2 Chronicles 1 : 2–6.

127. Solomon's Dream and Prayer for Wisdom.
        1 Kings 3 : 5–15.   2 Chronicles 1 : 7–13.

128. God's Gift of Wisdom manifest by Solomon's Judgment on the Harlots.
        1 Kings 3 : 16–28.

PART II.
SOLOMON IN ALL HIS GLORY.

129. Preparations for the Building of the Temple.

(1) The League with Hiram, King of Tyre.
        1 Kings 5 : 1–12 ; 7 : 13, 14.   2 Chronicles 2 : 1, 3–16.

(2) Solomon's Levy of Laborers.
        1 Kings 5 : 13–18.   2 Ch. 2 : 2.   2 Ch. 2 : 17, 18.

130. The Building of the Temple.

(1) Commencement of the Temple.
        1 Kings 6 : 1.   2 Chronicles 3 : 1, 2.

(2) God's Promise to Solomon.
        1 Kings 6 : 11–13.

(3) Dimensions of the Temple.
        1 Kings 6 : 2.   2 Chronicles 3 : 3.

(4) Materials of the Temple.
        1 Kings 6 : 7, 9b, 22a.   2 Chronicles 3 : 5–7a.

(5) The Porch.
        1 Kings 6 : 3.   2 Chronicles 3 : 4.

(6) The Windows.
        1 Kings 6 : 4.

(7) The Stories.
        1 Kings 6 : 5, 6, 8, 10.   2 Chronicles 3 : 9b.

(8) The Most Holy Place.
        1 Kings 6 : 16–21, 22b.   2 Chronicles 3 : 8, 9a.

(9) The Cherubim.
        1 Kings 6 : 23–28.   2 Chronicles 3 : 10–13.

(10) The Veil.

                                                    2 Chronicles 3 : 14.

(11) The Walls.

                   1 Kings 6 : 15*a*, 29.   2 Chronicles 3 : 7*b*.

(12) The Floor.

                   1 Kings 6 : 15*b*, 30.

(13) The Doors.

                   1 Kings 6 : 31–35.

(14) Completion of the Temple.

      1 Kings 6 : 9*a*.   1 Kings 6 : 14.   **1 Kings 6 : 37, 38.**

131. The Building of the Royal Palace.
    (1) The thirteen Years in Building.
                    1 Kings 7 : 1.
    (2) The House of the Forest of Lebanon.
                    1 Kings 7 : 2–5.
    (3) The Porch of Pillars.
                    1 Kings 7 : 6.
    (4) The Porch of the Throne.
                    1 Kings 7 : 7.
    (5) The King's own Dwelling House.
                    1 Kings 7 : 8*a*.
    (6) The House of Pharaoh's Daughter.
                    1 Kings 7 : 8*b*.
    (7) Materials of the Buildings.
                    1 Kings 7 : 9–11.
    (8) The great Court.
                    1 Kings 7 : 12.

132. The Making of the Vessels, etc., pertaining to the Temple.
    (1) Hiram the Artisan of Tyre.
                  [1 Kings 7 : 13, 14.]
    (2) The two Pillars.
                  1 Kings 7 : 15–22.   2 Chronicles 3 : 15–17.
    (3) The Altar of Brass.
                                          2 Chronicles 4 : 1.
    (4) The molten Sea.
                  1 Kings 7 : 23–26, 39*b*.   2 Chronicles 4 : 2–5, 10, 6*b*.
    (5) The ten Bases.
                  1 Kings 7 : 27–37.
    (6) The ten Lavers.
                  1 Kings 7 : 38, 39*a*.   2 Chronicles 4 : 6*a*.
    (7) The Courts.
                  1 Kings 6 : 36.   2 Chronicles 4 : 9.

   3

(8) Summary of Hiram's Work in Brass.

　　　　　　　1 Kings 7 : 40–47.　　　　　　2 Chronicles 4 : 11–18.

(9) Summary of the golden Vessels, etc.

　　　　　　　1 Kings 7 : 48–50.　　　2 Ch. 4 : 7, 8.　2 Ch. 4 : 19–22.

(10) Completion of the Work.

　　　　　　　1 Kings 7 : 51.　　　　　　2 Chronicles 5 : 1.

133. The Dedication of the Temple.

(1) Removal of the Tabernacle and its Contents from Zion to the Temple.

　　　　　　　1 Kings 8 : 1–11.　　　　　　2 Chronicles 5 : 2–14.

(2) Solomon's opening Address and Blessing.

　　　　　　　1 Kings 8 : 12–21.　　　　　2 Chronicles 6 : 1–11.

(3) Solomon's dedicatory Prayer.

A. God's constant Care invoked.

　　　　　　　1 Kings 8 : 22–30.　　　　　2 Chronicles 6 : 12–21.

B. When an Oath is made at the Altar.

　　　　　　　1 Kings 8 : 31, 32.　　　　　2 Chronicles 6 : 22, 23.

C. In Defeat.

　　　　　　　1 Kings 8 : 33, 34.　　　　　2 Chronicles 6 : 24, 25.

D. In Drouth.

　　　　　　　1 Kings 8 : 35, 36.　　　　　2 Chronicles 6 : 26, 27.

E. In Famine and Pestilence.

　　　　　　　1 Kings 8 : 37–40.　　　　　2 Chronicles 6 : 28–31.

F. For the Stranger.

　　　　　　　1 Kings 8 : 41–43.　　　　　2 Chronicles 6 : 32, 33.

G. In Battle.

　　　　　　　1 Kings 8 : 44, 45.　　　　　2 Chronicles 6 : 34, 35.

H. In Captivity.

　　　　　　　1 Kings 8 : 46–53.　　　　　2 Chronicles 6 : 36–39.

I. Close of the Prayer.

　　　　　　　　　　　　　　　　　　　2 Chronicles 6 : 40–42.

(4) Solomon's closing Benediction.

　　　　　　　1 Kings 8 : 54–61.

(5) The Divine Confirmation.

　　　　　　　　　　　　　　　　　　　2 Chronicles 7 : 1–3.

(6) The Sacrifice and public Festival.

　　　　　　　1 Kings 8 : 62–66.　　　　　2 Chronicles 7 : 4–10.

(7) God's second Appearance to Solomon.

　　　　　　　1 Kings 9 : 1–9.　　　　　　2 Chronicles 7 : 11–22.

134. Solomon's Activity and Fame.

(1) Solomon's and Hiram's Exchange of Cities.

　　　　　　　1 Kings 9 : 10–14.　　　　　2 Chronicles 8 : 1, 2.

(2) The Subjugation of Hamath.
$\qquad\qquad\qquad\qquad\qquad\qquad\qquad\qquad$ 2 Chronicles 8 : 3.
(3) The Removal of Pharaoh's Daughter to her own House.
$\qquad\qquad\qquad$ 1 Kings 9 : 24*a*. $\qquad\qquad\qquad$ 2 Chronicles 8 : 11.
(4) The Building of Millo : the Affair with Jeroboam.
$\quad$ 1 Kings 9 : 24*b*. $\qquad\qquad$ 1 Kings 11 : 27*b*, 28, 27*a*, 29–40.
(5) The Levy of forced Labor.
$\qquad\qquad\qquad$ 1 Kings 9 : 20–23, 15. $\qquad\qquad$ 2 Chronicles 8 : 7–10.
$\qquad\qquad\qquad$ 1 Kings 9 : 16—Footnote.
(6) The Building of the Cities.
$\qquad\qquad\qquad$ 1 Kings 9 : 17–19. $\qquad\qquad$ 2 Chronicles 8 : 4–6.
(7) Solomon's Worship.
$\qquad\qquad\qquad$ 1 Kings 9 : 25. $\qquad\qquad\qquad$ 2 Chronicles 8 : 12–16.
(8) The Navies of Solomon and Hiram.
$\qquad\qquad\qquad$ 1 Kings 9 : 26–28; 10 : 22. $\qquad$ 2 Chronicles 8 : 17,18; 9 : 21.
(9) The Visit of the Queen of Sheba.
$\qquad\qquad\qquad$ 1 Kings 10 : 1–13. $\qquad\qquad$ 2 Chronicles 9 : 1–12.
135. The Glory of Solomon.
$\quad$ (1) The Princes.
$\qquad\qquad\qquad$ 1 Kings 4 : 1–6.
$\quad$ (2) The Commissaries.
$\qquad\qquad\qquad$ 1 Kings 4 : 7–19, 22, 23, 27, 28.
$\quad$ (3) Solomon's Wisdom.
$\qquad\qquad\qquad$ 1 Kings 4 : 29–34.
$\quad$ (4) Solomon's Revenue and Splendor.
$\quad$ 1 Kings 10 : 14–21, 27, 23–25.   2 Chronicles 1 : 15. $\qquad$ 2 Ch 9 : 13–20, 27, 22–24.
$\quad$ (5) Solomon's Chariots, Horsemen, and Traffic.
$\quad$ 1 Kings 4 : 26. $\qquad$ 1 Kings 10 : 26, 28, 29.   2 Ch. 1 : 14, 16, 17.   2 Ch. 9 : 25, 28.
$\quad$ (6) The Extent and Security of the Kingdom.
$\qquad\qquad\qquad$ 1 Kings 4 : 21, 24, 20, 25. $\qquad\qquad$ 2 Chronicles 9 : 26.

PART III.

SOLOMON'S FALL AND END.

136. The strange Wives turn away Solomon's Heart.
$\qquad\qquad\qquad$ 1 Kings 11 : 1–8.
137. God's Anger and Threatening.
$\qquad\qquad\qquad$ 1 Kings 11 : 9–13.
138. Solomon's Adversaries.
$\quad$ (1) Hadad the Edomite.
$\qquad\qquad\qquad$ 1 Kings 11 : 14, 21, 22.

(2) Rezon the Son of Eliada.
1 Kings 11 : 23, 25.

(3) Jeroboam the Son of Nebat.
1 Kings 11 : 26.

139. The Death of Solomon.
1 Kings 11 : 41–43.   2 Chronicles 9 : 29–31.

BOOK FIFTH.

The Kingdoms of Judah and Israel.

PART I.

FROM THE YEAR OF THE DISRUPTION TO THE RISE OF JEHU.

Kingdom of Judah.	Kingdom of Israel.
140. Introduction: Accession of Rehoboam and Revolt of the Ten Tribes.	
1 Kings 12 : 1–19.	2 Chronicles 10 : 1–19.
141. The Reign of Rehoboam.	142. The Reign of Jeroboam.
(1) Rehoboam's Plans against Israel frustrated by the Prophet Shemaiah.	(1) Jeroboam is made King over Israel.
1 Kings 12 : 21–24. 2 Chronicles 11 : 1–4.	1 Kings 12 : 20.
	(2) Jeroboam takes Measures to establish his Kingdom.
	1 Kings 12 : 25–33. 2 Ch. 11 : 15.
(2) Adherence of the Levites in all Israel to Rehoboam.	
2 Chronicles 11 : 13, 14.	
(3) Rehoboam is further strengthened by the Immigration of other pious Israelites.	
2 Chronicles 11 : 16, 17.	
	(3) The "Man of God out of Judah."
	A. The Prophecy against Jeroboam's Altar in Beth-el.
	1 Kings 13 : 1–3.
	B. The Withering and Restoration of Jeroboam's Hand.
	1 Kings 13 : 4–6.

KINGDOM OF JUDAH.

KINGDOM OF ISRAEL.

C. The Disobedience of the Man of God.

1 Kings 13 : 7–22.

D. The Man of God is slain.

1 Kings 13 : 23, 24.

E. The " Old Prophet " buries the Man of God, and confirms his Words.

1 Kings 13 : 25–32.

(4) Jeroboam's Persistence in Evil.

1 Kings 13 : 33, 34.

(5) Ahijah's Prophecy against the House and Kingdom of Jeroboam.

A. Jeroboam's Inquiry concerning his sick Child.

1 Kings 14 : 1–4.

B. Ahijah's Prophecy and its partial Fulfillment.

1 Kings 14 : 5–18.

(4) Rehoboam's Fortifications.

2 Chronicles 11 : 5–12.

(5) Rehoboam's Family.

2 Chronicles 11 : 18–23.

(6) Judah's Apostasy under Rehoboam.

1 Kings 14 : 22–24.   2 Chronicles 12 : 1, 14.

(7) The Invasion of Shishak.

1 Kings 14 : 25–28.   2 Chronicles 12 : 2–12.

(8) The Constant Warfare between Rehoboam and Jeroboam. (6)

1 Kings 14 : 30.   1 Kings 15 : 6.   2 Chronicles 12 : 15*b*.

(9) The Death of Rehoboam.

1 Kings 14 : 21, 29, 31*a*. 2 Ch. 12 : 13, 15*a*, 16*a*.

143. The Reign of Abijah.

(1) Abijah's Accession to the Throne.

1 Kings 14:31*b*; 15:1, 2. 2 Ch. 12:16*b*; 13:1, 2*a*.

(2) The War between Abijah and Jeroboam. (7)

1 Kings 15 : 7*b*.   2 Chronicles 13 : 2*b*–20*a*.

(3) The Family of Abijah.

2 Chronicles 13 : 21.

KINGDOM OF JUDAH.	KINGDOM OF ISRAEL.

KINGDOM OF JUDAH.

(4) The Character of Abijah.
    I Kings 15 : 3-5.

(5) The Death of Abijah.
I Kings 15 : 7*a*, 8*a*. 2 Chronicles 13 : 22; 14 : 1*a*.

144. The Reign of Asa.

(1) Asa's Accession to the Throne.
I Kings 15 : 8*b*–10.   2 Chronicles 14 : 1*b*.

(2) The ten Years of Peace.
    2 Chronicles 14 : 1*c*.

(3) The Character of Asa : His first
    Reforms.
I Kings 15 : 11.   2 Chronicles 14 : 2-5.

(4) Asa's Policy of Defense.
    2 Chronicles 14 : 6-8.

(5) Asa's Victory over Zerah the
    Ethiopian.
    2 Chronicles 14 : 9-15.

(6) The Warning of the Prophet
    Azariah.
    2 Chronicles 15 : 1-7.

(7) The Second Reformation under
    Asa.

A. The four Years of Peace.
    2 Chronicles 15 : 19.

B. The Reforms in Worship.
I Kings 15:12, 14, 15. 2 Chronicles 15:8,17,18.

C. The Renewal of the Covenant.
    2 Chronicles 15 : 9-15.

D. The Removal of Maacah, the
    Queen Mother.
I Kings 15 : 13.   2 Chronicles 15 : 16.

KINGDOM OF ISRAEL.

(8) The Death of Jeroboam.
    I Kings 14 : 19, 20*a*.   2 Chronicles 13 : 20*b*.

145. The Reign of Nadab.

(1) Nadab's Accession to the Throne.
    I Kings 14 : 20*b*; 15 : 25.

(2) The Character of Nadab.
    I Kings 15 : 26.

(3) The Death of Nadab.
    I Kings 15 : 31, 27.

146. The Reign of Baasha.

(1) Baasha's Accession to the Throne.
    I Kings 15 : 28-30, 33, 34.

KINGDOM OF JUDAH. | KINGDOM OF ISRAEL.

(8) The War between Asa and Baasha. (2)

1 Kings 15:17–22, 16.   1 Kings 15:32.   2 Chronicles 16:1–6.

(9) The Warning of the Prophet Hanani.
2 Chronicles 16:7–9.

(10) Asa's Transgression.
2 Chronicles 16:10.

(3) The Prophecy of Jehu against Baasha and his House.
1 Kings 16:7, 1–4.

(4) The Death of Baasha.
1 Kings 16:5, 6a.

147. The Reign of Elah.
1 Kings 16:6b, 8, 14, 9, 10.

148. The Reign of Zimri.
1 Kings 16:15a, 11–13, 20, 15b–19.

149. The Reigns of Tibni and Omri.
(1) The Civil War.
1 Kings 16:21.
(2) Omri marries his Son Ahab to Jezebel of Zidon.
1 Kings 16:31a.
(3) Omri becomes sole King.
1 Kings 16:22.

150. The Reign of Omri.
(1) The first six Years in Tirzah.
1 Kings 16:23.
(2) Omri makes Samaria his Capital.
1 Kings 16:24.
(3) The Character of Omri.
1 Kings 16:25, 26.
(4) The Death of Omri.
1 Kings 16:27, 28a.

151. The Reign of Ahab.
(1) Ahab's Accession to the Throne.
1 Kings 16: 28b, 29.

KINGDOM OF JUDAH.	KINGDOM OF ISRAEL.

KINGDOM OF ISRAEL.

(2) The Character of Ahab.
    1 Ki. 16: 30, 31*b*–33. 1 Ki. 21: 25, 26.

(11) Asa's Illness.
1 Kings 15: 23*b*.   2 Chronicles 16: 12.

(12) The Death of Asa.
1 Kings 15: 23*a*, 24*a*. 2 Ch. 16: 11, 13, 14.

(3) The Rebuilding of Jericho.
    1 Kings 16: 34.

152. The Reign of Jehoshaphat.

(1) Jehoshaphat's Accession to the
    Throne.
1 Ki. 15: 24*b*; 22: 41, 42. 2 Ch. 17: 1*a*; 20: 31.

(2) The Character of Jehoshaphat.
1 Kings 22: 43, 46.   2 Chronicles 20: 32, 33.

(3) Jehoshaphat strengthens his King-
    dom.
                2 Chronicles 17: 1*b*–6.

(4) The Mission of the Princes, Le-
    vites, and Priests.
                2 Chronicles 17 · 7–9.

(5) Jehoshaphat's increasing Power.
                2 Ch. 17: 10–18: 1*a*.

(6) Jehoshaphat marries his Son Jehoram to Athaliah, Daughter of Ahab. (4)
        1 Kings 22: 44.   2 Chronicles 18: 1*b*.

(5) The Persecution of the Prophets.
        1 Kings 18: 3*b*, 4.

(6) Elijah the Tishbite.
    A. The Famine foretold.
        1 Kings 17: 1.
    B. Elijah hides by the Brook Cherith.
        1 Kings 17: 2–7.
    C. Elijah in Zarephath.
        1 Kings 17: 8–16.
    D. Elijah raises the Widow's Son.
        1 Kings 17: 17–24.
    E. Elijah goes to meet Ahab.
        1 Kings 18: 1–3*a*, 5–16.
    F. Elijah's Challenge.
        1 Kings 18: 17–24.

KINGDOM OF JUDAH.	KINGDOM OF ISRAEL.
	G. Jehovah *versus* Baal. 1 Kings 18 : 25–39.
	H. Baal's Priests are slain. 1 Kings 18 : 40.
	I. The Promise of Rain. 1 Kings 18 : 41–46.
	J. Elijah's Flight to Horeb. 1 Kings 19 : 1–8.
	K. God's Revelation to Elijah. 1 Kings 19 : 9–18.
	L. The Call of Elisha. 1 Kings 19 : 19–21.
	(7) Ahab's first Syrian Campaign. *A.* Ben-hadad besieges Samaria. 1 Kings 20 : 1. *B.* Ben-hadad's arrogant Claims. 1 Kings 20 : 2–12. *C.* God's Promise of Victory. 1 Kings 20 : 13, 14. *D.* Ahab's Victory over the Syrians. 1 Kings 20 : 15–21.
	(8) Ahab's second Syrian Campaign. *A.* The Prophet's Warning. 1 Kings 20 : 22. *B.* Ahab again victorious. 1 Kings 20 : 23–30*a.* *C.* Ahab spares Ben-hadad. 1 Kings 20 : 30*b*–34. *D.* The Prophet's Rebuke. 1 Kings 20 : 35–43.
	(9) The three Years of Peace. 1 Kings 22 : 1.
	(10) The Story of Naboth. *A.* Naboth's Vineyard is coveted by Ahab. 1 Kings 21 : 1–3. *B.* Jezebel causes Naboth's Death. 1 Kings 21 : 4–16.

KINGDOM OF JUDAH.	KINGDOM OF ISRAEL.

KINGDOM OF ISRAEL.

C. Ahab's Doom pronounced by Elijah.
> 1 Kings 21 : 17-24.

D. Ahab's Repentance gains him a Respite.
> 1 Kings 21 : 27-29.

(11) Ahaziah becomes co-regnant with Ahab.
> 1 Kings 22 : 51.

(7) Jehoshaphat joins Ahab in his third Syrian Campaign. (12)

A. Ahab resolves to recover Ramoth-gilead.
> 1 Kings 22 : 2-4.   2 Chronicles 18 : 2, 3.

B. Ahab's Prophets promise him the Victory.
> 1 Kings 22 : 5, 6, 10-12.   2 Chronicles 18 : 4, 5, 9-11.

C. Micaiah's Prophecy.
> 1 Kings 22 : 7-9, 13-28.   2 Chronicles 18 : 6-8, 12-27.

D. The Battle of Ramoth-gilead : Defeat and Death of Ahab.
> 1 Kings 22 : 29-40*a*.   2 Chronicles 18 : 28-34.

153. The Reign of Ahaziah.

(1) Ahaziah becomes sole King.
> 1 Kings 22 : 40*b*.

(2) The Character of Ahaziah.
> 1 Kings 22 : 52, 53.

(3) The Revolt of Moab.
> 2 Kings 1 : 1.   2 Kings 3 : 4, 5.

(8) **The Prophet Jehu's Judgment on Jehoshaphat.**
> 2 Chronicles 19 : 1-3.

(9) Jehoshaphat's further Reforms in Worship and Law.
> 2 Chronicles 19 : 4-11.

(10) **The wondrous Deliverance from the Children of Moab and Ammon and Mount Seir.**

A. The Invasion.
> 2 Chronicles 20 : 1, 2.

B. Jehoshaphat's Prayer.
> 2 Chronicles 20 : 3-12.

C. Jehovah's Answer through Jahaziel.
> 2 Chronicles 20 : 13-19.

D. The Annihilation of the Invading Armies.
> 2 Chronicles 20 : 20-24.

KINGDOM OF JUDAH.	KINGDOM OF ISRAEL.

KINGDOM OF JUDAH.

E. The Spoil.
　　2 Chronicles 20 : 25.
F. The triumphant Return to Jerusalem.
　　2 Chronicles 20 : 26–30.

(11) Jehoshaphat's Shipping Alliance with Ahaziah. (4)
　1 Kings 22 : 48, 47, 49.　　　2 Chronicles 20 : 35–37.

KINGDOM OF ISRAEL.

(5) Ahaziah's Illness.
　　2 Kings 1 : 2.

(6) Jehovah's Message by Elijah.
　　2 Kings 1 : 3-16.

(7) The Death of Ahaziah.
　　2 Kings 1 : 17*a*, 18.

154. The Reign of Jehoram.

(1) Jehoram's Accession to the Throne.
　　2 Kings 1 : 17*b*.　　2 Kings 3 : 1.

(2) The Character of Jehoram.
　　2 Kings 3 : 2, 3.

(3) Elisha the Son of Shaphat.

A. The Translation of Elijah.
　　2 Kings 2 : 1–11.

B. Elijah's Spirit rests upon Elisha.
　　2 Kings 2 : 12–18.

C. Elisha heals the noxious Waters at Jericho.
　　2 Kings 2 : 19–22.

D. The Cursing of the Children.
　　2 Kings 2 : 23, 24.

E. Elisha's Journeying.
　　2 Kings 2 : 25.

F. The Increase of the Widow's Oil.
　　2 Kings 4 : 1-7.

G. Elisha promises a Son to the hospitable Shunammite.
　　2 Kings 4 : 8-17.

H. Elisha heals the noxious Pottage at Gilgal.
　　2 Kings 4 : 38-41.

KINGDOM OF JUDAH.	KINGDOM OF ISRAEL.

KINGDOM OF ISRAEL.

I. Elisha feeds one hundred Men with twenty Loaves.
2 Kings 4:42–44.

J. Elisha restores the Life of the Shunammite's Son.
2 Kings 4:18–37.

K. The seven Years' Famine Foretold.
2 Kings 8:1, 2.

L. The Recovery of the lost Ax.
2 Kings 6:1–7.

KINGDOM OF JUDAH.

(12) Jehoram becomes co-regnant with Jehoshaphat.
2 Ki. 8:16, 17.   2 Ch. 21:5.   2 Ch. 21:20a.

(13) Jehoram's sixfold Fratricide.
2 Chronicles 21:2–4.

(14) Jehoshaphat joins Jehoram of Israel in an Expedition against the Moabites. (4)
A. The March.
2 Kings 3:6–9.
B. Elisha's Promise of Water and Victory.
2 Kings 3:10–19.
C. The Morning brings Water.
2 Kings 3:20.
D. The Moabites defeated by the allied Armies.
2 Kings 3:21–27.

(15) The Death of Jehoshaphat.
1 Kings 22:45, 50a.   2 Ch. 20:34; 21:1a.

155. The Reign of Jehoram.

(1) Jehoram becomes sole King.
1 Kings 22:50b.   2 Chronicles 21:1b.

(2) The Character of Jehoram.
2 Kings 8:18, 19.   2 Chronicles 21:6, 7, 11.

(3) The Revolt of Edom.
2 Kings 8:20–22a.   2 Chronicles 21:8–10a.

(4) The Revolt of Libnah.
2 Kings 8:22b.   2 Chronicles 21:10b.

KINGDOM OF JUDAH.

(5) The posthumous Message from Elijah.
    2 Chronicles 21 : 12–15.

(6) The Invasion of the Philistines and Arabians.
    2 Chronicles 21 : 16, 17.

(7) Jehoram's Illness.
    2 Chronicles 21 : 18.

KINGDOM OF ISRAEL.

(5) Elisha and the Syrians.
    A. Elisha reveals Ben-hadad's Plans.
        2 Kings 6 : 8–12.
    B. The Syrian Bands smitten with Blindness at Dothan.
        2 Kings 6 : 13–18.
    C. Elisha leads the blinded Syrians to Samaria.
        2 Kings 6 : 19–23.

(6) Jehoram restores the Shunammite's Land because of Elisha's Miracles.
        2 Kings 8 : 3–6.

(7) The Story of Naaman.
    A. The Healing of Naaman's Leprosy.
        2 Kings 5 : 1–14.
    B. Naaman's Gratitude.
        2 Kings 5 : 15–19.
    C. Gehazi's Sin and Punishment.
        2 Kings 5 : 20–27.

(8) The Siege of Samaria.
    A. Ben-hadad besieges Samaria.
        2 Kings 6 : 24.
    B. The Suffering from the Famine.
        2 Kings 6 : 25–31.
    C. The King's Messenger of Vengeance and Elisha's Promise of Plenty.
        2 Kings 6 : 32–7 : 2.

KINGDOM OF JUDAH.	KINGDOM OF ISRAEL.

KINGDOM OF ISRAEL.

D. The Discovery of the four Lepers.
2 Kings 7 : 3-11.

E. The Lepers' Report confirmed and Elisha's Promises fulfilled.
2 Kings 7 : 12-20.

KINGDOM OF JUDAH.

(8) The Death of Jehoram.
2 Kings 8 : 23, 24*a*. 2 Chronicles 21 : 19, 20*b*.

156. The Reign of Ahaziah.

(1) Ahaziah's Accession to the Throne.
2 Ki. 8 : 24*b*-26. 2 Ki. 9 : 29. 2 Ch. 22 : 1, 2.

(2) The Character of Ahaziah.
2 Kings 8 : 27.   2 Chronicles 22 : 3-5*a*.

(9) Elisha's Interview with Hazael.
2 Kings 8 : 7-15.

(3) Ahaziah aids Jehoram in the Defense of Ramoth-gilead. (10)
2 Kings 8 : 28.   2 Chronicles 22 : 5*b*.

(11) Jehoram goes for Healing to Jezreel.

2 Ki. 8 : 29*a*. 2 Ki. 9 : 14*b*, 15*a*. 2 Ch, 22 : 6*a*.

(4) Jehu's Successful Conspiracy. (12)

A. Ahaziah visits Jehoram in Jezreel.

2 Kings 8 : 29*b*.   2 Kings 9 : 16*b*.   2 Chronicles 22 : 6*b*.

B. At Elisha's Command, Jehu is anointed King over Israel, at Ramoth-gilead.
2 Kings 9 : 1-10.

C. Jehu is proclaimed King by his Brother Officers.
2 Kings 9 : 11-13.

D. Jehu proceeds to Jezreel and slays Jehoram.
2 Kings 9 : 14*a*, 15*b*, 16*a*, 17-26.   2 Chronicles 22 : 7.

E. Ahaziah is, in turn, also slain by Jehu's Command.
2 Kings 9 : 27, 28.   2 Chronicles 22 : 9*a*.

KINGDOM OF JUDAH.	KINGDOM OF ISRAEL.

KINGDOM OF ISRAEL.

F. The Fate of Jezebel.
2 Kings 9:30–37.
G. The Judgment on the House of Ahab.
2 Kings 10:1–11.

H. The Massacre of the Princes Royal of Judah.
2 Kings 10:12–14.　　　　2 Chronicles 22:8.

I. Jehu attaches Jehonadab to his Support.
2 Kings 10:15, 16.
J. The complete Success of the Usurper.
2 Kings 10:17.

PART II.

FROM THE RISE OF JEHU TO THE FALL OF THE KINGDOM OF ISRAEL.

157. The Reign of Jehu.
(1) Jehu's Destruction of Baal.
2 Kings 10:18–28.

158. The Reign of Athaliah.
(1) Having slain all the Seed Royal save Joash, Athaliah usurps the Throne.
2 Kings 11:1, 3*b*.　2 Ch. 22:9*b*, 10, 12*b*.
(2) The Rescue of Joash.
2 Kings 11:2, 3*a*.　2 Chronicles 22:11,12*a*.

(2) Jehovah's Promise to Jehu and his House.
2 Kings 10:30.
(3) Jehu walks in the Sins of Jeroboam.
2 Kings 10:29.　2 Kings 10:31.

(3) Jehoiada elevates Joash to the Throne.
2 Kings 11:4-12.　2 Chronicles 23:1-11.

(4) Athaliah meets with her Deserts.
2 Kings 11 : 13–16. 2 Chronicles 23 : 12–15.
2 Kings 11 : 20*b*.   2 Chronicles 23 : 21*b*.

159. The Reign of Joash.

(1) Joash's Accession to the Throne.
2 Ki. 11 : 21 ; 12 : 1. 2 Chronicles 24 : 1.
(2) The Covenant made by Jehoiada.
2 Kings 11 : 17–20*a*. 2 Ch. 23 : 16–21*a*.
(3) Joash's Character as influenced by
    Jehoiada.
2 Kings 12 : 2.   2 Chronicles 24 : 2.
(4) Spiritual Condition of the King-
    dom.
2 Kings 12 : 3.
(5) Joash's matrimonial Affairs.
            2 Chronicles 24 : 3.
(6) Joash's Commands to repair the
    Temple.
2 Kings 12 : 4, 5.   2 Chronicles 24 : 4, 5.

(4) The "Cutting short" of Israel.
        2 Kings 10 : 32, 33.
(5) The Death of Jehu.
        2 Kings 10 : 34, 35*a*, 36.
160. The Reign of Jehoahaz.
(1) The Accession of Jehoahaz.
        2 Kings 10 : 35*b* ; 13 : 1.
(2) The Character of Jehoahaz.
        2 Kings 13 : 2.
(3) The Oppression of the Syrians.
        2 Kings 13 : 22, 3.

(7) The Repairing of the Temple.
2 Kings 12 : 6–16.   2 Chronicles 24 : 6–14*a*.
(8) The Temple Worship.
            2 Chronicles 24 : 14*b*.
(9) The Death of Jehoiada.
            2 Chronicles 24 : 15, 16.
(10) The Sins of Joash.
            2 Chronicles 24 : 17–19.

(4) The Repentance of Jehoahaz.
        2 Kings 13 : 4.

KINGDOM OF JUDAH.

(11) The Stoning of Zechariah.
2 Chronicles 24 : 20–22.

(12) Hazael's Operations in Judah.
A. The Reverses of Judah.
2 Chronicles 24:23, 24.
B. Hazael subdues Gath.
2 Kings 12:17*a.*
C. Hazael bought off by Joash.
2 Kings 12:17*b*, 18.

(13) The Death of Joash.
2 Kings 12:20, 21*a*, 19.   2 Ch. 24:25–27*a*.

162. The Reign of Amaziah.

(1) Amaziah's Accession to the Throne.
2 Ki. 12:21*b*; 14:1, 2.   2 Ch. 24:27*b*; 25:1

(2) The Character of Amaziah.
2 Kings 14:3–6.   2 Chronicles 25:2–4.

KINGDOM OF ISRAEL.

(5) Jehoash becomes co-regnant with Jehoahaz.
2 Kings 13:10.

(6) Hazael reduces Israel low.
2 Kings 13:7.

(7) The Death of Jehoahaz.
2 Kings 13:8, 9*a.*

161. The Reign of Jehoash.

(1) Jehoash becomes sole King.
2 Kings 13:9*b.*

(2) The Character of Jehoash.
2 Kings 13:11.

(3) The encouraging Prophecy of Elisha on his Deathbed.
2 Kings 13:14–19.

(4) The Death of Elisha.
2 Kings 13:20*a.*

(5) The Miracle in Elisha's Tomb.
2 Kings 13:20*b*, 21.

KINGDOM OF JUDAH.	KINGDOM OF ISRAEL.

KINGDOM OF ISRAEL.

(6) The Fulfillment of Elisha's Prophecy : Success of Jehoash over Benhadad.
2 Kings 13 : 23–25.

KINGDOM OF JUDAH.

(3) Amaziah plans an Expedition against Edom.
2 Chronicles 25 : 5.

(4) Amaziah hires one hundred thousand Mercenaries out of Israel, but subsequently dismisses them. (7)
2 Chronicles 25 : 6–10.

(5) Amaziah's Success in Edom.
2 Kings 14 : 7.   2 Chronicles 25 : 11, 12.

(6) The dismissed Israelitish Mercenaries pillage the Cities of Judah. (8)
2 Chronicles 25 : 13.

(7) Amaziah's further Wickedness.
2 Chronicles 25 : 14–16.

(8) The War between Amaziah and Jehoash. (9)
2 Kings 14 : 8–14.   2 Chronicles 25 : 17–24.

(10) The Death of Jehoash.
2 Ki. 13 : 12, 13a, 13c.   2 Ki. 14 : 15, 16a.

163. The Reign of Jeroboam II.

(9) The last fifteen Years of Amaziah's Reign.
2 Kings 14 : 17.   2 Chronicles 25 : 25.

(1) The Accession of Jeroboam II.
2 Ki. 13 : 13b.   2 Ki. 14 : 16b, 23.

(2) The Character of Jeroboam II.
2 Kings 14 : 24.

(3) Jehovah saves Israel by the Hand of Jeroboam II.
2 Kings 13 : 5.   2 Kings 14 : 25–27.

(4) The continued Apostasy of Israel.
2 Kings 13 : 6.

(10) The Death of Amaziah.
2 Kings 14 : 18–20. 2 Chronicles 25 : 26–28.

INTERREGNUM OF ELEVEN YEARS.

164. The Reign of Uzziah.
(1) Uzziah's Accession to the Throne.
2 Kings 14 : 21 ; 15 : 1, 2.   2 Ch. 26 : 1, 3.

KINGDOM OF JUDAH.

(2) The Character of Uzziah.
2 Kings 15:3.   2 Chronicles 26:4, 5.
(3) Spiritual Condition of the Kingdom.
2 Kings 15:4.
(4) Uzziah's prosperous Years.
  A. The Building of Eloth.
2 Kings 14:22.   2 Chronicles 26:2.
  B. Uzziah's Success in War.
          2 Chronicles 26:6–8*a*.
  C. Uzziah's Building and Husbandry.
          2 Ch. 26:9, 10, 15*a*.
  D. Uzziah's Army.
          2 Chronicles 26:11–14.
  E. Uzziah's Fame.
2 Chronicles 26:8*b*. 2 Chronicles 26:15*b*.

(5) Uzziah's Sin and Punishment.
2 Kings 15:5*a*.   2 Chronicles 26:16–21*a*.
(6) The Regency of Jotham.
2 Kings 15:5*b*.   2 Chronicles 26:21*b*.

KINGDOM OF ISRAEL.

(5) The Death of Jeroboam II.
      2 Kings 14:28, 29*a*.

INTERREGNUM OF TWENTY-TWO YEARS.

165. The Reign of Zechariah.
    (1) Zechariah's Accession to the Throne.
          2 Kings 14:29*b*; 15:8.
    (2) The Character of Zechariah.
          2 Kings 15:9.
    (3) The Death of Zechariah.
          2 Kings 15:10, 11.
    (4) The Fulfillment of Jehovah's Promise to Jehu.
          2 Kings 15:12.
166. The Reign of Shallum.
          2 Kings 15:13–15.
167. The Reign of Menahem.
    (1) Menahem's Accession to the Throne.
          2 Kings 15:16, 17.
    (2) The Character of Menahem.
          2 Kings 15:18.

KINGDOM OF JUDAH.

KINGDOM OF ISRAEL.

(3) The Invasion of Pul, King of
    Assyria.
        2 Kings 15 : 19, 20.   [1 Ch. 5 : 26a.]
(4) The Death of Menahem.
        2 Kings 15 : 21, 22a.

168. The Reign of Pekahiah.
    (1) Pekahiah's Accession to the
        Throne.
            2 Kings 15 : 22b, 23.
    (2) The Character of Pekahiah.
            2 Kings 15 : 24.
    (3) The Death of Pekahiah.
            2 Kings 15 : 25, 26.

169. The Reign of Pekah.
    (1) Pekah's Accession to the Throne.
            2 Kings 15 : 27.
    (2) The Character of Pekah.
            2 Kings 15 : 28.

(7) The Death of Uzziah.
    2 Kings 15 : 6, 7a. 2 Chronicles 26 : 22, 23a.

170. The Reign of Jotham.
    (1) Jotham's Accession to the Throne.
    2 Ki. 15 : 7b, 32, 33. 2 Ch. 26 : 23b; 27 : 1.
                        2 Chronicles 27 : 8.
    (2) The Character of Jotham.
    2 Kings 15 : 34.   2 Chronicles 27 : 2a.
    (3) Spiritual Condition of the People.
    2 Kings 15 : 35a.   2 Chronicles 27 : 2b.
    (4) Jotham's Building.
    2 Kings 15 : 35b.   2 Chronicles 27 : 3, 4.
    (5) The Subjugation of the Ammon-
        ites.
                        2 Chronicles 27 : 5, 6.

(3) The Beginning of the Captivity.
    1 Ch. 5 : 25a, 26b, 25b, 26a, 26c, 6c, 6a, 6d.

(6) The War between Jotham and Rezin and Pekah. (4)
                2 Kings 15 : 37.

KINGDOM OF JUDAH.	KINGDOM OF ISRAEL.

KINGDOM OF JUDAH.

(7) The Death of Jotham.
2 Ki. 15 : 36, 38a.   2 Ch. 27 : 7, 9a.

171. The Reign of Ahaz.

(1) The Accession of Ahaz.
2 Ki. 15 : 38b; 16 : 1, 2a. 2 Ch. 27 : 9b; 28 : 1a.

(2) The Character of Ahaz.
2 Kings 16 : 2b–4.   2 Chronicles 28 : 1b–4.

(3) The War between Ahaz and Rezin and Pekah. (5)
    A. Ahaz is defeated by the allied Kings.
        2 Kings 16 : 5, 6.   2 Chronicles 28 : 5–8.
    B. Oded the Prophet procures the Release of the Jewish Captives.
        2 Chronicles 28 : 9–15.

(4) The Edomite and Philistine Invasions.
        2 Chronicles 28 : 17–19.

(5) Ahaz seeks Help from Tiglath-pileser.
2 Kings 16 : 7, 8.   2 Chronicles 28 : 16, 21.

(6) Tiglath-pileser captures Damascus.
2 Kings 16 : 9.

KINGDOM OF ISRAEL.

(6) Tiglath-pileser captures many Cities in northern Israel, and deports many Captives.
    2 Kings 15 : 29.

(7) Ahaz becomes Tributary to Tiglath-pileser.
2 Kings 16 : 10a.   2 Chronicles 28 : 20.

(8) Ahaz continues in his wicked Ways.
2 Kings 16 : 10b–18. 2 Chronicles 28 : 22–25.

(7) The Death of Pekah.
    2 Kings 15 : 31, 30.

INTERREGNUM OF NINE YEARS.

172. The Reign of Hoshea.
    (1) Hoshea's Accession to the Throne.
        2 Kings 17 : 1.

KINGDOM OF JUDAH.

(9) The Death of Ahaz.

2 Ki. 16:19, 20a.   2 Ch. 28:26, 27a.

173. The Reign of Hezekiah (first 6 years).

(1) Hezekiah's Accession to the Throne.

2 Ki. 16:20b; 18:1, 2.   2 Ch. 28:27b; 29.1.

(2) The Character of Hezekiah.

2 Kings 18:3-7a.   2 Chronicles 29:2.

(3) The Cleansing of the Temple.

2 Chronicles 29:3-19.

(4) The Reconsecration of the Temple.

2 Chronicles 29:20-36.

(5) Many of the Subjects of Hoshea unite with the People of Judah in Keeping the Passover. (3)

A. Preparations for the Passover.

2 Chronicles 30:1-12.

B. The Keeping of the Passover.

2 Chronicles 30:13-22.

C. The Keeping of "other seven Days."

2 Chronicles 30:23-27.

D. The Enthusiasm aroused results in widespread Iconoclasm.

2 Kings 18:4.   2 Chronicles 31:1.

(6) Hezekiah's further religious Reforms.

2 Chronicles 31:2-21.

KINGDOM OF ISRAEL.

(2) The Character of Hoshea.

2 Kings 17:2.

(4) Hoshea becomes Tributary to Shalmaneser.

2 Kings 17:3.

(5) The secret Alliance with Egypt.

2 Kings 17:4a.

(6) Shalmaneser besieges Samaria.

2 Kings 17:5.   2 Kings 18:9.

(7) The Fall of Samaria.

2 Kings 17:6. 2   Kings 18:10, 11.

KINGDOM OF JUDAH.	KINGDOM OF ISRAEL.
	(8) The Imprisonment of Hoshea.
	2 Kings 17 :4*b*.
	174. Appendix to the History of the Kingdom of Israel.
	(1) The Sins for which Israel was carried into Captivity.
	2 Kings 17 :7–23. 2 Kings 18 : 12.
	(2) The Peoples that were brought to inhabit Samaria.
	2 Kings 17 : 24.
	(3) The Plague of the Lions.
	2 Kings 17 : 25, 26.
	(4) The mixed Character of the Samaritans' Religion.
	2 Kings 17 : 27–41.

PART III.

THE KINGDOM OF JUDAH AFTER THE FALL OF THE KINGDOM OF ISRAEL.

175. The Reign of Hezekiah (last 23 years).
  (1) Hezekiah throws off the Assyrian Yoke.
        2 Kings 18: 7*b*.
  (2) Hezekiah's successful Philistine Campaign.
        2 Kings 18 : 8.
  (3) Sennacherib's first Invasion of Judah.
        2 Kings 18 : 13–16.
  (4) Hezekiah's Illness and Recovery.
        2 Kings 20 : 1–11.   2 Chronicles 32 : 24.
  (5) Hezekiah's Reception of the Babylonian Embassy.
        2 Kings 20 : 12–19.   2 Chronicles 32 : 31, 25, 26.
  (6) Hezekiah's Wealth and Building.

                                                          2 Chronicles 32 : 27–30.
  (7) Sennacherib's second Invasion of Judah.
      A. Sennacherib enters Judah.

                                                          2 Chronicles 32 : 1.

      B. Hezekiah's Precautions.

                                                          2 Chronicles 32 : 2–8.

      C. The Advance against Jerusalem : Rabshakeh's Message.
                  2 Kings 18 : 17–25.   2 Chronicles 32 : 9–15.
      D. The Reply of Hezekiah's Ministers.
                  2 Kings 18 : 26.
      E. The further Insolence of Rabshakeh.
                  2 Kings 18 : 27–35.   2 Chronicles 32 : 16, 18, 19.
      F. The Despair of Hezekiah's Ministers.
                  2 Kings 18 : 36, 37.
      G. Hezekiah's Message to Isaiah.
                  2 Kings 19 : 1–5.
      H. Isaiah's Answer.
                  2 Kings 19 : 6, 7.
      I. Rabshakeh's Departure.
                  2 Kings 19 : 8.
      J. Sennacherib's Letter to Hezekiah.
                  2 Kings 19 : 9–13.   2 Chronicles 32 : 17.
      K. Hezekiah's Prayer.
                  2 Kings 19 : 14–19.   2 Chronicles 32 : 20.
      L. Jehovah's Answer through Isaiah.
                  2 Kings 19 : 20–34.
      M. The Overthrow of the Assyrians.
                  2 Kings 19 : 35, 36.   2 Chronicles 32 : 21*a*, 22.
  (8) Hezekiah once more prosperous.
                                      2 Chronicles 32 : 23.
  (9) The Death of Hezekiah.
                  2 Kings 20 : 20, 21*a*.   2 Chronicles 32 : 32, 33*a*.
176. The Reign of Manasseh.
  (1) Manasseh's Accession to the Throne.
                  2 Kings 20 : 21*b*; 21 : 1.   2 Chronicles 32 : 33*b*; 33 : 1.
  (2) Manasseh's excessive Idolatries.
                  2 Kings 21 : 2–9.   2 Chronicles 33 : 2–9.
  (3) The Death of Sennacherib.
                  2 Kings 19 : 37*a*.   2 Chronicles 32 : 21*b*.
  (4) Accession of Esar-haddon as King of Assyria.
                  2 Kings 19 : 37*b*.
  (5) Jehovah's Message " by His Servants the Prophets."
                  2 Kings 21 : 10–15.   2 Chronicles 33 : 10.
  (6) Manasseh's further Crimes.
                  2 Kings 21 : 16.
  (7) Manasseh's Captivity.
                                      2 Chronicles 33 : 11.

(8) Manasseh's Repentance and Restoration.

             2 Chronicles 33 : 12, 13.

(9) The Acts of Manasseh after his Restoration.

             2 Chronicles 33 : 14–16.

(10) Spiritual Condition of the People.

             2 Chronicles 33 : 17.

(11) The Death of Manasseh.

    2 Kings 21 : 17, 18a.   2 Chronicles 33 : 18–20a.

177. The Reign of Amon.

 (1) Amon's Accession to the Throne.

    2 Kings 21 : 18b, 19.   2 Chronicles 33 : 20b, 21.

 (2) The Character of Amon.

    2 Kings 21 : 20–22.   2 Chronicles 33 : 22, 23.

 (3) The Death of Amon.

    2 Kings 21 : 25, 23, 26a.   2 Chronicles 33 : 24.

178. The Reign of Josiah.

 (1) Josiah's Accession to the Throne.

  2 Kings 21 : 24. 2 Kings 21 : 26b; 22, 1. 2 Chronicles 33 : 25 ; 34 : 1.

 (2) Josiah's godly Character.

    2 Kings 22 : 2; 23 : 25.   2 Chronicles 34 : 2.

 (3) Josiah's Life and Character not sufficient to atone for Judah's Sins.

    2 Kings 23 : 26, 27.

 (4) Josiah's early Reformations.

             2 Chronicles 34 : 3–7.

 (5) The Repairing of the Temple.

    2 Kings 22 : 3–7.   2 Chronicles 34 : 8–13.

 (6) The Book of the Law.

  A. The Finding of the Book of the Law.

    2 Kings 22 : 8.   2 Chronicles 34 : 14, 15.

  B. The Effect of the Discovery on Josiah.

    2 Kings 22 : 9–13.   2 Chronicles 34 : 16–21.

  C. The Words of Huldah the Prophetess.

    2 Kings 22 : 14–20.   2 Chronicles 34 : 22–28.

  D. The Reading of the Book of the Law.

    2 Kings 23 : 1, 2.   2 Chronicles 34 : 29, 30.

 (7) The Making of the Covenant.

    2 Kings 23 : 3.   2 Chronicles 34 : 31, 32.

 (8) Josiah's further Reformations.

    2 Kings 23 : 4–14, 24.   2 Chronicles 34 : 33.

(9) The Fulfillment of the Prophecy of the " Man of God out of Judah."

2 Kings 23:15-20.

(10) The Keeping of the Passover.

2 Kings 23:21, 23.	2 Chronicles 35:1-19.

(11) The Death of Josiah.

2 Kings 23:28-30a.	2 Chron. 35:26, 27, 20-25.

179. The Reign of Jehoahaz.

(1) The Accession of Jehoahaz.

2 Kings 23:30b, 31.	2 Chronicles 36:1, 2.

(2) The Character of Jehoahaz.

2 Kings 23:32.

(3) Jehoahaz is deposed by Pharaoh-necoh.

2 Kings 23:33.	2 Chronicles 36:3.

180. The Reign of Jehoiakim.

(1) Jehoiakim is made King by Pharaoh-necoh.

2 Kings 23:34a, 36.	2 Chronicles 36:4a, 5a.

(2) The Captivity of Jehoahaz.

2 Kings 23:34b.	2 Chronicles 36:4b.

(3) The Character of Jehoiakim.

2 Kings 23:37.	2 Chronicles 36:5b.

(4) Jehoiakim Tributary to Pharaoh-necoh.

2 Kings 23:35.

(5) Jehoiakim Tributary to Nebuchadnezzar.

2 Kings 24:1a, 7.	2 Chronicles 36:6, 7.

(6) Jehoiakim's Rebellion.

2 Kings 24:1b.

(7) Jehoiakim's many Adversaries.

2 Kings 24:2-4.

(8) The Death of Jehoiakim.

2 Kings 24:5, 6a.	2 Chronicles 36:8a.

181. The Reign of Jehoiachin.

(1) Jehoiachin's Accession to the Throne.

2 Kings 24:6b, 8.	2 Chronicles 36:8b, 9a.

(2) The Character of Jehoiachin.

2 Kings 24:9.	2 Chronicles 36:9b.

(3) Jehoiachin is taken Captive by Nebuchadnezzar.

2 Kings 24:10-12.

182. The Reign of Zedekiah.

(1) Zedekiah is made King by Nebuchadnezzar.

2 Kings 24:17, 18.	2 Chronicles 36:10b, 11.

(2) The great Deportation to Babylon.
    2 Kings 24:13-16.   2 Chronicles 36: 10*a*.
(3) The Character of Zedekiah.
    2 Kings 24:19.   2 Chronicles 36: 12.
(4) Zedekiah's Rebellion.
    2 Kings 24:20*b*.   2 Chronicles 36:13*a*.
(5) The Wickedness of the People the Cause of their Ruin.
    2 Kings 24:20*a*.   2 Chronicles 36:13*b*-16.
(6) The Siege of Jerusalem.
    2 Kings 25:1, 2.
(7) Zedekiah is taken Captive by Nebuchadnezzar.
    2 Kings 25:3-7.
183. Appendix to the History of the Kingdom of Judah.
    (1) The Overthrow of Jerusalem.
        2 Kings 25:8-10.   2 Chronicles 36:17, 19.
    (2) The remaining Nobles Slain.
        2 Kings 25:18-21*a*.
    (3) The Treasure taken by the Chaldeans.
        2 Kings 25:13-17.   2 Chronicles 36:18.
    (4) The last Deportation to Babylon.
        2 Kings 25:11.   2 Chronicles 36:20*a*.
        2 Kings 25:21*b*.   1 Chronicles 9:1*b*.
    (5) The Length of the Captivity.
                                   2 Chronicles 36:20*b*, 21.
    (6) Gedaliah is made Governor of Judah.
        2 Kings 25:12, 22.
    (7) The Murder of Gedaliah and Flight of the People.
        2 Kings 25:23-26.
    (8) Jehoiachin is set at Liberty.
        2 Kings 25:27-30.
    (9) The Proclamation of Cyrus permitting the Return from the Captivity.
                                   2 Chronicles 36:22, 23.

THE BOOKS OF THE KINGS OF JUDAH AND ISRAEL.

BOOK FIRST.
UNTIL THE FOUNDING OF THE MONARCHY.

PART I.
GENEALOGICAL TABLES, WITH BRIEF HISTORICAL STATEMENTS.

I. Genealogies of the Patriarchs.

1. THE GENEALOGY FROM ADAM TO NOAH.[a]

1 *Chronicles* 1 : 1-4.

1 Adam, Seth, Enosh, 2 Kenan, Mahalalel, Jared; 3 Enoch, Methuselah, Lamech; 4 Noah, Shem, Ham, and Japheth.

2. THE DESCENDANTS OF NOAH'S SONS.

1 *Chronicles* 1 : 5-23.

5 The sons of Japheth; Gomer, and Magog, and Madai, and Javan, and Tubal, and Meshech, and Tiras. 6 And the sons of Gomer; Ashkenaz, and [b]Diphath, and Togarmah. 7 And the sons of Javan; Elishah, and Tarshish, Kittim, and [c]Rodanim.

8 The sons of Ham; Cush, and Mizraim, Put, and Canaan. 9 And the sons of Cush; Seba, and Havilah, and Sabta, and Raama, and Sabteca. And the sons of Raamah; Sheba, and Dedan. 10 And Cush begat Nimrod: he began to be a mighty one in the earth. 11 And Mizraim begat Ludim, and Anamim, and Lehabim, and Naphtuhim, 12 and Pathrusim, and Casluhim (from whence came [d]the Philistines), and Caphtorim. 13 And Canaan begat Zidon his firstborn, and Heth; 14 and the Jebusite, and the Amorite, and Girgashite; 15 and the Hivite, and the Arkite, and the Sinite; 16 and the Arvadite, and the Zemarite, and the Hamathite.

17 The sons of Shem; Elam, and Asshur, and Arpachshad, and Lud, and Aram, and Uz, and Hul, and Gether, and [e]Meshech. 18 And Arpachshad begat Shelah, and Shelah begat Eber. 19 And unto Eber were born two sons: the name of the one was Peleg; for in his days the earth was divided; and his brother's name was Joktan. 20 And Joktan begat Almodad, and Sheleph, and Hazarmaveth, and Jerah; 21 and Hadoram, and Uzal, and Diklah; 22 and [f]Ebal, and Abimael, and Sheba; 23 and Ophir, and Havilah, and Jobab. All these were the sons of Joktan.

---

a With this and the following sections of Part I, cf. references in Genesis, Joshua, Ruth, Nehemiah, Matthew, and Luke, as suggested in the Appendix, §§1, 2, 3, 5, 9, and 10.   *b* In Genesis 10 : 3, " Riphath."   *c* In Genesis 10 : 4, " Dodanim."
d Heb. " Pelishtim."   *e* In Genesis 10 : 23, " Mash."   *f* In Genesis 10 : 28, " Obal."

3. FROM SHEM TO ABRAHAM.

1 Chronicles 1 : 24–27.

24 Shem, Arpachshad, Shelah ; 25 Eber, Peleg, Reu ; 26 Serug, Nahor, Terah ; 27 Abram (the same is Abraham).

4. THE DESCENDANTS OF ABRAHAM.

1 Chronicles 1 : 28–42.

28 The sons of Abraham ; Isaac, and Ishmael.

29 These are their generations : the firstborn of Ishmael, Nebaioth ; then Kedar, and Adbeel, and Mibsam 30 Mishma, and Dumah, Massa ; Hadad, and Tema, 31 Jetur, Naphish, and Kedemah. These are the sons of Ishmael.

32 And the sons of Keturah, Abraham's concubine: she bare Zimran, and Jokshan, and Medan, and Midian, and Ishbak, and Shuah. And the sons of Jokshan ; Sheba, and Dedan. 33 And the sons of Midian ; Ephah, and Epher, and Hanoch, and Abida, and Eldaah. All these were the sons of Keturah.

34 And Abraham begat Isaac. The sons of Isaac ; Esau, and Israel.

35 The sons of Esau ; Eliphaz, Reuel, and Jeush, and Jalam, and Korah. 36 The sons of Eliphaz ; Teman, and Omar, *a* Zephi, and Gatam, Kenaz, and Timna, and Amalek. 37 The sons of Reuel ; Nahath, Zerah, Shammah, and Mizzah. 38 And the sons of Seir ; Lotan and Shobal and Zibeon and Anah, and Dishon and Ezer and Dishan. 39 And the sons of Lotan ; Hori and *b* Homam : and Timna was Lotan's sister. 40 The sons of Shobal ; *c* Alian and Manahath and Ebal, *d* Shephi and Onam. And the sons of Zibeon ; Aiah and Anah. 41 The sons of Anah ; Dishon. And the sons of Dishon ; *e* Hamran and Eshban and Ithran and Cheran. 42 The sons of Ezer ; Bilhan and Zaavan, *f* Jaakan. The sons of Dishan ; Uz and Aran.

5. THE KINGS AND DUKES OF EDOM.

1 Chronicles 1 : 43–54.

43 Now these are the kings that reigned in the land of Edom, before there reigned any king over the children of Israel : Bela the son of Beor ; and the name of his city was Dinhabah. 44 And Bela died, and Jobab the son of Zerah of Bozrah reigned in his stead. 45 And Jobab died, and Husham of the land of the Temanites reigned in his stead. 46 And Husham died, and Hadad the son of Bedad, which smote Midian in the field of Moab, reigned in his stead : and the name of his city was Avith. 47 And Hadad died, and Samlah of Masrekah reigned in his stead. 48 And Samlah died, and Shaul of Rehoboth by the River reigned in his stead. 49 And Shaul died, and Baal-hanan the son of Achbor reigned in his stead. 50 And Baal-hanan died, and *g* Hadad reigned in his stead ; and the name of his city was *h* Pai : and his wife's name was Mehetabel, the daughter of Matred, the daughter of Me-zahab. 51 And Hadad died. And the dukes of Edom were ; duke Timna, duke *i* Aliah, duke Jetheth ; 52 duke Oholibamah, duke Elah, duke Pinon ; 53 duke Kenaz, duke Teman, duke Mibzar ; 54 duke Magdiel, duke Iram. These are the dukes of Edom.

6. THE TWELVE SONS OF ISRAEL.

1 Chronicles 2 : 1, 2.

1 These are the sons of Israel ; Reuben, Simeon, Levi, and Judah, Issachar and Zebulun ; 2 Dan, Joseph and Benjamin Naphtali, Gad and Asher.

---

a In Genesis 36: 11, ". Zepho." *b* In Genesis 36: 22, "Hemam." *c* In Genesis 36: 23, ". Alvan." *d* In Genesis 36: 23, "Shepho." *e* In Genesis 36: 26, "Hemdan." *f* In Genesis 36: 27, "and Akan." *g* In Genesis 36: 39, "Hadar." *h* In Genesis 36: 39, " Pau." *i* In Genesis 36: 40, "Alvah."

II. Genealogies of the Tribes of Israel.

7. THE TRIBE OF JUDAH.

(1) GENERAL GENEALOGIES OF THE TRIBE.

1 *Chronicles* 2 : 3–17, 21–41.

3 The sons of Judah; Er, and Onan, and Shelah: which three were born unto him of Bath-shua the Canaanitess. And Er, Judah's firstborn, was wicked in the sight of the LORD; and he slew him. 4 And Tamar his daughter in law bare him Perez and Zerah. All the sons of Judah were five. 5 The sons of Perez; Hezron and Hamul. 6 And the sons of Zerah; *a* Zimri, and Ethan, and Heman, and Calcol, and *b* Dara: five of them in all. 7 And the sons of Carmi; *c* Achar, the troubler of Israel, who committed a trespass in the devoted thing. 8 And the sons of Ethan; Azariah. 9 The sons also of Hezron, that were born unto him; Jerahmeel, and Ram, and Chelubai. 10 And Ram begat Amminadab; and Amminadab begat Nahshon, prince of the children of Judah; 11 and Nahshon begat Salma, and Salma begat Boaz; 12 and Boaz begat Obed, and Obed begat Jesse; 13 and Jesse begat his firstborn Eliab, and Abinadab the second, and Shimea the third; 14 Nethanel the fourth, Raddai the fifth; 15 Ozem the sixth, David the seventh: 16 and their sisters were Zeruiah and Abigail. And the sons of Zeruiah; *d* Abishai, and Joab, and Asahel, three. 17 And Abigail bare Amasa: and the father of Amasa was Jether the Ishmaelite. 21 And afterward Hezron went in to the daughter of Machir the father of Gilead; whom he took *to wife* when he was threescore years old; and she bare him Segub. 22 And Segub begat Jair, who had three and twenty cities in the land of Gilead. 23 And Geshur and Aram took *e* the towns of Jair from them, with Kenath, and the *f* villages thereof, even threescore cities. All these were the sons of Machir the father of Gilead. 24 And after that Hezron was dead in Caleb-ephrathah, then Abiah Hezron's wife bare him Ashhur the father of Tekoa. 25 And the sons of Jerahmeel the firstborn of Hezron were Ram the firstborn, and Bunah, and Oren, and Ozem, Ahijah. 26 And Jerahmeel had another wife, whose name was Atarah; she was the mother of Onam. 27 And the sons of Ram the

1 *Chronicles* 4 : 1–23.

1 The sons of Judah; Perez, Hezron, and Carmi, and Hur, and Shobal. 2 And Reaiah the son of Shobal begat Jahath; and Jahath begat Ahumai and Lahad. These are the families of the Zorathites. 3 And these were *the sons of* the father of Etam; Jezreel, and Ishma, and Idbash: and the name of their sister was Hazzelelponi: 4 and Penuel the father of Gedor, and Ezer the father of Hushah. These are the sons of Hur, the firstborn of Ephrathah, the father of Beth-lehem. 5 And Ashhur the father of Tekoa had two wives, Helah and Naarah. 6 And Naarah bare him Ahuzzam, and Hepher, and Temeni, and Haahashtari. These were the sons of Naarah. 7 And the sons of Helah were Zereth, *g* Izhar, and Ethnan. 8 And Hakkoz begat Anub, and Zobebah, and the families of Aharhel the son of Harum. 9 And Jabez was more honourable than his brethren: and his mother called his name Jabez, saying, Because I bare him with sorrow. 10 And Jabez called on the God of Israel, saying, Oh that thou wouldest bless me indeed, and enlarge my border, and that thine hand might be with me, and that thou wouldest keep me from evil, that it be not to my sorrow! And God granted him that which he requested. 11 And Chelub the brother of Shuhah begat Mehir, which was the father of Eshton. 12 And Eshton begat Beth-rapha, and Paseah, and Tehinnah the father of *h* Ir-nahash. These are the men of Recah. 13 And the sons of Kenaz; Othniel, and Seraiah: and the sons of Othniel; Hathath. 14 And Meonothai begat Ophrah: and Seraiah begat Joab the father of *i* Ge-harashim; for they were craftsmen. 15 And the sons of Caleb the son of Jephunneh; Iru, Elah, and Naam: and the sons of Elah; and Kenaz. 16 And the sons of Jehallelel; Ziph, and Ziphah, Tiria, and Asarel. 17 And the sons of Ezrah; Jether, and Mered, and Epher, and Jalon: and she bare Miriam, and Shammai, and Ishbah the father of Eshtemoa. 18 And his wife *k* the Jewess bare Jered the father of Gedor, and Heber the father

a In Joshua 7 : 1, " Zabdi."   *b* Many ancient authorities read, " Darda."   Cf. 1 Kings 4 : 31. See §135, (3).   *c* In Joshua 7 : 1, " Achan."   *d* Heb. " Abshai."   *e* Or, " Havvoth-jair."   *f* Heb. " daughters."   *g* Another reading is, " and Zohar."   *h* Or, " the city of Nahash."   *i* Or, " the valley of craftsmen."   *k* Or, " Ha-jehudijah."

1 *Chronicles* 2.

firstborn of Jerahmeel were Maaz, and Jamin, and Eker. 28 And the sons of Onam were Shammai, and Jada : and the sons of Shammai ; Nadab, and Abishur. 29 And the name of the wife of Abishur was Abihail ; and she bare him Ahban, and Molid. 30 And the sons of Nadab ; Seled, and Appaim : but Seled died without *a* children. 31 And the sons of Appaim ; Ishi. And the sons of Ishi ; Sheshan. And the sons of Sheshan ; Ahlai. 32 And the sons of Jada the brother of Shammai; Jether, and Jonathan : and Jether died without *a* children. 33 And the sons of Jonathan ; Peleth, and Zaza. These were the sons of Jerahmeel. 34 Now Sheshan had no sons, but daughters. And Sheshan had a servant, an Egyptian, whose name was Jarha. 35 And Sheshan gave his daughter to Jarha his servant to wife ; and she bare him Attai. 36 And Attai begat Nathan, and Nathan begat Zabad ; 37 and Zabad begat Ephlal, and Ephlal begat Obed ; 38 and Obed begat Jehu, and Jehu begat Azariah ; 39 and Azariah begat Helez, and Helez begat Eleasah ; 40 and Eleasah begat Sismai, and Sismai begat Shallum ; 41 and Shallum begat Jekamiah, and Jekamiah begat Elishama.

1 *Chronicles* 4.

of Soco, and Jekuthiel the father of Zanoah. And these are the sons of Bithiah the daughter of Pharaoh, which Mered took. 19 And the sons of the wife of Hodiah, the sister of Naham, were the father of Keilah the Garmite, and Eshtemoa the Maacathite. 20 And the sons of Shimon ; Amnon, and Rinnah, Ben-hanan, and Tilon. And the sons of Ishi ; Zoheth, and Ben-zoheth. 21 The sons of Shelah the son of Judah ; Er the father of Lecah, and Laadah the father of Mareshah, and the families of the house of them that wrought fine linen, of the house of Ashbea ; 22 and Jokim, and the men of Cozeba, and Joash, and Saraph, who had dominion in Moab, and Jashubi-lehem. And the *b* records are ancient. 23 These were the potters, and *c* the inhabitants of Netaim and Gederah : there they dwelt with the king for his work.

(2) THREE ACCOUNTS OF THE DESCENDANTS OF CALEB. *d*

1 *Chronicles* 2 : 18–20.

18 And Caleb the son of Hezron begat *children* of Azubah *his* wife, and of Jerioth : and these were her sons ; Jesher, and Shobab, and Ardon. 19 And Azubah died, and Caleb took unto him Ephrath, which bare him Hur. 20 And Hur begat Uri, and Uri begat Bezalel.

1 *Chronicles* 2 : 42–49.

42 And the sons of Caleb the brother of Jerahmeel were Mesha his firstborn, which was the father of Ziph ; and the sons of Mareshah the father of Hebron. 43 And the sons of Hebron ; Korah, and Tappuah, and Rekem, and Shema. 44 And Shema begat Raham, the father of Jorkeam ; and Rekem begat Shammai. 45 And the son of Shammai was Maon ; and Maon was the father of Bethzur. 46 And Ephah, Caleb's concubine, bare Haran, and Moza, and Gazez : and Haran begat Gazez. 47 And the sons of Jahdai ; Regem, and Jotham, and Geshan, and Pelet, and Ephah, and Shaaph. 48 Maacah, Caleb's concubine, bare Sheber and Tirhanah. 49 She

1 *Chronicles* 2 : 50–55.

50 These were the sons of Caleb ; the *e* son of Hur, the firstborn of Ephratah, Shobal the father of Kiriath-jearim ; 51 Salma the father of Beth-lehem, Hareph the father of Bethgader. 52 And Shobal the father of Kiriath-jearim had sons ; Haroeh, half of the Menuhoth. 53 And the families of Kiriath-jearim ; the Ithrites, and the Puthites, and the Shumathites, and the Mishraites ; of them came the Zorathites and the Eshtaolites. 54 The sons of Salma ; Beth-lehem, and the Netophathites, Atroth-beth-Joab, and half of the Manahathites, the Zorites. 55 And the families of scribes which dwelt at Jabez ; the Tirathites, the Shimeathites, the Sucathites. These

---

a Or, "sons." *b* Heb. "words." *c* Or, "those that dwelt among plantations and hedges." *d* To be distinguished from Caleb, the son of Jephunneh, in ch. 4 : 15. *e* The Sept. has, "sons," which is, doubtless, the correct reading.

1 *Chronicles* 2.	1 *Chronicles* 2.
bare also Shaaph the father of Madmannah, Sheva the father of Machbena, and the father of Gibea ; and the daughter of Caleb was Achsah.	are the Kenites that came of Hammath, the father of the house of Rechab.

(3) THE FAMILY OF DAVID.[a]

[1 *Chronicles* 3 : 1–9.]

1 Now these were the sons of David, which were born unto him in Hebron : the firstborn, Amnon, of Ahinoam the Jezreelitess ; the second, Daniel, of Abigail the Carmelitess ; 2 the third, Absalom the son of Maacah the daughter of Talmai king of Geshur; the fourth, Adonijah the son of Haggith ; 3 the fifth, Shephatiah of Abital ; the sixth, Ithream by Eglah his wife. 4 Six were born unto him in Hebron ; and there he reigned seven years and six months : and in Jerusalem he reigned thirty and three years. 5 And these were born unto him in Jerusalem : Shimea, and Shobab, and Nathan, and Solomon, four, of Bath-shua the daughter of Ammiel : 6 and Ibhar, and Elishama, and Eliphelet ; 7 and Nogah, and Nepheg, and Japhia; 8 and Elishama, and Eliada, and Eliphelet, nine. 9 All these were the sons of David, beside the sons of the concubines ; and Tamar was their sister.

(4) THE LINE OF DAVID, THROUGH SOLOMON.

1 *Chronicles* 3 : 10–24.

10 And Solomon's son was Rehoboam, Abijah his son, Asa his son, Jehoshaphat his son; 11 Joram his son, Ahaziah his son, Joash his son ; 12 Amaziah his son, Azariah his son, Jotham his son ; 13 Ahaz his son, Hezekiah his son, Manasseh his son ; 14 Amon his son, Josiah his son. 15 And the sons of Josiah ; the firstborn Johanan, the second Jehoiakim, the third Zedekiah, the fourth Shallum. 16 And the sons of Jehoiakim : Jeconiah his son, Zedekiah his son. 17 And the sons of Jeconiah, [b] the captive ; Shealtiel his son, 18 and Malchiram, and Pedaiah, and Shenazzar, Jekamiah, Hoshama, and Nedabiah. 19 And the sons of Pedaiah ; Zerubbabel, and Shimei : and the [c] sons of Zerubbabel ; Meshullam, and Hananiah ; and Shelomith was their sister : 20 and Hashubah, and Ohel, and Berechiah, and Hasadiah, Jushab-hesed, five. 21 And the [c] sons of Hananiah ; Pelatiah, and Jeshaiah : the sons of Rephaiah, the sons of Arnan, the sons of Obadiah, the sons of Shecaniah. 22 And the sons of Shecaniah ; Shemaiah : and the sons of Shemaiah ; Hattush, and Igal, and Bariah, and Neariah, and Shaphat, six. 23 And the [c] sons of Neariah ; Elioenai, and Hizkiah, and Azrikam, three. 24 And the sons of Elioenai ; Hodaviah, and Eliashib, and Pelaiah, and Akkub, and Johanan, and Delaiah, and Anani, seven.

8. THE TRIBE OF LEVI.

(1) THE LINE OF AARON.

1 *Chronicles* 6 : 1–15.	1 *Chronicles* 6 : 49–53.
1 [d] The sons of Levi ; [e] Gershon, Kohath, and Merari. 2 And the sons of Kohath; Amram, Izhar, and Hebron, and Uzziel. 3 And the children of Amram ; Aaron, and Moses, and Miriam. And the sons of Aaron ; Nadab and Abihu, Eleazar and Ithamar. 4 Eleazar begat	49 But Aaron and his sons [f] offered upon the altar of burnt offering, and upon the altar of incense, for all the work of the most holy place, and to make atonement for Israel, according to all that Moses the servant of God had commanded. 50 And these are the sons of Aaron ;

---

a Cf. §§70 and 98.   *b* Or, "Assir."   *c* Heb. "son."   *d* Ch. 5 : 27 in Heb.   *e* In ver. 16, "Gershom."   *f* Or, "burnt incense."

5

1 *Chronicles* 6.

Phinehas, Phinehas begat Abishua; 5 and Abishua begat Bukki, and Bukki begat Uzzi; 6 and Uzzi begat Zerahiah, and Zerahiah begat Meraioth; 7 Meraioth begat Amariah, and Amariah begat Ahitub; 8 and Ahitub begat Zadok, and Zadok begat Ahimaaz; 9 and Ahimaaz begat Azariah, and Azariah begat Johanan; 10 and Johanan begat Azariah, (he it is that executed the priest's office in the house that Solomon built in Jerusalem :) 11 and Azariah begat Amariah, and Amariah begat Ahitub; 12 and Ahitub begat Zadok, and Zadok begat *a* Shallum; 13 and Shallum begat Hilkiah, and Hilkiah begat Azariah; 14 and Azariah begat Seraiah, and Seraiah begat Jehozadak; 15 and Jehozadak went *into captivity*, when the LORD carried away Judah and Jerusalem by the hand of Nebuchadnezzar.

1 *Chronicles* 6.

Eleazar his son, Phinehas his son, Abishua his son; 51 Bukki his son, Uzzi his son, Zerahiah his son; 52 Meraioth his son, Amariah his son, Ahitub his son; 53 Zadok his son, Ahimaaz his son.

(2) THE DESCENDANTS OF GERSHOM, KOHATH, AND MERARI.

1 *Chronicles* 6 : 16–30.

16 *b* The sons of Levi; *c* Gershom, Kohath, and Merari. 17 And these be the names of the sons of Gershom; Libni and Shimei. 18 And the sons of Kohath were Amram, and Izhar, and Hebron, and Uzziel. 19 The sons of Merari; Mahli and Mushi. And these are the families of the Levites according to their fathers' *houses.* 20 Of Gershom; Libni his son, Jahath his son, Zimmah his son; 21 *d* Joah his son, *e* Iddo his son, Zerah his son, *f* Jeatherai his son. 22 The sons of Kohath; *g* Amminadab his son, Korah his son, Assir his son; 23 Elkanah his son, and Ebiasaph his son, and Assir his son; 24 Tahath his son, *h* Uriel his son, Uzziah his son, and Shaul his son. 25 And the sons of Elkanah; Amasai, and Ahimoth. 26 As for Elkanah: the sons of Elkanah; *i* Zophai his son, and *k* Nahath his son; 27 *l* Eliab his son, Jeroham his son, Elkanah his son. 28 And the sons of Samuel; the firstborn *m* Joel, and the second Abiah. 29 The sons of Merari; Mahli, Libni his son, Shimei his son, Uzzah his son; 30 Shimea his son, Haggiah his son, Asaiah his son.

(3) THE ANCESTORS OF THE SONGMASTERS, HEMAN, ASAPH, AND ETHAN.

1 *Chronicles* 6 : 31–48.

31 And these are they whom David set over the service of song in the house of the LORD, after that the ark had rest. 32 And they ministered with song before the tabernacle of the tent of meeting, until Solomon had built the house of the LORD in Jerusalem: and they *n* waited on their office according to their order. 33 And these are they that *n* waited, and their sons. Of the sons of the Kohathites: Heman the singer, the son of Joel, the son of Samuel; 34 the son of Elkanah, the son of Jeroham, the son of Eliel, the son of *o* Toah; 35 the son of *p* Zuph, the son of Elkanah, the son of Mahath, the son of Amasai; 36 the son of Elkanah, the son of *q* Joel, the son of Azariah, the son of Zephaniah; 37 the son of Tahath, the son of Assir, the son of Ebiasaph, the son of Korah; 38 the son of Izhar, the son of Kohath, the son of Levi, the son of Israel. 39 And his brother Asaph, who stood on his right hand, even Asaph the son of Berechiah, the

---

a In ch. 9 : 11, " Meshullam." See §19, (2). *b* Ch. 6 : 1 in Heb.   *c* In ver. 1, " Gershon."   *d* In ver. 42, " Ethan."
e In ver. 41, " Adaiah," *f* In ver. 41, " Ethni."   *g* In vv. 2, 18, 38, " Izhar."   *h* In ver. 36, " Zephaniah, Azariah, Joel."
i In ver. 35, " Zuph."   *k* In ver. 34, " Toah."   *l* In ver. 34, " Eliel."   *m* So the Syriac. See ver. 33, §8, (3), and 1 Samuel 8 : 2,
§29. The Hebrew text has, " Vashni, and Abiah."   *n* Heb. " stood."   *o* In ver. 26, " Nahath."   *p* In ver. 26, " Zophai."
q In ver. 24, " Shaul, Uzziah, Uriel."

1 *Chronicles* 6.

son of Shimea; 40 the son of Michael, the son of Baaseiah, the son of Malchijah; 41 the son of Ethni, the son of Zerah, the son of Adaiah; 42 the son of Ethan, the son of Zimmah, the son of Shimei; 43 the son of Jahath, the son of Gershom, the son of Levi. 44 And on the left hand their brethren the sons of Merari: *a* Ethan the son of *b* Kishi, the son of Abdi, the son of Malluch; 45 the son of Hashabiah, the son of Amaziah, the son of Hilkiah; 46 the son of Amzi, the son of Bani, the son of Shemer; 47 the son of Mahli, the son of Mushi, the son of Merari, the son of Levi. 48 And their brethren the Levites were *c* appointed for all the service of the tabernacle of the house of God.

(4) THE CITIES OF THE LEVITES.

1 *Chronicles* 6 : 54–81.

54 Now these are their dwelling places according to their encampments in their borders: to the sons of Aaron, of the families of the Kohathites, for theirs was the *d first* lot, 55 to them they gave Hebron in the land of Judah, and the suburbs thereof round about it; 56 but the fields of the city, and the villages thereof, they gave to Caleb the son of Jephunneh. 57 And *e* to the sons of Aaron they gave the cities of refuge, Hebron; Libnah also with her suburbs, and Jattir, and Eshtemoa with her suburbs; 58 and *f* Hilen with her suburbs, Debir with her suburbs; 59 and *g* Ashan with her suburbs, and Beth-shemesh with her suburbs: 60 and out of the tribe of Benjamin; Geba with her suburbs, and *h* Allemeth with her suburbs, and Anathoth with her suburbs. All their cities throughout their families were thirteen cities. 61 *i* And unto the rest of the sons of Kohath *were given* by lot, out of the family of the tribe, out of the half tribe, the half of Manasseh, ten cities. 62 And to the sons of Gershom, according to their families, out of the tribe of Issachar, and out of the tribe of Asher, and out of the tribe of Naphtali, and out of the tribe of Manasseh in Bashan, thirteen cities. 63 Unto the sons of Merari *were given* by lot, according to their families, out of the tribe of Reuben, and out of the tribe of Gad, and out of the tribe of Zebulun, twelve cities. 64 And the children of Israel gave to the Levites the cities with their suburbs. 65 And they gave by lot out of the tribe of the children of Judah, and out of the tribe of the children of Simeon, and out of the tribe of the children of Benjamin, these cities which are mentioned by name. 66 And some of the families of the sons of Kohath had cities of their borders out of the tribe of Ephraim. 67 And they gave unto them the cities of refuge, Shechem in the hill country of Ephraim with her suburbs; Gezer also with her suburbs; 68 *k* and Jokmeam with her suburbs, and Beth-horon with her suburbs; 69 and Aijalon with her suburbs, and Gathrimmon with her suburbs: 70 and out of the half tribe of Manasseh; Aner with her suburbs, and Bileam with her suburbs, for the rest of the family of the sons of Kohath. 71 Unto the sons of Gershom *were given*, out of the family of the half tribe of Manasseh, Golan in Bashan with her suburbs, and Ashtaroth with her suburbs: 72 and out of the tribe of Issachar; Kedesh with her suburbs, Daberath with her suburbs; 73 and Ramoth with her suburbs, and Anem with her suburbs: 74 and out of the tribe of Asher; Mashal with her suburbs, and Abdon with her suburbs; 75 and Hukok with her suburbs, and Rehob with her suburbs: 76 and out of the tribe of Naphtali; Kedesh in Galilee with her suburbs, and Hammon with her suburbs, and Kiriathaim with her suburbs. 77 Unto the rest of *the Levites*, the sons of Merari, *were given*, out of the tribe of Zebulun, Rimmono with her suburbs, Tabor with her suburbs: 78 and beyond the Jordan at Jericho on the east side of Jordan, *were given them*, out of the tribe of Reuben, Bezer in the wilderness with her suburbs, and Jahzah with her suburbs, 79 and Kedemoth with her suburbs, and Mephaath with her suburbs: 80 and out of the tribe of Gad; Ramoth in Gilead with her suburbs, and Mahanaim with her suburbs, 81 and Heshbon with her suburbs, and Jazer with her suburbs.

---

a In ch. 9 : 16, " Jeduthun." See §19, (2). *b* In ch. 15 : 17, " Kushaiah." See §94, (2). *c* Heb. " given." See Numbers 3 : 9. *d* See Joshua 21 : 4, 10. *e* See Joshua 21 : 13, etc. *f* In Joshua 21 : 15, " Holon." *g* In Joshua 21 : 16, " Ain." *h* In Joshua 21 : 18, "Almon." *i* See vv. 66–70, below, and Joshua 21 : 5. *k* See Joshua 21 : 22–39, where some of the names are different.

9. THE TRIBE OF REUBEN.

1 *Chronicles* 5 : 1–10.

1 And the sons of Reuben the firstborn of Israel, (for he was the firstborn ; but, forasmuch as he defiled his father's couch, his birthright was given unto the sons of Joseph the son of Israel ; and the genealogy is not to be reckoned after the birthright.   2 For Judah prevailed above his brethren, and of him came the *a* prince ; but the birthright was Joseph's :) 3 the sons of Reuben the firstborn of Israel ; Hanoch, and Pallu, Hezron, and Carmi.   4 The sons of Joel ; Shemaiah his son, Gog his son, Shimei his son ; 5 Micah his son, Reaiah his son, Baal his son ; 6 Beerah his son, whom *b* Tilgath-pilneser king of Assyria carried away captive : he was prince of the Reuben- ites.   7 And his brethren by their families, when the genealogy of their generations was reckoned ; the chief, Jeiel, and Zechariah, 8 and Bela the son of Azaz, the son of Shema, the son of Joel, who dwelt in Aroer, even unto Nebo and Baal-meon : 9 and eastward he dwelt even unto the entering in of the wilderness from the river Euphrates : because their cattle were multiplied in the land of Gilead.   10 And in the days of Saul they made war with the Hagrites, who fell by their hand : and they dwelt in their tents throughout all the *land* east of Gilead.

10. THE TRIBE OF GAD.

1 *Chronicles* 5 : 11–17.

11 And the sons of Gad dwelt over against them, in the land of Bashan unto Salecah : 12 Joel the chief, and Shapham the second, and Janai, and Shaphat in Bashan : 13 and their brethren of their fathers' houses ; Michael, and Meshullam, and Sheba, and Jorai, and Jacan, and Zia, and Eber, seven.   14 These were the sons of Abihail the son of Huri, the son of Jaroah, the son of Gilead, the son of Michael, the son of Jeshishai, the son of Jahdo, the son of Buz ; 15 Ahi the son of Ab- diel, the son of Guni, chief of their fathers' houses.   16 And they dwelt in Gilead in Bashan, and in her *c* towns, and in all the *d* suburbs of Sharon, as far as their *e* borders.   17 All these were reckoned by genealogies in the days of Jotham king of Judah, and in the days of Jeroboam king of Israel.

11. THE HALF-TRIBE OF MANASSEH (EAST OF JORDAN).

1 *Chronicles* 5 : 23, 24.

23 And the children of the half tribe of Manasseh dwelt in the land : they increased from Bashan unto Baal-hermon and Senir and mount Hermon.   24 And these were the heads of their fathers' houses ; even Epher, and Ishi, and Eliel, and Azriel, and Jeremiah, and Hodaviah, and Jahdiel, mighty men of valour, famous men, heads of their fathers' houses.

12. THE TRIBE OF SIMEON.

1 *Chronicles* 4 : 24–43.

24 The sons of Simeon ; *f* Nemuel, and Jamin, *g* Jarib, *h* Zerah, Shaul : 25 Shallum his son, Mibsam his son, Mishma his son.   26 And the sons of Mishma ; Hammuel his son, Zaccur his son, Shimei his son.   27 And Shimei had sixteen sons and six daughters ; but his brethren had not many children, neither did all their family multiply, like to the children of Judah.   28 And they dwelt at Beer-sheba, and Moladah, and Hazar-shual ; 29 and at Bilhah, and at Ezem, and at Tolad ; 30 and at Bethuel, and at Hormah, and at Ziklag ; 31 and at Beth-marcaboth, and Hazar- susim, and at Beth-biri, and at Shaaraim.   These were their cities unto the reign of David. 32 And their villages were Etam, and Ain, Rimmon, and Tochen, and Ashan, five cities : 33 and

---

a Or, "leader."   *b* In 2 Kings 15 : 29 and 16 : 7, "Tiglath-pileser." See §§169, (6), and 171, (5).   *c* Heb. "daughters." *d* Or, "pasture lands."   *e* Heb. "goings forth."   *f* In Genesis 46 : 10 and Exodus 6 : 15, "Jemuel."   *g* In Genesis 46 : 10, "Jachin."   *h* In Genesis 46 : 10, "Zohar."

1 Chronicles 4.

all their villages that were round about the same cities, unto Baal. These were their habitations, and they have their genealogy. 34 And Meshobab, and Jamlech, and Joshah the son of Amaziah; 35 and Joel, and Jehu the son of Joshibiah, the son of Seraiah, the son of Asiel; 36 and Elioenai, and Jaakobah, and Jeshohaiah, and Asaiah, and Adiel, and Jesimiel, and Benaiah; 37 and Ziza the son of Shiphi, the son of Allon, the son of Jedaiah, the son of Shimri, the son of Shemaiah; 38 these mentioned by name were princes in their families: and their fathers' houses increased greatly. 39 And they went to the entering in of Gedor, even unto the east side of the valley, to seek pasture for their flocks. 40 And they found there pasture and good, and the land was wide, and quiet, and peaceable; for they that dwelt there aforetime were of Ham. 41 And these written by name came in the days of Hezekiah king of Judah, and smote their tents, and the Meunim that were found there, and *a* destroyed them utterly, unto this day, and dwelt in their stead: because there was pasture there for their flocks. 42 And some of them, even of the sons of Simeon, five hundred men, went to mount Seir, having for their captains Pelatiah, and Neariah, and Rephaiah, and Uzziel, the sons of Ishi. 43 And they smote the remnant of the Amalekites that escaped, and dwelt there, unto this day.

13. THE TRIBE OF ISSACHAR.

1 Chronicles 7 : 1-5.

1 And of the sons of Issachar; Tola, and *b* Puah, Jashub, and Shimron, four. 2 And the sons of Tola; Uzzi, and Rephaiah, and Jeriel, and Jahmai, and Ibsam, and Shemuel, heads of their fathers' houses, *to wit*, of Tola; mighty men of valour in their generations: their number in the days of David was two and twenty thousand and six hundred. 3 And the sons of Uzzi; Izrahiah: and the sons of Izrahiah; Michael, and Obadiah, and Joel, Isshiah, five: all of them chief men. 4 And with them, by their generations, after their fathers' houses, were bands of the host for war, six and thirty thousand: for they had many wives and sons. 5 And their brethren among all the families of Issachar, mighty men of valour, reckoned in all by genealogy, were fourscore and seven thousand.

14. THE TRIBE OF NAPHTALI.

1 Chronicles 7 : 13.

13 The sons of Naphtali; *c* Jahziel, and Guni, and Jezer, and *d* Shallum, the sons of Bilhah.

15. THE HALF-TRIBE OF MANASSEH (WEST OF JORDAN).

1 Chronicles 7 : 14-19.

14 The sons of Manasseh; Asriel, *e* whom *his wife* bare: (his concubine the Aramitess bare Machir the father of Gilead: 15 and Machir took a wife *f* of Huppim and Shuppim, *g* whose sister's name was Maacah;) and the name of the second was Zelophehad: and Zelophehad had daughters. 16 And Maacah the wife of Machir bare a son, and she called his name Peresh; and the name of his brother was Sheresh; and his sons were Ulam and Rakem. 17 And the sons of Ulam; Bedan. These were the sons of Gilead the son of Machir, the son of Manasseh. 18 And his sister Hammolecheth bare Ishhod, and *h* Abiezer, and Mahlah. 19 And the sons of Shemida were Ahian, and Shechem, and Likhi, and Aniam.

16. THE TRIBE OF EPHRAIM.

1 Chronicles 7 : 20-29.

20 And the sons of Ephraim; Shuthelah, and Bered his son, and Tahath his son, and Eleadah his son, and Tahath his son, 21 and Zabad his son, and Shuthelah his son, and Ezer, and Elead,

---

a Heb. " devoted them." *b* In Genesis 46 : 13, " Puvah, and Iob." *c* In Genesis 46 : 24, " Jahzeel." *d* In Genesis 46 : 24, " Shillem." *e* Or, according to the Sept., " whom his concubine the Aramitess bare; she bare," etc. *f* Or, " for." *g* Or, " and his." *h* In Numbers 26 : 30, " Iezer."

1 *Chronicles* 7.

whom the men of Gath that were born in the land slew, because they came down to take away their cattle.   22 And Ephraim their father mourned many days, and his brethren came to comfort him.   23 And he went in to his wife, and she conceived, and bare a son, and he called his name Beriah, because it went evil with his house.   24 And his daughter was Sheerah, who built Beth-horon the nether and the upper, and Uzzen-sheerah.   25 And Rephah was his son, and Resheph, and Telah his son, and Tahan his son ; 26 Ladan his son, Ammihud his son, Elishama his son ; 27 *a* Nun his son, Joshua his son.   28 And their possessions and habitations were Beth-el and the *b* towns thereof, and eastward *c* Naaran, and westward Gezer, with the towns thereof ; Shechem also and the towns thereof, unto *d* Azzah and the towns thereof : 29 and by the borders of the children of Manasseh, Beth-shean and her towns, Taanach and her towns, Megiddo and her towns, Dor and her towns.   In these dwelt the children of Joseph the son of Israel.

17. THE TRIBE OF ASHER.

1 *Chronicles* 7 : 30–40.

30 The sons of Asher ; Imnah, and Ishvah, and Ishvi, and Beriah, and Serah their sister. 31 And the sons of Beriah ; Heber, and Malchiel, who was the father of Birzaith.   32 And Heber begat Japhlet, and *e* Shomer, and Hotham, and Shua their sister.   33 And the sons of Japhlet ; Pasach, and Bimhal, and Ashvath.   These are the children of Japhlet.   34 And the sons of *f* Shemer ; Ahi, and Rohgah, Jehubbah, and Aram.   35 And the *g* sons of Helem his brother ; Zophah, and Imna, and Shelesh, and Amal.   36 The sons of Zophah ; Suah, and Harnepher, and Shual, and Beri, and Imrah ; 37 Bezer, and Hod, and Shamma, and Shilshah, and Ithran, and Beera. 38 And the sons of Jether ; Jephunneh, and Pispah, and Ara.   39 And the sons of Ulla ; Arah, and Hanniel, and Rizia.   40 All these were the children of Asher, heads of the fathers' houses, choice and mighty men of valour, chief of the princes.   And the number of them reckoned by genealogy for service in war was twenty and six thousand men.

18. THE TRIBE OF BENJAMIN.

(1) GENERAL GENEALOGIES OF THE TRIBE.

1 *Chronicles* 7 : 6–12.	1 *Chronicles* 8 : 1–28.
6 *The sons of* Benjamin ; Bela, and Becher, and Jediael, three. 7 And the sons of Bela ; Ezbon, and Uzzi, and Uzziel, and Jerimoth, and Iri, five ; heads of fathers' houses, mighty men of valour ; and they were reckoned by genealogy twenty and two thousand and thirty and four. 8 And the sons of Becher ; Zemirah, and Joash, and Eliezer, and Elioenai, and Omri, and Jeremoth, and Abijah, and Anathoth, and Alemeth. All these were the sons of Becher. 9 And they were reckoned by genealogy, after their generations, heads of their fathers' houses, mighty men of valour, twenty thousand and two hundred. And the sons of Jediael ; 10 Bilhan ; and the sons of Bilhan ; Jeush, and Benjamin, and Ehud, and Chenaanah, and Zethan, and Tarshish, and Ahishahar. 11 All these were the sons of Jedi-	1 And Benjamin begat Bela his firstborn, Ashbel the second, and Aharah the third ; 2 Nohah the fourth, and Rapha the fifth. 3 And Bela had sons, *h* Addar, and Gera, and Abihud ; 4 and Abishua, and Naaman, and Ahoah ; 5 and Gera, and *i* Shephuphan, and Huram. 6 And these are the sons of Ehud : these are the heads of fathers' *houses* of the inhabitants of Geba, and they carried them captive to Manahath : 7 and Naaman, and Ahijah, and Gera, he carried them captive ; and he begat Uzza and Ahihud. 8 And Shaharaim begat children in the field of Moab, after he had *k* sent them away ; Hushim and Baara were his wives. 9 And he begat of Hodesh his wife, Jobab, and Zibia, and Mesha, and Malcam ; 10 and Jeuz, and Shachia, and Mirmah. These were his sons, heads of

---

a Heb. " Non."   *b* Heb. " daughters."   *c* In Joshua 16 : 7, " Naarah."   *d* Many MSS. read, "Ayyah."   *e* In ver. 34, " Shemer."   *f* In ver. 32, " Shomer."   *g* Heb. " son."   *h* In Genesis 46 : 21, " Ard."   *i* In Numbers 26 : 39, " Shephupham." *k* Or, " sent away Hushim and Baara his wives."

1 Chronicles 7.

ael, according to the heads of their fathers' *houses*, mighty men of valour, seventeen thousand and two hundred, that were able to go forth in the host for war. 12 *a* Shuppim also, and Huppim, the sons of *b* Ir, Hushim, the sons of *c* Aher.

1 Chronicles 8.

fathers' *houses*. 11 And of Hushim he begat Abitub and Elpaal. 12 And the sons of Elpaal; Eber, and Misham, and Shemed, who built Ono and Lod, with the towns thereof ; 13 and Beriah, and Shema, who were heads of fathers' *houses* of the inhabitants of Aijalon, who put to flight the inhabitants of Gath ; 14 and Ahio, Shashak, and Jeremoth ; 15 and Zebadiah, and Arad, and Eder ; 16 and Michael, and Ishpah, and Joha, the sons of Beriah ; 17 and Zebadiah, and Meshullam, and Hizki, and Heber ; 18 and Ishmerai, and Izliah, and Jobab, the sons of Elpaal ; 19 and Jakim, and Zichri, and Zabdi ; 20 and Elienai, and Zillethai, and Eliel ; 21 and Adaiah, and Beraiah, and Shimrath, the sons of *d* Shimei ; 22 and Ishpan, and Eber, and Eliel ; 23 and Abdon, and Zichri, and Hanan ; 24 and Hananiah, and Elam, and Anthothijah ; 25 and Iphdeiah, and Penuel, the sons of Shashak ; 26 and Shamsherai, and Shehariah, and Athaliah ; 27 and Jaareshiah, and Elijah, and Zichri, the sons of Jeroham. 28 These were heads of fathers' *houses* throughout their generations, chief men : these dwelt in Jerusalem.

(2) THE HOUSE OF SAUL.

[1 Samuel 14 : 49–51.]	1 Chronicles 8 : 29–40.	1 Chronicles 9 : 35–44.
	29 And in Gibeon there dwelt the father of Gibeon, *Jeiel*, whose wife's name was Maacah : 30 and his firstborn son Abdon, and Zur, and Kish, and Baal, and Nadab ; 31 and Gedor, and Ahio, and Zecher. 32 And Mikloth begat Shimeah. And they also dwelt with their brethren in Jerusalem, over against their brethren. 33 And Ner begat Kish ; and Kish begat Saul ; and Saul begat Jonathan, and Malchi-shua, and Abinadab, and *e* Eshbaal. 34 And the son of Jonathan was *f* Merib-baal ; and Merib-baal begat Micah. 35 And the sons of Micah ; Pithon, and Melech, and Tarea, and Ahaz. 36 And Ahaz begat Jehoaddah ;	35 And in Gibeon there dwelt the father of Gibeon, Jeiel, whose wife's name was Maacah : 36 and his firstborn son Abdon, and Zur, and Kish, and Baal, and Ner, and Nadab ; 37 and Gedor, and Ahio, and Zechariah, and Mikloth. 38 And Mikloth begat Shimeam. And they also dwelt with their brethren in Jerusalem, over against their brethren. 39 And Ner begat Kish ; and Kish begat Saul ; and Saul begat Jonathan, and Malchi-shua, and Abinadab, and Eshbaal. 40 And the son of Jonathan was Merib-baal ; and Merib-baal begat Micah. 41 And the sons of Micah ; Pithon, and Melech, and Tahrea, *and Ahaz.*
49 Now the sons of Saul were Jonathan, and Ishvi, and Malchi-shua : and the names of his two daughters were these ; the name of the firstborn Merab, and the name of the younger Michal : 50 and the name of Saul's wife was Ahinoam the daughter of		

---

a In Numbers 26 : 39, "Shephupham *and* Hupham."   *b* In ver. 7, "Iri."   *c* In Numbers 26 : 38, "Ahiram."   *d* In ver. 13, "Shema."   *e* In 2 Samuel 2 : 8, "Ish-bosheth."   See §68.   *f* In 2 Samuel 4 : 4, and 9 : 6, 10, "Mephibosheth."   See §§63 and 96.

1 *Chronicles* 14.	1 *Chronicles* 8.	1 *Chronicles* 9.
Ahimaaz: and the name of the captain of his host was Abner the son of Ner, Saul's uncle. 51 *a* And Kish was the father of Saul; and Ner the father of Abner was the son of Abiel.	and Jehoaddah begat Alemeth, and Azmaveth, and Zimri; and Zimri begat Moza: 37 and Moza begat Binea; Raphah was his son, Eleasah his son, Azel his son: 38 and Azel had six sons, whose names are these; Azrikam, Bocheru, and Ishmael, and Sheariah, and Obadiah, and Hanan. All these were the sons of Azel. 39 And the sons of Eshek his brother; Ulam his firstborn, Jeush the second, and Eliphelet the third. 40 And the sons of Ulam were mighty men of valour, archers, and had many sons, and sons' sons, an hundred and fifty. All these were the sons of Benjamin.	42 And Ahaz begat Jarah; and Jarah begat Alemeth, and Azmaveth, and Zimri; and Zimri begat Moza: 43 and Moza begat Binea; and Rephaiah his son, Eleasah his son, Azel his son: 44 and Azel had six sons, whose names are these; Azrikam, Bocheru, and Ishmael, and Sheariah, and Obadiah, and Hanan: these were the sons of Azel.

19. APPENDIX: ADDITIONAL HISTORICAL STATEMENTS.

(1) War of the Three Transjordanic Tribes with Arab Nations.

1 *Chronicles* 5: 18–22.

18 The sons of Reuben, and the Gadites, and the half tribe of Manasseh, of valiant men, men able to bear buckler and sword, and to shoot with bow, and skilful in war, were forty and four thousand seven hundred and threescore, that were able to go forth to war.   19 And they made war with the Hagrites, with Jetur, and Naphish, and Nodab.   20 And they were helped against them, and the Hagrites were delivered into their hand, and all that were with them: for they cried to God in the battle, and he was intreated of them; because they put their trust in him.   21 And they took away their cattle; of their camels fifty thousand, and of sheep two hundred and fifty thousand, and of asses two thousand, and of *b* men an hundred thousand.   22 For there fell many slain, because the war was of God.   And they dwelt in their stead until the captivity.

(2) The Inhabitants of Jerusalem.

1 *Chronicles* 9: 2–34, 1*a*.

2 *c* Now the first inhabitants that dwelt in their possessions in their cities were, Israel, the priests, the Levites, and the Nethinim.   3 And in Jerusalem dwelt of the children of Judah, and of the children of Benjamin, and of the children of Ephraim and Manasseh; 4 Uthai the son of Ammihud, the son of Omri, the son of Imri, the son of Bani, of the children of Perez the son of Judah.   5 And of the Shilonites; Asaiah the firstborn, and his sons. 6 And of the sons of Zerah; Jeuel, and their brethren, six hundred and ninety.   7 And of the sons of Benjamin; Sallu the son of Meshullam, the son of Hodaviah, the son of Hassenuah; 8 and Ibneiah the son of Jeroham, and Elah the son of Uzzi, the son of Michri, and Meshullam the son of Shephatiah, the son of Reuel, the son of Ibnijah; 9 and their brethren, according to their generations, nine hundred and fifty and six.   All these men were heads of fathers' *houses* by their fathers' houses.

10 And of the priests; Jedaiah, and Jehoiarib, and Jachin; 11 and *d* Azariah the son of Hilkiah, the son of Meshullam, the son of Zadok, the son of Meraioth, the son of Ahitub, the ruler of

---

a According to some ancient authorities, "And Kish the father of Saul and Ner ... were the sons of Abiel."   *b* Heb. "souls of men."   *c* See Nehemiah 11: 3, etc.   *d* In Nehemiah 11: 11, "Seraiah."

1 *Chronicles* 9.

the house of God; 12 and Adaiah the son of Jeroham, the son of Pashhur, the son of Malchijah, and Maasai the son of Adiel, the son of Jahzerah, the son of Meshullam, the son of Meshillemith, the son of Immer; 13 and their brethren, heads of their fathers' houses, a thousand and seven hundred and threescore; very able men for the work of the service of the house of God. 14 And of the Levites; Shemaiah the son of Hasshub, the son of Azrikam, the son of Hashabiah, of the sons of Merari; 15 and Bakbakkar, Heresh, and Galal, and Mattaniah the son of Mica, the son of *a* Zichri, the son of Asaph; 16 and *b* Obadiah the son of *c* Shemaiah, the son of Galal, the son of Jeduthun, and Berechiah the son of Asa, the son of Elkanah, that dwelt in the villages of the Netophathites. 17 And the porters; Shallum, and Akkub, and Talmon, and Ahiman, and their brethren: Shallum was the chief; 18 who hitherto *waited* in the king's gate eastward: they were the porters for the camp of the children of Levi. 19 And Shallum the son of Kore, the son of Ebiasaph, the son of Korah, and his brethren, of his father's house, the Korahites, were over the work of the service, keepers of the *d* gates of the *e* tabernacle: and their fathers had been over the camp of the LORD, keepers of the entry; 20 and Phinehas the son of Eleazar was ruler over them in time past, *and* the LORD was with him. 21 Zechariah the son of Meshelemiah was porter of the door of the tent of meeting. 22 All these which were chosen to be porters in the *d* gates were two hundred and twelve. These were reckoned by genealogy in their villages, whom David and Samuel the seer did ordain in their *f* set office. 23 So they and their children had the oversight of the gates of the house of the LORD, even the house of the *e* tabernacle, by wards. 24 *g* On the four sides were the porters, toward the east, west, north, and south. 25 And their brethren, in their villages, were to come in every seven days from time to time to be with them: 26 for the four chief porters, who were Levites, were in a set office, and were over the chambers and over the treasuries in the house of God. 27 And they lodged round about the house of God, because the charge *thereof* was upon them, and to them pertained the opening thereof morning by morning. 28 And certain of them had charge of the vessels of service; for by tale were they brought in and by tale were they taken out. 29 Some of them also were appointed over the furniture, and over all the vessels of the sanctuary, and over the fine flour, and the wine, and the oil, and the frankincense, and the spices. 30 And some of the sons of the priests prepared the confection of the spices. 31 And Mattithiah, one of the Levites, who was the firstborn of Shallum the Korahite, had the set office over the things that were baked in pans. 32 And some of their brethren, of the sons of the Kohathites, were over the shewbread, to prepare it every sabbath. 33 And these are the singers, heads of fathers' *houses* of the Levites, *who dwelt* in the chambers *and were* free *from other service:* for they were employed in their work day and night. 34 These were heads of fathers' *houses* of the Levites, throughout their generations, chief men: these dwelt at Jerusalem.

1*a* So all Israel were reckoned by genealogies; and, behold, they are written in the book of the kings of Israel.

---

a In Nehemiah 11:17, "Zabdi."   *b* In Nehemiah 11:17, "Abda."   *c* In Nehemiah 11:17, "Shammua."   *d* Heb. "thresholds."   *e* Heb. "Tent."   *f* Or, "trust."   *g* Heb. "Towards the four winds."

PART II.

THE CLOSE OF THE THEOCRACY.

I. The Early Life of Samuel.

20. SAMUEL'S BIRTH AND INFANCY.

(1) SAMUEL'S BIRTH IN ANSWER TO PRAYER.[a]

1 *Samuel* I : 1–20.

1 Now there was a certain man of Ramathaim-zophim, of the hill country of Ephraim, and his name was Elkanah, the son of Jeroham, the son of Elihu, the son of Tohu, the son of Zuph, an Ephraimite : 2 and he had two wives ; the name of the one was Hannah, and the name of the other Peninnah : and Peninnah had children, but Hannah had no children. 3 And this man went up out of his city from year to year to worship and to sacrifice unto the LORD of hosts in Shiloh. And the two sons of Eli, Hophni and Phinehas, priests unto the LORD, were there. 4 And when the day came that Elkanah sacrificed, he gave to Peninnah his wife, and to all her sons and her daughters, portions : 5 but unto Hannah he gave [b] a double portion : for he loved Hannah, but the LORD had shut up her womb. 6 And her rival provoked her sore, for to make her fret, because the LORD had shut up her womb. 7 And *as* he did so year by year, when she went up to the house of the LORD, so she provoked her ; therefore she wept, and did not eat. 8 And Elkanah her husband said unto her, Hannah, why weepest thou ? and why eatest thou not ? and why is thy heart grieved ? am not I better to thee than ten sons ? 9 So Hannah rose up after they had eaten in Shiloh, and after they had drunk. Now Eli the priest sat upon his seat by the door post of the temple of the LORD. 10 And she was in bitterness of soul, and prayed unto the LORD, and wept sore. 11 And she vowed a vow, and said, O LORD of hosts, if thou wilt indeed look on the affliction of thine handmaid, and remember me, and not forget thine handmaid, but wilt give unto thine handmaid [c] a man child, then I will give him unto the LORD all the days of his life, and there shall no razor come upon his head. 12 And it came to pass, as she continued praying before the LORD, that Eli marked her mouth. 13 Now Hannah, she spake in her heart ; only her lips moved, but her voice was not heard : therefore Eli thought she had been drunken. 14 And Eli said unto her, How long wilt thou be drunken ? put away thy wine from thee. 15 And Hannah answered and said, No, my lord, I am a woman of a sorrowful spirit : I have drunk neither wine nor strong drink, but I poured out my soul before the LORD. 16 Count not thine handmaid for [d] a daughter of [e] Belial : for out of the abundance of my complaint and my provocation have I spoken hitherto. 17 Then Eli answered and said, Go in peace: and the God of Israel grant thy petition that thou hast asked of him. 18 And she said, Let thy servant find grace in thy sight. So the woman went her way, and did eat, and her countenance was no more *sad*. 19 And they rose up in the morning early, and worshipped before the LORD, and returned, and came to their house to Ramah : and Elkanah knew Hannah his wife; and the LORD remembered her. 20 And it came to pass, when the time was come about, that Hannah conceived, and bare a son ; and she called his name Samuel, *saying*, Because I have asked him of the LORD.

(2) SAMUEL'S CONSECRATION TO THE LORD.

1 *Samuel* I : 21–28.

21 And the man Elkanah, and all his house, went up to offer unto the LORD the yearly sacrifice, and his vow. 22 But Hannah went not up ; for she said unto her husband, *I will not go up* until the child be weaned, and then I will bring him, that he may appear before the LORD,

---

a The Story of Ruth was very nearly synchronous with the birth of Samuel.   *b* The Sept. reads, "a single portion, because she had no child ; howbeit Elkanah loved," etc.   *c* Heb. "seed of men."   *d* Or, "a wicked woman."   *e* I. e., "worthlessness."

1 *Samuel* 1.

and there abide for ever. 23 And Elkanah her husband said unto her, Do what seemeth thee good ; tarry until thou have weaned him ; only the LORD establish his word. So the woman tarried and gave her son suck, until she weaned him. 24 And when she had weaned him, she took him up with her, with *a* three bullocks, and one ephah of meal, and a *b* bottle of wine, and brought him unto the house of the LORD in Shiloh : and the child was young. 25 And they slew the bullock, and brought the child to Eli. 26 And she said, Oh my lord, as thy soul liveth, my lord, I am the woman that stood by thee here, praying unto the LORD. 27 For this child I prayed ; and the LORD hath given me my petition which I asked of him : 28 therefore I also have *c* granted him to the LORD ; as long as he liveth he is granted to the LORD. And *d* he worshipped the LORD there.

(3) HANNAH'S SONG OF THANKSGIVING.

1 *Samuel* 2 : 1–10.

1 And Hannah prayed, and said:
>   My heart exulteth in the LORD,
>   Mine horn is exalted in the LORD :
>   My mouth is enlarged over mine enemies ;
>   Because I rejoice in thy salvation.

2   There is none holy as the LORD;
>   For there is none beside thee :
>   Neither is there any rock like our God.

3   Talk no more so exceeding proudly ;
>   Let not arrogancy come out of your mouth :
>   For the LORD is a God of knowledge,
>   *e* And by him actions are weighed.

4   The bows of the mighty men are broken,
>   And they that stumbled are girded with strength.

5   They that were full have hired out themselves for bread ;
>   And they that were hungry *f* have ceased :
>   Yea, the barren hath borne seven ;
>   And she that hath many children languisheth.

6   The LORD killeth, and maketh alive :
>   He bringeth down to *g* the grave, and bringeth up.

7   The LORD maketh poor, and maketh rich :
>   He bringeth low, he also lifteth up.

8   He raiseth up the poor out of the dust,
>   He lifteth up the needy from the dunghill,
>   To make them sit with princes,
>   And inherit the throne of glory :
>   For the pillars of the earth are the LORD'S,
>   And he hath set the world upon them.

9   He will keep the feet of his *h* holy ones,
>   But the wicked shall be put to silence in darkness ;
>   For by strength shall no man prevail.

10   They that strive with the LORD shall be broken to pieces ;
>   Against them shall he thunder in heaven :
>   The LORD shall judge the ends of the earth ;
>   And he shall give strength unto his king,
>   And exalt the horn of his anointed.

---

a The Sept. and Syriac have, " a bullock of three years old." *b* Or, " skin." *c* Or, " lent." *d* According to several ancient authorities, " they." *e* According to another reading, " Though actions be not weighed." *f* Or, "have rest." *g* Heb. " Sheol." *h* Or, " godly ones." Another reading is, " holy one."

21. SAMUEL AT SHILOH.

(1) THE FAITHLESS PRIESTS.

1 *Samuel* 2 : 12–17.

12 Now the sons of Eli were *a* sons of *b* Belial ; *c* they knew not the LORD. 13 And the custom of the priests with the people was, that, when any man offered sacrifice, the priest's servant came, while the flesh was in seething, with a fleshhook of three teeth in his hand ; 14 and he struck it into the pan, or kettle, or caldron, or pot ; all that the fleshhook brought up the priest took *d* therewith. So they did in Shiloh unto all the Israelites that came thither. 15 Yea, before they burnt the fat, the priest's servant came, and said to the man that sacrificed, Give flesh to roast for the priest ; for he will not have sodden flesh of thee, but raw. 16 And if the man said unto him, They will surely burn the fat *e* presently, and then take as much as thy soul desireth ; then *f* he would say, Nay, but thou shalt give it me now : and if not, I will take it by force. 17 And the sin of the young men was very great before the LORD : for *g* men abhorred the offering of the LORD.

(2) ELI'S EXPOSTULATIONS WITH HIS SONS.

1 *Samuel* 2 : 22–25.

22 Now Eli was very old ; and he heard all that his sons did unto all Israel, and how that they lay with the women that *h* did service at the door of the tent of meeting. 23 And he said unto them, Why do ye such things? for I hear of your evil dealings from all this people. 24 Nay, my sons ; for it is no good report *i* that I hear : ye make the LORD'S people to transgress. 25 If one man sin against another, *k* God shall judge him : but if a man sin against the LORD, who shall intreat for him ? Notwithstanding they hearkened not unto the voice of their father, because the LORD would slay them.

(3) SAMUEL'S MINISTRY BEFORE THE LORD.

1 *Samuel* 2 : 11.	1 *Samuel* 2 : 18–21.
11 And Elkanah went to Ramah to his house. And the child did minister unto the LORD before Eli the priest.	18 But Samuel ministered before the LORD, being a child, girded with a linen ephod. 19 Moreover his mother made him a little robe, and brought it to him from year to year, when she came up with her husband to offer the yearly sacrifice. 20 And Eli blessed Elkanah and his wife, and said, The LORD give thee seed of this woman *l* for the loan which was lent to the LORD. And they went unto their own home. 21 *m* And the LORD visited Hannah and she conceived, and bare three sons and two daughters. And the child Samuel grew before the LORD.
26 And the child Samuel grew on, and was in favour both with the LORD, and also with men.	

(4) THE FALL OF ELI'S HOUSE FORETOLD.

1 *Samuel* 2 : 27–36.

27 And there came a man of God unto Eli, and said unto him, Thus saith the LORD, Did I reveal myself unto the house of thy father, when they were in Egypt *n in bondage* to Pharaoh's house ? 28 *o* And did I choose him out of all the tribes of Israel to be my priest, to *p* go up unto mine altar, to burn incense, to wear an ephod before me ? *q* and did I give unto the house of thy father all the offerings of the children of Israel made by fire ? 29 Wherefore *r* kick ye at my

a Or, "wicked men." *b* I. e., "worthlessness." *c* Or, "they knew not the LORD, nor the due of the priests from the people. When any man,"etc. *d* Some ancient authorities read, "for himself." *e* Or, "first." *f* Another reading is, "he would say unto him, Thou," etc. *g* Or, "the men despised." *h* See Exodus 38 : 8. *i* Or, "which I hear the LORD's people do spread abroad." *k* Or, "the judge." *l* Or, "for the petition which was asked for the LORD." *m* The Hebrew has, "For." *n* Or, "in Pharaoh's house." *o* Or, "And I chose." *p* Or, "offer upon." *q* Or, "and gave." *r* Or, "trample ye upon . . . and upon."

1 *Samuel* 2.

sacrifice and at mine offering, which I have commanded in *my* habitation; and honourest thy sons above me, to make yourselves fat with the chiefest of all the offerings of Israel my people? 30 Therefore the LORD, the God of Israel, saith, I said indeed that thy house, and the house of thy father, should walk before me for ever: but now the LORD saith, Be it far from me; for them that honour me I will honour, and they that despise me shall be lightly esteemed. 31 Behold, the days come, that I will cut off thine arm, and the arm of thy father's house, that there shall not be an old man in thine house. 32 And thou shalt behold *a* the affliction of *my* habitation, in all the wealth which *God* shall give Israel: and there shall not be an old man in thine house for ever. 33 *b* And the man of thine, *whom* I shall not cut off from mine altar, *shall be* to consume thine eyes, and to grieve thine heart: and all the increase of thine house shall die *c* in the flower of their age. 34 And this shall be the sign unto thee, that shall come upon thy two sons, on Hophni and Phinehas; in one day they shall die both of them. 35 And I will raise me up a faithful priest, that shall do according to that which is in mine heart and in my mind: and I will build him a sure house; and he shall walk before mine anointed for ever. 36 And it shall come to pass, that every one that is left in thine house shall come and bow down to him for a piece of silver and a loaf of bread, and shall say, Put me, I pray thee, into one of the priests' offices, that I may eat a morsel of bread.

(5) SAMUEL'S CALL.

1 *Samuel* 3: 1–18.

1 *d* And the child Samuel ministered unto the LORD before Eli. And the word of the LORD was *e* precious in those days; there was no *f* open vision. 2 And it came to pass at that time, when Eli was laid down in his place, (now his eyes had begun to wax dim, that he could not see,) 3 and the lamp of God was not yet gone out, and Samuel was laid down *to sleep*, in the temple of the LORD, where the ark of God was; 4 that the LORD called Samuel: and he said, Here am I. 5 And he ran unto Eli, and said, Here am I; for thou calledst me. And he said, I called not; lie down again. And he went and lay down. 6 And the LORD called yet again, Samuel. And Samuel arose and went to Eli, and said, Here am I; for thou calledst me. And he answered, I called not, my son; lie down again. 7 Now Samuel did not yet know the LORD, neither was the word of the LORD yet revealed unto him. 8 And the LORD called Samuel again the third time. And he arose and went to Eli, and said, Here am I; for thou calledst me. And Eli perceived that the LORD had called the child. 9 Therefore Eli said unto Samuel, Go, lie down: and it shall be, if he call thee, that thou shalt say, Speak, LORD; for thy servant heareth. So Samuel went and lay down in his place. 10 And the LORD came, and stood, and called as at other times, Samuel, Samuel. Then Samuel said, Speak; for thy servant heareth. 11 And the LORD said to Samuel, Behold, I will do a thing in Israel, at which both the ears of every one that heareth it shall tingle. 12 In that day I will perform against Eli all that I have spoken concerning his house, from the beginning even unto the end. 13 For I have told him that I will judge his house for ever, for the iniquity which he knew, because his sons *g* did bring a curse upon themselves, and he restrained them not. 14 And therefore I have sworn unto the house of Eli, that the iniquity of Eli's house shall not be *h* purged with sacrifice nor offering for ever. 15 And Samuel lay until the morning, and opened the doors of the house of the LORD. And Samuel feared to shew Eli the vision. 16 Then Eli called Samuel, and said, Samuel, my son. And he said, Here am I. 17 And he said, What is the thing that *the LORD* hath spoken unto thee? I pray thee hide it not from me: God do so to thee, and more also, if thou hide any thing from me of all the things that he spake unto thee. 18 And Samuel told him every whit, and hid nothing from him. And he said, It is the LORD: let him do what seemeth him good.

---

a Or, " an adversary in *my* habitation." *b* Or, " Yet will I not cut off every man of thine from mine altar, to consume," etc. *c* Heb. "*when they be* men." The Sept. has, " by the sword of men." *d* Cf. § 21, (3), above. The first word of this division might, with equal propriety, be translated " Now." It is better so to regard it, than to place the verse in subsection (3), parallel with vv. 11 and 18 of 1 Samuel 2. *e* Or, " rare." *f* Or, " frequent." Heb. " widely spread." *g* The Sept. has, " speak evil of God." *h* Or, " expiated."

(6) Samuel established as a Prophet.

1 *Samuel* 3 : 19–4 : 1*a*.

19 And Samuel grew, and the LORD was with him, and did let none of his words fall to the ground. 20 And all Israel from Dan even to Beer-sheba knew that Samuel was established to be a prophet of the LORD. 21 And the LORD appeared again in Shiloh : for the LORD revealed himself to Samuel in Shiloh by the word of the LORD. 1*a* And the word of Samuel came to all Israel.

II. The Period of National Disaster.

22. ISRAEL'S DEFEAT AND LOSS OF THE ARK.

1 *Samuel* 4 : 1*b*–11*a*.

1*b* Now Israel went out against the Philistines to battle, and pitched beside *b* Eben-ezer : and the Philistines pitched in Aphek. 2 And the Philistines put themselves in array against Israel : and when *c* they joined battle, Israel was smitten before the Philistines : and they slew of the *d* army in the field about four thousand men. 3 And when the people were come into the camp, the elders of Israel said, Wherefore hath the LORD smitten us to-day before the Philistines ? Let us fetch the ark of the covenant of the LORD out of Shiloh unto us, that it may come among us, and save us out of the hand of our enemies. 4 So the people sent to Shiloh, and they brought from thence the ark of the covenant of the LORD of hosts, which *e* sitteth upon the cherubim : and the two sons of Eli, Hophni and Phinehas, were there with the ark of the covenant of God. 5 And when the ark of the covenant of the LORD came into the camp, all Israel shouted with a great shout, so that the earth rang again. 6 And when the Philistines heard the noise of the shout, they said, What meaneth the noise of this great shout in the camp of the Hebrews ? And they understood that the ark of the LORD was come into the camp. 7 And the Philistines were afraid, for they said, God is come into the camp. And they said, Woe unto us ! for there hath not been such a thing heretofore. 8 Woe unto us ! who shall deliver us out of the hand of these mighty gods ? these are the gods that smote the Egyptians with all manner of *f* plagues in the wilderness. 9 Be strong, and quit yourselves like men, O ye Philistines, that ye be not servants unto the Hebrews, as they have been to you : quit yourselves like men, and fight. 10 And the Philistines fought, and Israel was smitten, and they fled every man to his tent : and there was a very great slaughter ; for there fell of Israel thirty thousand footmen. 11*a* And the ark of God was taken.

23. THE FALL OF THE HOUSE OF ELI.

1 *Samuel* 4 : 11*b*–22.

11*b* And the two sons of Eli, Hophni and Phinehas, were slain. 12 And there ran a man of Benjamin out of the *d* army, and came to Shiloh the same day with his clothes rent, and with earth upon his head. 13 And when he came, lo, Eli sat upon his seat *g* by the way side watching : for his heart trembled for the ark of God. And when the man came into the city, and told it, all the city cried out. 14 And when Eli heard the noise of the crying, he said, What meaneth the noise of this tumult ? And the man hasted, and came and told Eli. 15 Now Eli was ninety and eight years old ; and his eyes were *h* set, that he could not see. 16 And the man said unto Eli, I am he that came out of the *d* army, and I fled to-day out of the *d* army. And he said, How went the matter, my son ? 17 And he that brought the tidings answered and said, Israel is fled before the Philistines, and there hath been also a great slaughter among the people, and thy two sons also, Hophni and Phinehas, are dead, and the ark of God is taken. 18 And it came to pass, when he

---

a It is to be remembered that this period of disaster had begun fully forty years before the time of the text.   *b* Cf. 1 Samuel 7 : 12.   See §27.   *c* Or, "the battle was spread."   *d* Heb. "array."   *e* Or, "dwelleth between."   *f* Heb. "smiting."   *g* The Sept. has, "beside the gate, watching the way."   *h* Cf. 1 Kings 14 : 4.   See §142, (5), *A*.

1 *Samuel* 4.

made mention of the ark of God, that he fell from off his seat backward by the side of the gate, and his neck brake, and he died : for he was an old man, and heavy. And he had judged Israel forty years. 19 And his daughter in law, Phinehas' wife, was with child, near to be delivered : and when she heard the tidings that the ark of God was taken, and that her father in law and her husband were dead, she bowed herself and brought forth; for her pains came upon her. 20 And about the time of her death the women that stood by her said unto her, Fear not ; for thou hast brought forth a son. But she answered not, neither did she regard it. 21 And she named the child *a* Ichabod, saying, The glory is departed from Israel : because the ark of God was taken, and because of her father in law and her husband. 22 And she said, The glory is departed from Israel ; for the ark of God is taken.

24. THE ARK OF GOD.

(1) The Chastisement of the Philistines for the Removal of the Ark.

1 *Samuel* 5 : 1-12.

1 Now the Philistines had taken the ark of God, and they brought it from Eben-ezer unto Ashdod. 2 And the Philistines took the ark of God, and brought it into the house of Dagon. and set it by Dagon. 3 And when they of Ashdod arose early on the morrow, behold, Dagon was fallen *b* upon his face to the ground before the ark of the LORD. And they took Dagon, and set him in his place again. 4 And when they arose early on the morrow morning, behold, Dagon was fallen *b* upon his face to the ground before the ark of the LORD ; and the head of Dagon and both the palms of his hands *lay* cut off upon the threshold ; only *the stump of* Dagon was left to him. 5 Therefore neither the priests of Dagon, nor any that come into Dagon's house, tread on the threshold of Dagon in Ashdod, unto this day.

6 But the hand of the LORD was heavy upon them of Ashdod, and he destroyed them, and smote them with *c* tumours, *d* even Ashdod and the borders thereof. 7 And when the men of Ashdod saw that it was so, they said, The ark of the God of Israel shall not abide with us : for his hand is sore upon us, and upon Dagon our god. 8 They sent therefore and gathered all the lords of the Philistines unto them, and said, What shall we do with the ark of the God of Israel? And they answered, Let the ark of the God of Israel be carried about unto Gath. And they carried the ark of the God of Israel about *thither*. 9 And it was so, that, after they had carried it about, the hand of the LORD was against the city with a very great discomfiture: and he smote the men of the city, both small and great, and tumours brake out upon them. 10 So they sent the ark of God to Ekron. And it came to pass, as the ark of God came to Ekron, that the Ekronites cried out, saying, They have brought about the ark of the God of Israel to us, to slay us and our people. 11 They sent therefore and gathered together all the lords of the Philistines, and they said, Send away the ark of the God of Israel, and let it go again to its own place, that it slay us not, and our people : for there was a deadly discomfiture throughout all the city; the hand of God was very heavy there. 12 And the men that died not were smitten with the tumours : and the cry of the city went up to heaven.

(2) The Restoration of the Ark with expiatory Gifts.

1 *Samuel* 6 : 1-11.

1 And the ark of the LORD was in the *e* country of the Philistines seven months*f*. 2 And the Philistines called for the priests and the diviners, saying, What shall we do with the ark of the LORD ? shew us wherewith we shall send it to its place. 3 And they said, If ye send away the ark of the God of Israel, send it not empty ; but in any wise return him a *g* guilt offering : then ye shall be healed, and it shall be known to you why his hand is not removed from you. 4 Then

---

a I. e., " *There is* no glory." *b* Or, " before it." *c* Or, " plague boils." As read by the Jews, " emerods." *d* The Sept. has instead, " and in the midst of the land thereof mice were brought forth, and there was a great and deadly destruction in the city." *e* Heb. " field." *f* The Sept. adds, " and their land swarmed with mice." *g* Or, " trespass offering."

I *Samuel* 6.

said they, What shall be the guilt offering which we shall return to him ?   And they said, Five golden tumours, and five golden mice, *according to* the number of the lords of the Philistines : for one plague was on *ª* you all, and on your lords.   5 Wherefore ye shall make images of your tumours, and images of your mice that mar the land ; and ye shall give glory unto the God of Israel : peradventure he will lighten his hand from off you, and from off your gods, and from off your land.   6 Wherefore then do ye harden your hearts, as the Egyptians and Pharaoh hardened their hearts ? when he had *ᵇ* wrought wonderfully among them, did they not let *ª* the people go, and they departed ?   7 Now therefore take and prepare you a new cart, and two milch kine, on which there hath come no yoke, and tie the kine to the cart, and bring their calves home from them : 8 and take the ark of the LORD, and lay it upon the cart ; and put the jewels of gold, which ye return him for a guilt offering, in a coffer by the side thereof ; and send it away, that it may go.   9 And see, if it goeth up by the way of its own border to Beth-shemesh, then he hath done us this great evil : but if not, then we shall know that it is not his hand that smote us ; it was a chance that happened to us.   10 And the men did so ; and took two milch kine, and tied them to the cart, and shut up their calves at home ; 11 and they put the ark of the LORD upon the cart, and the coffer with the mice of gold and the images of their tumours.

(3) THE RECEPTION AND SETTLEMENT OF THE ARK IN ISRAEL.
I *Samuel* 6 : 12-7 : 1.

12 And the kine took the straight way by the way to Beth-shemesh ; they went along *ᵉ* the high way, lowing as they went, and turned not aside to the right hand or to the left ; and the lords of the Philistines went after them unto the border of Beth-shemesh.   13 And they of Beth-shemesh were reaping their wheat harvest in the valley : and they lifted up their eyes, and saw the ark, and rejoiced to see it.   14 And the cart came into the field of Joshua the Beth-shemite, and stood there, where there was a great stone : and they clave the wood of the cart, and offered up the kine for a burnt offering unto the LORD.   15 And the Levites took down the ark of the LORD, and the coffer that was with it, wherein the jewels of gold were, and put them on the great stone : and the men of Beth-shemesh offered burnt offerings and sacrificed sacrifices the same day unto the LORD.   16 And when the five lords of the Philistines had seen it, they returned to Ekron the same day.

17 And these are the golden tumours which the Philistines returned for a guilt offering unto the LORD ; for Ashdod one, for Gaza one, for Ashkelon one, for Gath one, for Ekron one ; 18 and the golden mice, according to the number of all the cities of the Philistines belonging to the five lords, both of fenced cities and of country villages : even unto the great *ᵈ* stone, whereon they set down the ark of the LORD, *which stone remaineth* unto this day in the field of Joshua the Beth-shemite.   19 *ᵉ* And he smote of the men of Beth-shemesh, because they had looked into the ark of the LORD, even he smote of the people seventy men, *and* fifty thousand men : and the people mourned, because the LORD had smitten the people with a great slaughter.   20 And the men of Beth-shemesh said, Who is able to stand before the LORD, this holy God ? and to whom shall he go up from us ?   21 And they sent messengers to the inhabitants of Kiriath-jearim, saying, The Philistines have brought again the ark of the LORD ; come ye down, and fetch it up to you. I And the men of Kiriath-jearim came, and fetched up the ark of the LORD, and brought it into the house of Abinadab in *ᶠ* the hill, and sanctified Eleazar his son to keep the ark of the LORD.

25. THE TWENTY YEARS OF WAITING.
I *Samuel* 7 : 2.

2 And it came to pass, from the day that the ark abode in Kiriath-jearim, that the time was long ; for it was twenty years : and all the house of Israel *ᵍ* lamented after the LORD.

a Heb. " them."   *b* Or, " made a mock of."   *c* Heb. " one raised way."   *d* So the Sept. and Targum. The Hebrew text has, "Abel" (i. e., " a meadow ").   *e* The Sept. has, "And the sons of Jeconiah rejoiced not among the men of Beth-shemesh, because they saw the ark of the LORD ; and he smote among them seventy men, and fifty thousand men."
ƒ Or, " Gibeah."   *g* Or, " was drawn together."

III. Samuel, the Last of the Judges.

26. NATIONAL REPENTANCE THROUGH SAMUEL'S LABORS.

1 *Samuel* 7 : 3–6.

3 And Samuel spake unto all the house of Israel, saying, If ye do return unto the LORD with all your heart, then put away the strange gods and the Ashtaroth from among you, and *a* prepare your hearts unto the LORD, and serve him only : and he will deliver you out of the hand of the Philistines. 4 Then the children of Israel did put away the Baalim and the Ashtaroth, and served the LORD only.

5 And Samuel said, Gather all Israel to Mizpah, and I will pray for you unto the LORD. 6 And they gathered together to Mizpah, and drew water, and poured it out before the LORD, and fasted on that day, and said there, We have sinned against the LORD. And Samuel judged the children of Israel in Mizpah.

27. ISRAEL'S VICTORY OVER THE PHILISTINES.

1 *Samuel* 7 : 7–12.

7 And when the Philistines heard that the children of Israel were gathered together to Mizpah, the lords of the Philistines went up against Israel. And when the children of Israel heard it, they were afraid of the Philistines. 8 And the children of Israel said to Samuel, Cease not to cry unto the LORD our God for us, that he will save us out of the hand of the Philistines. 9 And Samuel took a sucking lamb, and offered it for a whole burnt offering unto the LORD : and Samuel cried unto the LORD for Israel ; and the LORD answered him. 10 And as Samuel was offering up the burnt offering, the Philistines drew near to battle against Israel : but the LORD thundered with a great *b* thunder on that day upon the Philistines, and discomfited them ; and they were smitten down before Israel. 11 And the men of Israel went out of Mizpah, and pursued the Philistines, and smote them, until they came under Beth-car. 12 Then Samuel took a stone, and set it between Mizpah and Shen, and called the name of it *c* Eben-ezer, saying, Hitherto hath the LORD helped us.

28. SUMMARY STATEMENT OF SAMUEL'S WORK AS JUDGE.*d*

1 *Samuel* 7 : 13–17.

13 So the Philistines were subdued, and they came no more within the border of Israel : and the hand of the LORD was against the Philistines all the days of Samuel. 14 And the cities which the Philistines had taken from Israel were restored to Israel, from Ekron even unto Gath ; and the border thereof did Israel deliver out of the hand of the Philistines. And there was peace between Israel and the Amorites. 15 And Samuel judged Israel all the days of his life. 16 And he went from year to year in circuit to Beth-el, and Gilgal, and Mizpah ; and he judged Israel in all those places. 17 And his return was to Ramah, for there was his house ; and there he judged Israel : and he built there an altar unto the LORD.

---

a Or, "direct." *b* Heb. "voice." *c* I. e., "The stone of help." *d* It is to be remembered that this is a very meagre statement of Samuel's work as judge. One needs to look well at the words, and even beneath them, to gain a clear conception of what Samuel's influence and power meant to Israel.

6

BOOK SECOND.

The Reign of Saul.

PART I.

ESTABLISHMENT BY SAMUEL OF SAUL AS FIRST KING OF ISRAEL.

29. THE PERSISTENT DEMAND OF THE PEOPLE FOR A KING.

1 *Samuel* 8 : 1-22.

1 And it came to pass, when Samuel was old, that he made his sons judges over Israel. 2 Now the name of his firstborn was Joel; and the name of his second, Abijah: they were judges in Beer-sheba. 3 And his sons walked not in his ways, but turned aside after lucre, and took bribes, and perverted judgement.

4 Then all the elders of Israel gathered themselves together, and came to Samuel unto Ramah: 5 and they said unto him, Behold, thou art old, and thy sons walk not in thy ways: now make us a king to judge us like all the nations. 6 But the thing displeased Samuel, when they said, Give us a king to judge us. And Samuel prayed unto the LORD. 7 And the LORD said unto Samuel, Hearken unto the voice of the people in all that they say unto thee: for they have not rejected thee, but they have rejected me, that I should not be king over them. 8 According to all the works which they have done since the day that I brought them up out of Egypt even unto this day, in that they have forsaken me, and served other gods, so do they also unto thee. 9 Now therefore hearken unto their voice: howbeit thou shalt protest solemnly unto them, and shalt shew them the manner of the king that shall reign over them.

10 And Samuel told all the words of the LORD unto the people that asked of him a king. 11 And he said, This will be the manner of the king that shall reign over you: he will take your sons, and appoint them unto him, *a* for his chariots, and to be his horsemen; and they shall run before his chariots: 12 and he will appoint them unto him for captains of thousands, and captains of fifties; and *he will set some* to plow his ground, and to reap his harvest, and to make his instruments of war, and the instruments of his chariots. 13 And he will take your daughters to be *b* confectionaries, and to be cooks, and to be bakers. 14 And he will take your fields, and your vineyards, and your oliveyards, even the best of them, and give them to his servants. 15 And he will take the tenth of your seed, and of your vineyards, and give to his *c* officers, and to his servants. 16 And he will take your menservants, and your maidservants, and your goodliest *d* young men, and your asses, and put them to his work. 17 He will take the tenth of your flocks: and ye shall be his servants. 18 And ye shall cry out in that day because of your king which ye shall have chosen you; and the LORD will not answer you in that day. 19 But the people refused to hearken unto the voice of Samuel; and they said, Nay; but we will have a king over us; 20 that we also may be like all the nations; and that our king may judge us, and go out before us, and fight our battles. 21 And Samuel heard all the words of the people, and he rehearsed them in the ears of the LORD. 22 And the LORD said to Samuel, Hearken unto their voice, and make them a king. And Samuel said unto the men of Israel, Go ye every man unto his city.

---

a Or, "over his chariots, and over his horses."   *b* Or, "perfumers."   See Exodus 30: 25.   *c* Or, "eunuchs."   *d* The Sept. has, "herds."

30. SAMUEL MEETS SAUL, WHO IS DESTINED BY JEHOVAH TO BE KING OVER ISRAEL.

1 *Samuel* 9 : 1–25.

1 Now there was a man of Benjamin, whose name was Kish, the son of Abiel, the son of Zeror, the son of Becorath, the son of Aphiah, the son of a Benjamite, a mighty man of ᵃ valour. 2 And he had a son, whose name was Saul, a ᵇ young man and a goodly : and there was not among the children of Israel a goodlier person than he : from his shoulders and upward he was higher than any of the people. 3 And the asses of Kish Saul's father were lost. And Kish said to Saul his son, Take now one of the servants with thee, and arise, go seek the asses. 4 And he passed through the hill country of Ephraim, and passed through the land of Shalishah, but they found them not : then they passed through the land of Shaalim, and there they were not : and he passed through the land of the Benjamites, but they found them not. 5 When they were come to the land of Zuph, Saul said to his servant that was with him, Come and let us return ; lest my father leave caring for the asses, and take thought for us. 6 And he said unto him, Behold now, there is in this city a man of God, and he is a man that is held in honour ; all that he saith cometh surely to pass : now let us go thither ; peradventure he can tell us concerning our journey whereon we go. 7 Then said Saul to his servant, But, behold, if we go, what shall we bring the man ? for the bread is spent in our vessels, and there is not a present to bring to the man of God : what have we ? 8 And the servant answered Saul again, and said, Behold, I have in my hand the fourth part of a shekel of silver : that will I give to the man of God, to tell us our way. 9 (Beforetime in Israel, when a man went to inquire of God, thus he said, Come and let us go to the seer : for he that is now called a Prophet was beforetime called a Seer.) 10 Then said Saul to his servant, Well said ; come, let us go. So they went unto the city where the man of God was. 11 As they went up the ascent to the city, they found young maidens going out to draw water, and said unto them, Is the seer here ? 12 And they answered them, and said, He is ; behold, *he is* before thee : make haste now, for he is come to-day into the city ; for the people have a sacrifice to-day in the high place : 13 as soon as ye come into the city, ye shall straightway find him, before he go up to the high place to eat : for the people will not eat until he come, because he doth bless the sacrifice ; *and* afterwards they eat that be bidden. Now therefore get you up ; for at this time ye shall find him. 14 And they went up to the city ; *and* as they came within the city, behold, Samuel came out against them, for to go up to the high place.

15 Now the LORD had ᶜ revealed unto Samuel a day before Saul came, saying, 16 To-morrow about this time I will send thee a man out of the land of Benjamin, and thou shalt anoint him to be ᵈ prince over my people Israel, and he shall save my people out of the hand of the Philistines : for I have looked upon my people, because their cry is come unto me. 17 And when Samuel saw Saul, the LORD ᵉ said unto him, Behold the man ᶠ of whom I spake to thee ! this same shall have authority over my people. 18 Then Saul drew near to Samuel in the gate, and said, Tell me, I pray thee, where the seer's house is. 19 And Samuel answered Saul, and said, I am the seer ; go up before me unto the high place, for ye shall eat with me to-day : and in the morning I will let thee go, and will tell thee all that is in thine heart. 20 And as for thine asses that were lost three days ago, set not thy mind on them ; for they are found. And ᵍ for whom is all that is desirable in Israel ? Is it not for thee, and for all thy father's house ? 21 And Saul answered and said, Am not I a Benjamite, of the smallest of the tribes of Israel ? and my family the least of all the families of the ʰ tribe of Benjamin ? wherefore then speakest thou to me after this manner ? 22 And Samuel took Saul and his servant, and brought them into the guest-chamber, and made them sit in the chiefest place among them that were bidden, which were about thirty persons. 23 And Samuel said unto the cook, Bring the portion which I gave thee, of which I said unto thee, Set it by thee. 24 And the cook took up the ⁱ thigh, and that which was upon it, and set it

---

ᵃ Or, "wealth." ᵇ Or, " choice." ᶜ Heb. "uncovered the ear of Samuel." ᵈ Or, " leader." ᵉ Heb. "answered him." ᶠ Or, " of whom I said unto thee, This same," etc. ᵍ Or, " on whom is all the desire of Israel ? Is it not on thee, and on all," etc. ʰ Heb. " tribes." ⁱ Or, " shoulder."

before Saul. And *Samuel* said, Behold that which hath been reserved! set it before thee and eat; because unto the appointed time hath it been kept for thee, *a* for I said, I have invited the people. So Saul did eat with Samuel that day. 25 And when they were come down from the high place into the city, *b* he communed with Saul upon the housetop.

31. SAUL IS PRIVATELY ANOINTED BY SAMUEL.

1 *Samuel* 9 : 26–10 : 1.

26 And they arose early : and it came to pass about the spring of the day, that Samuel called to Saul on the housetop, saying, Up, that I may send thee away. And Saul arose, and they went out, both of them, he and Samuel, abroad. 27 As they were going down at the end of the city, Samuel said to Saul, Bid the servant pass on before us, (and he passed on,) but stand thou still at this time, that I may cause thee to hear the word of God. 1 Then Samuel took the vial of oil, and poured it upon his head, and kissed him, and said, Is it not that the LORD hath anointed thee to be prince over his inheritance ?

32. THE SIGNS OF THE DIVINE CONFIRMATION.

1 *Samuel* 10 : 2–16.

2 When thou art departed from me to-day, then thou shalt find two men by Rachel's sepulchre, in the border of Benjamin at Zelzah ; and they will say unto thee, The asses which thou wentest to seek are found : and, lo, thy father hath left the care of the asses, and taketh thought for you, saying, What shall I do for my son ? 3 Then shalt thou go on forward from thence, and thou shalt come to the *c* oak of Tabor, and there shall meet thee there three men going up to God to Beth-el, one carrying three kids, and another carrying three loaves of bread, and another carrying a *d* bottle of wine : 4 and they will salute thee, and give thee two loaves of bread ; which thou shalt receive of their hand. 5 After that thou shalt come to *e* the hill of God, where is the garrison of the Philistines : and it shall come to pass, when thou art come thither to the city, that thou shalt meet a band of prophets coming down from the high place with a psaltery, and a timbrel, and a pipe, and a harp, before them ; and they shall be prophesying : 6 and the spirit of the LORD will come mightily upon thee, and thou shalt prophesy with them, and shalt be turned into another man. 7 And *f* let it be, when these signs are come unto thee, *g* that thou do as occasion serve thee ; for God is with thee. 8 And thou shalt go down before me to Gilgal ; and, behold, I will come down unto thee, to offer burnt offerings, and to sacrifice sacrifices of peace offerings : seven days shalt thou tarry, till I come unto thee, and shew thee what thou shalt do. 9 And it was so, that when he had turned his back to go from Samuel, God *h* gave him another heart : and all those signs came to pass that day.

10 And when they came hither to *e* the hill, behold, a band of prophets met him ; and the spirit of God came mightily upon him, and he prophesied among them. 11 And it came to pass, when all that knew him beforetime saw that, behold, he prophesied with the prophets, then the people said one to another, What is this that is come unto the son of Kish ? Is Saul also among the prophets ? 12 And one of the same place answered and said, And who is their father ? Therefore it became a proverb, Is Saul also among the prophets ? 13 And when he had made an end of prophesying, he came to the high place.

14 And Saul's uncle said unto him and to his servant, Whither went ye ? And he said, To seek the asses : and when we saw that they were not found, we came to Samuel. 15 And Saul's uncle said, Tell me, I pray thee, what Samuel said unto you. 16 And Saul said unto his uncle, He told us plainly that the asses were found. But concerning the matter of the kingdom, whereof Samuel spake, he told him not.

---

a Heb. " saying."   *b* The Sept. has, " they spread a couch for Saul on the housetop, and he lay down. And it came to pass," etc.   *c* Or, " terebinth."   *d* Or, " skin."   *e* Or, " Gibeah."   *f* Heb. " it shall come to pass, that when these signs," etc.   *g* Heb. " do for thee as thine hand shall find."   *h* Heb. " turned."

33. THE CHOICE OF SAUL BY LOT AT MIZPAH.
1 *Samuel* 10: 17-21.

17 And Samuel called the people together unto the LORD to Mizpah; 18 and he said unto the children of Israel, Thus saith the LORD, the God of Israel, I brought up Israel out of Egypt, and I delivered you out of the hand of the Egyptians, and out of the hand of all the kingdoms that oppressed you: 19 but ye have this day rejected your God, who himself saveth you out of all your calamities and your distresses; and ye have said unto him, *Nay*, but set a king over us. Now therefore present yourselves before the LORD by your tribes, and by your thousands. 20 So Samuel brought all the tribes of Israel near, and the tribe of Benjamin was taken. 21 And he brought the tribe of Benjamin near by their families, and the family of the Matrites was taken *a* : and Saul the son of Kish was taken; but when they sought him, he could not be found.

34. THE INSTALLATION OF SAUL AS KING.
1 *Samuel* 10: 22-25.

22 Therefore they asked of the LORD further, *b* Is there yet a man to come hither? And the LORD answered, Behold, he hath hid himself among the stuff. 23 And they ran and fetched him thence; and when he stood among the people, he was higher than any of the people from his shoulders and upward. 24 And Samuel said to all the people, See ye him whom the LORD hath chosen, that there is none like him among all the people? And all the people shouted, and said, *c* God save the king.

25 Then Samuel told the people the manner of the kingdom, and wrote it in *d* a book, and laid it up before the LORD. And Samuel sent all the people away, every man to his house.

35. SAUL'S BRIEF RETIREMENT TO PRIVATE LIFE.
1 *Samuel* 10: 26, 27.

26 And Saul also went to his house to Gibeah; and there went with him the *e* host, whose hearts God had touched. 27 But certain *f* sons of *g* Belial said, How shall this man save us? And they despised him, and brought him no present. *h* But he held his peace.

PART II.
SAUL'S REIGN UNTIL HIS REJECTION.

36. A GENERIC ACCOUNT OF THE WHOLE OF SAUL'S REIGN.
1 *Samuel* 14: 47-52.

47 Now when Saul had taken the kingdom over Israel, he fought against all his enemies on every side, against Moab, and against the children of Ammon, and against Edom, and against the kings of Zobah, and against the Philistines: and whithersoever he turned himself, *i* he vexed *them*. 48 And he did valiantly, and smote the Amalekites, and delivered Israel out of the hands of them that spoiled them.

49 Now the sons of Saul were Jonathan, and Ishvi, and Malchi-shua: and the names of his two daughters were these; the name of the firstborn Merab, and the name of the younger Michal: 50 and the name of Saul's wife was Ahinoam the daughter of Ahimaaz: and the name of the captain of his host was Abner the son of Ner, Saul's uncle. 51 *k* And Kish was the father of Saul; and Ner the father of Abner was the son of Abiel.

52 And there was sore war against the Philistines all the days of Saul: and when Saul saw any mighty man, or any valiant man, he *l* took him unto him.

---

a The Sept. adds, " and the family of the Matrites was brought near man by man." *b* Or, " Is the man yet come hither?" *c* Heb. " Let the king live." *d* Or, " the." *e* Or, " men of valour." *f* Or, " base fellows." *g* I. e., " worthlessness." *h* Or, " But he was as though he had been deaf." *i* Or, " he put *them* to the worse." The Sept. has, " he was victorious." *k* According to some ancient authorities, " And Kish the father of Saul and Ner. . . . were the sons of Abiel." *l* Heb. " gathered."

37. CONFIRMATION AND GENERAL RECOGNITION OF SAUL AS KING.

(1) SAUL'S VICTORY OVER THE AMMONITES.

1 *Samuel* 11 : 1–11.

1 Then *a* Nahash the Ammonite came up, and encamped against Jabesh-gilead : and all the men of Jabesh said unto Nahash, Make a covenant with us, and we will serve thee. 2 And Nahash the Ammonite said unto them, On this condition will I make it with you, that all your right eyes be put out; and I will lay it for a reproach upon all Israel. 3 And the elders of Jabesh said unto him, Give us seven days' respite, that we may send messengers unto all the borders of Israel : and then, if there be none to save us, we will come out to thee. 4 Then came the messengers to Gibeah of Saul, and spake these words in the ears of the people : and all the people lifted up their voice, and wept. 5 And, behold, Saul came following the oxen out of the field ; and Saul said, What aileth the people that they weep ? And they told him the words of the men of Jabesh. 6 And the spirit of God came mightily upon Saul when he heard those words, and his anger was kindled greatly. 7 And he took a yoke of oxen, and cut them in pieces, and sent them through-out all the borders of Israel by the hand of messengers, saying, Whosoever cometh not forth after Saul and after Samuel, so shall it be done unto his oxen. And *b* the dread of the LORD fell on the people, and they came out as one man. 8 And he numbered them in Bezek ; and the children of Israel were three hundred thousand, and the men of Judah thirty thousand. 9 And they said unto the messengers that came, Thus shall ye say unto the men of Jabesh-gilead, To-morrow, by the time the sun is hot, ye shall have deliverance. And the messengers came and told the men of Jabesh ; and they were glad. 10 Therefore the men of Jabesh said, To-morrow we will come out unto you, and ye shall do with us all that seemeth good unto you. 11 And it was so on the morrow, that Saul put the people in three companies ; and they came into the midst of the camp in the morning watch, and smote the Ammonites until the heat of the day : and it came to pass, that they which remained were scattered, so that two of them were not left together.

(2) CONFIRMATION OF SAUL AS KING AT GILGAL.

1 *Samuel* 11 : 12–15.

12 And the people said unto Samuel, Who is he that said, Shall Saul reign over us ? bring the men, that we may put them to death. 13 And Saul said, There shall not a man be put to death this day : for to-day the LORD hath wrought *c* deliverance in Israel.

14 Then said Samuel to the people, Come, and let us go to Gilgal, and renew the kingdom there. 15 And all the people went to Gilgal ; and there they made Saul king before the LORD in Gilgal ; and there they sacrificed sacrifices of peace offerings before the LORD ; and there Saul and all the men of Israel rejoiced greatly.

(3) SAMUEL'S LAST TRANSACTION WITH THE PEOPLE AT GILGAL.

1 *Samuel* 12 : 1–25.

1 And Samuel said unto all Israel, Behold, I have hearkened unto your voice in all that ye said unto me, and have made a king over you. 2 And now, behold, the king walketh before you : and I am old and grayheaded ; and, behold, my sons are with you : and I have walked before you from my youth unto this day. 3 Here I am : witness against me before the LORD, and before his anointed : whose ox have I taken ? or whose ass have I taken ? or whom have I defrauded ? whom have I oppressed ? or of whose hand have I taken a *d* ransom *e* to blind mine eyes therewith ? and I will restore it you. 4 And they said, Thou hast not defrauded us, nor oppressed us, neither hast thou taken aught of any man's hand. 5 And he said unto them, The LORD is witness against

---

a The Sept. has, " And it came to pass after about a month, that Nahash," etc.   *b* Or, " a terror from the LORD."
c Heb. " salvation."   *d* Or, " bribe."   *e* Or, " that I should hide mine eyes at him."   The Sept. has, " even a pair of
shoes ? answer against me and I will," etc.   See Ecclesiasticus 46 : 19.

1 *Samuel* 12.

you, and his anointed is witness this day, that ye have not found aught in my hand. And they said, He is witness. 6 And Samuel said unto the people, It is the LORD that *a* appointed Moses and Aaron, and that brought your fathers up out of the land of Egypt. 7 Now therefore stand still, that I may plead with you before the LORD concerning all the righteous acts of the LORD, which he did to you and to your fathers. 8 When Jacob was come into Egypt, and your fathers cried unto the LORD, then the LORD sent Moses and Aaron, who brought forth your fathers out of Egypt, and made them to dwell in this place. 9 But they forgat the LORD their God, and he sold them into the hand of Sisera, captain of the host of Hazor, and into the hand of the Philistines, and into the hand of the king of Moab, and they fought against them. 10 And they cried unto the LORD, and said, We have sinned, because we have forsaken the LORD, and have served the Baalim and the Ashtaroth: but now deliver us out of the hand of our enemies, and we will serve thee. 11 And the LORD sent Jerubbaal, and *b* Bedan, and Jephthah, and Samuel, and delivered you out of the hand of your enemies on every side, and ye dwelled in safety. 12 And when ye saw that Nahash the king of the children of Ammon came against you, ye said unto me, Nay, but a king shall reign over us: when the LORD your God was your king. 13 Now therefore behold the king whom ye have chosen, and whom ye have asked for: and, behold, the LORD hath set a king over you. 14 If ye will fear the LORD, and serve him, and hearken unto his voice, and not rebel against the commandment of the LORD, *c* and both ye and also the king that reigneth over you be followers of the LORD your God, *well:* 15 but if ye will not hearken unto the voice of the LORD, but rebel against the commandment of the LORD, then shall the hand of the LORD be against you, *d* as it was against your fathers. 16 Now therefore stand still and see this great thing, which the LORD will do before your eyes. 17 Is it not wheat harvest to-day? I will call unto the LORD, that he may send thunder and rain; and ye shall know and see that your wickedness is great, which ye have done in the sight of the LORD, in asking you a king. 18 So Samuel called unto the LORD; and the LORD sent thunder and rain that day: and all the people greatly feared the LORD and Samuel. 19 And all the people said unto Samuel, Pray for thy servants unto the LORD thy God, that we die not: for we have added unto all our sins *this* evil, to ask us a king. 20 And Samuel said unto the people, Fear not: ye have indeed done all this evil: yet turn not aside from following the LORD, but serve the LORD with all your heart; 21 *e* and turn ye not aside: for *then should ye go* after vain things which cannot profit nor deliver, for they are vain. 22 For the LORD will not forsake his people for his great name's sake: because it hath pleased the LORD to make you a people unto himself. 23 Moreover as for me, God forbid that I should sin against the LORD in ceasing to pray for you: but I will instruct you in the good and the right way. 24 Only fear the LORD, and serve him in truth with all your heart: for consider how great things he hath done for you. 25 But if ye shall still do wickedly, ye shall be consumed, both ye and your king.

38. THE BEGINNINGS OF ROYALTY.

1 *Samuel* 13 : 1, 2.

1 Saul was [*f thirty*] years old when he began to reign; and he reigned two years over Israel. 2 And Saul chose him three thousand men of Israel; whereof two thousand were with Saul in Michmash and in the mount of Beth-el, and a thousand were with Jonathan in Gibeah of Benjamin: and the rest of the people he sent every man to his tent.

---

a Or, "made." *b* Some ancient authorities read, "Barak." *c* Or, "then shall both ye . . . the LORD your God: but," etc. *d* The Sept. has, "and against your king." *e* The Sept. has, "and turn ye not aside after the vanities which," etc. *f* The Hebrew text has, "Saul was a year old." The whole verse is omitted in the unrevised Sept., but in a later recension the number "thirty" is inserted.

39. THE WAR AGAINST THE PHILISTINES.[a]

(1) Jonathan's Exploit in Gibeah.

1 *Samuel* 13 : 3*a*.

3*a* And Jonathan smote the garrison of the Philistines that was in Geba, and the Philistines heard of it.

(2) Saul summons Israel to Gilgal.

1 *Samuel* 13 : 3*b*, 4.

3*b* And Saul blew the trumpet throughout all the land, saying, Let the Hebrews hear.   4 And all Israel heard say that Saul had smitten the garrison of the Philistines, and that Israel also was had in abomination with the Philistines.   And the people were gathered together after Saul to Gilgal.

(3) The Philistines encamp in Michmash.

1 *Samuel* 13 : 5.

5 And the Philistines assembled themselves together to fight with Israel, thirty thousand chariots, and six thousand horsemen, and people as the sand which is on the sea shore in multitude : and they came up, and pitched in Michmash, eastward of Beth-aven.

(4) The Distress of Israel.

1 *Samuel* 13 : 6, 7, 19–23.

6 When the men of Israel saw that they were in a strait, (for the people were distressed,) then the people did hide themselves in caves, and in thickets, and in rocks, and in [b] holds, and in [c] pits. 7 Now some of the Hebrews had gone over Jordan to the land of Gad and Gilead ; but as for Saul, he was yet in Gilgal, and all the people followed him trembling.

19 Now there was no smith found throughout all the land of Israel : for the Philistines said, Lest the Hebrews make them swords or spears : 20 but all the Israelites went down to the Philistines, to sharpen every man his share, and his coulter, and his axe, and his mattock ; 21 [d] yet they had a file for the mattocks, and for the coulters, and for the forks, and for the axes ; and to set the goads.   22 So it came to pass in the day of battle, that there was neither sword nor spear found in the hand of any of the people that were with Saul and Jonathan : but with Saul and with Jonathan his son was there found.   23 And the garrison of the Philistines went out unto the pass of Michmash.

(5) Saul wrongly offers Sacrifice.

1 *Samuel* 13 : 8, 9.

8 And he tarried seven days, according to the set time that Samuel *had appointed :* but Samuel came not to Gilgal ; and the people were scattered from him.   9 And Saul said, Bring hither the burnt offering to me, and the peace offerings.   And he offered the burnt offering.

(6) Samuel's Prophecy of Retribution.

1 *Samuel* 13 : 10–14.

10 And it came to pass that, as soon as he had made an end of offering the burnt offering, behold, Samuel came ; and Saul went out to meet him, that he might [e] salute him.   11 And Samuel said, What hast thou done ?   And Saul said, Because I saw that the people were scattered from me, and that thou camest not within the days appointed, and that the Philistines assembled them-

---

a Fifteen years, at least, and perhaps twenty, have been passed over in silence, since the last event mentioned in §38 ; for Saul was a very young man at the time of his accession to the throne, and time enough must have elapsed between the events of vv. 2 and 3 of 1 Samuel 13, so that Jonathan could have meanwhile grown to manhood.   *b* Or, "holes."   *c* Or, "cisterns."   *d* Or, "when the edges of the mattocks . . . and of the axes were blunt."   The Hebrew text is obscure.   *e* Or, "bless."

1 *Samuel* 13.

selves together at Michmash; 12 therefore said I, Now will the Philistines come down upon me to Gilgal, and I have not intreated the favour of the LORD: I forced myself therefore, and offered the burnt offering. 13 And Samuel said to Saul, Thou hast done foolishly: thou hast not kept the commandment of the LORD thy God, which he commanded thee: for now would the LORD have established thy kingdom upon Israel for ever. 14 But now thy kingdom shall not continue: the LORD hath sought him a man after his own heart, and the LORD hath appointed him to be prince over his people, because thou hast not kept that which the LORD commanded thee.

(7) Saul moves his Headquarters to Gibeah.

1 *Samuel* 13 : 15, 16.

15 And Samuel arose, and gat him up from Gilgal unto Gibeah of Benjamin. And Saul numbered the people that were present with him, about six hundred men. 16 And Saul, and Jonathan his son, and the people that were present with them, abode in Geba of Benjamin: but the Philistines encamped in Michmash.

(8) The three marauding Bands of the Philistines.

1 *Samuel* 13 : 17, 18.

17 And the spoilers came out of the camp of the Philistines in three companies: one company turned unto the way that leadeth to Ophrah, unto the land of Shual: 18 and another company turned the way to Beth-horon: and another company turned the way of the border that looketh down upon the valley of Zeboim toward the wilderness.

(9) Jonathan's bold Attack on the Philistines.

1 *Samuel* 14 : 1–16.

1 Now it fell upon a day, that Jonathan the son of Saul said unto the young man that bare his armour, Come and let us go over to the Philistines' garrison, that is on yonder side. But he told not his father. 2 And Saul abode in the uttermost part of Gibeah under the pomegranate tree which is in Migron: and the people that were with him were about six hundred men; 3 and Ahijah, the son of Ahitub, Ichabod's brother, the son of Phinehas, the son of Eli, the priest of the LORD in Shiloh, wearing an ephod. And the people knew not that Jonathan was gone. 4 And between the passes, by which Jonathan sought to go over unto the Philistines' garrison, there was a rocky crag on the one side, and a rocky crag on the other side: and the name of the one was Bozez, and the name of the other Seneh. 5 The one crag rose up on the north in front of Michmash, and the other on the south in front of Geba. 6 And Jonathan said to the young man that bare his armour, Come and let us go over unto the garrison of these uncircumcised: it may be that the LORD will work for us: for there is no restraint to the LORD to save by many or by few. 7 And his armourbearer said unto him, Do all that is in thine heart: turn thee, behold I am with thee according to thy heart. 8 Then said Jonathan, Behold, we will pass over unto the men, and we will discover ourselves unto them. 9 If they say thus unto us, Tarry until we come to you; then we will stand still in our place, and will not go up unto them. 10 But if they say thus, Come up unto us; then we will go up: for the LORD hath delivered them into our hand: and this shall be the sign unto us. 11 And both of them discovered themselves unto the garrison of the Philistines: and the Philistines said, Behold, the Hebrews come forth out of the holes where they had hid themselves. 12 And the men of the garrison answered Jonathan and his armourbearer, and said, Come up to us, and we will shew you a thing. And Jonathan said unto his armourbearer, Come up after me: for the LORD hath delivered them into the hand of Israel. 13 And Jonathan climbed up upon his hands and upon his feet, and his armourbearer after him: and they fell before Jonathan; and his armourbearer slew them after him. 14 And that first slaughter, which Jonathan and his armourbearer made, was about twenty men, within as it were *a* half a furrow's length in an

---

a Or, " half an acre of land."

1 *Samuel* 14.

acre of land.   15 And there was a trembling in the camp, in the field, and among all the people ; the garrison, and the spoilers, they also trembled : and the earth quaked ; so there was *a* an exceeding great trembling.   16 And the watchmen of Saul in Gibeah of Benjamin looked ; and, behold, the multitude melted away, and they went *hither* and thither.

(10) FLIGHT AND OVERTHROW OF THE PHILISTINES.

1 *Samuel* 14 : 17–23.

17 Then said Saul unto the people that were with him, Number now, and see who is gone from us.   And when they had numbered, behold, Jonathan and his armourbearer were not there. 18 And Saul said unto Ahijah, *b* Bring hither the ark of God.   For the ark of God was *there* at that time *c* with the children of Israel.   19 And it came to pass, while Saul talked unto the priest, that the tumult that was in the camp of the Philistines went on and increased : and Saul said unto the priest, Withdraw thine hand.   20 And Saul and all the people that were with him were gathered together, and came to the battle : and, behold, every man's sword was against his fellow, *and there was* a very great discomfiture.   21 Now the Hebrews that were with the Philistines as beforetime, which went up with them *d* into the camp *e from the country* round about ; even they also *turned* to be with the Israelites that were with Saul and Jonathan.   22 Likewise all the men of Israel which had hid themselves in the hill country of Ephraim, when they heard that the Philistines fled, even they also followed hard after them in the battle.   23 So the LORD saved Israel that day : and the battle passed over by Beth-aven.

(11) SAUL'S RASH CURSE AND ITS CONSEQUENCES.

1 *Samuel* 14 : 24–46.

24 And the men of Israel were distressed that day : but Saul adjured the people, saying, Cursed be the man that eateth any food until it be evening, and I be avenged on mine enemies.   So none of the people tasted food.   25 And all *f* the people came into the forest ; and there was honey upon the ground.   26 And when the people were come unto the forest, behold, *g* the honey dropped : but no man put his hand to his mouth ; for the people feared the oath.   27 But Jonathan heard not when his father charged the people with the oath : wherefore he put forth the end of the rod that was in his hand, and dipped it in the honeycomb, and put his hand to his mouth ; and his eyes were enlightened.   28 Then answered one of the people, and said, Thy father straitly charged the people with an oath, saying, Cursed be the man that eateth food this day.   And the people were faint.   29 Then said Jonathan, My father hath troubled the land ; see, I pray you, how mine eyes have been enlightened, because I tasted a little of this honey.   30 How much more, if haply the people had eaten freely to-day of the spoil of their enemies which they found ? *h* for now hath there been no great slaughter among the Philistines.   31 And they smote of the Philistines that day from Michmash to Aijalon : and the people were very faint.   32 And the people flew upon the spoil, and took sheep, and oxen, and calves, and slew them on the ground : and the people did eat them with the blood.   33 Then they told Saul, saying, Behold, the people sin against the LORD, in that they eat with the blood.   And he said, Ye have dealt treacherously : roll a great stone unto me this day.   34 And Saul said, Disperse yourselves among the people, and say unto them, Bring me hither every man his ox, and every man his sheep, and slay them here, and eat ; and sin not against the LORD in eating with the blood.   And all the people brought every man his ox with him that night, and slew them there.   35 And Saul built an altar unto the LORD : the same was the first altar that he built unto the LORD.

36 And Saul said, Let us go down after the Philistines by night, and spoil them until the morning light, and let us not leave a man of them.   And they said, Do whatsoever seemeth good unto thee.

---

a Heb. " a trembling of God."   *b* The Sept. has, " Bring hither the ephod.   For he wore the ephod at that time before Israel."   *c* Heb. " and."   *d* Or, " in the camp, round about."   *e* The Sept. has, " they also turned to be," etc.   *f* Heb. " the land."   *g* Or, " a stream of honey."   *h* Or, " for had there not been now a much greater slaughter ? " etc.

1 *Samuel* 14.

Then said the priest, Let us draw near hither unto God. 37 And Saul asked counsel of God, Shall I go down after the Philistines? wilt thou deliver them into the hand of Israel? But he answered him not that day. 38 And Saul said, Draw nigh hither, all ye *a* chiefs of the people: and know and see wherein this sin hath been this day. 39 For, as the LORD liveth, which saveth Israel, though it be in Jonathan my son, he shall surely die. But there was not a man among all the people that answered him. 40 Then said he unto all Israel, Be ye on one side, and I and Jonathan my son will be on the other side. And the people said unto Saul, Do what seemeth good unto thee. 41 Therefore Saul said unto the LORD, the God of Israel, *b* Shew the right. And Jonathan and Saul were taken *by lot:* but the people escaped. 42 And Saul said, Cast *lots* between me and Jonathan my son. 43 And Jonathan was taken. Then Saul said to Jonathan, Tell me what thou hast done. And Jonathan told him, and said, I did certainly taste a little honey with the end of the rod that was in mine hand; and, lo, I must die. 44 And Saul said, God do so and more also: for thou shalt surely die, Jonathan. 45 And the people said unto Saul, Shall Jonathan die, who hath wrought this great salvation in Israel? God forbid: as the LORD liveth, there shall not one hair of his head fall to the ground; for he hath wrought with God this day. So the people *c* rescued Jonathan, that he died not. 46 Then Saul went up from following the Philistines: and the Philistines went to their own place.

40. JEHOVAH'S REJECTION OF SAUL.

(1) THE COMMISSION TO DESTROY AMALEK.

1 *Samuel* 15: 1-3.

1 And Samuel said unto Saul, The LORD sent me to anoint thee to be king over his people, over Israel: now therefore hearken thou unto the voice of the words of the LORD. 2 Thus saith the LORD of hosts, I *d* have marked that which Amalek did to Israel, how he set himself against him in the way, when he came up out of Egypt. 3 Now go and smite Amalek, and *e* utterly destroy all that they have, and spare them not; but slay both man and woman, infant and suckling, ox and sheep, camel and ass.

(2) SAUL'S DISOBEDIENCE.

1 *Samuel* 15: 4-9.

4 And Saul summoned the people, and numbered them in Telaim, two hundred thousand footmen, and ten thousand men of Judah. 5 And Saul came to the city of Amalek, and *f* laid wait in the valley. 6 And Saul said unto the Kenites, Go, depart, get you down from among the Amalekites, lest I destroy you with them: for ye shewed kindness to all the children of Israel, when they came up out of Egypt. So the Kenites departed from among the Amalekites. 7 And Saul smote the Amalekites, from Havilah as thou goest to Shur, that is before Egypt. 8 And he took Agag the king of the Amalekites alive, and utterly destroyed all the people with the edge of the sword. 9 But Saul and the people spared Agag, and the best of the sheep, and of the oxen, and of the fatlings, and the lambs, and all that was good, and would not utterly destroy them: but every thing that was vile and refuse, that they destroyed utterly.

(3) THE PENALTY OF DISOBEDIENCE.

1 *Samuel* 15: 10-31.

10 Then came the word of the LORD unto Samuel, saying, 11 It repenteth me that I have set up Saul to be king: for he is turned back from following me, and hath not performed my commandments. And Samuel was wroth; and he cried unto the LORD all night. 12 And Samuel rose early to meet Saul in the morning; and it was told Samuel, saying, Saul came to Carmel, and, behold, he set him up a *g* monument, and is gone about, and passed on, and gone down to Gilgal.

---

a Heb. "corners."   *b* Or, "Give a perfect lot."   *c* Heb. "ransomed."   *d* Or, "will visit."   *e* Heb. "devote."
f Or, "strove."   *g* Heb. "hand."

1 *Samuel* 15.

13 And Samuel came to Saul: and Saul said unto him, Blessed be thou of the LORD: I have performed the commandment of the LORD.   14 And Samuel said, What meaneth then this bleating of the sheep in mine ears, and the lowing of the oxen which I hear?   15 And Saul said, They have brought them from the Amalekites: for the people spared the best of the sheep and of the oxen, to sacrifice unto the LORD thy God; and the rest we have *a* utterly destroyed.   16 Then Samuel said unto Saul, Stay, and I will tell thee what the LORD hath said to me this night.   And he said unto him, Say on.   17 And Samuel said, *b* Though thou wast little in thine own sight, wast thou not made the head of the tribes of Israel?   And the LORD anointed thee king over Israel; 18 and the LORD sent thee on a journey, and said, Go and utterly destroy the sinners the Amalekites, and fight against them until they be consumed.   19 Wherefore then didst thou not obey the voice of the LORD, but didst fly upon the spoil, and didst that which was evil in the sight of the LORD?   20 And Saul said unto Samuel, Yea, I have obeyed the voice of the LORD, and have gone the way which the LORD sent me, and have brought Agag the king of Amalek, and have *a* utterly destroyed the Amalekites.   21 But the people took of the spoil, sheep and oxen, the chief of the devoted things, to sacrifice unto the LORD thy God in Gilgal.   22 And Samuel said, Hath the LORD as great delight in burnt offerings and sacrifices, as in obeying the voice of the LORD?   Behold, to obey is better than sacrifice, and to hearken than the fat of rams.   23 For rebellion is as the sin of *c* witchcraft, and stubbornness is as *d* idolatry and *e* teraphim.   Because thou hath rejected the word of the LORD, he hath also rejected thee from being king.   24 And Saul said unto Samuel, I have sinned: for I have transgressed the commandment of the LORD, and thy words: because I feared the people, and obeyed their voice.   25 Now therefore, I pray thee, pardon my sin, and turn again with me, that I may worship the LORD.   26 And Samuel said unto Saul, I will not return with thee: for thou hast rejected the word of the LORD, and the LORD hath rejected thee from being king over Israel.   27 And as Samuel turned about to go away, he laid hold upon the skirt of his robe, and it rent.   28 And Samuel said unto him, The LORD hath rent the kingdom of Israel from thee this day, and hath given it to a neighbour of thine, that is better than thou.   29 And also the *f* Strength of Israel will not lie nor repent: for he is not a man, that he should repent.   30 Then he said, I have sinned: yet honour me now, I pray thee, before the elders of my people, and before Israel, and turn again with me, that I may worship the LORD thy God.   31 So Samuel turned again after Saul; and Saul worshipped the LORD.

(4) THE FATE OF AGAG.

1 *Samuel* 15: 32, 33.

32 Then said Samuel, Bring ye hither to me Agag the king of the Amalekites.   And Agag came unto him *g* delicately.   And Agag said, Surely the bitterness of death is past.   33 And Samuel said, As thy sword hath made women childless, so shall thy mother be childless among women.   And Samuel hewed Agag in pieces before the LORD in Gilgal.

(5) SAMUEL AND SAUL PART.

1 *Samuel* 15: 34, 35.

34 Then Samuel went to Ramah; and Saul went up to his house to Gibeah of Saul.   35 And Samuel came no more to see Saul until the day of his death; *h* for Samuel mourned for Saul: and the LORD repented that he had made Saul king over Israel.

---

a Heb. "devoted."   *b* Or, " Though thou be little . . . art thou not head of the tribes of Israel?"   *c* Heb. " divination."   *d* Or, " iniquity."   *e* See Genesis 31: 19, 34.   *f* Or, " Victory." Or, " Glory."   *g* Or, "cheerfully."   *h* Or, " but."

PART III.

THE DECLINE OF SAUL AND THE RISE OF DAVID.

I. The Early History of David.

41. DAVID CHOSEN AND ANOINTED AS SAUL'S SUCCESSOR BY SAMUEL.

1 Samuel 16 : 1–13.

1 And the LORD said, unto Samuel, How long wilt thou mourn for Saul, seeing I have rejected him from being king over Israel? fill thine horn with oil, and go, I will send thee to Jesse the Beth-lehemite: for I have provided me a king among his sons. 2 And Samuel said, How can I go? if Saul hear it, he will kill me. And the LORD said, Take an heifer with thee, and say, I am come to sacrifice to the LORD. 3 And call Jesse to the sacrifice, and I will shew thee what thou shalt do: and thou shalt anoint unto me him whom I name unto thee. 4 And Samuel did that which the LORD spake, and came to Beth-lehem. And the elders of the city came to meet him trembling, and said, Comest thou peaceably? 5 And he said, Peaceably: I am come to sacrifice unto the LORD: sanctify yourselves, and come with me to the sacrifice. And he sanctified Jesse and his sons, and called them to the sacrifice. 6 And it came to pass, when they were come, that he looked on *a* Eliab, and said, Surely the LORD's anointed is before him. 7 But the LORD said unto Samuel, Look not on his countenance, or on the height of his stature; because I have rejected him: for *the LORD seeth* not as man seeth; for man looketh on the outward appearance, but the LORD looketh on the heart. 8 Then Jesse called Abinadab, and made him pass before Samuel. And he said, Neither hath the LORD chosen this. 9 Then Jesse made *b* Shammah to pass by. And he said, Neither hath the LORD chosen this. 10 And Jesse made seven of his sons to pass before Samuel. And Samuel said unto Jesse, The LORD hath not chosen these. 11 And Samuel said unto Jesse, Are here all thy children? And he said, There remaineth yet the youngest, and, behold, he keepeth the sheep. And Samuel said unto Jesse, Send and fetch him: for we will not sit *c* down till he come hither. 12 And he sent, and brought him in. Now he was ruddy, and withal *d* of a beautiful countenance, and goodly to look upon. And the LORD said, Arise, anoint him: for this is he. 13 Then Samuel took the horn of oil, and anointed him in the midst of his brethren: and the spirit of the LORD came mightily upon David from that day forward. So Samuel rose up, and went to Ramah.

42. DAVID'S INTRODUCTION TO THE COURT OF SAUL.

1 Samuel 16 : 14–23.

14 Now the spirit of the LORD had departed from Saul, and an evil spirit from the LORD *e* troubled him. 15 And Saul's servants said unto him, Behold now, an evil spirit from God troubleth thee. 16 Let our lord now command thy servants, which are before thee, to seek out a man who is a cunning player on the harp: and it shall come to pass, when the evil spirit from God is upon thee, that he shall play with his hand, and thou shalt be well. 17 And Saul said unto his servants, Provide me now a man that can play well, and bring him to me. 18 Then answered one of the young men, and said, Behold, I have seen a son of Jesse the Beth-lehemite, that is cunning in playing, and a mighty man of valour, and a man of war, and *f* prudent in *g* speech, and a comely person, and the LORD is with him. 19 Wherefore Saul sent messengers unto Jesse, and said, Send me David thy son, which is with the sheep. 20 And Jesse took an ass *laden* with bread, and a *h* bottle of wine, and a kid, and sent them by David his son unto Saul. 21 And David

---

a In 1 Chronicles 27 : 18, " Elihu." See §107, (2), *J*. *b* In 2 Samuel 13 : 3, " Shimeah." In 1 Chronicles 2 : 13, " Shimea." See §§7, (1), and 99. *c* Heb. " around." *d* Heb. " fair of eyes." *e* Or, " terrified." *f* Or, " skilful." *g* Or, " business." *h* Or, " skin."

1 *Samuel* 16.

came to Saul, and stood before him : and he loved him greatly ; and he became his armourbearer.
22 And Saul sent to Jesse, saying, Let David, I pray thee, stand before me ; for he hath found
favour in my sight.   23 And it came to pass, when the *evil* spirit from God was upon Saul, that
David took the harp, and played with his hand : so Saul was refreshed, and was well, and the evil
spirit departed from him.

II. David's Advancement and Saul's growing Jealousy.

43. THE STORY OF DAVID AND GOLIATH.

(1) THE INVASION OF THE PHILISTINES.

1 *Samuel* 17 : 1–3.

1 Now the Philistines gathered together their armies to battle, and they were gathered together
at Socoh, which belongeth to Judah, and pitched between Socoh and Azekah, in Ephes-dammim.
2 And Saul and the men of Israel were gathered together, and pitched in the vale of *a* Elah, and
set the battle in array against the Philistines.   3 And the Philistines stood on the mountain on
the one side, and Israel stood on the mountain on the other side : and there was a valley between
them.

(2) THE CHALLENGE OF GOLIATH.

1 *Samuel* 17 : 4–11.

4 And there went out a champion out of the camp of the Philistines, named Goliath, of Gath,
whose height was six cubits and a span.   5 And he had an helmet of brass upon his head, and he
was clad with a coat of mail ; and the weight of the coat was five thousand shekels of brass.
6 And he had greaves of brass upon his legs, and a *b* javelin of brass between his shoulders.   7 And
the *c* staff of his spear was like a weaver's beam ; and his spear's head *weighed* six hundred shekels
of iron : and his shieldbearer went before him.   8 And he stood and cried unto the *d* armies of
Israel, and said unto them, Why are ye come out to set your battle in array ? am not I a Philistine, and ye servants to Saul ? choose you a man for you, and let him come down to me.   9 If
he be able to fight with me, and kill me, then will we be your servants : but if I prevail against
him, and kill him, then shall ye be our servants, and serve us.   10 And the Philistine said, I *e* defy
the armies of Israel this day ; give me a man, that we may fight together.   11 And when Saul and
all Israel heard those words of the Philistine, they were dismayed, and greatly afraid.

(3) DAVID IS SENT BY HIS FATHER TO HIS BRETHREN IN THE ARMY.

1 *Samuel* 17 : 12–22.

12 *f* Now David was the son of that Ephrathite of Beth-lehem-judah, whose name was Jesse ;
and he had eight sons : and the man was an old man in the days of Saul, stricken *in years* among
men.   13 And the three eldest sons of Jesse had gone after Saul to the battle : and the names of
his three sons that went to the battle were Eliab the firstborn, and next unto him Abinadab, and
the third Shammah.   14 And David was the youngest : and the three eldest followed Saul.   15 Now
David went to and fro from Saul to feed his father's sheep at Beth-lehem.   16 And the Philistine
drew near morning and evening, and presented himself forty days.

17 And Jesse said unto David his son, Take now for thy brethren an ephah of this parched corn,
and these ten loaves, and carry *them* quickly to the camp to thy brethren ; 18 and bring these ten
cheeses unto the captain of their thousand, and look how thy brethren fare, and take their pledge.
19 Now Saul, and they, and all the men of Israel, *g* were in the vale of Elah, fighting with the
Philistines.   20 And David rose up early in the morning, and left the sheep with a keeper, and

---

a Or, " the terebinth."   *b* The Sept. and Vulgate have, " target."   *c* Or, according to another reading, "blade."
d Heb. " ranks," and in vv. 10, 21, 22, 26, etc.   *e* Or, " reproach."   *f* The Sept. omits vv. 12–31 and 55–18 : 5.   *g* Or,
" are."

1 *Samuel* 17.

took, and went, as Jesse had commanded him ; and he came to the *a* place of the wagons, as the host which was going forth to the *b* fight shouted for the battle. 21 And Israel and the Philistines put the battle in array, army against army. 22 And David left his baggage in the hand of the keeper of the baggage, and ran to the army, and came and saluted his brethren.

(4) DAVID ACCEPTS GOLIATH'S CHALLENGE.

1 *Samuel* 17 : 23–37.

23 And as he talked with them, behold, there came up the champion, the Philistine of Gath, Goliath by name, out of the ranks of the Philistines, and spake according to the same words : and David heard them. 24 And all the men of Israel, when they saw the man, fled from him, and were sore afraid. 25 And the men of Israel said, Have ye seen this man that is come up ? surely to defy Israel is he come up : and it shall be, that the man who killeth him, the king will enrich him with great riches, and will give him his daughter, and make his father's house free in Israel. 26 And David spake to the men that stood by him, saying, What shall be done to the man that killeth this Philistine, and taketh away the reproach from Israel ? for who is this uncircumcised Philistine, that he should defy the armies of the living God ? 27 And the people answered him after this manner, saying, So shall it be done to the man that killeth him. 28 And Eliab his eldest brother heard when he spake unto the men ; and Eliab's anger was kindled against David, and he said, Why art thou come down ? and with whom hast thou left those few sheep in the wilderness ? I know thy pride, and the naughtiness of thine heart; for thou art come down that thou mightest see the battle. 29 And David said, What have I now done ? *c* Is there not a cause ? 30 And he turned away from him toward another, and spake after the same manner : and the people answered him again after the former manner. 31 And when the words were heard which David spake, they rehearsed them before Saul; and he sent for him. 32 And David said to Saul, Let no man's heart fail *d* because of him ; thy servant will go and fight with this Philistine. 33 And Saul said to David, Thou art not able to go against this Philistine to fight with him : for thou art but a youth, and he a man of war from his youth. 34 And David said unto Saul, Thy servant kept his father's sheep ; *e* and when there came a lion, or a bear, and took a lamb out of the flock, 35 I went out after him, and smote him, and delivered it out of his mouth : and when he arose against me, I caught him by his beard, and smote him, and slew him. 36 Thy servant smote both the lion and the bear : and this uncircumcised Philistine shall be as one of them, seeing he hath *f* defied the armies of the living God. 37 And David said, The LORD that delivered me out of the paw of the lion, and out of the paw of the bear, he will deliver me out of the hand of this Philistine. And Saul said unto David, Go, and the LORD shall be with thee.

(5) DAVID'S CONTEST WITH GOLIATH.

1 *Samuel* 17 : 38–51.

38 And Saul clad David with his apparel, and he put an helmet of brass upon his head, and he clad him with a coat of mail. 39 And David girded his sword upon his apparel, and he assayed to go ; for he had not proved it. And David said unto Saul, I cannot go with these; for I have not proved them. And David put them off him. 40 And he took his staff in his hand, and chose him five smooth stones out of the *g* brook, and put them in the shepherd's bag which he had, even in his scrip ; and his sling was in his hand : and he drew near to the Philistine. 41 And the Philistine came on and drew near unto David ; and the man that bare the shield went before him. 42 And when the Philistine looked about, and saw David, he disdained him : for he was but a youth, and ruddy, and withal of a fair countenance. 43 And the Philistine said unto David, Am I a dog, that thou comest to me with staves ? And the Philistine cursed David by his gods. 44 And the Philistine said to David, Come to me, and I will give thy flesh unto the fowls of the air, and to

---

a Or, " barricade." *b* Or, " battle ground." *c* Or, " Was it not *but* a word ? " *d* Or, " within him." *e* Or, " and there came a lion and a bear . . . and I went out," etc. *f* Or, " reproached." *g* Or, " torrent bed."

1 *Samuel* 17.

the beasts of the field.   45 Then said David to the Philistine, Thou comest to me with a sword, and with a spear, and with a javelin : but I come to thee in the name of the LORD of hosts, the God of the armies of Israel, which thou hast defied.   46 This day will the LORD deliver thee into mine hand ; and I will smite thee, and take thine head from off thee ; and I will give the carcases of the hosts of the Philistines this day unto the fowls of the air, and to the wild beasts of the earth ; that all the earth may know that there is a God in Israel : 47 and that all this assembly may know that the LORD saveth not with sword and spear : for the battle is the LORD'S, and he will give you into our hand.   48 And it came to pass, when the Philistine arose, and came and drew nigh to meet David, that David hastened, and ran toward the army to meet the Philistine.   49 And David put his hand in his bag, and took thence a stone, and slang it, and smote the Philistine in his forehead ; and the stone sank into his forehead, and he fell upon his face to the earth.   50 So David prevailed over the Philistine with a sling and with a stone, and smote the Philistine, and slew him ; but there was no sword in the hand of David.   51 Then David ran, and stood over the Philistine, and took his sword, and drew it out of the sheath thereof, and slew him, and cut off his head therewith.   And when the Philistines saw that their *a* champion was dead, they fled.

(6) DAVID ONCE MORE IN THE ROYAL PRESENCE.

1 *Samuel* 17 : 55–58.

55 And when Saul saw David go forth against the Philistine, he said unto Abner, the captain of the host, Abner, whose son is this youth ?   And Abner said, As thy soul liveth, O king, I cannot tell.   56 And the king said, Inquire thou whose son the stripling is.   57 And as David returned from the slaughter of the Philistine, Abner took him, and brought him before Saul with the head of the Philistine in his hand.   58 And Saul said to him, Whose son art thou, thou young man ?   And David answered, I am the son of thy servant Jesse the Beth-lehemite.

(7) THE DEED OF SHAMMAH. *b*

[2 *Samuel* 23 : 11*b*, 12.]	[1 *Chronicles* 11 : 13, 14.]
11*b* And the Philistines were gathered together *c* into a troop, where was a plot of ground full of lentils ; and the people fled from the Philistines. 12 But he stood in the midst of the plot, and defended it, and slew the Philistines : and the LORD wrought a great *d* victory.	13 He was with David at *e* Pas-dammim, and there the Philistines were gathered together to battle, where was a plot of ground full of barley ; and the people fled from before the Philistines. 14 And they stood in the midst of the plot, and defended it, and slew the Philistines ; and the LORD saved them by a great *d* victory.

(8) THE ROUT OF THE PHILISTINES.

1 *Samuel* 17 : 52–54.

52 And the men of Israel and of Judah arose, and shouted, and pursued the Philistines, until thou comest to *f* Gai, and to the gates of Ekron.   And the wounded of the Philistines fell down by the way to *g* Shaaraim, even unto Gath, and unto Ekron.   53 And the children of Israel returned from chasing after the Philistines, and they spoiled their camp.   54 And David took the head of the Philistine, and brought it to Jerusalem ; but he put his armour in his tent.

44. DAVID AT THE COURT OF SAUL.

(1) SAUL ATTACHES DAVID TO HIS SUIT.

1 *Samuel* 18 : 2.

2 And Saul took him that day, and would let him go no more home to his father's house.

---

a Or, " mighty man."   *b* Cf. §91, (1), *C.*   *c* Or, " for foraging."   *d* Heb. " salvation."   *e* In 1 Samuel 17 : 1, " Ephes-dammim."   See above §43, (1).   *f* The Sept. has, " Gath."   *g* Or, " the two gates."

(2) Jonathan's Friendship for David.

1 *Samuel* 18 : 1, 3, 4.

1 And it came to pass, when he had made an end of speaking unto Saul, that the soul of Jonathan was knit with the soul of David, and Jonathan loved him as his own soul.   3 Then Jonathan and David made a covenant, because he loved him as his own soul.   4 And Jonathan stripped himself of the robe that was upon him, and gave it to David, and his apparel, even to his sword, and to his bow, and to his girdle.

(3) David's Popularity.

1 *Samuel* 18 : 5.

5 And David *a* went out whithersoever Saul sent him, *and b* behaved himself wisely: and Saul set him over the men of war, and it was good in the sight of all the people, and also in the sight of Saul's servants.

(4) Saul's Hatred toward David.

1 *Samuel* 18 : 6–16.

6 And it came to pass as they came, when David returned from the slaughter of the *c* Philistine, that the women came out of all the cities of Israel, singing and dancing, to meet king Saul, with timbrels, with joy, and with *d* instruments of music.   7 And the women *e* sang one to another in their play, and said,

Saul hath slain his thousands,
And David his ten thousands.

8 And Saul was very wroth, and this saying displeased him; and he said, They have ascribed unto David ten thousands, and to me they have ascribed but thousands: and what can he have more but the kingdom?   9 And Saul eyed David from that day and forward.

10 And it came to pass on the morrow, that an evil spirit from God came mightily upon Saul, and he *f* prophesied in the midst of the house: and David played with his hand, as he did day by day: and Saul had his spear in his hand.   11 And Saul cast the spear; for he said, I will smite David even to the wall.   And David avoided out of his presence twice.   12 And Saul was afraid of David, because the LORD was with him, and was departed from Saul.   13 Therefore Saul removed him from him, and made him his captain over a thousand; and he went out and came in before the people.   14 And David *b* behaved himself wisely in all his ways; and the LORD was with him.   15 And when Saul saw that he behaved himself very wisely, he stood in awe of him.   16 But all Israel and Judah loved David; for he went out and came in before them.

(5) Saul's artful Attempt against David's Life.

1 *Samuel* 18 : 17–29.

17 And Saul said to David, Behold, my elder daughter Merab, her will I give thee to wife: only be thou valiant for me, and fight the LORD's battles.   For Saul said, Let not mine hand be upon him, but let the hand of the Philistines be upon him.   18 And David said unto Saul, Who am I, and *g* what is my life, *or* my father's family in Israel, that I should be son in law to the king?   19 But it came to pass at the time Merab Saul's daughter should have been given to David, that she was given unto Adriel the Meholathite to wife.   20 And Michal Saul's daughter loved David: and they told Saul, and the thing pleased him.   21 And Saul said, I will give him her, that she may be a snare to him, and that the hand of the Philistines may be against him.   Wherefore Saul said to David, Thou shalt this day be my son in law a second time.   22 And Saul commanded his servants, *saying,* Commune with David secretly, and say, Behold, the king hath delight in thee, and all his servants love thee: now therefore be the king's son in law.   23 And Saul's servants

---

a Or, " went out; whithersoever Saul sent him, he," etc.   *b* Or, " prospered."   *c* Or, " Philistines."   *d* Or, " triangles."   Or, " three-stringed instruments."   *e* Or, " answered one another."   *f* Or, " raved."   *g* Or, " who are my kinsfolk."

7

1 *Samuel* 18.

spake those words in the ears of David.   And David said, Seemeth it to you a light thing to be the king's son in law, seeing that I am a poor man, and lightly esteemed ?   24 And the servants of Saul told him, saying, On this manner spake David.   25 And Saul said, Thus shall ye say to David, The king desireth not any dowry, but an hundred foreskins of the Philistines, to be avenged of the king's enemies.   Now Saul thought to make David fall by the hand of the Philistines.   26 And when his servants told David these words, it pleased David well to be the king's son in law.   And the days were not expired ;   27 and David arose and went, he and his men, and slew of the Philistines two hundred men ;   and David brought their foreskins, and they gave them in full tale to the king, that he might be the king's son in law.   And Saul gave him Michal his daughter to wife.   28 And Saul saw and knew that the LORD was with David ;   and Michal Saul's daughter loved him.   29 And Saul was yet the more afraid of David ;   and Saul was David's enemy continually.

(6) DAVID'S INCREASING POPULARITY.

1 *Samuel* 18 : 30.

30 Then the princes of the Philistines went forth : and it came to pass, as often as they went forth, that David *a* behaved himself more wisely than all the servants of Saul ; so that his name was much *b* set by.

(7) JONATHAN PROVES HIS FRIENDSHIP FOR DAVID.

1 *Samuel* 19 : 1-7.

1 And Saul spake to Jonathan his son, and to all his servants, that they should slay David.   2 But Jonathan Saul's son delighted much in David.   And Jonathan told David, saying, Saul my father seeketh to slay thee : now therefore, I pray thee, take heed to thyself in the morning, and abide in a secret place, and hide thyself :   3 and I will go out and stand beside my father in the field where thou art, and I will commune with my father of thee ; and if I see aught, I will tell thee.   4 And Jonathan spake good of David unto Saul his father, and said unto him, Let not the king sin against his servant, against David ; because he hath not sinned against thee, and because his works have been to thee-ward very good :   5 for he put his life in his hand, and smote the Philistine, and the LORD wrought a great *c* victory for all Israel : thou sawest it, and didst rejoice : wherefore then wilt thou sin against innocent blood, to slay David without a cause ?   6 And Saul hearkened unto the voice of Jonathan : and Saul sware, As the LORD liveth, he shall not be put to death.   7 And Jonathan called David, and Jonathan shewed him all those things.   And Jonathan brought David to Saul, and he was in his presence, as beforetime.

45. DAVID IS FORCED TO LEAVE COURT.

(1) DAVID ESCAPES BY MICHAL'S HELP.

1 *Samuel* 19 : 8-17.

8 And there was war again : and David went out, and fought with the Philistines, and slew them with a great slaughter ; and they fled before him.   9 And *d* an evil spirit from the LORD was upon Saul, as he sat in his house with his spear in his hand ; and David played with his hand.   10 And Saul sought to smite David even to the wall with the spear ; but he slipped away out of Saul's presence, and he smote the spear into the wall : and David fled, and escaped that night.   11 And Saul sent messengers unto David's house, to watch him, and to slay him in the morning : and Michal David's wife told him, saying, If thou save not thy life to-night, to-morrow thou shalt be slain.   12 So Michal let David down through the window : and he went, and fled, and escaped.   13 And Michal took the teraphim, and laid it in the bed, and put a *e* pillow of goats' *hair* at the head thereof, and covered it with the clothes.   14 And when Saul sent messengers to take David,

---

a Or, " prospered more than."   *b* Heb. " precious."   *c* Heb. " salvation."   *d* Or, " the spirit of the LORD was evil toward Saul."   *e* Or, " quilt."   Or, " network."

1 *Samuel* 19.

she said, He is sick.   15 And Saul sent the messengers to see David, saying, Bring him up to me in the bed, that I may slay him.   16 And when the messengers came in, behold, the teraphim was in the bed, with the pillow of goats' *hair* at the head thereof.   17 And Saul said unto Michal, Why hast thou deceived me thus, and let mine enemy go, that he is escaped?   And Michal answered Saul, He said unto me, Let me go; why should I kill thee?

(2) David's Flight to Ramah and Saul's Pursuit.

1 *Samuel* 19: 18–24.

18 Now David fled, and escaped, and came to Samuel to Ramah, and told him all that Saul had done to him.   And he and 'Samuel went and dwelt in Naioth.   19 And it was told Saul, saying, Behold, David is at Naioth in Ramah.   20 And Saul sent messengers to take David : and when they saw the company of the prophets prophesying, and Samuel standing as head over them, the spirit of God came upon the messengers of Saul, and they also prophesied.   21 And when it was told Saul, he sent other messengers, and they also prophesied.   And Saul sent messengers again the third time, and they also prophesied.   22 Then went he also to Ramah, and came to *a* the great *b* well that is in Secu: and he asked and said, Where are Samuel and David ?   And one said, Behold, they be at Naioth in Ramah.   23 And he went thither to Naioth in Ramah: and the spirit of God came upon him also, and he went on, and prophesied, until he came to Naioth in Ramah. 24 And he also stripped off his clothes, and he also prophesied before Samuel, and *e* lay down naked all that day and all that night.   Wherefore they say, Is Saul also among the prophets?

(3) The Conference between David and Jonathan.

1 *Samuel* 20: 1–23.

1 And David fled from Naioth in Ramah, and came and said before Jonathan, What have I done? what is mine iniquity? and what is my sin before thy father, that he seeketh my life?   2 And he said unto him, God forbid ; thou shalt not die: behold, my father doeth nothing either great or small, but that he *d* discloseth it unto me : and why should my father hide this thing from me? it is not so.   3 And David sware moreover, and said, Thy father knoweth well that I have found grace in thine eyes, and he saith, Let not Jonathan know this, lest he be grieved : but truly as the LORD liveth, as thy soul liveth, there is but a step between me and death.   4 Then said Jonathan unto David, *e* Whatsoever thy soul *f* desireth, I will even do it for thee.   5 And David said unto Jonathan, Behold, to-morrow is the new moon, and I should not fail to sit with the king at meat : but let me go, that I may hide myself in the field unto the third day at even.   6 If thy father miss me at all, then say, David earnestly asked leave of me that he might run to Beth-lehem his city : for it is the yearly sacrifice there for all the family.   7 If he say thus, It is well; thy servant shall have peace : but if he be wroth, then know that evil is determined by him.   8 Therefore deal kindly with thy servant ; for thou hast brought thy servant into a covenant of the LORD with thee: but if there be in me iniquity, slay me thyself; for why shouldest thou bring me to thy father?   9 And Jonathan said, Far be it from thee : for if I should at all know that evil were determined by my father to come upon thee, then would not I tell it thee?   10 Then said David to Jonathan, Who shall tell me if perchance thy father answer thee roughly?   11 And Jonathan said unto David, Come and let us go out into the field.   And they went out both of them into the field.

12 And Jonathan said unto David, The LORD, the God of Israel, *be witness;* when I have sounded my father about this time to-morrow, *or* the third day, behold, if there be good toward David, shall I not then send unto thee, and disclose it unto thee?   13 The LORD do so to Jonathan, and more also, should it please my father to do thee evil, if I disclose it not unto thee, and send thee away, that thou mayest go in peace: and the LORD be with thee, as he hath been with my father.   14 And thou shalt not only while yet I live shew me the kindness of the LORD, that I

---

a The Sept. has, " the well of the threshing-floor that is," etc.   *b* Or, " cistern."   *c* Or, " fell."   *d* Heb." uncovereth mine ear."   *e* Or, " What doth thy soul desire, that I should do it for thee ? "   *f* Heb. " saith."

1 *Samuel* 20.

die not : 15 but also thou shalt not cut off thy kindness from my house for ever : no, not when the LORD hath cut off the enemies of David every one from the face of the earth. 16 So Jonathan made a covenant with the house of David, *saying*, And the LORD shall require it at the hand of David's enemies. 17 And Jonathan caused David to swear again, *a* for the love that he had to him : for he loved him as he loved his own soul. 18 Then Jonathan said unto him, To-morrow is the new moon : and thou shalt be missed, because thy seat will be *b* empty. 19 And when thou hast stayed three days, thou shalt go down *c* quickly, and come to the place where thou didst hide thyself *d* when the business was in hand, and shalt remain by *e* the stone Ezel. 20 And I will shoot three arrows on the side thereof, as though I shot at a mark. 21 And, behold, I will send the lad, *saying*, Go, find the arrows. If I say unto the lad, Behold, the arrows are on this side of thee : take *f* them, and come ; for there is peace to thee and *g* no hurt, as the LORD liveth. 22 But if I say thus unto the boy, Behold, the arrows are beyond thee : go thy way ; for the LORD hath sent thee away. 23 And as touching the matter which thou and I have spoken of, behold, the LORD is between thee and me forever.

(4) JONATHAN LEARNS OF HIS FATHER'S INTENTIONS TOWARDS DAVID.

1 *Samuel* 20 : 24–34.

24 So David hid himself in the field : and when the new moon was come, the king sat him down to eat meat. 25 And the king sat upon his seat, as at other times, even upon the seat by the wall ; and Jonathan stood up, and Abner sat by Saul's side : but David's place was empty. 26 Nevertheless Saul spake not any thing that day : for he thought, Something hath befallen him, he is not clean ; surely he is not clean. 27 And it came to pass on the morrow after the new moon, *which was* the second *day*, that David's place was empty : and Saul said unto Jonathan his son, Wherefore cometh not the son of Jesse to meat, neither yesterday, nor to-day ? 28 And Jonathan answered Saul, David earnestly asked leave of me to go to Beth-lehem : 29 And he said, Let me go, I pray thee ; for our family hath a sacrifice in the city ; and my brother, he hath commanded me *to be there :* and now, if I have found favour in thine eyes, let me get away, I pray thee, and see my brethren. Therefore he is not come unto the king's table. 30 Then Saul's anger was kindled against Jonathan, and he said unto him, Thou son of a perverse rebellious woman, do not I know that thou hast chosen the son of Jesse to thine own shame, and unto the shame of thy mother's nakedness ? 31 For as long as the son of Jesse liveth upon the ground, thou shalt not be stablished, nor thy kingdom. Wherefore now send and fetch him unto me, for he *h* shall surely die. 32 And Jonathan answered Saul his father, and said unto him, Wherefore should he be put to death ? what hath he done ? 33 And Saul cast his spear at him to smite him : whereby Jonathan knew that it was determined of his father to put David to death. 34 So Jonathan arose from the table in fierce anger, and did eat no meat the second day of the month : for he was grieved for David, because his father had done him shame.

(5) THE PARTING BETWEEN DAVID AND JONATHAN.

1 *Samuel* 20 : 35–42.

35 And it came to pass in the morning, that Jonathan went out into the field at the time appointed by David, and a little lad with him. 36 And he said unto his lad, Run, find now the arrows which I shoot. And as the lad ran, he shot an arrow *k* beyond him. 37 And when the lad was come to the place of the arrow which Jonathan had shot, Jonathan cried after the lad, and said, Is not the arrow beyond thee ? 38 And Jonathan cried after the lad, Make speed, haste, stay not. And Jonathan's lad gathered up the arrows, and came to his master. 39 But the lad knew not anything : only Jonathan and David knew the matter. 40 And Jonathan gave his weapons unto the lad, and said unto him, Go, carry them to the city. 41 And as soon as the lad was gone,

---

a Or, " by his love toward him."   *b* Heb. " missed."   *c* Heb. " greatly."   *d* Heb. " in the day of the business." Cf. 1 Samuel 19 : 2. See §44, (7).   *e* Or, as read by the Sept., " this mound."   *f* Or, " him."   *g* Heb. " not *any* thing." *h* Or, " is worthy to die." Heb. " is a son of death."   *i* Or, " to the place."   *k* Heb. " making it pass over him "

1 *Samuel* 20.

David arose *a* out of *a place* toward the South, and fell on his face to the ground, and bowed himself three times : and they kissed one another, and wept one with another, until David exceeded. 42 And Jonathan said to David, Go in peace, forasmuch as we have sworn both of us in the name of the LORD, saying, The LORD shall be between me and thee, and between my seed and thy seed, for ever. *b* And he arose and departed : and Jonathan went into the city.

III. David's Outlaw Life.

46. DAVID'S FLIGHT.

(1) TO NOB, TO AHIMELECH, THE HIGH PRIEST.

1 *Samuel* 21 : 1–9.

1 Then came David to Nob to Ahimelech the priest : and Ahimelech came to meet David trembling, and said unto him, Why art thou alone, and no man with thee ? 2 And David said unto Ahimelech the priest, The king hath commanded me a business, and hath said unto me, Let no man know any thing of the business whereabout I send thee, and what I have commanded thee : and I have appointed the young men to such and such a place. 3 Now therefore what is under thine hand ? give me five loaves of bread in mine hand, or whatsoever there is present. 4 And the priest answered David, and said, There is no common bread under mine hand, but there is holy bread ; if only the young men have kept themselves from women. 5 And David answered the priest, and said unto him, Of a truth women have been kept from us about these three days ; when I came out, the vessels of the young men were holy, *c* though it was but a common journey ; how much more then to-day shall their vessels be holy ? 6 So the priest gave him holy *bread :* for there was no bread there but the shewbread, that was taken from before the LORD, to put hot bread in the day it was taken away. 7 Now a certain man of the servants of Saul was there that day, detained before the LORD ; and his name was Doeg the Edomite, the *d* chiefest of the herdmen that belonged to Saul. 8 And David said unto Ahimelech, And is there not here under thine hand spear or sword ? for I have neither brought my sword nor my weapons with me, because the king's business required haste. 9 And the priest said, The sword of Goliath the Philistine, whom thou slewest in the vale of *e* Elah, behold, it is here wrapped in a cloth behind the ephod : if thou wilt take that, take it : for there is none other save that here. And David said, There is none like that ; give it me.

(2) TO ACHISH, KING OF GATH.

1 *Samuel* 21 : 10–15.

10 And David arose, and fled that day for fear of Saul, and went to Achish the king of Gath. 11 And the servants of Achish said unto him, Is not this David the king of the land ? did they not sing one to another of him in dances, saying,

Saul hath slain his thousands,
And David his ten thousands ?

12 And David laid up these words in his heart, and was sore afraid of Achish the king of Gath. 13 And he changed his behaviour before them, and feigned himself mad in their hands, and *f* scrabbled on the doors of the gate, and let his spittle fall down upon his beard. 14 Then said Achish unto his servants, Lo, ye see the man is mad : wherefore then have ye brought him to me ? 15 Do I lack mad men, that ye have brought this fellow to play the mad man in my presence ? shall this fellow come into my house ?

---

a Heb. "from beside the South." Or, as read by the Sept., "from beside the mound." *b* Ch. 21 : 1 in Heb. *c* Or, "and it may be used as common *bread ;* and especially since to-day it will be holy in respect of their vessels." *d* Or, "mightiest." *e* Or, "the terebinth." *f* Or, "made marks." " Scribbled " would be a very sensible English rendering.

(3) To the Cave of Adullam.

1 Samuel 22: 1, 2.

1 David therefore departed thence, and escaped to the cave of Adullam : and when his brethren and all his father's house heard it, they went down thither to him. 2 And every one that was in distress, and every one that was in debt, and every one that was *a* discontented, gathered themselves unto him ; and he became captain over them : and there were with him about four hundred men.

1 Chronicles 12: 16–18.

16 And there came of the children of Benjamin and Judah to the hold unto David. 17 And David went out to meet them, and answered and said unto them, If ye be come peaceably unto me to help me, mine heart shall be knit unto you : but if *ye be come* to betray me to mine adversaries, seeing there is no *b* wrong in mine hands, the God of our fathers look thereon, and rebuke it. 18 Then the spirit *c* came upon Amasai, who was chief of the *d* thirty, *and he said*, Thine are we, David, and on thy side, thou son of Jesse : peace, peace be unto thee, and peace be to thine helpers ; for thy God helpeth thee. Then David received them, and made them captains of the band.

(4) To Mizpeh of Moab, where he finds Asylum for his Parents.

1 Samuel 22: 3, 4.

3 And David went thence to Mizpeh of Moab : and he said unto the king of Moab, Let my father and my mother, I pray thee, come forth, *and be* with you, till I know what God will do for me. 4 And he brought them before the king of Moab : and they dwelt with him all the while that David was in the hold.

(5) To the Forest of Hereth, in Judah.

1 Samuel 22 : 5.

5 And the prophet Gad said unto David, Abide not in the hold ; depart, and get thee into the land of Judah. Then David departed, and came into the forest of Hereth.

47. SAUL'S VENGEANCE ON THE PRIESTS OF NOB.

1 Samuel 22 : 6–20.

6 And Saul heard that David was discovered, and the men that were with him : now Saul was sitting in Gibeah, under the tamarisk tree *e* in Ramah, with his spear in his hand, and all his servants were standing about him. 7 And Saul said unto his servants that stood about him, Hear now, ye Benjamites ; will the son of Jesse give every one of you fields and vineyards, will he make you all captains of thousands and captains of hundreds ; 8 that all of you have conspired against me, and *f* there is none that discloseth to me when my son maketh a league with the son of Jesse, and there is none of you that is sorry for me, or discloseth unto me that my son hath stirred up my servant against me, to lie in wait, as at this day? 9 Then answered Doeg the Edomite, which *g* stood by the servants of Saul, and said, I saw the son of Jesse coming to Nob, to Ahimelech the son of Ahitub. 10 And he inquired of the LORD for him, and gave him victuals, and gave him the sword of Goliath the Philistine. 11 Then the king sent to call Ahimelech the priest, the son of Ahitub, and all his father's house, the priests that were in Nob : and they came all of them to the king. 12 And Saul said, Hear now, thou son of Ahitub. And he answered, Here I am, my lord. 13 And Saul said unto him, Why have ye conspired against me, thou and the son of Jesse, in that thou hast given him bread, and a sword, and hast inquired of God for him, that he should

---

a Heb. "bitter of soul."   *b* Or, "violence."   *c* Heb. "clothed."   *d* Another reading is, "captains."   *e* Or, "on the height."   *f* Or, "there was none that disclosed it to me when my son made," etc.   *g* Or, "was set over."

1 *Samuel* 22.

rise against me, to lie in wait, as at this day ?   14 Then Ahimelech answered the king, and said, And who among all thy servants is so faithful as David, which is the king's son in law, and is taken into thy council, and is honourable in thine house ?   15 Have I to-day begun to inquire of God for him ? be it far from me : let not the king impute any thing unto his servant, nor to all the house of my father : for thy servant knoweth nothing of all this, less or more.   16 And the king said, Thou shalt surely die, Ahimelech, thou, and all thy father's house.   17 And the king said unto the *a* guard that stood about him, Turn, and slay the priests of the LORD ; because their hand also is with David, and because they knew that he fled, and did not disclose it to me.   But the servants of the king would not put forth their hand to fall upon the priests of the LORD.   18 And the king said to Doeg, Turn thou, and fall upon the priests.   And Doeg the Edomite turned, and he fell upon the priests, and he slew on that day fourscore and five persons that did wear a linen ephod. 19 And Nob, the city of the priests, smote he with the edge of the sword, both men and women, children and sucklings, and oxen and asses and sheep, with the edge of the sword.   20 And one of the sons of Ahimelech the son of Ahitub, named Abiathar, escaped, and fled after David.

48. DAVID IN KEILAH.

(1) DAVID RESCUES KEILAH.

1 *Samuel* 23 : 1–5.

1 And they told David, saying, Behold, the Philistines are fighting against Keilah, and they rob the threshing-floors.   2 Therefore David inquired of the LORD, saying, Shall I go and smite these Philistines?   And the LORD said unto David, Go, and smite the Philistines, and save Keilah. 3 And David's men said unto him, Behold, we be afraid here in Judah : how much more then if we go to Keilah against the armies of the Philistines?   4 Then David inquired of the LORD yet again.   And the LORD answered him and said, Arise, go down to Keilah; for I will deliver the Philistines into thine hand.   5 And David and his men went to Keilah, and fought with the Philistines, and brought away their cattle, and slew them with a great slaughter.   So David saved the inhabitants of Keilah.

(2) ABIATHAR JOINS DAVID.

1 *Samuel* 22 : 21–23 ; 23 : 6.

21 And Abiathar told David that Saul had slain the LORD'S priests.   22 And David said unto Abiathar, I knew on that day, when Doeg the Edomite was there, that he would surely tell Saul : I have occasioned *the death* of all the persons of thy father's house.   23 Abide thou with me, fear not ; for he that seeketh my life seeketh thy life : for with me thou shalt be in safeguard.

6 And it came to pass, when Abiathar the son of Ahimelech fled to David to Keilah, that he came down with an ephod in his hand.

(3) DAVID ESCAPES FROM KEILAH.

1 *Samuel* 23 : 7–13.

7 And it was told Saul that David was come to Keilah.   And Saul said, God hath *b* delivered him into mine hand ; for he is shut in, by entering into a town that hath gates and bars.   8 And Saul summoned all the people to war, to go down to Keilah, to besiege David and his men.   9 And David knew that Saul devised mischief against him; and he said to Abiathar the priest, Bring hither the ephod.   10 Then said David, O LORD, the God of Israel, thy servant hath surely heard that Saul seeketh to come to Keilah, to destroy the city for my sake.   11 Will the men of Keilah deliver me up into his hand? will Saul come down, as thy servant hath heard ?   O LORD, the God of Israel, I beseech thee, tell thy servant.   And the LORD said, He will come down.   12 Then said

a Heb. "runners."   *b* Heb. " alienated him."   The Sept. has, " sold."

1 *Samuel* 23.

David, Will the men of Keilah deliver up me and my men into the hand of Saul? And the LORD said, They will deliver thee up. 13 Then David and his men, which were about six hundred, arose and departed out of Keilah, and went whithersoever they could go. And it was told Saul that David was escaped from Keilah ; and he forbare to go forth.

49. DAVID'S LAST MEETING WITH JONATHAN.

1 *Samuel* 23 : 14–18.

14 And David abode in the wilderness in the strong holds, and remained in the hill country in the wilderness of Ziph. And Saul sought him every day, but God delivered him not into his hand. 15 And David saw that Saul was come out to seek his life : and David was in the wilderness of Ziph in *a* the wood. 16 And Jonathan Saul's son arose, and went to David into *a* the wood, and strengthened his hand in God. 17 And he said unto him, Fear not : for the hand of Saul my father shall not find thee ; and thou shalt be king over Israel, and I shall be next unto thee ; and that also Saul my father knoweth. 18 And they two made a covenant before the LORD : and David abode in *a* the wood, and Jonathan went to his house.

50. DAVID'S BETRAYAL BY THE ZIPHITES.

1 *Samuel* 23 : 19–24a.

19 Then came up the Ziphites to Saul to Gibeah, saying, Doth not David hide himself with us in the strong holds in *a* the wood, in the hill of Hachilah, which is on the south of *b* the desert ? 20 Now therefore, O king, come down, according to all the desire of thy soul to come down ; and our part shall be to deliver him up into the king's hand. 21 And Saul said, Blessed be ye of the LORD ; for ye have had compassion on me. 22 Go, I pray you, make yet more sure, and know and see his place where his *c* haunt is, *and* who hath seen him there : for it is told me that he dealeth very subtilly. 23 See therefore, and take knowledge of all the lurking places where he hideth himself, and come ye again to me *d* of a certainty, and I will go with you : and it shall come to pass, if he be in the land, that I will search him out among all the *e* thousands of Judah. 24a And they arose, and went to Ziph before Saul.

51. DAVID'S ESCAPE FROM SAUL IN THE WILDERNESS OF MAON.

1 *Samuel* 23 : 24b–28.

24b But David and his men were in the wilderness of Maon, in the *f* Arabah on the south of *b* the desert. 25 And Saul and his men went to seek him. And they told David : wherefore he came down to the rock, and abode in the wilderness of Maon. And when Saul heard *that*, he pursued after David in the wilderness of Maon. 26 And Saul went on this side of the mountain, and David and his men on that side of the mountain : and David made haste to get away for fear of Saul ; for Saul and his men compassed David and his men round about to take them. 27 But there came a messenger unto Saul, saying, Haste thee, and come ; for the Philistines have made a raid upon the land. 28 So Saul returned from pursuing after David, and went against the Philistines : therefore they called that place *g* Sela-hammahlekoth.

52. DAVID IN THE WILDERNESS OF ENGEDI : HE SPARES SAUL IN THE CAVE.

1 *Samuel* 23 : 29–24 : 22.

29 *i* And David went up from thence, and dwelt in the strong holds of En-gedi.

---

a Or, "Horesh."   *b* Or, " Jeshimon."   *c* Heb. "foot."   *d* Or, "with the certainty." Or, "to a set place."   *e* Or, "families."   *f* Cf. Deuteronomy 1 : 1.   *g* I. e., " The rock of divisions ," or, " The rock of escape."   *i* Ch. 24 : 1 in Heb.

I *Samuel* 24.

I And it came to pass, when Saul was returned from following the Philistines, that it was told him, saying, Behold, David is in the wilderness of En-gedi. 2 Then Saul took three thousand chosen men out of all Israel, and went to seek David and his men upon the rocks of the wild goats. 3 And he came to the sheepcotes by the way, where was a cave ; and Saul went in to cover his feet. Now David and his men were *a* abiding in the innermost parts of the cave. 4 And the men of David said unto him, Behold, the day of which the LORD said unto thee, Behold, I will deliver thine enemy into thine hand, and thou shalt do to him as it shall seem good unto thee. Then David arose, and cut off the skirt of Saul's robe privily. 5 And it came to pass afterward, that David's heart smote him, because he had cut off Saul's skirt. 6 And he said unto his men, The LORD forbid that I .should do this thing unto my lord, the LORD'S anointed, to put forth mine hand against him, seeing he is the LORD'S anointed. 7 So David checked his men with these words, and suffered them not to rise against Saul. And Saul rose up out of the cave, and went on his way. 8 David also arose afterward, and went out of the cave, and cried after Saul, saying, My lord the king. And when Saul looked behind him, David bowed with his face to the earth, and did obeisance. 9 And David said unto Saul, Wherefore hearkenest thou to men's words, saying, Behold, David seeketh thy hurt ? 10 Behold, this day thine eyes have seen how that the LORD had delivered thee to-day into mine hand in the cave : and some bade me kill thee : but *mine eye* spared thee ; and I said, I will not put forth mine hand against my lord ; for he is the LORD'S anointed. 11 Moreover, my father, see, yea, see the skirt of thy robe in my hand : for in that I cut off the skirt of thy robe, and killed thee not, know thou and see that there is neither evil nor transgression in mine hand, and I have not sinned against thee, though thou *b* huntest after my soul to take it. 12 The LORD judge between me and thee, and the LORD avenge me of thee : but mine hand shall not be upon thee. 13 As saith the proverb of the ancients, Out of the wicked cometh forth wickedness : but mine hand shall not be upon thee. 14 After whom is the king of Israel come out ? after whom dost thou pursue ? after a dead dog, after a flea. 15 The LORD therefore be judge, and give sentence between me and thee, and see, and plead my cause, and *c* deliver me out of thine hand. 16 And it came to pass, when David had made an end of speaking these words unto Saul, that Saul said, Is this thy voice, my son David ? And Saul lifted up his voice, and wept. 17 And he said to David, Thou art more righteous than I : for thou hast rendered unto me good, whereas I have rendered unto thee evil. 18 And thou hast declared this day how that thou hast dealt well with me : forasmuch as when the LORD had delivered me up into thine hand, thou killedst me not. 19 For if a man find his enemy, will he let him go well away ? wherefore the LORD reward thee good for that thou hast done unto me this day. 20 And now, behold, I know that thou shalt surely be king, and that the kingdom of Israel shall be established in thine hand. 21 Swear now therefore unto me by the LORD, that thou wilt not cut off my seed after me, and that thou wilt not destroy my name out of my father's house. 22 And David sware unto Saul. And Saul went home , but David and his men gat them up unto the hold.

53. THE DEATH OF SAMUEL.

I *Samuel* 25 : 1a.

1a And Samuel died ; and all Israel gathered themselves together, and lamented him, and buried him in his house at Ramah.

54. DAVID IN THE WILDERNESS OF PARAN : THE HISTORY OF NABAL AND ABIGAIL.

I *Samuel* 25 : 1b–38.

1b And David arose, and went down to the wilderness of Paran. 2 And there was a man in Maon, whose *d* possessions were in Carmel ; and the man was very

---

a Or, "sitting." *b* Or, " layest wait for." *c* Heb. " give sentence for me." *d* Or, " business was."

1 Samuel 25.

great, and he had three thousand sheep, and a thousand goats : and he was shearing his sheep in Carmel. 3 Now the name of the man was Nabal ; and the name of his wife Abigail : and the woman was of good understanding, and of a beautiful countenance : but the man was churlish and evil in his doings ; and he was of the house of Caleb. 4 And David heard in the wilderness that Nabal did shear his sheep. 5 And David sent ten young men, and David said unto the young men, Get you up to Carmel, and go to Nabal, and greet him in my name : 6 and *a* thus shall ye say *b*to him that liveth *in prosperity,* Peace be both unto thee, and peace be to thine house, and peace be unto all that thou hast. 7 And now I have heard that thou hast shearers : thy shepherds have now been with us, and we*c* did them no hurt, neither was there aught missing unto them, all the while they were in Carmel 8 Ask thy young men, and they will tell thee : wherefore let the young men find favour in thine eyes ; for we come in a good day : give, I pray thee, whatsoever cometh to thine hand, unto thy servants, and to thy son David. 9 And when David's young men came, they spake to Nabal according to all those words in the name of David, and *d* ceased. 10 And Nabal answered David's servants, and said, Who is David? and who is the son of Jesse ? there be many servants now a days that break away every man from his master. 11 Shall I then take my bread, and my water, and my *e* flesh that I have killed for my shearers, and give it unto men of whom I know not whence they be ? 12 So David's young men turned on their way, and went back, and came and told him according to all these words. 13 And David said unto his men, Gird ye on every man his sword. And they girded on every man his sword ; and David also girded on his sword : and there went up after David about four hundred men ; and two hundred abode by the stuff. 14 But one of the young men told Abigail, Nabal's wife, saying, Behold, David sent messengers out of the wilderness to *f* salute our master ; and he *g* flew upon them. 15 But the men were very good unto us, and we were not *h* hurt, neither missed we any thing, as long as we were conversant with them, when we were in the fields : 16 they were a wall unto us both by night and by day, all the while we were with them keeping the sheep. 17 Now therefore know and consider what thou wilt do ; for evil is determined against our master, and against all his house : for he is such a *i* son of *k* Belial, that one cannot speak to him. 18 Then Abigail made haste, and took two hundred loaves, and two *l* bottles of wine, and five sheep ready dressed, and five measures of parched corn, and an hundred clusters of raisins, and two hundred cakes of figs, and laid them on asses. 19 And she said unto her young men, Go on before me ; behold, I come after you. But she told not her husband Nabal. 20 And it was so, as she rode on her ass, and came down by the covert of the mountain, that, behold, David and his men came down against her ; and she met them. 21 Now David had said, Surely in vain have I kept all that this fellow hath in the wilderness, so that nothing was missed of all that pertained unto him : and he hath returned me evil for good. 22 God do so *m* unto the enemies of David, and more also, if I leave of all that pertain to him by the morning light so much as one man child. 23 And when Abigail saw David, she hasted, and lighted off her ass, and fell before David on her face, and bowed herself to the ground. 24 And she fell at his feet, and said, Upon me, my lord, upon me be the iniquity : and let thine handmaid, I pray thee, speak in thine ears, and hear thou the words of thine handmaid. 25 Let not my lord, I pray thee, regard this man of Belial, even Nabal : for as his name is, so is he ; *n* Nabal is his name, and folly is with him : but I thine handmaid saw not the young men of my lord, whom thou didst send. 26 Now therefore, my lord, as the LORD liveth, and as thy soul liveth, seeing the LORD hath withholden thee *o* from bloodguiltiness, and from *p* avenging thyself with thine own hand, now therefore let thine enemies, and them that seek evil to my lord, be as Nabal. 27 And now this *q* present which thy servant hath brought unto my lord, let it be given unto the young men that follow my lord. 28 Forgive, I pray thee, the trespass of thine handmaid : for the LORD will certainly make my lord a sure house, because my lord fighteth the battles of the LORD ; and evil shall not be found in thee all

---

a Or, "thus shall ye say, All hail! and peace be unto thee," etc.   *b* The Vulgate has, "to my brethren."   *c* Heb. "put them not to shame."   *d* Or, "remained quiet."   *e* Heb. "slaughter."   *f* Heb. "bless."   *g* Or, "railed on." *h* Heb. "put to shame."   *i* Or, "base fellow."   *k* I. e. "worthlessness."   *l* Or, "skins."   *m* The Sept. has, "unto David."   *n* I. e., "Fool."   *o* Heb. "from coming into blood."   *p* Heb. "thine own hand saving thee."   *q* Heb. "blessing."

1 *Samuel* 25.

thy days.   29 And though man be risen up to pursue thee, and to seek thy soul, yet the soul of my lord shall be bound in the bundle of *ᵃ* life with the LORD thy God ; and the souls of thine enemies, them shall he sling out, as from the hollow of a sling.   30 And it shall come to pass, when the LORD shall have done to my lord according to all the good that he hath spoken concerning thee, and shall have appointed thee prince over Israel; 31 that this shall be no *ᵇ* grief unto thee, nor offence of heart unto my lord, *ᶜ* either that thou hast shed blood causeless, or that my lord hath avenged himself : and when the LORD shall have dealt well with my lord, then remember thine handmaid.   32 And David said to Abigail, Blessed be the LORD, the God of Israel, which sent thee this day to meet me : 33 and blessed be thy *ᵈ* wisdom, and blessed be thou, which hast kept me this day from bloodguiltiness, and from avenging myself with mine own hand.   34 For in very deed, as the LORD, the God of Israel, liveth, which hath withholden me from hurting thee, except thou hadst hasted and come to meet me, surely there had not been left unto Nabal by the morning light so much as one man child.   35 So David received of her hand that which she had brought him : and he said unto her, Go up in peace to thine house ; see, I have hearkened to thy voice, and have accepted thy person.   36 And Abigail came to Nabal ; and, behold, he held a feast in his house, like the feast of a king ; and Nabal's heart was merry within him, for he was very drunken : wherefore she told him nothing, less or more, until the morning light.   37 And it came to pass in the morning, when the wine was gone out of Nabal, that his wife told him these things, and his heart died within him, and he became as a stone.   38 And it came to pass about ten days after, that the LORD smote Nabal, that he died.

55. DAVID'S MATRIMONIAL RELATIONS.

1 *Samuel* 25 : 39–44.

39 And when David heard that Nabal was dead, he said, Blessed be the LORD, that hath pleaded the cause of my reproach from the hand of Nabal, and hath kept back his servant from evil : and the evil-doing of Nabal hath the LORD returned upon his own head.   And David sent and *ᵉ* spake concerning Abigail, to take her to him to wife.   40 And when the servants of David were come to Abigail to Carmel, they spake unto her, saying, David hath sent us unto thee, to take thee to him to wife.   41 And she arose, and bowed herself with her face to the earth, and said, Behold, thine handmaid is a servant to wash the feet of the servants of my lord.   42 And Abigail hasted, and arose, and rode upon an ass, with five damsels of hers that followed her ; and she went after the messengers of David, and became his wife.   43 David also took Ahinoam of Jezreel ; and they became both of them his wives.   44 Now Saul had given Michal his daughter, David's wife, to *ᶠ* Palti the son of Laish, which was of Gallim.

56. DAVID, BETRAYED AGAIN BY THE ZIPHITES, SPARES SAUL THE SECOND TIME.

1 *Samuel* 26 : 1–25.

1 And the Ziphites came unto Saul to Gibeah, saying, Doth not David hide himself in the hill of Hachilah, which is before *ᵍ* the desert ?   2 Then Saul arose, and went down to the wilderness of Ziph, having three thousand chosen men of Israel with him, to seek David in the wilderness of Ziph.   3 And Saul pitched in the hill of Hachilah, which is before *ᵍ* the desert, by the way.   But David abode in the wilderness, and he saw that Saul came after him into the wilderness.   4 David therefore sent out spies, and understood that Saul was come *ʰ* of a certainty.   5 And David arose, and came to the place where Saul had pitched : and David beheld the place where Saul lay, and Abner the son of Ner, the captain of his host : and Saul lay within the *ⁱ* place of the wagons, and

---

1 *Samuel* 26.

the people pitched round about him.   6 Then answered David and said to Ahimelech the Hittite, and to Abishai the son of Zeruiah, brother to Joab, saying, Who will go down with me to Saul to the camp?   And Abishai said, I will go down with thee.   7 So David and Abishai came to the people by night : and, behold, Saul lay sleeping within the *a* place of the wagons, with his spear stuck in the ground at his head : and Abner and the people lay round about him.   8 Then said Abishai to David, God hath delivered up thine enemy into thine hand this day : now therefore let me smite him, I pray thee, with the spear to the earth at one stroke, and I will not smite him the second time.   9 And David said to Abishai, Destroy him not : for who can put forth his hand against the LORD'S anointed, and be guiltless ?   10 And David said, As the LORD liveth, the LORD shall smite him ; *b* or his day shall come to die ; or he shall go down into battle, and perish.   11 The LORD forbid that I should put forth mine hand against the LORD'S anointed : but now take, I pray thee, the spear that is at his head, and the cruse of water, and let us go.   12 So David took the spear and the cruse of water from Saul's head ; and they gat them away, and no man saw it, nor knew it, neither did any awake : for they were all asleep ; because a deep sleep from the LORD was fallen upon them.   13 Then David went over to the other side, and stood on the top of the mountain afar off ; a great space being between them : 14 and David cried to the people, and to Abner the son of Ner, saying, Answerest thou not, Abner ?   Then Abner answered and said, Who art thou that criest to the king ?   15 And David said to Abner, Art not thou a *valiant* man ? and who is like to thee in Israel ? wherefore then hast thou not kept watch over thy lord the king ? for there came one of the people in to destroy the king thy lord.   16 This thing is not good that thou hast done.   As the LORD liveth, ye are *c* worthy to die, because ye have not kept watch over your lord, the LORD'S anointed.   And now, see, where the king's spear is, and the cruse of water that was at his head.   17 And Saul knew David's voice, and said, Is this thy voice, my son David ? And David said, It is my voice, my lord, O king.   18 And he said, Wherefore doth my lord pursue after his servant ? for what have I done ? or what evil is in mine hand ?   19 Now therefore, I pray thee, let my lord the king hear the words of his servant.   If it be the LORD that hath stirred thee up against me, let him *d* accept an offering : but if it be the children of men, cursed be they before the LORD ; for they have driven me out this day that I should *e* not cleave unto the inheritance of the LORD, saying, Go, serve other gods.   20 Now therefore, let not my blood fall to the earth away from the presence of the LORD : for the king of Israel is come out to seek *f* a flea, as when one doth hunt a partridge in the mountains.   21 Then said Saul, I have sinned : return, my son David : for I will no more do thee harm, because my life was precious in thine eyes this day : behold, I have played the fool, and have erred exceedingly.   22 And David answered and said, Behold *g* the spear, O king ! let then one of the young men come over and fetch it.   23 And the LORD shall render to every man his righteousness and his faithfulness : forasmuch as the LORD delivered thee into my hand to-day, and I would not put forth mine hand against the LORD'S anointed.   24 And, behold, as thy life was much set by this day in mine eyes, so let my life be much set by in the eyes of the LORD, and let him deliver me out of all tribulation.   25 Then Saul said to David, Blessed be thou, my son David : thou shalt both do mightily, and shalt surely prevail.   So David went his way, and Saul returned to his place.

57. DAVID AGAIN IN THE LAND OF THE PHILISTINES.

(1) DAVID ONCE MORE FLEES TO ACHISH, KING OF GATH.

1 *Samuel* 27 : 1–4.

1 And David said in his heart, I shall now perish one day by the hand of Saul : there is nothing better for me than that I should escape into the land of the Philistines ; and Saul shall despair of me, to seek me any more in all the borders of Israel : so shall I escape out of his hand.   2 And David arose, and passed over, he and the six hundred men that were with him, unto Achish the

---

a Or, "barricade."   *b* Or, "either."   *c* Heb. "sons of death."   *d* Heb. "smell."   *e* Or, "have no share in."
f The Sept. has, "my life."   *g* Another reading is, "the king's spear."

1 Samuel 27.

son of Maoch, king of Gath. 3 And David dwelt with Achish at Gath, he and his men, every man with his household, even David with his two wives, Ahinoam the Jezreelitess, and Abigail the Carmelitess, Nabal's wife. 4 And it was told Saul that David was fled to Gath : and he sought no more again for him.

(2) ACHISH GRANTS ZIKLAG TO DAVID.

1 Samuel 27 : 5, 6.

5 And David said unto Achish, If now I have found grace in thine eyes, let them give me a place in one of the cities in the *a* country, that I may dwell there : for why should thy servant dwell in the royal city with thee ? 6 Then Achish gave him Ziklag that day : wherefore Ziklag pertaineth unto the kings of Judah unto this day.

(3) DAVID'S OPERATIONS WHILE AT ZIKLAG.

1 Samuel 27 : 7-12.

7 And the number of the days that David dwelt in the *a* country of the Philistines was a full year and four months. 8 And David and his men went up, and made a raid upon the Geshurites, and the *b* Girzites, and the Amalekites : for those *nations* were the inhabitants of the land, *c* which were of old, as thou goest to Shur, even unto the land of Egypt. 9 And David smote the land, and saved neither man nor woman alive, and took away the sheep, and the oxen, and the asses, and the camels, and the apparel ; and he returned, and came to Achish. 10 And Achish said, *d* Whither have ye made a raid to-day ? And David said, Against the South of Judah, and against the South of the Jerahmeelites, and against the South of the Kenites. 11 And David saved neither man nor woman alive, to bring them to Gath, saying, Lest they should tell on us, saying, So did David, and so hath been his manner all the while he hath dwelt in the *a* country of the Philistines. 12 And Achish believed David, saying, He hath made his people Israel utterly to abhor him ; therefore he shall be my servant for ever.

(4) LIST OF THE MEN WHO CAME TO DAVID AT ZIKLAG.

1 Chronicles 12 : 1-7.

1 Now these are they that came to David to Ziklag, *e* while he yet kept himself close because of Saul the son of Kish : and they were among the mighty men, his helpers in war. 2 They *f* were armed with bows, and could use both the right hand and the left in slinging stones and in shooting arrows from the bow ; they were of Saul's brethren of Benjamin. 3 The chief was Ahiezer, then Joash, the sons of Shemaah the Gibeathite ; and Jeziel, and Pelet, the sons of Azmaveth ; and Beracah, and Jehu the Anathothite ; 4 and Ishmaiah the Gibeonite, a mighty man among the thirty, and over the thirty ; and Jeremiah, and Jahaziel, and Johanan, and Jozabad the Gederathite ; 5 Eluzai, and Jerimoth, and Bealiah, and Shemariah, and Shephatiah the Haruphite ; 6 Elkanah, and Isshiah, and Azarel, and Joezer, and Jashobeam, the Korahites ; 7 and Joelah, and Zebadiah, the sons of Jeroham of Gedor.

IV. Saul's Downfall in War with the Philistines.

58. THE PHILISTINES PREPARE FOR A CAMPAIGN AGAINST ISRAEL.

1 Samuel 28 : 1a.

1a And it came to pass in those days, that the Philistines gathered their *g* hosts together for warfare, to fight with Israel.

---

a Heb. "field." *b* Another reading is, "Gizrites." *c* Some copies of the Sept. have, "from Telam." *d* So some ancient authorities. Others read, "Against whom." *e* Heb. "*being* yet shut up." *f* Or, "drew the bow." *g* Heb. "camps."

59. DAVID AND THE PHILISTINE INVASION OF ISRAEL.

(1) Achish places Confidence in David.

1 *Samuel* 28 : 1*b*, 2.

1*b* And Achish said unto David, Know thou assuredly, that thou shalt go out with me in the host, thou and thy men.   2 And David said to Achish, Therefore thou shalt know what thy servant will do.   And Achish said to David, Therefore will I make thee keeper of mine head for ever.

(2) David encamps with the Philistines in Aphek: the Israelites pitch in Jezreel.

1 *Samuel* 29 : 1, 2.

1 Now the Philistines gathered together all their hosts to Aphek : and the Israelites pitched by the fountain which is in Jezreel.   2 And the lords of the Philistines passed on by hundreds, and by thousands : and David and his men passed on in the rearward with Achish.

(3) David, dismissed from the Philistine Army, starts for Ziklag.

1 *Samuel* 29 : 3–11*a*.

3 Then said the princes of the Philistines, What *do* these Hebrews *here ?*   And Achish said unto the princes of the Philistines, Is not this David, the servant of Saul the king of Israel, which hath been with me these days or these years, and I have found no fault in him since he fell away *unto me* unto this day ?   4 But the princes of the Philistines were wroth with him ; and the princes of the Philistines said unto him, Make the man return, that he may go back to his place where thou hast appointed him, and let him not go down with us to battle, lest in the battle he become an adversary to us : for wherewith should this *fellow* reconcile himself unto his lord ? should it not be with the heads of these men ?   5 Is not this David, of whom they sang one to another in dances, saying,

Saul hath slain his thousands,
And David his ten thousands ?

6 Then Achish called David, and said unto him, As the LORD liveth, thou hast been upright, and thy going out and thy coming in with me in the host is good in my sight : for I have not found evil in thee since the day of thy coming unto me unto this day : nevertheless the lords favour thee not.   7 Wherefore now return, and go in peace, that thou displease not the lords of the Philistines.   8 And David said unto Achish, But what have I done ? and what hast thou found in thy servant so long as I have been before thee unto this day, that I may not go and fight against the enemies of my lord the king ?   9 And Achish answered and said to David, I know that thou art good in my sight, as an angel of God : notwithstanding the princes of the Philistines have said, He shall not go up with us to the battle.   10 Wherefore now rise up early in the morning with the servants of thy lord that are come with thee : and as soon as ye be up early in the morning, and have light, depart.   11*a* So David rose up early, he and his men, to depart in the morning, to return into the land of the Philistines.

(4) The Philistines march toward Jezreel.

1 *Samuel* 29 : 11*b*.

11*b* And the Philistines went up to Jezreel.

(5) List of the Men who joined David on his Way to Ziklag.

1 *Chronicles* 12 : 19–22.

19 Of Manasseh also there fell away some to David, when he came with the Philistines against Saul to battle, but they helped them not : for the lords of the Philistines upon advisement

sent him away, saying, He will fall away to his master Saul to the jeopardy of our heads. 20 As he went to Ziklag, there fell to him of Manasseh, Adnah, and Jozabad, and Jediael, and Michael, and Jozabad, and Elihu, and Zillethai, captains of thousands that were of Manasseh. 21 And they helped David against *a* the band of rovers : for they were all mighty men of valour, and were captains in the host. 22 For from day to day there came to David to help him, until it was a great host, like the host of God.

60. DAVID'S VICTORY OVER THE AMALEKITES WHO HAD DE-STROYED ZIKLAG.

1 *Samuel* 30 : 1-31.

1 And it came to pass, when David and his men were come to Ziklag on the third day, that the Amalekites had made a raid upon the South, and upon Ziklag, and had smitten Ziklag, and burned it with fire ; 2 and had taken captive the women *and all* that were therein, both small and great : they slew not any, but carried them off, and went their way. 3 And when David and his men came to the city, behold, it was burned with fire ; and their wives, and their sons, and their daughters, were taken captives. 4 Then David and the people that were with him lifted up their voice and wept, until they had no more power to weep. 5 And David's two wives were taken captives, Ahinoam the Jezreelitess, and Abigail the wife of Nabal the Carmelite. 6 And David was greatly distressed ; for the people spake of stoning him, because the soul of all the people was grieved, every man for his sons and for his daughters : but David strengthened himself in the LORD his God.

7 And David said to Abiathar the priest, the son of Ahimelech, I pray thee, bring me hither the ephod. And Abiathar brought thither the ephod to David. 8 And David inquired of the LORD, saying, *b* If I pursue after this troop, shall I overtake them ? And he answered him, Pursue : for thou shalt surely overtake *them*, and shalt without fail recover *all*. 9 So David went, he and the six hundred men that were with him, and came to the brook Besor, where those that were left behind stayed. 10 But David pursued, he and four hundred men : for two hundred stayed behind, which were so faint that they could not go over the brook Besor : 11 and they found an Egyptian in the field, and brought him to David, and gave him bread, and he did eat ; and they gave him water to drink : 12 and they gave him a piece of a cake of figs, and two clusters of raisins ; and when he had eaten, his spirit came again to him : for he had eaten no bread, nor drunk any water, three days and three nights. 13 And David said unto him, To whom belongest thou ? and whence art thou ? And he said, I am a young man of Egypt, servant to an Amalekite ; and my master left me, because three days agone I fell sick. 14 We made a raid upon the South of the Cherethites, and upon that which belongeth to Judah, and upon the South of Caleb ; and we burned Ziklag with fire. 15 And David said to him, Wilt thou bring me down to this troop ? And he said, Swear unto me by God, that thou wilt neither kill me, nor deliver me up into the hands of my master, and I will bring thee down to this troop. 16 And when he had brought him down, behold, they were spread abroad over all the ground, eating and drinking, and feasting, *c* because of all the great spoil that they had taken out of the land of the Philistines, and out of the land of Judah. 17 And David smote them from the twilight even unto the evening of the next day : and there escaped not a man of them, save four hundred young men, which rode upon camels and fled. 18 And David recovered all that the Amalekites had taken : and David rescued his two wives. 19 And there was nothing lacking to them, neither small nor great, neither sons nor daughters, neither spoil, nor any thing that they had taken to them : and David brought back all. 20 And David took all the flocks and the herds, *which* they drave before those *other* cattle, and said, This is David's spoil. 21 And David came to the two hundred men, which were so faint that they could not follow David, whom also they had made to abide at the brook Besor : and

---

a See §60, below.   *b* Or, "Shall I pursue."   *c* Or, "amidst."

1 Samuel 30.

they went forth to meet David, and to meet the people that were with him : and when David came near ^a to the people, he ^b saluted them.   22 Then answered all the wicked men and ^c men of ^d Belial, of those that went with David, and said, Because they went not with us, we will not give them aught of the spoil that we have recovered, save to every man his wife and his children, that they may lead them away, and depart.   23 Then said David, Ye shall not do so, my brethren, with that which the LORD hath given unto us, who hath preserved us, and delivered the troop that came against us into our hand.   24 And who will hearken unto you in this matter ? for as his share is that goeth down to the battle, so shall his share be that tarrieth by the stuff : they shall share alike.   25 And it was so from that day forward, that he made it a statute and an ordinance for Israel, unto this day.

26 And when David came to Ziklag, he sent of the spoil unto the elders of Judah, even to his friends, saying, Behold a ^e present for you of the spoil of the enemies of the LORD ; 27 to them which were in Beth-el, and to them which were in Ramoth of the South, and to them which were in Jattir ; 28 and to them which were in Aroer, and to them which were in Siphmoth, and to them which were in Eshtemoa ; 29 and to them which were in Racal, and to them which were in the cities of the Jerahmeelites, and to them which were in the cities of the Kenites ; 30 and to them which were in Hormah, and to them which were in ^f Cor-ashan, and to them which were in Athach ; 31 and to them which were in Hebron, and to all the places where David himself and his men were wont to haunt.

61. THE PHILISTINES PITCH IN SHUNEM : THE ISRAELITES IN GILBOA.

1 <i>Samuel</i> 28 : 4.

4 And the Philistines gathered themselves together, and came and pitched in Shunem : and Saul gathered all Israel together, and they pitched in Gilboa.

62. SAUL'S VISIT TO THE WITCH OF EN-DOR.

1 <i>Samuel</i> 28 : 3, 5–25.

3 Now ^g Samuel was dead, and all Israel had lamented him, and buried him in Ramah, even in his own city.   And Saul had put away those that had familiar spirits, and the wizards, out of the land.   5 And when Saul saw the host of the Philistines, he was afraid, and his heart trembled greatly.   6 And when Saul inquired of the LORD, the LORD answered him not, neither by dreams, nor by Urim, nor by prophets.   7 Then said Saul unto his servants, Seek me a woman that hath a familiar spirit, that I may go to her, and inquire of her.   And his servants said to him, Behold, there is a woman that hath a familiar spirit at En-dor.   8 And Saul disguised himself, and put on other raiment, and went, he and two men with him, and they came to the woman by night : and he said, Divine unto me, I pray thee, by the familiar spirit, and bring me up whomsoever I shall name unto thee.   9 And the woman said unto him, Behold, thou knowest what Saul hath done, how he hath cut off those that have familiar spirits, and the wizards, out of the land : wherefore then layest thou a snare for my life, to cause me to die ?   10 And Saul sware to her by the LORD, saying, As the LORD liveth, there shall no ^h punishment happen to thee for this thing.   11 Then said the woman, Whom shall I bring up unto thee ?   And he said, Bring me up Samuel.   12 And when the woman saw Samuel, she cried with a loud voice : and the woman spake to Saul, saying, Why hast thou deceived me ? for thou art Saul.   13 And the king said unto her, Be not afraid : for what seest thou ?   And the woman said unto Saul, I see ⁱ a god coming up out of the earth.   14 And he said unto her, What form is he of ?   And she said, An old man cometh up ; and he is

---

^a Or, " with."   ^b Or, " asked them of their welfare."   ^c Or, " base fellows."   ^d I. e., " worthlessness."   ^e Heb. " blessing."   ^f According to many MSS. and versions, " Bor-ashan."   ^g Cf. 1 Samuel 25 : 1a.   See §53.   ^h Or, " guilt come upon thee."   ⁱ Or, " gods."

1 *Samuel* 28.

covered with a robe. And Saul perceived that it was Samuel, and he bowed with his face to the ground, and did obeisance. 15 And Samuel said to Saul, Why hast thou disquieted me, to bring me up? And Saul answered, I am sore distressed; for the Philistines make war against me, and God is departed from me, and answereth me no more, neither by prophets, nor by dreams: therefore I have called thee, that thou mayest make known unto me what I shall do. 16 And Samuel said, Wherefore then dost thou ask of me, seeing the LORD is departed from thee, and *a* is become thine adversary? 17 And the LORD hath *b* wrought for himself, as he spake by me: and the LORD hath rent the kingdom out of thine hand, and given it to thy neighbour, even to David. 18 Because thou obeyedst not the voice of the LORD, and didst not execute his fierce wrath upon Amalek, therefore hath the LORD done this thing unto thee this day. 19 Moreover the LORD will deliver Israel also with thee into the hand of the Philistines: and to-morrow shalt thou and thy sons be with me: the LORD shall deliver the host of Israel also into the hand of the Philistines. 20 Then Saul fell straightway his full length upon the earth, and was sore afraid, because of the words of Samuel: and there was no strength in him; for he had eaten no bread all the day, nor all the night. 21 And the woman came unto Saul, and saw that he was sore troubled, and said unto him, Behold, thine handmaid hath hearkened unto thy voice, and I have put my life in my hand, and have hearkened unto thy words which thou spakest unto me. 22 Now therefore, I pray thee, hearken thou also unto the voice of thine handmaid, and let me set a morsel of bread before thee; and eat, that thou mayest have strength, when thou goest on thy way. 23 But he refused, and said, I will not eat. But his servants, together with the woman, constrained him; and he hearkened unto their voice. So he arose from the earth, and sat upon the bed. 24 And the woman had a fatted calf in the house; and she hasted, and killed it; and she took flour, and kneaded it, and did bake unleavened bread thereof: 25 and she brought it before Saul, and before his servants; and they did eat. Then they rose up, and went away that night.

63. THE FALL OF THE HOUSE OF SAUL.

(1) THE BATTLE OF MOUNT GILBOA.

1 *Samuel* 31 : 1–13.	1 *Chronicles* 10 : 1–14.
1 Now the Philistines fought against Israel: and the men of Israel fled from before the Philistines, and fell down *c* slain in mount Gilboa. 2 And the Philistines followed hard upon Saul and upon his sons; and the Philistines slew Jonathan, and *d* Abinadab, and Malchi-shua, the sons of Saul. 3 And the battle went sore against Saul, and the archers overtook him; and he was greatly distressed by reason of the archers. 4 Then said Saul to his armourbearer, Draw thy sword, and thrust me through therewith; lest these uncircumcised come and thrust me through, and *e* abuse me. But his armourbearer would not; for he was sore afraid. Therefore Saul took his sword, and fell upon it. 5 And when his armourbearer saw that Saul was dead, he likewise fell upon his sword, and died with him. 6 So Saul died, and his three sons, and his armourbearer, and all his men, that same	1 Now the Philistines fought against Israel: and the men of Israel fled from before the Philistines, and fell down *c* slain in mount Gilboa. 2 And the Philistines followed hard after Saul and after his sons; and the Philistines slew Jonathan, and *d* Abinadab, and Malchi-shua, the sons of Saul. 3 And the battle went sore against Saul, and the archers overtook him; and he was distressed by reason of the archers. 4 Then said Saul unto his armourbearer, Draw thy sword, and thrust me through therewith; lest these uncircumcised come and *e* abuse me. But his armourbearer would not; for he was sore afraid. Therefore Saul took his sword, and fell upon it. 5 And when his armourbearer saw that Saul was dead, he likewise fell upon his sword, and died. 6 So Saul died, and his three sons; and all his house died together. 7 And when all the men of Israel that were in the valley saw that they

a The Sept. has, "is on the side of thy neighbour."   *b* Or, "done unto him."   Some ancient authorities read, "done unto thee."   *c* Or, "wounded."   *d* In 1 Samuel 14: 49, "Ishvi." See §18, (2).   *e* Or, "make a mock of me."

8

1 *Samuel* 31.	1 *Chronicles* 10.
day together. 7 And when the men of Israel that were on the other side of the valley, and they that were beyond Jordan, saw that the men of Israel fled, and that Saul and his sons were dead, they forsook the cities, and fled ; and the Philistines came and dwelt in them. 8 And it came to pass on the morrow, when the Philistines came to strip the slain, that they found Saul and his three sons fallen in mount Gilboa. 9 And they cut off his head, and stripped off his armour, and sent into the land of the Philistines round about, to carry the tidings unto the house of their idols, and to the people. 10 And they put his armour in the house of the Ashtaroth : and they fastened his body to the wall of Beth-shan. 11 And when the inhabitants of Jabesh-gilead heard concerning him that which the Philistines had done to Saul, 12 all the valiant men arose, and went all night, and took the body of Saul and the bodies of his sons from the wall of Beth-shan ; and they came to Jabesh, and burnt them there. 13 And they took their bones, and buried them under the tamarisk tree in Jabesh, and fasted seven days.	fled, and that Saul and his sons were dead, they forsook their cities, and fled ; and the Philistines came and dwelt in them. 8 And it came to pass on the morrow, when the Philistines came to strip the slain, that they found Saul and his sons fallen in mount Gilboa. 9 And they stripped him, and took his head, and his armour, and sent into the land of the Philistines round about, to carry the tidings unto their idols, and to the people. 10 And they put his armour in the house of their gods, and fastened his head in the house of Dagon. 11 And when all Jabesh-gilead heard all that the Philistines had done to Saul, 12 all the valiant men arose, and took away the body of Saul, and the bodies of his sons, and brought them to Jabesh, and buried their bones under the *a* oak in Jabesh, and fasted seven days. 13 So Saul died *b* for his trespass which he committed against the LORD, because of the word of the LORD, which he kept not ; and also for that he asked counsel of one that had a familiar spirit, to inquire *thereby*, 14 and inquired not of the LORD : therefore he slew him, and turned the kingdom unto David the son of Jesse.

(2) THE ACCIDENT TO MEPHIBOSHETH.[c]

2 *Samuel* 4 : 4.

4 Now Jonathan, Saul's son, had a son that was lame of his feet. He was five years old when the tidings came of Saul and Jonathan out of Jezreel, and his nurse took him up, and fled : and it came to pass, as she made haste to flee, that he fell, and became lame. And his name was [d] Mephibosheth.

---

a Or, " terebinth."   *b* Or, " in."   *c* Cf. 2 Samuel 9 : 1-13. See §96.   *d* In 1 Chronicles 8 : 34 and 9 : 40, Merib-baal. See §18, (2).

BOOK THIRD.

The Reign of David.

PART I.

THE SEVEN AND A HALF YEARS IN HEBRON.

I. David's Behavior on Hearing of Saul's Death.

64. THE NEWS OF SAUL'S DEATH IS BROUGHT TO DAVID.

2 Samuel 1 : 1-16.

1 And it came to pass after the death of Saul, when David was returned from the slaughter of the Amalekites, and David had abode two days in Ziklag ; 2 it came even to pass on the third day, that, behold, a man came out of the camp from Saul with his clothes rent, and earth upon his head : and so it was, when he came to David, that he fell to the earth, and did obeisance. 3 And David said unto him, From whence comest thou ? And he said unto him, Out of the camp of Israel am I escaped. 4 And David said unto him, How went the matter ? I pray thee, tell me. And he answered, The people are fled from the battle, and many of the people also are fallen and dead ; and Saul and Jonathan his son are dead also. 5 And David said unto the young man that told him, How knowest thou that Saul and Jonathan his son be dead ? 6 And the young man that told him said, As I happened by chance upon mount Gilboa, behold, Saul leaned upon his spear ; and, lo, the chariots and the horsemen followed hard after him. 7 And when he looked behind him, he saw me, and called unto me. And I answered, Here am I. 8 And he said unto me, Who art thou ? And I answered him, I am an Amalekite. 9 And he said unto me, Stand, I pray thee, *a* beside me, and slay me, for *b* anguish hath taken hold of me ; because my life is yet whole in me. 10 So I stood *a* beside him, and slew him, because I was sure that he could not live after that he was fallen : and I took the crown that was upon his head, and the bracelet that was on his arm, and have brought them thither unto my lord. 11 Then David took hold on his clothes, and rent them ; and likewise all the men that were with him : 12 and they mourned, and wept, and fasted until even, for Saul, and for Jonathan his son, and for the people of the LORD, and for the house of Israel ; because they were fallen by the sword. 13 And David said unto the young man that told him, Whence art thou ? And he answered, I am the son of a stranger, an Amalekite. 14 And David said unto him, How wast thou not afraid to put forth thine hand to destroy the LORD'S anointed ? 15 And David called one of the young men, and said, Go near, and fall upon him. And he smote him that he died. 16 And David said unto him, Thy blood be upon thy head ; for thy mouth hath testified against thee, saying, I have slain the LORD'S anointed.

65. DAVID'S LAMENTATION FOR SAUL AND JONATHAN.

2 Samuel 1 : 17-27.

17 And David lamented with this lamentation over Saul and over Jonathan his son : 18 and he bade them teach the children of Judah *the song of* the bow : behold, it is written in the book of *c* Jashar.

---

a Or, " over."   *b* Or, " giddiness."   *c* Or, " The Upright."

2 *Samuel* 1.

19 *a*Thy glory, O Israel, is slain upon thy high places!
　　How are the mighty fallen!
20 Tell it not in Gath,
　　Publish it not in the streets of Ashkelon,
　　Lest the daughters of the Philistines rejoice,
　　Lest the daughters of the uncircumcised triumph.
21 Ye mountains of Gilboa,
　　Let there be no dew nor rain upon you, neither fields of offerings:
　　For there the shield of the mighty was *b*vilely cast away,
　　The shield of Saul, *c* not anointed with oil.
22 From the blood of the slain, from the fat of the mighty,
　　The bow of Jonathan turned not back,
　　And the sword of Saul returned not empty.
23 Saul and Jonathan were lovely and pleasant in their lives,
　　And in their death they were not divided;
　　They were swifter than eagles,
　　They were stronger than lions.
24 Ye daughters of Israel, weep over Saul,
　　Who clothed you in scarlet *d* delicately,
　　Who put ornaments of gold upon your apparel.
25 How are the mighty fallen in the midst of the battle!
　　*e*Jonathan is slain upon thy high places.
26 I am distressed for thee, my brother Jonathan:
　　Very pleasant hast thou been unto me:
　　Thy love to me was wonderful,
　　Passing the love of women.
27 How are the mighty fallen,
　　And the weapons of war perished!

II. The Rival Kingdoms.

66. DAVID IS ANOINTED KING OVER JUDAH.

2 *Samuel* 2 : 1–4*a*.

1 And it came to pass after this, that David inquired of the Lord, saying, Shall I go up into any of the cities of Judah? And the Lord said unto him, Go up. And David said, Whither shall I go up? And he said, Unto Hebron.   2 So David went up thither, and his two wives also, Ahinoam the Jezreelitess, and Abigail the wife of Nabal the Carmelite.   3 And his men that were with him did David bring up, every man with his household: and they dwelt in the city of Hebron.   4 And the men of Judah came, and there they anointed David king over the house of Judah.

67. DAVID'S MESSAGE TO THE MEN OF JABESH-GILEAD.

2 *Samuel* 2 : 4*b*–7.

4*b* And they told David, saying, The men of Jabesh-gilead were they that buried Saul.   5 And David sent messengers unto the men of Jabesh-gilead, and said unto them, Blessed be ye of the Lord, that ye have shewed this kindness unto your lord, even unto Saul, and have buried him.   6 And now the Lord shew kindness and truth unto you: and I also will requite you this kindness, because ye have done this thing.   7 Now therefore let your hands be strong, and be ye valiant: for Saul your lord is dead, and also the house of Judah have anointed me king over them.

---

a Or, " The gazelle."   *b* Or, "defiled."   *c* Or," *as of one* not anointed."   *d* Heb." with delights."   *e* Or, " O Jonathan, slain," etc.

68. ISH-BOSHETH IS MADE KING OVER ISRAEL.

2 *Samuel* 2 : 8–11.

8 Now Abner the son of Ner, captain of Saul's host, had taken *a* Ish-bosheth the son of Saul, and brought him over to Mahanaim ; 9 and he made him king over Gilead, and over the *b* Ashurites, and over Jezreel, and over Ephraim, and over Benjamin, and over all Israel. 10 (Ish-bosheth Saul's son was forty years old when he began to reign over Israel, and he reigned two years.) But the house of Judah followed David. 11 And the time that David was king in Hebron over the house of Judah was seven years and six months.

69. THE CIVIL WAR.

2 *Samuel* 2 : 12–3 : 1.

12 And Abner the son of Ner, and the servants of Ish-bosheth the son of Saul, went out from Mahanaim to Gibeon. 13 And Joab the son of Zeruiah, and the servants of David, went out, and met *c* them by the pool of Gibeon ; and they sat down, the one on the one side of the pool, and the other on the other side of the pool. 14 And Abner said to Joab, Let the young men, I pray thee, arise and play before us. And Joab said, Let them arise. 15 Then they arose and went over by number ; twelve for Benjamin, and for Ish-bosheth the son of Saul, and twelve of the servants of David. 16 And they caught every one his fellow by the head, and *thrust* his sword in his fellow's side ; so they fell down together : wherefore that place was called *d* Helkath-hazzurim, which is in Gibeon. 17 And the battle was very sore that day ; and Abner was beaten, and the men of Israel, before the servants of David. 18 And the three sons of Zeruiah were there, Joab, and Abishai, and Asahel : and Asahel was as light of foot *e* as a wild roe. 19 And Asahel pursued after Abner ; and in going he turned not to the right hand nor to the left from following Abner. 20 Then Abner looked behind him, and said, Is it thou, Asahel? And he answer, It is I. 21 And Abner said to him, Turn thee aside to thy right hand or to thy left, and lay thee hold on one of the young men, and take thee his *f* armour. But Asahel would not turn aside from following of him. 22 And Abner said again to Asahel, Turn thee aside from following me : wherefore should I smite thee to the ground ? how then should I hold up my face to Joab thy brother ? 23 Howbeit he refused to turn aside : wherefore Abner with the hinder end of the spear smote him in the belly, that the spear came out behind him ; and he fell down there, and died in the same place : and it came to pass, that as many as came to the place where Asahel fell down and died stood still. 24 But Joab and Abishai pursued after Abner : and the sun went down when they were come to the hill of Ammah, that lieth before Giah by the way of the wilderness of Gibeon. 25 And the children of Benjamin gathered themselves together after Abner, and became one band, and stood on the top of an hill. 26 Then Abner called to Joab, and said, Shall the sword devour for ever ? knowest thou not that it will be bitterness in the latter end ? how long shall it be then, ere thou bid the people return from following their brethren ? 27 And Joab said, As God liveth, *g* if thou hadst not spoken, surely then *h* in the morning the people had gone away, nor followed every one his brother. 28 So Joab blew the trumpet, and all the people stood still, and pursued after Israel no more, neither fought they any more. 29 And Abner and his men went all that night through the Arabah ; and they passed over Jordan, and went through all Bithron, and came to Mahanaim. 30 And Joab returned from following Abner : and when he had gathered all the people together, there lacked of David's servants nineteen men and Asahel. 31 But the servants of David had smitten of Benjamin, and of Abner's men, *so that* three hundred and threescore men died. 32 And they took up Asahel, and buried him in the sepulchre of his father, which was in Beth-lehem. And Joab and his men went all night, and the day brake upon them at Hebron. 1 Now there was long war between the house of Saul and the house of David : and David waxed stronger and stronger, but the house of Saul waxed weaker and weaker.

---

a In 1 Chronicles 8 : 33 and 9 : 39, " Eshbaal." See §18, (2).   *b* The Vulgate and Syriac have, " Geshurites."   *c* Heb. " them together."   *d* I. e., " The field of the sharp knives."   *e* Heb. " as one of the roes that are in the field."   *f* Or, " spoil." See Judges 14 : 19.   *g* See ver. 14, above.   *h* Heb. " from the morning."

70. DAVID'S FAMILY IN HEBRON. [a]

2 *Samuel* 3 : 2–5.	1 *Chronicles* 3 : 1–4a.
2 And unto David were sons born in Hebron : and his firstborn was Amnon, of Ahinoam the Jezreelitess ; 3 and his second, Chileab, of Abigail the wife of Nabal the Carmelite ; and the third, Absalom the son of Maacah the daughter of Talmai king of Geshur; 4 and the fourth, Adonijah the son of Haggith ; and the fifth, Shephatiah the son of Abital ; 5 and the sixth, Ithream, of Eglah David's wife. These were born to David in Hebron.	1 Now these were the sons of David, which were born unto him in Hebron : the firstborn, Amnon, of Ahinoam the Jezreelitess ; the second, Daniel, of Abigail the Carmelitess ; 2 the third, Absalom the son of Maacah the daughter of Talmai king of Geshur ; the fourth, Adonijah the son of Haggith ; 3 the fifth, Shephatiah of Abital ; the sixth, Ithream by Eglah his wife. 4a Six were born unto him in Hebron.

III. Events leading to David's Elevation to the Throne of Israel.

71. ABNER'S QUARREL WITH ISH-BOSHETH.

2 *Samuel* 3 : 6–11.

6 And it came to pass, while there was war between the house of Saul and the house of David, that Abner [b] made himself strong in the house of Saul. 7 Now Saul had a concubine, whose name was Rizpah, the daughter of Aiah : and *Ish-bosheth* said to Abner, Wherefore hast thou gone in unto my father's concubine ? 8 Then was Abner very wroth for the words of Ish-bosheth, and said, Am I a dog's head that belongeth to Judah ? This day do I shew kindness unto the house of Saul thy father, to his brethren, and to his friends, and have not delivered thee into the hand of David, and yet thou chargest me this day with [c] a fault concerning this woman. 9 God do so to Abner, and more also, if as the LORD hath sworn to David, I do not even so to him ; 10 to translate the kingdom from the house of Saul, and to set up the throne of David over Israel and over Judah, from Dan even to Beer-sheba. 11 And he could not answer Abner another word, because he feared him.

72. ABNER'S DESERTION TO DAVID : MICHAL RESTORED TO DAVID.

2 *Samuel* 3 : 12–21.

12 And Abner sent messengers to David [d] on his behalf, saying, Whose is the land ? saying *also*, Make thy league with me, and, behold, my hand shall be with thee, to bring about all Israel unto thee. 13 And he said, Well ; I will make a league with thee : but one thing I require of thee, that is, thou shalt not see my face, except thou first bring Michal Saul's daughter, when thou comest to see my face. 14 And David sent messengers to Ish-bosheth Saul's son, saying, Deliver me my wife Michal, whom I betrothed to me for an hundred foreskins of the Philistines. 15 And Ish-bosheth sent, and took her from her husband, even from [e] Paltiel the son of Laish. 16 And her husband went with her, weeping as he went, and followed her to Bahurim. Then said Abner unto him, Go, return : and he returned.

17 And Abner had communication with the elders of Israel, saying, In times past ye sought for David to be king over you : 18 now then do it : for the LORD hath spoken of David, saying, By the hand of my servant David I will save my people Israel out of the hand of the Philistines, and out of the hand of all their enemies. 19 And Abner also spake in the ears of Benjamin : and Abner went also to speak in the ears of David in Hebron all that seemed good to Israel, and to

---

a Cf. §98.   *b* Or, "shewed himself strong for."   *c* Or, "the fault of this woman."   *d* Or, "where he was."   *e* In 1 Samuel 25 : 44, "Palti." See §55.

2 *Samuel* 3.

the whole house of Benjamin. 20 So Abner came to David to Hebron, and twenty men with him. And David made Abner and the men that were with him a feast. 21 And Abner said unto David, I will arise and go, and will gather all Israel unto my lord the king, that they may make a covenant with thee, and that thou mayest reign over all that thy soul desireth. And David sent Abner away; and he went in peace.

73. JOAB'S MURDER OF ABNER: DAVID'S LAMENTATION.

2 *Samuel* 3: 22–39.

22 And, behold, the servants of David and Joab came from *a* a foray, and brought in a great spoil with them: but Abner was not with David in Hebron; for he had sent him away, and he was gone in peace. 23 When Joab and all the host that was with him were come, they told Joab, saying, Abner the son of Ner came to the king, and he hath sent him away, and he is gone in peace. 24 Then Joab came to the king, and said, What hast thou done? behold, Abner came unto thee; why is it that thou hast sent him away, and he is quite gone? 25 Thou knowest Abner the son of Ner, that he came to deceive thee, and to know thy going out and thy coming in, and to know all that thou doest. 26 And when Joab was come out from David, he sent messengers after Abner, and they brought him back from the *b* well of Sirah: but David knew it not. 27 And when Abner was returned to Hebron, Joab took him aside into the midst of the gate to speak with him quietly, and smote him there in the belly, that he died, for the blood of Asahel his brother. 28 And afterward when David heard it, he said, I and my kingdom are guiltless before the LORD for ever from the blood of Abner the son of Ner: 29 let it fall upon the head of Joab, and upon all his father's house; and let there not fail from the house of Joab one that hath an issue, or that is a leper, or that leaneth on a staff, or that falleth by the sword, or that lacketh bread. 30 So Joab and Abishai his brother slew Abner, because he had killed their brother Asahel at Gibeon in the battle.

31 And David said to Joab, and to all the people that were with him, Rend your clothes, and gird you with sackcloth, and mourn before Abner. And king David followed the bier. 32 And they buried Abner in Hebron: and the king lifted up his voice, and wept at the grave of Abner; and all the people wept. 33 And the king lamented for Abner, and said,

Should Abner die as a fool dieth?

34 Thy hands were not bound, nor thy feet put into fetters:

As a man falleth before the children of iniquity, so didst thou fall.

And all the people wept again over him. 35 And all the people came to cause David to eat bread while it was yet day; but David sware, saying, God do so to me, and more also, if I taste bread, or aught else, till the sun be down. 36 And all the people took notice of it, and it pleased them: as whatsoever the king did pleased all the people. 37 So all the people and all Israel understood that day that it was not of the king to slay Abner the son of Ner. 38 And the king said unto his servants, Know ye not that there is a prince and a great man fallen this day in Israel? 39 And I am this day weak, though anointed king; and these men the sons of Zeruiah be too hard for me: the LORD reward the wicked doer according to his wickedness.

74. THE MURDER OF ISH-BOSHETH.

2 *Samuel* 4: 1–3, 5–7.

1 And when *Ish-bosheth*, Saul's son, heard that Abner was dead in Hebron, his hands became feeble, and all the Israelites were troubled. 2 And *Ish-bosheth*, Saul's son, *had* two men that were captains of bands: the name of the one was Baanah, and the name of the other Rechab, the sons of Rimmon the Beerothite, of the children of Benjamin: (for Beeroth also is reckoned to Benjamin: 3 and the Beerothites fled to Gittaim, and have been sojourners there until this day.)

---

a Heb. "the troop."   *b* Or, "cistern."

2 Samuel 4.

5 And the sons of Rimmon the Beerothite, Rechab and Baanah, went, and came about the heat of the day to the house of Ish-bosheth, as he took his rest at noon: 6 *a* And *b* they came thither into the midst of the house, as though they would have fetched wheat ; and they smote him in the belly : and Rechab and Baanah his brother escaped.   7 Now when they came into the house, as he lay on his bed in his bedchamber, they smote him, and slew him, and beheaded him, and took his head, and went by the way of the Arabah all night.

75. DAVID PUNISHES THE MURDERERS OF ISH-BOSHETH.

2 Samuel 4: 8–12.

8 And they brought the head of Ish-bosheth unto David to Hebron, and said to the king, Behold the head of Ish-bosheth the son of Saul thine enemy, which sought thy life ; and the LORD hath avenged my lord the king this day of Saul, and of his seed.   9 And David answered Rechab and Baanah his brother, the sons of Rimmon the Beerothite, and said unto them, As the LORD liveth, who hath redeemed my soul out of all adversity, 10 when one told me, saying, Behold, Saul is dead, thinking to have brought good tidings, I took hold of him, and slew him in Ziklag, which was the reward I gave him for his tidings.   11 How much more, when wicked men have slain a righteous person in his own house upon his bed, shall I not now require his blood of your hand, and take you away from the earth ?   12 And David commanded his young men, and they slew them, and cut off their hands and their feet, and hanged them up beside the pool in Hebron.   But they took the head of Ish-bosheth, and buried it in the grave of Abner in Hebron.

PART II.

THE PERIOD OF DAVID'S WARS.

76. DAVID IS MADE KING OVER ISRAEL.

2 Samuel 5 : 1–3.

1 Then came all the tribes of Israel to David unto Hebron, and spake, saying, Behold, we are thy bone and thy flesh.   2 In times past, when Saul was king over us, it was thou that leddest out and broughtest in Israel : and the LORD said to thee, Thou shalt feed my people Israel, and thou shalt be *c* prince over Israel.   3 So all the elders of Israel came to the king to Hebron ; and king David made a covenant with them in Hebron before the LORD : and they anointed David king over Israel.

1 Chronicles 11 : 1–3.

1 Then all Israel gathered themselves to David unto Hebron, saying, Behold, we are thy bone and thy flesh.   2 In times past, even when Saul was king, it was thou that leddest out and broughtest in Israel : and the LORD thy God said unto thee, Thou shalt feed my people Israel, and thou shalt be *c* prince over my people Israel.   3 So all the elders of Israel came to the king to Hebron ; and David made a covenant with them in Hebron before the LORD ; and they anointed David king over Israel, according to the word of the LORD by the hand of Samuel.

77. DATA CONCERNING THE NUMBER OF WARRIORS WHO MADE DAVID KING.

1 Chronicles 12 : 23–40.

23 And these are the numbers of the heads of them that were armed for war, which came to David to Hebron, to turn the kingdom of Saul to him, according to the word of the LORD.   24 The

a The Sept. has, " And, behold, the woman that kept the door of the house was winnowing wheat, and she slumbered and slept ; and the brethren, Rechab and Baanah, went privily into the house."   *b* Or, " There came . . . men fetching wheat. *c* Or, " leader."

1 *Chronicles* 12.

children of Judah that bare shield and spear were six thousand and eight hundred, armed for war. 25 Of the children of Simeon, mighty men of valour for the war, seven thousand and one hundred. 26 Of the children of Levi four thousand and six hundred. 27 And Jehoiada was the leader of *the house of* Aaron, and with him were three thousand and seven hundred ; 28 and Zadok, a young man mighty of valour, and of his father's house twenty and two captains. 29 And of the children of Benjamin, the brethren of Saul, three thousand : for hitherto the greatest part of them had *a* kept their allegiance to the house of Saul. 30 And of the children of Ephraim twenty thousand and eight hundred, mighty men of valour, famous men in their fathers' houses. 31 And of the half tribe of Manasseh eighteen thousand, which were expressed by name, to come and make David king. 32 And of the children of Issachar, men that had understanding of the times, to know what Israel ought to do ; the heads of them were two hundred ; and all their brethren were at their commandment. 33 Of Zebulun, such as were able to go out in the host, that could set the battle in array, with all manner of instruments of war, fifty thousand ; and that could order *the battle array, and were* not of double heart. 34 And of Naphtali a thousand captains, and with them with shield and spear thirty and seven thousand. 35 And of the Danites that could set the battle in array, twenty and eight thousand and six hundred. 36 And of Asher, such as were able to go out in the host, that could set the battle in array, forty thousand. 37 And on the other side of Jordan, of the Reubenites, and the Gadites, and of the half tribe of Manasseh, with all manner of instruments of war for the battle, an hundred and twenty thousand. 38 All these, being men of war, that could order the battle array, came with a perfect heart to Hebron, to make David king over all Israel : and all the rest also of Israel were of one heart to make David king. 39 And they were there with David three days, eating and drinking : for their brethren had made preparation for them. 40 Moreover they that were nigh unto them, *even* as far as Issachar and Zebulun and Naphtali, brought bread on asses, and on camels, and on mules, and on oxen, victual of meal, cakes of figs, and clusters of raisins, and wine, and oil, and oxen, and sheep in abundance : for there was joy in Israel.

78. JERUSALEM CAPTURED AND MADE THE CAPITAL.

2 *Samuel* 5 : 6–10.

6 And the king and his men went to Jerusalem against the Jebusites, the inhabitants of the land : which spake unto David, saying, *b* Except thou take away the blind and the lame, thou shalt not come in hither : thinking, David cannot come in hither. 7 Nevertheless David took the strong hold of Zion ; the same is the city of David. 8 And David said on that day, Whosoever smiteth the Jebusites, let him go up to the watercourse, *c* and *smite* the lame and the blind, *d* that are hated of David's soul. Wherefore they say, *e* There are the blind and the lame ; he cannot come into the house. 9 And David dwelt in the strong hold, and called it the city of David. And David built round about from Millo and inward. 10 And David waxed greater and greater ; for the LORD, the God of hosts, was with him.

1 *Chronicles* 11 : 4–9.

4 And David and all Israel went to Jerusalem (the same is Jebus) ; and the Jebusites, the inhabitants of the land, were there. 5 And the inhabitants of Jebus said to David, Thou shalt not come in hither. Nevertheless David took the strong hold of Zion ; the same is the city of David. 6 And David said, Whosoever smiteth the Jebusites first shall be chief and captain. And Joab the son of Zeruiah went up first, and was made chief. 7 And David dwelt in the strong hold ; therefore they called it the city of David. 8 And he built the city round about, from Millo even round about : and Joab *f* repaired the rest of the city. 9 And David waxed greater and greater ; for the LORD of hosts was with him.

---

a Heb. " kept the charge of the house." *b* Or, " Thou shalt not come in hither, but the blind and the lame shall turn thee away." *c* Or, " and as for the lame and the blind, that are hated of David's soul—." *d* Another reading is, " that hate David's soul." *e* Or, " The blind and the lame shall not come into the house." *f* Heb. " revived."

79. DEFENSIVE WARS AGAINST THE PHILISTINES.

(1) THE FIRST CAMPAIGN.

A. DAVID GOES "DOWN TO THE HOLD."

2 *Samuel* 5 : 17.	1 *Chronicles* 14 : 8.
17 And when the Philistines heard that they had anointed David king over Israel, all the Philistines went up to seek David; and David heard of it, and went down to the hold.	8 And when the Philistines heard that David was anointed king over all Israel, all the Philistines went up to seek David: and David heard of it, and went out against them.

B. THE GADITES WHO "SEPARATED THEMSELVES UNTO DAVID."

1 *Chronicles* 12 : 8–15.

8 And of the Gadites there separated themselves unto David to the hold in the wilderness, mighty men of valour, men trained for war, that could handle shield and spear; whose faces were like the faces of lions, and they were as swift as the roes upon the mountain; 9 Ezer the chief, Obadiah the second, Eliab the third; 10 Mishmannah the fourth, Jeremiah the fifth; 11 Attai the sixth, Eliel the seventh; 12 Johanan the eighth, Elzabad the ninth; 13 Jeremiah the tenth, Machbannai the eleventh. 14 These of the sons of Gad were captains of the host: he that was least was *a* equal to an hundred, and the greatest *a* to a thousand. 15 These are they that went over Jordan in the first month, when it had overflown all its banks; and they put to flight all them of the valleys, both toward the east, and toward the west.

C. THE DEED OF "THE THREE MIGHTY MEN." *b*

2 *Samuel* 5 : 18.	2 *Samuel* 23 : 13–17.	1 *Chronicles* 11 : 15–19.	1 *Chronicles* 14 : 9.
18 Now the Philistines had come and spread themselves in the valley of Rephaim.	13 And three of the thirty chief went down, and came to David in the harvest time unto the cave of Adullam; and the troop of the Philistines were encamped in the valley of Rephaim. 14 And David was then in the hold, and the garrison of the Philistines was then in Beth-lehem. 15 And David longed, and said, Oh that one would give me water to drink of the well of Beth-lehem, which is by the gate! 16 And the three mighty men brake through the host of the Philistines, and drew water out of the well of Beth-lehem, that was	15 And three of the thirty chief went down to the rock to David, into the cave of Adullam; and the host of the Philistines were encamped in the valley of Rephaim. 16 And David was then in the hold, and the garrison of the Philistines was then in Beth-lehem. 17 And David longed, and said, Oh that one would give me water to drink of the well of Beth-lehem, which is by the gate! 18 And the three brake through the host of the Philistines, and drew water out of the well of Beth-lehem, that was by the gate, and took it, and brought it to	9 Now the Philistines had come and made a raid in the valley of Rephaim.

a Or, "over." *b* Cf. §91, (2), *A*.

2 *Samuel* 23.	1 *Chronicles* 11.
by the gate, and took it, and brought it to David: but he would not drink thereof, but poured it out unto the LORD. 17 And he said, Be it far from me, O LORD, that I should do this: *shall I drink* the blood of the men that went *a* in jeopardy of their lives? therefore he would not drink it. These things did the three mighty men.	David: but David would not drink thereof, but poured it out unto the LORD, and said, 19 My God forbid it me, that I should do this: shall I drink the blood of these men *a* that have put their lives in jeopardy? for with *the jeopardy of* their lives they brought it. Therefore he would not drink it. These things did the three mighty men.

D. DAVID'S VICTORY AT BAAL-PERAZIM.

2 *Samuel* 5 : 19-21.	1 *Chronicles* 14 : 10-12.
19 And David inquired of the LORD, saying, Shall I go up against the Philistines? wilt thou deliver them into mine hand? And the LORD said unto David, Go up: for I will certainly deliver the Philistines into thine hand. 20 And David came to Baal-perazim, and David smote them there; and he said, The LORD hath *b* broken mine enemies before me, like the breach of waters. Therefore he called the name of that place *c* Baal-perazim. 21 And they left their images there, and David and his men took them away.	10 And David inquired of God, saying, Shall I go up against the Philistines? and wilt thou deliver them into mine hand? And the LORD said unto him, Go up; for I will deliver them into thine hand. 11 So they came up to Baal-perazim, and David smote them there; and David said, God hath *b* broken mine enemies by mine hand, like the breach of waters. Therefore they called the name of that place *c* Baal-perazim. 12 And they left their gods there; and David gave commandment, and they were burned with fire.

(2) THE SECOND CAMPAIGN.

2 *Samuel* 5 : 22-25.	1 *Chronicles* 14 : 13-17.
22 And the Philistines came up yet again, and spread themselves in the valley of Rephaim. 23 And when David inquired of the LORD, he said, Thou shalt not go up: make a circuit behind them, and come upon them over against the *d* mulberry trees. 24 And it shall be, when thou hearest the sound of marching in the tops of the mulberry trees, that then thou shalt bestir thyself: for then is the LORD gone out before thee to smite the host of the Philistines. 25 And David did so, as the LORD commanded him; and smote the Philistines from Geba until thou come to Gezer.	13 And the Philistines yet again made a raid in the valley. 14 And David inquired again of God; and God said unto him, Thou shalt not go up after them: turn away from them, and come upon them over against the *d* mulberry trees. 15 And it shall be, when thou hearest the sound of marching in the tops of the mulberry trees, that then thou shalt go out to battle: for God is gone out before thee to smite the host of the Philistines. 16 And David did as God commanded him: and they smote the host of the Philistines from Gibeon even to Gezer. 17 And the fame of David went out into all lands; and the LORD brought the fear of him upon all nations.

---

a Heb. " with their lives."   *b* Or, " broken forth upon mine enemies."   *c* I. e., " The place of breakings forth."   *d* Or " balsam trees."

80. DAVID'S ALLIANCE WITH HIRAM OF TYRE.

2 *Samuel* 5 . 11, 12.

11 And Hiram king of Tyre sent messengers to David, and cedar trees, and carpenters, and masons : and they built David an house.   12 And David perceived that the LORD had established him king over Israel, and that he had exalted his kingdom for his people Israel's sake.

1 *Chronicles* 14 : 1, 2.

1 And Hiram king of Tyre sent messengers to David, and cedar trees, and masons, and carpenters, to build him an house.   2 And David perceived that the LORD had established him king over Israel, for his kingdom was exalted on high, for his people Israel's sake.

81. OFFENSIVE WARS AGAINST THE PHILISTINES.

(1) A SUMMARY OF THESE WARS.

2 *Samuel* 8 : 1.

1 And after this it came to pass, that David smote the Philistines, and subdued them : and David took *a* the bridle of the mother city out of the hand of the Philistines.

1 *Chronicles* 18 : 1.

1 And after this it came to pass, that David smote the Philistines, and subdued them, and took Gath and her towns out of the hand of the Philistines.

(2) THE FIRST CAMPAIGN.
2 *Samuel* 21 : 15-17*a*.

15 And the Philistines had war again with Israel ; and David went down, and his servants with him, and fought against the Philistines : and David waxed faint.   16 And Ishbi-benob, which was of the sons of the *b* giant, the weight of whose spear was three hundred *shekels* of brass in weight, he being girded with *c* a new *sword*, thought to have slain David.   17*a* But Abishai the son of Zeruiah succoured him, and smote the Philistine, and killed him.

(3) WITHDRAWAL OF DAVID FROM ACTIVE MILITARY SERVICE.
2 *Samuel* 21 : 17*b*.

17*b* Then the men of David sware unto him, saying, Thou shalt go no more out with us to battle, that thou quench not the lamp of Israel.

(4) THE SECOND CAMPAIGN.

2 *Samuel* 21 : 18.

18 And it came to pass after this, that there was again war with the Philistines at Gob : then Sibbecai the Hushathite slew Saph, which was of the sons of the *b* giant.

1 *Chronicles* 20 : 4.

4 And it came to pass after this, that there arose war at Gezer with the Philistines : then Sibbecai the Hushathite slew Sippai, of the sons of the *d* giant : and they were subdued.

(5) THE THIRD CAMPAIGN.

2 *Samuel* 21 : 19.

19 And there was again war with the Philistines at Gob ; and Elhanan the son of Jaare-oregim the Beth-lehemite slew Goliath the Gittite, the staff of whose spear was like a weaver's beam.

1 *Chronicles* 20 : 5.

5 And there was again war with the Philistines ; and Elhanan the son of Jair slew Lahmi the brother of Goliath the Gittite, the staff of whose spear was like a weaver's beam.

---

a Or, "Metheg-ammah."   *b* Heb. "Raphah."   *c* Or, "new *armour*."   *d* Heb. "Rapha." According to another reading, "giants." Heb. "Rephaim."

(6) THE FOURTH CAMPAIGN.

2 *Samuel* 21 : 20-22.

20 And there was again war at Gath, where was a man of great stature, that had on every hand six fingers, and on every foot six toes, four and twenty in number ; and he also was born to the *a* giant. 21 And when he *b* defied Israel, Jonathan the son of *c* Shimei David's brother slew him. 22 These four were born to the *a* giant in Gath ; and they fell by the hand of David, and by the hand of his servants.

1 *Chronicles* 20 : 6-8.

6 And there was again war at Gath, where was a man of great stature, whose fingers and toes were four and twenty, six *on each hand,*and six *on each foot;* and he also was born unto the *d* giant. 7 And when he *b* defied Israel, Jonathan the son of *c* Shimea David's brother slew him. 8 These were born unto the *d* giant in Gath ; and they fell by the hand of David, and by the hand of his servants.

82. THE AMMONITE-SYRIAN CAMPAIGN.

(1) DAVID'S AMBASSADORS INSULTED BY THE AMMONITES.

2 *Samuel* 10 : 1-5.

1 And it came to pass after this, that the king of the children of Ammon died, and Hanun his son reigned in his stead. 2 And David said, I will shew kindness unto Hanun the son of Nahash, as his father shewed kindness unto me. So David sent by the hand of his servant to comfort him concerning his father. And David's servants came into the land of the children of Ammon. 3 But the princes of the children of Ammon said unto Hanun their lord, Thinkest thou that David doth honour thy father, that he hath sent comforters unto thee ? hath not David sent his servants unto thee to search the city, and to spy it out, and to overthrow it ? 4 So Hanun took David's servants, and shaved off the one half of their beards, and cut off their garments in the middle, even to their buttocks, and sent them away. 5 When they told it unto David, he sent to meet them ; for the men were greatly ashamed. And the king said, Tarry at Jericho until your beards be grown, and then return.

1 *Chronicles* 19 : 1-5.

1 And it came to pass after this, that Nahash the king of the children of Ammon died, and his son reigned in his stead. 2 And David said, I will shew kindness unto Hanun the son of Nahash, because his father shewed kindness to me. So David sent messengers to comfort him concerning his father. And David's servants came into the land of the children of Ammon to Hanun, to comfort him. 3 But the princes of the children of Ammon said unto Hanun, Thinkest thou that David dost honour thy father, that he hath sent comforters unto thee ? are not his servants come unto thee for to search, and to overthrow, and to spy out the land ? 4 So Hanun took David's servants, and shaved them, and cut off their garments in the middle, even to their buttocks, and sent them away. 5 Then there went certain, and told David how the men were served. And he sent to meet them ; for the men were greatly ashamed. And the king said, Tarry at Jericho until your beards be grown, and then return.

(2) THE ISRAELITISH VICTORY UNDER THE LEADERSHIP OF JOAB.

2 *Samuel* 10 : 6-14.

6 And when the children of Ammon saw that they were become odious to David, the children of Ammon sent and hired the Syrians of Bethrehob, and the Syrians of Zobah, twenty thousand footmen, and the king of Maacah with a thousand men, and the men of Tob twelve thousand men. 7 And when David heard of it, he sent Joab, and all the host of the mighty men.

1 *Chronicles* 19 : 6-15.

6 And when the children of Ammon saw that they had made themselves odious to David, Hanun and the children of Ammon sent a thousand talents of silver to hire them chariots and horsemen out of Mesopotamia, and out of Aram-maacah,and out of Zobah. 7 So they hired them thirty and two thousand chariots, and the king of Maacah and his people ; who came and

---

a Heb "Raphah." *b* Or "reproached." *c* In 1 Samuel 16 : 9, "Shammah." See §41. *d* Heb. "Rapha."

2 *Samuel* 10.

8 And the children of Ammon came out, and put the battle in array at the entering in of the gate: and the Syrians of Zobah, and of Rehob, and the men of Tob and Maacah, were by themselves in the field. 9 Now when Joab saw that *a* the battle was set against him before and behind, he chose of all the choice men of Israel, and put them in array against the Syrians: 10 and the rest of the people he committed into the hand of *b* Abishai his brother, and he put them in array against the children of Ammon. 11 And he said, If the Syrians be too strong for me, then thou shalt help me: but if the children of Ammon be too strong for thee, then I will come and help thee. 12 Be of good courage, and let us play the men for our people, and for the cities of our God: and the LORD do that which seemeth him good. 13 So Joab and the people that were with him drew nigh unto the battle against the Syrians: and they fled before him. 14 And when the children of Ammon saw that the Syrians were fled, they likewise fled before Abishai, and entered into the city. Then Joab returned from the children of Ammon, and came to Jerusalem.

1 *Chronicles* 19.

pitched before Medeba. And the children of Ammon gathered themselves together from their cities, and came to battle. 8 And when David heard of it, he sent Joab, and all the host of the mighty men. 9 And the children of Ammon came out, and put the battle in array at the gate of the city: and the kings that were come were by themselves in the field. 10 Now when Joab saw that *a* the battle was set against him before and behind, he chose of all the choice men of Israel, and put them in array against the Syrians. 11 And the rest of the people he committed into the hand of *b* Abishai his brother, and they put themselves in array against the children of Ammon. 12 And he said, If the Syrians be too strong for me, then thou shalt help me: but if the children of Ammon be too strong for thee, then I will help thee. 13 Be of good courage, and let us play the men for our people, and for the cities of our God: and the LORD do that which seemeth him good. 14 So Joab and the people that were with him drew nigh before the Syrians unto the battle; and they fled before him. 15 And when the children of Ammon saw that the Syrians were fled, they likewise fled before Abishai his brother, and entered into the city. Then Joab came to Jerusalem.

83. THE SYRIAN CAMPAIGN.

2 *Samuel* 10 : 15-19.

15 And when the Syrians saw that they were put to the worse before Israel, they gathered themselves together. 16 And *c* Hadarezer sent, and brought out the Syrians that were beyond the River: and they came to Helam, with Shobach the captain of the host of Hadarezer at their head. 17 And it was told David; and he gathered all Israel together, and passed over Jordan, and came to Helam. And the Syrians set themselves in array against David, and fought with him. 18 And the Syrians fled before Israel; and David slew of the Syrians *the men of* seven hundred chariots, and forty thousand horsemen, and smote Shobach the captain of their hosts, that he died there. 19 And when all the kings that were servants to Hadarezer saw that they were put to the worse before Israel, they made peace with Israel, and served them. So the Syrians feared to help the children of Ammon any more.

1 *Chronicles* 19 : 16-19.

16 And when the Syrians saw that they were put to the worse before Israel, they sent messengers, and drew forth the Syrians that were beyond the River, with Shophach the captain of the host of Hadarezer at their head. 17 And it was told David; and he gathered all Israel together, and passed over Jordan, and came upon them, and set the battle in array against them. So when David had put the battle in array against the Syrians, they fought with him. 18 And the Syrians fled before Israel; and David slew of the Syrians *the men of* seven thousand chariots, and forty thousand footmen, and killed Shophach the captain of the host. 19 And when the servants of Hadarezer saw that they were put to the worse before Israel, they made peace with David, and served him: neither would the Syrians help the children of Ammon any more.

---

a Heb. " the face of the battle was against."   *b* Heb. " Abshai."   *c* In 2 Samuel 8 : 3, " Hadadezer." See §86.

84. THE SECOND AMMONITE CAMPAIGN.

(1) JOAB LAYS SIEGE TO RABBAH.

2 Samuel 11 : 1.

1 And it came to pass, at the return of the year, at the time when kings go out *to battle,* that David sent Joab, and his servants with him, and all Israel ; and they destroyed the children of Ammon, and besieged Rabbah. But David tarried at Jerusalem.

1 Chronicles 20 : 1a.

1a And it came to pass, at the time of the return of the year, at the time when kings go out *to battle,* that Joab led forth the power of the army, and wasted the country of the children of Ammon, and came and besieged Rabbah. But David tarried at Jerusalem.

(2) DAVID'S FALL.

2 Samuel 11 : 2–27.

2 And it came to pass at eventide, that David arose from off his bed, and walked upon the roof of the king's house : and from the roof he saw a woman bathing ; and the woman was very beautiful to look upon. 3 And David sent and inquired after the woman. And one said, Is not this Bath-sheba, the daughter of Eliam, the wife of Uriah the Hittite ? 4 And David sent messengers, and took her ; and she came in unto him, and he lay with her ; (for she was purified from her uncleanness ;) and she returned unto her house. 5 And the woman conceived ; and she sent and told David, and said, I am with child. 6 And David sent to Joab, *saying,* Send me Uriah the Hittite. And Joab sent Uriah to David. 7 And when Uriah was come unto him, David asked of him how Joab did, and how the people fared, and how the war prospered. 8 And David said to Uriah, Go down to thy house and wash thy feet. And Uriah departed out of the king's house, and there followed him a *a* mess *of meat* from the king. 9 But Uriah slept at the door of the king's house with all the servants of his lord, and went not down to his house. 10 And when they had told David, saying, Uriah went not down unto his house, David said unto Uriah, Art thou not come from a journey ? wherefore didst thou not go down unto thine house ? 11 And Uriah said unto David, The ark, and Israel, and Judah, abide in booths ; and my lord Joab, and the servants of my lord, are encamped in the open field ; shall I then go into mine house, to eat and to drink, and to lie with my wife ? as thou livest, and as thy soul liveth, I will not do this thing. 12 And David said to Uriah, Tarry here to-day also, and to-morrow I will let thee depart. So Uriah abode in Jerusalem *b* that day, and the morrow. 13 And when David did call him, he did eat and drink before him ; and he made him drunk : and at even he went out to lie on his bed with the servants of his lord, but went not down to his house. 14 And it came to pass in the morning, that David wrote a letter to Joab, and sent it by the hand of Uriah. 15 And he wrote in the letter, saying, Set ye Uriah in the forefront of the *c* hottest battle, and retire ye from him, that he may be smitten, and die. 16 And it came to pass, when Joab *d* kept watch upon the city, that he assigned Uriah unto the place where he knew that valiant men were. 17 And the men of the city went out, and fought with Joab : and there fell some of the people, even of the servants of David ; and Uriah the Hittite died also. 18 Then Joab sent and told David all the things concerning the war ; 19 and he charged the messenger, saying, When thou hast made an end of telling all the things concerning the war unto the king, 20 it shall be that, if the king's wrath arise, and he say unto thee, Wherefore went ye so nigh unto the city to fight ? knew ye not that they would shoot from the wall ? 21 who smote Abimelech the son of *e* Jerubbesheth ? did not a woman cast an upper millstone upon him from the wall, that he died at Thebez ? why went ye so nigh the wall ? then shalt thou say, Thy servant Uriah the Hittite is dead also. 22 So the messenger went, and came and shewed David all that Joab had sent him for. 23 And the messenger said unto David, The men prevailed against us, and came out unto us into the field, and we were upon them even unto the entering of the gate.

---

a Or, " present from." *b* Or, " that day. And on the morrow David called him, and he," etc. *c* Heb. " strong." *d* Or, " observed." *e* In Judges 6 : 32, " Jerubbaal."

2 *Samuel* 11.

24 And the shooters shot at thy servants from off the wall; and some of the king's servants be dead, and thy servant Uriah the Hittite is dead also.   25 Then David said unto the messenger, Thus shalt thou say unto Joab, Let not this thing displease thee, for the sword devoureth one as well as another: make thy battle more strong against the city, and overthrow it: and encourage thou him.   26 And when the wife of Uriah heard that Uriah her husband was dead, she made lamentation for her husband.   27 And when the mourning was past, David sent and took her home to his house, and she became his wife, and bare him a son.   But the thing that David had done displeased the LORD.

(3) DAVID'S REPENTANCE.

2 *Samuel* 12 : 1–24*a*.

1 And the LORD sent Nathan unto David.   And he came unto him, and said unto him, There were two men in one city; the one rich, and the other poor.   2 The rich man had exceeding many flocks and herds: 3 but the poor man had nothing save one little ewe lamb, which he had bought and nourished up: and it grew up together with him, and with his children; it did eat of his own morsel, and drank of his own cup, and lay in his bosom, and was unto him as a daughter.   4 And there came a traveller unto the rich man, and he spared to take of his own flock and of his own herd, to dress for the wayfaring man that was come unto him, but took the poor man's lamb, and dressed it for the man that was come to him.   5 And David's anger was greatly kindled against the man; and he said to Nathan, As the LORD liveth, the man that hath done this is *a* worthy to die: 6 and he shall restore the lamb fourfold, because he did this thing, and because he had no pity.

7 And Nathan said to David, Thou art the man.   Thus saith the LORD, the God of Israel, I anointed thee king over Israel, and I delivered thee out of the hand of Saul, 8 and I gave thee thy master's house, and thy master's wives into thy bosom, and gave thee the house of Israel and of Judah; and if that had been too little, I would have added unto thee such and such things.   9 Wherefore hast thou despised the word of the LORD, to do that which is evil in his sight? thou hast smitten Uriah the Hittite with the sword, and hast taken his wife to be thy wife, and hast slain him with the sword of the children of Ammon.   10 Now therefore, the sword shall never depart from thine house; because thou hast despised me, and hast taken the wife of Uriah the Hittite to be thy wife.   11 Thus saith the LORD, Behold, I will raise up evil against thee out of thine own house, and I will take thy wives before thine eyes, and give them unto thy neighbour, and he shall lie with thy wives in the sight of this sun.   12 For thou didst it secretly: but I will do this thing before all Israel, and before the sun.   13 And David said unto Nathan, I have sinned against the LORD.   And Nathan said unto David, The LORD also hath put away thy sin; thou shalt not die.   14 Howbeit, because by this deed thou hast given great occasion to the enemies of the LORD to blaspheme, the child also that is born unto thee shall surely die.   15 And Nathan departed unto his house.

And the LORD struck the child that Uriah's wife bare unto David, and it was very sick.   16 David therefore besought God for the child; and David fasted, and went in, and lay all night upon the earth.   17 And the elders of his house arose, *and stood* beside him, to raise him up from the earth: but he would not, neither did he eat bread with them.   18 And it came to pass on the seventh day, that the child died.   And the servants of David feared to tell him that the child was dead: for they said, Behold, while the child was yet alive, we spake unto him, and he hearkened not unto our voice: *b* how will he then vex himself, if we tell him that the child is dead?   19 But when David saw that his servants whispered together, David perceived that the child was dead: and David said unto his servants, Is the child dead?   And they said, He is dead.   20 Then David arose from the earth, and washed, and anointed himself, and changed his apparel; and he came into the house of the LORD, and worshipped: then he came to his own house; and when he required they set bread before him, and he did eat.   21 Then said his servants unto him, What thing

---

a Heb. " a son of death."   *b* Or, " how then shall we tell him that the child is dead, so that he do himself some harm ? "

2 *Samuel* 12.

is this that thou hast done? thou didst fast and weep for the child, while it was alive; but when the child was dead, thou didst rise and eat bread. 22 And he said, While the child was yet alive, I fasted and wept: for I said, Who knoweth whether the LORD will not be gracious to me, that the child may live? 23 But now he is dead, wherefore should I fast? can I bring him back again? I shall go to him, but he shall not return to me. 24*a* And David comforted Bath-sheba his wife, and went in unto her, and lay with her.

(4) THE CAPTURE OF RABBAH.

2 *Samuel* 12:26–31.	1 *Chronicles* 20:1*b*–3.
26 Now Joab fought against Rabbah of the children of Ammon, and took the royal city. 27 And Joab sent messengers to David, and said, I have fought against Rabbah, yea, I have taken the city of waters. 28 Now therefore gather the rest of the people together, and encamp against the city, and take it: lest I take the city, and *a* it be called after my name. 29 And David gathered all the people together, and went to Rabbah, and fought against it, and took it. 30 And he took the crown of *b* their king from off his head; and the weight thereof was a talent of gold, and *in it were* precious stones; and it was set on David's head. And he brought forth the spoil of the city, exceeding much. 31 And he brought forth the people that were therein, and put them *c* under saws, and *c* under harrows of iron, and *c* under axes of iron, and *d* made them pass through the *e* brickkiln: and thus did he unto all the cities of the children of Ammon. And David and all the people returned unto Jerusalem.	1*b* And Joab smote Rabbah, and overthrew it. 2 And David took the crown of *b* their king from off his head, and found it to weigh a talent of gold, and there were precious stones in it; and it was set upon David's head: and he brought forth the spoil of the city, exceeding much. 3 And he brought forth the people that were therein, and cut *them* with saws, and with harrows of iron, and with axes. And thus did David unto all the cities of the children of Ammon. And David and all the people returned to Jerusalem.

85. THE CAMPAIGN AGAINST MOAB.

(1) THE CONQUEST BY DAVID.

2 *Samuel* 8:2.	1 *Chronicles* 18:2.
• 2 And he smote Moab, and measured them with the line, making them to lie down on the ground; and he measured two lines to put to death, and one full line to keep alive. And the Moabites became servants to David, and brought presents.	2 And he smote Moab; and the Moabites became servants to David, and brought presents.

(2) THE EXPLOIT OF BENAIAH.

2 *Samuel* 23:20*a*.	1 *Chronicles* 11:22*a*.
20*a* And Benaiah the son of Jehoiada, the son of *f* a valiant man of Kabzeel, who had done mighty deeds, he slew the two *sons of* Ariel of Moab.	22*a* Benaiah the son of Jehoiada, the son of a valiant man of Kabzeel, who had done mighty deeds, he slew the two *sons of* Ariel of Moab.

a Heb. " my name be called upon it."   *b* Or, " Malcam."   See Zephaniah 1:5.   *c* Or, " to."   *d* Or, with a slight change in the Hebrew text, " made them labour at."   *e* Or, " brickmould."   *f* According to another reading, " Ish-hai."

86. DECISIVE CAMPAIGN AGAINST HADADEZER.

2 *Samuel* 8 : 3, 4, 7, 8.	1 *Kings* 11 : [23*b*], 24*a*.	1 *Chronicles* 18 : 3, 4, 7, 8.
3 David smote also Hadadezer the son of Rehob, king of Zobah, as he went to recover his dominion at *a* the River. 4 And David took from him a thousand and seven hundred horsemen, and twenty thousand footmen : and David houghed all the chariot horses, but reserved of them for an hundred chariots. 7 And David took the shields of gold that were on the servants of Hadadezer, and brought them to Jerusalem. 8 And from Betah and from Berothai, cities of Hadadezer, king David took exceeding much brass.		3 And David smote Hadarezer king of Zobah *e* unto Hamath, as he went to stablish his dominion by the river Euphrates. 4 And David took from him a thousand chariots, and seven thousand horsemen, and twenty thousand footmen : and David houghed all the chariot horses, but reserved of them for an hundred chariots. 7 And David took the shields of gold that were on the servants of Hadarezer, and brought them to Jerusalem. 8 And from Tibhath and from Cun, cities of Hadarezer, David took very much brass, wherewith Solomon made the brasen sea, and the pillars, and the vessels of brass.
	23*b* Rezon the son of Eliada, . . . fled from his lord Hadadezer king of Zobah : 24*a* and he gathered men unto him, and became captain over a troop, when David slew them *of Zobah.*[b]	

87. SUBJUGATION OF DAMASCUS.

2 *Samuel* 8 : 5, 6.	1 *Chronicles* 18 : 5, 6.
5 And when *d* the Syrians of Damascus came to succour Hadadezer king of Zobah, David smote of *d* the Syrians two and twenty thousand men. 6 Then David put garrisons in *d* Syria of Damascus : and *d* the Syrians became servants to David, and brought presents. And the LORD *c* gave victory to David whithersoever he went.	5 And when *d* the Syrians of *f* Damascus came to succour Hadarezer king of Zobah, David smote of *d* the Syrians two and twenty thousand men. 6 Then David put *garrisons* in *d* Syria of *f* Damascus ; and *d* the Syrians became servants to David, and brought presents. And the LORD *c* gave victory to David whithersoever he went.

88. SUBMISSION OF HAMATH.

2 *Samuel* 8 : 9-11.	1 *Chronicles* 18 : 9-11*a*.
9 And when Toi king of Hamath heard that David had smitten all the host of Hadadezer, 10 then Toi sent Joram his son unto king David,	9 And when Tou king of Hamath heard that David had smitten all the host of Hadarezer king of Zobah, 10 he sent Hadoram his son to

---

a Another reading is, "the river Euphrates."   *b* And they went to Damascus, and dwelt therein, and reigned in Damascus.—1 Kings 11 : 24*b*. This fact occurred, of course, years after David's campaign against Hadadezer, for in §87 we note David's subjugation of Damascus. Rezon probably became king of Damascus about the time of the accession of Solomon. *c* Or, "by." *d* Heb. "Aram." *e* Or, "saved David." Cf. §90. *f* Heb. "Darmesek."

2 *Samuel* 8.	1 *Chronicles* 18.
to *a* salute him, and to bless him, because he had fought against Hadadezer and smitten him : for Hadadezer *b* had wars with Toi. And *c Joram* brought with him vessels of silver, and vessels of gold, and vessels of brass : 11 these also did king David dedicate unto the LORD, with the silver and gold that he dedicated of all the nations which he subdued.	king David, to salute him, and to bless him, be- cause he had fought against Hadarezer and smitten him ; for Hadarezer had wars with Tou ; and *he had with him* all manner of vessels of gold and silver and brass. 11*a* These also did king David dedicate unto the LORD, with the silver and the gold that he carried away from all the nations.

· 89. SUBJUGATION OF EDOM.

2 *Samuel* 8 : 13, 14*a*.	1 *Kings* 11 : 15-17, [14*b*], 18.	1 *Chronicles* 18 : 12, 13*a*.
13 And David gat him a name when he returned from smiting of *d* the Syrians in the Valley of Salt, even eighteen thousand men. 14*a* And he put garrisons in Edom ; throughout all Edom put he garrisons, and all the Edomites became servants to David.		12 Moreover *g* Abishai the son of Zeruiah smote of the Edom- ites in the Valley of Salt eighteen thousand. 13*a* And he put gar- risons in Edom ; and all the Edomites became servants to David.
	15 For it came to pass when David *e* was in Edom, and Joab the captain of the host was gone up to bury the slain, and had smitten every male in Edom ; 16 (for Joab and all Israel remained there six months, until he had cut off every male in Edom ;) 17 that Hadad fled, he and certain Edomites of his fa- ther's servants with him, to go into Egypt ; Hadad being yet a little child : 14*b* he was of the king's seed in Edom. 18 And they arose out of Midian, and came to Paran : and they took men with them out of Paran, and they came to Egypt, unto Pha- raoh king of Egypt ; which gave him an house, and appointed him victuals, and gave him land.*f*	

90. SUMMARY OF DAVID'S WARS : THE NATIONS CONQUERED.

2 *Samuel* 8 : [11*d*], 12, [11*b*], 14*b*.	1 *Chronicles* 18 : 11*c*, 11*b*, 13*b*.
11*d* The silver and gold of all the nations which he subdued ; 12 of *d* Syria, and of Moab, and of the children of Ammon, and of the Philis-	11*c* The silver and the gold that he carried away from all the nations ; from Edom, and from Moab, and from the children of Ammon, and

a Heb. " ask him of his welfare."   *b* Heb. " was a man of wars."   *c* Heb. " in his hand were."   *d* Heb. " Aram."
According to some ancient authorities, " Edom."   *e* The Sept. and Syr. read, " destroyed Edom."   *f* 1 Kings 11 : 19,
20.—19 And Hadad found great favour in the sight of Pharaoh, so that he gave him to wife the sister of his own wife, the sister
of Tahpenes the queen. 20 And the sister of Tahpenes bare him Genubath his son, whom Tahpenes weaned in Pharaoh's
house : and Genubath was in Pharaoh's house among the sons of Pharaoh.   *g* Heb. " Abshai."

2 *Samuel* 8.	1 *Chronicles* 18.
tines, and of Amalek, and of the spoil of Hadad-ezer, son of Rehob, king of Zobah, 11*b* did king David dedicate unto the LORD. 14*b* And the LORD *a* gave victory to David whithersoever he went.	from the Philistines, and from Amalek, 11*b* did king David dedicate unto the LORD. 13*b* And the LORD *a* gave victory to David whithersoever he went.

91. LIST OF DAVID'S HEROES.

(1) THE "FIRST" THREE.

A. JASHOBEAM.

2 *Samuel* 23 : 8.	1 *Chronicles* 11 : 10, 11.
	10 Now these are the chief of the mighty men whom David had, who *c* shewed themselves strong with him in his kingdom, together with all Israel, to make him king, according to the word of the LORD concerning Israel. 11 And
8 These be the names of the mighty men whom David had : *b* Josheb-basshebeth a Tahchemo-nite, chief of the captains ; the same was Adino the Eznite, against eight hundred slain at one time.	this is the number of the mighty men whom David had : Jashobeam, the son of a Hachmo-nite, the chief of the *d* thirty ; he lifted up his spear against three hundred *e* and slew them at one time.

B. ELEAZER.

2 *Samuel* 23 : 9, 10.	1 *Chronicles* 11 : 12.
9 And after him was Eleazar the son of Dodai the son of an Ahohite, one of the three mighty men with David, when they defied the Philis-tines that were there gathered together to battle, and the men of Israel *f* were gone away : 10 he arose, and smote the Philistines until his hand was weary, and his hand clave unto the sword : and the LORD wrought a great *g* victory that day ; and the people returned after him only to spoil.	12 And after him was Eleazar the son of Dodo, the Ahohite, who was one of the three mighty men.

C. SHAMMAH. *h*

2 *Samuel* 23 : 11, 12.	1 *Chronicles* 11 : 13, 14.
11 And after him was Shammah the son of Agee a Hararite. And the Philistines were gathered together *i* into a troop, where was a plot of ground full of lentils ; and the people fled from the Philistines. 12 But he stood in the midst of the plot, and defended it, and slew the Philistines : and the LORD wrought a great *g* victory.	13 *k* He was with David at *l* Pas-dammim, and there the Philistines were gathered together to battle, where was a plot of ground full of barley ; and the people fled from before the Philistines. 14 And they stood in the midst of the plot, and defended it, and slew the Philistines ; and the LORD saved them by a great *g* victory.

a Or, " saved David." Cf. §87.   *b* This verse is probably corrupt.   *c* Or, " held strongly with him."   *d* Another read-ing is, " captains."   *e* Heb. " slain."   *f* Heb. " went up."   *g* Heb. " salvation."   *h* For historical setting, see §43, (7).
i Or, " for foraging."   *k* The Chronicler in transcribing has doubtless omitted the name of Shammah.   *l* In 1 Samuel 17 : 1, " Ephes-dammim." See §43, (1).

(2) The "three mighty men."

A. THEIR EXPLOIT AT BETHLEHEM.[a]

[2 Samuel 23 : 13-17.]

13 And three of the thirty chief went down, and came to David in the harvest time unto the cave of Adullam ; and the troop of the Philistines were encamped in the valley of Rephaim. 14 And David was then in the hold, and the garrison of the Philistines was then in Beth-lehem. 15 And David longed, and said, Oh that one would give me water to drink of the well of Beth-lehem, which is by the gate ! 16 And the three mighty men brake through the host of the Philistines, and drew water out of the well of Beth-lehem, that was by the gate, and took it, and brought it to David : but he would not drink thereof, but poured it out unto the LORD. 17 And he said, Be it far from me, O LORD, that I should do this : *shall I drink* the blood of the men that went [b] in jeopardy of their lives ? therefore he would not drink it. These things did the three mighty men.

[1 Chronicles 11 : 15-19.]

15 And three of the thirty chief went down to the rock to David, into the cave of Adullam ; and the host of the Philistines were encamped in the valley of Rephaim. 16 And David was then in the hold, and the garrison of the Philistines was then in Beth-lehem. 17 And David longed, and said, Oh that one would give me water to drink of the well of Beth-lehem, which is by the gate ! 18 And the three brake through the host of the Philistines, and drew water out of the well of Beth-lehem, that was by the gate, and took it, and brought it to David : but David would not drink thereof, but poured it out unto the LORD, and said, 19 My God forbid it me, that I should do this : shall I drink the blood of these men [b] that have put their lives in jeopardy ? for with *the jeopardy of* their lives they brought it. Therefore he would not drink it. These things did the three mighty men.

B. ABISHAI.

2 Samuel 23 : 18, 19.

18 And Abishai, the brother of Joab, the son of Zeruiah, was chief of the three. And he lifted up his spear against three hundred [c] and slew them, and had a name among the three. 19 Was he not most honourable of the three ? therefore he was made their captain : howbeit he attained not unto the *first* three.

1 Chronicles 11 : 20, 21.

20 And [d] Abishai, the brother of Joab, he was chief of the three : for he lifted up his spear against three hundred [c] and slew them, and had a name among the three. 21 [e] Of the three, he was more honourable than the two, and was made their captain : howbeit he attained not to the *first* three.

C. BENAIAH.

2 Samuel 23 : [20a], 20b-23.

20 And Benaiah the son of Jehoiada, the son of [f] a valiant man of Kabzeel, who had done mighty deeds, he slew the two *sons of* Ariel of Moab : he went down also and slew a lion in the midst of a pit in time of snow : 21 and he slew an Egyptian, a goodly man : and the Egyptian had a spear in his hand ; but he went down to him with a staff, and plucked the spear out of the Egyptian's hand, and slew him with his own spear. 22 These things did Benaiah the son of Jehoiada, and had a name among the three mighty men. 23 He was more honourable than the thirty, but he attained not to the *first* three. And David set him over his [g] guard.

1 Chronicles 11 : [22a], 22b-25.

22 Benaiah the son of Jehoiada, the son of a valiant man of Kabzeel, who had done mighty deeds, he slew the two *sons of* Ariel of Moab : he went down also and slew a lion in the midst of a pit in time of snow. 23 And he slew an Egyptian, a man of great stature, five cubits high ; and in the Egyptian's hand was a spear like a weaver's beam ; and he went down to him with a staff, and plucked the spear out of the Egyptian's hand, and slew him with his own spear. 24 These things did Benaiah the son of Jehoiada, and had a name among the three mighty men. 25 Behold, he was more honourable than the thirty, but he attained not to the *first* three : and David set him over his [g] guard.

---

a For historical setting, see §79, (1), C.   *b* Heb. "with their lives."   *c* Heb. "slain."   *d* Heb. "Abshai."   *e* Or, "Of the three in the second rank he was the most honourable."   *f* According to another reading, "Ish-hai."   *g* Or, "council."

(3) The remaining Heroes.

2 Samuel 23 : 24–39.

24 Asahel the brother of Joab was one of the thirty ; Elhanan the son of Dodo of Beth-lehem ; 25 Shammah the Harodite, Elika the Harodite ; 26 Helez the Paltite, Ira the son of Ikkesh the Tekoite ; 27 Abiezer the Anathothite, Mebunnai the Hushathite ; 28 Zalmon the Ahohite, Maharai the Netophathite ; 29 Heleb the son of Baanah the Netophathite, Ittai the son of Ribai of Gibeah of the children of Benjamin ; 30 Benaiah a Pirathonite, Hiddai of the brooks of Gaash ; 31 Abi-albon the Arbathite, Azmaveth the Barhumite ; 32 Eliahba the Shaalbonite, the sons of Jashen, Jonathan ; 33 Shammah the Hararite, Ahiam the son of Sharar the Ararite ; 34 Eliphelet the son of Ahasbai, the son of Maacathite, Eliam the son of Ahithophel the Gilonite ; 35 *a* Hezro the Carmelite, Paarai the Arbite ; 36 Igal the son of Nathan of Zobah, Bani the Gadite ; 37 Zelek the Ammonite, Naharai the Beerothite, *b* armourbearers to Joab the son of Zeruiah ; 38 Ira the Ithrite, Gareb the Ithrite ; 39 Uriah the Hittite : thirty and seven in all.

1 Chronicles 11 : 26–47.

26 Also the mighty men of the armies ; Asahel the brother of Joab, Elhanan the son of Dodo of Beth-lehem ; 27 Shommoth the Harorite, Helez the Pelonite ; 28 Ira the son of Ikkesh the Tekoite, Abiezer the Anathothite ; 29 Sibbecai the Hushathite, Ilai the Ahohite ; 30 Maharai the Netophathite, Heled the son of Baanah the Netophathite ; 31 Ithai the son of Ribai of Gibeah of the children of Benjamin, Benaiah the Pirathonite ; 32 Hurai of the brooks of Gaash, Abiel the Arbathite ; 33 Azmaveth the Baharumite, Eliahba the Shaalbonite ; 34 the sons of Hashem the Gizonite, Jonathan the son of Shage the Hararite ; 35 Ahiam the son of Sacar the Hararite, Eliphal the son of Ur ; 36 Hepher the Mecherathite, Ahijah the Pelonite ; 37 Hezro the Carmelite, Naarai the son of Ezbai ; 38 Joel the brother of Nathan, Mibhar the son of Hagri ; 39 Zelek the Ammonite, Naharai the Berothite, the armourbearer of Joab the son of Zeruiah ; 40 Ira the Ithrite, Gareb the Ithrite ; 41 Uriah the Hittite, Zabad the son of Ahlai ; 42 Adina the son of Shiza the Reubenite, a chief of the Reubenites, and thirty with him ; 43 Hanan the son of Maacah, and Joshaphat the Mithnite ; 44 Uzzia the Ashterathite, Shama and Jeiel the sons of Hotham the Aroerite ; 45 Jediael the son of Shimri, and Joha his brother, the Tizite ; 46 Eliel the Mahavite, and Jeribai, and Joshaviah, the sons of Elnaam, and Ithmah the Moabite ; 47 Eliel, and Obed, and Jaasiel the Mezobaite.

92. THE ADMINISTRATION AND OFFICERS OF THE KINGDOM DURING THIS PERIOD.*c*

2 Samuel 8 : 15–18.

15 And David reigned over all Israel ; and David executed judgement and justice unto all his people. 16 And Joab the son of Zeruiah was over the host ; and Jehoshaphat the son of Ahilud was *d* recorder : 17 and Zadok the son of Ahitub, and Ahimelech the son of Abiathar, were priests ; and Seraiah was *e* scribe ; 18 And Benaiah the son of Jehoiada *f was over* the Cherethites and the Pelethites ; and David's sons were *g* priests.

1 Chronicles 18 : 14–17.

14 And David reigned over all Israel ; and he executed judgement and justice unto all his people. 15 And Joab the son of Zeruiah was over the host ; and Jehoshaphat the son of Ahilud was *d* recorder. 16 And Zadok the son of Ahitub, and Abimelech the son of Abiathar, were priests ; and Shavsha was *e* scribe ; 17 and Benaiah the son of Jehoiada was overt he Cherethites and the Pelethites ; and the sons of David were chief about the king.

---

a Or, " Hezrai."   *b* Another reading is "armourbearer."   *c* Cf. §§107, (2), *L*, and 116.   *d* Or, " chronicler."
e Or, "secretary."   *f* The Hebrew text has, " and the Cherethites," etc.   *g* Or, " chief ministers."

93. DAVID'S SONG OF THANKSGIVING.[a]

2 *Samuel* 22 : 1-51.

1 And David spake unto the LORD the words of this song in the day that the LORD delivered him out of the hand of all his enemies, and out of the hand of Saul : 2 and he said,
> The LORD is my rock, and my fortress, and my deliverer, even mine ;
> 3 The God of my rock, in him will I trust ;
> My shield, and the horn of my salvation, my high tower, and my refuge ;
> My saviour, thou savest me from violence.
> 4 I will call upon the LORD, who is worthy to be praised :
> So shall I be saved from mine enemies.
> 5 For the waves of death compassed me,
> The floods of [b] ungodliness made me afraid.
> 6 The cords of [c] Sheol were round about me :
> The snares of death came upon me.
> 7 In my distress I called upon the LORD,
> Yea, I called unto my God :
> And he heard my voice out of his temple,
> And my cry *came* into his ears.
> 8 Then the earth shook and trembled,
> The foundations of heaven moved
> And were shaken, because he was wroth.
> 9 There went up a smoke [d] out of his nostrils,
> And fire out of his mouth devoured :
> Coals were kindled by it.
> 10 He bowed the heavens also, and came down ;
> And thick darkness was under his feet.
> 11 And he rode upon a cherub, and did fly :
> Yea, he was seen upon the wings of the wind.
> 12 And he made darkness pavilions round about him,
> Gathering of waters, thick clouds of the skies.
> 13 At the brightness before him
> Coals of fire were kindled.
> 14 The LORD thundered from heaven,
> And the Most High uttered his voice.
> 15 And he sent out arrows, and scattered them ;
> Lightning, and discomfited them.
> 16 Then the channels of the sea appeared,
> The foundations of the world were laid bare,
> By the rebuke of the LORD,
> At the blast of the breath of his nostrils.
> 17 He sent from on high, he took me ;
> He drew me out of [e] many waters ;
> 18 He delivered me from my strong enemy,
> From them that hated me ; for they were too mighty for me.
> 19 They came upon me in the day of my calamity :
> But the LORD was my stay.
> 20 He brought me forth also into a large place :
> He delivered me. because he delighted in me.
> 21 The LORD rewarded me according to my righteousness :
> According to the cleanness of my hands hath he recompensed me.

---

a Cf. Psalm 18. See Appendix, §6.   *b* Heb. " Belial."   *c* See Genesis 37 : 35.   *d* Or, " in his wrath."   *e* Or, " great."

2 Samuel 22.

22 For I have kept the ways of the LORD,
   And have not wickedly departed from my God.
23 For all his judgements were before me:
   And as for his statutes, I did not depart from them.
24 I was also perfect toward him,
   And I kept myself from mine iniquity.
25 Therefore hath the LORD recompensed me according to my righteousness;
   According to my cleanness in his eyesight.
26 With the merciful thou wilt shew thyself merciful,
   With the perfect man thou wilt shew thyself perfect;
27 With the pure thou wilt shew thyself pure;
   And with the perverse thou wilt shew thyself *a* froward.
28 And the afflicted people thou wilt save:
   But thine eyes are upon the haughty, *b* that thou mayest bring them down.
29 For thou art my lamp, O LORD:
   And the LORD will lighten my darkness.
30 For by thee I run *c* upon a troop:
   By my God do I leap over a wall.
31 As for God, his way is perfect:
   The word of the LORD is tried;
   He is a shield unto all them that trust in him.
32 For who is God, save the LORD?
   And who is a rock, save our God?
33 God is my strong fortress:
   And he *d* guideth the perfect in his way.
34 He maketh *e* his feet like hinds' *feet*:
   And setteth me upon my high places.
35 He teacheth my hands to war;
   So that mine arms do bend a bow of brass.
36 Thou hast also given me the shield of thy salvation:
   And thy *f* gentleness hath made me great.
37 Thou hast enlarged my steps under me,
   And my *g* feet have not slipped.
38 I have pursued mine enemies, and destroyed them;
   Neither did I turn again till they were consumed.
39 And I have consumed them, and smitten them through, that they cannot arise:
   Yea, they are fallen under my feet.
40 For thou hast girded me with strength unto the battle:
   Thou hast *h* subdued under me those that rose up against me.
41 Thou hast also made mine enemies turn their backs unto me,
   That I might cut off them that hate me.
42 They looked, but there was none to save;
   Even unto the LORD, but he answered them not.
43 Then did I beat them small as the dust of the earth,
   I did stamp them as the mire of the streets, and did spread them abroad.
44 Thou also hast delivered me from the strivings of my people;
   Thou *i* hast kept me to be the head of the nations:
   A people whom I have not known shall serve me.

---

a So Psalm 18 : 26.   The text has, "unsavoury."   *b* Or, "whom thou wilt bring down."   *c* Or, "through."   *d* Or,
"setteth free."   According to another reading, "guideth my way in perfectness."   *e* Another reading is, "my."   *f* Or,
"condescension."   *g* Heb. "ankles."   *h* Heb. "caused to bow."   *i* Or, "wilt keep."

2 *Samuel* 22.

45 The strangers shall *a* submit themselves unto me:
As soon as they hear of me, they shall obey me.
46 The strangers shall fade away,
And shall *b* come trembling out of their close places.
47 The LORD liveth; and blessed be my rock;
And exalted be the God of the rock of my salvation:
48 Even the God that executeth vengeance for me,
And bringeth down peoples under me,
49 And that bringeth me forth from mine enemies:
Yea, thou liftest me up above them that rise up against me:
Thou deliverest me from the violent man.
50 Therefore I will give thanks unto thee, O LORD, among the nations,
And will sing praises unto thy name.
51 *c* Great *d* deliverance giveth he to his king:
And sheweth lovingkindness to his anointed,
To David and to his seed, for evermore.

PART III.

THE PERIOD OF REST.

94. REMOVAL OF THE ARK FROM KIRJATH-JEARIM. *e*

(1) To THE HOUSE OF OBED-EDOM.

2 *Samuel* 6:1-11.

1 *Chronicles* 13:1-14.

1 And David consulted with the captains of thousands and of hundreds, even with every leader. 2 And David said unto all the assembly of Israel, If it seem good unto you, and if it be of the LORD our God, let us send abroad every where unto our brethren that are left in all the *i* land of Israel, *k* with whom the priests and Levites are in their cities that have *l* suburbs, that they may gather themselves unto us: 3 and let us bring again the ark of our God to us: for we sought not unto it in the days of Saul. 4 And all the assembly said that they would do so: for the thing was right in the eyes of all the people. 5 So David assembled all Israel together, from Shihor *the brook* of Egypt even unto the entering in of Hamath, to bring the ark of God from Kiriath-jearim. 6 And David went up, and all Israel, to Baalah, *that is*, to Kiriath-jearim, which belonged to Judah, to bring up from thence the ark of God, the LORD that *g* sitteth

1 And David again gathered together all the chosen men of Israel, thirty thousand. 2 And David arose, and went with all the people that were with him, from Baale Judah, to bring up from thence the ark of God, *f* which is called by the Name, even the name of the LORD of hosts that *g* sitteth upon the cherubim. 3 And they set the ark of God upon a new cart, and brought it out of the house of Abinadab that was in *h* the hill: and Uzzah and Ahio, the sons of Abinadab, drave the new cart. 4 And they

---

a Or, " yield feigned obedience." Heb. " lie." *b* So Psalm 18:45. The text has, " gird themselves." *c* Another reading is, "He is a tower of deliverance." *d* Heb. "salvations." *e* For this, according to 1 Chronicles 13:5, " David assembled all Israel together, from Shihor of Egypt, even unto the entering in of Hamath." Hence the date must have been after the wars of conquest. *f* Heb. " whereupon is called the Name." *g* Or, " dwelleth between." *h* Or, " Gibeah." *i* Heb. " lands." *k* Or, " and with them to the priests and Levites which are," etc. *l* Or, " pasture lands."

2 Samuel 6.

brought it out of the house of Abinadab, which was in the hill, with the ark of God: and Ahio went before the ark. 5 And David and all the house of Israel played before the LORD with all manner of *instruments made of* ^a fir wood, and with harps, and with psalteries, and with timbrels, and with ^b castanets, and with cymbals. 6 And when they came to the threshing-floor of Nacon, Uzzah put forth *his hand* to the ark of God, and took hold of it; for the oxen ^c stumbled. 7 And the anger of the LORD was kindled against Uzzah; and God smote him there for his ^d error; and there he died by the ark of God. 8 And David was displeased, because the LORD had broken forth upon Uzzah: and he called that place ^e Perez-uzzah, unto this day. 9 And David was afraid of the LORD that day; and he said, How shall the ark of the LORD come unto me? 10 So David would not remove the ark of the LORD unto him into the city of David; but David carried it aside into the house of Obed-edom the Gittite. 11 And the ark of the LORD remained in the house of Obed-edom the Gittite three months: and the LORD blessed Obed-edom, and all his house.

1 Chronicles 13.

upon the cherubim, ^f which is called by the Name. 7 And they carried the ark of God upon a new cart, *and brought it* out of the house of Abinadab: and Uzza and Ahio drave the cart. 8 And David and all Israel played before God with all their might: even with songs, and with harps, and with psalteries, and with timbrels, and with cymbals, and with trumpets. 9 And when they came unto the threshing-floor of Chidon, Uzza put forth his hand to hold the ark; for the oxen ^c stumbled. 10 And the anger of the LORD was kindled against Uzza, and he smote him, because he put forth his hand to the ark: and there he died before God. 11 And David was displeased, because the LORD had broken forth upon Uzza: and he called that place ^e Perez-uzza, unto this day. 12 And David was afraid of God that day, saying, How shall I bring the ark of God home to me? 13 So David removed not the ark unto him into the city of David, but carried it aside into the house of Obed-edom the Gittite. 14 And the ark of God remained with the family of Obed-edom in his house three months: and the LORD blessed the house of Obed-edom, and all that he had.

(2) TO JERUSALEM.

2 Samuel 6: 12–19a.

12a And it was told king David, saying, The LORD hath blessed the house of Obed-edom, and all that pertaineth unto him, because of the ark of God.

1 Chronicles 15: 1–16: 3.

1 And *David* made him houses in the city of David; and he prepared a place for the ark of God, and pitched for it a tent. 2 Then David said, None ought to carry the ark of God but the Levites: for them hath the LORD chosen to carry the ark of God, and to minister unto him for ever. 3 And David assembled all Israel at Jerusalem, to bring up the ark of the LORD unto its place, which he had prepared for it. 4 And David gathered together the sons of Aaron, and the Levites: 5 of the sons of Kohath; Uriel the chief, and his brethren an hundred and twenty: 6 of the sons of Merari; Asaiah the chief, and his brethren two hundred and twenty: 7 of the sons of Gershom; Joel the chief, and his brethren an hundred and thirty: 8 of the sons of Elizaphan; Shemaiah the chief, and his brethren two hundred: 9 of the sons of Hebron; Eliel the chief, and his brethren fourscore: of the sons of Uzziel; 10 Amminadab the chief, and his brethren an hundred and twelve. 11 And David

^a Or, "cypress."   ^b Or, "sistra."   ^c Or, "were restive." Or, "threw *it* down."   ^d Or, "rashness."   ^e I. e. "The breach of Uzzah."   ^f Heb. "whereupon is called the Name."

2 *Samuel* 6.

1 *Chronicles* 15.

called for Zadok and Abiathar the priests, and for the Levites, for Uriel, Asaiah, and Joel, Shemaiah, and Eliel, and Amminadab, and said unto them, 12 Ye are the heads of the fathers' *houses* of the Levites : sanctify yourselves, both ye and your brethren, that ye may bring up the ark of the LORD, the God of Israel, unto *the place* that I have prepared for it. 13 For because ye *bare it* not at the first, the LORD our God made a breach upon us, for that we sought him not according to the ordinance. 14 So the priests and the Levites sanctified themselves to bring up the ark of the LORD, the God of Israel. 15 And the children of the Levites bare the ark of God upon their shoulders with the staves thereon, as Moses commanded according to the word of the LORD. 16 And David spake to the chief of the Levites to appoint their brethren the singers, with instruments of music, psalteries and harps and cymbals, sounding aloud and lifting up the voice with joy. 17 So the Levites appointed Heman the son of Joel ; and of his brethren, Asaph the son of Berechiah ; and of the sons of Merari their brethren, Ethan the son of Kushaiah ; 18 and with them their brethren of the second degree, Zechariah, Ben, and Jaaziel, and Shemiramoth, and Jehiel, and Unni, Eliab, and Benaiah, and Maaseiah, and Mattithiah, and Eliphelehu, and Mikneiah, and Obededom, and Jeiel, the doorkeepers. 19 So the singers, Heman, Asaph, and Ethan, *were appointed*, with cymbals of brass to sound aloud ; 20 and Zechariah, and Aziel, and Shemiramoth, and Jehiel, and Unni, and Eliab, and Maaseiah, and Benaiah, with psalteries set to *ª* Alamoth ; 21 and Mattithiah, and Eliphelehu, and Mikneiah, and Obed-edom, and Jeiel, and Azaziah, with harps set to *ᵇ* the Sheminith, to lead. 22 And Chenaniah, chief of the Levites, was over *ᶜ* the song : he instructed about *ᶜ* the song, because he was skilful. 23 And Berechiah and Elkanah were doorkeepers for the ark. 24 And Shebaniah, and Joshaphat, and Nethanel, and Amasai, and Zechariah, and Benaiah, and Eliezer, the priests, did blow with the trumpets before the ark of God : and Obed-edom and Jehiah were doorkeepers for the ark. 25 So David, and the elders over Israel, and the captains over thousands, went to bring up the ark of the covenant of the LORD out of the house of Obed-edom with

a See Psalm 46, title.   *b* See Psalm 6, title.   *c* Or, " the carrying *of the ark.*"   Heb. " the lifting up."

2 *Samuel* 6.

12b And David went and brought up the ark of God from the house of Obed-edom into the city of David with joy. 13 And it was so, that when they that bare the ark of the LORD had gone six paces, he sacrificed an ox and a fatling. 14 And David danced before the LORD with all his might; and David was girded with a linen ephod. 15 So David and all the house of Israel brought up the ark of the LORD with shouting, and with the sound of the trumpet. 16 And it was so, as the ark of the LORD came into the city of David, that Michal the daughter of Saul looked out at the window, and saw king David leaping and dancing before the LORD ; and she despised him in her heart. 17 And they brought in the ark of the LORD, and set it in its place, in the midst of the tent that David had pitched for it: and David offered burnt offerings and peace offerings before the LORD. 18 And when David had made an end of offering the burnt offering and the peace offerings, he blessed the people in the name of the LORD of hosts. 19a And he dealt among all the people, even among the whole multitude of Israel, both to men and women, to every one a cake of bread and a portion *a of flesh*, and a cake of raisins.

1 *Chronicles* 15.

joy : 26 and it came to pass, when God helped the Levites that bare the ark of the covenant of the LORD, that they sacrificed seven bullocks and seven rams. 27 And David was clothed with a robe of fine linen, and all the Levites that bare the ark, and the singers, and Chenaniah the master of *b* the song *with* the singers : and David had upon him an ephod of linen. 28 Thus all Israel brought up the ark of the covenant of the LORD with shouting, and with sound of the cornet, and with trumpets, and with cymbals, sounding aloud with psalteries and harps. 29 And it came to pass, as the ark of the covenant of the LORD came to the city of David, that Michal the daughter of Saul looked out at the window, and saw king David dancing and playing ; and she despised him in her heart. 1 And they brought in the ark of God, and set it in the midst of the tent that David had pitched for it : and they offered burnt offerings and peace offerings before God. 2 And when David had made an end of offering the burnt offering and the peace offerings, he blessed the people in the name of the LORD. 3 And he dealt to every one of Israel, both man and woman, to every one a loaf of bread, and a portion *a of flesh*, and a cake of raisins.

(3) DAVID'S HYMN OF PRAISE. *c*

1 *Chronicles* 16 : 4-36.

4 And he appointed certain of the Levites to minister before the ark of the LORD, and to celebrate and to thank and praise the LORD, the God of Israel : 5 Asaph the chief, and second to him Zechariah, *d* Jeiel, and Shemiramoth, and Jehiel, and Mattithiah, and Eliab, and Benaiah, and Obed-edom, and Jeiel, with psalteries and with harps ; and Asaph with cymbals, sounding aloud ; 6 and Benaiah and Jahaziel the priests with trumpets continually, before the ark of the covenant of God.

7 Then on that day did David *e* first ordain to give thanks unto the LORD, by the hand of Asaph and his brethren.

    8 O give thanks unto the LORD, call upon his name ;
      Make known his doings among the peoples.
    9 Sing unto him, sing praises unto him ;
      f Talk ye of all his marvellous works.
    10 Glory ye in his holy name :
      Let the heart of them rejoice that seek the LORD.
    11 Seek ye the LORD and his strength ;
      Seek his face evermore.
    12 Remember his marvellous works that he hath done ;
      His wonders, and the judgements of his mouth ;

---

a Or, "*of wine.*"   *b* Or, "the carrying *of the ark.*"   Heb. "the lifting up."   *c* Cf. Psalms 105 : 1-15 ; 96 : 1-13 ; 106 : 1, 47. 48. See Appendix §6.   *d* In 1 Chronicles 15 : 18, "Jaaziel."   *e* Or, "make it the chief work."   *f* Or, "Meditate."

1 *Chronicles* 16.

13 O ye seed of Israel his servant,
Ye children of Jacob, his chosen ones.

14 He is the LORD our God:
His judgements are in all the earth.

15 Remember his covenant for ever,
The word which he commanded to a thousand generations;

16 *The covenant* which he made with Abraham,
And his oath unto Isaac;

17 And confirmed the same unto Jacob for a statute,
To Israel for an everlasting covenant:

18 Saying, Unto thee will I give the land of Canaan,
The *a* lot of your inheritance:

19 When ye were but a few men in number;
Yea, very few, and sojourners in it;

20 And they went about from nation to nation,
And from one kingdom to another people.

21 He suffered no man to do them wrong;
Yea, he reproved kings for their sakes;

22 *Saying*, Touch not mine anointed ones,
And do my prophets no harm.

23 *b* Sing unto the LORD, all the earth;
Shew forth his salvation from day to day.

24 Declare his glory among the nations,
His marvellous works among all the peoples.

25 For great is the LORD, and highly to be praised:
He also is to be feared above all gods.

26 For all the gods of the peoples are *c* idols:
But the LORD made the heavens.

27 Honour and majesty are before him:
Strength and gladness are in his place.

28 Give unto the LORD, ye kindreds of the peoples,
Give unto the LORD glory and strength.

29 Give unto the LORD the glory due unto his name:
Bring an offering, and come before him:
Worship the LORD *d* in the beauty of holiness.

30 Tremble before him, all the earth:
The world also is stablished that it cannot be moved.

31 Let the heavens be glad, and let the earth rejoice;
And let them say among the nations, The LORD reigneth.

32 Let the sea roar, and the fulness thereof;
Let the field exult, and all that is therein;

33 Then shall the trees of the wood sing for joy before the LORD,
For he cometh to judge the earth.

34 *e* O give thanks unto the LORD; for he is good:
For his mercy *endureth* for ever.

35 *f* And say ye, Save us, O God of our salvation,
And gather us together and deliver us from the nations,
To give thanks unto thy holy name,
And to triumph in thy praise.

---

a Heb. "cord," or, "line."   *b* Cf. Psalm 96:1.   *c* Or, "things of nought."   *d* Or, "in holy array."   *e* Cf. Psalm 106:1.   *f* Cf. Psalm 106:47, 48.

1 *Chronicles* 16.

36 Blessed be the LORD, the God of Israel,
From everlasting even to everlasting.
And all the people said, Amen, and praised the LORD.

(4) CONCLUDING STATEMENTS.

2 *Samuel* 6 : 19*b*–23.

1 *Chronicles* 16 : 37–43.

37 So he left there, before the ark of the covenant of the LORD, Asaph and his brethren, to minister before the ark continually, as every day's work required : 38 and Obed-edom with their brethren, threescore and eight ; Obed-edom also the son of Jeduthun and Hosah to be doorkeepers : 39 and Zadok the priest, and his brethren the priests, before the tabernacle of the LORD in the high place that was at Gibeon, 40 to offer burnt offerings unto the LORD upon the altar of burnt offering continually morning and evening, even according to all that is written in the law of the LORD, which he commanded unto Israel ; 41 and with them Heman and Jeduthun, and the rest that were chosen, who were expressed by name, to give thanks to the LORD, because his mercy *endureth* for ever ; 42 and with them Heman and Jeduthun *with* trumpets and cymbals for those that should sound aloud, and *with* instruments for *a* the songs of God : and the sons of Jeduthun to be at the gate.   43 And all the people departed every man to his house : and David returned to bless his house.

19*b* So all the people departed every one to his house.   20 Then David returned to bless his household.   And Michal the daughter of Saul came out to meet David, and said, How glorious was the king of Israel to-day, who uncovered himself to-day in the eyes of the handmaids of his servants, as one of the vain fellows shamelessly uncovereth himself !   21 And David said unto Michal, *It was* before the LORD, which chose me above thy father, and above all his house, to appoint me prince over the people of the LORD, over Israel : therefore will I play before the LORD.   22 And I will be yet more vile than thus, and will be base in mine own sight : but of the handmaids which thou hast spoken of, of them shall I be had in honour. 23 And Michal the daughter of Saul had no child unto the day of her death.

---

a Cf. 1 Chronicles 25 : 7 : 2 Chronicles 7 : 6 and 29 : 27.   See §§107, (2), *E*, 133, (6), and 173, (4.)

95. THE PROMISE OF ETERNAL DOMINION TO THE HOUSE OF DAVID.

(1) David's Purpose to build a Temple to Jehovah.

2 Samuel 7 : 1-3.

1 And it came to pass, when the king dwelt in his house, and the Lord had given him rest from all his enemies round about, 2 that the king said unto Nathan the prophet, See now, I dwell in an house of cedar, but the ark of God dwelleth within curtains. ʹ3 And Nathan said to the king, Go, do all that is in thine heart ; for the Lord is with thee.

1 Chronicles 17 : 1, 2.

1 And it came to pass, when David dwelt in his house, that David said to Nathan the prophet, Lo, I dwell in an house of cedar, but the ark of the covenant of the Lord *dwelleth* under curtains. 2 And Nathan said unto David, Do all that is in thine heart ; for God is with thee.

(2) The Lord's Answer through Nathan.

2 Samuel 7 : 4-17.

4 And it came to pass the same night, that the word of the Lord came unto Nathan, saying, 5 Go and tell my servant David, Thus saith the Lord, Shalt thou build me an house for me to dwell in ? 6 For I have not dwelt in an house since the day that I brought up the children of Israel out of Egypt, even to this day, but have walked in a tent and in a tabernacle. 7 In all places wherein I have walked with all the children of Israel, spake I a word with any of the tribes of Israel, whom I commanded to feed my people Israel, saying, Why have ye not built me an house of cedar ? 8 Now therefore thus shalt thou say unto my servant David, Thus saith the Lord of hosts, I took thee from the ᵃ sheepcote, from following the sheep, that thou shouldest be ᵇ prince over my people, over Israel : 9 and I have been with thee withersoever thou wentest, and have cut off all thine enemies from before thee ; and I will make thee a great name, like unto the name of the great ones that are in the earth. 10 And I will appoint a place for my people Israel, and will plant them, that they may dwell in their own place, and be moved no more ; neither shall the children of wickedness afflict them any more, as at the first, 11 and *as* from the day that I commanded judges to be over my people Israel ; and I ᶜ will cause thee to rest from all thine enemies. Moreover the Lord telleth thee that the Lord will make thee an house. 12 When thy days be fulfilled, and thou shalt sleep with thy fathers, I will set up thy seed after thee, which shall proceed out of thy bowels, and I will establish his kingdom.

1 Chronicles 17 : 3-15.

3 And it came to pass the same night, that the word of God came to Nathan, saying, 4 Go and tell David my servant, Thus saith the Lord, Thou shalt not build me an house to dwell in : 5 for I have not dwelt in an house since the day that I brought up Israel, unto this day ; but ᵈ have gone from tent to tent, and from. *one* tabernacle *to another*. 6 In all places wherein I have walked with all Israel, spake I a word with any of the judges of Israel, whom I commanded to feed my people, saying, Why have ye not built me an house of cedar ? 7 Now therefore thus shalt thou say unto my servant David, Thus saith the Lord of hosts, I took thee from the ᵃ sheepcote, from following the sheep, that thou shouldest be ᵇ prince over my people Israel : 8 and I have been with thee whithersoever thou wentest, and have cut off all thine enemies from before thee ; and I will make thee a name, like unto the name of the great ones that are in the earth. 9 And I will appoint a place for my people Israel, and will plant them, that they may dwell in their own place, and be moved no more ; neither shall children of wickedness waste them any more, as at the first, 10 and *as* from the day that I commanded judges to be over my people Israel ; and I ᵉ will subdue all thine enemies. Moreover I tell thee that the Lord will build thee an house. 11 And it shall come to pass, when thy days be fulfilled that thou must go to be with thy fathers, that I will set up thy seed after thee, which shall be of thy sons ; and I will establish his kingdom. 12 He shall build me

---

ᵃ Or, " pasture."   ᵇ Or, " leader."   ᶜ Or, " have caused."   ᵈ Heb. " have been."   ᵉ Or, " have subdued."

2 *Samuel* 7.	1 *Chronicles* 17.
13 He shall build an house for my name, and I will establish the throne of his kingdom for ever. 14 I will be his father, and he shall be my son: if he commit iniquity, I will chasten him with the rod of men, and with the stripes of the children of men; 15 but my mercy shall not depart from him, as I took it from Saul, whom I put away before thee. 16 And thine house and thy kingdom shall be made sure forever before thee: thy throne shall be established for ever. 17 According to all these words, and according to all this vision, so did Nathan speak unto David.	an house, and I will establish his throne for ever. 13 I will be his father, and he shall be my son: and I will not take my mercy away from him, as I took it from him that was before thee: 14 but I will settle him in mine house and in my kingdom for ever: and his throne shall be established for ever. 15 According to all these words, and according to all this vision, so did Nathan speak unto David.

(3) David's Prayer and Thanksgiving.

2 *Samuel* 7 : 18–29.	1 *Chronicles* 17 : 16–27.
18 Then David the king went in, and sat before the LORD; and he said, Who am I, O Lord GOD, and what is my house, that thou hast brought me thus far? 19 And this was yet a small thing in thine eyes, O Lord GOD; but thou hast spoken also of thy servant's house for a great while to come; *a* and this *too* after the manner of men, O Lord GOD! 20 And what can David say more unto thee? for thou knowest thy servant, O Lord GOD. 21 For thy word's sake, and according to thine own heart, hast thou wrought all this greatness, to make thy servant know it. 22 Wherefore thou art great, O LORD God: for there is none like thee, neither is there any God beside thee, according to all that we have heard with our ears. 23 *b* And what one nation in the earth is like thy people, even like Israel, whom God went to redeem unto himself for a people, and to make him a name, and to do great things for you, and terrible things for thy land, before thy people, which thou redeemedst to thee out of Egypt, *from* the nations and their gods? 24 And thou didst establish to thyself thy people Israel to be a people unto thee for ever; and thou, LORD, becamest their God. 25 And now, O LORD God, the word that thou hast spoken concerning thy servant, and concerning his house, confirm thou it for ever, and do as thou hast spoken. 26 And let thy name be magnified for ever, saying, The LORD of hosts is God over Israel: and the house of thy servant David shall be established before thee. 27 For thou, O LORD of hosts, the	16 Then David the king went in, and sat before the LORD; and he said, Who am I, O LORD God, and what is my house, that thou hast brought me thus far? 17 And this was a small thing in thine eyes, O God; but thou hast spoken of thy servant's house for a great while to come, and hast regarded me according to the estate of a man of high degree, O LORD God. 18 What can David *say* yet more unto thee concerning the honour which is done to thy servant? for thou knowest thy servant. 19 O LORD, for thy servant's sake, and according to thine own heart, hast thou wrought all this greatness, to make known all *these* great things. 20 O LORD, there is none like thee, neither is there any God beside thee, according to all that we have heard with our ears. 21 *c* And what one nation in the earth is like thy people Israel, whom God went to redeem unto himself for a people, to make thee a name by great and terrible things, in driving out nations from before thy people, which thou redeemedst out of Egypt? 22 For thy people Israel didst thou make thine own people for ever; and thou, LORD, becamest their God. 23 And now, O LORD, let the word that thou hast spoken concerning thy servant, and concerning his house, be established for ever, and do as thou hast spoken. 24 *d* And let thy name be established and magnified for ever, saying, The LORD of hosts is the God of Israel, even a God to Israel: and the house of David thy servant is established before thee. 25 For thou, O my God, hast revealed to thy servant

---

a Or, " and is this the law of man, O Lord GOD?"   *b* Or, " And who is like thy people, like Israel, a nation that is alone in the earth," etc.   *c* Or, "And who is like thy people Israel, a nation that is alone in the earth," etc.   *d* Or, ' Yea, let it be established, and let thy name be magnified," etc.

2 *Samuel* 7.	1 *Chronicles* 17.
God of Israel, hast revealed to thy servant, saying, I will build thee an house: therefore hath thy servant ᵃ found in his heart to pray this prayer unto thee. 28 And now, O Lord GOD, thou art God, and thy words are truth, and thou hast promised this good thing unto thy servant: 29 now therefore ᵇ let it please thee to bless the house of thy servant, that it may continue for ever before thee: for thou, O Lord GOD, hast spoken it: and with thy blessing let the house of thy servant be blessed for ever.	that thou wilt build him an house: therefore hath thy servant found *in his heart* to pray before thee. 26 And now, O LORD, thou art God, and hast promised this good thing unto thy servant: 27 and now it hath pleased thee to bless the house of thy servant, that it may continue for ever before thee: for thou, O LORD, hast blessed, and it is blessed for ever.

96. DAVID'S KINDNESS TOWARDS JONATHAN'S SON, MEPHIBOSHETH.ᶜ

2 *Samuel* 9: 1–13.

1 And David said, Is there yet any that is left of the house of Saul, that I may shew him kindness for Jonathan's sake? 2 And there was of the house of Saul a servant whose name was Ziba, and they called him unto David; and the king said unto him, Art thou Ziba? And he said, Thy servant is he. 3 And the king said, Is there not yet any of the house of Saul, that I may shew the kindness of God unto him? And Ziba said unto the king, Jonathan hath yet a son, which is lame on his feet. 4 And the king said unto him, Where is he? And Ziba said unto the king, Behold, he is in the house of Machir the son of Ammiel, in Lo-debar. 5 Then king David sent, and fetched him out of the house of Machir the son of Ammiel, from Lo-debar. 6 And Mephibosheth, the son of Jonathan, the son of Saul, came unto David, and fell on his face, and did obeisance. And David said, Mephibosheth. And he answered, Behold thy servant! 7 And David said unto him, Fear not: for I will surely shew thee kindness for Jonathan thy father's sake, and will restore thee all the ᵈ land of Saul thy father; and thou shalt eat bread at my table continually. 8 And he did obeisance, and said, What is thy servant, that thou shouldest look upon such a dead dog as I am? 9 Then the king called to Ziba, Saul's servant, and said unto him, All that pertained to Saul and to all his house have I given unto thy master's son. 10 And thou shalt till the land for him, thou, and thy sons, and thy servants; and thou shalt bring in *the fruits*, that thy master's son may have bread to eat: but Mephibosheth thy master's son shall eat bread alway at my table. Now Ziba had fifteen sons and twenty servants. 11 Then said Ziba unto the king, According to all that my lord the king commandeth his servant, so shall thy servant do. ᵉ As for Mephibosheth, *said the king*, he shall eat at my table, as one of the king's sons. 12 And Mephibosheth had a young son, whose name was Mica. And all that dwelt in the house of Ziba were servants unto Mephibosheth. 13 So Mephibosheth dwelt in Jerusalem: for he did eat continually at the king's table; and he was lame on both his feet.

97. THE BIRTH OF SOLOMON.

2 *Samuel* 12: 24b, 25.

24b And she [i. e., Bath-sheba] bare a son, and ᶠ he called his name Solomon. And the LORD loved him; 25 and he sent by the hand of Nathan the prophet, and he called his name ᵍ Jedidiah, for the LORD's sake.

ᵃ Or, "been bold." ᵇ Or, "begin and bless." ᶜ Mephibosheth was five years old at David's accession. Cf. 2 Samuel 4: 4. See §63, (2). 2 Samuel 9: 1-13, could not have occurred, therefore, until this period. ᵈ Heb. "field." ᵉ Or, "But Mephibosheth eateth," etc. ᶠ Another reading is, "she called." ᵍ I. e., "Beloved of Jah."

10

98. DAVID'S FAMILY IN JERUSALEM. *a*

2 *Samuel* 5 : 13-16.	1 *Chronicles* 3 : 5-9.	1 *Chronicles* 14 : 3-7.
13 And David took him more concubines and wives out of Jerusalem, after he was come from Hebron: and there were yet sons and daughters born to David. 14 And these be the names of those that were born unto him in Jerusalem ; Shammua, and Shobab, and Nathan, and Solomon, 15 and Ibhar, and Elishua ; and Nepheg, and Japhia ; 16 and Elishama, and Eliada, and Eliphelet.	5 And these were born unto him in Jerusalem : Shimea, and Shobab, and Nathan, and Solomon, four, of Bath-shua the daughter of Ammiel : 6 and Ibhar, and Elishama, and Eliphelet ; 7 and Nogah, and Nepheg, and Japhia ; 8 and Elishama, and Eliada, and Eliphelet, nine. 9 All these were the sons of David, beside the sons of the concubines ; and Tamar was their sister.	3 And David took more wives at Jerusalem : and David begat more sons and daughters. 4 And these are the names of the children which he had in Jerusalem ; Shammua, and Shobab, Nathan, and Solomon ; 5 and Ibhar, and Elishua, and Elpelet ; 6 and Nogah, and Nepheg, and Japhia ; 7 and Elishama, and Beeliada, and Eliphelet.

PART IV.
THE PERIOD OF INTERNAL DISSENSIONS.

I. Family Troubles.

99. AMNON'S CRIME.

2 *Samuel* 13 : 1-22.

1 And it came to pass after this, that Absalom the son of David had a fair sister, whose name was Tamar ; and Amnon the son of David loved her. 2 And Amnon was so vexed that he fell sick because of his sister Tamar ; for she was a virgin ; and it seemed hard to Amnon to do any thing unto her. 3 But Amnon had a friend, whose name was Jonadab, the son of Shimeah David's brother : and Jonadab was a very subtil man. 4 And he said unto him, Why, O son of the king, art thou thus lean *b* from day to day ? wilt thou not tell me ? And Amnon said unto him, I love Tamar, my brother Absalom's sister. 5 And Jonadab said unto him, Lay thee down on thy bed, and feign thyself sick : and when thy father cometh to see thee, say unto him, Let my sister Tamar come, I pray thee, and give me bread to eat, and dress the food in my sight, that I may see it, and eat it at her hand. 6 So Amnon lay down, and feigned himself sick : and when the king was come to see him, Amnon said unto the king, Let my sister Tamar come, I pray thee, and make me a couple of cakes in my sight, that I may eat at her hand. 7 Then David sent home to Tamar, saying, Go now to thy brother Amnon's house, and dress him food. 8 So Tamar went to her brother Amnon's house ; and he was laid down. And she took dough, and kneaded it, and made cakes in his sight, and did bake the cakes. 9 And she took the pan, and poured them out before him ; but he refused to eat. And Amnon said, Have out all men from me. And they went out every man from him. 10 And Amnon said unto Tamar, Bring the food into the chamber, that I may eat of thine hand. And Tamar took the cakes which she had made, and brought them into the chamber to Amnon her brother. 11 And when she had brought them near unto him to eat, he took hold of her, and said unto her, Come lie with me, my sister. 12 And she answered him, Nay, my brother, do not *c* force me ; for no such thing ought to be done in Israel : do not thou this

---

a Cf. §§ 7, (3), and 70.   *b* Heb. " morning by morning."   *c* Heb. " humble."

2 Samuel 13.

folly. 13 And I, whither shall I carry my shame? and as for thee, thou shalt be as one of the fools in Israel. Now therefore, I pray thee, speak unto the king; for he will not withhold me from thee. 14 Howbeit he would not hearken unto her voice: but being stronger than she, he forced her, and lay with her. 15 Then Amnon hated her with exceeding great hatred; for the hatred wherewith he hated her was greater than the love wherewith he had loved her. And Amnon said unto her, Arise, be gone. 16 And she said unto him, *a* Not so, because this great wrong in putting me forth is *worse* than the other that thou didst unto me. But he would not hearken unto her. 17 Then he called his servant that ministered unto him, and said, Put now this woman out from me, and bolt the door after her. 18 And she had a *b* garment of divers colours upon her: for with such robes were the king's daughters that were virgins apparelled. Then his servant brought her out, and bolted the door after her. 19 And Tamar put ashes on her head, and rent her garment of divers colours that was on her; and she laid her hand on her head, and went her way, crying aloud as she went. 20 And Absalom her brother said unto her, Hath *c* Amnon thy brother been with thee? but now hold thy peace, my sister: he is thy brother: take not this thing to heart. So Tamar remained desolate in her brother Absalom's house. 21 But when king David heard of all these things, he was very wroth. 22 And Absalom spake unto Amnon neither good nor bad: for Absalom hated Amnon, because he had forced his sister Tamar.

100. ABSALOM'S VENGEANCE.

2 Samuel 13: 23-36.

23 And it came to pass after two full years, that Absalom had sheepshearers in Baal-hazor, which is beside Ephraim: and Absalom invited all the king's sons. 24 And Absalom came to the king, and said, Behold now, thy servant hath sheepshearers; let the king, I pray thee, and his servants go with thy servant. 25 And the king said to Absalom, Nay, my son, let us not all go, lest we be burdensome unto thee. And he pressed him: howbeit he would not go, but blessed him. 26 Then said Absalom, If not, I pray thee, let my brother Amnon go with us. And the king said unto him, Why should he go with thee? 27 But Absalom pressed him, that he let Amnon and all the king's sons go with him. 28 And Absalom commanded his servants, saying, Mark ye now, when Amnon's heart is merry with wine; and when I say unto you, Smite Amnon, then kill him, fear not: have not I commanded you? be courageous, and be valiant. 29 And the servants of Absalom did unto Amnon as Absalom had commanded. Then all the king's sons arose, and every man gat him up upon his mule, and fled. 30 And it came to pass, while they were in the way, that the tidings came to David, saying, Absalom hath slain all the king's sons, and there is not one of them left. 31 Then the king arose, and rent his garments, and lay on the earth; and all his servants stood by with their clothes rent. 32 And Jonadab, the son of Shimeah David's brother, answered and said, Let not my lord suppose that they have killed all the young men the king's sons; for Amnon only is dead: for by the appointment of Absalom this hath been determined from the day that he forced his sister Tamar. 33 Now therefore let not my lord the king take the thing to his heart, to think that all the king's sons are dead: for Amnon only is dead. 34 But Absalom fled. And the young man that kept the watch lifted up his eyes, and looked, and, behold, there came much people by the way of the hill side behind him. 35 And Jonadab said unto the king, Behold, the king's sons are come: as thy servant said, so it is. 36 And it came to pass, as soon as he had made an end of speaking, that, behold, the king's sons came, and lifted up their voice, and wept: and the king also and all his servants wept *d* very sore.

---

a Or, " *Think* not there is occasion for this great wrong in putting me forth, *which is worse*," etc.   *b* Or, " a long garment with sleeves."   *c* Heb. " Aminon."   *d* Heb. " with a very great weeping."

101. ABSALOM'S FLIGHT AND SOJOURN IN GESHUR.

2 *Samuel* 13 : 37–39.

37 But Absalom fled, and went to Talmai the son of *ªAmmihur, king of Geshur. And *David* mourned for his son every day.

38 So Absalom fled, and went to Geshur, and was there three years. 39 And *the soul of* king David longed to go forth unto Absalom : for he was comforted concerning Amnon, seeing he was dead.

102. THE RECALL OF ABSALOM.

(1) JOAB'S STRATAGEM.

2 *Samuel* 14 : 1–20.

1 Now Joab the son of Zeruiah perceived that the king's heart was toward Absalom. 2 And Joab sent to Tekoa, and fetched thence a wise woman, and said unto her, I pray thee, feign thyself to be a mourner, and put on mourning apparel, I pray thee, and anoint not thyself with oil, but be as a woman that had a long time mourned for the dead : 3 and go in to the king, and speak on this manner unto him. So Joab put the words in her mouth. 4 And when the woman of Tekoa spake to the king, she fell on her face to the ground, and did obeisance, and said, Help, O king. 5 And the king said unto her, What aileth thee ? And she answered, Of a truth I am a widow woman, and mine husband is dead. 6 And thy handmaid had two sons, and they two strove together in the field, and there was none to part them, but the one smote the other, and killed him. 7 And, behold, the whole family is risen against thine handmaid, and they said, Deliver him that smote his brother, that we may kill him for the life of his brother whom he slew, and so destroy the heir also : thus shall they quench my coal which is left, and shall leave to my husband neither name nor remainder upon the face of the earth. 8 And the king said unto the woman, Go to thine house, and I will give charge concerning thee. 9 And the woman of Tekoa said unto the king, My lord, O king, the iniquity be on me, and on my father's house : and the king and his throne be guiltless. 10 And the king said, Whosoever saith aught unto thee, bring him to me, and he shall not touch thee any more. 11 Then said she, I pray thee, let the king remember the LORD thy God, that the avenger of blood destroy not any more, lest they destroy my son. And he said, As the LORD liveth, there shall not one hair of thy son fall to the earth. 12 Then the woman said, Let thine handmaid, I pray thee, speak a word unto my lord the king. And he said, Say on. 13 And the woman said, Wherefore then hast thou devised such a thing against the people of God ? for in speaking this word the king is as one which is guilty, in that the king doth not fetch home again his banished one. 14 For we must needs die, and are as water spilt on the ground, which cannot be gathered up again ; neither doth God take away life, but deviseth means, that he that is banished be not an outcast from him. 15 Now therefore seeing that I am come to speak this word unto my lord the king, it is because the people have made me afraid : and thy handmaid said, I will now speak unto the king ; it may be that the king will perform the request of his servant. 16 For the king will hear, to deliver his servant out of the hand of the man that would destroy me and my son together out of the inheritance of God. 17 Then thine handmaid said, Let, I pray thee, the word of my lord the king be *b* comfortable : for as *c* an angel of God, so is my lord the king *d* to discern good and bad : and the LORD thy God be with thee. 18 Then the king answered and said unto the woman, Hide not from me, I pray thee, aught that I shall ask thee. And the woman said, Let my lord the king now speak. 19 And the king said, Is the hand of Joab with thee in all this ? And the woman answered and said, As thy soul liveth, my lord the king, none can turn to the right hand or to the left from aught that my lord the king hath spoken : for thy servant Joab, he bade me, and he put all these words in the mouth of thine handmaid : 20 to change the face of the matter hath thy servant Joab done this thing : and my lord is wise, according to the wisdom of *c* an angel of God, to know all things that are in the earth.

---

a Another reading is, " Ammihud."   *b* Heb. " for rest."   *c* Or, " the."   *d* Heb. " to hear."

(2) ABSALOM'S RETURN.

2 Samuel 14 : 21–24.

21 And the king said unto Joab, Behold now, *a* I have done this thing : go therefore, bring the young man Absalom again. 22 And Joab fell to the ground on his face, and did obeisance, and blessed the king : and Joab said, To-day thy servant knoweth that I have found grace in thy sight, my lord, O king, in that the king hath performed the request of *b* his servant. 23 So Joab arose and went to Geshur, and brought Absalom to Jerusalem. 24 And the king said, Let him turn to his own house, but let him not see my face. So Absalom turned to his own house, and saw not the king's face.

(3) ABSALOM AND HIS FAMILY.

2 Samuel 14 : 25–27.

25 Now in all Israel there was none to be so much praised as Absalom for his beauty : from the sole of his foot even to the crown of his head there was no blemish in him. 26 And when he polled his head, (now it was at every year's end that he polled it : because *the hair* was heavy on him, therefore he polled it :) he weighed the hair of his head at two hundred shekels, after the king's weight. 27 And unto Absalom there were born three sons, and one daughter, whose name was Tamar : she was a woman of a fair countenance.

(4) ABSALOM'S WAITING IN JERUSALEM.

2 Samuel 14 : 28.

28 And Absalom dwelt two full years in Jerusalem ; and he saw not the king's face.

(5) ABSALOM'S READMISSION TO COURT.

2 Samuel 14 : 29–33.

29 Then Absalom sent for Joab, to send him to the king; but he would not come to him : and he sent again a second time, but he would not come. 30 Therefore he said unto his servants, See, Joab's field is near mine, and he hath barley there ; go and set it on fire. And Absalom's servants set the field on fire. 31 Then Joab arose, and came to Absalom unto his house, and said unto him, Wherefore have thy servants set my field on fire ? 32 And Absalom answered Joab, Behold, I sent unto thee, saying, Come hither, that I may send thee to the king, to say, Wherefore am I come from Geshur ? it were better for me to be there still : now therefore let me see the king's face ; and if there be iniquity in me, let him kill me. 33 So Joab came to the king, and told him : and when he had called for Absalom, he came to the king, and bowed himself on his face to the ground before the king : and the king kissed Absalom.

103. ABSALOM STEALING THE HEARTS OF THE MEN OF ISRAEL.

2 Samuel 15 : 1–6.

1 And it came to pass after this, that Absalom prepared him a chariot and horses, and fifty men to run before him. 2 And Absalom rose up early, and stood beside the way of the gate : and it was so, that when any man had a suit which should come to the king for judgement, then Absalom called unto him, and said, Of what city art thou ? And he said, Thy servant is of one of the tribes of Israel. 3 And Absalom said unto him, See, thy matters are good and right ; but there is no man deputed of the king to hear thee. Absalom said moreover, 4 Oh that I were made judge in the land, that every man which hath any suit or cause might come unto me, and I would do him justice ! 5 And it was so, that when any man came nigh to do him obeisance, he put forth his hand, and took hold of him, and kissed him. 6 And on this manner did Absalom to all Israel that came to the king for judgement : so Absalom stole the hearts of the men of Israel.

a Another reading is, " thou hast done." *b* Another reading is, " thy."

II. National Calamities.

104. THE THREE YEARS' FAMINE.[a]

(1) THE EXECUTION OF SAUL'S GRANDSONS.

2 *Samuel* 21 : 1–10.

1 And there was a famine in the days of David three years, year after year; and David sought the face of the LORD.   And the LORD said, It is for Saul, and for his bloody house, because he put to death the Gibeonites.   2 And the king called the Gibeonites, and said unto them; (now the Gibeonites were not of the children of Israel, but of the remnant of the Amorites; and the children of Israel had sworn unto them: and Saul sought to slay them in his zeal for the children of Israel and Judah:) 3 and David said unto the Gibeonites, What shall I do for you? and wherewith shall I make atonement, that ye may bless the inheritance of the LORD?   4 And the Gibeonites said unto him, It is no matter of silver or gold between us and Saul, or his house; [b] neither is it for us to put any man to death in Israel.   And he said, What ye shall say, that will I do for you.   5 And they said unto the king, The man that consumed us, and that devised against us, [c] *that* we should be destroyed from remaining in any of the borders of Israel, 6 let seven men of his sons be delivered unto us, and we will hang them up unto the LORD in Gibeah of Saul, the chosen of the LORD. And the king said, I will give them.   7 But the king spared Mephibosheth, the son of Jonathan the son of Saul, because of the LORD'S oath that was between them, between David and Jonathan the son of Saul.   8 But the king took the two sons of Rizpah the daughter of Aiah, whom she bare unto Saul, Armoni and Mephibosheth; and the five sons of [d] Michal the daughter of Saul, whom she bare to Adriel the son of Barzillai the Meholathite: 9 and he delivered them into the hands of the Gibeonites, and they hanged them in the mountain before the LORD, and they fell *all* seven together: and they were put to death in the days of harvest, in the first days, at the beginning of barley harvest.   10 And Rizpah the daughter of Aiah took sackcloth, and spread it for her upon the rock, from the beginning of harvest until water was poured upon them from heaven; and she suffered neither the birds of the air to rest on them by day, nor the beasts of the field by night.

(2) THE BURIAL OF SAUL AND HIS SONS.

2 *Samuel* 21 : 11–14.

11 And it was told David what Rizpah the daughter of Aiah, the concubine of Saul, had done. 12 And David went and took the bones of Saul and the bones of Jonathan his son from the men of Jabesh-gilead, which had stolen them from the [e] street of Beth-shan, where the Philistines had hanged them, in the day that the Philistines slew Saul in Gilboa: 13 and he brought up from thence the bones of Saul and the bones of Jonathan his son; and they gathered the bones of them that were hanged.   14 And they buried the bones of Saul and Jonathan his son in the country of Benjamin in Zela, in the sepulchre of Kish his father: and they performed all that the king commanded.   And after that God was intreated for the land.

105. THE THREE DAYS' PESTILENCE.

(1) DAVID'S SIN IN NUMBERING THE PEOPLE.

2 *Samuel* 24 : 1–9.	1 *Chronicles* 21 : 1–6.
1 And again the anger of the LORD was kindled against Israel, and he moved David against	1 And [f] Satan stood up against Israel, and moved David to number Israel. 2 And David

---

[a] Doubtless this section may not be in its perfect chronological place.   But all things considered, it has seemed best to put it here.   [b] Or, "neither for us shalt thou put any man to death in Israel."   [c] Or, "*so that* we have been destroyed." [d] In 1 Samuel 18: 19, "Merab."   See §44, (5).   [e] Or, "broad place."   [f] Or, "an adversary."

2 Samuel 24.

them, saying, Go, number Israel and Judah. 2 And the king said to Joab the captain of the host, which was with him, Go now to and fro through all the tribes of Israel, from Dan even to Beer-sheba, and number ye the people, that I may know the sum of the people. 3 And Joab said unto the king, Now the LORD thy God add unto the people, how many soever they be, an hundredfold, and may the eyes of my lord the king see it: but why doth my lord the king delight in this thing? 4 Notwithstanding the king's word prevailed against Joab, and against the captains of the host. And Joab and the captains of the host went out from the presence of the king, to number the people of Israel. 5 And they passed over Jordan, and pitched in Aroer, on the right side of the city that is in the middle of the valley *a* of Gad, and unto Jazer: 6 then they came to Gilead, and to the land of Tahtim-hodshi; and they came to Dan-jaan, and round about to Zidon, 7 and came to the strong hold of Tyre, and to all the cities of the Hivites, and of the Canaanites: and they went out to the south of Judah, at Beer-sheba. 8 So when they had gone to and fro through all the land, they came to Jerusalem at the end of nine months and twenty days. 9 And Joab gave up the sum of the numbering of the people unto the king: and there were in Israel eight hundred thousand valiant men that drew the sword; and the men of Judah were five hundred thousand men.

1 Chronicles 21.

said to Joab and to the princes of the people, Go, number Israel from Beer-sheba even to Dan; and bring me word, that I may know the sum of them. 3 And Joab said, The LORD make his people an hundred times so many more as they be: but, my lord the king, are they not all my lord's servants? why doth my lord require this thing? why will he be a cause of guilt unto Israel? 4 Nevertheless the king's word prevailed against Joab. Wherefore Joab departed, and went throughout all Israel, and came to Jerusalem. 5 And Joab gave up the sum of the numbering of the people unto David. And all they of Israel were a thousand thousand and an hundred thousand men that drew sword: and Judah was four hundred threescore and ten thousand men that drew sword. 6 But Levi and Benjamin counted he not among them: for the king's word was abominable to Joab.

(2) THE CHOICE OF PUNISHMENTS.

2 Samuel 24: 10–14.

10 And David's heart smote him after that he had numbered the people. And David said unto the LORD, I have sinned greatly in that I have done: but now, O LORD, put away, I beseech thee, the iniquity of thy servant; for I have done very foolishly. 11 And when David rose up in the morning, the word of the LORD came unto the prophet Gad, David's seer, saying, 12 Go and speak unto David, Thus saith the Lord, I *b* offer thee three things; choose thee one of them, that I may do it unto thee. 13 So Gad came to David, and told him, and said unto him, Shall seven years of famine come unto thee in thy land? or wilt thou flee three months before thy foes while they pursue thee? or shall there be three days' pestilence in thy land? now advise thee, and

1 Chronicles 21: 7–13.

7 And God was displeased with this thing; therefore he smote Israel. 8 And David said unto God, I have sinned greatly, in that I have done this thing: but now, put away, I beseech thee, the iniquity of thy servant; for I have done very foolishly. 9 And the LORD spake unto Gad, David's seer, saying, 10 Go and speak unto David, saying, Thus saith the LORD, I *c* offer thee three things; choose thee one of them, that I may do it unto thee. 11 So Gad came to David, and said unto him, Thus saith the LORD, Take which thou wilt; 12 either three years of famine; or three months to be consumed before thy foes, while that the sword of thine enemies overtaketh thee; or else three days the sword of the LORD, *d* even pestilence in the land, and the angel of

---

a Or, "toward."   *b* Or, "lay upon."   *c* Heb. "stretch out unto."   *d* Or, "and."

2 *Samuel* 24.	1 *Chronicles* 21.
consider what answer I shall return to him that sent me. 14 And David said unto Gad, I am in a great strait: let us fall now into the hand of the LORD; for his mercies are *great: and let me not fall into the hand of man.	the LORD destroying throughout all the coasts of Israel. Now therefore consider what answer I shall return to him that sent me. 13 And David said unto Gad, I am in a great strait: let me fall now into the hand of the LORD; for very *great are his mercies: and let me not fall into the hand of man.

(3) THE PESTILENCE.

2 *Samuel* 24: 15-17.	1 *Chronicles* 21: 14-17.
15 So the LORD sent a pestilence upon Israel from the morning even to the time appointed: and there died of the people from Dan even to Beer-sheba seventy thousand men. 16 And when the angel stretched out his hand toward Jerusalem to destroy it, the LORD repented him of the evil, and said to the angel that destroyed the people, It is enough; now stay thine hand. And the angel of the LORD was by the threshing-floor of Araunah the Jebusite. 17 And David spake unto the LORD when he saw the angel that smote the people, and said, Lo, I have sinned, and I have done perversely: but these sheep, what have they done? let thine hand, I pray thee, be against me, and against my father's house.	14 So the LORD sent a pestilence upon Israel: and there fell of Israel seventy thousand men. 15 And God sent an angel unto Jerusalem to destroy it: and as he was about to destroy, the LORD beheld, and he repented him of the evil, and said to the destroying angel, It is enough; now stay thine hand. And the angel of the LORD stood by the threshing-floor of Ornan the Jebusite. 16 And David lifted up his eyes, and saw the angel of the LORD stand between the earth and the heaven, having a drawn sword in his hand stretched out over Jerusalem. Then David and the elders, clothed in sackcloth, fell upon their faces. 17 And David said unto God, Is it not I that commanded the people to be numbered? even I it is that have sinned and done very wickedly; but these sheep, what have they done? let thine hand, I pray thee, O LORD my God, be against me, and against my father's house; but not against thy people, that they should be plagued.

(4) DAVID PURCHASES ARAUNAH'S THRESHING-FLOOR AND ERECTS AN ALTAR.

2 *Samuel* 24: 18-25.	1 *Chronicles* 21: 18-30.
18 And Gad came that day to David, and said unto him, Go up, rear an altar unto the LORD in the threshing-floor of Araunah the Jebusite. 19 And David went up according to the saying of Gad, as the LORD commanded. 20 And Araunah looked forth, and saw the king and his servants *b* coming on toward him: and Araunah went out, and bowed himself before the king with his face to the ground. 21 And Araunah said, Wherefore is my lord the king come to his servant? And David said, To buy the threshing-floor of thee, to build an altar unto the LORD, that the plague may be stayed from the people. 22 And Araunah said unto David, Let my lord the king take and offer up what seemeth good	18 Then the angel of the LORD commanded Gad to say to David, that David should go up, and rear an altar unto the LORD in the threshing-floor of Ornan the Jebusite. 19 And David went up at the saying of Gad, which he spake in the name of the LORD. 20 And Ornan turned back, and saw the angel; and his four sons that were with him hid themselves. Now Ornan was threshing wheat. 21 And as David came to Ornan, Ornan looked and saw David, and went out of the threshing-floor, and bowed himself to David with his face to the ground. 22 Then David said to Ornan, Give me the place of this threshing-floor, that I may build thereon an altar unto the LORD: for the full price shalt thou give

---

a Or, "many."   *b* Or, "passing over."

2 *Samuel* 24.

unto him : behold, the oxen for the burnt offering, and the threshing instruments and the furniture of the oxen for the wood : 23 [a] all this, O king, doth Araunah give unto the king. And Araunah said unto the king, The LORD thy God accept thee. 24 And the king said unto Araunah, Nay; but I will verily buy it of thee at a price : neither will I offer burnt offerings unto the LORD my God which cost me nothing. So David bought the threshing-floor and the oxen for fifty shekels of silver. 25 And David built there an altar unto the LORD, and offered burnt offerings and peace offerings. So the LORD was intreated for the land, and the plague was stayed from Israel.

1 *Chronicles* 21.

it me : that the plague may be stayed from the people. 23 And Ornan said unto David, Take it to thee, and let my lord the king do that which is good in his eyes : lo, I give *thee* the oxen for burnt offerings, and the threshing instruments for wood, and the wheat for the meal offering; I give it all. 24 And king David said to Ornan, Nay; but I will verily buy it for the full price : for I will not take that which is thine for the LORD, nor offer a burnt offering without cost. 25 So David gave to Ornan for the place six hundred shekels of gold by weight. 26 And David built there an altar unto the LORD, and offered burnt offerings and peace offerings, and called upon the LORD; and he answered him from heaven by fire upon the altar of burnt offering. 27 And the LORD commanded the angel; and he put up his sword again into the sheath thereof.

28 At that time, when David saw that the LORD had answered him in the threshing-floor of Ornan the Jebusite, then he sacrificed there. 29 For the tabernacle of the LORD, which Moses made in the wilderness, and the altar of burnt offering, were at that time in the high place at Gibeon. 30 But David could not go before it to inquire of God : for he was afraid because of the sword of the angel of the LORD.

III. David's Final [b]Arrangements.

106. PREPARATIONS FOR THE BUILDING OF THE TEMPLE.[c]

(1) THE TEMPLE SITE CHOSEN.

1 *Chronicles* 22 : 1.

1 Then David said, This is the house of the LORD God, and this is the altar of burnt offering for Israel.

(2) DAVID'S PLANS AND FORESIGHT.

1 *Chronicles* 22 : 2–5.

2 And David commanded to gather together the strangers that were in the land of Israel ; and he set masons to hew wrought stones to build the house of God. 3 And David prepared iron in abundance for the nails for the doors of the gates, and for the couplings; and brass in abundance without weight; 4 and cedar trees without number : for the Zidonians and they of Tyre brought cedar trees in abundance to David. 5 And David said, Solomon my son is young and tender, and the house that is to be builded for the LORD must be exceeding magnifical, of fame and of glory throughout all countries : I will therefore make preparation for it. So David prepared abundantly before his death.

---

a Or, "all this did Araunah the king give," etc.   *b* I. e., the arrangements which David thought to be final, and which, as the sequel shows, §§108–123, were final, notwithstanding Absalom, Sheba, and Adonijah.   *c* Cf. §129.

(3) DAVID'S CHARGE TO SOLOMON.

I *Chronicles* 22 : 6-16.

6 Then he called for Solomon his son, and charged him to build an house for the LORD, the God of Israel. 7 And David said to Solomon *a* his son, As for me, it was in my heart to build an house unto the name of the LORD my God. 8 But the word of the LORD came to me, saying, Thou hast shed blood abundantly, and hast made great wars : thou shalt not build an house unto my name, because thou hast shed much blood upon the earth in my sight ; 9 behold, a son shall be born to thee, who shall be a man of rest ; and I will give him rest from all his enemies round about : for his name shall be *b* Solomon, and I will give peace and quietness unto Israel in his days : 10 he shall build an house for my name ; and he shall be my son, and I will be his father ; and I will establish the throne of his kingdom over Israel for ever. 11 Now, my son, the LORD be with thee ; and prosper thou, and build the house of the LORD thy God, as he hath spoken concerning thee. 12 Only the LORD give thee discretion and understanding, and give thee charge concerning Israel ; that so thou mayest keep the law of the LORD thy God. 13 Then shalt thou prosper, if thou observe to do the statutes and the judgements which the LORD charged Moses with concerning Israel : be strong, and of good courage ; fear not, neither be dismayed. 14 Now, behold, in my *c* affliction I have prepared for the house of the LORD an hundred thousand talents of gold, and a thousand thousand talents of silver ; and of brass and iron without weight ; for it is in abundance : timber also and stone have I prepared ; and thou mayest add thereto. 15 Moreover there are workmen with thee in abundance, hewers and workers of stone and timber, and all men that are cunning in any manner of work ; 16 of the gold, the silver, and the brass, and the iron, there is no number ; arise and be doing, and the LORD be with thee.

(4) DAVID'S CHARGE TO THE PRINCES.

I *Chronicles* 22 : 17-19.

17 David also commanded all the princes of Israel to help Solomon his son, *saying*, 18 Is not the LORD your God with you ? and hath he not given you rest on every side ? for he hath delivered the inhabitants of the land into mine hand ; and the land is subdued before the LORD, and before his people. 19 Now set your heart and your soul to seek after the LORD your God ; arise therefore, and build ye the sanctuary of the LORD God, to bring the ark of the covenant of the LORD, and the holy vessels of God, into the house that is to be built to the name of the LORD.

107. THE NATIONAL CONVENTION.

(1) THE CONVENTION SUMMONED.

I *Chronicles* 23 : 1a, 2.

1a Now David was old and full of days. 2 And he gathered together all the princes of Israel, with the priests and the Levites.

(2) DATA CONCERNING THE OFFICIALS "GATHERED."

A. THE NUMBER AND DISTRIBUTION OF THE LEVITES.

I *Chronicles* 23 · 3-5.

3 And the Levites were numbered from thirty years old and upward : and their number by their polls, man by man, was thirty and eight thousand. 4 Of these, twenty and four thousand were to oversee the work of the house of the LORD ; and six thousand were officers and judges : 5 and four thousand were doorkeepers ; and four thousand praised the LORD with the instruments which I made, *said David*, to praise therewith.

---

a According to another reading, "My son, as for me," etc.   *b* I. e., "Peaceful."   *c* Or, "low estate."

B. THE TWENTY-FOUR HOUSES OF THE LEVITES.

1 Chronicles 23 : 6–23.

6 And David divided them into ᵃ courses according to the sons of Levi; Gershon, Kohath, and Merari. 7 Of the Gershonites; ᵇ Ladan and Shimei. 8 The sons of Ladan; Jehiel the chief, and Zetham, and Joel, three. 9 The sons of Shimei; Shelomoth, and Haziel, and Haran, three. These were the heads of the fathers' *houses* of Ladan. 10 And the sons of Shimei; Jahath, ᶜ Zina, and Jeush, and Beriah. These four were the sons of Shimei. 11 And Jahath was the chief, and Zizah the second: but Jeush and Beriah had not many sons; therefore they became a fathers' house in one reckoning. 12 The sons of Kohath; Amram, Izhar, Hebron, and Uzziel, four. 13 The sons of Amram; Aaron and Moses: and Aaron was separated, ᵈ that he should sanctify the most holy things, he and his sons, for ever, to burn incense before the LORD, to minister unto him, and to bless in his name, for ever. 14 But as for Moses the man of God, his sons were named among the tribe of Levi. 15 The sons of Moses; Gershom and Eliezer. 16 The sons of Gershom; Shebuel the chief. 17 And the sons of Eliezer were, Rehabiah the chief. And Eliezer had none other sons; but the sons of Rehabiah were very many. 18 The sons of Izhar; Shelomith the chief. 19 The sons of Hebron; Jeriah the chief, Amariah the second, Jahaziel the third, and Jekameam the fourth. 20 The sons of Uzziel; Micah the chief, and Isshiah the second. 21 The sons of Merari; Mahli and Mushi. The sons of Mahli; Eleazar and Kish. 22 And Eleazar died, and had no sons, but daughters only: and their brethren the sons of Kish took them *to wife*. 23 The sons of Mushi; Mahli, and Eder, and Jeremoth, three.

1 Chronicles 24 : 20–30a.

20 And of the rest of the sons of Levi: of the sons of Amram, Shubael; of the sons of Shubael, Jehdeiah. 21 Of Rehabiah: of the sons of Rehabiah, Isshiah the chief. 22 Of the Izharites, Shelomoth; of the sons of Shelomoth, Jahath. 23 And the sons *of Hebron;* Jeriah *the chief*, Amariah the second, Jahaziel the third, Jakameam the fourth. 24 The sons of Uzziel, Micah; of the sons of Micah, Shamir. 25 The brother of Micah, Isshiah: of the sons of Isshiah, Zechariah. 26 The sons of Merari; Mahli and Mushi: the sons of Jaaziah; Beno. 27 The sons of Merari; of Jaaziah, Beno, and Shoham, and Zaccur, and Ibri. 28 Of Mahli; Eleazar, who had no sons. 29 Of Kish; the sons of Kish, Jerahmeel. 30a And the sons of Mushi; Mahli, and Eder, and Jerimoth.

C. THE DUTIES OF THE LEVITES.

1 Chronicles 23 : 24–32.

24 These were the sons of Levi after their fathers' houses, even the heads of the fathers' *houses* of those of them that were counted, in the number of names by their polls, who did the work for the service of the house of the LORD, from twenty years old and upward. 25 For David said, The LORD, the God of Israel, hath given rest unto his people; and he dwelleth in

1 Chronicles 24 : 30b, 31.

30b These were the sons of the Levites after their fathers' houses. 31 These likewise cast lots even as their brethren the sons of Aaron in the presence of David the king, and Zadok, and Ahimelech, and the heads of the fathers' *houses* of the priests and of the Levites; the fathers' *houses* of the chief even as those of his younger brother.

ᵃ Heb. "divisions."   ᵇ In 1 Chronicles 6 : 17, "Libni." See § 8, (2).   ᶜ In ver. 11, "Zizah."   ᵈ Or, "to sanctify as most holy him," etc.

1 *Chronicles* 23.

Jerusalem for ever: 26 and also the Levites shall no more have need to carry the tabernacle and all the vessels of it for the service thereof. 27 For *a* by the last words of David the sons of Levi were numbered, from twenty years old and upward. 28 For *b* their office was to wait on the sons of Aaron for the service of the house of the LORD, in the courts, and in the chambers, and in the purifying of all holy things, even the work of the service of the house of God; 29 for the shewbread also, and for the fine flour for a meal offering, whether of unleavened wafers, or of that which is baked in the pan, or of that which is soaked, and for all manner of measure and size; 30 and to stand every morning to thank and praise the LORD, and likewise at even; 31 and to offer all burnt offerings unto the LORD, in the sabbaths, in the new moons, and on the set feasts, in number according to the ordinance concerning them, continually before the LORD: 32 and that they should keep the charge of the tent of meeting, and the charge of the holy place, and the charge of the sons of Aaron their brethren, for the service of the house of the LORD.

D. THE TWENTY-FOUR COURSES OF PRIESTS.

1 *Chronicles* 24 : 1-19.

1 And the courses of the sons of Aaron *were these.* The sons of Aaron; Nadab and Abihu, Eleazar and Ithamar. 2 But Nadab and Abihu died before their father, and had no children: therefore Eleazar and Ithamar executed the priest's office. 3 *c* And David with Zadok of the sons of Eleazar, and Ahimelech of the sons of Ithamar, divided them according to their ordering in their service. 4 And there were more chief men found of the sons of Eleazar than of the sons of Ithamar; and *thus* were they divided: of the sons of Eleazar there were sixteen, heads of fathers' houses; and of the sons of Ithamar, according to their fathers' houses, eight. 5 Thus were they divided by lot, one sort with another; for there were princes of the sanctuary, and princes of God, both of the sons of Eleazar, and of the sons of Ithamar. 6 And Shemaiah the son of Nethanel the scribe, who was of the Levites, wrote them in the presence of the king, and the princes, and Zadok the priest, and Ahimelech the son of Abiathar, and the heads of the fathers' *houses* of the priests and of the Levites: one fathers' house being taken for Eleazar, and *d* one taken for Ithamar. 7 Now the first lot came forth to Jehoiarib, the second to Jedaiah; 8 the third to Harim, the fourth to Seorim; 9 the fifth to Malchijah, the sixth to Mijamin; 10 the seventh to Hakkoz, the eighth to Abijah; 11 the ninth to Jeshua, the tenth to Shecaniah; 12 the eleventh to Eliashib, the twelfth to Jakim; 13 the thirteenth to Huppah, the fourteenth to Jeshebeab; 14 the fifteenth to Bilgah, the sixteenth to Immer; 15 the seventeenth to Hezir, the eighteenth to Happizzez; 16 the nineteenth to Pethahiah, the twentieth to Jehezkel; 17 the one and twentieth to Jachin, the two and twentieth to Gamul; 18 the three and twentieth to Delaiah, the four and twentieth to Maaziah. 19 This was the ordering of them in their service, to come into the house of the LORD according to the ordinance *given* unto them by the hand of Aaron their father, as the LORD, the God of Israel, had commanded him.

---

a Or, "in the last acts."   *b* Heb. "their station was at the hand of the sons of Aaron." Cf. Nehemiah 11 : 24.   *c* Or, "And David divided them, even Zadok," etc.   *d* The Heb. text has, "taken, taken."

E. THE TWENTY-FOUR CLASSES OF SINGERS.

1 *Chronicles* 25 : 1-31.

1 Moreover David and the captains of the host separated for the service certain of the sons of Asaph, and of Heman, and of Jeduthun, who should prophesy with harps, with psalteries, and with cymbals : and the number of them that did the work according to their service was : 2 of the sons of Asaph ; Zaccur, and Joseph, and Nethaniah, and *a* Asharelah, the sons of Asaph ; under the hand of Asaph, who prophesied *b* after the order of the king. 3 Of Jeduthun : the sons of Jeduthun ; Gedaliah, and *c* Zeri, and Jeshaiah, Hashabiah, and Mattithiah, *d* six ; under the hands of their father Jeduthun with the harp, who prophesied in giving thanks and praising the LORD. 4 Of Heman : the sons of Heman ; Bukkiah, Mattaniah, *e* Uzziel, *f* Shebuel, and Jerimoth, Hananiah, Hanani, Eliathah, Giddalti, and Romamti-ezer, Joshbekashah, Mallothi, Hothir, Mahazioth : 5 all these were the sons of Heman the king's seer in the words of God, to lift up the horn. And God gave to Heman fourteen sons and three daughters. 6 All these were under the hands of their father for song in the house of the LORD, with cymbals, psalteries, and harps, for the service of the house of God ; *g* Asaph, Jeduthun, and Heman being under the order of the king. 7 And the number of them, with their brethren that were instructed in singing unto the LORD, even all that were skilful, was two hundred fourscore and eight. 8 And they cast lots *h* for their charges, all alike, as well the small as the great, the teacher as the scholar. 9 Now the first lot came forth for Asaph to Joseph : the second to Gedaliah ; he and his brethren and sons were twelve : 10 the third to Zaccur, his sons and his brethren, twelve : 11 the fourth to Izri, his sons and his brethren, twelve : 12 the fifth to Nethaniah, his sons and his brethren, twelve : 13 the sixth to Bukkiah, his sons and his brethren, twelve : 14 the seventh to Jesharelah, his sons and his brethren, twelve : 15 the eighth to Jeshaiah, his sons and his brethren, twelve : 16 the ninth to Mattaniah, his sons and his brethren, twelve : 17 the tenth to Shimei, his sons and his brethren, twelve : 18 the eleventh to Azarel, his sons and his brethren, twelve : 19 the twelfth to Hashabiah, his sons and his brethren, twelve : 20 for the thirteenth, Shubael, his sons and his brethren, twelve : 21 for the fourteenth, Mattithiah, his sons and his brethren, twelve : 22 for the fifteenth to Jeremoth, his sons and his brethren, twelve : 23 for the sixteenth to Hananiah, his sons and his brethren, twelve : 24 for the seventeenth to Joshbekashah, his sons and his brethren, twelve : 25 for the eighteenth to Hanani, his sons and his brethren, twelve : 26 for the nineteenth to Mallothi, his sons and his brethren, twelve : 27 for the twentieth to Eliathah, his sons and his brethren, twelve : 28 for the one and twentieth to Hothir, his sons and his brethren, twelve : 29 for the two and twentieth to Giddalti, his sons and his brethren, twelve : 30 for the three and twentieth to Mahazioth, his sons and his brethren, twelve : 31 for the four and twentieth to Romamti-ezer, his sons and his brethren, twelve.

F. THE COURSES OF THE DOORKEEPERS.

1 *Chronicles* 26 : 1-19.

1 For the courses of the doorkeepers : of the Korahites ; *i* Meshelemiah the son of Kore, of the sons of *k* Asaph. 2 And Meshelemiah had sons ; Zechariah the firstborn, Jediael the second, Zebadiah the third, Jathniel the fourth ; 3 Elam the fifth, Jehohanan the sixth, Eliehoenai the seventh. 4 And Obed-edom had sons ; Shemaiah the firstborn, Jehozabad the second, Joah the third, and Sacar the fourth, and Nethanel the fifth ; 5 Ammiel the sixth, Issachar the seventh, Peullethai the eighth : for God blessed him. 6 Also unto Shemaiah his son were sons born, that ruled over the house of their father : for they were mighty men of valour. 7 The sons of Shemaiah ; Othni, and Rephael, and Obed, Elzabad, whose brethren were valiant men, Elihu, and Semachiah. 8 All these were of the sons of Obed-edom : they and their sons and their brethren, able men in strength for the service ; threescore and two of Obed-edom. 9 And Meshelemiah had sons and brethren, valiant men, eighteen. 10 Also Hosah, of the children of Merari, had sons ; Shimri the

---

a In ver. 14, " Jesharelah."   *b* Heb. " by the hands of the king."   *c* In ver. 11, " Izri."   *d* With Shimei, mentioned in ver. 17.   *e* In ver. 18, " Azarel."   *f* In ver. 20, " Shubael."   *g* Or, " after the order of the king, *even* Asaph," etc.   *h* Or, " ward against *ward*, as well," etc.   *i* In ver. 14, " Shelemiah."   *k* In 1 Chronicles 9 : 19, Ebiasaph. See §19, (2).

1 Chronicles 26.

chief, (for though he was not the firstborn, yet his father made him chief ;) 11 Hilkiah the second, Tebaliah the third, Zechariah the fourth : all the sons and brethren of Hosah were thirteen. 12 Of these were the courses of the doorkeepers, even of the chief men, having a charges like as their brethren, to minister in the house of the LORD. 13 And they cast lots, as well the small as the great, according to their fathers' houses, for every gate. 14 And the lot eastward fell to Shelemiah. Then for Zechariah his son, a discreet counsellor, they cast lots ; and his lot came out northward. 15 To Obed-edom southward ; and to his sons the storehouse. 16 To Shuppim and Hosah westward, by the gate of b Shallecheth, at the causeway that goeth up, ward against ward. 17 Eastward were six Levites, northward four a day, southward four a day, and for the storehouse two and two. 18 For c Parbar westward, four at the causeway, and two at c Parbar. 19 These were the courses of the doorkeepers ; of the sons of the Korahites, and of the sons of Merari.

G. THE OFFICERS OF THE TREASURIES OF "THE HOUSE OF GOD."

1 Chronicles 26: 20–28.

20 And d of the Levites, Ahijah was over the treasuries of the house of God, and over the treasuries of the e dedicated things. 21 The sons of f Ladan ; the sons of the Gershonites belonging to Ladan, the heads of the fathers' houses belonging to Ladan the Gershonite ; g Jehieli. 22 The sons of Jehieli ; Zetham, and Joel his brother, over the treasuries of the house of the LORD. 23 Of the Amramites, of the Izharites, of the Hebronites, of the Uzzielites : 24 and Shebuel the son of Gershom, the son of Moses, was ruler over the treasuries. 25 And his brethren ; of Eliezer came Rehabiah his son, and Jeshaiah his son, and Joram his son, and Zichri his son, and Shelomoth his son. 26 This Shelomoth and his brethren were over all the treasuries of the dedicated things, which David the king, and the heads of the fathers' houses, the captains over thousands and hundreds, and the captains of the host, had dedicated. 27 h Out of the spoil won in battles did they dedicate to repair the house of the LORD. 28 And all that Samuel the seer, and Saul the son of Kish, and Abner the son of Ner, and Joab the son of Zeruiah, had dedicated ; whosoever had dedicated any thing, it was under the hand of i Shelomoth, and of his brethren.

H. THE OFFICERS AND JUDGES "FOR THE OUTWARD BUSINESS."

1 Chronicles 26 : 29–32.

29 Of the Izharites, Chenaniah and his sons were for the outward business over Israel, for officers and judges. 30 Of the Hebronites, Hashabiah and his brethren, men of valour, a thousand and seven hundred, had the oversight of Israel beyond Jordan westward ; for all the business of the LORD, and for the service of the king. 31 Of the Hebronites was Jerijah the chief, even of the Hebronites, according to their generations by fathers' houses. In the fortieth year of the reign of David they were sought for, and there were found among them mighty men of valour at Jazer of Gilead. 32 And his brethren, men of valour, were two thousand and seven hundred, heads of fathers' houses, whom king David made overseers over the Reubenites, and the Gadites, and the half tribe of the Manassites, for every matter pertaining to God, and for the affairs of the king.

I. THE TWELVE CAPTAINS OF THE ARMY.

1 Chronicles 27 : 1–15.

1 Now the children of Israel after their number, to wit, the heads of fathers' houses and the captains of thousands and of hundreds, and their officers that served the king, in any matter of the courses which came in and went out month by month throughout all the months of the year, of every course were twenty and four thousand. 2 Over the first course for the first month was

---

a Or, "wards over against their brethren."   b I. e., "Casting forth."   c Or, "the Precinct."   d According to the Sept., "And the Levites their brethren were over," etc.   e Heb. "holy things."   f In 1 Chronicles 6 : 17, "Libni." See §8, (2).   g In 1 Chronicles 23 : 8, "Jehiel." See §107, (2), B.   h Heb. "Out of the battles and the spoil."   i Heb. "Shelomith."

I *Chronicles* 27.

Jashobeam the son of Zabdiel: and in his course were twenty and four thousand. 3 *He was* of the children of Perez, the chief of all the captains of the host for the first month. 4 And over the course of the second month was Dodai the Ahohite, and his course; and Mikloth the ruler: and in his course were twenty and four thousand. 5 The third captain of the host for the third month was Benaiah, the son of Jehoiada the *a* priest, chief: and in his course were twenty and four thousand. 6 This is that Benaiah, who was the mighty man of the thirty, and over the thirty: and *of* his course was Ammizabad his son. 7 The fourth *captain* for the fourth month was Asahel the brother of Joab, and Zebadiah his son after him: and in his course were twenty and four thousand. 8 The fifth captain for the fifth month was Shamhuth the Izrahite: and in his course were twenty and four thousand. 9 The sixth *captain* for the sixth month was Ira the son of Ikkesh the Tekoite: and in his course were twenty and four thousand. 10 The seventh *captain* for the seventh month was Helez the Pelonite, of the children of Ephraim: and in his course were twenty and four thousand. 11 The eighth *captain* for the eighth month was Sibbecai the Hushathite, of the Zerahites: and in his course were twenty and four thousand. 12 The ninth *captain* for the ninth month was Abiezer the Anathothite, of the Benjamites: and in his course were twenty and four thousand. 13 The tenth *captain* for the tenth month was Maharai the Netophathite, of the Zerahites: and in his course were twenty and four thousand. 14 The eleventh *captain* for the eleventh month was Benaiah the Pirathonite, of the children of Ephraim: and in his course were twenty and four thousand. 15 The twelfth *captain* for the twelfth month was *b* Heldai the Netophathite, of Othniel: and in his course were twenty and four thousand.

J. THE CHIEFS OF THE TWELVE TRIBES.

I *Chronicles* 27: 16–24.

16 Furthermore over the tribes of Israel: of the Reubenites was Eliezer the son of Zichri the ruler: of the Simeonites, Shephatiah the son of Maacah: 17 of Levi, Hashabiah the son of Kemuel: of Aaron, Zadok: 18 of Judah, *c* Elihu, one of the brethren of David: of Issachar, Omri the son of Michael: 19 of Zebulun, Ishmaiah the son of Obadiah: of Naphtali, Jeremoth the son of Azriel: 20 of the children of Ephraim, Hoshea the son of Azaziah: of the half tribe of Manasseh, Joel the son of Pedaiah: 21 of the half *tribe* of Manasseh in Gilead, Iddo the son of Zechariah: of Benjamin, Jaasiel the son of Abner: 22 of Dan, Azarel the son of Jeroham. These were the captains of the tribes of Israel. 23 But David took not the number of them from twenty years old and under: because the LORD had said he would increase Israel like to the stars of heaven. 24 Joab the son of Zeruiah began to number, but finished not; and there came wrath for this upon Israel; neither was the number put into the account in the chronicles of king David.

K. THE OVERSEERS OF THE KING'S TREASURIES AND POSSESSIONS.

I *Chronicles* 27: 25–31.

25 And over the king's treasures was Azmaveth the son of Adiel: and over the treasuries in the fields, in the cities, and in the villages, and in the castles, was Jonathan the son of Uzziah: 26 and over them that did the work of the field for tillage of the ground was Ezri the son of Chelub: 27 and over the vineyards was Shimei the Ramathite: and over the increase of the vineyards for the wine cellars was Zabdi the Shiphmite: 28 and over the olive trees and the sycomore trees that were in the lowland was Baal-hanan the Gederite: and over the cellars of oil was Joash: 29 and over the herds that fed in Sharon was Shitrai the Sharonite: and over the herds that were in the valleys was Shaphat the son of Adlai: 30 and over the camels was Obil the Ishmaelite: and over the asses was Jehdeiah the Meronothite: 31 and over the flocks was Jaziz the Hagrite. All these were the rulers of the substance which was king David's.

---

a Or, "chief minister." Cf. 2 Samuel 8:18. See §92.   *b* In 2 Samuel 23:29, "Heleb." In 1 Chronicles 11:30, "Heled." See §91, (3).   *c* In 1 Samuel 16:6, "Eliab." See §41.

L. THE OFFICERS OF STATE.[a]

1 *Chronicles* 27 : 32–34.

32 Also Jonathan David's [b] uncle was a counsellor, a man of understanding, and a scribe : and Jehiel the son of Hachmoni was with the king's sons : 33 and Ahithophel was the king's counsellor : and Hushai the Archite was the king's friend : 34 and after Ahithophel was Jehoiada the son of Benaiah, and Abiathar : and the captain of the king's host was Joab.

(3) THE CONVENING INTO AN ASSEMBLY OF THE SECULAR OFFICIALS "GATHERED."

1 *Chronicles* 28 : 1.

1 And David assembled all the princes of Israel, the princes of the tribes, and the captains of the companies that served the king by course, and the captains of thousands, and the captains of hundreds, and the rulers over all the substance and [c] possessions of the king and of his sons, with the [d] officers, and the mighty men, even all the mighty men of valour, unto Jerusalem.

(4) THE PUBLIC ACTS IN NATIONAL CONVENTION.

A. DAVID CAUSES SOLOMON TO BE MADE KING (FIRST TIME).[e]

1 *Chronicles* 23 : 1b.

1b And he made Solomon his son king over Israel.

B. DAVID'S ADDRESS.

1 *Chronicles* 28 : 2–8.

2 Then David the king stood up upon his feet, and said, Hear me, my brethren, and my people : as for me, it was in mine heart to build an house of rest for the ark of the covenant of the LORD, and for the footstool of our God ; and I had made ready for the building. 3 But God said unto me, Thou shalt not build an house for my name, because thou art a man of war, and hast shed blood. 4 Howbeit the LORD, the God of Israel, chose me out of all the house of my father to be king over Israel for ever : for he hath chosen Judah to be [f] prince ; and in the house of Judah, the house of my father ; and among the sons of my father he took pleasure in me to make me king over all Israel : 5 and of all my sons, (for the LORD hath given me many sons,) he hath chosen Solomon my son to sit upon the throne of the kingdom of the LORD over Israel. 6 And he said unto me, Solomon thy son, he shall build my house and my courts : for I have chosen him to be my son, and I will be his father. 7 And I will establish his kingdom for ever, if he be constant to do my commandments and my judgements, as at this day. 8 Now therefore, in the sight of all Israel, the congregation of the LORD, and in the audience of our God, observe and seek out all the commandments of the LORD your God : that ye may possess this good land, and leave it for an inheritance to your children after you for ever.

C. DAVID DIRECTS SOLOMON CONCERNING THE BUILDING OF THE TEMPLE.

1 *Chronicles* 28 : 9–21.

9 And thou, Solomon my son, know thou the God of thy father, and serve him with a perfect heart and with a willing mind : for the LORD searcheth all hearts, and understandeth all the imaginations of the thoughts : if thou seek him, he will be found of thee ; but if thou forsake him, he will cast thee off for ever. 10 Take heed now ; for the LORD hath chosen thee to build an house for the sanctuary : be strong, and do it. 11 Then David gave to Solomon his son the pattern of the porch *of the temple*, and of the houses thereof, and of the treasuries thereof, and of the upper rooms thereof, and of the inner chambers thereof, and of the [g] place of the mercy-seat : 12 and the pattern of all that he had [h] by the spirit,

---

a Cf. §§92 and 116.   *b* Or, "brother's son."   *c* Or, "cattle."   *d* Or, "eunuchs."   *e* This making of Solomon king was not an abdication on the part of David, but the public associating of Solomon with himself as sharing the throne and having exclusive succession to it. It doubtless hastened Absalom's rebellion, and was thereby rendered practically inoperative, as the sequel shows.   *f* Or, "leader."   *g* Heb. "house."   *h* Or, "in his spirit."

1 *Chronicles* 28.

for the courts of the house of the LORD, and for all the chambers round about, for the treasuries of the house of God, and for the treasuries of the dedicated things : 13 also for the courses of the priests and the Levites, and for all the work of the service of the house of the LORD, and for all the vessels of service in the house of the LORD : 14 of gold by weight for the *vessels of* gold, for all vessels of every kind of service ; *of silver* for all the vessels of silver by weight, for all vessels of every kind of service : 15 by weight also for the candlesticks of gold, and for the lamps thereof, of gold, by weight for every candlestick and for the lamps thereof : and for the candlesticks of silver, *silver* by weight for *every* candlestick and for the lamps thereof, according to the use of every candlestick : 16 and the gold by weight for the tables of shewbread, for every table ; and silver for the tables of silver : 17 and the fleshhooks, and the basons, and the cups, of pure gold : and for the golden bowls by weight for every bowl ; and for the silver bowls by weight for every bowl : 18 and for the altar of incense refined gold by weight : and gold for the pattern of the chariot, *even* the cherubim, that spread out *their wings*, and covered the ark of the covenant of the LORD. 19 All this, *said David,* ᵃ have I been made to understand in writing from the hand of the LORD, even all the works of this pattern. 20 And David said to Solomon his son, Be strong and of good courage, and do it : fear not, nor be dismayed : for the LORD God, even my God, is with thee : he will not fail thee, nor forsake thee, until all the work for the service of the house of the LORD be finished. 21 And, behold, there are the courses of the priests and the Levites, for all the service of the house of God : and there shall be with thee in all manner of work every willing man that hath skill, for any manner of service : also the captains and all the people will be wholly at thy commandment.

D. CONTRIBUTIONS OF DAVID AND THE OFFICIALS FOR THE BUILDING OF THE TEMPLE.

1 *Chronicles* 29 : 1–9.

1 And David the king said unto all the congregation, Solomon my son, whom alone God hath chosen, is yet young and tender, and the work is great : for the palace is not for man, but for the LORD God. 2 Now I have prepared with all my might for the house of my God the gold for the *things of* gold, and the silver for the *things of* silver, and the brass for the *things of* brass, the iron for the *things of* iron, and wood for the *things of* wood ; ᵇ onyx stones, and *stones* to be set, stones for inlaid work, and of divers colours, and all manner of precious stones, and marble stones in abundance. 3 Moreover also, because I have set my affection to the house of my God, seeing that I have a treasure of mine own of gold and silver, I give it unto the house of my God, over and above all that I have prepared for the holy house ; 4 even three thousand talents of gold, of the gold of Ophir, and seven thousand talents of refined silver, to overlay the walls of the houses withal : 5 of gold for the *things of* gold, and of silver for the *things of* silver, and for all manner of work *to be made* by the hands of artificers. Who then offereth willingly ᶜ to consecrate himself this day unto the LORD ? 6 Then the princes of the fathers' *houses*, and the princes of the tribes of Israel, and the captains of thousands and of hundreds, with the rulers over the king's work, offered willingly ; 7 and they gave for the service of the house of God of gold five thousand talents and ten thousand darics, and of silver ten thousand talents, and of brass eighteen thousand talents, and of iron a hundred thousand talents. 8 And they with whom *precious* stones were found gave them to the treasure of the house of the LORD, under the hand of Jehiel the Gershonite. 9 Then the people rejoiced, for that they offered willingly, because with a perfect heart they offered willingly to the LORD : and David the king also rejoiced with great joy.

E. DAVID'S THANKSGIVING AND PRAYER.

1 *Chronicles* 29 : 10–19.

10 Wherefore David blessed the LORD before all the congregation : and David said, Blessed be thou, O LORD, the God of Israel our father, for ever and ever. 11 Thine, O LORD, is the great-

---

a Or, " the LORD made me understand in writing by his hand upon me, even," etc. *b* Or, " beryl." *c* Heb. " to fill his hand."

1 *Chronicles* 29.

ness, and the power, and the glory, and the victory, and the majesty : for all that is in the heaven and in the earth *is thine ;* thine is the kingdom, O LORD, and thou art exalted as head above all. 12 Both riches and honour come of thee, and thou rulest over all ; and in thine hand is power and might ; and in thine hand it is to make great, and to give strength unto all.　13 Now therefore, our God, we thank thee, and praise thy glorious name.　14 But who am I, and what is my people, that we should *a* be able to offer so willingly after this sort ? for all things come of thee, and *b* of thine own have we given thee.　15 For we are strangers before thee, and sojourners, as all our fathers were : our days on the earth are as a shadow, and there is no *c* abiding.　16 O LORD our God, all this store that we have prepared to build thee an house for thine holy name cometh of thine hand, and is all thine own.　17 I know also, my God, that thou triest the heart, and hast pleasure in uprightness.　As for me, in the uprightness of mine heart I have willingly offered all these things : and now have I seen with joy thy people, which are present here, to offer willingly unto thee. 18 O LORD, the God of Abraham, of Isaac, and of Israel, our fathers, keep this for ever in the imagination of the thoughts of the heart of thy people, and *d* prepare their heart unto thee : 19 and give unto Solomon my son a perfect heart, to keep thy commandments, thy testimonies, and thy statutes, and to do all these things, and to build the palace, for the which I have made provision.

(5) CLOSE OF THE CONVENTION.

1 *Chronicles* 29 : 20–22*a*.

20 And David said to all the congregation, Now bless the LORD your God.　And all the congregation blessed the LORD, the God of their fathers, and bowed down their heads, and worshipped the LORD, and the king.　21 And they sacrificed sacrifices unto the LORD, and offered burnt offerings unto the LORD, on the morrow after that day, even a thousand bullocks, a thousand rams, and a thousand lambs, with their drink offerings, and sacrifices in abundance for all Israel, 22*a* and did eat and drink before the LORD on that day with great gladness.

IV.　Absalom's Rebellion.

108.　THE OUTBREAK OF THE REBELLION.

2 *Samuel* 15 : 7–12.

7 And it came to pass at the end of *e* forty years, that Absalom said unto the king, I pray thee, let me go and pay my vow, which I have vowed unto the LORD, in Hebron.　8 For thy servant vowed a vow while I abode at Geshur in *f* Syria, saying, If the LORD shall indeed bring me again to Jerusalem, then I will *g* serve the LORD.　9 And the king said unto him, Go in peace.　So he arose, and went to Hebron.　10 But Absalom sent spies throughout all the tribes of Israel, saying, As soon as ye hear the sound of the trumpet, then ye shall say, Absalom is king in Hebron.　11 And with Absalom went two hundred men out of Jerusalem, that were invited, and went in their simplicity ; and they knew not any thing.　12 And Absalom *h* sent for Ahithophel the Gilonite, David's counsellor, from his city, even from Giloh, while he offered the sacrifices.　And the conspiracy was strong ; for the people increased continually with Absalom.

109.　DAVID'S FLIGHT.

(1) HE HASTILY LEAVES JERUSALEM.

2 *Samuel* 15 : 13–18.

13 And there came a messenger to David, saying, The hearts of the men of Israel are after Absalom.　14 And David said unto all his servants that were with him at Jerusalem, Arise, and

---

a Heb. " retain strength."　　*b* Heb. " of thine hand."　　*c* Heb. " hope."　　*d* Or, " establish."　　*e* According to some ancient authorities, " four ; " but without doubt the text is correct, for it is most natural to consider the meaning here to be, " at the end of forty years of David's reign."　　*f* Heb. " Aram."　　*g* Or, " worship."　　*h* Or, " sent Ahithophel."

2 *Samuel* 15.

let us flee; for else none of us shall escape from Absalom : make speed to depart, lest he overtake us quickly, and bring down evil upon us, and smite the city with the edge of the sword. 15 And the king's servants said unto the king, Behold, thy servants are ready to do whatsoever my lord the king shall choose. 16 And the king went forth, and all his household after him. And the king left ten women, which were concubines, to keep the house. 17 And the king went forth, and all the people after him ; and they tarried *a* in Beth-merhak. 18 And all his servants passed on beside him ; and all the Cherethites, and all the Pelethites, and all the Gittites, six hundred men which came after him from Gath, passed on before the king.

(2) ITTAI'S FIDELITY.

2 *Samuel* 15 : 19-23.

19 Then said the king to Ittai the Gittite, Wherefore goest thou also with us ? return, and abide with the king : for thou art a stranger, and also an exile; *return* to thine own place. 20 Whereas thou camest but yesterday, should I this day make thee go up and down with us, seeing I go whither I may ? return thou, and take back thy brethren ; mercy and truth be with thee. 21 And Ittai answered the king, and said, As the LORD liveth, and as my lord the king liveth, surely in what place my lord the king shall be, whether for death or for life, even there also will thy servant be. 22 And David said to Ittai, Go and pass over. And Ittai the Gittite passed over, and all his men, and all the little ones that were with him. 23 And all the country wept with a loud voice, and all the people passed over : the king also himself passed over the brook Kidron, and all the people passed over, toward the way of the wilderness.

(3) THE PRIESTS AND THE ARK.

2 *Samuel* 15 : 24-29.

24 And, lo, Zadok also *came,* and all the Levites with him, bearing the ark of the covenant of God ; and they set down the ark of God, and Abiathar went up, until all the people had done passing out of the city. 25 And the king said unto Zadok, Carry back the ark of God into the city : if I shall find favour in the eyes of the LORD, he will bring me again, and shew me both it, and his habitation : 26 but if he say thus, I have no delight in thee ; behold, here am I, let him do to me as seemeth good unto him. 27 The king said also unto Zadok the priest, *b* Art thou *not* a seer ? return into the city in peace, and your two sons with you, Ahimaaz thy son, and Jonathan the son of Abiathar. 28 See, I will tarry *c* at the fords of the wilderness, until there come word from you to certify me. 29 Zadok therefore and Abiathar carried the ark of God again to Jerusalem : and they abode there.

(4) HUSHAI IS SENT BACK TO THE CITY.

2 *Samuel* 15 : 30-37*a.*

30 And David went up by the ascent of the *mount of* Olives, and wept as he went up ; and he had his head covered, and went barefoot : and all the people that were with him covered every man his head, and they went up, weeping as they went up. 31 And one told David, saying, Ahithophel is among the conspirators with Absalom. And David said, O LORD, I pray thee, turn the counsel of Ahithophel into foolishness. 32 And it came to pass, that when David was come to the top *of the ascent,* *d* where God was worshipped, behold, Hushai the Archite came to meet him with his coat rent, and earth upon his head : 33 and David said unto him, If thou passest on with me, then thou shalt be a burden unto me : 34 but if thou return to the city, and say unto Absalom, I will be thy servant, O king ; as I have been thy father's servant in time past, so will I now be thy servant : then shalt thou defeat for me the counsel of Ahithophel. 35 And hast thou not there with thee Zadok and Abiathar the priests ? therefore it shall be, that what thing soever

---

a Or, " at the Far House."   *b* Or, " Seest thou ?"   *c* Another reading is, " in the plains."   *d* Or, " where he was wont to worship God."

2 Samuel 15.

thou shalt hear out of the king's house, thou shalt tell it to Zadok and Abiathar the priests. 36 Behold, they have there with them their two sons, Ahimaaz Zadok's son, and Jonathan Abiathar's son; and by them ye shall send unto me every thing that ye shall hear.   37 a So Hushai David's friend came into the city.

(5) THE LYING ZIBA AND HIS PRESENT.

2 Samuel 16 : 1–4.

1 And when David was a little past the top *of the ascent*, behold, Ziba the servant of Mephibosheth met him, with a couple of asses saddled, and upon them two hundred loaves of bread, and an hundred clusters of raisins, and an hundred of summer fruits, and a *a* bottle of wine. 2 And the king said unto Ziba, What meanest thou by these? And Ziba said, The asses be for the king's household to ride on; and the bread and summer fruit for the young men to eat; and the wine, that such as be faint in the wilderness may drink. 3 And the king said, And where is thy master's son? And Ziba said unto the king, Behold, he abideth at Jerusalem: for he said, To-day shall the house of Israel restore me the kingdom of my father. 4 Then said the king to Ziba, Behold, thine is all that pertaineth unto Mephibosheth. And Ziba said, I do obeisance; let me find favour in thy sight, my lord, O king.

(6) THE CURSING OF SHIMEI.

2 Samuel 16 : 5–14.

5 And when king David came to Bahurim, behold, there came out thence a man of the family of the house of Saul, whose name was Shimei, the son of Gera: he came out, and cursed still as he came. 6 And he cast stones at David, and at all the servants of king David: and all the people and all the mighty men were on his right hand and on his left. 7 And thus said Shimei when he cursed, Begone, begone, thou man of blood, and man of *b* Belial: 8 the LORD hath returned upon thee all the blood of the house of Saul, in whose stead thou hast reigned; and the LORD hath delivered the kingdom into the hand of Absalom thy son: and, behold, thou art *taken* in thine own mischief, because thou art a man of blood. 9 Then said Abishai the son of Zeruiah unto the king, Why should this dead dog curse my lord the king? let me go over, I pray thee, and take off his head. 10 And the king said, What have I to do with you, ye sons of Zeruiah ? *c* Because he curseth, and because the LORD hath said unto him, Curse David; who then shall say, Wherefore hast thou done so? 11 And David said to Abishai, and to all his servants, Behold, my son, which came forth of my bowels, seeketh my life: how much more *may* this Benjamite now *do it?* let him alone, and let him curse; for the LORD hath bidden him. 12 It may be that the LORD will look on *d* the wrong done unto me, and that the LORD will requite me good for *his* cursing of me this day. 13 So David and his men went by the way: and Shimei went along on the hill side over against him, and cursed as he went, and threw stones *e* at him, and cast dust. 14 And the king, and all the people that were with him, came *f* weary; and he refreshed himself there.

110. ABSALOM IN JERUSALEM.

(1) HIS ENTRANCE INTO THE CITY.

2 *Samuel* 15: 37*b*.	2 *Samuel* 16: 15.
37*b* And Absalom came into Jerusalem.	15 And Absalom, and all the people the men of Israel, came to Jerusalem, and Ahithophel with him.

---

a Or, "skin."   *b* I. e., "worthlessness."   *c* Or, "When he curseth, and when," etc.   Another reading is, "So let him curse, because."   *d* Some ancient versions read, "my affliction."   *e* Heb. "over against."   *f* Or, "to Ayephim."

(2) HUSHAI MEETS ABSALOM.

2 *Samuel* 16 : 16–19.

16 And it came to pass, when Hushai the Archite, David's friend, was come unto Absalom, that Hushai said unto Absalom, *a* God save the king, God save the king. 17 And Absalom said to Hushai, Is this thy kindness to thy friend? why wentest thou not with thy friend? 18 And Hushai said unto Absalom, Nay; but whom the LORD, and this people, and all the men of Israel have chosen, his will I be, and with him will I abide. 19 And again, whom should I serve? *should I* not *serve* in the presence of his son? as I have served in thy father's presence, so will I be in thy presence.

(3) THE COUNSELS OF AHITHOPHEL.

2 *Samuel* 16 : 20–17 : 4.

20 Then said Absalom to Ahithophel, Give your counsel what we shall do. 21 And Ahithophel said unto Absalom, Go in unto thy father's concubines, which he hath left to keep the house; and all Israel shall hear that thou art abhorred of thy father: then shall the hands of all that are with thee be strong. 22 So they spread Absalom a tent upon the top of the house; and Absalom went in unto his father's concubines in the sight of all Israel. 23 And the counsel of Ahithophel, which he counselled in those days, was as if a man inquired at the *b* oracle of God: so was all the counsel of Ahithophel both with David and with Absalom.

1 Moreover Ahithophel said unto Absalom, Let me now choose out twelve thousand men, and I will arise and pursue after David this night: 2 and I will come upon him while he is weary and weak handed, and will make him afraid: and all the people that are with him shall flee; and I will smite the king only: 3 and I will bring back all the people unto thee: the man whom thou seekest is as if all returned: *so* all the people shall be in peace. 4 And the saying pleased Absalom well, and all the elders of Israel.

(4) AHITHOPHEL'S COUNSEL IS THWARTED BY HUSHAI.

2 *Samuel* 17 : 5–14.

5 Then said Absalom, Call now Hushai the Archite also, and let us hear likewise what he saith. 6 And when Hushai was come to Absalom, Absalom spake unto him, saying, Ahithophel hath spoken after this manner: shall we do *after* his saying? if not, speak thou. 7 And Hushai said unto Absalom, The counsel that Ahithophel hath given this time is not good. 8 Hushai said moreover, Thou knowest thy father and his men, that they be mighty men, and they be *c* chafed in their minds, as a bear robbed of her whelps in the field: and thy father is a man of war, and will not lodge with the people. 9 Behold, he is hid now in some pit, or in some *other* place: and it will come to pass, *d* when some of them be fallen at the first, that whosoever heareth it will say, There is a slaughter among the people that follow Absalom. 10 And even he that is valiant, whose heart is as the heart of a lion, shall utterly melt: for all Israel knoweth that thy father is a mighty man, and they which be with him are valiant men. 11 But I counsel that all Israel be gathered together unto thee, from Dan even to Beer-sheba, as the sand that is by the sea for multitude; and *e* that thou go to battle in thine own person. 12 So shall we come upon him in some place where he shall be found, and we will light upon him as the dew falleth on the ground: and of him and of all the men that are with him we will not leave so much as one. 13 Moreover, if he *f* be gotten into a city, then shall all Israel bring ropes to that city, and we will draw it into the river, until there be not one small stone found there. 14 And Absalom and all the men of Israel said, The counsel of Hushai the Archite is better than the counsel of Ahithophel. For the LORD had ordained to defeat the good counsel of Ahithophel, to the intent that the LORD might bring evil upon Absalom.

---

a Heb. " Let the king live."   *b* Heb. " word."   *c* Heb. " bitter of soul."   *d* Or, " when he falleth upon them."
e Or, " that thy presence (Heb. face) go to the battle."   *f* Or, " withdraw himself."

(5) HUSHAI'S MESSAGE TO DAVID.

2 *Samuel* 17 : 15–22.

15 Then said Hushai unto Zadok and to Abiathar the priests, Thus and thus did Ahithophel counsel Absalom and the elders of Israel ; and thus and thus have I counselled. 16 Now therefore send quickly, and tell David, saying, Lodge not this night *a* at the fords of the wilderness, but in any wise pass over ; lest the king be swallowed up, and all the people that are with him. 17 *b* Now Jonathan and Ahimaaz stayed by En-rogel ; and a maidservant used to go and tell them ; and they went and told king David : for they might not be seen to come into the city. 18 But a lad saw them, and told Absalom : and they went both of them away quickly, and came to the house of a man in Bahurim, who had a well in his court ; and they went down thither. 19 And the woman took and spread the covering over the well's mouth, and strewed bruised corn thereon ; and nothing was known. 20 And Absalom's servants came to the woman to the house ; and they said, Where are Ahimaaz and Jonathan ? And the woman said unto them, They be gone over the brook of water. And when they had sought and could not find them, they returned to Jerusalem. 21 And it came to pass, after they were departed, that they came up out of the well, and went and told king David ; and they said unto David, Arise ye, and pass quickly over the water : for thus hath Ahithophel counselled against you. 22 Then David arose, and all the people that were with him, and they passed over Jordan : by the morning light there lacked not one of them that was not gone over Jordan.

(6) AHITHOPHEL'S SUICIDE.

2 *Samuel* 17 : 23.

23 And when Ahithophel saw that his counsel was not followed, he saddled his ass, and arose, and gat him home, unto his city, and set his house in order, and hanged himself ; and he died, and was buried in the sepulchre of his father.

III. THE CIVIL WAR.

(1) ABSALOM'S PURSUIT.

2 *Samuel* 17 : 24–26.

24 Then David came to Mahanaim. And Absalom passed over Jordan, he and all the men of Israel with him. 25 And Absalom set Amasa over the host instead of Joab. Now Amasa was the son of a man, whose name was *c* Ithra the Israelite, that went in to *d* Abigal the daughter of Nahash, sister to Zeruiah Joab's mother. 26 And Israel and Absalom pitched in the land of Gilead.

(2) THE RECEPTION OF DAVID AT MAHANAIM.

2 *Samuel* 17 : 27–29.

27 And it came to pass, when David was come to Mahanaim, that Shobi the son of Nahash of Rabbah of the children of Ammon, and Machir the son of Ammiel of Lo-debar, and Barzillai the Gileadite of Rogelim, 28 brought beds, and basons, and earthen vessels, and wheat, and barley, and meal, and parched *corn*, and beans, and lentils, and parched *pulse*, 29 and honey, and butter, and sheep, and cheese of kine, for David, and for the people that were with him, to eat : for they said, The people is hungry, and weary, and thirsty, in the wilderness.

(3) THE BATTLE OF MOUNT EPHRAIM.

2 *Samuel* 18 : 1–8.

1 And David numbered the people that were with him, and set captains of thousands and captains of hundreds over them. 2 And David sent forth the people, a third part under the hand

---

a Another reading is, " in the plains." *b* Or, " Now Jonathan and Ahimaaz stayed by En-rogel ; so let the maidservant go and tell them, and let them go and tell king David ;' for they may not be seen to come into the city." *c* In 1 Chronicles 2 : 17. " Jether the Ishmaelite." See §7, (1). *d* In 1 Chronicles 2 : 16, 17, " Abigail." See §7, (1).

2 *Samuel* 18.

of Joab, and a third part under the hand of Abishai the son of Zeruiah, Joab's brother, and a third part under the hand of Ittai the Gittite. And the king said unto the people, I will surely go forth with you myself also. 3 But the people said, Thou shalt not go forth: for if we flee away, they will not care for us; neither if half of us die, will they care for us: *a* but thou art worth ten thousand of us: therefore now it is better that thou be ready to succour us out of the city. 4 And the king said unto them, What seemeth you best I will do. And the king stood by the gate side, and all the people went out by hundreds and by thousands. 5 And the king commanded Joab and Abishai and Ittai, saying, Deal gently for my sake with the young man, even with Absalom. And all the people heard when the king gave all the captains charge concerning Absalom. 6 So the people went out into the field against Israel: and the battle was in the forest of Ephraim. 7 And the people of Israel were smitten there before the servants of David, and there was a great slaughter there that day of twenty thousand men. 8 For the battle was there spread over the face of all the country: and the forest devoured more people that day than the sword devoured.

(4) ABSALOM IS MURDERED BY JOAB.
2 *Samuel* 18 : 9–18.

9 And Absalom chanced to meet the servants of David. And Absalom rode upon his mule, and the mule went under the thick boughs of a great *b* oak, and his head caught hold of the oak, and he was taken up between the heaven and the earth; and the mule that was under him went on. 10 And a certain man saw it, and told Joab, and said, Behold, I saw Absalom hanging in an oak. 11 And Joab said unto the man that told him, And, behold, thou sawest it, and why didst thou not smite him there to the ground? and I would have given thee ten *pieces of* silver, and a girdle. 12 And the man said unto Joab, Though I should receive a thousand *pieces of* silver in mine hand, yet would I not put forth mine hand against the king's son: for in our hearing the king charged thee and Abishai and Ittai, saying, *c* Beware that none touch the young man Absalom. 13 Otherwise if I had dealt falsely against *d* his life, (and there is no matter hid from the king,) then thou thyself *c* wouldest have stood aloof. 14 Then said Joab, I may not tarry thus with thee. And he took three *f* darts in his hand, and thrust them through the heart of Absalom, while he was yet alive in the midst of the oak. 15 And ten young men that bare Joab's armour compassed about and smote Absalom, and slew him. 16 And Joab blew the trumpet, and the people returned from pursuing after Israel: for Joab *g* held back the people. 17 And they took Absalom, and cast him into the great pit in the forest, and raised over him a very great heap of stones: and all Israel fled every one to his tent. 18 Now Absalom in his life time had taken and reared up for himself the pillar, which is in the king's dale: for he said, I have no son to keep my name in remembrance: and he called the pillar after his own name: and it is called Absalom's monument, unto this day.

(5) THE TIDINGS BROUGHT TO DAVID: HIS GRIEF FOR ABSALOM.
2 *Samuel* 18 : 19–33.

19 Then said Ahimaaz the son of Zadok, Let me now run, and bear the king tidings, how that the LORD hath *h* avenged him of his enemies. 20 And Joab said unto him, Thou shalt not be the bearer of tidings this day, but thou shalt bear tidings another day: but this day thou shalt bear no tidings, because the king's son is dead. 21 Then said Joab to the Cushite, Go tell the king what thou hast seen. And the Cushite bowed himself unto Joab, and ran. 22 Then said Ahimaaz the son of Zadok yet again to Joab, But come what may, let me, I pray thee, also run after the Cushite. And Joab said, Wherefore wilt thou run, my son, seeing that thou *i* wilt have no reward for the tidings? 23 But come what may, *said he,* I will run. And he said unto him, Run. Then Ahimaaz ran by the way of the Plain, and overran the Cushite.

---

a So some ancient authorities. The Heb. text has, " for now are there ten thousand such as we."   *b* Or, " terebinth."
c Heb. " Have a care, whosoever ye be, of," etc.   *d* Another reading is, " my."   *e* Or, " wouldest have set thyself against me."   *f* Heb. " staves."   *g* Or, " spared."   *h* Heb. " judged him from the hand," etc.   *i* Or, " hast no sufficient tidings."

2 *Samuel* 18.

24 Now David sat between the two gates and the watchman went up to the roof of the gate unto the wall, and lifted up his eyes, and looked, and, behold, a man running alone.   25 And the watchman cried, and told the king.   And the king said, if he be alone, there is tidings in his mouth.   And he came apace, and drew near.   26 And the watchman saw another man running : and the watchman called unto the porter, and said, Behold, *another* man running alone.   And the king said, He also bringeth tidings.   27 And the watchman said, Me thinketh the running of the foremost is like the running of Ahimaaz the son of Zadok.   And the king said, He is a good man, and cometh with good tidings.   28 And Ahimaaz called, and said unto the king, *a* All is well.   And he bowed himself before the king with his face to the earth, and said, Blessed be the LORD thy God, which hath delivered up the men that lifted up their hand against my lord the king.   29 And the king said, *b* Is it well with the young man Absalom ?   And Ahimaaz answered, When Joab sent the king's servant, *c* even me thy servant, I saw a great tumult, but I knew not what it was.   30 And the king said, Turn aside, and stand here.   And he turned aside, and stood still.   31 And, behold, the Cushite came ; and the Cushite said, Tidings for my lord the king : for the LORD hath avenged thee this day of all them that rose up against thee.   32 And the king said unto the Cushite, Is it well with the young man Absalom ?   And the Cushite answered, The enemies of my lord the king, and all that rise up against thee to do thee hurt, be as that young man is.   33 *d* And the king was much moved, and went up to the chamber over the gate, and wept : and as he went, thus he said, O my son Absalom, my son, my son Absalom ! would God I had died for thee, O Absalom, my son, my son !

V.   The Restoration of David's Authority.

112. JOAB'S REPROVAL OF DAVID'S UNWORTHY GRIEF.

2 *Samuel* 19 : 1–8a.

1 And it was told Joab, Behold, the king weepeth and mourneth for Absalom.   2 And the *e* victory that day was turned into mourning unto all the people : for the people heard say that day, The king grieveth for his son.   3 And the people gat them by stealth that day into the city, as people that are ashamed steal away when they flee in battle.   4 And the king covered his face, and the king cried with a loud voice, O my son Absalom, O Absalom, my son, my son !   5 And Joab came into the house to the king, and said, Thou hast shamed this day the faces of all thy servants, which this day have saved thy life, and the lives of thy sons and of thy daughters, and the lives of thy wives, and the lives of thy concubines ; 6 in that thou lovest them that hate thee, and hatest them that love thee.   For thou hast declared this day, that princes and servants are nought unto thee : for this day I perceive, that if Absalom had lived, and all we had died this day, then it had pleased thee well.   7 Now therefore arise, go forth, and speak comfortably unto thy servants : for I swear by the LORD, if thou go not forth, there will not tarry a man with thee this night : and that will be worse unto thee than all the evil that hath befallen thee from thy youth until now.   8a Then the king arose, and sat in the gate.   And they told unto all the people, saying, Behold, the king doth sit in the gate : and all the people came before the king.

113. NEGOTIATIONS FOR DAVID'S RECALL.

2 *Samuel* 19 : 8b–14.

8b Now Israel had fled every man to his tent.   9 And all the people were at strife throughout all the tribes of Israel, saying, The king delivered us out of the hand of our enemies, and he saved us out of the hand of the Philistines ; and now he is fled out of the land from Absalom.   10 And Absalom, whom we anointed over us, is dead in battle.   Now therefore why speak ye not a word of bringing the king back ?

---

a Heb. " Peace."   *b* Heb. "*Is there* peace with ?" etc.   *c* Or, " and."   *d* Ch. 19 : 1, in Heb.   *e* Heb. " salvation."

2 *Samuel* 19.

11 And king David sent to Zadok and to Abiathar the priests, saying, Speak unto the elders of Judah, saying, Why are ye the last to bring the king back to his house? seeing the speech of all Israel is come to the king, *to bring him* to his house. 12 Ye are my brethren, ye are my bone and my flesh: wherefore then are ye the last to bring back the king? 13 And say ye to Amasa, Art thou not my bone and my flesh? God do so to me, and more also, if thou be not captain of the host before me continually in the room of Joab. 14 And he bowed the heart of all the men of Judah, even as *the heart of* one man; so that they sent unto the king, *saying*, Return thou, and all thy servants.

114. DAVID'S RETURN.

(1) THE HOMEWARD MARCH BEGINS.

2 *Samuel* 19: 15.

15 So the king returned, and came to Jordan. And Judah came to Gilgal, to go to meet the king, to bring the king over Jordan.

(2) SHIMEI IS PARDONED.

2 *Samuel* 19 : 16–23.

16 And Shimei the son of Gera, the Benjamite, which was of Bahurim, hasted and came down with the men of Judah to meet king David. 17 And there were a thousand men of Benjamin with him, and Ziba the servant of the house of Saul, and his fifteen sons and his twenty servants with him; and they went through Jordan in the presence of the king. 18 And there went over *a* a ferry boat to bring over the king's household, and to do what he thought good. And Shimei the son of Gera fell down before the king, when he *b* was come over Jordan. 19 And he said unto the king, Let not my lord impute iniquity unto me, neither do thou remember that which thy servant did perversely the day that my lord the king went out of Jerusalem, that the king should take it to his heart. 20 For thy servant doth know that I have sinned: therefore, behold, I am come this day the first of all the house of Joseph to go down to meet my lord the king. 21 But Abishai the son of Zeruiah answered and said, Shall not Shimei be put to death for this, because he cursed the LORD'S anointed? 22 And David said, What have I to do with you, ye sons of Zeruiah, that ye should this day be adversaries unto me? shall there any man be put to death this day in Israel? for do not I know that I am this day king over Israel? 23 And the king said unto Shimei, Thou shalt not die. And the king sware unto him.

(3) THE MEETING WITH MEPHIBOSHETH.

2 *Samuel* 19: 24–30.

24 And Mephibosheth the son of Saul came down to meet the king; and he had neither dressed his feet, nor trimmed his beard, nor washed his clothes, from the day the king departed until the day he came home in peace. 25 And it came to pass, *c* when he was come to Jerusalem to meet the king, that the king said unto him, Wherefore wentest not thou with me, Mephibosheth? 26 And he answered, My lord, O king, my servant deceived me: for thy servant said, I will saddle me an ass, that I may ride thereon, and go *d* with the king; because thy servant is lame. 27 And he hath slandered thy servant unto my lord the king; but my lord the king is as *e* an angel of God: do therefore what is good in thine eyes. 28 For all my father's house were but *f* dead men before my lord the king: yet didst thou set thy servant among them that did eat at thine own table. What right therefore have I yet that I should cry any more unto the king? 29 And the king said unto him, Why speakest thou any more of thy matters? I say, Thou and Ziba divide the land. 30 And Mephibosheth said unto the king, Yea, let him take all, forasmuch as my lord the king is come in peace unto his own house.

---

a Or, " the convoy."   *b* Or, " would go over."   *c* Or, " when Jerusalem was come."   *d* Another reading is, " to."
e Or, " the."   *f* Heb. " men of death."

(4) BARZILLAI'S FAREWELL.

2 Samuel 19 : 31–40a.

31 And Barzillai the Gileadite came down from Rogelim ; and he went over Jordan with the king, to conduct him over Jordan. 32 Now Barzillai was a very aged man, even fourscore years old : and he had provided the king with sustenance while he lay at Mahanaim ; for he was a very great man. 33 And the king said unto Barzillai, Come thou over with me, and I will sustain thee with me in Jerusalem. 34 And Barzillai said unto the king, How many are the days of the years of my life, that I should go up with the king unto Jerusalem ? 35 I am this day fourscore years old : can I discern between good and bad ? can thy servant taste what I eat or what I drink ? can I hear any more the voice of singing men and singing women ? wherefore then should thy servant be yet a burden unto my lord the king ? 36 Thy servant would but just go over Jordan with the king : and why should the king recompense it me with such a reward ? 37 Let thy servant, I pray thee, turn back again, that I may die in mine own city, by the grave of my father and my mother. But behold, thy servant Chimham ; let him go over with my lord the king ; and do to him what shall seem good unto thee. 38 And the king answered, Chimham shall go over with me, and I will do to him that which shall seem good unto thee : and whatsoever thou shalt *a* require of me, that will I do for thee. 39 And all the people went over Jordan, and the king went over : and the king kissed Barzillai, and blessed him ; and he returned unto his own place. 40a So the king went over to Gilgal, and Chimham went over with him.

(5) THE STRIFE BETWEEN JUDAH AND ISRAEL.

2 Samuel 19 : 40b–43.

40b And all the people of Judah brought the king over, and also half the people of Israel. 41 And, behold, all the men of Israel came to the king, and said unto the king, Why have our brethren the men of Judah stolen thee away, and brought the king, and his household, over Jordan, and all David's men with him ? 42 And all the men of Judah answered the men of Israel, Because the king is near of kin to us : wherefore then be ye angry for this matter ? have we eaten at all of the king's cost ? or hath he given us any gift ? 43 And the men of Israel answered the men of Judah, and said, We have ten parts in the king, and we have also more *right* in David than ye : why then did ye despise us, *b* that our advice should not be first had in bringing back our king ? And the words of the men of Judah were fiercer than the words of the men of Israel.

115. SHEBA'S INSURRECTION.

(1) THE OUTBREAK OF THE REVOLT.

2 Samuel 20 : 1, 2.

1 And there happened to be there a man of *c* Belial, whose name was Sheba, the son of Bichri, a Benjamite : and he blew the trumpet, and said, We have no portion in David, neither have we inheritance in the son of Jesse : every man to his tents, O Israel. 2 So all the men of Israel went up from following David, and followed Sheba the son of Bichri : but the men of Judah clave unto their king, from Jordan even to Jerusalem.

(2) DAVID RE-ENTERS JERUSALEM.

2 Samuel 20 : 3.

3 And David came to his house at Jerusalem ; and the king took the ten women his concubines, whom he had left to keep the house, and put them in ward, and provided them with sustenance, but went not in unto them. So they were shut up unto the day of their death, *d* living in widowhood.

---

a Heb. " choose *to lay* upon."   *b* Or, " and were not we the first to speak of bringing back our king ? "   *c* I. e., "worthlessness."   *d* Heb. " in widowhood of life."

(3) Joab, after murdering Amasa, pursues Sheba.

2 Samuel 20 : 4–14.

4 Then said the king to Amasa, Call me the men of Judah together within three days, and be thou here present. 5 So Amasa went to call *the men of* Judah together : but he tarried longer than the set time which he had appointed him. 6 And David said to Abishai, Now shall Sheba the son of Bichri do us more harm than did Absalom : take thou thy lord's servants, and pursue after him, lest he get him fenced cities, and escape out of our sight. 7 And there went out after him Joab's men, and the Cherethites and the Pelethites, and all the mighty men : and they went out of Jerusalem, to pursue after Sheba the son of Bichri. 8 When they were at the great stone which is in Gibeon, Amasa came to meet them. And Joab was girded with his apparel of war that he had put on, and thereon was a girdle with a sword fastened upon his loins in the sheath thereof ; and as he went forth it fell out. 9 And Joab said to Amasa, Is it well with thee, my brother? And Joab took Amasa by the beard with his right hand to kiss him. 10 But Amasa took no heed to the sword that was in Joab's hand : so he smote him therewith in the belly, and shed out his bowels to the ground, and struck him not again ; and he died. And Joab and Abishai his brother pursued after Sheba the son of Bichri. 11 And there stood by him one of Joab's young men, and said, He that favoureth Joab, and he that is for David, let him follow Joab. 12 And Amasa lay wallowing in his blood in the midst of the high way. And when the man saw that all the people stood still, he carried Amasa out of the high way into the field, and cast a garment over him, when he saw that every one that came by him stood still. 13 When he was removed out of the high way, all the people went on after Joab, to pursue after Sheba the son of Bichri. 14 And he went through all the tribes of Israel unto Abel, and to Beth-maacah, and all the Berites : and they were gathered together, and went also after him.

(4) Siege of Abel of Beth-maacah, Death of Sheba, and End of the Rebellion.

2 Samuel 20 : 15–22.

15 And they came and besieged him in Abel of Beth-maacah, and they cast up a mount against the city, and it stood against the rampart : and all the people that were with Joab *a* battered the wall, to throw it down. 16 Then cried a wise woman out of the city, Hear, hear ; say, I pray you, unto Joab, Come near hither, that I may speak with thee. 17 And he came near unto her ; and the woman said, Art thou Joab? And he answered, I am. Then she said unto him, Hear the words of thine handmaid. And he answered, I do hear. 18 Then she spake, saying, They were wont to speak in old time, saying, They shall surely ask *counsel* at Abel : and so they ended *the matter*. 19 I am of them that are peaceable and faithful in Israel : thou seekest to destroy a city and a mother in Israel : why wilt thou swallow up the inheritance of the Lord? 20 And Joab answered and said, Far be it, far be it from me, that I should swallow up or destroy. 21 The matter is not so : but a man of the hill country of Ephraim, Sheba the son of Bichri by name, hath lifted up his hand against the king, even against David · deliver him only, and I will depart from the city. And the woman said unto Joab, Behold, his head shall be thrown to thee over the wall. 22 Then the woman went unto all the people in her wisdom. And they cut off the head of Sheba the son of Bichri, and threw it out to Joab. And he blew the trumpet, and they were dispersed from the city, every man to his tent. And Joab returned to Jerusalem unto the king.

116. THE OFFICERS OF STATE AFTER THE RESTORATION.*b*

2 Samuel 20 : 23–26.

23 Now Joab was over all the host of Israel : and Benaiah the son of Jehoiada was over the *c* Cherethites and over the Pelethites : 24 And Adoram was over the *d* tribute : and Jehoshaphat the son of Ahilud was the *e* recorder : 25 and Sheva was *f* scribe : and Zadok and Abiathar were priests : 26 and Ira also the Jairite was *g* priest unto David.

---

a Or, " undermined."   *b* Cf. §§92 and 107, (2), *L.*   *c* Another reading is," Carites." Cf. 2 Kings 11 : 4. See §158, (3).   *d* Or, " levy."   *e* Or, "chronicler."   *f* Or, " secretary."   *g* Or, " a chief minister." Cf. 1 Chronicles 18 :17. See §92.

VI. The Closing Days of David's Life.

117. DAVID'S FAILING HEALTH: ABISHAG THE SHUNAMMITE.

1 *Kings* 1 : 1–4.

1 Now king David was old and stricken in years ; and they covered him with clothes, but he gat no heat.   2 Wherefore his servants said unto him, Let there be sought for my lord the king a young virgin : and let her stand before the king, and cherish him ; and let her lie in thy bosom, that my lord the king may get heat.   3 So they sought for a fair damsel throughout all the coasts of Israel, and found Abishag the Shunammite, and brought her to the king.   4 And the damsel was very fair ; and she cherished the king, and ministered to him ; but the king knew her not.

118. SOLOMON IS MADE KING "THE SECOND TIME."

(1) Adonijah attempts to seize the Kingdom.

1 *Kings* 1 : 5–10.

5 Then Adonijah the son of Haggith exalted himself, saying, I will be king : and he prepared him chariots and horsemen, and fifty men to run before him.   6 And his father had not displeased him *a* at any time in saying, Why hast thou done so ? and he was also a very goodly man ; and he was born after Absalom.   7 And he conferred with Joab the son of Zeruiah, and with Abiathar the priest : and they following Adonijah helped him.   8 But Zadok the priest, and Benaiah the son of Jehoiada, and Nathan the prophet, and Shimei, and Rei, and the mighty men which belonged to David, were not with Adonijah.   9 And Adonijah *b* slew sheep and oxen and fatlings by the stone of Zoheleth, which is beside En-rogel; and he called all his brethren the king's sons, and all the men of Judah the king's servants : 10 but Nathan the prophet, and Benaiah, and the mighty men, and Solomon his brother, he called not.

(2) Nathan and Bath-sheba's counter Coup d'état.

1 *Kings* 1 : 11–37.

11 Then Nathan spake unto Bath-sheba the mother of Solomon, saying, Hast thou not heard that Adonijah the son of Haggith doth reign, and David our lord knoweth it not ?   12 Now therefore come, let me, I pray thee, give thee counsel, that thou mayest save thine own life, and the life of thy son Solomon.   13 Go and get thee in unto king David, and say unto him, Didst not thou, my lord, O king, swear unto thine handmaid, saying, Assuredly Solomon thy son shall reign after me, and he shall sit upon my throne ? why then doth Adonijah reign ?   14 Behold, while thou yet talkest there with the king, I also will come in after thee, and confirm thy words. 15 And Bath-sheba went in unto the king into the chamber : and the king was very old ; and Abishag the Shunammite ministered unto the king.   16 And Bath-sheba bowed, and did obeisance unto the king.   And the king said, What wouldest thou ?   17 And she said unto him, My lord, thou swarest by the LORD thy God unto thine handmaid, *saying*, Assuredly Solomon thy son shall reign after me, and he shall sit upon my throne.   18 And now, behold, Adonijah reigneth ; *c* and thou, my lord the king, knowest it not : 19 and he hath *b* slain oxen and fatlings and sheep in abundance, and hath called all the sons of the king, and Abiathar the priest, and Joab the captain of the host : but Solomon thy servant hath he not called.   20 And *d* thou, my lord the king, the eyes of all Israel are upon thee, that thou shouldest tell them who shall sit on the throne of my lord the king after him.   21 Otherwise it shall come to pass, when my lord the king shall sleep with his fathers, that I and my son Solomon shall be counted *e* offenders.   22 And, lo, while she yet talked with the

---

a Or, " all his life."   *b* Or, " sacrificed."   *c* Another reading is, " and now, my lord the king, thou," etc.   *d* Another reading is, " now."   *e* Heb. " sinners."

1 *Kings* 1.

king, Nathan the prophet came in. 23 And they told the king, saying, Behold, Nathan the prophet. And when he was come in before the king, he bowed himself before the king with his face to the ground. 24 And Nathan said, My lord, O king, hast thou said, Adonijah shall reign after me, and he shall sit upon my throne? 25 For he is gone down this day, and hath *a* slain oxen and fatlings and sheep in abundance, and hath called all the king's sons, and the captains of the host, and Abiathar the priest; and, behold, they eat and drink before him, and say, God save king Adonijah. 26 But me, even me thy servant, and Zadok the priest, and Benaiah the son of Jehoiada, and thy servant Solomon, hath he not called. 27 Is this thing done by my lord the king, and thou hast not shewed unto thy *b* servants who should sit on the throne of my lord the king after him? 28 Then king David answered and said, Call me Bath-sheba. And she came into the king's presence, and stood before the king. 29 And the king sware, and said, As the LORD liveth, who hath redeemed my soul out of all adversity, 30 verily as I sware unto thee by the LORD, the God of Israel, saying, Assuredly Solomon thy son shall reign after me, and he shall sit upon my throne in my stead; verily so will I do this day. 31 Then Bath-sheba bowed with her face to the earth, and did obeisance to the king, and said, Let my lord king David live for ever. 32 And king David said, Call me Zadok the priest, and Nathan the prophet, and Benaiah the son of Jehoiada. And they came before the king. 33 And the king said unto them, Take with you the servants of your lord, and cause Solomon my son to ride upon mine own mule, and bring him down to Gihon: 34 and let Zadok the priest and Nathan the prophet anoint him there king over Israel: and blow ye with the trumpet, and say, God save king Solomon. 35 Then ye shall come up after him, and he shall come and sit upon my throne; for he shall be king in my stead: and I have appointed him to be *c* prince over Israel and over Judah. 36 And Benaiah the son of Jehoiada answered the king, and said, Amen: the LORD, the God of my lord the king, say so *too*. 37 As the LORD hath been with my lord the king, even so be he with Solomon, and make his throne greater than the throne of my lord king David.

(3) SOLOMON'S SECOND ANOINTING.

1 *Kings* 1 : 38–40.	1 *Chronicles* 29 : 22*b*.
38 So Zadok the priest, and Nathan the prophet, and Benaiah the son of Jehoiada, and the Cherethites and the Pelethites, went down, and caused Solomon to ride upon king David's mule, and brought him to Gihon. 39 And Zadok the priest took the horn of oil out of the Tent, and anointed Solomon. And they blew the trumpet; and all the people said, God save king Solomon. 40 And all the people came up after him, and the people piped with pipes, and rejoiced with great joy, so that the earth rent with the sound of them.	22*b* And they made Solomon the son of David king the second time, and anointed him unto the LORD to be *c* prince, and Zadok to be priest.

(4) ADONIJAH'S ALARM AND SUBMISSION.

1 *Kings* 1 : 41–53.

41 And Adonijah and all the guests that were with him heard it as they had made an end of eating. And when Joab heard the sound of the trumpet, he said, Wherefore is this noise of the city being in an uproar? 42 While he yet spake, behold, Jonathan the son of Abiathar the priest came: and Adonijah said, Come in; for thou art a worthy man, and bringest good tidings. 43 And Jonathan answered and said to Adonijah, Verily our lord king David hath made Solomon king: 44 and the king hath sent with him Zadok the priest, and Nathan the prophet, and Benaiah the son of Jehoiada, and the Cherethites and the Pelethites, and they have caused him to ride upon the king's mule: 45 and Zadok the priest and Nathan the prophet have anointed him king in

---

a Or, "sacrificed."   *b* Another reading is, "servant."   *c* Or, "leader."

1 *Kings* 1.

Gihon : and they are come up from thence rejoicing, so that the city rang again. This is the noise that ye have heard. 46 And also Solomon sitteth on the throne of the kingdom. 47 And moreover the king's servants came to bless our lord king David, saying, *a* Thy God make the name of Solomon better than thy name, and make his throne greater than thy throne : and the king bowed himself upon the bed.   48 And also thus said the king, Blessed be the LORD, the God of Israel, which hath given one to sit on my throne this day, mine eyes even seeing it. 49 And all the guests of Adonijah were afraid, and rose up, and went every man his way.   50 And Adonijah feared because of Solomon ; and he arose, and went, and caught hold on the horns of the altar.   51 And it was told Solomon, saying, Behold, Adonijah feareth king Solomon : for, lo, he hath laid hold on the horns of the altar, saying, Let king Solomon swear unto me *b* this day that he will not slay his servant with the sword.   52 And Solomon said, If he shall shew himself a worthy man, there shall not an hair of him fall to the earth : but if wickedness be found in him, he shall die.   53 So king Solomon sent, and they brought him down from the altar.   And he came and did obeisance to king Solomon : and Solomon said unto him, Go to thine house.

119. DAVID'S LAST PROPHETIC WORDS.

2 *Samuel* 23 : 1-7.

1 Now these be the last words of David.
>   David the son of Jesse saith,
>   And the man who was raised on high saith,
>   The anointed of the God of Jacob,
>   And *c* the sweet psalmist of Israel :
2   The spirit of the LORD spake *d* by me,
>   And his word was upon my tongue.
3   The God of Israel said,
>   The Rock of Israel spake to me :
>   *c* One that ruleth over men *f* righteously,
>   That ruleth in the fear of God,
4   *He shall be* as the light of the morning, when the sun riseth,
>   A morning without clouds ;
>   *When* the tender grass *springeth* out of the earth,
>   Through clear shining after rain.
5   *g* Verily my house is not so with God ;
>   Yet he hath made with me an everlasting covenant,
>   Ordered in all things, and sure :
>   For it is all my salvation, and all *my* desire,
>   Although he maketh it not to grow.
6   But *h* the ungodly shall be all of them as thorns to be thrust away,
>   For they cannot be taken with the hand :
7   But the man that toucheth them
>   Must be *i* armed with iron and the staff of a spear
>   And they shall be utterly burned with fire in *their* place.

120. DAVID'S LAST WORDS TO SOLOMON.

1 *Kings* 2 : 1-9.

1 Now the days of David drew nigh that he should die ; and he charged Solomon his son, saying, 2 I go the way of all the earth : be thou strong therefore, and shew thyself a man ; 3 and keep

---

a Another reading omits " Thy."   *b* Or, " first of all."   *c* Heb. " pleasant in the psalms of Israel."   *d* Or, " in."
e Or, " *There shall be* one . . . and *it shall be* as," etc.   *f* Heb. " a righteous one."   *g* Or, " For is not my house so with God ? for he . . . for all my salvation, and all *my* desire, will he not make it to grow ? "   *h* Heb. " Belial," i. e., " worthlessness."   *i* Heb. " filled."

1 *Kings* 2.

the charge of the LORD thy God, to walk in his ways, to keep his statutes, *and* his commandments, and his judgements, and his testimonies, according to that which is written in the law of Moses, that thou mayest *a* prosper in all that thou doest, and whithersoever thou turnest thyself : 4 that the LORD may establish his word which he spake concerning me, saying, If thy children take heed to their way, to walk before me in truth with all their heart and with all their soul, there shall not fail thee (said he) a man on the throne of Israel. 5 Moreover thou knowest also what Joab the son of Zeruiah did unto me, even what he did to the two captains of the hosts of Israel, unto Abner the son of Ner, and unto Amasa the son of Jether, whom he slew, and *b* shed the blood of war in peace, and put the blood of war upon his girdle that was about his loins, and in his shoes that were on his feet. 6 Do therefore according to thy wisdom, and let not his hoar head go down to *c* the grave in peace. 7 But shew kindness unto the sons of Barzillai the Gileadite, and let them be of those that eat at thy table : for so they came to me when I fled from Absalom thy brother. 8 And, behold, there is with thee Shimei the son of Gera, the Benjamite, of Bahurim, who cursed me with a grievous curse in the day when I went to Mahanaim : but he came down to meet me at Jordan, and I sware to him by the LORD, saying, I will not put thee to death with the sword. 9 Now therefore hold him not guiltless, for thou art a wise man ; and thou wilt know what thou oughtest to do unto him, and thou shalt bring his hoar head down to *c* the grave with blood.

121. THE DEATH OF DAVID.

2 *Samuel* 5 : 4, 5.	1 *Kings* 2 : 11, 10.	1 *Chronicles* 3 : 4b.	1 *Chronicles* 29 : 26–30.
4 David was thirty years old when he began to reign, and he reigned forty years. 5 In Hebron he reigned over Judah seven years and six months : and in Jerusalem he reigned thirty and three years over all Israel and Judah.	11 And the days that David reigned over Israel were forty years : seven years reigned he in Hebron, and thirty and three years reigned he in Jerusalem. 10 And David slept with his fathers, and was buried in the city of David.	4b And there [i. e., in Hebron] he reigned seven years and six months : and in Jerusalem he reigned thirty and three years.	26 Now David the son of Jesse reigned over all Israel. 27 And the time that he reigned over Israel was forty years ; seven years reigned he in Hebron, and thirty and three *years* reigned he in Jerusalem. 28 And he died in a good old age, full of days, riches, and honour : and Solomon his son reigned in his stead. 29 Now the acts of David the king, first and last, behold, they are written in the *d* history of Samuel the seer, and in the *d* history of Nathan the prophet, and in the *d* history of Gad the seer ; 30 with all his reign and his might, and the times that went over him, and over Israel, and over all the kingdoms of the countries.

a Or, " do wisely."   *b* Heb. " set."   *c* Heb. " Sheol."   *d* Heb. " words."

BOOK FOURTH.
The Reign of Solomon.

PART I.
THE BEGINNING OF SOLOMON'S REIGN.

122. SOLOMON'S ACCESSION TO THE THRONE.[a]

1 *Kings* 2 : 12.	1 *Chronicles* 29 : 23-25.	2 *Chronicles* 1 : 1.
12 And Solomon sat upon the throne of David his father; and his kingdom was established greatly.	23 Then Solomon sat on the throne of the LORD as king instead of David his father, and prospered; and all Israel obeyed him. 24 And all the princes, and the mighty men, and all the sons likewise of king David,[b] submitted themselves unto Solomon the king. 25 And the LORD magnified Solomon exceedingly in the sight of all Israel, and bestowed upon him such royal majesty as had not been on any king before him in Israel.	1 And Solomon the son of David was strengthened in his kingdom, and the LORD his God was with him, and magnified him exceedingly.

123. SOLOMON'S REMOVAL OF HIS ADVERSARIES.
(1) Adonijah, asking Abishag to Wife, is put to Death.
1 *Kings* 2 : 13-25.

13 Then Adonijah the son of Haggith came to Bath-sheba the mother of Solomon. And she said, Comest thou peaceably? And he said, Peaceably. 14 He said moreover, I have somewhat to say unto thee. And she said, Say on. 15 And he said, Thou knowest that the kingdom was mine, and that all Israel set their faces on me, that I should reign: howbeit the kingdom is turned about, and is become my brother's: for it was his from the LORD. 16 And now I ask one petition of thee, [c] deny me not. And she said unto him, Say on. 17 And he said, Speak, I pray thee, unto Solomon the king, (for he will not say thee nay,) that he give me Abishag the Shunammite to wife. 18 And Bath-sheba said, Well; I will speak for thee unto the king. 19 Bath-sheba therefore went unto king Solomon, to speak unto him for Adonijah. And the king rose up to meet her, and bowed himself unto her, and sat down on his throne, and caused a throne to be set for the king's mother; and she sat on his right hand. 20 Then she said, I ask one small petition of thee; deny me not. And the king said unto her, Ask on, my mother: for I will not deny thee. 21 And she said, Let Abishag the Shunammite be given to Adonijah thy brother to wife. 22 And king

---

a Cf. §§107, (4), *A*, and 118.   *b* Heb. "gave the hand under Solomon."   *c* Heb. "turn not away my face."

1 *Kings* 2.

Solomon answered and said unto his mother, And why dost thou ask Abishag the Shunammite for Adonijah? ask for him the kingdom also; for he is mine elder brother; even for him, and for Abiathar the priest, and for Joab the son of Zeruiah.   23 Then king Solomon sware by the LORD, saying, God do so to me, and more also, if Adonijah have not spoken this word against his own life.   24 Now therefore as the LORD liveth, who hath established me, and set me on the throne of David my father, and who hath made me an house, as he promised, surely Adonijah shall be put to death this day.   25 And king Solomon sent by the hand of Benaiah the son of Jehoiada; and he fell upon him, that he died.

(2) ABIATHAR IS DEGRADED FROM THE PRIESTHOOD.

1 *Kings* 2 : 26, 27.

26 And unto Abiathar the priest said the king, Get thee to Anathoth, unto thine own fields; for thou *a* art worthy of death: but I will not at this time put thee to death, because thou barest the ark of the Lord GOD before David my father, and because thou wast afflicted in all wherein my father was afflicted.   27 So Solomon thrust out Abiathar from being priest unto the LORD; that he might fulfil *b* the word of the LORD, which he spake concerning the house of Eli in Shiloh.

(3) JOAB'S FLIGHT AND DEATH.

1 *Kings* 2 : 28–34.

28 And the tidings came to Joab: for Joab had turned after Adonijah, though he turned not after Absalom.   And Joab fled unto the Tent of the LORD, and caught hold on the horns of the altar.   29 And it was told king Solomon, Joab is fled unto the Tent of the LORD, and, behold, he is by the altar.   Then Solomon sent Benaiah the son of Jehoiada, saying, Go, fall upon him.   30 And Benaiah came to the Tent of the LORD, and said unto him, Thus saith the king, Come forth.   And he said, Nay; but I will die here.   And Benaiah brought the king word again, saying, Thus said Joab, and thus he answered me.   31 And the king said unto him, Do as he hath said, and fall upon him, and bury him; that thou mayest take away the blood, which Joab shed without cause, from me and from my father's house.   32 And the LORD shall return his blood upon his own head, because he fell upon two men more righteous and better than he, and slew them with the sword, and my father David knew it not, *to wit*, Abner the son of Ner, captain of the host of Israel, and Amasa the son of Jether, captain of the host of Judah.   33 So shall their blood return upon the head of Joab, and upon the head of his seed for ever: but unto David, and unto his seed, and unto his house, and unto his throne, shall there be peace for ever from the LORD.   34 Then Benaiah the son of Jehoiada went up, and fell upon him, and slew him; and he was buried in his own house in the wilderness.

(4) THE ELEVATION OF BENAIAH AND ZADOK.*c*

1 *Kings* 2 : 35.

35 And the king put Benaiah the son of Jehoiada in his room over the host: and Zadok the priest did the king put in the room of Abiathar.

(5) SHIMEI MEETS WITH HIS DESERTS.

1 *Kings* 2 : 36–46.

36 And the king sent and called for Shimei, and said unto him, Build thee an house in Jerusalem, and dwell there, and go not forth thence any whither.   37 For on the day thou goest out, and passest over the brook Kidron, know thou for certain that thou shalt surely die: thy blood shall be upon thine own head.   38 And Shimei said unto the king, The saying is good: as my lord the king hath said, so will thy servant do.   And Shimei dwelt in Jerusalem many days.   39 And it

---

a Heb. "a man of."   *b* Cf. 1 Samuel 2 : 27–36.   See §21, (4).   *c* Cf. §118, (3).

12

1 *Kings* 2.

came to pass at the end of three years, that two of the servants of Shimei ran away unto Achish, son of Maacah, king of Gath. And they told Shimei, saying, Behold, thy servants be in Gath. 40 And Shimei arose, and saddled his ass, and went to Gath to Achish, to seek his servants : and Shimei went, and brought his servants from Gath. 41 And it was told Solomon that Shimei had gone from Jerusalem to Gath, and was come again. 42 And the king sent and called for Shimei, and said unto him, Did I not make thee to swear by the LORD, and protested unto thee, saying, Know for certain, that on the day thou goest out, and walkest abroad any whither, thou shalt surely die ? and thou saidst unto me, The saying that I have heard is good. 43 Why then hast thou not kept the oath of the LORD, and the commandment that I have charged thee with ? 44 The king said moreover to Shimei, Thou knowest all the wickedness which thine heart is privy to, that thou didst to David my father : therefore the LORD shall return thy wickedness upon thine own head. 45 But king Solomon shall be blessed, and the throne of David shall be established before the LORD for ever. 46 So the king commanded Benaiah the son of Jehoiada ; and he went out, and fell upon him, that he died. And the kingdom was established in the hand of Solomon.

124. SOLOMON MARRIES PHARAOH'S DAUGHTER.

1 *Kings* 3: 1.

1 And Solomon made affinity with Pharaoh king of Egypt, and took Pharaoh's daughter, and brought her into the city of David, until he had made an end of building his own house, and the house of the LORD, and the wall of Jerusalem round about.

125. SPIRITUAL CONDITION OF SOLOMON AND HIS KINGDOM.

1 *Kings* 3 : 2, 3.

2 Only the people sacrificed in the high places, because there was no house built for the name of the LORD until those days. 3 And Solomon loved the LORD, walking in the statutes of David his father : only he sacrificed and burnt incense in the high places.

126. SOLOMON'S SACRIFICE AT GIBEON.

1 *Kings* 3: 4.

4 And the king went to Gibeon to sacrifice there ; for that was the great high place : a thousand burnt offerings did Solomon offer upon that altar.

2 *Chronicles* 1 : 2–6.

2 And Solomon spake unto all Israel, to the captains of thousands and of hundreds, and to the judges, and to every prince in all Israel, the heads of the fathers' *houses*. 3 So Solomon, and all the congregation with him, went to the high place that was at Gibeon ; for there was the tent of meeting of God, which Moses the servant of the LORD had made in the wilderness. 4 But the ark of God had David brought up from Kiriath-jearim to *the place* that David had prepared for it : for he had pitched a tent for it at Jerusalem. 5 Moreover the brasen altar, that Bezalel the son of Uri, the son of Hur, had made, *a* was there before the tabernacle of the LORD : and Solomon and the congregation sought unto it. 6 And Solomon *b* went up thither to the brasen altar before the LORD, which was at the tent of meeting, and offered a thousand burnt offerings upon it.

---

a Or, as otherwise read, " he had put."   *b* Or, " offered there, upon . . . yea, he offered."

127. SOLOMON'S DREAM AND PRAYER FOR WISDOM.

1 *Kings* 3 : 5-15.

5 In Gibeon the LORD appeared to Solomon in a dream by night: and God said, Ask what I shall give thee. 6 And Solomon said, Thou hast shewed unto thy servant David my father great kindness, according as he walked before thee in truth, and in righteousness, and in uprightness of heart with thee; and thou hast kept for him this great kindness, that thou hast given him a son to sit on his throne, as it is this day. 7 And now, O LORD my God, thou hast made thy servant king instead of David my father: and I am but a little child; I know not how to go out or come in. 8 And thy servant is in the midst of thy people which thou hast chosen, a great people, that cannot be numbered nor counted for multitude. 9 Give thy servant therefore an *a* understanding heart to judge thy people, that I may discern between good and evil; for who is able to judge this thy *b* great people? 10 And the speech pleased the Lord, that Solomon had asked this thing. 11 And God said unto him, Because thou hast asked this thing, and hast not asked for thyself *c* long life; neither hast asked riches for thyself, nor hast asked the life of thine enemies; but hast asked for thyself understanding to *d* discern judgement; 12 behold, I have done according to thy word: lo, I have given thee a wise and an *a* understanding heart; so that there hath been none like thee before thee, neither after thee shall any arise like unto thee. 13 And I have also given thee that which thou hast not asked, both riches and honour, so that there *e* shall not be any among the kings like unto thee, all thy days. 14 And if thou wilt walk in my ways, to keep my statutes and my commandments, as thy father David did walk, then I will lengthen thy days. 15 And Solomon awoke, and, behold, it was a dream: and he came to Jerusalem, and stood before the ark of the covenant of the LORD, and offered up burnt offerings, and offered peace offerings, and made a feast to all his servants.

2 *Chronicles* 1 : 7-13.

7 In that night did God appear unto Solomon, and said unto him, Ask what I shall give thee. 8 And Solomon said unto God, Thou hast shewed great kindness unto David my father, and hast made me king in his stead. 9 Now, O LORD God, let thy promise unto David my father be established: for thou hast made me king over a people like the dust of the earth in multitude. 10 Give me now wisdom and knowledge, that I may go out and come in before this people: for who can judge this thy people, that is so great? 11 And God said to Solomon, Because this was in thine heart, and thou hast not asked riches, wealth, or honour, nor the life of them that hate thee, neither yet hast asked long life; but hast asked wisdom and knowledge for thyself, that thou mayest judge my people, over whom I have made thee king: 12 wisdom and knowledge is granted unto thee; and I will give thee riches, and wealth, and honour, such as none of the kings have had that have been before thee, neither shall there any after thee have the like. 13 So Solomon *f* came *from his journey* to the high place that was at Gibeon, from before the tent of meeting, unto Jerusalem; and he reigned over Israel.

---

a Heb. "hearing."　　*b* Heb. "heavy."　　*c* Heb. "many days."　　*d* Heb. "hear."　　*e* Or, "hath not been."　　*f* The Sept. and Vulgate have, "came from the high place."

128. GOD'S GIFT OF WISDOM MANIFEST BY SOLOMON'S JUDGMENT ON THE HARLOTS.

1 *Kings* 3 : 16–28.

16 Then came there two women, that were harlots, unto the king, and stood before him. 17 And the one woman said, Oh my lord, I and this woman dwell in one house; and I was delivered of a child with her in the house. 18 And it came to pass the third day after I was delivered, that this woman was delivered also ; and we were together ; there was no stranger with us in the house, save we two in the house. 19 And this woman's child died in the night ; because she overlaid it. 20 And she arose at midnight, and took my son from beside me, while thine handmaid slept, and laid it in her bosom, and laid her dead child in my bosom. 21 And when I rose in the morning to give my child suck, behold, it was dead : but when I had considered it in the morning, behold, it was not my son, which I did bear. 22 And the other woman said, Nay ; but the living is my son, and the dead is thy son. And this said, No ; but the dead is thy son, and the living is my son. Thus they spake before the king. 23 Then said the king, The one saith, This is my son that liveth, and thy son is the dead : and the other saith, Nay ; but thy son is the dead, and my son is the living. 24 And the king said, Fetch me a sword. And they brought a sword before the king. 25 And the king said, Divide the living child in two, and give half to the one, and half to the other. 26 Then spake the woman whose the living child was unto the king, for her bowels yearned upon her son, and she said, Oh my lord, give her the living child, and in no wise slay it. But the other said, It shall be neither mine nor thine ; divide it. 27 Then the king answered and said, Give her the living child, and in no wise slay it : she is the mother thereof. 28 And all Israel heard of the judgement which the king had judged ; and they feared the king : for they saw that the wisdom of God was in him, to do judgement.

PART II.

SOLOMON IN ALL HIS GLORY.

129. PREPARATIONS FOR THE BUILDING OF THE TEMPLE.[a]

(1) THE LEAGUE WITH HIRAM, KING OF TYRE.

1 *Kings* 5 : 1–12 ; 7 : 13, 14.	2 *Chronicles* 2 : 1, 3–16.
1 [b] And Hiram king of Tyre sent his servants unto Solomon ; for he had heard that they had anointed him king in the room of his father : for Hiram was ever a lover of David. 2 And Solomon sent to Hiram, saying, 3 Thou knowest how that David my father could not build an house for the name of the LORD his God for the wars which were about him on every side, until the LORD put them under the soles of his feet. 4 But now the LORD my God hath given me rest on every side ; there is neither adversary, nor evil occurrent. 5 And, behold, I purpose to build an house for the name of the LORD my God, as the LORD spake unto David my father, saying,	1 [c] Now Solomon purposed to build an house for the name of the LORD, and an house for his kingdom. 3 [d] And Solomon sent to Huram the king of Tyre, saying, As thou didst deal with David my father, and didst send him cedars to build him an house to dwell therein, *even so deal with me.* 4 Behold, I build an house for the name of the LORD my God, to dedicate it to him, and to burn before him incense of sweet spices, and for the continual shewbread, and for the burnt offerings morning and evening, on the sabbaths, and on the new moons, and on the set feasts of the LORD our God. This is *an ordinance* for ever to Israel. 5 And the house

a Cf. §106.　　*b* Ch. 5 : 15 in Heb.　　*c* Ch. 1 : 18 in Heb.　　*d* Ch. 2 : 2 in Heb.

1 *Kings* 5.

Thy son, whom I will set upon thy throne in thy room, he shall build the house for my name. 6 Now therefore command thou that they hew me cedar trees out of Lebanon; and my servants shall be with thy servants; and I will give thee hire for thy servants according to all that thou shalt say: for thou knowest that there is not among us any that can skill to hew timber like unto the Zidonians. 7 And it came to pass, when Hiram heard the words of Solomon, that he rejoiced greatly, and said, Blessed be the LORD this day, which hath given unto David a wise son over this great people. 8 And Hiram sent to Solomon, saying, I have heard *the message* which thou hast sent unto me: I will do all thy desire concerning timber of cedar, and concerning timber of *a* fir. 9 My servants shall bring them down from Lebanon unto the sea: and I will make them into rafts to go by sea unto the place that thou shalt appoint me, and will cause them to be broken up there, and thou shalt *b* receive them: and thou shalt accomplish my desire, in giving food for my household. 10 So *c* Hiram gave Solomon timber of cedar and timber of fir according to all his desire. 11 And Solomon gave Hiram twenty thousand *d* measures of wheat for food to his household, and twenty measures of *e* pure oil; thus gave Solomon to Hiram year by year. 12 And the LORD gave Solomon wisdom, as he promised him; and there was peace between Hiram and Solomon; and they two made a league together. 13 And king Solomon sent and fetched Hiram out of Tyre. 14 He was the son of a widow woman of the tribe of Naphtali, and his father was a man of Tyre, a worker in brass; and he was filled with wisdom and understanding and cunning, to work all works in brass. And he came to king Solomon, and wrought all his work.

2 *Chronicles* 2.

which I build is great: for great is our God above all gods. 6 But who *f* is able to build him an house, seeing the heaven and the heaven of heavens cannot contain him? who am I then, that I should build him an house, save only to burn incense before him? 7 Now therefore send me a man cunning to work in gold, and in silver, and in brass, and in iron, and in purple, and crimson, and blue, and that can skill to grave *all manner of* gravings, *to be* with the cunning men that are with me in Judah and in Jerusalem, whom David my father did provide. 8 Send me also cedar trees, *a* fir trees, and *g* algum trees, out of Lebanon: for I know that thy servants can skill to cut timber in Lebanon; and, behold, my servants shall be with thy servants, 9 even to prepare me timber in abundance: for the house which I am about to build shall be wonderful great. 10 And, behold, I will give to thy servants, the hewers that cut timber, twenty thousand *h* measures of beaten wheat, and twenty thousand *h* measures of barley, and twenty thousand baths of wine, and twenty thousand baths of oil. 11 Then Huram the king of Tyre answered in writing, which he sent to Solomon, Because the LORD loveth his people, he hath made thee king over them. 12 Huram said moreover, Blessed be the LORD, the God of Israel, that made heaven and earth, who hath given to David the king a wise son, endued with discretion and understanding, that should build an house for the LORD, and an house for his kingdom. 13 And now I have sent a cunning man, endued with understanding, *i* of Huram my father's, 14 the son of a woman of the daughters of Dan, and his father was a man of Tyre, skilful to work in gold, and in silver, in brass, in iron, in stone, and in timber, in purple, in blue, and in fine linen, and in crimson; also to grave any manner of graving, and to devise any device: that there may be *a place* appointed unto him with thy cunning men, and with the cunning men of my lord David thy father. 15 Now therefore the wheat and the barley, the oil and the wine, which my lord hath spoken of, let him send unto his servants: 16 and we will cut wood out of Lebanon, as much as thou shalt need: and we will bring it to thee in floats by sea to *k* Joppa; and thou shalt carry it up to Jerusalem.

---

a Or, " cypress."   *b* Or, " carry them away."   *c* Heb. " Hirom."   *d* Heb. " cor."   *e* Or, " beaten."   *f* Heb. " retaineth strength."   *g* In 1 Kings 10: 11, " almug trees." See §134, (9).   *h* Heb. " cors."   *i* Or, " even Huram, my father." Cf. 2 Chronicles 4: 16. See §132, (8).   *k* Heb. " Japho."

(2) Solomon's Levy of Laborers.[a]

1 *Kings* 5 : 13-18.	2 *Chronicles* 2 : 2.	2 *Chronicles* 2 : 17, 18.
13 And king Solomon raised a levy out of all Israel; and the levy was thirty thousand men. 14 And he sent them to Lebanon, ten thousand a month by courses: a month they were in Lebanon, and two months at home: and Adoniram was over the levy. 15 And Solomon had threescore and ten thousand that bare burdens, and fourscore thousand that were hewers in the mountains; 16 besides Solomon's chief officers that were over the work, three thousand and three hundred, which bare rule over the people that wrought in the work. 17 And the king commanded, and they [b] hewed out great stones, costly stones, to lay the foundation of the house with wrought stone. 18 And Solomon's builders and [c] Hiram's builders and the Gebalites did fashion them, and prepared the timber and the stones to build the house.	2 And Solomon told out threescore and ten thousand men to bear burdens, and fourscore thousand men that were hewers in the mountains, and three thousand and six hundred to oversee them.	17 And Solomon numbered all the strangers that were in the land of Israel, after the numbering wherewith David his father had numbered them; and they were found an hundred and fifty thousand and three thousand and six hundred. 18 And he set threescore and ten thousand of them to bear burdens, and fourscore thousand that were hewers in the mountains, and three thousand and six hundred overseers to set the people awork.

130. THE BUILDING OF THE TEMPLE.

(1) Commencement of the Temple.

1 *Kings* 6 : 1.	2 *Chronicles* 3 : 1, 2.
1 And it came to pass in the four hundred and eightieth year after the children of Israel were come out of the land of Egypt, in the fourth year of Solomon's reign over Israel, in the month Ziv, which is the second month, that he [d] began to build the house of the LORD.	1 Then Solomon began to build the house of the LORD at Jerusalem in mount Moriah, where *the LORD* appeared unto David his father, [e] which he made ready [f] in the place that David had appointed, in the threshing-floor of [g] Ornan the Jebusite. 2 And he began to build in the second *day* of the second month, in the fourth year of his reign.

(2) God's Promise to Solomon.

1 *Kings* 6 : 11-13.

11 And the word of the LORD came to Solomon, saying, 12 Concerning this house which thou art in building, if thou wilt walk in my statutes, and execute my judgements, and keep all my commandments to walk in them; then will I establish my word with thee, which I spake unto David thy father. 13 And I will dwell among the children of Israel, and will not forsake my people Israel.

---

a Cf. §134, (5). *b* Or, "brought away." *c* Heb. "Hirom's." *d* Heb. "built." *e* The Sept .and Vulgate have,"in the place which David had prepared, in the threshing-floor," etc. *f* Heb. " in the place of David." *g* In 2 Samuel 24 : 16, 18, etc., "Araunah." See §105, (3) and (4).

(3) DIMENSIONS OF THE TEMPLE.

1 *Kings* 6 : 2.

2 And the house which king Solomon built for the LORD, the length thereof was threescore cubits, and the breadth thereof twenty *cubits*, and the height thereof thirty cubits.

2 *Chronicles* 3 : 3.

3 Now *a* these are the foundations which Solomon laid for the building of the house of God. The length by cubits after the first measure was threescore cubits, and the breadth twenty cubits.

(4) MATERIALS OF THE TEMPLE.

1 *Kings* 6 : 7, 9*b*, 22*a*.

7 And the house, when it was in building, was built of stone made ready *b* at the quarry: and there was neither hammer nor axe nor any tool of iron heard in the house, while it was in building 9*b* And he covered the house with beams and *c* planks of cedar. 22*a* And the whole house he overlaid with gold, until all the house was finished.

2 *Chronicles* 3 : 5–7*a*.

5 And the greater house he cieled with *d* fir tree, which he overlaid with fine gold, and wrought thereon palm trees and chains. 6 And he garnished the house with precious stones for beauty: and the gold was gold of Parvaim. 7*a* He overlaid also the house, the beams, the thresholds, and the walls thereof, and the doors thereof, with gold.

(5) THE PORCH.

1 *Kings* 6 : 3.

3 And the porch before *e* the temple of the house, twenty cubits was the length thereof, according to the breadth of the house ; *and* ten cubits was the breadth thereof before the house.

2 *Chronicles* 3 : 4.

4 And the porch that was before *the house*, the length of it, according to the breadth of the house, was twenty cubits, and the height an hundred and twenty : and he overlaid it within with pure gold.

(6) THE WINDOWS.

1 *Kings* 6 : 4.

4 And for the house he made *f* windows of fixed lattice-work.

(7) THE STORIES.

1 *Kings* 6 : 5, 6, 8, 10.

5 And against the wall of the house he built stories round about, against the walls of the house round about, both of the temple and of *g* the oracle : and he made side-chambers round about : 6 the nethermost story was five cubits broad, and the middle was six cubits broad, and the third was seven cubits broad : for on the outside he made rebatements *in the wall* of the house round about, that *the beams* should not have hold in the walls of the house. 8 The door for the *h* middle side-chambers was in the right *i* side of the house : and they went up by winding stairs into the middle *chambers*, and out of the middle into the third. 10 And he built the stories against all the house, each five cubits high : and *k* they rested on the house with timber of cedar.

2 *Chronicles* 3 : 9*b*.

9*b* And he overlaid the upper chambers with gold.

---

a Or, " these are the things wherein Solomon was instructed for," etc. *b* Or, " when it was brought away." *c* Heb. " rows." *d* Or, " cypress." *e* I. e., the holy place. *f* Or, " windows broad *within, and* narrow *without*." *g* I. e., " the most holy place." *h* The Sept. and Targum have, " lowest." *i* Heb. " shoulder." *k* Or, " he fastened the house."

(8) The Most Holy Place.

1 *Kings* 6 : 16–21, 22*b*.

16 And he built twenty cubits on the hinder part of the house with boards of cedar from the floor unto the *a* walls : he even built *them* for it within, for an oracle, even for the most holy place. 17 And the house, that is, the temple before *the oracle*, was forty cubits *long*. 18 And there was cedar on the house within, carved with *b* knops and open flowers : all was cedar ; there was no stone seen. 19 And he prepared an oracle in the midst of the house within, to set there the ark of the covenant of the LORD. 20 And within the oracle was *a space of* twenty cubits in length, and twenty cubits in breadth, and twenty cubits in the height thereof ; and he overlaid it with pure gold : *c* and he covered the altar with cedar. 21 So Solomon overlaid the house within with pure gold : and he drew chains of gold across before the oracle ; and he overlaid it with gold. 22*b* Also the whole altar that belonged to the oracle he overlaid with gold.

2 *Chronicles* 3 : 8, 9*a*.

8 And he made the most holy house ; the length thereof, according to the breadth of the house, was twenty cubits, and the breadth thereof twenty cubits : and he overlaid it with fine gold, amounting to six hundred talents. 9*a* And the weight of the nails was fifty shekels of gold.

(9) The Cherubim.

1 *Kings* 6 : 23–28.

23 And in the oracle he made two cherubim of olive wood, each ten cubits high. 24 And five cubits was the one wing of the cherub, and five cubits the other wing of the cherub : from the uttermost part of the one wing unto the uttermost part of the other were ten cubits. 25 And the other cherub was ten cubits : both the cherubim were of one measure and one form. 26 The height of the one cherub was ten cubits, and so was it of the other cherub. 27 And he set the cherubim within the inner house : and the wings of the cherubim were stretched forth, so that the wing of the one touched the one wall, and the wing of the other cherub touched the other wall ; and their wings touched one another in the midst of the house. 28 And he overlaid the cherubim with gold.

2 *Chronicles* 3 : 10–13.

10 And in the most holy house he made two cherubim of image work ; and they overlaid them with gold. 11 And the wings of the cherubim were twenty cubits long : the wing of the one *cherub* was five cubits, reaching to the wall of the house ; and the other wing was *likewise* five cubits, reaching to the wing of the other cherub. 12 And the wing of the other cherub was five cubits, reaching to the wall of the house : and the other wing was five cubits *also*, joining to the wing of the other cherub. 13 The wings of these cherubim spread themselves forth twenty cubits : and they stood on their feet, and their faces were *d* toward the house.

(10) The Veil.

2 *Chronicles* 3 : 14.

14 And he made the veil of blue, and purple, and crimson, and fine linen, and wrought cherubim thereon.

---

a The Sept. has, "beams."   *b* Or, "gourds."   *c* Or, " he overlaid the altar also, *which was of* cedar."   *d* Or, "inward."

(11) THE WALLS.

1 *Kings* 6 : 15a, 29.

15a And he built the walls of the house within with boards of cedar; *a* from the floor of the house unto the walls of the cieling, he covered them on the inside with wood. 29 And he carved all the walls of the house round about with carved figures of cherubim and palm trees and open flowers, within and without.

2 *Chronicles* 3 : 7b.

7b And [he] graved cherubim on the walls.

(12) THE FLOOR.

1 *Kings* 6 : 15b, 30.

15b And he covered the floor of the house with boards of *b* fir. 30 And the floor of the house he overlaid with gold, within and without.

(13) THE DOORS.

1 *Kings* 6 : 31–35.

31 And for the entering of the oracle he made doors of olive wood : the *c* lintel *and* door posts were a fifth part *of the wall.* 32 So *he made* two doors of olive wood ; and he carved upon them carvings of cherubim and palm trees and open flowers, and overlaid them with gold ; and he spread the gold upon the cherubim, and upon the palm trees. 33 So also made he for the entering of the temple door posts of olive wood, out of a fourth part *of the wall ;* 34 and two doors of *b* fir wood ; the two leaves of the one door were folding, and the two leaves of the other door were folding. 35 And he carved *thereon* cherubim and palm trees and open flowers : and he overlaid them with gold fitted upon the graven work.

(14) COMPLETION OF THE TEMPLE.

1 *Kings* 6 : 9a.

9a So he built the house, and finished it.

1 *Kings* 6 : 14.

14 So Solomon built the house, and finished it.

1 *Kings* 6 : 37, 38.

37 In the fourth year was the foundation of the house of the LORD laid, in the month Ziv. 38 And in the eleventh year, in the month Bul, which is the eighth month, was the house finished *d* throughout all the parts thereof, and according to all the fashion of it. So was he seven years in building it.

131. THE BUILDING OF THE ROYAL PALACE.*e*

(1) THE THIRTEEN YEARS IN BUILDING.

1 *Kings* 7 : 1.

1 And Solomon was building his own house thirteen years, and he finished all his house.

(2) THE HOUSE OF THE FOREST OF LEBANON.

1 *Kings* 7 : 2–5.

2 For he built the house of the forest of Lebanon ; the length thereof was an hundred cubits, and the breadth thereof fifty cubits, and the height thereof thirty cubits, upon four rows of

---

a Or, "both the floor of the house and the walls," etc. *b* Or, "cypress." *c* Or, "posts." *d* Or, "with all the appurtenances thereof, and with all the ordinances thereof." *e* In our judgment there are not sufficient reasons for putting this section out of the Bible order. Doubtless, some of these thirteen years were synchronous with the seven years of the building of the temple. Doubtless, too, the temple may have been dedicated ere these thirteen years were past ; but cf. 1 Kings 9 : 1. See §133, (7).

1 *Kings* 7.

cedar pillars, with cedar beams upon the pillars.   3 And it was covered with cedar above over the forty and five *a* beams, that were upon the pillars; fifteen in a row.   4 And there were *b* prospects in three rows, and light was over against light in three ranks.   5 And all the doors and posts *c* were square in prospect : and light was over against light in three ranks.

(3) The Porch of Pillars.

1 *Kings* 7 : 6.

6 And he made the porch of pillars; the length thereof was fifty cubits, and the breadth thereof thirty cubits ; and a porch before them ; and pillars and *d* thick beams before them.

(4) The Porch of the Throne.

1 *Kings* 7 : 7.

7 And he made the porch of the throne where he might judge, even the porch of judgement : and it was covered with cedar from floor to floor.

(5) The King's own Dwelling House.

1 *Kings* 7 : 8*a*.

8*a* And his house where he might dwell, the other court within the porch, was of the like work.

(6) The House of Pharaoh's Daughter.

1 *Kings* 7 : 8*b*.

8*b* He made also an house for Pharaoh's daughter, (whom Solomon had taken to wife,) like unto this porch.

(7) Material of the Buildings.

1 *Kings* 7 : 9–11.

9 All these were of costly stones, even of hewn stone, *e* according to measure, sawed with saws, within and without, even from the foundation unto the coping, and so on the outside unto the great court.   10 And the foundation was of costly stones, even great stones, stones of ten cubits, and stones of eight cubits.   11 And above were costly stones, even hewn stone, according to measure, and cedar wood.

(8) The Great Court.

1 *Kings* 7 : 12.

12 And the great court round about had three rows of hewn stone, and a row of cedar beams ; *f* like as the inner court of the house of the LORD, and the porch of the house.

132. THE MAKING OF THE VESSELS, ETC., PERTAINING TO THE TEMPLE.*g*

(1) Hiram, the Artisan of Tyre.

[1 *Kings* 7 : 13, 14.]

13 And king Solomon sent and fetched Hiram out of Tyre.   14 He was the son of a widow woman of the tribe of Naphtali, and his father was a man of Tyre, a worker in brass ; and he was filled with wisdom and understanding and cunning, to work all works in brass.   And he came to king Solomon, and wrought all his work.

---

a Or, "side-chambers." Heb. "ribs."   *b* Or, "beams."   *c* Or, "were made square with beams."   *d* Or, "a threshold."   *e* Or, "after *divers* measures."   *f* Or, "both for . . . and for."   *g* Without doubt, synchronous with the building of the temple ; for cf. §129, (1), latter part.

(2) The two Pillars.

1 *Kings* 7 : 15-22.

15 For he fashioned the two pillars of brass, [a] of eighteen cubits high apiece : and a line of twelve cubits compassed [b] either of them about. 16 And he made two chapiters of molten brass, to set upon the tops of the pillars : the height of the one chapiter was five cubits, and the height of the other chapiter was five cubits. 17 There were nets of checker work, and wreaths of chain work, for the chapiters which were upon the top of the pillars ; seven for the one chapiter, and seven for the other chapiter. 18 So he made the pillars ; and there were two rows round about upon the one network, to cover the chapiters that were upon the top of the [c] pillars : and so did he for the other chapiter. 19 And the chapiters that were upon the top of the pillars in the porch were of lily work, four cubits. 20 And there were chapiters above also upon the two pillars, close by the belly which was beside the network : and the pomegranates were two hundred, in rows round about upon the other chapiter. 21 And he set up the pillars at the porch of the temple : and he set up the right pillar, and called the name thereof [d] Jachin : and he set up the left pillar, and called the name thereof [e] Boaz. 22 And upon the top of the pillars was lily work : so was the work of the pillars finished.

2 *Chronicles* 3 : 15-17.

15 Also he made before the house two pillars of thirty and five cubits high, and the chapiter that was on the top of each of them was five cubits. 16 And he made chains in the oracle, and put *them* on the tops of the pillars ; and he made an hundred pomegranates, and put them on the chains.

17 And he set up the pillars before the temple, one on the right hand, and the other on the left ; and called the name of that on the right hand [d] Jachin, and the name of that on the left [e] Boaz.

(3) The Altar of Brass.

2 *Chronicles* 4 : 1.

1 Moreover he made an altar of brass, twenty cubits the length thereof, and twenty cubits the breadth thereof, and ten cubits the height thereof.

(4) The molten Sea.

1 *Kings* 7 : 23-26, 39b.

23 And he made the molten sea of ten cubits from brim to brim, round in compass, and the height thereof was five cubits : and a line of thirty cubits compassed it round about. 24 And under the brim of it round about there were knops which did compass it, [f] for ten cubits, compassing the sea round about : the knops were in two rows, cast when it was cast. 25 It stood upon twelve oxen, three looking toward the north, and three looking toward the west, and three looking toward the south, and three

2 *Chronicles* 4 : 2-5, 10, 6b.

2 Also he made the molten sea of ten cubits from brim to brim, round in compass, and the height thereof was five cubits ; and a line of thirty cubits compassed it round about. 3 And under it was the similitude of oxen, which did compass it round about, [f] for ten cubits, compassing the sea round about. The oxen were in two rows, cast when it was cast. 4 It stood upon twelve oxen, three looking toward the north, and three looking toward the west, and three looking toward the south, and three look-

---

[a] Heb. " eighteen cubits was the height of one pillar." [b] Heb. " the other pillar." [c] So some of the ancient authorities. The text has, " pomegranates." [d] I. e., " He shall establish." [e] I. e., " In it is strength." [f] Or, " ten in a cubit."

1 *Kings* 7.	2 *Chronicles* 4.
looking toward the east : and the sea was set upon them above, and all their hinder parts were inward. 26 And it was an handbreadth thick ; and the brim thereof was wrought like the brim of a cup, like the flower of a lily : it held two thousand baths. 39*b* And he set the sea on the right side of the house eastward, toward the south.	ing toward the east : and the sea was set upon them above, and all their hinder parts were inward. 5 And it was an handbreadth thick ; and the brim thereof was wrought like the brim of a cup, like the flower of a lily : it received and held three thousand baths. 10 And he set the sea on the right side *of the house* eastward, toward the south. 6*b* But the sea was for the priests to wash in.

(5) The ten Bases.

1 *Kings* 7 : 27–37.

27 And he made the ten bases of brass ; four cubits was the length of one base, and four cubits the breadth thereof, and three cubits the height of it. 28 And the work of the bases was on this manner : they had *a* borders ; and *b* there were borders between the ledges : 29 and on the borders that were between the ledges were lions, oxen, and cherubim ; and upon the ledges *c* there was a pedestal above : and beneath the lions and oxen were wreaths of hanging work. 30 And every base had four brasen wheels, and axles of brass : and the four feet thereof had *d*undersetters : beneath the laver were the undersetters molten, with wreaths at the side of each. 31 And the mouth of it within the chapiter and above was a cubit : and the mouth thereof was round after the work of a pedestal, a cubit and a half : and also upon the mouth of it were gravings, and their borders were foursquare, not round. 32 And the four wheels were underneath the borders ; and the axletrees of the wheels were in the base : and the height of a wheel was a cubit and half a cubit. 33 And the work of the wheels was like the work of a chariot wheel : their axletrees, and their felloes, and their spokes, and their naves, were all molten. 34 And there were four under- setters at the four corners of each base : the undersetters thereof were of the base itself. 35 And in the top of the base was there a round compass of half a cubit high : and on the top of the base the *e* stays thereof and the borders thereof were of the same. 36 And on the plates of the stays thereof, and on the borders thereof, he graved cherubim, lions, and palm trees, according to the space of each, with wreaths round about. 37 After this manner he made the ten bases : all of them had one casting, one measure, and one form.

(6) The ten Lavers.

1 *Kings* 7 : 38, 39*a*.	2 *Chronicles* 4 : 6*a*.
38 And he made ten lavers of brass : one laver contained forty baths : and every laver was four cubits : and upon every one of the ten bases one laver. 39*a* And he set the bases, five on the right *f* side of the house, and five on the left side of the house.	6*a* He made also ten lavers, and put five on the right hand, and five on the left, to wash in them ; such things as belonged to the burnt offering they washed in them.

(7) The Courts.

1 *Kings* 6 : 36.	2 *Chronicles* 4 : 9.
36 And he built the inner court with three rows of hewn stone, and a row of cedar beams.	9 Fur'hermore he made the court of the priests, and the great court, and doors for the court, and overlaid the doors of them with brass.

---

a Or, " panels ; " and so in ver. 29. etc.   *b* Or, " even borders."   *c* Or, " it was in like manner above."   *d* Heb.
" shoulders."   *e* Heb. " hands."   *f* Heb. " shoulder."

(8) Summary of Hiram's Work in Brass.

1 *Kings* 7 : 40–47.

40 And *a* Hiram made the *b* lavers, and the shovels, and the basons. So Hiram made an end of doing all the work that he wrought for king Solomon in the house of the LORD : 41 the two pillars, and the two bowls of the chapiters that were on the top of the pillars ; and the two networks to cover the two bowls of the chapiters that were on the top of the pillars ; 42 and the four hundred pomegranates for the two networks ; two rows of pomegranates for each network, to cover the two bowls of the chapiters that were *c* upon the pillars ; 43 and the ten bases, and the ten lavers on the bases ; 44 and the one sea, and the twelve oxen under the sea ; 45 and the pots, and the shovels, and the basons : even all *d* these vessels, which Hiram made for king Solomon, in the house of the LORD, were of burnished brass. 46 In the plain of Jordan did the king cast them, in the clay ground between Succoth and Zarethan. 47 And Solomon left all the vessels *unweighed*, because they were exceeding many : the weight of the brass *e* could not be found out.

2 *Chronicles* 4 : 11–18.

11 And Huram made the pots, and the shovels, and the basons. So Huram made an end of doing the work that he wrought for king Solomon in the house of God : 12 the two pillars, and the bowls, and the two chapiters which were on the top of the pillars ; and the two networks to cover the two bowls of the chapiters that were on the top of the pillars ; 13 and the four hundred pomegranates for the two networks ; two rows of pomegranates for each network, to cover the two bowls of the chapiters that were *c* upon the pillars. 14 He made also the bases, and the lavers made he upon the bases ; 15 one sea, and the twelve oxen under it. 16 The pots also, and the shovels, and the fleshhooks, and all the vessels thereof, did *f* Huram his father make for king Solomon for the house of the LORD of bright brass. 17 In the plain of Jordan did the king cast them, in the clay ground between Succoth and Zeredah. 18 Thus Solomon made all these vessels in great abundance : for the weight of the brass *e* could not be found out.

(9) Summary of the golden Vessels, etc.

1 *Kings* 7 : 48–50.

48 And Solomon made all the vessels that were in the house of the LORD : the golden altar, and the table whereupon the shewbread was, of gold ; 49 and the candlesticks, five on the right side, and five on the left, before the oracle, of pure gold ; and the flowers, and the lamps, and the tongs, of gold ; 50 and the cups, and the snuffers, and the basons, and the spoons, and the firepans, of pure gold ; and the hinges, both for the doors of the inner house, the most holy place, and for the doors of the house, *to wit*, of the temple, of gold.

2 *Chronicles* 4 : 7, 8.

7 And he made the ten candlesticks of gold according to the ordinance concerning them; and he set them in the temple, five on the right hand, and five on the left. 8 He made also ten tables, and placed them in the temple, five on the right side, and five on the left. And he made an hundred basons of gold.

2 *Chronicles* 4 : 19–22.

19 And Solomon made all the vessels that were in the house of God, the golden altar also, and the tables whereon was the shewbread ; 20 And the candlesticks with their lamps, that they should burn according to the ordinance before the oracle, of pure gold ; 21 and the flowers, and the lamps, and the tongs, of gold, and that perfect gold ; 22 and the snuffers, and the basons, and the spoons, and the firepans, of pure gold : and as for the entry of the house, the inner doors thereof for the most holy place, and the doors of the house, *to wit*, of the temple, were of gold.

---

a Heb. " Hirom." *b* Many ancient authorities read, " pots." *c* Heb. " upon the face of the pillars." *d* Another reading is, " the vessels of the Tent." *e* Or, " was not searched out." *f* Cf. 2 Chronicles 2 : 13. See §129 (1).

(10) COMPLETION OF THE WORK.

1 *Kings* 7 : 51.	2 *Chronicles* 5 : 1.
51 Thus all the work that king Solomon wrought in the house of the LORD was finished. And Solomon brought in the things which David his father had dedicated, *even* the silver, and the gold, and the vessels, and put them in the treasuries of the house of the LORD.	1 Thus all the work that Solomon wrought for the house of the LORD was finished. And Solomon brought in the things that David his father had dedicated; even the silver, and the gold, and all the vessels, and put them in the treasuries of the house of God.

133. THE DEDICATION OF THE TEMPLE.ᵃ

(1) REMOVAL OF THE TABERNACLE AND ITS CONTENTS FROM ZION TO THE TEMPLE.

1 *Kings* 8 : 1-11.	2 *Chronicles* 5 : 2-14.
1 Then Solomon assembled the elders of Israel, and all the heads of the tribes, the princes of the fathers' *houses* of the children of Israel, unto king Solomon in Jerusalem, to bring up the ark of the covenant of the LORD out of the city of David, which is Zion. 2 And all the men of Israel assembled themselves unto king Solomon at the feast, in the month Ethanim, which is the seventh month. 3 And all the elders of Israel came, and the priests took up the ark. 4 And they brought up the ark of the LORD, and the tent of meeting, and all the holy vessels that were in the Tent ; even these did the priests and the Levites bring up. 5 And king Solomon and all the congregation of Israel, that were assembled unto him, were with him before the ark, sacrificing sheep and oxen, that could not be told nor numbered for multitude. 6 And the priests brought in the ark of the covenant of the LORD unto its place, into the oracle of the house, to the most holy place, even under the wings of the cherubim. 7 For the cherubim spread forth their wings over the place of the ark, and the cherubim covered the ark and the staves thereof above. 8 And ᵇ the staves were so long that the ends of the staves were seen from the holy place before the oracle ; but they were not seen without : and there they are, unto this day. 9 There was nothing in the ark save the two tables of stone which Moses put there at Horeb, ᶜ when the LORD made a covenant with the children of Israel, when they came out of the land of Egypt. 10 And it came to pass, when the priests were come out of the holy place, that the cloud filled the house of the LORD, 11 so that the priests could not stand to minister by reason of the cloud : for the glory of the LORD filled the house of the LORD.	2 Then Solomon assembled the elders of Israel, and all the heads of the tribes, the princes of the fathers' *houses* of the children of Israel, unto Jerusalem, to bring up the ark of the covenant of the LORD out of the city of David, which is Zion. 3 And all the men of Israel assembled themselves unto the king at the feast, which was *in* the seventh month. 4 And all the elders of Israel came, and the Levites took up the ark. 5 And they brought up the ark, and the tent of meeting, and all the holy vessels that were in the Tent ; these did the priests the Levites bring up. 6 And king Solomon and all the congregation of Israel, that were assembled unto him, were before the ark, sacrificing sheep and oxen, that could not be told nor numbered for multitude. 7 And the priests brought in the ark of the covenant of the LORD unto its place, into the oracle of the house, to the most holy place, even under the wings of the cherubim. 8 For the cherubim spread forth their wings over the place of the ark, and the cherubim covered the ark and the staves thereof above. 9 And ᵇ the staves were so long that the ends of the staves were seen from the ark before the oracle ; but they were not seen without : and there it is, unto this day. 10 There was nothing in the ark save the two tables which Moses put *there* at Horeb, ᶜ when the LORD made a covenant with the children of Israel, when they came out of Egypt. 11 And it came to pass, when the priests were come out of the holy place, (for all the priests that were present had sanctified themselves, and did not keep their courses ; 12 also the Levites which were the singers, all of them, even Asaph, Heman, Jeduthun, and their sons and their brethren, arrayed in fine linen, with

ᵃ See chronological note under §131.   ᵇ Or, " they drew out the staves, so that," etc.   ᶜ Or, " where."

2 *Chronicles* 5.

cymbals and psalteries and harps, stood at the east end of the altar, and with them an hundred and twenty priests sounding with trumpets:) 13 it came even to pass, when the trumpeters and singers were as one, to make one sound to be heard in praising and thanking the LORD; and when they lifted up their voice with the trumpets and cymbals and instruments *a* of music, and praised the LORD, *saying*, For he is good; for his mercy *endureth* for ever: that then the house was filled with a cloud, even the house of the LORD, 14 so that the priests could not stand to minister, by reason of the cloud: for the glory of the LORD filled the house of God.

(2) SOLOMON'S OPENING ADDRESS AND BLESSING.

1 *Kings* 8: 12–21.

12 Then spake Solomon, The LORD hath said that he would dwell in the thick darkness. 13 I have surely built thee an house of habitation, a place for thee to dwell in for ever. 14 And the king turned his face about, and blessed all the congregation of Israel: and all the congregation of Israel stood. 15 And he said, Blessed be the LORD, the God of Israel, which spake with his mouth unto David my father, and hath with his hand fulfilled it, saying, 16 Since the day that I brought forth my people Israel out of Egypt, I chose no city out of all the tribes of Israel to build an house, that my name might be there; but I chose David to be over my people Israel. 17 Now it was in the heart of David my father to build an house for the name of the LORD, the God of Israel. 18 But the LORD said unto David my father, Whereas it was in thine heart to build an house for my name, thou didst well that it was in thine heart: 19 nevertheless thou shalt not build the house; but thy son that shall come forth out of thy loins, he shall build the house for my name. 20 And the LORD hath established his word that he spake; for I am risen up in the room of David my father, and sit on the throne of Israel, as the LORD promised, and have built the house for the name of the LORD, the God of Israel. 21 And there have I set a place for the ark, wherein is the covenant of the LORD, which he made with our fathers, when he brought them out of the land of Egypt.

2 *Chronicles* 6: 1–11.

1 Then spake Solomon, The LORD hath said that he would dwell in the thick darkness. 2 But I have built thee an house of habitation, and a place for thee to dwell in for ever. 3 And the king turned his face, and blessed all the congregation of Israel: and all the congregation of Israel stood. 4 And he said, Blessed be the LORD, the God of Israel, which spake with his mouth unto David my father, and hath with his hands fulfilled it, saying, 5 Since the day that I brought forth my people out of the land of Egypt, I chose no city out of all the tribes of Israel to build an house in, that my name might be there; neither chose I any man to be *b* prince over my people Israel: 6 but I have chosen Jerusalem, that my name might be there; and have chosen David to be over my people Israel. 7 Now it was in the heart of David my father to build an house for the name of the LORD, the God of Israel. 8 But the LORD said unto David my father, Whereas it was in thine heart to build an house for my name, thou didst well that it was in thine heart: 9 nevertheless thou shalt not build the house; but thy son that shall come forth out of thy loins, he shall build the house for my name. 10 And the LORD hath performed his word that he spake; for I am risen up in the room of David my father, and sit on the throne of Israel, as the LORD promised, and have built the house for the name of the LORD, the God of Israel. 11 And there have I set the ark, wherein is the covenant of the LORD, which he made with the children of Israel.

a Or, "for song." *b* Or, "leader."

(3) SOLOMON'S DEDICATORY PRAYER.

A. GOD'S CONSTANT CARE INVOKED.

1 *Kings* 8 : 22–30.

22 And Solomon stood before the altar of the LORD in the presence of all the congregation of Israel, and spread forth his hands toward heaven : 23 and he said, O LORD, the God of Israel, there is no God like thee, in heaven above, or on earth beneath ; who keepest covenant and mercy *a* with thy servants, that walk before thee with all their heart : 24 who hast kept with thy servant David my father that which thou didst promise him : yea, thou spakest with thy mouth, and hast fulfilled it with thine hand, as it is this day. 25 Now therefore, O LORD, the God of Israel, keep with thy servant David my father that which thou hast promised him, saying, *b* There shall not fail thee a man in my sight to sit on the throne of Israel ; if only thy children take heed to their way, to walk before me as thou hast walked before me. 26 Now therefore, O God of Israel, let thy word, I pray thee, be verified, which thou spakest unto thy servant David my father. 27 But will God in very deed dwell on the earth ? behold, heaven and the heaven of heavens cannot contain thee ; how much less this house that I have builded ! 28 Yet have thou respect unto the prayer of thy servant, and to his supplication, O LORD my God, to hearken unto the cry and to the prayer which thy servant prayeth before thee this day : 29 that thine eyes may be open toward this house night and day, even toward the place whereof thou hast said, My name shall be there : to hearken unto the prayer which thy servant shall pray toward this place. 30 And hearken thou to the supplication of thy servant, and of thy people Israel, when they shall pray toward this place : yea, hear thou in heaven thy dwelling place ; and when thou hearest, forgive.

2 *Chronicles* 6 : 12–21.

12 And he stood before the altar of the LORD in the presence of all the congregation of Israel, and spread forth his hands : 13 (for Solomon had made a brasen scaffold, of five cubits long, and five cubits broad, and three cubits high, and had set it in the midst of the court ; and upon it he stood, and kneeled down upon his knees before all the congregation of Israel, and spread forth his hands toward heaven :) 14 and he said, O LORD, the God of Israel, there is no God like thee, in the heaven, or in the earth ; who keepest covenant and mercy *a* with thy servants, that walk before thee with all their heart : 15 who hast kept with thy servant David my father that which thou didst promise him : yea, thou spakest with thy mouth, and hast fulfilled it with thine hand, as it is this day. 16 Now therefore, O LORD, the God of Israel, keep with thy servant David my father that which thou hast promised him, saying, *b* There shall not fail thee a man in my sight to sit on the throne of Israel ; if only thy children take heed to their way, to walk in my law as thou hast walked before me. 17 Now therefore, O LORD, the God of Israel, let thy word be verified, which thou spakest unto thy servant David. 18 But will God in very deed dwell with men on the earth ? behold, heaven and the heaven of heavens cannot contain thee ; how much less this house which I have builded ! 19 Yet have thou respect unto the prayer of thy servant, and to his supplication, O LORD my God, to hearken unto the cry and to the prayer which thy servant prayeth before thee : 20 that thine eyes may be open toward this house day and night, even toward the place whereof thou hast said that thou wouldest put thy name there ; to hearken unto the prayer which thy servant shall pray toward this place. 21 And hearken thou to the supplications of thy servant, and of thy people Israel, when they shall pray toward this place : yea, hear thou from thy dwelling place, even from heaven ; and when thou hearest, forgive.

B. WHEN AN OATH IS MADE AT THE ALTAR.

1 *Kings* 8 : 31, 32.

31 *c* If a man sin against his neighbour, and an oath be laid upon him to cause him to swear,

2 *Chronicles* 6 : 22, 23.

22 *c* If a man sin against his neighbour, and an oath be laid upon him to cause him to swear,

---

a Or, " for."   *b* Heb. " There shall not be cut off unto thee a man from my sight."   *c* Or, " Whereinsoever a man shall sin."

1 *Kings* 8.	2 *Chronicles* 6.
and he come *and* swear before thine altar in this house . 32 then hear thou in heaven, and do, and judge thy servants, condemning the wicked, to bring his way upon his own head ; and justifying the righteous, to give him according to his righteousness.	and he come *and* swear before thine altar in this house : 23 then hear thou from heaven, and do, and judge thy servants, requiting the wicked, to bring his way upon his own head ; and justifying the righteous, to give him according to his righteousness.

C. IN DEFEAT.

1 *Kings* 8 : 33, 34.	2 *Chronicles* 6 : 24, 25.
33 When thy people Israel be smitten down before the enemy, because they have sinned against thee ; if they turn again to thee, and confess thy name, and pray and make supplication unto thee in this house : 34 then hear thou in heaven, and forgive the sin of thy people Israel, and bring them again unto the land which thou gavest unto their fathers.	24 And if thy people Israel be smitten down before the enemy, because they have sinned against thee ; and shall turn again and confess thy name, and pray and make supplication before thee in this house : 25 then hear thou from heaven, and forgive the sin of thy people Israel, and bring them again unto the land which thou gavest to them and to their fathers.

D. IN DROUTH.

1 *Kings* 8 : 35, 36.	2 *Chronicles* 6 : 26, 27.
35 When heaven is shut up, and there is no rain, because they have sinned against thee ; if they pray toward this place, and confess thy name, and turn from their sin, *a* when thou *b* dost afflict them : 36 then hear thou in heaven, and forgive the sin of thy servants, and of thy people Israel, *a* when thou teachest them the good way wherein they should walk ; and send rain upon thy land, which thou hast given to thy people for an inheritance.	26 When the heaven is shut up, and there is no rain, because they have sinned against thee ; if they pray toward this place, and confess thy name, and turn from their sin, *a* when thou *b* dost afflict them : 27 then hear thou in heaven, and forgive the sin of thy servants, and of thy people Israel, *a* when thou teachest them the good way wherein they should walk ; and send rain upon thy land, which thou hast given to thy people for an inheritance.

E. IN FAMINE AND PESTILENCE.

1 *Kings* 8 : 37-40.	2 *Chronicles* 6 : 28-31.
37 If there be in the land famine, if there be pestilence, if there be blasting *or* mildew, locust *or* caterpiller ; if their enemy besiege them in the land of their *c* cities ; whatsoever plague, whatsoever sickness there be ; 38 what prayer and supplication soever be made by any man, *or* by all thy people Israel, which shall know every man the plague of his own heart, and spread forth his hands toward this house : 39 then hear thou in heaven thy dwelling place, and forgive, and do, and render unto every man according to all his ways, whose heart thou knowest ; (for thou, even thou only, knowest the hearts of all the children of men ;) 40 that they may fear thee all the days that they live in the land which thou gavest unto our fathers.	28 If there be in the land famine, if there be pestilence, if there be blasting or mildew, locust or caterpiller ; if their enemies besiege them in the land of their *c* cities ; whatsoever plague or whatsoever sickness there be ; 29 what prayer and supplication soever be made by any man, or by all thy people Israel, which shall know every man his own plague and his own sorrow, and shall spread forth his hands toward this house : 30 then hear thou from heaven thy dwelling place, and forgive, and render unto every man according to all his ways, whose heart thou knowest ; (for thou, even thou only, knowest the hearts of the children of men ;) 31 that they may fear thee, to walk in thy ways, so long as they live in the land which thou gavest unto our fathers.

a Or, " because."   *b* Or, " answerest."   *c* Heb. " gates."

13

F. FOR THE STRANGER.

1 *Kings* 8:41–43.	2 *Chronicles* 6:32, 33.
41 Moreover concerning the stranger, that is not of thy people Israel, when he shall come out of a far country for thy name's sake; 42 (for they shall hear of thy great name, and of thy mighty hand, and of thy stretched out arm;) when he shall come and pray toward this house; 43 hear thou in heaven thy dwelling place, and do according to all that the stranger calleth to thee for; that all the peoples of the earth may know thy name, to fear thee, as doth thy people Israel, and that they may know that *a* this house which I have built is called by thy name.	32 Moreover concerning the stranger, that is not of thy people Israel, when he shall come from a far country for thy great name's sake, and thy mighty hand, and thy stretched out arm; when they shall come and pray toward this house: 33 then hear thou from heaven, even from thy dwelling place, and do according to all that the stranger calleth to thee for; that all the peoples of the earth may know thy name, and fear thee, as doth thy people Israel, and that they may know that *a* this house which I have built is called by thy name.

G. IN BATTLE.

1 *Kings* 8:44, 45.	2 *Chronicles* 6:34, 35.
44 If thy people go out to battle against their enemy, by whatsoever way thou shalt send them, and they pray unto the LORD toward the city which thou hast chosen, and toward the house which I have built for thy name: 45 then hear thou in heaven their prayer and their supplication, and maintain their *b* cause.	34 If thy people go out to battle against their enemies, by whatsoever way thou shalt send them, and they pray unto thee toward this city which thou hast chosen, and the house which I have built for thy name: 35 then hear thou from heaven their prayer and their supplication, and maintain their *b* cause.

H. IN CAPTIVITY.

1 *Kings* 8:46–53.	2 *Chronicles* 6:36–39.
46 If they sin against thee, (for there is no man that sinneth not,) and thou be angry with them, and deliver them to the enemy, so that *c* they carry them away captive unto the land of the enemy, far off or near; 47 yet if they shall bethink themselves in the land whither they are carried captive, and turn again, and make supplication unto thee in the land of them that carried them captive, saying, We have sinned, and have done perversely, we have dealt wickedly; 48 if they return unto thee with all their heart and with all their soul in the land of their enemies, which carried them captive, and pray unto thee toward their land, which thou gavest unto their fathers, the city which thou hast chosen, and the house which I have built for thy name: 49 then hear thou their prayer and their supplication in heaven thy dwelling place, and maintain their *b* cause; 50 and forgive thy people which have sinned against thee, and all their transgressions wherein they have	36 If they sin against thee, (for there is no man that sinneth not,) and thou be angry with them, and deliver them to the enemy, so that *c* they carry them away captive unto a land far off or near; 37 yet if they shall bethink themselves in the land whither they are carried captive, and turn again, and make supplication unto thee in the land of their captivity, saying, We have sinned, we have done perversely, and have dealt wickedly; 38 if they return unto thee with all their heart and with all their soul in the land of their captivity, whither they have carried them captive, and pray toward their land, which thou gavest unto their fathers, and the city which thou hast chosen, and toward the house which I have built for thy name: 39 then hear thou from heaven, even from thy dwelling place, their prayer and their supplications, and maintain their *b* cause; and forgive thy people which have sinned against thee.

---

a Or, "thy name is called upon this house," etc.   *b* Or, "right."   *c* Heb. "they that take them captive carry them away."

1 *Kings* 8.

transgressed against thee ; and give them *a* compassion before those who carried them captive, that they may have compassion on them : 51 for they be thy people, and thine inheritance, which thou broughtest forth out of Egypt, from the midst of the furnace of iron : 52 that thine eyes may be open unto the supplication of thy servant, and unto the supplication of thy people Israel, to hearken unto them whensoever they cry unto thee. 53 For thou didst separate them from among all the peoples of the earth, to be thine inheritance, as thou spakest by the hand of Moses thy servant, when thou broughtest our fathers out of Egypt, O Lord GOD.

I. CLOSE OF THE PRAYER.

2 *Chronicles* 6 : 40–42.

40 Now, O my God, let, I beseech thee, thine eyes be open, and let thine ears be attent, unto the prayer that is made in this place. 41 *b* Now therefore arise, O LORD God, into thy resting place, thou, and the ark of thy strength : let thy priests, O LORD God, be clothed with salvation, and let thy saints rejoice in *c* goodness. 42 O LORD God, turn not away the face of thine anointed : remember the *d* mercies of David thy servant.

(4) SOLOMON'S CLOSING BENEDICTION.

1 *Kings* 8 : 54–61.

54 And it was so, that when Solomon had made an end of praying all this prayer and supplication unto the LORD, he arose from before the altar of the LORD, from kneeling on his knees with his hands spread forth toward heaven. 55 And he stood, and blessed all the congregation of Israel with a loud voice, saying, 56 Blessed be the LORD, that hath given rest unto his people Israel, according to all that he promised : there hath not *e* failed one word of all his good promise, which he promised by the hand of Moses his servant. 57 The LORD our God be with us, as he was with our fathers : let him not leave us, nor forsake us : 58 that he may incline our hearts unto him, to walk in all his ways, and to keep his commandments, and his statutes, and his judgements, which he commanded our fathers. 59 And let these my words, wherewith I have made supplication before the LORD, be nigh unto the LORD our God day and night, that he maintain the cause of his servant, and the cause of his people Israel, *f* as every day shall require : 60 that all the peoples of the earth may know that the LORD, he is God ; there is none else. 61 Let your heart therefore be perfect with the LORD our God, to walk in his statutes, and to keep his commandments, as at this day.

(5) THE DIVINE CONFIRMATION.

2 *Chronicles* 7 : 1–3.

1 Now when Solomon had made an end of praying, the fire came down from heaven, and consumed the burnt offering and the sacrifices ; and the glory of the LORD filled the house. 2 And the priests could not enter into the house of the LORD, because the glory of the LORD filled the LORD'S house. 3 And all the children of Israel looked on, when the fire came down, and the glory of the LORD was upon the house ; and they bowed themselves with their faces to the ground upon the pavement, and worshipped, and gave thanks unto the LORD, *saying*, For he is good ; for his mercy *endureth* for ever.

---

a Heb. " to be for compassion."   *b* Cf. Psalm 132 : 8–10.   *c* Or, "good."   *d* Or, "good deeds."   Cf. 2 Chronicles 32 : 32. See §175, (9).   *e* Heb. " fallen."   *f* Heb. " the thing of a day in its day."

(6) THE SACRIFICE AND PUBLIC FESTIVAL.

1 *Kings* 8 : 62–66.

62 And the king, and all Israel with him, offered sacrifice before the LORD. 63 And Solomon offered for the sacrifice of peace offerings, which he offered unto the LORD, two and twenty thousand oxen, and an hundred and twenty thousand sheep. So the king and all the children of Israel dedicated the house of the LORD. 64 The same day did the king hallow the middle of the court that was before the house of the LORD ; for there he offered the burnt offering, and the meal offering, and the fat of the peace offerings: because the brasen altar that was before the LORD was too little to receive the burnt offering, and the meal offering, and the fat of the peace offerings. 65 So Solomon held the feast at that time, and all Israel with him, a great congregation, from the entering in of Hamath unto the brook of Egypt, before the LORD our God, seven days and seven days, even fourteen days. 66 On the eighth day he sent the people away, and they blessed the king, and went unto their tents joyful and glad of heart for all the goodness that the LORD had shewed unto David his servant, and to Israel his people.

2 *Chronicles* 7 : 4–10.

4 Then the king and all the people offered sacrifice before the LORD. 5 And king Solomon offered a sacrifice of twenty and two thousand oxen, and an hundred and twenty thousand sheep. So the king and all the people dedicated the house of God. 6 And the priests stood, according to their offices ; the Levites also with instruments *a* of music of the LORD, which David the king had made to give thanks unto the LORD, for his mercy *endureth* for ever, when David praised by their ministry : and the priests sounded trumpets before them ; and all Israel stood. 7 Moreover Solomon hallowed the middle of the court that was before the house of the LORD ; for there he offered the burnt offerings, and the fat of the peace offerings : because the brasen altar which Solomon had made was not able to receive the burnt offering, and the meal offering, and the fat. 8 So Solomon held the feast at that time seven days, and all Israel with him, a very great congregation, from the entering in of Hamath unto the brook of Egypt. 9 And on the eighth day they held a *b* solemn assembly : for they kept the dedication of the altar seven days, and the feast seven days. 10 And on the three and twentieth day of the seventh month he sent the people away unto their tents, joyful and glad of heart for the goodness that the LORD hath shewed unto David, and to Solomon, and to Israel his people.

(7) GOD'S SECOND APPEARANCE TO SOLOMON.

1 *Kings* 9 : 1–9.

1 And it came to pass, when Solomon had finished the building of the house of the LORD, and the king's house, and all Solomon's *c* desire which he was pleased to do, 2 that the LORD appeared to Solomon the second time, as he had appeared unto him at Gibeon. 3 And the LORD said unto him, I have heard thy prayer and thy supplication, that thou hast made before me : I have hallowed this house, which thou hast built, to put my name there for ever ; and mine eyes and mine heart shall be there perpetually. 4 And as for thee, if thou wilt walk before me, as David thy father walked, in integrity of heart, and in uprightness, to do according to all that I have

2 *Chronicles* 7 : 11–22.

11 Thus Solomon finished the house of the LORD, and the king's house : and all that came into Solomon's heart to make in the house of the LORD, and in his own house, he prosperously effected. 12 And the LORD appeared to Solomon by night, and said unto him, I have heard thy prayer, and have chosen this place to myself for an house of sacrifice. 13 If I shut up heaven that there be no rain, or if I command the locust to devour the land, or if I send pestilence among my people ; if my people, 14 *d* which are called by my name, shall humble themselves, and pray, and seek my face, and turn from their wicked ways ; then will I hear from heaven, and will

---

a Or, " for the song of the LORD."   *b* Or, " closing festival."   *c* Or, " delight."   *d* Heb. " upon whom my name is called."

1 *Kings* 9.

commanded thee, and wilt keep my statutes and my judgements ; 5 then I will establish the throne of thy kingdom over Israel for ever ; according as I *a* promised to David thy father, saying, There shalt not fail thee a man upon the throne of Israel. 6 But if ye shall turn away from following me, ye or your children, and not keep my commandments and my statutes which I have set before you, but shall go and serve other gods, and worship them : 7 then will I cut off Israel out of the land which I have given them ; and this house, which I have hallowed for my name, will I cast out of my sight ; and Israel shall be a proverb and a byword among all peoples : 8 *b* and though this house be so high, yet shall every one that passeth by it be astonished, and shall hiss ; and they shalt say, Why hath the LORD done thus unto this land, and to this house ? 9 And they shall answer, Because they forsook the LORD their God, which brought forth their fathers out of the land of Egypt, and laid hold on other gods, and worshipped them, and served them : therefore hath the LORD brought all this evil upon them.

2 *Chronicles* 9.

forgive their sin, and will heal their land. 15 Now mine eyes shall be open, and mine ears attent, unto the prayer that is made in this place. 16 For now have I chosen and hallowed this house, that my name may be there for ever : and mine eyes and mine heart shall be there perpetually. 17 And as for thee, if thou wilt walk before me as David thy father walked, and do according to all that I have commanded thee, and wilt keep my statutes and my judgements ; 18 then I will establish the throne of thy kingdom, according as I covenanted with David thy father, saying, There shall not fail thee a man to be ruler in Israel. 19 But if ye turn away, and forsake my statutes and my commandments which I have set before you, and shall go and serve other gods, and worship them : 20 then will I pluck them up by the roots out of my land which I have given them ; and this house, which I have hallowed for my name, will I cast out of my sight, and I will make it a proverb and a byword among all peoples. 21 And this house, which is so high, every one that passeth by it shall be astonished, and shall say, Why hath the LORD done this unto this land, and to this house ? 22 And they shall answer, Because they forsook the LORD, the God of their fathers, which brought them forth out of the land of Egypt, and laid hold on other gods, and worshipped them, and served them : therefore hath he brought all this evil upon them.

134. SOLOMON'S ACTIVITY AND FAME.

(1) SOLOMON'S AND HIRAM'S EXCHANGE OF CITIES.

1 *Kings* 9 : 10-14.

10 And it came to pass at the end of twenty years, wherein Solomon had built the two houses, the house of the LORD and the king's house, 11 (now Hiram the king of Tyre had furnished Solomon with cedar trees and fir trees, and with gold, according to all his desire,) that then king Solomon gave Hiram twenty cities in the land of Galilee. 12 And Hiram came out from Tyre to see the cities which Solomon had given him ; and they pleased him not. 13 And he said, What cities are these which thou hast given me, my brother ? And *c* he called them the land of Cabul, unto this day. And Hiram sent to the king sixscore talents of gold.

2 *Chronicles* 8 : 1, 2.

1 And it came to pass at the end of twenty years, wherein Solomon had built the house of the LORD, and his own house, 2 that the cities which Huram had given to Solomon, Solomon built them, and caused the children of Israel to dwell there.

---

a Or, " spake concerning."   *b* Or, " and this house shall be high ; every one," etc.   *c* Or, " they were called."

(2) The Subjugation of Hamath.

2 Chronicles 8 : 3.

3 And Solomon went to Hamath-zobah, and prevailed against it.

(3) The Removal of Pharaoh's Daughter to her own House.

1 Kings 9 : 24a.	2 Chronicles 8 : 11.
24a But Pharaoh's daughter came up out of the city of David unto her house which *Solomon* had built for her.	11 And Solomon brought up the daughter of Pharaoh out of the city of David unto the house that he had built for her : for he said, My wife shall not dwell in the house of David king of Israel, because *a* the places are holy, whereunto the ark of the LORD hath come.

(4) The Building of Millo : the Affair with Jeroboam.

1 Kings 9 : 24b.	1 Kings 11 : 27b, 28, 27a, 29–40.
24b Then did he build Millo.	27b Solomon built Millo, and *b* repaired the breach of the city of David his father. 28 And the man Jeroboam was a mighty man of valour : and Solomon saw the young man that he was industrious, and he gave him charge over all the *c* labour of the house of Joseph. 27a And this was the cause that he lifted up his hand against the king. 29 And it came to pass at that time, when Jeroboam went out of Jerusalem, that the prophet Ahijah the Shilonite found him in the way ; now *Ahijah* had clad himself with a new garment ; and they two were alone in the field. 30 And Ahijah laid hold of the new garment that was on him, and rent it in twelve pieces. 31 And he said to Jeroboam, Take thee ten pieces : for thus saith the LORD, the God of Israel, Behold, I will rend the kingdom out of the hand of Solomon, and will give ten tribes to thee : 32 (but he shall have one tribe, for my servant David's sake, and for Jerusalem's sake, the city which I have chosen out of all the tribes of Israel :) 33 because that they have forsaken me, and have worshipped Ashtoreth the goddess of the Zidonians, Chemosh the god of Moab, and Milcom the god of the children of Ammon ; and they have not walked in my ways, to do that which is right in mine eyes, and *to keep* my statutes and my judgements, as did David his father. 34 Howbeit I will not take the whole kingdom out of his hand : but I will make him prince all the days of his life, for David my servant's sake, whom I chose, *d* because he kept my commandments and my statutes : 35 but I will take the kingdom out of his son's

---

a Heb. "they are."   *b* Heb. "closed up."   *c* Heb. "burden."   *d* Or. "who kept."

I *Kings* 11.

hand, and will give it unto thee, even ten tribes. 36 And unto his son will I give one tribe, that David my servant may have a lamp alway before me in Jerusalem, the city which I have chosen me to put my name there. 37 And I will take thee, and thou shalt reign *a* according to all that thy soul desireth, and shalt be king over Israel. 38 And it shall be, if thou wilt hearken unto all that I command thee, and wilt walk in my ways, and do that which is right in mine eyes, to keep my statutes and my commandments, as David my servant did ; that I will be with thee, and will build thee a sure house, as I built for David, and will give Israel unto thee. 39 And I will for this afflict the seed of David, but not for ever. 40 Solomon sought therefore to kill Jeroboam : but Jeroboam arose, and fled into Egypt, unto Shishak king of Egypt, and was in Egypt until the death of Solomon.

(5) The Levy of forced Labor.*b*

I *Kings* 9 : 20–23, 15.

20 As for all the people that were left of the Amorites, the Hittites, the Perizzites, the Hivites, and the Jebusites, which were not of the children of Israel ; 21 their children that were left after them in the land, whom the children of Israel were not able utterly to destroy, of them did Solomon raise a levy of bondservants, unto this day. 22 But of the children of Israel did Solomon make no bondservants : but they were the men of war, and his servants, and his princes, and his captains, and rulers of his chariots and of his horsemen. 23 These were the chief officers that were over Solomon's work, five hundred and fifty, which bare rule over the people that wrought in the work.

15 And this is the *c* reason of the levy which king Solomon raised; for to build the house of the LORD, and his own house, and Millo, and the wall of Jerusalem, and Hazor, and Megiddo, and *d* Gezer.

2 *Chronicles* 8 : 7–10.

7 As for all the people that were left of the Hittites, and the Amorites, and the Perizzites, and the Hivites, and the Jebusites, which were not of Israel ; 8 of their children that were left after them in the land, whom the children of Israel consumed not, of them did Solomon raise a levy *of bondservants*, unto this day. 9 But of the children of Israel did Solomon make no servants for his work ; but they were men of war, and chief of his captains, and rulers of his chariots and of his horsemen. 10 And these were the chief officers of king Solomon, even two hundred and fifty, that bare rule over the people.

(6) The Building of the Cities.

I *Kings* 9 : 17–19.

17 And Solomon built Gezer, and Beth-horon the nether, 18 and Baalath, and *e* Tamar in the

2 *Chronicles* 8 : 4–6.

4 And he built Tadmor in the wilderness, and all the store cities, which he built in Hamath.

---

a Or, "over all." *b* Cf. §129, (2). *c* Or, "account." *d* [For] Pharaoh king of Egypt had gone up, and taken Gezer, and burnt it with fire, and slain the Canaanites that dwelt in the city, and given it for a portion unto his daughter, Solomon's wife.—1 Kings 9 : 16. It cannot be, or at least, as yet it has not been, determined, when Pharaoh's taking of Gezer occurred : it has seemed best, therefore, to place this account in a footnote. *e* Another reading is, "Tadmor."

1 *Kings* 9.	2 *Chronicles* 8.
wilderness, in the land, 19 and all the store cities that Solomon had, and the cities for his chariots, and the cities for his horsemen, and that which Solomon desired to build for his pleasure in Jerusalem, and in Lebanon, and in all the land of his dominion.	5 Also he built Beth-horon the upper, and Beth-horon the nether, fenced cities, with walls, gates, and bars; 6 and Baalath, and all the store cities that Solomon had, and all the cities for his chariots, and the cities for his horsemen, and all that Solomon desired to build for his pleasure in Jerusalem, and in Lebanon, and in all the land of his dominion.

(7) Solomon's Worship.

1 *Kings* 9 : 25.	2 *Chronicles* 8 : 12–16.
25 And three times in a year did Solomon offer burnt offerings and peace offerings upon the altar which he built unto the LORD, burning incense therewith, *upon the altar* that was before the LORD. So he finished the house.	12 Then Solomon offered burnt offerings unto the LORD on the altar of the LORD, which he had built before the porch, 13 even as the duty of every day required, offering according to the commandment of Moses, on the sabbaths, and on the new moons, and on the set feasts, three times in the year, *even* in the feast of unleavened bread, and in the feast of weeks, and in the feast of tabernacles. 14 And he appointed, according to the ordinance of David his father, the courses of the priests to their service, and the Levites to their charges, to praise, and to minister before the priests, as the duty of every day required: the doorkeepers also by their courses at every gate: for so had David the man of God commanded. 15 And they departed not from the commandment of the king unto the priests and Levites concerning any matter, or concerning the treasures. 16 Now all the work of Solomon was prepared unto the day of the foundation of the house of the LORD, and until it was finished. *So* the house of the LORD was perfected.

(8) The Navies of Solomon and Hiram.

1 *Kings* 9 : 26–28 ; 10 : 22.	2 *Chronicles* 8 : 17, 18 ; 9 : 21.
26 And king Solomon made a navy of ships in Ezion-geber, which is beside Eloth, on the shore of the Red Sea, in the land of Edom. 27 And Hiram sent in the navy his servants, shipmen that had knowledge of the sea, with the servants of Solomon. 28 And they came to Ophir, and fetched from thence gold, four hundred and twenty talents, and brought it to king Solomon. 22 For the king had at sea a navy of Tarshish with the navy of Hiram: once every three years came the navy of Tarshish, bringing gold, and silver, ivory, and apes, and peacocks.	17 Then went Solomon to Ezion-geber, and to Eloth, on the sea shore in the land of Edom. 18 And Huram sent him by the hands of his servants ships, and servants that had knowledge of the sea; and they came with the servants of Solomon to Ophir, and fetched from thence four hundred and fifty talents of gold, and brought them to king Solomon. 21 For the king had ships that went to Tarshish with the servants of Huram: once every three years came the ships of Tarshish, bringing gold, and silver, ivory, and apes, and peacocks.

(9) THE VISIT OF THE QUEEN OF SHEBA.

1 *Kings* 10 : 1–13.	2 *Chronicles* 9 : 1–12.
1 And when the queen of Sheba heard of the fame of Solomon concerning the name of the LORD, she came to prove him with hard questions. 2 And she came to Jerusalem with a very great train, with camels that bare spices, and very much gold, and precious stones : and when she was come to Solomon, she communed with him of all that was in her heart. 3 And Solomon told her all her questions : there was not any thing hid from the king which he told her not. 4 And when the queen of Sheba had seen all the wisdom of Solomon, and the house that he had built, 5 and the meat of his table, and the sitting of his servants, and the *a* attendance of his ministers, and their apparel, and his cupbearers, and *b* his ascent by which he went up into the house of the LORD ; there was no more spirit in her. 6 And she said to the king, It was a true report that I heard in mine own land of thine *c* acts, and of thy wisdom. 7 Howbeit I believed not the words, until I came, and mine eyes had seen it : and, behold, the half was not told me : *d* thy wisdom and prosperity exceedeth the fame which I heard. 8 Happy are thy men, happy are these thy servants, which stand continually before thee, *and* that hear thy wisdom. 9 Blessed be the LORD thy God, which delighted in thee, to set thee on the throne of Israel : because the LORD loved Israel for ever, therefore made he thee king, to do judgement and justice. 10 And she gave the king an hundred and twenty talents of gold, and of spices very great store, and precious stones : there came no more such abundance of spices as these which the queen of Sheba gave to king Solomon. 11 And the navy also of Hiram, that brought gold from Ophir, brought in from Ophir great plenty of *e* almug trees and precious stones. 12 And the king made of the almug trees *f* pillars for the house of the LORD, and for the king's house, harps also and psalteries for the singers : there came no such almug trees, nor were seen, unto this day. 13 And king Solomon gave to the queen of Sheba all her desire, whatsoever she asked, beside that *g* which Solomon gave her of his royal bounty. So she turned, and went to her own land, she and her servants.	1 And when the queen of Sheba heard of the fame of Solomon, she came to prove Solomon with hard questions at Jerusalem, with a very great train, and camels that bare spices, and gold in abundance, and precious stones : and when she was come to Solomon, she communed with him of all that was in her heart. 2 And Solomon told her all her questions : and there was not any thing hid from Solomon which he told her not. 3 And when the queen of Sheba had seen the wisdom of Solomon, and the house that he had built, 4 and the meat of his table, and the sitting of his servants, and the *a* attendance of his ministers, and their apparel ; his cupbearers also, and their apparel ; and his ascent by which he went up unto the house of the LORD ; there was no more spirit in her. 5 And she said to the king, It was a true report that I heard in mine own land of thine *e* acts, and of thy wisdom. 6 Howbeit I believed not their words, until I came, and mine eyes had seen it : and, behold, the half of the greatness of thy wisdom was not told me : thou exceedest the fame that I heard. 7 Happy are thy men, and happy are these thy servants, which stand continually before thee, and hear thy wisdom. 8 Blessed be the LORD thy God, which delighted in thee, to set thee on his throne, to be king for the LORD thy God : because thy God loved Israel, to establish them for ever, therefore made he thee king over them, to do judgement and justice. 9 And she gave the king an hundred and twenty talents of gold, and spices in great abundance, and precious stones : neither was there any such spice as the queen of Sheba gave to king Solomon. 10 And the servants also of Huram, and the servants of Solomon, which brought gold from Ophir, brought *e* algum trees and precious stones. 11 And the king made of the algum trees terraces for the house of the LORD, and for the king's house, and harps and psalteries for the singers : and there were none such seen before in the land of Judah. 12 And king Solomon gave to the queen of Sheba all her desire, whatsoever she asked, beside that which she had brought unto the king. So she turned, and went to her own land, she and her servants.

a Heb. " standing."   *b* Or, " his burnt offering which he offered in," etc.   *c* Or, "sayings."   *d* Heb. "thou hast added wisdom and goodness to the fame."   *e* Perhaps, "sandal wood."   *f* Or, " a railing." Heb. " a prop."   *g* Heb. " which he gave her according to the hand of king Solomon."

135. THE GLORY OF SOLOMON.

(1) THE PRINCES.

1 *Kings* 4 : 1–6.

1 And king Solomon was king over all Israel.   2 And these were the princes which he had ;
Azariah the son of Zadok, *a* the priest ; 3 Elihoreph and Ahijah, the sons of Shisha, *b* scribes ;
Jehoshaphat the son of Ahilud, the *c* recorder ; 4 and Benaiah the son of Jehoiada was over the
host ; and Zadok and Abiathar were priests ; 5 and Azariah the son of Nathan was over *d* the
officers ; and Zabud the son of Nathan was *e* priest, *and* the king's friend ; 6 and Ahishar was
over the household ; and Adoniram the son of Abda was over the levy.

(2) THE COMMISSARIES.

1 *Kings* 4 : 7–19, 22, 23, 27, 28.

7 And Solomon had twelve officers over all Israel, which provided victuals for the king and
his household : each man had to make provision for a month in the year.   8 And these are their
names : Ben-hur, in the hill country of Ephraim : 9 Ben-deker, in Makaz, and in Shaalbim, and
Beth-shemesh, and Elon-beth-hanan : 10 Ben-hesed, in Arubboth ; to him *pertained* Socoh, and
all the land of Hepher : 11 Ben-abinadab, in all *f* the *g* height of Dor ; he had Taphath the daughter
of Solomon to wife : 12 Baana the son of Ahilud, in Taanach and Megiddo, and all Beth-shean
which is beside Zarethan, beneath Jezreel, from Beth-shean to Abel-meholah, as far as *h* beyond
Jokmeam : 13 Ben-geber, in Ramoth-gilead ; to him *pertained* *i* the towns of Jair the son of
Manasseh, which are in Gilead ; *even* to him *pertained* the region of Argob, which is in Bashan,
threescore great cities with walls and brasen bars : 14 Ahinadab the son of Iddo, in Mahanaim :
Ahimaaz, in Naphtali ; 15 he also took Basemath the daughter of Solomon to wife : 16 Baana the
son of Hushai, in Asher and *k* Bealoth : 17 Jehoshaphat the son of Paruah, in Issachar : 18 Shimei
the son of Ela, in Benjamin : 19 Geber the son of Uri, in the land of Gilead, the country of Sihon
king of the Amorites and of Og king of Bashan ; *l* and *he was* the only officer which was in the
land.
22 And Solomon's provision for one day was thirty *m* measures of fin : flour, and threescore
measures of meal ; 23 ten fat oxen, and twenty oxen out of the pastures, and an hundred sheep,
beside harts, and gazelles, and roebucks, and fatted fowl.   27 And those officers provided victual
for king Solomon, and for all that came unto king Solomon's table, every man in his month : they
let nothing be lacking.   28 Barley also and straw for the horses and swift steeds brought they unto
the place *n* where *the officers* were, every man according to his charge.

(3) SOLOMON'S WISDOM.

1 *Kings* 4 : 29–34.

29 And God gave Solomon wisdom and understanding exceeding much, and largeness of
heart, even as the sand that is on the sea shore.   30 And Solomon's wisdom excelled the wisdom
of all the children of the east, and all the wisdom of Egypt.   31 For he was wiser than all men ;
than Ethan the Ezrahite, and Heman, and Calcol, and Darda, the sons of Mahol : and his fame
was in all the nations round about.   32 And he spake three thousand proverbs : and his songs
were a thousand and five.   33 And he spake of trees, from the cedar that is in Lebanon even unto
the hyssop that springeth out of the wall : he spake also of beasts, and of fowl, and of creeping
things, and of fishes.   34 And there came of all peoples to hear the wisdom of Solomon, from all
kings of the earth, which had heard of his wisdom.

---

a Cf. 1 Chronicles 6 : 10.   See §8, (1).   *b* Or, " secretaries."   *c* Or, " chronicler."   *d* Cf. ver. 7, below.   See §135, (2).
e Or, " chief minister."   Cf. 2 Samuel 8 : 18.   See §92.   *f* Or, " Naphathdor."   *g* Or, " region."   *h* Or, " over against."
i Or, " Havvoth-jair."   *k* Or, " in Aloth."   *l* Heb. " and one officer."   *m* Heb. " cor."   *n* Or, " where he (i. e., the
king) was."   Or, " where it should be."

(4) Solomon's Revenue and Splendor.

1 Kings 10: 14-21, 27, 23-25.

14 Now the weight of gold that came to Solomon in one year was six hundred threescore and six talents of gold, 15 beside *that which* the chapmen *brought*, and the traffic of the merchants, and of all the kings of the mingled people, and of the governors of the country. 16 And king Solomon made two hundred targets of beaten gold: six hundred *shekels* of gold went to one target. 17 And *he made* three hundred shields of beaten gold; three *a* pound of gold went to one shield : and the king put them in the house of the forest of Lebanon. 18 Moreover the king made a great throne of ivory, and overlaid it with the finest gold. 19 There were six steps to the throne, and the top of the throne was round behind : and there were *b* stays on either side by the place of the seat, and two lions standing beside the stays. 20 And twelve lions stood there on the one side and on the other upon the six steps : there was not the like made in any kingdom. 21 And all king Solomon's drinking vessels were of gold, and all the vessels of the house of the forest of Lebanon were of pure gold : none were of silver ; it was nothing accounted of in the days of Solomon.

27 And the king made silver to be in Jerusalem as stones, and cedars made he to be as the sycomore trees that are in the lowland, for abundance.

23 So king Solomon exceeded all the kings of the earth in riches and in wisdom. 24 And all the earth sought the presence of Solomon, to hear his wisdom,

2 Chronicles 1 : 15.

15 And the king made silver and gold to be in Jerusalem as stones, and cedars made he to be as the sycomore trees that are in the lowland, for abundance.

2 Chronicles 9 : 13-20, 27, 22-24.

13 Now the weight of gold that came to Solomon in one year was six hundred and threescore and six talents of gold; 14 beside that which the chapmen and merchants brought : and all the kings of Arabia and the governors of the country brought gold and silver to Solomon. 15 And king Solomon made two hundred targets of beaten gold : six hundred *shek- els* of beaten gold went to one target. 16 And *he made* three hundred shields of beaten gold ; three hundred *shekels* of gold went to one shield : and the king put them in the house of the forest of Lebanon. 17 More- over the king made a great throne of ivory, and overlaid it with pure gold. 18 And there were six steps to the throne, with a footstool of gold, which were fastened to the throne, and *b*stays on either side by the place of the seat, and two lions standing be- side the stays. 19 And twelve lions stood there on the one side and on the other upon the six steps : there was not the like made in any kingdom. 20 And all king Solomon's drinking ves- sels were of gold, and all the vessels of the house of the forest of Lebanon were of pure gold : silver was nothing accounted of in the days of Solomon.

27 And the king made silver to be in Jerusalem as stones, and cedars made he to be as the sycomore trees that are in the lowland, for abundance. 22 So king Solomon exceeded all the kings of the earth in riches and wisdom. 23 And all the kings of the earth sought the presence of Solomon, to hear his

a Heb. " maneh."   *b* Or, " arms."   Heb. " hands."

1 *Kings* 10.			2 *Chronicles* 9.
which God had put in his heart. 25 And they brought every man his present, vessels of silver, and vessels of gold, and raiment, and armour, and spices, horses, and mules, a rate year by year.			wisdom, which God had put in his heart. 24 And they brought every man his present, vessels of silver, and vessels of gold, and raiment, armour, and spices, horses, and mules, a rate year by year.

(5) SOLOMON'S CHARIOTS, HORSEMEN, AND TRAFFIC.

1 *Kings* 4 : 26.	1 *Kings* 10 : 26, 28, 29.	2 *Chronicles* 1 : 14, 16, 17.	2 *Chronicles* 9 : 25, 28.
26 And Solomon had forty thousand stalls of horses for his chariots, and twelve thousand horsemen.	26 And Solomon gathered together chariots and horsemen : and he had a thousand and four hundred chariots, and twelve thousand horsemen, which he bestowed in the chariot cities, and with the king at Jerusalem. 28 And the horses which Solomon had were brought out of Egypt ; and the king's merchants received them in droves, each drove at a price. 29 And a chariot came up and went out of Egypt for six hundred *shekels* of silver, and an horse for an hundred and fifty : and so for all the kings of the Hittites, and for the kings of Syria, did they bring them out *a* by their means.	14 And Solomon gathered chariots and horsemen: and he had a thousand and four hundred chariots, and twelve thousand horsemen, which he placed in the chariot cities, and with the king at Jerusalem. 16 And the horses which Solomon had were brought out of Egypt ; the king's merchants received them in droves, each drove at a price. 17 And they fetched up, and brought out of Egypt a chariot for six hundred *shekels* of silver, and an horse for an hundred and fifty : and so for all the kings of the Hittites, and the kings of Syria, did they bring them out *a* by their means.	25 And Solomon had four thousand stalls for horses and chariots, and twelve thousand horsemen, which he bestowed in the chariot cities, and with the king at Jerusalem. 28 And they brought horses for Solomon out of Egypt, and out of all lands.

(6) THE EXTENT AND SECURITY OF THE KINGDOM.

1 *Kings* 4 : 21, 24, 20, 25.	2 *Chronicles* 9 : 26.
21 *b* And Solomon ruled over all the kingdoms from the River unto the land of the Philistines, and unto the border of Egypt : they brought presents, and served Solomon all the days of his life. 24 For he had dominion over all *the region* *c* on this side the River, from Tiphsah even to Gaza, over all the kings *c* on this side the River : and he had peace *d* on all sides round about him. 20 Judah and Israel were many, as the sand which is by the sea in multitude, eating and drinking and making merry. 25 And Judah and Israel dwelt safely, every man under his vine and under his fig tree, from Dan even to Beer-sheba, all the days of Solomon.	26 And he ruled over all the kings from the River even unto the land of the Philistines, and to the border of Egypt.

a Heb. "in their hand."   *b* Ch. 5 : 1 in Heb.   *c* Or, "beyond the River."   *d* Some authorities read, "with all his servants,"

PART III.

SOLOMON'S FALL AND END.

136. THE STRANGE WIVES TURN AWAY SOLOMON'S HEART.

1 *Kings* 11 : 1–8.

1 Now king Solomon loved many strange women, *a* together with the daughter of Pharaoh, women of the Moabites, Ammonites, Edomites, Zidonians, and Hittites ; 2 of the nations concerning which the LORD said unto the children of Israel, Ye shall not go among them, neither shall they come among you : for surely they will turn away your heart after their gods : Solomon clave unto these in love. 3 And he had seven hundred wives, princesses, and three hundred concubines : and his wives turned away his heart. 4 For it came to pass, when Solomon was old, that his wives turned away his heart after other gods : and his heart was not perfect with the LORD his God, as was the heart of David his father. 5 For Solomon went after Ashtoreth the goddess of the Zidonians, and after Milcom the abomination of the Ammonites. 6 And Solomon did that which was evil in the sight of the LORD, and went not fully after the LORD, as did David his father. 7 Then did Solomon build an high place for Chemosh the abomination of Moab, in the mount that is before Jerusalem, and for Molech the abomination of the children of Ammon. 8 And so did he for all his strange wives, which burnt incense and sacrificed unto their gods.

137. GOD'S ANGER AND THREATENING.

1 *Kings* 11 : 9–13.

9 And the LORD was angry with Solomon, because his heart was turned away from the LORD, the God of Israel, which had appeared unto him twice, 10 and had commanded him concerning this thing, that he should not go after other gods : but he kept not that which the LORD commanded. 11 Wherefore the LORD said unto Solomon, Forasmuch as this *b* is done of thee, and thou hast not kept my covenant and my statutes, which I have commanded thee, I will surely rend the kingdom from thee, and will give it to thy servant. 12 Notwithstanding in thy days I will not do it, for David thy father's sake : but I will rend it out of the hand of thy son. 13 Howbeit I will not rend away all the kingdom : but I will give one tribe to thy son, for David my servant's sake, and for Jerusalem's sake which I have chosen.

138. SOLOMON'S ADVERSARIES.

(1) HADAD THE EDOMITE. *c*

1 *Kings* 11 : 14, 21, 22.

14 And the LORD raised up an adversary unto Solomon, Hadad the Edomite : he was of the king's seed in Edom. 21 And when Hadad heard in Egypt that David slept with his fathers, and that Joab the captain of the host was dead, Hadad said to Pharaoh, Let me depart, that I may go to mine own country. 22 Then Pharaoh said unto him, But what hast thou lacked with me, that, behold, thou seekest to go to thine own country ? And he answered, Nothing : howbeit let me depart in any wise.

(2) REZON THE SON OF ELIADA. *d*

1 *Kings* 11 : 23, 25.

23 And God raised up *another* adversary unto him, Rezon the son of Eliada, which had fled from his lord Hadadezer king of Zobah. 25 And he was an adversary to Israel all the days of Solomon, beside the mischief that Hadad *did :* and he abhorred Israel, and reigned over Syria.

a Or, " besides." *b* Heb. " is with thee." *c* For a fuller account of Hadad, cf. 1 Kings 11 : 15-20. It will be found in its chronological setting in §89 and accompanying footnote. *d* For a fuller account of Rezon, cf. 1 Kings 11 : 24. See §86, with accompanying footnote.

(3) JEROBOAM THE SON OF NEBAT. [a]

1 *Kings* 11 : 26.

26 And Jeroboam the son of Nebat, an Ephraimite of Zeredah, a servant of Solomon, whcse mother's name was Zeruah, a widow woman, he also lifted up his hand against the king.

139. THE DEATH OF SOLOMON.

1 *Kings* 11 : 41–43.	2 *Chronicles* 9 : 29–31.
41 Now the rest of the [b] acts of Solomon, and all that he did, and his wisdom, are they not written in the book of the [b] acts of Solomon? 42 And the time that Solomon reigned in Jerusalem over all Israel was forty years. 43 And Solomon slept with his fathers, and was buried in the city of David his father: and Rehoboam his son reigned in his stead.	29 Now the rest of the [b] acts of Solomon, first and last, are they not written in the [b] history of Nathan the prophet, and in the prophecy of Ahijah the Shilonite, and in the visions of [c] Iddo the seer concerning Jeroboam the son of Nebat? 30 And Solomon reigned in Jerusalem over all Israel forty years. 31 And Solomon slept with his fathers, and he was buried in the city of David his father: and Rehoboam his son reigned in his stead.

[a] For the account of Jeroboam's "lifting up his hand against the king," cf. 1 Kings 11 : 27-40. See §134, (4).   [b] Heb. "words."   [c] Heb. "Jedai," or "Jedo."

BOOK FIFTH.

The Kingdoms of Judah and Israel.

PART I.

FROM THE YEAR OF THE DISRUPTION TO THE RISE OF JEHU.

Kingdom of Judah.		Kingdom of Israel.

140. INTRODUCTION : ACCESSION OF REHOBOAM AND REVOLT OF THE TEN TRIBES.

1 Kings 12 : 1–19.	*2 Chronicles* 10 : 1–19.
1 And Rehoboam went to Shechem : for all Israel were come to Shechem to make him king. 2 And it came to pass, when Jeroboam the son of Nebat heard of it, (for he was yet in Egypt, whither he had fled from the presence of king Solomon, and Jeroboam dwelt in Egypt, 3 and they sent and called him ;) that Jeroboam and all the congregation of Israel came, and spake unto Rehoboam, saying, 4 Thy father made our yoke grievous : now therefore make thou the grievous service of thy father, and his heavy yoke which he put upon us, lighter, and we will serve thee. 5 And he said unto them, Depart yet for three days, then come again to me. And the people departed. 6 And king Rehoboam took counsel with the old men, that had stood before Solomon his father while he yet lived, saying, What counsel give ye me to return answer to this people ? 7 And they spake unto him, saying, If thou wilt be a servant unto this people this day, and wilt serve them, and answer them, and speak good words to them, then they will be thy servants for ever. 8 But he forsook the counsel of the old men which they had given him, and took counsel with the young men that were grown up with him, that stood be-	1 And Rehoboam went to Shechem : for all Israel were come to Shechem to make him king. 2 And it came to pass, when Jeroboam the son of Nebat heard of it, (for he was in Egypt, whither he had fled from the presence of king Solomon,) that Jeroboam returned out of Egypt. 3 And they sent and called him ; and Jeroboam and all Israel came, and they spake to Rehoboam, saying, 4 Thy father made our yoke grievous : now therefore make thou the grievous service of thy father, and his heavy yoke which he put upon us, lighter, and we will serve thee. 5 And he said unto them, Come again unto me after three days. And the people departed. 6 And king Rehoboam took counsel with the old men, that had stood before Solomon his father while he yet lived, saying, What counsel give ye me to return answer to this people ? 7 And they spake unto him, saying, If thou be kind to this people, and please them, and speak good words to them, then they will be thy servants for ever. 8 But he forsook the counsel of the old men which they had given him, and took counsel with the young men that were grown up with him, that stood before him. 9 And he said unto them,

Kingdom of Judah.	Kingdom of Israel.
1 *Kings* 12.	2 *Chronicles* 10.

fore him. 9 And he said unto them, What counsel give ye, that we may return answer to this people, who have spoken to me, saying, Make the yoke that thy father did put upon us lighter? 10 And the young men that were grown up with him spake unto him, saying, Thus shalt thou say unto this people that spake unto thee, saying, Thy father made our yoke heavy, but make thou it lighter unto us; thus shalt thou speak unto them, My little finger is thicker than my father's loins. 11 And now whereas my father did lade you with a heavy yoke, I will add to your yoke: my father chastised you with whips, but I will chastise you with scorpions. 12 So Jeroboam and all the people came to Rehoboam the third day, as the king bade, saying, Come to me again the third day. 13 And the king answered the people roughly, and forsook the counsel of the old men which they had given him; 14 and spake to them after the counsel of the young men, saying, My father made your yoke heavy, but I will add to your yoke: my father chastised you with whips, but I will chastise you with scorpions. 15 So the king hearkened not unto the people; for it was a thing brought about of the LORD, that he might establish his word, which the LORD spake by the hand of Ahijah the Shilonite to Jeroboam the son of Nebat. 16 And when all Israel saw that the king hearkened not unto them, the people answered the king, saying, What portion have we in David? neither have we inheritance in the son of Jesse: to your tents, O Israel: now see to thine own house, David. So Israel departed unto their tents. 17 But as for the children of Israel which dwelt in the cities of Judah, Rehoboam reigned over them. 18 Then king Rehoboam sent Adoram, who was over the levy; and all Israel stoned him with stones, that he died. And king Rehoboam made speed to get him up to his chariot, to flee to Jerusalem. 19 So Israel rebelled against the house of David, unto this day.

What counsel give ye, that we may return answer to this people, who have spoken to me, saying, Make the yoke that thy father did put upon us lighter? 10 And the young men that were grown up with him spake unto him, saying, Thus shalt thou say unto the people that spake unto thee, saying, Thy father made our yoke heavy, but make it lighter unto us; thus shalt thou say unto them, My little finger is thicker than my father's loins. 11 And now whereas my father did lade you with a heavy yoke, I will add to your yoke: my father chastised you with whips, but I *will chastise you* with scorpions. 12 So Jeroboam and all the people came to Rehoboam the third day, as the king bade, saying, Come to me again the third day. 13 And the king answered them roughly; and king Rehoboam forsook the counsel of the old men, 14 and spake to them after the counsel of the young men, saying, My father made your yoke heavy, but I will add thereto: my father chastised you with whips, but I *will chastise you* with scorpions. 15 So the king hearkened not unto the people; for it was brought about of God, that the LORD might establish his word, which he spake by the hand of Ahijah the Shilonite to Jeroboam the son of Nebat. 16 And when all Israel saw that the king hearkened not unto them, the people answered the king, saying, What portion have we in David? neither have we inheritance in the son of Jesse: every man to your tents, O Israel: now see to thine own house, David. So all Israel departed unto their tents. 17 But as for the children of Israel that dwelt in the cities of Judah, Rehoboam reigned over them. 18 Then king Rehoboam sent Hadoram, who was over the levy; and the children of Israel stoned him with stones, that he died. And king Rehoboam made speed to get him up to his chariot, to flee to Jerusalem. 19 So Israel rebelled against the house of David, unto this day.

141. THE REIGN OF REHOBOAM.

(1) REHOBOAM'S PLANS AGAINST ISRAEL FRUSTRATED BY THE PROPHET SHEMAIAH.

1 *Kings* 12:21-24.	2 *Chronicles* 11:1-4.
21 And when Rehoboam was come to Jeru-	1 And when Rehoboam was come to Jeru-

142. THE REIGN OF JEROBOAM.

(1) JEROBOAM IS MADE KING OVER ISRAEL.

1 *Kings* 12: 20.

20 And it came to pass, when all Israel heard that Jeroboam was returned, that they sent and called him unto the congregation, and made him

Kingdom of Judah.

1 *Kings* 12.	2 *Chronicles* 11.
salem, he assembled all the house of Judah, and the tribe of Benjamin, an hundred and fourscore thousand chosen men, which were warriors, to fight against the house of Israel, to bring the kingdom again to Rehoboam the son of Solomon. 22 But the word of God came unto Shemaiah the man of God, saying, 23 Speak unto Rehoboam the son of Solomon, king of Judah, and unto all the house of Judah and Benjamin, and to the *a* rest of the people, saying, 24 Thus saith the LORD, Ye shall not go up, nor fight against your brethren the children of Israel : return every man to his house ; for this thing is of me. So they hearkened unto the word of the LORD, and returned and went their way, according to the word of the LORD.	salem, he assembled the house of Judah and Benjamin, an hundred and fourscore thousand chosen men, which were warriors, to fight against Israel, to bring the kingdom again to Rehoboam. 2 But the word of the LORD came to Shemaiah the man of God, saying, 3 Speak unto Rehoboam the son of Solomon, king of Judah, and to all Israel in Judah and Benjamin, saying, 4 Thus saith the LORD, Ye shall not go up, nor fight against your brethren : return every man to his house ; for this thing is of me. So they hearkened unto the words of the LORD, and returned from going against Jeroboam.

Kingdom of Israel.

1 *Kings* 12.

king over all Israel : there was none that followed the house of David, but the tribe of Judah only.

(2) JEROBOAM TAKES MEASURES TO ESTAB-
LISH HIS KINGDOM.

1 *Kings* 12:25-33.	2 *Chronicles* 11 : 15.
25 Then Jeroboam built Shechem in the hill country of Ephraim, and dwelt therein; and he went out from thence, and built Penuel. 26 And Jeroboam said in his heart, Now shall the kingdom return to the house of David : 27 if this people go up to offer sacrifices in the house of the LORD at Jerusalem, then shall	

---

a Cf. 1 Kings 12 : 17. See, §140.
14

Kingdom of Judah.	Kingdom of Israel.

Kingdom of Israel.

1 *Kings* 12.

the heart of this people turn again unto their lord, even unto Rehoboam king of Judah; and they shall kill me, and return to Rehoboam king of Judah. 28 Whereupon the king took counsel, and made two calves of gold; and he said unto them, *b* It is too much for you to go up to Jerusalem; behold thy gods, O Israel, which brought thee up out of the land of Egypt. 29 And he set the one in Beth-el, and the other put he in Dan. 30 And this thing became a sin: for the people went *to worship* before *c* the one, even unto Dan. 31 And he made houses of high places, and made priests from among all the people, which were not of the sons of Levi. 32 And Jeroboam ordained a feast in the eighth month, on the fifteenth day of the month, like unto the feast that is in Judah, and he *d* went up unto the altar; so did he in Beth-el, *e* sacrificing unto the calves that he had made: and he placed in Beth-el the priests of the high places which he had made. 33 And he *d* went up unto the altar which he had made in Beth-el on the fifteenth day in the

2 *Chronicles* 11.

15 And he appointed him priests for the high places, and for the *f* he-goats, and for the calves which he had made.

(2) Adherence of the Levites in all Israel to Rehoboam.*a*

2 *Chronicles* 11 : 13, 14.

13 And the priests and the Levites that were in all Israel resorted to him out of all their border. 14 For the Levites left their suburbs and their possession, and came to Judah and Jerusalem : for Jeroboam and his sons cast them off, that they should not execute the priest's office unto the LORD.

(3) Rehoboam is further strengthened by the Immigration of other pious Israelites.

2 *Chronicles* 11 : 16, 17.

16 And after them, out of all the tribes of Israel, such as set their hearts to seek the LORD, the God of Israel, came to Jerusalem to sacrifice unto the LORD, the God of their fathers. 17 So they strengthened the kingdom

a With almost equal propriety, this sub-section, and the following, (3), could have been placed as equally belonging to each kingdom, as, e. g., subsection (8). But as they are synchronous, or very nearly synchronous with §142, (2), it has been thought best to place them as they are in the text.   *b* Or, " Ye have gone up long enough."   *c* Or, " each of hem."   *d* Or, " offered upon."   *e* Or, " to sacrifice."   *f* Or, " satyrs."   See Leviticus 17:7.

Kingdom of Judah.	Kingdom of Israel.

Kingdom of Judah.

2 *Chronicles* 11.

of Judah, and made Rehoboam the son of Solomon strong, three years: for they walked three years in the way of David and Solomon.

Kingdom of Israel.

1 *Kings* 12.

eighth month, even in the month which he had devised *a* of his own heart: and he ordained a feast for the children of Israel, and *b* went up unto the altar, to burn incense.

(3) THE "MAN OF GOD OUT OF JUDAH."

A. THE PROPHECY AGAINST JEROBOAM'S ALTAR IN BETH-EL.*c*

1 *Kings* 13 : 1-3.

1 And, behold, there came a man of God out of Judah by the word of the LORD unto Bethel: and Jeroboam was standing by the altar to burn incense. 2 And he cried against the altar by the word of the LORD, and said, O altar, altar, thus saith the LORD: Behold, a child shall be born unto the house of David, Josiah by name; and upon thee shall he sacrifice the priests of the high places that burn incense upon thee, and men's bones shall they burn upon thee. 3 And he gave a sign the same day, saying, This is the sign which the LORD hath spoken: Behold, the altar shall be rent, and the ashes that are upon it shall be poured out.

B. THE WITHERING AND RESTORATION OF JEROBOAM'S HAND.

1 *Kings* 13 : 4-6.

4 And it came to pass, when the king heard the saying of the man of God, which he cried against the altar in Beth-el, that Jeroboam put forth his hand from the altar, saying, Lay hold on him. And his hand, which he put forth against him, dried up, so that he could not draw it back again to him. 5 The altar also was rent, and the ashes poured out from the altar, according to the sign which the man of God had given by the word of the LORD. 6 And the king answered and said unto the man of God, Intreat now the favour of the LORD thy God, and pray for me, that my hand may be restored me again. And the man of God intreated the LORD, and the king's hand was restored him again, and became as it was before.

---

a Another reading is, "apart."   *b* Or, "offered upon."   *c* Cf. 2 Kings 23 : 15-20. See §178, (9).

Kingdom of Judah.	Kingdom of Israel.
	C. THE DISOBEDIENCE OF THE MAN OF GOD.

Kingdom of Israel.

C. THE DISOBEDIENCE OF THE MAN OF GOD.

1 *Kings* 13:7–22.

7 And the king said unto the man of God, Come home with me, and refresh thyself, and I will give thee a reward. 8 And the man of God said unto the king, If thou wilt give me half thine house, I will not go in with thee, neither will I eat bread nor drink water in this place: 9 for so was it charged me by the word of the LORD, saying, Thou shalt eat no bread, nor drink water, neither return by the way that thou camest. 10 So he went another way, and returned not by the way that he came to Beth-el.

11 Now there dwelt an old prophet in Beth-el; and *a* one of his sons came and told him all the works that the man of God had done that day in Beth-el: the words which he had spoken unto the king, them also they told unto their father. 12 And their father said unto them, What way went he? *b* Now his sons had seen what way the man of God went, which came from Judah. 13 And he said unto his sons, Saddle me the ass. So they saddled him the ass: and he rode thereon. 14 And he went after the man of God, and found him sitting under an *c* oak: and he said unto him, Art thou the man of God that camest from Judah? And he said, I am. 15 Then he said unto him, Come home with me, and eat bread. 16 And he said, I may not return with thee, nor go in with thee: neither will I eat bread nor drink water with thee in this place: 17 for it was said to me by the word of the LORD, Thou shalt eat no bread nor drink water there, nor turn again to go by the way that thou camest. 18 And he said unto him, I also am a prophet as thou art; and an angel spake unto me by the word of the LORD, saying, Bring him back with thee into thine house, that he may eat bread and drink water. *But* he lied unto him. 19 So he went back with him, and did eat bread in his house, and drank water. 20 And it came to pass, as they sat at the table, that the word of the LORD came unto the prophet that brought him back: 21 and he cried unto the man of God that came from Judah, saying, Thus saith the LORD, Forasmuch as thou hast *d* been disobedient unto the mouth of the LORD, and hast not kept the com-

---

a Heb. " his son."   *b* According to some ancient versions, " And his sons shewed him."   *c* Or, " terebinth."   *d* Or, " rebelled against the word."

Kingdom of Judah.	Kingdom of Israel.

Kingdom of Israel.

1 *Kings* 13.

mandment which the LORD thy God commanded thee, 22 but camest back, and hast eaten bread and drunk water in the place of the which he said to thee, Eat no bread, and drink no water; thy carcase shall not come unto the sepulchre of thy fathers.

D. THE MAN OF GOD IS SLAIN.

1 *Kings* 13:23, 24.

23 And it came to pass, after he had eaten bread, and after he had drunk, that he saddled for him the ass, *to wit,* for the prophet whom he had brought back. 24 And when he was gone, a lion met him by the way, and slew him: and his carcase was cast in the way, and the ass stood by it; the lion also stood by the carcase.

E. THE "OLD PROPHET" BURIES THE MAN OF GOD, AND CONFIRMS HIS WORDS.

1 *Kings* 13:25-32.

25 And, behold, men passed by, and saw the carcase cast in the way, and the lion standing by the carcase: and they came and told it in the city where the old prophet dwelt. 26 And when the prophet that brought him back from the way heard thereof, he said, It is the man of God, who *ª* was disobedient unto the mouth of the LORD: therefore the LORD hath delivered him unto the lion, which hath torn him, and slain him, according to the word of the LORD, which he spake unto him. 27 And he spake to his sons, saying, Saddle me the ass. And they saddled it. 28 And he went and found his carcase cast in the way, and the ass and the lion standing by the carcase: the lion had not eaten the carcase, nor torn the ass. 29 And the prophet took up the carcase of the man of God, and laid it upon the ass, and brought it back: and he came to the city of the old prophet, to mourn, and to bury him. 30 And he laid his carcase in his own grave; and they mourned over him, *saying,* Alas, my brother! 31 And it came to pass, after he had buried him, that he spake to his sons, saying, When I am dead, then bury me in the sepulchre wherein the man of God is buried; lay my bones beside his bones. 32 For the saying which he cried by the word of the LORD against the altar in Beth-el,

---

ª Or, " rebelled against the word."

Kingdom of Judah.	Kingdom of Israel.

Kingdom of Israel.

1 *Kings* 13.

and against all the houses of the high places which are in the cities of Samaria, shall surely come to pass.

(4) JEROBOAM'S PERSISTENCE IN EVIL.

1 *Kings* 13 : 33, 34.

33 After this thing Jeroboam returned not from his evil way, but made again from among all the people priests of the high places: *a* whosoever would, he consecrated him, that there might be priests of the high places.   34 And *b* this thing became sin unto the house of Jeroboam, even to cut it off, and to destroy it from off the face of the earth.

(5) AHIJAH'S PROPHECY AGAINST THE HOUSE AND KINGDOM OF JEROBOAM.

A. JEROBOAM'S INQUIRY CONCERNING HIS SICK CHILD.

1 *Kings* 14 : 1–4.

1 At that time Abijah the son of Jeroboam fell sick.   2 And Jeroboam said to his wife, Arise, I pray thee, and disguise thyself, that thou be not known to be the wife of Jeroboam: and get thee to Shiloh; behold, there is Ahijah the prophet, which spake concerning me that I should be king over this people.   3 And take with thee ten loaves, and cracknels, and a *c* cruse of honey, and go to him: he shall tell thee what shall become of the child.   4 And Jeroboam's wife did so, and arose, and went to Shiloh, and came to the house of Ahijah.   Now Ahijah could not see; for his eyes were set by reason of his age.

B. AHIJAH'S PROPHECY AND ITS PARTIAL FULFILLMENT.

1 *Kings* 14 : 5–18.

5 And the LORD said unto Ahijah, Behold, the wife of Jeroboam cometh to inquire of thee concerning her son; for he is sick: thus and thus shalt thou say unto her: for it shall be, when she cometh in, that she shall feign herself to be another woman.   6 And it was so, when Ahijah heard the sound of her feet, as she came in at the door, that he said, Come in, thou wife

---

a Or, "whomsoever he would."   *b* Or, "by this thing he became."   *c* Or, "bottle."

Kingdom of Judah.

Kingdom of Israel.

1 *Kings* 14.

of Jeroboam; why feignest thou thyself to be another? for I am sent to thee with heavy tidings. 7 Go, tell Jeroboam, Thus saith the LORD, the God of Israel: Forasmuch as I exalted thee from among the people, and made thee *a* prince over my people Israel, 8 and rent the kingdom away from the house of David, and gave it thee: and yet thou hast not been as my servant David, who kept my commandments, and who followed me with all his heart, to do that only which was right in mine eyes; 9 but hast done evil above all that were before thee, and hast gone and made thee other gods, and molten images, to provoke me to anger, and hast cast me behind thy back: 10 therefore, behold, I will bring evil upon the house of Jeroboam, and will cut off from Jeroboam every man child, him that is shut up and him that is left at large in Israel, and will utterly sweep away the house of Jeroboam, as a man sweepeth away dung, till it be all gone. 11 Him that dieth of Jeroboam in the city shall the dogs eat; and him that dieth in the field shall the fowls of the air eat: for the LORD hath spoken it. 12 Arise thou therefore, get thee to thine house: *and* when thy feet enter into the city, the child shall die. 13 And all Israel shall mourn for him, and bury him; for he only of Jeroboam shall come to the grave: because in him there is found some good thing toward the LORD, the God of Israel, in the house of Jeroboam. 14 Moreover the LORD shall raise him up a king over Israel, who shall cut off the house of Jeroboam that day: *b* but what? even now. 15 For the LORD shall smite Israel, as a reed is shaken in the water; and he shall root up Israel out of this good land, which he gave to their fathers, and shall scatter them beyond the River; because they have made their Asherim, provoking the LORD to anger. 16 And he shall give Israel up because of the sins of Jeroboam, *c* which he hath sinned, and wherewith he hath made Israel to sin. 17 And Jeroboam's wife arose, and departed, and came to Tirzah: *and* as she came to the threshold of the house, the child died. 18 And all Israel buried him, and mourned for him; according to the word of the LORD, which he spake by the hand of his servant Ahijah the prophet.

---

a Or, "leader."   *b* Or, "and what even now?"   *c* Or, "who did sin, and who made," etc.

Kingdom of Judah.

(4) REHOBOAM'S FORTIFICATIONS.

2 Chronicles 11 : 5-12.

5 And Rehoboam dwelt in Jerusalem, and built cities for defence in Judah. 6 He built even Beth-lehem, and Etam, and Tekoa, 7 and Beth-zur, and Soco, and Adullam, 8 and Gath, and Mareshah, and Ziph, 9 and Adoraim, and Lachish, and Azekah, 10 and Zorah, and Aijalon, and Hebron, which are in Judah and in Benjamin, fenced cities. 11 And he fortified the strong holds, and put captains in them, and store of victual, and oil and wine. 12 And in every several city *he put* shields and spears, and made them exceeding strong.   And Judah and Benjamin belonged to him.

(5) REHOBOAM'S FAMILY.

2 Chronicles 11 : 18-23.

18 And Rehoboam took him a wife, Mahalath the daughter of Jerimoth the son of David, *a and of* Abihail the daughter of Eliab the son of Jesse ; 19 and she bare him sons ; Jeush, and Shemariah, and Zaham. 20 And after her he took *b* Maacah the daughter of Absalom ; and she bare him Abijah, and Attai, and Ziza, and Shelomith. 21 And Rehoboam loved Maacah the daughter of Absalom above all his wives and his concubines : (for he took eighteen wives, and threescore concubines, and begat twenty and eight sons and threescore daughters.) 22 And Rehoboam appointed Abijah the son of Maacah to be chief, *even* the prince among his brethren : for *he was minded* to make him king. 23 And he dealt wisely, and dispersed of all his sons throughout all the lands of Judah and Benjamin, unto every fenced city : and he gave them victual in abundance.   And he *c* sought *for them* many wives.

(6) JUDAH'S APOSTASY UNDER REHOBOAM.

1 Kings 14 : 22-24.	*2 Chronicles* 12 : 1, 14.
22 And Judah did that which was evil in the sight of the LORD ; and they provoked him to jealousy with their sins which they com-	1 And it came to pass, when the kingdom of Rehoboam was established, and he was strong, that he forsook the law of the LORD,

Kingdom of Israel.

---

a Or, " *and* Abihail."   *b* In 2 Chronicles 13 : 2, " Micaiah the daughter of Uriel."   See §143, (1).   *c* Or, "sought a multitude of wives."

Kingdom of Judah.

1 *Kings* 14.

mitted, above all that their fathers had done. 23 For they also built them high places, and *a* pillars, and Asherim, on every high hill, and under every green tree; 24 and there were also *b* sodomites in the land : they did according to all the abominations of the nations which the LORD drave out before the children of Israel.

2 *Chronicles* 12.

and all Israel with him. 14 And he did that which was evil, because he set not his heart to seek the LORD.

(7) THE INVASION OF SHISHAK.

1 *Kings* 14 : 25-28.

25 And it came to pass in the fifth year of king Rehoboam, that Shishak king of Egypt came up against Jerusalem.

2 *Chronicles* 12 : 2-12.

2 And it came to pass in the fifth year of king Rehoboam, that Shishak king of Egypt came up against Jerusalem, because they had trespassed against the LORD, 3 with twelve hundred chariots, and threescore thousand horsemen : and the people were without number that came with him out of Egypt; the Lubim, the Sukkiim, and the Ethiopians. 4 And he took the fenced cities which pertained to Judah, and came unto Jerusalem. 5 Now Shemaiah the prophet came to Rehoboam, and to the princes of Judah, that were gathered together to Jerusalem because of Shishak, and said unto them, Thus saith the LORD, Ye have forsaken me, therefore have I also left you in

a Or, " obelisks."   *b* See Deuteronomy 23 : 17.

Kingdom of Judah.

1 *Kings* 14.

2 *Chronicles* 12.

the hand of Shishak. 6 Then the princes of Israel and the king humbled themselves; and they said, The LORD is righteous. 7 And when the LORD saw that they h u m b l e d themselves, the word of the LORD came to Shemaiah, saying, They have humbled themselves; I will not destroy them: but I will grant them *b* some deliverance, a n d m y wrath s h a l l n o t be poured out upon Jerusalem by the hand of Shishak. 8 Nevertheless they shall be his servants; that they may know my service, and the service of the kingdoms of the countries. 9 So Shishak king of Egypt came up against

26 And he took away the treasures o f t h e house of the LORD, and the treasures of the king's house; he even took away all: and he took away all the shields of gold which Solomon had made. 27 And king Rehoboam m a d e in their stead shields of brass, and committed them to the hands of the c a p t a i n s of the *a* guard, which kept the door of the king's house. 28 And it was so, that as oft as the king went into the house of the LORD, the guard bare them, and brought them back into the guard chamber.

Jerusalem, a n d t o o k away the treasures of the house of the LORD, and the treasures of the king's house; he took all away: he took away also the shields of gold which Solomon h a d made. 10 And king Rehoboam m a d e i n their stead shields of brass, and committed them to the hands of the captains o f t h e *a* guard, that kept the door of the king's house. 11 And it was so, that as oft as the king entered into the house of the LORD, the guard came and bare them, and brought them back into the guard chamber.

Kingdom of Israel.

---

a Heb. "runners."   *b* Or, "deliverance within a little while."   Or, "a few that shall escape."

Kingdom of Judah.	Kingdom of Israel.

2 Chronicles 12.

12 And when he humbled himself, the wrath of the LORD turned from him, that he would not destroy him altogether : and moreover in Judah *a* there were good things *found*.

(8) THE CONSTANT WARFARE BETWEEN REHOBOAM AND JEROBOAM. (6)

1 *Ki.* 14: 30.	1 *Kings* 15 : 6.	2 *Chronicles* 12 : 15*b*.
30 And there was war between Rehoboam and Jeroboam continually.	6 Now there was war between *b* Rehoboam and Jeroboam all the days of his *c* life.	15*b* And there were wars between Rehoboam and Jeroboam continually.

(9) THE DEATH OF REHOBOAM.

1 *Ki.* 14 : 21, 29, 31*a*.	2 *Ch.* 12 : 13, 15*a*, 16*a*.
21 And Rehoboam the son of Solomon reigned in Judah. Rehoboam was forty and one years old when he began to reign, and he reigned seventeen years in Jerusalem, the city which the LORD had chosen out of all the tribes of Israel, to put his name there: and his mother's name was Naamah the Ammonitess.	13 So king Rehoboam strengthened himself in Jerusalem, and reigned: for Rehoboam was forty and one years old when he began to reign, and he reigned seventeen years in Jerusalem, the city which the LORD had chosen out of all the tribes of Israel, to put his name there : and his mother's name was Naamah the Ammonitess.
29 Now the rest of the acts of Rehoboam, and all that he did, are they not written in the book of the chronicles of the kings of Judah?	15*a* Now the acts of Rehoboam, first and last, are they not written in the *d* histories of Shemaiah the prophet and of Iddo the seer, *e* after the manner of genealogies?
31*a* And Rehoboam slept with his fathers, and was buried with his fathers in the city of David: and his mother's name was Naamah the Ammonitess.	16*a* And Rehoboam slept with his fathers, and was buried in the city of David.

---

a Cf. 2 Chronicles 19:3. See §152. (8). *b* According to some authorities, "Abijam." *c* I. e., Abijah's life. See 1 Kings 15:1-8. *d* Heb. "words." *e* Or, "in reckoning the genealogies."

Kingdom of Judah.	Kingdom of Israel.

143. THE REIGN OF ABIJAH.

(1) ABIJAH'S ACCESSION TO THE THRONE.

1 *Ki.* 14:31*b*; 15: 1, 2.	2 *Ch.* 12:16*b*; 13:1, 2*a*.
31*b* And Abijam his son reigned in his stead.	16*b* And Abijah his son reigned in his stead.
1 Now in the eighteenth year of king Jeroboam the son of Nebat began Abijam to reign over Judah. 2 Three years reigned he in Jerusalem : and his mother's name was Maacah the daughter of *a*Abishalom.	1 In the eighteenth year of king Jeroboam began Abijah to reign over Judah. 2*a* Three years reigned he in Jerusalem : and his mother's name was *b* Micaiah the daughter of Uriel of Gibeah.

(2) THE WAR BETWEEN ABIJAH AND JEROBOAM. (7)

1 *Kings* 15:7*b*.	2 *Chronicles* 13: 2*b*–20*a*.

7*b* And there was war between Abijam and Jeroboam.

2*b* And there was war between Abijah and Jeroboam. 3 And Abijah joined battle with an army of valiant men of war, even four hundred thousand chosen men : and Jeroboam set the battle in array against him with eight hundred thousand chosen men, who were mighty men of valour. 4 And Abijah stood up upon mount Zemaraim, which is in the hill country of Ephraim, and said, Hear me, O Jeroboam and all Israel ; 5 ought ye not to know that the LORD, the God of Israel, gave the kingdom over Israel to David for ever, even to him and to his sons by a covenant of salt ? 6 Yet Jeroboam the son of Nebat, the servant of Solomon the son of David, rose up, and rebelled against his lord. 7 And there were gathered unto him vain men, sons of *c* Belial, which strengthened themselves against Rehoboam the son of Solomon, when Rehoboam was young and tenderhearted, and could not withstand them. 8 And now ye think to withstand the kingdom of the LORD in the hand of the sons of David ; and ye be a great multitude, and there are with you the golden calves which Jeroboam made you for gods. 9 Have ye not driven out the priests of the LORD, the sons of Aaron, and the Levites, and have made you priests after the manner of the peoples of *other* lands ? so that whosoever cometh to

---

a In 2 Chronicles 11 : 20, 21, "Absalom."   See §141, (4).   *b* Cf. 2 Chronicles 11 : 20.   See §141, (4).   *c* I. e., "worthlessness."

Kingdom of Judah.	Kingdom of Israel.

2 *Chronicles* 13.

consecrate himself with a young bullock and seven rams, the same may be a priest of *them that are* no gods. 10 But as for us, the LORD is our God, and we have not forsaken him; and *we have* priests ministering unto the LORD, the sons of Aaron, and the Levites in their work: 11 and they burn unto the LORD every morning and every evening burnt offerings and sweet incense: the shewbread also *set they* in order upon the pure table; and the candlestick of gold with the lamps thereof, to burn every evening: for we keep the charge of the LORD our God; but ye have forsaken him. 12 And, behold, God is with us at our head, and his priests with the trumpets of alarm to sound an alarm against you. O children of Israel, fight ye not against the LORD, the God of your fathers; for ye shall not prosper. 13 But Jeroboam caused an ambushment to come about behind them: so they were before Judah, and the ambushment was behind them. 14 And when Judah looked back, behold, the battle was before and behind them: and they cried unto the LORD, and the priests sounded with the trumpets. 15 Then the men of Judah gave a shout: and as the men of Judah shouted, it came to pass, that God smote Jeroboam and all Israel before Abijah and Judah. 16 And the children of Israel fled before Judah: and God delivered them into their hand. 17 And Abijah and his people slew them with a great slaughter: so there fell down slain of Israel five hundred thousand chosen men. 18 Thus the children of Israel were brought under at that time, and the children of Judah prevailed, because they relied upon the LORD, the God of their fathers. 19 And Abijah pursued after Jeroboam, and took cities from him, Beth-el with the towns thereof, and Jeshanah with the towns thereof, and ª Ephron with the towns thereof. 20ª Neither did Jeroboam recover strength again in the days of Abijah.

(3) THE FAMILY OF ABIJAH.

2 *Chronicles* 13: 21.

21 But Abijah waxed mighty, and took unto himself fourteen wives, and begat twenty and two sons, and sixteen daughters.

---

a Another reading is, "Ephrain."

Kingdom of Judah.

(4) THE CHARACTER OF ABIJAH.

1 *Kings* 15 : 3–5.

3 And he walked in all the sins of his father, which he had done before him : and his heart was not perfect with the LORD his God, as the heart of David his father. 4 Nevertheless for David's sake did the LORD his God give him a lamp in Jerusalem, to set up his son after him, and to establish Jerusalem : 5 because David did that which was right in the eyes of the LORD, and turned not aside from any thing that he commanded him all the days of his life, save only in the matter of Uriah the Hittite.

(5) THE DEATH OF ABIJAH.

1 *Ki.* 15 : 7a, 8a.	2 *Ch.* 13 : 22 ; 14 : 1a.
7a And the rest of the acts of Abijam, and all that he did, are they not written in the book of the chronicles of the kings of Judah ?	22 And the rest of the acts of Abijah, and his ways, and his sayings, are written in the commentary of the prophet Iddo.
8a And Abijam slept with his fathers ; and they buried him in the city of David.	1a *a* So Abijah slept with his fathers, and they buried him in the city of David.

144. THE REIGN OF ASA.

(1) ASA'S ACCESSION TO THE THRONE.

1 *Kings* 15 : 8b–10.	2 *Chronicles* 14 : 1b.
8b And Asa his son reigned in his stead.	1b And Asa his son reigned in his stead.
9 And in the twentieth year of Jeroboam king of Israel began Asa to reign over Judah. 10 And forty and one years reigned he in Jerusalem : and his mother's name was Maacah the daughter of Abishalom.	

(2) THE TEN YEARS OF PEACE.

2 *Chronicles* 14 : 1c.

1c In his days the land was quiet ten years.

a Ch. 13 : 23 in Heb.

Kingdom of Judah.

(3) THE CHARACTER OF ASA: HIS FIRST REFORMS.

I *Kings* 15:11.	2 *Chronicles* 14:2–5.
11 And Asa did that which was right in the eyes of the LORD, as did David his father.	2 *a* And Asa did that which was good and right in the eyes of the LORD his God: 3 for he took away the strange altars, and the high places, and brake down the *b* pillars, and hewed down the *c* Asherim; 4 and commanded Judah to seek the LORD, the God of their fathers, and to do the law and the commandment. 5 Also he took away out of all the cities of Judah the high places and the sun-images: and the kingdom was quiet before him.

(4) ASA'S POLICY OF DEFENSE.

2 *Chronicles* 14:6–8.

6 And he built fenced cities in Judah: for the land was quiet, and he had no war in those years; because the LORD had given him rest. 7 For he said unto Judah, Let us build these cities, and make about them walls, and towers, gates, and bars; the land is yet before us, because we have sought the LORD our God; we have sought him, and he hath given us rest on every side. So they built and prospered. 8 And Asa had an army that bare bucklers and spears, out of Judah three hundred thousand; and out of Benjamin, that bare shields and drew bows, two hundred and fourscore thousand: all these were mighty men of valour.

Kingdom of Israel.

(8) THE DEATH OF JEROBOAM.

I *Kings* 14:19, 20a.	2 *Chronicles* 13:20b.
19 And the rest of the acts of Jeroboam, how he warred, and how he reigned, behold, they are written in the book of the chronicles of the kings of Israel. 20a And the days which Jeroboam reigned were two and twenty years: and he slept with his fathers.	20b And the LORD smote him, and he died.

145. THE REIGN OF NADAB.

(1) NADAB'S ACCESSION TO THE THRONE.

I *Kings* 14:20b; 15:25.

20b And Nadab his son reigned in his stead. 25 And Nadab the son of Jeroboam began to reign over Israel in the second year of Asa king of Judah, and he reigned over Israel two years.

(2) THE CHARACTER OF NADAB.

I *Kings* 15:26.

26 And he did that which was evil in the sight of the LORD, and walked in the way of his father, and in his sin wherewith he made Israel to sin.

(3) THE DEATH OF NADAB.

I *Kings* 15:31, 27.

31 Now the rest of the acts of Nadab, and all that he did, are they not written in the book of the chronicles of the kings of Israel? 27 And Baasha the son of Ahijah, of the house of Issachar, conspired against him; and Baasha smote him at Gibbethon, which belonged to the Philistines; for Nadab and all Israel were laying siege to Gibbethon.

a Ch. 14:1 in Heb. - *b* Or, "obelisks." *c* See Exodus 34:13.

Kingdom of Judah.

Kingdom of Israel.

146. THE REIGN OF BAASHA.

(1) BAASHA'S ACCESSION TO THE THRONE.

1 *Kings* 15 : 28–30, 33, 34.

28 Even in the third year of Asa king of Judah did Baasha slay him, and reigned in his stead. 29 And it came to pass that, as soon as he was king, he smote all the house of Jeroboam ; he left not to Jeroboam any that breathed, until he had destroyed him ; according unto the saying of the LORD, which he spake by the hand of his servant Ahijah the Shilonite : 30 for the sins of Jeroboam which he sinned, and wherewith he made Israel to sin ; because of his provocation wherewith he provoked the LORD, the God of Israel, to anger.

33 In the third year of Asa king of Judah began Baasha the son of Ahijah to reign over all Israel in Tirzah, *and reigned* twenty and four years. 34 And he did that which was evil in the sight of the LORD, and walked in the way of Jeroboam, and in his sin wherewith he made Israel to sin.

(5) ASA'S VICTORY OVER ZERAH THE ETHIOPIAN.

2 *Chronicles* 14 : 9–15.

9 And there came out against them Zerah the Ethiopian with an army of a thousand thousand, and three hundred chariots ; and he came unto Mareshah. 10 Then Asa went out to meet him, and they set the battle in array in the valley of Zephathah at Mareshah. 11 And Asa cried unto the LORD his God, and said, LORD, *a* there is none *b* beside thee to help, between the mighty and him that hath no strength : help us, O LORD our God ; for we rely on thee, and in thy name are we come against this multitude. O LORD, thou art our God ; let not man prevail against thee. 12 So the LORD smote the Ethiopians before Asa, and before Judah ; and the Ethiopians fled. 13 And Asa and the people that were with him pursued them unto Gerar : and there fell of the Ethiopians *c* so many that they could not recover themselves ; for they were *d* destroyed before the LORD, and before his host ; and they carried away very much booty. 14 And they smote all the cities round about Gerar ; for *e* the fear of the LORD came upon them : and they

---

a Or, " there is no difference with thee to help, whether the mighty or him," etc.   *b* Or, " like."   *c* Or, " so that none remained alive."   *d* Heb. " broken."   *e* Or, " a terror from the LORD."

Kingdom of Judah.

2 *Chronicles* 14.

spoiled all the cities; for there was much spoil in them. 15 They smote also the tents of cattle, and carried away sheep in abundance and camels, and returned to Jerusalem.

(6) THE WARNING OF THE PROPHET AZARIAH.

2 *Chronicles* 15:1-7.

1 And the spirit of God came upon Azariah the son of Oded: 2 and he went out to meet Asa, and said unto him, Hear ye me, Asa, and all Judah and Benjamin: the LORD is with you, while ye be with him; and if ye seek him, he will be found of you; but if ye forsake him he will forsake you. 3 Now for *a* long seasons Israel hath been without the true God, and without a teaching priest, and without law: 4 but when in their distress they turned unto the LORD, the God of Israel, and sought him, he was found of them. 5 And in those times there was no peace to him that went out, nor to him that came in, but great vexations were upon all the inhabitants of the lands. 6 And they were broken in pieces, nation against nation, and city against city: for God did vex them with all adversity. 7 But be ye strong, and let not your hands be slack: for your work shall be rewarded.

(7) THE SECOND REFORMATION UNDER ASA.*b*

A. THE FOUR YEARS OF PEACE.*c*

2 *Chronicles* 15:19.

19 And there was no more war unto the five and thirtieth year of the reign of Asa.

B. THE REFORMS IN WORSHIP.

1 *Ki* 15:12, 14, 15.	2 *Ch*. 15:8, 17, 18.
	8 And when Asa heard these words, *d* and the prophecy of Oded the prophet, he took courage, and put away the abominations out of all the land of Judah and Benjamin, and out of the cities which he had
12 And he put away the sodomites out of the land, and removed all the idols that his fathers had made.	

Kingdom of Israel.

---

a Or, "a long season." *b* For the first reformation, see under (3). *c* Determined thus: The first ten years of Asa's reign were years of peace, 2 Chronicles 14:1*c*, §144, (2). Then came the victory over Zerah in the eleventh year. Understand in 2 Chronicles 15:19, "the five and thirtieth year of the kingdom of Asa"—i. e., his fifteenth year. Or, it may be, that in the earlier MSS. the numeral ל (30) was taken for י (10); hence, the "five and thirtieth," instead of "fifteenth." By either interpretation, 2 Chronicles 15:19 means the "fifteenth year of the reign of Asa." Hence, the four years of peace. *d* Or, "even."

15

Kingdom of Judah.	Kingdom of Israel.

Kingdom of Judah.

1 *Kings* 15.	2 *Chronicles* 15.
	taken from the hill country of Ephraim ; and he renewed the altar of the LORD, that was before the porch of the LORD.
14 But the high places were not taken away : nevertheless the heart of Asa was perfect with the LORD all his days. 15 And he brought into the house of the LORD the things that his father had dedicated, and the things that himself had dedicated, silver, and gold, and vessels.	17 But the high places were not taken away out of Israel : nevertheless the heart of Asa was perfect all his days. 18 And he brought into the house of God the things that his father had dedicated, and that he himself had dedicated, silver, and gold, and vessels.

C. THE RENEWAL OF THE COVENANT.

2 *Chronicles* 15 : 9–15.

9 And he gathered all Judah and Benjamin, and them that sojourned with them out of Ephraim and Manasseh, and out of Simeon : for they fell to him out of Israel in abundance, when they saw that the LORD his God was with him. 10 So they gathered themselves together at Jerusalem in the third month, in the fifteenth *a* year of the reign of Asa. 11 And they sacrificed unto the LORD in that day, of the spoil which they had brought, seven hundred oxen and seven thousand sheep. 12 And they entered into the covenant to seek the LORD, the God of their fathers, with all their heart and with all their soul ; 13 and that whosoever would not seek the LORD, the God of Israel, should be put to death, whether small or great, whether man or woman. 14 And they sware unto the LORD with a loud voice, and with shouting, and with trumpets, and with cornets. 15 And all Judah rejoiced at the oath : for they had sworn with all their heart, and sought him with their whole desire ; and he was found of them : and the LORD gave them rest round about.

D. THE REMOVAL OF MAACAH, THE QUEEN MOTHER.

1 *Kings* 15 : 13.	2 *Chronicles* 15 : 16.
13 And also Maacah his mother he removed	16 And also Maacah the mother of Asa the

a Cf. note under (7), *A*.

Kingdom of Judah.

1 *Kings* 15.	2 *Chronicles* 15.
from being *a* queen, because she had made an abominable image *b* for an Asherah; and Asa cut down her image, and burnt it at the brook Kidron.	king, he removed her from being *a* queen, because she had made an abominable image *b* for an Asherah; and Asa cut down her image, and made dust of it, and burnt it at the brook Kidron.

Kingdom of Israel.

(8) THE WAR BETWEEN ASA AND BAASHA. (2)

1 *Kings* 15 : 17–22, 16.	1 *Kings* 15 : 32.	2 *Chronicles* 16 : 1–6.
17 And Baasha king of Israel went up against Judah, and built Ramah, that he might not suffer any to go out or come in to Asa king of Judah. 18 Then Asa took all the silver and the gold that were left in the treasures of the house of the LORD, and the treasures of the king's house, and delivered them into the hand of his servants : and king Asa sent them to Ben-hadad, the son of Tabrimmon, the son of Hezion, king of Syria, that dwelt at Damascus, saying, 19 *c There is* a league between me and thee, between my father and thy father : behold, I have sent unto thee a present of silver and gold ; go, break thy league with Baasha king of Israel, that he may depart from me. 20 And Ben-hadad hearkened unto king Asa, and sent the captains of his armies against the cities of Israel, and smote Ijon, and Dan, and Abel-beth-maacah, and all Chinneroth, with all the land of Naphtali. 21 And it came to pass, when Baasha heard thereof, that he left off building of Ramah, and dwelt in Tirzah. 22 Then king Asa made a proclamation		1 In the six and thirtieth *d* year of the reign of Asa, Baasha king of Israel went up against Judah, and built Ramah, that he might not suffer any to go out or come in to Asa king of Judah. 2 Then Asa brought out silver and gold out of the treasures of the house of the LORD and of the king's house, and sent to Ben-hadad king of Syria, that dwelt at *e* Damascus, saying, 3 *c There is* a league between thee and me, as *there was* between my father and thy father : behold, I have sent thee silver and gold ; go, break thy league with Baasha king of Israel, that he may depart from me. 4 And Ben-hadad hearkened unto king Asa, and sent the captains of his armies against the cities of Israel ; and they smote Ijon, and Dan, and Abel-maim, and all the *f* store cities of Naphtali. 5 And it came to pass, when Baasha heard thereof, that he left off building of Ramah, and let his work cease. 6 Then Asa the king took all Judah ; and they carried away the stones of Ramah, and the timber thereof, wherewith Baasha had builded ; and

a Or, "queen mother."   *b* Or, "for Asherah."   *c* Or, "*Let there be.*"   *d* Read, "the six and thirtieth year of the kingdom of Asa"—i. e., the fifteenth year of Asa's reign. Cf. note under §144, (7), *A*.   *e* Heb. "Darmesek."   *f* Heb. "storehouses of the cities."

Kingdom of Judah.		Kingdom of Israel.

1 *Kings* 15.

unto all Judah ; none was exempted : and they carried away the stones of Ramah, and the timber thereof, wherewith Baasha had builded ; and king Asa built therewith Geba of Benjamin, and Mizpah.

16 And there was war between Asa and Baasha king of Israel all their days.

1 *Kings* 15.

32 And there was war between Asa and Baasha king of Israel all their days.

2 *Chronicles* 16.

he built therewith Geba and Mizpah.

(9) The Warning of the Prophet Hanani.

2 *Chronicles* 16 : 7–9.

7 And at that time Hanani the seer came to Asa king of Judah, and said unto him, Because thou hast relied on the king of Syria, and hast not relied on the Lord thy God, therefore is the host of the king of Syria escaped out of thine hand.   8 Were not the Ethiopians and the Lubim a huge host, with chariots and horsemen exceeding many ? yet, because thou didst rely on the Lord, he delivered them into thine hand.   9 For the eyes of the Lord run to and fro throughout the whole earth, to shew himself strong in the behalf of them whose heart is perfect toward him. Herein thou hast done foolishly ; for from henceforth thou shalt have wars.

(10) Asa's Transgression.

2 *Chronicles* 16 : 10.

10 Then Asa was wroth with the seer, and put him in the *a* prison house ; for he was in a rage with him because of this thing.   And Asa oppressed some of the people the same time.

(3) The Prophecy of Jehu against Baasha and his House.

1 *Kings* 16 : 7, 1–4.

7 And moreover by the hand of the prophet Jehu the son of Hanani came the word of the Lord against Baasha, and against his house, both because of all the evil that he did in the sight of the Lord, to provoke him to anger with the work of his hands, in being like the house of Jeroboam, and because he smote *b* him.   1 And the word of the Lord came to Jehu the son of Hanani against Baasha, saying,

---

a Heb. " house of the stocks."   *b* Or, " it."

Kingdom of Judah.

Kingdom of Israel.

1 *Kings* 16.

2 Forasmuch as I exalted thee out of the dust, and made thee *a* prince over my people Israel; and thou hast walked in the way of Jeroboam, and hast made my people Israel to sin, to provoke me to anger with their sins; 3 behold, I will utterly sweep away Baasha and his house; and I will make thy house like the house of Jeroboam the son of Nebat. 4 Him that dieth of Baasha in the city shall the dogs eat; and him that dieth of his in the field shall the fowls of the air eat.

(4) THE DEATH OF BAASHA.

1 *Kings* 16 : 5, 6a.

5 Now the rest of the acts of Baasha, and what he did, and his might, are they not written in the book of the chronicles of the kings of Israel? 6a And Baasha slept with his fathers, and was buried in Tirzah.

147. THE REIGN OF ELAH.

1 *Kings* 16 : 6b, 8, 14, 9, 10.

6b And Elah his son reigned in his stead.

8 In the twenty and sixth year of Asa king of Judah began Elah the son of Baasha to reign over Israel in Tirzah, *and reigned* two years. 14 Now the rest of the acts of Elah, and all that he did, are they not written in the book of the chronicles of the kings of Israel? 9 And his servant Zimri, captain of half his chariots, conspired against him: now he was in Tirzah, drinking himself drunk in the house of Arza, which was over the household in Tirzah: 10 and Zimri went in and smote him, and killed him, in the twenty and seventh year of Asa king of Judah, and reigned in his stead.

148. THE REIGN OF ZIMRI.

1 *Kings* 16 : 15a, 11-13, 20, 15b-19.

15a In the twenty and seventh year of Asa king of Judah did Zimri reign seven days in Tirzah. 11 And it came to pass, when he began to reign, as soon as he sat on his throne, that he smote all the house of Baasha: he left him not a single man child, neither of his kinsfolks, nor of his friends. 12 Thus did Zimri destroy all the

---

a Or, " leader."

Kingdom of Judah.	Kingdom of Israel.

Kingdom of Israel.

1 *Kings* 16.

house of Baasha, according to the word of the LORD, which he spake against Baasha by Jehu the prophet, 13 for all the sins of Baasha, and the sins of Elah his son, which they sinned, and wherewith they made Israel to sin, to provoke the LORD, the God of Israel, to anger with their vanities. 20 Now the rest of the acts of Zimri, and his treason that he wrought, are they not written in the book of the chronicles of the kings of Israel?

15*b* Now the people were encamped against Gibbethon, which belonged to the Philistines. 16 And the people that were encamped heard say, Zimri hath conspired, and hath also smitten the king: wherefore all Israel made Omri, the captain of the host, king over Israel that day in the camp. 17 And Omri went up from Gibbethon, and all Israel with him, and they besieged Tirzah. 18 And it came to pass, when Zimri saw that the city was taken, that he went into the *a* castle of the king's house, and burnt the king's house over him with fire, and died, 19 for his sins which he sinned in doing that which was evil in the sight of the LORD, in walking in the way of Jeroboam, and in his sin which he did, to make Israel to sin.

149. THE REIGNS OF TIBNI AND OMRI.

(1) THE CIVIL WAR.

1 *Kings* 16 : 21.

21 Then were the people of Israel divided into two parts : half of the people followed Tibni the son of Ginath, to make him king; and half followed Omri.

(2) OMRI MARRIES HIS SON AHAB TO JEZEBEL OF ZIDON.*b*

1 *Kings* 16 : 31*a*.

31*a* And it came to pass, as if it had been a light thing for him to walk in the sins of Jeroboam the son of Nebat, that he [i. e., Ahab] took to wife *c* Jezebel the daughter of Ethbaal king of the Zidonians.

---

a Or, "palace."   *b* This marriage could not have occurred before Omri's accession.   It could not have occurred many years after his accession, for Ahaziah, the grandson of Ahab and Jezebel, was twenty-two years old at the beginning of A. Di. 90. Cf. 2 Kings 8 : 26. See §156, (1). It is to be remembered, too, that Ahaziah was the youngest son of Jehoram. 2 Chronicles 22 : 1, §156, (1).   *c* Heb. "Izebel."

| Kingdom of Judah. | Kingdom of Israel. |

Kingdom of Israel.

(3) Omri becomes sole King.

1 *Kings* 16: 22.

22 But the people that followed Omri prevailed against the people that followed Tibni the son of Ginath: so Tibni died, and Omri reigned.

150. THE REIGN OF OMRI.

(1) The first six Years in Tirzah.

1 *Kings* 16: 23.

23 In the thirty and first year of Asa king of Judah began Omri to reign over Israel, *and reigned* twelve years: six years reigned he in Tirzah.

(2) Omri makes Samaria his Capital.

1 *Kings* 16: 24.

24 And he bought the hill *a* Samaria of Shemer for two talents of silver; and he *b* built on the hill, and he called the name of the city which he built, after the name of Shemer, the owner of the hill, *a* Samaria.

(3) The Character of Omri.

1 *Kings* 16: 25, 26.

25 And Omri did that which was evil in the sight of the LORD, and dealt wickedly above all that were before him. 26 For he walked in all the way of Jeroboam the son of Nebat, and in his sins wherewith he made Israel to sin, to provoke the LORD, the God of Israel, to anger with their vanities.

(4) The Death of Omri.

1 *Kings* 16: 27, 28a.

27 Now the rest of the acts of Omri which he did, and his might that he shewed, are they not written in the book of the chronicles of the kings of Israel? 28a So Omri slept with his fathers, and was buried in Samaria.

151. THE REIGN OF AHAB.

(1) Ahab's Accession to the Throne.

1 *Kings* 16: 28b, 29.

28b And Ahab his son reigned in his stead.
29 And in the thirty and eighth year of Asa king of Judah began Ahab the son of Omri to

---

a Heb. "Shomeron."   *b* Or, "fortified the hill."

Kingdom of Judah.	Kingdom of Israel.

Kingdom of Israel.

1 Kings 16.

reign over Israel: and Ahab the son of Omri reigned over Israel in Samaria twenty and two years.

(2) THE CHARACTER OF AHAB.

1 *Kings* 16: 30, 31*b*–33.	1 *Kings* 21 : 25, 26.
30 And Ahab the son of Omri did that which was evil in the sight of the LORD above all that were before him. 31*b* And [he] went and served Baal, and worshipped him. 32 And he reared up an altar for Baal in the house of Baal, which he had built in Samaria. 33 And Ahab made *a* the Asherah; and Ahab did yet more to provoke the LORD, the God of Israel, to anger than all the kings of Israel that were before him.	25 But there was none like unto Ahab, which did sell himself to do that which was evil in the sight of the LORD, whom Jezebel his wife stirred up. 26 And he did very abominably in following idols, according to all that the Amorites did, whom the LORD cast out before the children of Israel.

(11) ASA'S ILLNESS.

1 *Kings* 15 : 23*b*.	2 *Chronicles* 16 : 12.
23*b* But in the time of his old age he was diseased in his feet.	12 And in the thirty and ninth year of his reign Asa was diseased in his feet; his disease was exceeding great : yet in his disease he sought not to the LORD, but to the physicians.

(12) THE DEATH OF ASA.

1 *Ki.* 15 : 23*a*, 24*a*.	2 *Ch.* 16 : 11, 13, 14.
23*a* Now the rest of all the acts of Asa, and all his might, and all that he did, and the cities which he built, are they not written in the book of the chronicles of the kings of Judah ?	11 And, behold, the acts of Asa, first and last, lo, they are written in the book of the kings of Judah and Israel. 13 And Asa slept with his fathers, and died in the one and fortieth year

(3) THE REBUILDING OF JERICHO.

1 *Kings* 16 : 34.

34 In his days *b* did Hiel the Beth-elite build Jericho : he laid the foundation thereof with the loss of Abiram his firstborn, and set up the gates thereof with the loss of his youngest son Segub ; according to the word of the LORD, which he spake by the hand of Joshua the son of Nun.

---

a Cf. 2 Kings 13 : 6. See §163, (4).   *b* See Joshua 6 : 26.

Kingdom of Judah.		Kingdom of Israel.

Kingdom of Judah.

1 *Kings* 15.

24a And Asa slept with his fathers, and was buried with his fathers in the city of David his father.

2 *Chronicles* 16.

of his reign. 14 And they buried him in his own sepulchres, which he had hewn out for himself in the city of David, and laid him in the bed which was filled with sweet odours and divers kinds *of spices* prepared by the apothecaries' art : and they made a very great burning for him.

152. THE REIGN OF JEHOSHA-PHAT.

(1) JEHOSHAPHAT'S ACCESSION TO THE THRONE.

1 *Kings* 15 : 24b ; 22 : 41, 42.

24b And Jehoshaphat his son reigned in his stead.

41 And Jehoshaphat the son of Asa began to reign over Judah in the fourth year of Ahab king of Israel. 42 Jehoshaphat was thirty and five years old when he began to reign ; and he reigned twenty and five years in Jerusalem. And his mother's name was Azubah the daughter of Shilhi.

2 *Chronicles* 17 : 1a ; 20 : 31.

1a And Jehoshaphat his son reigned in his stead.

31 And Jehoshaphat reigned over Judah : he was thirty and five years old when he began to reign : and he reigned twenty and five years in Jerusalem : and his mother's name was Azubah the daughter of Shilhi.

(2) THE CHARACTER OF JEHOSHAPHAT.

1 *Kings* 22 : 43, 46.

43 And he walked in all the way of Asa his father ; he turned not aside from it, doing that which was right in the eyes of the LORD : howbeit the high places were not taken away ;

2 *Chronicles* 20 : 32, 33.

32 And he walked in the way of Asa his father, and turned not aside from it, doing that which was right in the eyes of the LORD. 33 Howbeit the high places were not taken

Kingdom of Judah.		Kingdom of Israel.

Kingdom of Judah.

1 *Kings* 22.

the people still sacri-
ficed and burnt incense
in the h i g h places.
46 And the remnant of
the sodomites, which
remained in the days of
his father Asa, he put
away out of the land.

2 *Chronicles* 20.

away; neither as yet
had the people set their
hearts unto the God of
their fathers.

(3) JEHOSHAPHAT STRENGTHENS HIS KINGDOM.

2 *Chronicles* 17 : 1b–6.

1b And [he] strengthened himself against Israel. 2 And he placed forces in all the fenced
cities of Judah, and set garrisons in the land
of Judah, and in the cities of Ephraim, which
Asa his father had taken. 3 And the LORD
was with Jehoshaphat, because he walked in
the first ways of his father David, and sought
not unto the Baalim; 4 but sought to the God
of his father, and walked in his commandments,
and not after the doings of Israel. 5 Therefore
the LORD stablished the kingdom in his hand;
and all Judah brought to Jehoshaphat presents;
and he had riches and honour in abundance.
6 And his heart was lifted up in the ways of the
LORD: and furthermore he took away the high
places and the Asherim out of Judah.

(4) THE MISSION OF THE PRINCES, LEVITES, AND PRIESTS.

2 *Chronicles* 17 : 7–9.

7 Also in the third year of his reign he sent
his princes, even Ben-hail, and Obadiah, and
Zechariah, and Nethanel, and Micaiah, to teach
in the cities of Judah; 8 and with them the
Levites, even Shemaiah, and Nethaniah, and
Zebadiah, and Asahel, and Shemiramoth, and
Jehonathan, and Adonijah, and Tobijah, and
Tob-adonijah, the Levites; and with them Elishama and Jehoram, the priests. 9 And they
taught in Judah, having the book of the law of
the LORD with them; and they went about
throughout all the cities of Judah, and taught
among the people.

Kingdom of Judah.

(5) Jehoshaphat's increasing Power.

2 *Chronicles* 17 : 10–18 : 1*a*.

10 And *ᵃ* the fear of the LORD fell upon all the kingdoms of the lands that were round about Judah, so that they made no war against Jehoshaphat. 11 And some of the Philistines brought Jehoshaphat presents, and silver for tribute; the Arabians also brought him flocks, seven thousand and seven hundred rams, and seven thousand and seven hundred he-goats. 12 And Jehoshaphat waxed great exceedingly; and he built in Judah castles and cities of store. 13 And he had many works in the cities of Judah; and men of war, mighty men of valour, in Jerusalem. 14 And this was the numbering of them according to their fathers' houses: of Judah, the captains of thousands; Adnah the captain, and with him mighty men of valour three hundred thousand: 15 and next to him Jehohanan the captain, and with him two hundred and fourscore thousand: 16 and next to him Amasiah the son of Zichri, who willingly offered himself unto the LORD; and with him two hundred thousand mighty men of valour: 17 and of Benjamin; Eliada a mighty man of valour, and with him two hundred thousand armed with bow and shield: 18 and next to him Jehozabad, and with him an hundred and fourscore thousand ready prepared for war. 19 These were they that waited on the king, beside those whom the king put in the fenced cities throughout all Judah.

1*a* Now Jehoshaphat had riches and honour in abundance.

Kingdom of Israel.

(6) Jehoshaphat marries his Son Iehoram to Athaliah, Daughter of Ahab. (4)

1 *Kings* 22:44.

44 And Jehoshaphat made peace with the king of Israel.

2 *Chronicles* 18 : 1*b*.

1*b* And he joined affinity with Ahab.

(5) The Persecution of the Prophets.

1 *Kings* 18 : 3*b*, 4.

3*b* Now Obadiah feared the LORD greatly: 4 for it was so, when Jezebel cut off the prophets of the LORD, that Obadiah took an hundred prophets, and hid them by fifty in a cave, and fed them with bread and water.

a Or, "a terror from the LORD."

Kingdom of Judah.	Kingdom of Israel.

Kingdom of Israel.

(6) ELIJAH THE TISHBITE.

A. THE FAMINE FORETOLD.

1 *Kings* 17 : 1.

1 And Elijah the Tishbite, who was [a] of the sojourners of Gilead, said unto Ahab, As the LORD, the God of Israel, liveth, before whom I stand, there shall not be dew nor rain these years, but according to my word.

B. ELIJAH HIDES BY THE BROOK CHERITH.

1 *Kings* 17 : 2–7.

2 And the word of the LORD came unto him, saying, 3 Get thee hence, and turn thee eastward, and hide thyself by the brook Cherith, that is before Jordan. 4 And it shall be, that thou shalt drink of the brook ; and I have commanded the ravens to feed thee there. 5 So he went and did according unto the word of the LORD : for he went and dwelt by the brook Cherith, that is before Jordan. 6 And the ravens brought him bread and flesh in the morning, and bread and flesh in the evening ; and he drank of the brook. 7 And it came to pass after a while, that the brook dried up, because there was no rain in the land.

C. ELIJAH IN ZAREPHATH.

1 *Kings* 17 : 8–16.

8 And the word of the LORD came unto him, saying, 9 Arise, get thee to Zarephath, which belongeth to Zidon, and dwell there : behold, I have commanded a widow woman there to sustain thee. 10 So he arose and went to Zarephath ; and when he came to the gate of the city, behold, a widow woman was there gathering sticks : and he called to her, and said, Fetch me, I pray thee, a little water in a vessel, that I may drink. 11 And as she was going to fetch it, he called to her, and said, Bring me, I pray thee, a morsel of bread in thine hand. 12 And she said, As the LORD thy God liveth, I have not a cake, but an handful of meal in the barrel, and a little oil in the cruse : and, behold, I am gathering two sticks, that I may go in and dress it for me and my son, that we may eat it, and die. 13 And Elijah said unto her, Fear not ; go and do as thou hast said : but make me thereof a little cake first, and bring it forth unto me, and after-

---

[a] According to the Sept., " of Tishbeh of Gilead."

Kingdom of Judah.	Kingdom of Israel.

Kingdom of Israel.

1 *Kings* 17.

ward make for thee and for thy son. 14 For thus saith the LORD, the God of Israel, The barrel of meal shall not waste, neither shall the cruse of oil fail, until the day that the LORD sendeth rain upon the earth. 15 And she went and did according to the saying of Elijah : and she, and he, and her house, did eat *many* days. 16 The barrel of meal wasted not, neither did the cruse of oil fail, according to the word of the LORD, which he spake by Elijah.

D. ELIJAH RAISES THE WIDOW'S SON.

1 *Kings* 17 : 17–24.

17 And it came to pass after these things, that the son of the woman, the mistress of the house, fell sick ; and his sickness was so sore, that there was no breath left in him. 18 And she said unto Elijah, What have I to do with thee, O thou man of God ? *a* thou art come unto me to bring my sin to remembrance, and to slay my son ! 19 And he said unto her, Give me thy son.. And he took him out of her bosom, and carried him up into the chamber, where he abode, and laid him upon his own bed. 20 And he cried unto the LORD, and said, O LORD my God, hast thou also brought evil upon the widow with whom I sojourn, by slaying her son ? 21 And he stretched himself upon the child three times, and cried unto the LORD, and said, O LORD my God, I pray thee, let this child's soul come into him again. 22 And the LORD hearkened unto the voice of Elijah ; and the soul of the child came into him again, and he revived. 23 And Elijah took the child, and brought him down out of the chamber into the house, and delivered him unto his mother : and Elijah said, See, thy son liveth. 24 And the woman said to Elijah, Now I know that thou art a man of God, and that the word of the LORD in thy mouth is truth.

E. ELIJAH GOES TO MEET AHAB.

1 *Kings* 18 : 1–3*a*, 5–16.

1 And it came to pass after many days, that the word of the LORD came to Elijah, in the third year, saying, Go, shew thyself unto Ahab ; and I will send rain upon the earth. 2 And Elijah went to shew himself unto Ahab. And

a Or, " art thou," etc.

Kingdom of Judah.	Kingdom of Israel.

Kingdom of Israel.

1 *Kings* 18.

the famine was sore in Samaria.   3a And Ahab called Obadiah, which was over the household. 5 And Ahab said unto Obadiah, Go through the land, unto all the fountains of water, and unto all the brooks : peradventure we may find grass and save the horses and mules alive, *a* that we lose not all the beasts.   6 So they divided the land between them to pass throughout it : Ahab went one way by himself, and Obadiah went another way by himself.   7 And as Obadiah was in the way, behold, Elijah met him : and he knew him, and fell on his face, and said, Is it thou, my lord Elijah ?   8 And he answered him, It is I : go, tell thy lord, Behold, Elijah *is here.*   9 And he said, Wherein have I sinned, that thou wouldest deliver thy servant into the hand of Ahab, to slay me ?   10 As the LORD thy God liveth, there is no nation or kingdom, whither my lord hath not sent to seek thee : and when they said, He is not here, he took an oath of the kingdom and nation, that they found thee not.   11 And now thou sayest, Go, tell thy lord, Behold, Elijah *is here.*   12 And it shall come to pass, as soon as I am gone from thee, that the spirit of the LORD shall carry thee whither I know not ; and so when I come and tell Ahab, and he cannot find thee, he shall slay me : but I thy servant fear the LORD from my youth. 13 Was it not told my lord what I did when Jezebel slew the prophets of the LORD, how I hid an hundred men of the LORD'S prophets by fifty in a cave, and fed them with bread and water ?   14 And now thou sayest, Go, tell thy lord, Behold, Elijah *is here :* and he shall slay me.   15 And Elijah said, As the LORD of hosts liveth, before whom I stand, I will surely shew myself unto him to-day.   16 So Obadiah went to meet Ahab, and told him : and Ahab went to meet Elijah.

F. ELIJAH'S CHALLENGE.

1 *Kings* 18 : 17-24.

17 And it came to pass, when Ahab saw Elijah, that Ahab said unto him, Is it thou, thou troubler of Israel ?   18 And he answered, I have not troubled Israel ; but thou, and thy father's house, in that ye have forsaken the commandments of the LORD, and thou hast followed the Baalim.   19 Now therefore send, and gather to

a Or, "and lose none of."

Kingdom of Judah.	Kingdom of Israel.

Kingdom of Israel.

1 *Kings* 18.

me all Israel unto mount Carmel, and the prophets of Baal four hundred and fifty, and the prophets of the Asherah four hundred, which eat at Jezebel's table. 20 So Ahab sent unto all the children of Israel, and gathered the prophets together unto mount Carmel. 21 And Elijah came near unto all the people, and said, How long halt ye between two opinions? If the LORD be God, follow him: but if Baal, then follow him. And the people answered him not a word. 22 Then said Elijah unto the people, I, even I only, am left a prophet unto the LORD; but Baal's prophets are four hundred and fifty men. 23 Let them therefore give us two bullocks; and let them choose one bullock for themselves, and cut it in pieces, and lay it on the wood, and put no fire under: and I will dress the other bullock, and lay it on the wood, and put no fire under. 24 And call ye on the name of your god, and I will call on the name of the LORD: and the God that answereth by fire, let him be God. And all the people answered and said, It is well spoken,

G. JEHOVAH *versus* BAAL.

1 *Kings* 18: 25–39.

25 And Elijah said unto the prophets of Baal, Choose you one bullock for yourselves, and dress it first; for ye are many; and call on the name of your god, but put no fire under. 26 And they took the bullock which was given them, and they dressed it, and called on the name of Baal from morning even until noon, saying, O Baal, *a* hear us. But there was no voice, nor any that answered. And they *b* leaped about the altar which was made. 27 And it came to pass at noon, that Elijah mocked them, and said, Cry aloud: for he is a god; either he is musing, or he is gone aside, or he is in a journey, or peradventure he sleepeth, and must be awaked. 28 And they cried aloud, and cut themselves after their manner with *c* knives and lances, till the blood gushed out upon them. 29 And it was so, when midday was past, that they prophesied until the time of the offering of the *evening* oblation; but there was neither voice, nor any to answer, nor any *d* that regarded. 30 And Elijah said unto all the people, Come near unto me;

a Or, "answer."   *b* Or, "limped."   *c* Or, "swords."   *d* Heb. "attention."

Kingdom of Judah.	Kingdom of Israel.

Kingdom of Israel.

1 Kings 18.

and all the people came near unto him. And he repaired the altar of the LORD that was thrown down. 31 And Elijah took twelve stones, according to the number of the tribes of the sons of Jacob, unto whom the word of the LORD came, saying, Israel shall be thy name. 32 And with the stones he built an altar in the name of the LORD; and he made a trench about the altar, as great as would contain *a* two measures of seed. 33 And he put the wood in order, and cut the bullock in pieces, and laid it on the wood. And he said, Fill four barrels with water, and pour it on the burnt offering, and on the wood. 34 And he said, Do it the second time; and they did it the second time. And he said, Do it the third time; and they did it the third time. 35 And the water ran round about the altar; and he filled the trench also with water. 36 And it came to pass at the time of the offering of the *evening* oblation, that Elijah the prophet came near, and said, O LORD, the God of Abraham, of Isaac, and of Israel, let it be known this day that thou art God in Israel, and that I am thy servant, and that I have done all these things at thy word. 37 Hear me, O LORD, hear me, that this people may know that thou, LORD, art God, *b* and *that* thou hast turned their heart back again. 38 Then the fire of the LORD fell, and consumed the burnt offering, and the wood, and the stones, and the dust, and licked up the water that was in the trench. 39 And when all the people saw it, they fell on their faces: and they said, The LORD, he is God; the LORD, he is God.

H. BAAL'S PRIESTS ARE SLAIN.

1 Kings 18 : 40.

40 And Elijah said unto them, Take the prophets of Baal; let not one of them escape. And they took them: and Elijah brought them down to the brook Kishon, and slew them there.

I. THE PROMISE OF RAIN.

1 Kings 18 : 41–46.

41 And Elijah said unto Ahab, Get thee up, eat and drink; for there is the sound of abundance of rain. 42 So Ahab went up to eat and to

---

a Or, " a two-seah measure."   *b* Or, " for thou didst turn their heart backward."

Kingdom of Judah.	Kingdom of Israel.

Kingdom of Israel.

1 *Kings* 18.

drink. And Elijah went up to the top of Carmel; and he bowed himself down upon the earth, and put his face between his knees. 43 And he said to his servant, Go up now, look toward the sea. And he went up, and looked, and said, There is nothing. And he said, Go again seven times. 44 And it came to pass at the seventh time, that he said, Behold, there ariseth a cloud out of the sea, as small as a man's hand. And he said, Go up, say unto Ahab, *a* Make ready *thy chariot*, and get thee down, that the rain stop thee not. 45 And it came to pass in a little while, that the heaven grew black with clouds and wind, and there was a great rain. And Ahab rode, and went to Jezreel. 46 And the hand of the LORD was on Elijah; and he girded up his loins, and ran before Ahab to the entrance of Jezreel.

J. ELIJAH'S FLIGHT TO HOREB.

1 *Kings* 19: 1–8.

1 And Ahab told Jezebel all that Elijah had done, and withal how he had slain all the prophets with the sword. 2 Then Jezebel sent a messenger unto Elijah, saying, So let the gods do to me, and more also, if I make not thy life as the life of one of them by to-morrow about this time. 3 *b* And when he saw that, he arose, and went for his life, and came to Beer-sheba, which belongeth to Judah, and left his servant there. 4 But he himself went a day's journey into the wilderness, and came and sat down under a *c* juniper tree: and he requested for himself that he might die; and said, It is enough; now, O LORD, take away my life; for I am not better than my fathers. 5 And he lay down and slept under a juniper tree; and, behold, an angel touched him, and said unto him, Arise and eat. 6 And he looked, and, behold, there was at his head a cake baken on the *d* coals, and a cruse of water. And he did eat and drink, and laid him down again. 7 And the angel of the LORD came again the second time, and touched him, and said, Arise and eat; because the journey is too great for thee. 8 And he arose, and did eat and drink, and went in the strength of that meat forty days and forty nights unto Horeb the mount of God.

---

a Or, "Yoke."   *b* According to some ancient authorities, "And he was afraid, and arose."   *c* Or, "broom."   *d* Or, "hot stones."

16

Kingdom of Judah.	Kingdom of Israel.

Kingdom of Israel.

K. GOD'S REVELATION TO ELIJAH.

1 *Kings* 19 : 9–18.

9 And he came thither unto a cave, and lodged there ; and, behold, the word of the LORD came to him, and he said unto him, What doest thou here, Elijah ? 10 And he said, I have been very jealous for the LORD, the God of hosts ; for the children of Israel have forsaken thy covenant, thrown down thine altars, and slain thy prophets with the sword : and I, even I only, am left ; and they seek my life, to take it away. 11 And he said, Go forth, and stand upon the mount before the LORD. And, behold, the LORD passed by, and a great and strong wind rent the mountains, and brake in pieces the rocks before the LORD ; but the LORD was not in the wind : and after the wind an earthquake ; but the LORD was not in the earthquake : 12 and after the earthquake a fire ; but the LORD was not in the fire : and after the fire *a* a still small voice. 13 And it was so, when Elijah heard it, that he wrapped his face in his mantle, and went out, and stood in the entering in of the cave. And, behold, there came a voice unto him, and said, What doest thou here, Elijah ? 14 And he said, I have been very jealous for the LORD, the God of hosts ; for the children of Israel have forsaken thy covenant, thrown down thine altars, and slain thy prophets with the sword ; and I, even I only, am left ; and they seek my life, to take it away. 15 And the LORD said unto him, Go, return on thy way *b* to the wilderness of Damascus : and when thou comest, thou shalt anoint Hazael to be king over Syria : 16 and Jehu the son of Nimshi shalt thou anoint to be king over Israel : and Elisha the son of Shaphat of Abel-meholah shalt thou anoint to be prophet in thy room. 17 And it shall come to pass, that him that escapeth from the sword of Hazael shall Jehu slay : and him that escapeth from the sword of Jehu shall Elisha slay. 18 Yet will I leave *me* seven thousand in Israel, all the knees which have not bowed unto Baal, and every mouth which hath not kissed him.

L. THE CALL OF ELISHA.

1 *Kings* 19 : 19–21.

19 So he departed thence, and found Elisha the son of Shaphat, who was plowing, with

---

a Heb. " a sound of gentle stillness."   *b* Or, "by the wilderness to."

Kingdom of Judah.

Kingdom of Israel.

1 *Kings* 19.

twelve yoke *of oxen* before him, and he with the twelfth: and Elijah passed over unto him, and cast his mantle upon him. 20 And he left the oxen, and ran after Elijah, and said, Let me, I pray thee, kiss my father and my mother, and then I will follow thee. And he said unto him, Go back again; for what have I done to thee? 21 And he returned from following him, and took the yoke of oxen, and slew them, and *a* boiled their flesh with the instruments of the oxen, and gave unto the people, and they did eat. Then he arose, and went after Elijah, and ministered unto him.

(7) AHAB'S FIRST SYRIAN CAMPAIGN.

A. BEN-HADAD BESIEGES SAMARIA.

1 *Kings* 20: 1.

1 And Ben-hadad the king of Syria gathered all his host together: and there were thirty and two kings with him, and horses and chariots: and he went up and besieged Samaria, and fought against it.

B. BEN-HADAD'S ARROGANT CLAIMS.

1 *Kings* 20: 2–12.

2 And he sent messengers to Ahab king of Israel, into the city, and said unto him, Thus saith Ben-hadad, 3 Thy silver and thy gold is mine; thy wives also and thy children, even the goodliest, are mine. 4 And the king of Israel answered and said, It is according to thy saying, my lord, O king; I am thine, and all that I have. 5 And the messengers came again, and said, Thus speaketh Ben-hadad, saying, I sent indeed unto thee, saying, Thou shalt deliver me thy silver, and thy gold, and thy wives, and thy children; 6 but I will send my servants unto thee to-morrow about this time, and they shall search thine house, and the houses of thy servants; and it shall be, that *b* whatsoever is pleasant in thine eyes, they shall put it in their hand, and take it away. 7 Then the king of Israel called all the elders of the land, and said, Mark, I pray you, and see how this man seeketh mischief: for he sent unto me for my wives, and for my children, and for my silver, and for my gold; and I denied

---

a Or, "roasted." *b* Heb. "all the desire of thine eyes."

Kingdom of Judah.	Kingdom of Israel.

Kingdom of Israel.

1 *Kings* 20.

him not. 8 And all the elders and all the people said unto him, Hearken thou not, neither consent. 9 Wherefore he said unto the messengers of Ben-hadad, Tell my lord the king, All that thou didst send for to thy servant at the first I will do : but this thing I may not do. And the messengers departed, and brought him word again. 10 And Ben-hadad sent unto him, and said, The gods do so unto me, and more also, if the dust of Samaria shall suffice for handfuls for all the people that *a* follow me. 11 And the king of Israel answered and said, Tell him, Let not him that girdeth on *his armour* boast himself as he that putteth it off. 12 And it came to pass, when *Ben-hadad* heard this message, as he was drinking, he and the kings, in the *b* pavilions, that he said unto his servants, *c* Set *yourselves in array.* And· they set *themselves in array* against the city.

C. GOD'S PROMISE OF VICTORY.

1 *Kings* 20 : 13, 14.

13 And, behold, a prophet came near unto Ahab king of Israel, and said, Thus saith the LORD, Hast thou seen all this great multitude ? behold, I will deliver it into thine hand this day ; and thou shalt know that I am the LORD. 14 And Ahab said, By whom ? And he said, Thus saith the LORD, By the *d* young men of the princes of the provinces. Then he said, Who shall *e* begin the battle ? And he answered, Thou.

D. AHAB'S VICTORY OVER THE SYRIANS.

1 *Kings* 20 : 15-21.

15 Then he mustered the young men of the princes of the provinces, and they were two hundred and thirty two : and after them he mustered all the people, even all the children of Israel, being seven thousand. 16 And they went out at noon. But Ben-hadad was drinking himself drunk in the pavilions, he and the kings, the thirty and two kings that helped him. 17 And the young men of the princes of the provinces went out first ; and Ben-hadad sent out, and they told him, saying, There are men come out from Samaria. 18 And he said, Whether they

a Heb. "are at my feet."   *b* Or, "huts."   *c* Or, "Place *the engines*. And they placed *the engines*."   *d* Or, "servants."   *e* Heb. " bind."

Kingdom of Judah.

Kingdom of Israel.

1 *Kings* 20.

be come out for peace, take them alive; or whether they be come out for war, take them alive. 19 So these went out of the city, the young men of the princes of the provinces, and the army which followed them. 20 And they slew every one his man; and the Syrians fled, and Israel pursued them: and Ben-hadad the king of Syria escaped *a* on an horse with horsemen. 21 And the king of Israel went out, and smote the horses and chariots, and slew the Syrians with a great slaughter.

(8) AHAB'S SECOND SYRIAN CAMPAIGN.

A. THE PROPHET'S WARNING.

1 *Kings* 20:22.

22 And the prophet came near to the king of Israel, and said unto him, Go, strengthen thyself, and mark, and see what thou doest: for at the return of the year the king of Syria will come up against thee.

B. AHAB AGAIN VICTORIOUS.

1 *Kings* 20:23–30*a*.

23 And the servants of the king of Syria said unto him, Their god is a god of the hills; therefore they were stronger than we: but let us fight against them in the plain, and surely we shall be stronger than they. 24 And do this thing; take the kings away, every man out of his place, and put *b* captains in their room: 25 and number thee an army, like the army that thou hast lost, horse for horse, and chariot for chariot: and we will fight against them in the plain, and surely we shall be stronger than they. And he hearkened unto their voice, and did so. 26 And it came to pass at the return of the year, that Ben-hadad mustered the Syrians, and went up to Aphek, to fight against Israel. 27 And the children of Israel were mustered, and were victualled, and went against them: and the children of Israel encamped before them like two little flocks of kids; but the Syrians filled the country. 28 And *c* a man of God came near and spake unto the king of Israel, and said, Thus saith the LORD, Because the Syrians have said, The LORD is a god of the hills, but he is not a god of the val-

---

a Or, " with horse and horsemen."   *b* Or, " governors."   Cf. 1 Kings 10 : 15.   See §135, (4).   *c* Or, "the."

Kingdom of Judah.	Kingdom of Israel.

Kingdom of Israel.

1 *Kings* 20.

leys ; therefore will I deliver all this great multitude into thine hand, and ye shall know that I am the LORD. 29 And they encamped one over against the other seven days. And so it was, that in the seventh day the battle was joined ; and the children of Israel slew of the Syrians an hundred thousand footmen in one day. 30*a* But the rest fled to Aphek, into the city ; and the wall fell upon twenty and seven thousand men that were left.

C. AHAB SPARES BEN-HADAD.

1 *Kings* 20: 30*b*–34.

30*b* And Ben-hadad fled, and came into the city, *a* into an inner chamber. 31 And his servants said unto him, Behold now, we have heard that the kings of the house of Israel are merciful kings : let us, we pray thee, put sackcloth on our loins, and ropes upon our heads, and go out to the king of Israel : peradventure he will save thy life. 32 So they girded sackcloth on their loins, and *put* ropes on their heads, and came to the king of Israel, and said, Thy servant Ben-hadad saith, I pray thee, let me live. And he said, Is he yet alive? he is my brother. 33 Now the men *b* observed diligently and hasted *c* to catch whether it were *d* his mind ; and they said, Thy brother Ben-hadad. Then he said, Go ye, bring him. Then Ben-hadad came forth to him ; and he caused him to come up into the chariot. 34 And *Ben-hadad* said unto him, The cities which my father took from thy father I will restore ; and thou shalt make streets for thee in Damascus, as my father made in Samaria. And I, *said Ahab,* will let thee go with this covenant. So he made a covenant with him, and let him go.

D. THE PROPHET'S REBUKE.

1 *Kings* 20: 35–43.

35 And a certain man of the sons of the prophets said unto his fellow by the word of the LORD, Smite me, I pray thee. And the man refused to smite him. 36 Then said he unto him, Because thou hast not obeyed the voice of the LORD, behold, as soon as thou art departed from me, a lion shall slay thee. And as soon as he was departed from him, a lion found him,

---

a Or, " from chamber to chamber."   *b* Or, " took it as an omen (Heb. divined), and hasted."   *c* Another reading is, "to catch it from him."   *d* Heb. " from him."

Kingdom of Judah.	Kingdom of Israel.

Kingdom of Israel.

1 *Kings* 20.

and slew him. 37 Then he found another man, and said, Smite me, I pray thee. And the man smote him, smiting and wounding him. 38 So the prophet departed, and waited for the king by the way, and disguised himself with his headband over his eyes. 39 And as the king passed by, he cried unto the king: and he said, Thy servant went out into the midst of the battle; and, behold, a man turned aside, and brought a man unto me, and said, Keep this man: if by any means he be missing, then shall thy life be for his life, or else thou shalt pay a talent of silver. 40 And as thy servant was busy here and there, he was gone. And the king of Israel said unto him, So shall thy judgement be; thyself hast decided it. 41 And he hasted, and took the headband away from his eyes; and the king of Israel discerned him that he was of the prophets. 42 And he said unto him, Thus saith the LORD, Because thou hast let go out of thy hand the man whom I had devoted to destruction, therefore thy life shall go for his life, and thy people for his people. 43 And the king of Israel went to his house heavy and displeased, and came to Samaria.

(9) THE THREE YEARS OF PEACE.

1 *Kings* 22 : 1.

1 And they continued three years without war between Syria and Israel.

(10) THE STORY OF NABOTH.

A. NABOTH'S VINEYARD IS COVETED BY AHAB.

1 *Kings* 21 : 1–3.

1 And it came to pass after these things, that Naboth the Jezreelite had a vineyard, which was in Jezreel, hard by the palace of Ahab king of Samaria. 2 And Ahab spake unto Naboth, saying, Give me thy vineyard, that I may have it for a garden of herbs, because it is near unto my house; and I will give thee for it a better vineyard than it: or, if it seem good to thee, I will give thee the worth of it in money. 3 And Naboth said to Ahab, The LORD forbid it me, that I should give the inheritance of my fathers unto thee.

Kingdom of Judah.	Kingdom of Israel.
	B. JEZEBEL CAUSES NABOTH'S DEATH.

1 *Kings* 21 : 4–16.

4 And Ahab came into his house heavy and displeased because of the word which Naboth the Jezreelite had spoken to him : for he had said, I will not give thee the inheritance of my fathers. And he laid him down upon his bed, and turned away his face, and would eat no bread. 5 But Jezebel his wife came to him, and said unto him, Why is thy spirit so sad, that thou eatest no bread ? 6 And he said unto her, Because I spake unto Naboth the Jezreelite, and said unto him, Give me thy vineyard for money ; or else, if it please thee, I will give thee *another* vineyard for it : and he answered, I will not give thee my vineyard. 7 And Jezebel his wife said unto him, Dost thou now govern the kingdom of Israel? arise, and eat bread, and let thine heart be merry : I will give thee the vineyard of Naboth the Jezreelite. 8 So she wrote *a* letters in Ahab's name, and sealed them with his seal, and sent the letters unto the elders and to the nobles that were in his city, *and* that dwelt with Naboth. 9 And she wrote in the letters, saying, Proclaim a fast, and set Naboth *b* on high among the people : 10 and set two men, sons of *c* Belial, before him, and let them bear witness against him, saying, Thou didst *d* curse God and the king. And then carry him out, and stone him, that he die. 11 And the men of his city, even the elders and the nobles who dwelt in his city, did as Jezebel had sent unto them, according as it was written in the letters which she had sent unto them. 12 They proclaimed a fast, and set Naboth *b* on high among the people. 13 And the two men, sons of Belial, came in and sat before him : and the men of Belial bare witness against him, even against Naboth, in the presence of the people, saying, Naboth did *d* curse God and the king. Then they carried him forth out of the city, and stoned him with stones, that he died. 14 Then they sent to Jezebel, saying, Naboth is stoned, and is dead. 15 And it came to pass, when Jezebel heard that Naboth was stoned, and was dead, that Jezebel said to Ahab, Arise, take possession of the vineyard of Naboth the Jezreelite, which he refused to give thee for money : for Naboth is not alive, but dead. 16 And

---

a Or, " a letter."   *b* Or, " at the head of."   *c* I. e., " worthlessness."   *d* Or, " renounce."

Kingdom of Judah.	Kingdom of Israel.

Kingdom of Israel.

1 *Kings* 21.

it came to pass, when Ahab heard that Naboth was dead, that Ahab rose up to go down to the vineyard of Naboth the Jezreelite, to take possession of it.

C. AHAB'S DOOM PRONOUNCED BY ELIJAH.

1 *Kings* 21 : 17-24.

17 And the word of the LORD came to Elijah the Tishbite, saying, 18 Arise, go down to meet Ahab king of Israel, which dwelleth in Samaria: behold, he is in the vineyard of Naboth, whither he is gone down to take possession of it. 19 And thou shalt speak unto him, saying, Thus saith the LORD, Hast thou killed, and also taken possession? and thou shalt speak unto him, saying, Thus saith the LORD, In the place where dogs licked the blood of Naboth shall dogs lick thy blood, even thine. 20 And Ahab said to Elijah, Hast thou found me, O mine enemy? And he answered, I have found thee: because thou hast sold thyself to do that which is evil in the sight of the LORD. 21 Behold, I will bring evil upon thee, and will utterly sweep thee away, and will cut off from Ahab every man child, and him that is shut up and him that is left at large in Israel: 22 and I will make thine house like the house of Jeroboam the son of Nebat, and like the house of Baasha the son of Ahijah, for the provocation wherewith thou hast provoked me to anger, and hast made Israel to sin. 23 And of Jezebel also spake the LORD, saying, The dogs shall eat Jezebel [a] by the rampart of Jezreel. 24 Him that dieth of Ahab in the city the dogs shall eat; and him that dieth in the field shall the fowls of the air eat.

D. AHAB'S REPENTANCE GAINS HIM A RESPITE.

1 *Kings* 21 : 27-29.

27 And it came to pass, when Ahab heard those words, that he rent his clothes, and put sackcloth upon his flesh, and fasted, and lay in sackcloth, and went softly. 28 And the word of the LORD came to Elijah the Tishbite, saying, 29 Seest thou how Ahab humbleth himself before me? because he humbleth himself before me, I will not bring the evil in his days: but in his son's days will I bring the evil upon his house.

---

[a] According to some ancient authorities, " in the portion," as in 2 Kings 9: 10, 36. See §155, (12), B and F.

Kingdom of Judah.	Kingdom of Israel.

Kingdom of Israel.

(11) AHAZIAH BECOMES CO-REGNANT WITH AHAB.

1 *Kings* 22 : 51.

51 Ahaziah the son of Ahab began to reign over Israel in Samaria in the seventeenth year of Jehoshaphat king of Judah, and he reigned two years over Israel.

(7) JEHOSHAPHAT JOINS AHAB IN HIS THIRD SYRIAN CAMPAIGN. (12)

A. AHAB RESOLVES TO RECOVER RAMOTH-GILEAD.

1 *Kings* 22 : 2-4.	2 *Chronicles* 18 : 2, 3.

2 And it came to pass in the third year, that Jehoshaphat the king of Judah came down to the king of Israel. 3 And the king of Israel said unto his servants, Know ye that Ramoth-gilead is ours, and we *a* be still, and take it not out of the hand of the king of Syria? 4 And he said unto Jehoshaphat, Wilt thou go with me to battle to Ramoth-gilead? And Jehoshaphat said to the king of Israel, I am as thou art, my people as thy people, my horses as thy horses.

2 And after certain years he went down to Ahab to Samaria. And Ahab killed sheep and oxen for him in abundance, and for the people that were with him, and moved him to go up *with him* to Ramoth-gilead. 3 And Ahab king of Israel said unto Jehoshaphat king of Judah, Wilt thou go with me to Ramoth-gilead? And he answered him, I am as thou art, and my people as thy people; and *we will be* with thee in the war.

B. AHAB'S PROPHETS PROMISE HIM THE VICTORY.

1 *Kings* 22 : 5, 6, 10-12.	2 *Chronicles* 18 : 4, 5, 9-11.

5 And Jehoshaphat said unto the king of Israel, Inquire, I pray thee, at the word of the LORD to-day. 6 Then the king of Israel gathered the prophets together, about four hundred men, and said unto them, Shall I go against Ramoth-gilead to battle, or shall I forbear? And they said, Go up; for the Lord shall deliver it into the hand of the king. 10 Now the king of Israel and Jehoshaphat the king of Judah sat each on his throne, arrayed in their robes, in *b* an open place at the entrance of the gate of Samaria; and all the prophets prophesied before them. 11 And Zedekiah the son of Chenaanah made him horns of iron, and said, Thus saith the LORD, With these shalt thou push the Syrians, until they be consumed. 12 And all the prophets prophesied so, saying, Go up to Ramoth-gilead, and prosper: for the LORD shall deliver it into the hand of the king.

4 And Jehoshaphat said unto the king of Israel, Inquire, I pray thee, at the word of the LORD to-day. 5 Then the king of Israel gathered the prophets together, four hundred men, and said unto them, Shall we go to Ramoth-gilead to battle, or shall I forbear? And they said, Go up; for God shall deliver it into the hand of the king. 9 Now the king of Israel and Jehoshaphat the king of Judah sat each on his throne, arrayed in their robes, and they sat in *b* an open place at the entrance of the gate of Samaria; and all the prophets prophesied before them. 10 And Zedekiah the son of Chenaanah made him horns of iron, and said, Thus saith the LORD, With these shalt thou push the Syrians, until they be consumed. 11 And all the prophets prophesied so, saying, Go up to Ramoth-gilead, and prosper: for the LORD shall deliver it into the hand of the king.

---

a Or, " keep silence."   *b* Heb. " a threshing-floor."

Kingdom of Judah.	Kingdom of Israel.

C. MICAIAH'S PROPHECY.

1 *Kings* 22 : 7–9, 13–28.	2 *Chronicles* 18 : 6–8, 12–27.
7 But Jehoshaphat said, Is there not here besides a prophet of the LORD, that we might inquire of him? 8 And the king of Israel said unto Jehoshaphat, There is yet one man by whom we may inquire of the LORD, Micaiah the son of Imlah : but I hate him ; for he doth not prophesy good concerning me, but evil. And Jehoshaphat said, Let not the king say so. 9 Then the king of Israel called an *a* officer, and said, Fetch quickly Micaiah the son of Imlah. 13 And the messenger that went to call Micaiah spake unto him, saying, Behold now, the words of the prophets *declare* good unto the king with one mouth : let thy word, I pray thee, be like the word of one of them, and speak thou good. 14 And Micaiah said, As the LORD liveth, what the LORD saith unto me, that will I speak. 15 And when he was come to the king, the king said unto him, Micaiah, shall we go to Ramoth-gilead to battle, or shall we forbear? And he answered him, Go up, and prosper; and the LORD shall deliver it into the hand of the king. 16 And the king said unto him, How many times shall I adjure thee that thou speak unto me nothing but the truth in the name of the LORD? 17 And he said, I saw all Israel scattered upon the mountains, as sheep that have no shepherd : and the LORD said, These have no master ; let them return every man to his house in peace. 18 And the king of Israel said to Jehoshaphat, Did I not tell thee that he would not prophesy good concerning me, but evil? 19 And he said, Therefore hear thou the word of the LORD : I saw the LORD sitting on his throne, and all the host of heaven standing by him on his right hand and on his left. 20 And the LORD said, Who shall *b* entice Ahab, that he may go up and fall at Ramoth-gilead? And one said on this manner; and another said on that manner. 21 And there came forth *c* a spirit, and stood before the LORD, and said, I will entice him. 22 And the LORD said unto him, Wherewith? And he said, I will go forth, and will be a lying spirit in the mouth of all his prophets. And he said, Thou shalt entice him, and shalt prevail also : go forth, and do so. 23 Now	6 But Jehoshaphat said, Is there not here besides a prophet of the LORD, that we might inquire of him? 7 And the king of Israel said unto Jehoshaphat, There is yet one man by whom we may inquire of the LORD : but I hate him ; for he never prophesieth good concerning me, but always evil : the same is Micaiah the son of Imla. And Jehoshaphat said, Let not the king say so. 8 Then the king of Israel called an *a* officer, and said, Fetch quickly Micaiah the son of Imla. 12 And the messenger that went to call Micaiah spake to him, saying, Behold, the words of the prophets *declare* good to the king with one mouth : let thy word therefore, I pray thee, be like one of theirs, and speak thou good. 13 And Micaiah said, As the LORD liveth, what my God saith, that will I speak. 14 And when he was come to the king, the king said unto him, *d* Micaiah, shall we go to Ramoth-gilead to battle, or shall I forbear? And he said, Go ye up, and prosper; and they shall be delivered into your hand. 15 And the king said to him, How many times shall I adjure thee that thou say unto me nothing but the truth in the name of the LORD? 16 And he said, I saw all Israel scattered upon the mountains, as sheep that have no shepherd : and the LORD said, These have no master ; let them return every man to his house in peace. 17 And the king of Israel said to Jehoshaphat, Did I not tell thee that he would not prophesy good concerning me, but evil? 18 And he said, Therefore hear ye the word of the LORD : I saw the LORD sitting upon his throne, and all the host of heaven standing on his right hand and on his left. 19 And the LORD said, Who shall *b* entice Ahab king of Israel that he may go up and fall at Ramoth-gilead? And one spake saying after this manner, and another saying after that manner. 20 And there came forth *c* a spirit, and stood before the LORD, and said, I will entice him. And the LORD said unto him, Wherewith? 21 And he said, I will go forth, and will be a lying spirit in the mouth of all his prophets. And he said, Thou shalt entice him, and shalt prevail also : go forth, and do so. 22 Now

a Or, "eunuch."   *b* Or, "deceive."   *c* Heb. "the spirit."   *d* Heb. "Micah."

Kingdom of Judah.	Kingdom of Israel.
1 *Kings* 22.	2 *Chronicles* 18.

therefore, behold, the LORD hath put a lying spirit in the mouth of all these thy prophets; and the LORD hath spoken evil concerning thee. 24 Then Zedekiah the son of Chenaanah came near, and smote Micaiah on the cheek, and said, Which way went the spirit of the LORD from me to speak unto thee? 25 And Micaiah said, Behold, thou shalt see on that day, when thou shalt go *a* into an inner chamber to hide thyself. 26 And the king of Israel said, Take Micaiah, and carry him back unto Amon the governor of the city, and to Joash the king's son; 27 and say, Thus saith the king, Put this fellow in the prison, and feed him with bread of affliction and with water of affliction, until I come in peace. 28 And Micaiah said, If thou return at all in peace, the LORD hath not spoken by me. And he said, *b* Hear, ye peoples, all of you.

therefore, behold, the LORD hath put a lying spirit in the mouth of these thy prophets; and the LORD hath spoken evil concerning thee. 23 Then Zedekiah the son of Chenaanah came near, and smote Micaiah upon the cheek, and said, Which way went the spirit of the LORD from me to speak unto thee? 24 And Micaiah said, Behold, thou shalt see on that day, when thou shalt go *a* into an inner chamber to hide thyself. 25 And the king of Israel said, Take ye Micaiah and carry him back unto Amon the governor of the city, and to Joash the king's son; 26 and say, Thus saith the king, Put this fellow in the prison, and feed him with bread of affliction and with water of affliction, until I return in peace. 27 And Micaiah said, If thou return at all in peace, the LORD hath not spoken by me. And he said, *b* Hear, ye peoples, all of you.

D. THE BATTLE OF RAMOTH-GILEAD: DEFEAT AND DEATH OF AHAB.

1 *Kings* 22 : 29–40a.	2 *Chronicles* 18 : 28–34.

29 So the king of Israel and Jehoshaphat the king of Judah went up to Ramoth-gilead. 30 And the king of Israel said unto Jehoshaphat, I will disguise myself, and go into the battle; but put thou on thy robes. And the king of Israel disguised himself, and went into the battle. 31 Now the king of Syria had commanded the thirty and two captains of his chariots, saying, Fight neither with small nor great, save only with the king of Israel. 32 And it came to pass, when the captains of the chariots saw Jeposhaphat, that they said, Surely it is the king of Israel; and they turned aside to fight against him: and Jehoshaphat cried out. 33 And it came to pass, when the captains of the chariots saw that it was not the king of Israel, that they turned back from pursuing him. 34 And a certain man drew his bow *c* at a venture, and smote the king of Israel between *d* the joints of the harness: wherefore he said unto the driver of his chariot, Turn thine hand, and carry me out of the host; for I am sore wounded. 35 And the battle increased that day: and the king was stayed up in his chariot against the Syrians, and died at even: and the blood ran out of the wound into the bottom of the chariot. 36 And there went a cry throughout the host about the going down of the sun, say-

28 So the king of Israel and Jehoshaphat the king of Judah went up to Ramoth-gilead. 29 And the king of Israel said unto Jehoshaphat, I will disguise myself, and go into the battle; but put thou on thy robes. So the king of Israel disguised himself; and they went into the battle. 30 Now the king of Syria had commanded the captains of his chariots, saying, Fight neither with small nor great, save only with the king of Israel. 31 And it came to pass, when the captains of the chariots saw Jehoshaphat, that they said, It is the king of Israel. Therefore they turned about to fight against him: but Jehoshaphat cried out, and the LORD helped him; and God moved them *to depart* from him. 32 And it came to pass, when the captains of the chariots saw that it was not the king of Israel, that they turned back from pursuing him. 33 And a certain man drew his bow *c* at a venture, and smote the king of Israel between *d* the joints of the harness: wherefore he said to the driver of the chariot, Turn thine hand, and carry me out of the host; for I am sore wounded. 34 And the battle increased that day: howbeit the king of Israel stayed himself up in his chariot against the Syrians until the even: and about the time of the going down of the sun he died.

---

a Or, "from chamber to chamber."   *b* Cf. Micah 1 : 2.   *c* Heb. "in his simplicity."   *d* Or, "the lower armour and the breastplate."

Kingdom of Judah.	Kingdom of Israel.

1 Kings 22.

ing, Every man to his city, and every man to his country. 37 So the king died, and was brought to Samaria ; and they buried the king in Samaria. 38 And they washed the chariot by the pool of Samaria ; and the dogs licked up his blood ; (*a*now the harlots washed themselves *there ;*) according unto the word of the LORD which he spake. 39 Now the rest of the acts of Ahab, and all that he did, and the ivory house which he built, and all the cities that he built, are they not written in the book of the chronicles of the kings of Israel ? 40*a* So Ahab slept with his fathers.

153. THE REIGN OF AHAZIAH.

(1) AHAZIAH BECOMES SOLE KING.

1 Kings 22 : 40*b*.

40*b* And Ahaziah his son reigned in his stead.

(8) THE PROPHET JEHU'S JUDGMENT ON JEHOSHAPHAT.

2 Chronicles 19 : 1–3.

1 And Jehoshaphat the king of Judah returned to his house in peace to Jerusalem. 2 And Jehu the son of Hanani the seer went out to meet him, and said to king Jehoshaphat, Shouldest thou help the wicked, and love them that hate the LORD? for this thing wrath is upon thee from before the LORD. 3 Nevertheless there are good things found in thee, in that thou hast put away the Asheroth out of the land, and hast set thine heart to seek God.

(2) THE CHARACTER OF AHAZIAH.

1 Kings 22 : 52, 53.

52 And he did that which was evil in the sight of the LORD, and walked in the way of his father, and in the way of his mother, and in the way of Jeroboam the son of Nebat, *b* wherein he made Israel to sin. 53 And he served Baal, and worshipped him, and provoked to anger the LORD, the God of Israel, according to all that his father had done.

(9) JEHOSHAPHAT'S FURTHER REFORMS IN WORSHIP AND LAW.

2 Chronicles 19 : 4–11.

4 And Jehoshaphat dwelt at Jerusalem : and he went out again among the people from Beersheba to the hill country of Ephraim, and brought them back unto the LORD, the God of their fathers. 5 And he set judges in the land throughout all the fenced cities of Judah, city by city, and said to the judges, 6 Consider what ye do : for ye judge not for man, but for the LORD ; and *he is* with you *c* in the judgement. 7 Now therefore let the fear of the LORD be upon you ; take heed and do it : for there is no iniquity with the

(3) THE REVOLT OF MOAB.

2 Kings 1 : 1.	2 Kings 3 : 4, 5.
	4 Now Mesha king of Moab was a sheepmaster; and he rendered unto the king of Israel *d*the wool of an hundred thousand lambs, and of an hundred thousand rams. 5 But it came to pass, when Ahab was
1 And Moab rebelled against Israel after the death of Ahab.	dead, that the king of Moab rebelled against the king of Israel.

---

a Or, " and they washed the armour."   *b* Or, "who made."   *c* Or, "in giving judgement."   Heb. "in the matter of judgement."   *d* Or, "an hundred thousand lambs, and an hundred thousand rams, *with* the wool."

Kingdom of Judah.

2 *Chronicles* 19.

LORD our God, nor respect of persons, nor taking of gifts. 8 Moreover in Jerusalem did Jehoshaphat set of the Levites and the priests, and of the heads of the fathers' *houses* of Israel, for the judgement of the LORD, and for controversies. And they returned to Jerusalem. 9 And he charged them, saying, Thus shall ye do in the fear of the LORD, faithfully, and with a perfect heart. 10 And whensoever any controversy shall come to you from your brethren that dwell in their cities, between blood and blood, between law and commandment, statutes and judgements, ye shall warn them, that they be not guilty towards the LORD, and so wrath come upon you and upon your brethren : this do, and ye shall not be guilty. 11 And, behold, Amariah the chief priest is over you in all matters of the LORD ; and Zebadiah the son of Ishmael, the ruler of the house of Judah, in all the king's matters : also the Levites shall be officers before you. *a* Deal courageously, and the LORD be with the good.

(10) THE WONDROUS DELIVERANCE FROM THE CHILDREN OF MOAB AND AMMON AND MOUNT SEIR.

A. THE INVASION.

2 *Chronicles* 20 : 1, 2.

1 And it came to pass after this, that the children of Moab, and the children of Ammon, and with them some of the *b* Ammonites, came against Jehoshaphat to battle. 2 Then there came some that told Jehoshaphat, saying, There cometh a great multitude against thee from beyond the sea from Syria ; and, behold, they be in Hazazon-tamar (the same is En-gedi).

B. JEHOSHAPHAT'S PRAYER.

2 *Chronicles* 20 : 3–12.

3 And Jehoshaphat feared, and set himself to seek unto the LORD ; and he proclaimed a fast throughout all Judah. 4 And Judah gathered themselves together, to seek *help* of the LORD : even out of all the cities of Judah they came to seek the LORD. 5 And Jehoshaphat stood in

Kingdom of Israel.

---

a Heb. " Be strong and do."   *b* Perhaps an error for " Meunim."   So the Sept.   Cf. 2 Chronicles 26 : 7.   See §164, (4), *D.*

Kingdom of Judah.	Kingdom of Israel.

2 *Chronicles* 20.

the congregation of Judah and Jerusalem, in the house of the LORD, before the new court ; 6 and he said, O LORD, the God of our fathers, art not thou God in heaven ? and art not thou ruler over all the kingdoms of the nations ? and in thine hand is power and might, so that none is able to withstand thee. 7 Didst not thou, O our God, drive out the inhabitants of this land before thy people Israel, and gavest it to the seed of Abraham thy friend for ever ? 8 And they dwelt therein, and have built thee a sanctuary therein for thy name, saying, 9 If evil come upon us, *a* the sword, judgement, or pestilence, or famine, we will stand before this house, and before thee, (for thy name is in this house,) and cry unto thee in our affliction, and thou wilt hear and save. 10 And now, behold, the children of Ammon and Moab and mount Seir, whom thou wouldest not let Israel invade, when they came out of the land of Egypt, but they turned aside from them, and destroyed them not ; 11 behold, how they reward us, to come to cast us out of thy possession, which thou hast given us to inherit. 12 O our God, wilt thou not judge them ? for we have no might against this great company that cometh against us ; neither know we what to do : but our eyes are upon thee.

C. JEHOVAH'S ANSWER THROUGH JAHAZIEL.

2 *Chronicles* 20 : 13-19.

13 And all Judah stood before the LORD with their little ones, their wives, and their children. 14 Then upon Jahaziel the son of Zechariah, the son of Benaiah, the son of Jeiel, the son of Mattaniah, the Levite, of the sons of Asaph, came the spirit of the LORD in the midst of the congregation ; 15 and he said, Hearken ye, all Judah, and ye inhabitants of Jerusalem, and thou king Jehoshaphat : thus saith the LORD unto you, Fear not ye, neither be dismayed by reason of this great multitude ; for the battle is not yours, but God's. 16 To-morrow go ye down against them : behold, they come up by the ascent of Ziz ; and ye shall find them at the end of the valley, before the wilderness of Jeruel. 17 Ye shall not need to fight in this *battle :* set yourselves, stand ye still, and see the salvation

---

a Or, " the sword of judgement."

Kingdom of Judah.	Kingdom of Israel.

2 *Chronicles* 20.

of the LORD with you, O Judah and Jerusalem : fear not, nor be dismayed : to-morrow go out against them; for the LORD is with you. 18 And Jehoshaphat bowed his head with his face to the ground : and all Judah and the inhabitants of Jerusalem fell down before the LORD, worshipping the LORD. 19 And the Levites, of the children of the Kohathites and of the children of the Korahites, stood up to praise the LORD, the God of Israel, with an exceeding loud voice.

D. THE ANNIHILATION OF THE INVADING ARMIES.

2 *Chronicles* 20 : 20-24.

20 And they rose early in the morning, and went forth into the wilderness of Tekoa : and as they went forth, Jehoshaphat stood and said, Hear me, O Judah, and ye inhabitants of Jerusalem ; believe in the LORD your God, so shall ye be established ; believe his prophets, so shall ye prosper. 21 And when he had taken counsel with the people, he appointed them that should sing unto the LORD, and praise *a* the beauty of holiness, as they went out before the army, and say, Give thanks unto the LORD ; for his mercy *endureth* for ever. 22 And when they began to sing and to praise, the LORD set liers in wait against the children of Ammon, Moab, and mount Seir, which were come against Judah ; and they were smitten. 23 For the children of Ammon and Moab stood up against the inhabitants of mount Seir, utterly to slay and destroy them : and when they had made an end of the inhabitants of Seir, every one helped to destroy another. 24 And when Judah came to the watch-tower of the wilderness, they looked upon the multitude ; and, behold, they were dead bodies fallen to the earth, and there were none that escaped.

E. THE SPOIL.

2 *Chronicles* 20 : 25.

25 And when Jehoshaphat and his people came to take the spoil of them, they found among them in abundance both riches and *b* dead bodies, and precious jewels, which they stripped off for themselves, more than they could carry away : and they were three days in taking of the spoil, it was so much.

---

a Or, " in the beauty of holiness."   *b* According to some ancient authorities, "garments."

Kingdom of Judah.	Kingdom of Israel.

Kingdom of Judah.

F. THE TRIUMPHANT RETURN TO JERUSALEM.

2 *Chronicles* 20 : 26–30.

26 And on the fourth day they assembled themselves in the valley of *ª* Beracah ; for there they blessed the LORD : therefore the name of that place was called The valley of Beracah, unto this day. 27 Then they returned, every man of Judah and Jerusalem, and Jehoshaphat in the forefront of them, to go again to Jerusalem with joy ; for the LORD had made them to rejoice over their enemies. 28 And they came to Jerusalem with psalteries and harps and trumpets unto the house of the LORD. 29 And the fear of God was on all the kingdoms of the countries, when they heard that the LORD fought against the enemies of Israel. 30 So the realm of Jehoshaphat was quiet : for his God gave him rest round about.

(11) JEHOSHAPHAT'S SHIPPING ALLIANCE WITH AHAZIAH. (4)

1 *Kings* 22 : 48, 47, 49.

48 Jehoshaphat made ships of Tarshish to go to Ophir for gold : but they went not ; for the ships were broken at Ezion-geber. 47 And there was no king in Edom : a deputy was king. 49 Then said Ahaziah the son of Ahab unto Jehoshaphat, Let my servants go with thy servants in the ships. But Jehoshaphat would not.

2 *Chronicles* 20 : 35–37.

35 And after this did Jehoshaphat king of Judah join himself with Ahaziah king of Israel ; the same did very wickedly : 36 and he joined himself with him to make ships to go to Tarshish : and they made the ships in Ezion-geber. 37 Then Eliezer the son of Dodavahu of Mareshah prophesied against Jehoshaphat, saying, Because thou hast joined thyself with Ahaziah, the LORD hath *ᵇ* destroyed thy works. And the ships were broken, that they were not able to go to Tarshish.

(5) AHAZIAH'S ILLNESS.

2 *Kings* 1 : 2.

2 And Ahaziah fell down through the lattice in his upper chamber that was in Samaria, and was sick : and he sent messengers, and said unto them, Go, inquire of Baal-zebub the god of Ekron whether I shall recover of this sickness.

(6) JEHOVAH'S MESSAGE BY ELIJAH.

2 *Kings* 1 : 3–16.

3 But the angel of the LORD said to Elijah the Tishbite, Arise, go up to meet the messengers of the king of Samaria, and say unto them,

a I. e., " Blessing."   *b* Or, " made a breach in."

17

Kingdom of Judah.	Kingdom of Israel.

Kingdom of Israel.

2 Kings 1.

Is it because there is no God in Israel, that ye go to inquire of Baal-zebub the god of Ekron? 4 Now therefore thus saith the LORD, Thou shalt not come down from the bed whither thou art gone up, but shalt surely die. 5 And Elijah departed. And the messengers returned unto him, and he said unto them, Why is it that ye are returned? 6 And they said unto him, There came up a man to meet us, and said unto us, Go, turn again unto the king that sent you, and say unto him, Thus saith the LORD, Is it because there is no God in Israel, that thou sendest to inquire of Baal-zebub the god of Ekron? therefore thou shalt not come down from the bed whither thou art gone up, but shalt surely die. 7 And he said unto them, What manner of man was he which came up to meet you, and told you these words? 8 And they answered him, He was *a* an hairy man, and girt with a girdle of leather about his loins. And he said, It is Elijah the Tishbite. 9 Then *the king* sent unto him a captain of fifty with his fifty. And he went up to him: and, behold, he *b* sat on the top of the hill. And he spake unto him, O man of God, the king hath said, Come down. 10 And Elijah answered and said to the captain of fifty, If I be a man of God, let fire come down from heaven, and consume thee and thy fifty. And there came down fire from heaven, and consumed him and his fifty. 11 And again he sent unto him another captain of fifty with his fifty. And he answered and said unto him, O man of God, thus hath the king said, Come down quickly. 12 And Elijah answered and said unto them, If I be a man of God, let fire come down from heaven, and consume thee and thy fifty. And the fire of God came down from heaven, and consumed him and his fifty. 13 And again he sent the captain of a third fifty with his fifty. And the third captain of fifty went up, and came and fell on his knees before Elijah, and besought him, and said unto him, O man of God, I pray thee, let my life, and the life of these fifty thy servants, be precious in thy sight. 14 Behold, there came fire down from heaven, and consumed the two former captains of fifty with their fifties: but now let my life be precious in thy sight. 15 And the angel of the LORD said

---

a Or, " a man with *a garment of* hair."   *b* Or, " dwelt."

Kingdom of Judah.	Kingdom of Israel.

Kingdom of Israel.

2 *Kings* 1.

unto Elijah, Go down with him : be not afraid of him. And he arose, and went down with him unto the king. 16 And he said unto him, Thus saith the LORD, Forasmuch as thou hast sent messengers to inquire of Baal-zebub the god of Ekron, is it because there is no God in Israel to inquire of his word ? therefore thou shalt not come down from the bed whither thou art gone up, but shalt surely die.

(7) THE DEATH OF AHAZIAH.

2 *Kings* 1 : 17*a*, 18.

17*a* So he died according to the word of the LORD which Elijah had spoken. 18 Now the rest of the acts of Ahaziah which he did, are they not written in the book of the chronicles of the kings of Israel ?

154. THE REIGN OF JEHORAM.

(1) JEHORAM'S ACCESSION TO THE THRONE.

2 *Kings* 1 : 17*b*.	2 *Kings* 3 : 1.
17*b* And Jehoram began to reign in his stead in the second year of Jehoram*a* the son of Jehoshaphat king of Judah; because he had no son.	1 Now Jehoram the son of Ahab began to reign over Israel in Samaria in the eighteenth year of Jehoshaphat king of Judah, and reigned twelve years.

(2) THE CHARACTER OF JEHORAM.

2 *Kings* 3 : 2, 3.

2 And he did that which was evil in the sight of the LORD ; but not like his father, and like his mother : for he put away the *b* pillar of Baal that his father had made. 3 Nevertheless he cleaved unto the sins of Jeroboam the son of Nebat, wherewith he made Israel to sin ; he departed not therefrom.

(3) ELISHA THE SON OF SHAPHAT.

A. THE TRANSLATION OF ELIJAH.

2 *Kings* 2 : 1–11.

1 And it came to pass, when the LORD would take up Elijah by a whirlwind into heaven, that

---

a If this date be correct, it undoubtedly points to two separate accessions of Jehoram of Judah, to co-regnancy with his father, the first of which is only noticed here, and which lasted but a very few years. *b* Or, " obelisk."

Kingdom of Judah.

Kingdom of Israel.

2 *Kings* 2.

Elijah went with Elisha from Gilgal. 2 And Elijah said unto Elisha, Tarry here, I pray thee ; for the LORD hath sent me as far as Beth-el. And Elisha said, As the LORD liveth, and as thy soul liveth, I will not leave thee. So they went down to Beth-el. 3 And the sons of the prophets that were at Beth-el came forth to Elisha, and said unto him, Knowest thou that the LORD will take away thy master from thy head to-day ? And he said, Yea, I know it ; hold ye your peace. 4 And Elijah said unto him, Elisha, tarry here, I pray thee ; for the LORD hath sent me to Jericho. And he said, As the LORD liveth, and as thy soul liveth, I will not leave thee. So they came to Jericho. 5 And the sons of the prophets that were at Jericho came near to Elisha, and said unto him, Knowest thou that the LORD will take away thy master from thy head to-day ? And he answered, Yea, I know it ; hold ye your peace. 6 And Elijah said unto him, Tarry here, I pray thee ; for the LORD hath sent me to Jordan. And he said, As the LORD liveth, and as thy soul liveth, I will not leave thee. And they two went on. 7 And fifty men of the sons of the prophets went, and stood over against them afar off : and they two stood by Jordan. 8 And Elijah took his mantle, and wrapped it together, and smote the waters, and they were divided hither and thither, so that they two went over on dry ground. 9 And it came to pass, *a* when they were gone over, that Elijah said unto Elisha, Ask what I shall do for thee, before I be taken from thee. And Elisha said, I pray thee, let *b* a double portion of thy spirit be upon me. 10 And he said, Thou hast asked a hard thing : *nevertheless,* if thou see me when I am taken from thee, it shall be so unto thee ; but if not, it shall not be so. 11 And it came to pass, as they still went on, and talked, that, behold, *there appeared* *c* a chariot of fire, and horses of fire, which parted them both asunder ; and Elijah went up by a whirlwind into heaven.

B. ELIJAH'S SPIRIT RESTS UPON ELISHA.

2 *Kings* 2 : 12–18.

12 And Elisha saw it, and he cried, My father, my father, the *d* chariots of Israel and the horsemen thereof ! And he saw him no more :

---

a Or, "as they went."   *b* I. e., the portion of the firstborn. See Deuteronomy 21 : 17.   *c* Or, "chariots."   *d* Or, "chariot."

Kingdom of Judah.	Kingdom of Israel.
	2 *Kings* 2.

and he took hold of his own clothes, and rent them in two pieces. 13 He took up also the mantle of Elijah that fell from him, and went back, and stood by the bank of Jordan. 14 And he took the mantle of Elijah that fell from him, and smote the waters, and said, Where is the LORD, *a* the God of Elijah? and when he also had smitten the waters, they were divided hither and thither : and Elisha went over. 15 And when the sons of the prophets which were at Jericho over against him saw him, they said, The spirit of Elijah doth rest on Elisha. And they came to meet him, and bowed themselves to the ground before him. 16 And they said unto him, Behold now, there be with thy servants fifty strong men ; let them go, we pray thee, and seek thy master : lest peradventure the spirit of the LORD hath taken him up, and cast him upon some mountain, or into some valley. And he said, Ye shall not send. 17 And when they urged him till he was ashamed, he said, Send. They sent therefore fifty men ; and they sought three days, but found him not. 18 And they came back to him, while he tarried at Jericho ; and he said unto them, Did I not say unto you, Go not ?

C. ELISHA HEALS THE NOXIOUS WATERS AT JERICHO.

2 *Kings* 2 : 19–22.

19 And the men of the city said unto Elisha, Behold, we pray thee, the situation of this city is pleasant, as my lord seeth : but the water is naught, and the land *b* miscarrieth. 20 And he said, Bring me a new cruse, and put salt therein. And they brought it to him. 21 And he went forth unto the spring of the waters, and cast salt therein, and said, Thus saith the LORD, I have healed these waters ; there shall not be from thence any more death or *c* miscarrying. 22 So the waters were healed unto this day, according to the word of Elisha which he spake.

D. THE CURSING OF THE CHILDREN.

2 *Kings* 2 : 23, 24.

23 And he went up from thence unto Beth-el : and as he was going up by the way, there came

---

a Or, " the God of Elijah, even he ? and when he had smitten," etc.   *b* Or, " casteth her fruit."   *c* Or, " casting of fruit."

Kingdom of Judah.	Kingdom of Israel.

Kingdom of Israel.

2 *Kings* 2.

forth *a* little children out of the city, and mocked him, and said unto him, Go up, thou bald head ; go up, thou bald head.   24 And he looked behind him and saw them, and cursed them in the name of the LORD.   And there came forth two she-bears out of the wood, and tare forty and two children of them.

E. ELISHA'S JOURNEYING.

2 *Kings* 2 : 25.

25 And he went from thence to mount Carmel, and from thence he returned to Samaria.

F. THE INCREASE OF THE WIDOW'S OIL.

2 *Kings* 4 : 1–7.

1 Now there cried a certain woman of the wives of the sons of the prophets unto Elisha, saying, Thy servant my husband is dead : and thou knowest that thy servant did fear the LORD : and the creditor is come to take unto him my two children to be bondmen.   2 And Elisha said unto her, What shall I do for thee ? tell me ; what hast thou in the house ?   And she said, Thine handmaid hath not any thing in the house, save a pot of oil.   3 Then he said, Go, borrow thee vessels abroad of all thy neighbours, even empty vessels ; borrow not a few.   4 And thou shalt go in, and shut the door upon thee and upon thy sons, and pour out into all those vessels ; and thou shalt set aside that which is full. 5 So she went from him, and shut the door upon her and upon her sons ; they brought *the vessels* to her, and she poured out.   6 And it came to pass, when the vessels were full, that she said unto her son, Bring me yet a vessel.   And he said unto her, There is not a vessel more.   And the oil stayed.   7 Then she came and told the man of God.   And he said, Go, sell the oil, and pay thy debt, and live thou and thy sons of the rest.

G. ELISHA PROMISES A SON TO THE HOSPITABLE SHUNAMMITE.

2 *Kings* 4 : 8–17.

8 And it fell on a day, that Elisha passed to Shunem, where was a great woman ; and she constrained him to eat bread.   And so it was,

---

a Or, "young lads."

Kingdom of Judah.	Kingdom of Israel.

Kingdom of Israel.

2 *Kings* 4.

that as oft as he passed by, he turned in thither to eat bread. 9 And she said unto her husband, Behold now, I perceive that this is an holy man of God, which passeth by us continually. 10 Let us make, I pray thee, a little chamber *a* on the wall; and let us set for him there a bed, and a table, and a stool, and a candlestick: and it shall be, when he cometh to us, that he shall turn in thither. 11 And it fell on a day, that he came thither, and he turned into the chamber and lay there. 12 And he said to Gehazi his servant, Call this Shunammite. And when he had called her, she stood before him. 13 And he said unto him, Say now unto her, Behold, thou hast *b* been careful for us with all this care; what is to be done for thee? wouldest thou be spoken for to the king, or to the captain of the host? And she answered, I dwell among mine own people. 14 And he said, What then is to be done for her? And Gehazi answered, Verily she hath no son, and her husband is old. 15 And he said, Call her. And when he had called her, she stood in the door. 16 And he said, At this season, when the time *c* cometh round, thou shalt embrace a son. And she said, Nay, my lord, thou man of God, do not lie unto thine handmaid. 17 And the woman conceived, and bare a son at that season, when the time came round, as Elisha had said unto her.

H. ELISHA HEALS THE NOXIOUS POTTAGE AT GILGAL.*d*

2 *Kings* 4 : 38–41.

38 And Elisha came again to Gilgal: and there was a dearth in the land; and the sons of the prophets were sitting before him: and he said unto his servant, Set on the great pot, and seethe pottage for the sons of the prophets. 39 And one went out into the field to gather herbs, and found a wild vine, and gathered thereof wild gourds his lap full, and came and shred them into the pot of pottage: for they knew them not. 40 So they poured out for the men to eat. And it came to pass, as they were eating of the pottage, that they cried out, and said, O man of God, there is death in the pot. And they could not eat thereof. 41 But he said,

---

a Or, "with walls."   *b* Or, "shewed us all this reverence."   *c* Heb. "liveth," or, "reviveth."   *d* Divisions *H* and *I* are placed here because *J* must have occurred at least three years after *G*.

Kingdom of Judah.	Kingdom of Israel.

Kingdom of Israel.

2 *Kings* 4.

Then bring meal. And he cast it into the pot; and he said, Pour out for the people, that they may eat. And there was no *a* harm in the pot.

I. ELISHA FEEDS ONE HUNDRED MEN WITH TWENTY LOAVES.*b*

2 *Kings* 4 : 42-44.

42 And there came a man from Baal-shal-ishah, and brought the man of God bread of the first fruits, twenty loaves of barley, and fresh ears of corn in *c* his sack. And he said, Give unto the people, that they may eat. 43 And his *d* serv-ant said, What, should I set this before an hun-dred men? But he said, Give the people, that they may eat; for thus saith the LORD, They shall eat, and shall leave thereof. 44 So he set it before them, and they did eat, and left thereof, according to the word of the LORD.

J. ELISHA RESTORES THE LIFE OF THE SHUNAMMITE'S SON.*e*

2 *Kings* 4 : 18-37.

18 And when the child was grown, it fell on a day, that he went out to his father to the reapers. 19 And he said unto his father, My head, my head. And he said to his servant, Carry him to his mother. 20 And when he had taken him, and brought him to his mother, he sat on her knees till noon, and then died. 21 And she went up, and laid him on the bed of the man of God, and shut *the door* upon him, and went out. 22 And she called unto her hus-band, and said, Send me, I pray thee, one of the servants, and one of the asses, that I may run to the man of God, and come again. 23 And he said, Wherefore wilt thou go to him to-day? it is neither new moon nor sabbath. And she said, *f* It shall be well. 24 Then she saddled an ass, and said to her servant, Drive, and go forward; slacken me not the riding, except I bid thee. 25 So she went, and came unto the man of God to mount Carmel. And it came to pass, when the man of God saw her afar off, that he said to Gehazi his servant, Behold, yonder is the Shunammite: 26 run, I pray thee, now to meet her, and say unto her, Is it well with thee? is it well with thy husband? is it well with the child? And she answered, It is

---

a Heb. " evil thing."   *b* Divisions *H* and *I* are placed here because *J* must have occurred at least three years after *G*.
c Or, " the husk thereof."   *d* Or, " minister."   *e* Cf. §154, (6).   *f* Heb. "Peace."

Kingdom of Judah.	Kingdom of Israel.

Kingdom of Israel.

2 *Kings* 4.

well. 27 And when she came to the man of God to the hill, she caught hold of his feet. And Gehazi came near to thrust her away; but the man of God said, Let her alone: for her soul is *a* vexed within her; and the LORD hath hid it from me, and hath not told me. 28 Then she said, Did I desire a son of my lord? did I not say, Do not deceive me? 29 Then he said to Gehazi, Gird up thy loins, and take my staff in thine hand, and go thy way: if thou meet any man, salute him not; and if any salute thee, answer him not again: and lay my staff upon the face of the child. 30 And the mother of the child said, As the LORD liveth, and as thy soul liveth, I will not leave thee. And he arose, and followed her. 31 And Gehazi passed on before them, and laid the staff upon the face of the child; but there was neither voice, nor *b* hearing. Wherefore he returned to meet him, and told him, saying, The child is not awaked. 32 And when Elisha was come into the house, behold, the child was dead, and laid upon his bed. 33 He went in therefore, and shut the door upon them twain, and prayed unto the LORD. 34 And he went up, and lay upon the child, and put his mouth upon his mouth, and his eyes upon his eyes, and his hands upon his hands: and he *c* stretched himself upon him; and the flesh of the child waxed warm. 35 Then he returned, and walked in the house once to and fro; and went up, and *c* stretched himself upon him: *d* and the child sneezed seven times, and the child opened his eyes. 36 And he called Gehazi, and said, Call this Shunammite. So he called her. And when she was come in unto him, he said, Take up thy son. 37 Then she went in, and fell at his feet, and bowed herself to the ground; and she took up her son, and went out.

K. THE SEVEN YEARS' FAMINE FORETOLD.

2 *Kings* 8:1, 2.

1 Now Elisha had spoken unto the woman, whose son he had restored to life, saying, Arise, and go thou and thine household, and sojourn wheresoever thou canst sojourn: for the LORD hath called for a famine; and it shall also come upon the land seven years. 2 And the woman

---

a Heb. "bitter."   *b* Heb. "attention."   *c* Or, "bowed himself."   *d* Or, "and embraced the child."

Kingdom of Judah.	Kingdom of Israel.

Kingdom of Israel.

2 Kings 8.

arose, and did according to the word of the man of God : and she went with her household, and sojourned in the land of the Philistines seven years.

L. THE RECOVERY OF THE LOST AXE.

2 Kings 6: 1-7.

1 And the sons of the prophets said unto Elisha, Behold now, the place where we dwell before thee is too strait for us.   2 Let us go, we pray thee, unto Jordan, and take thence every man a beam, and let us make us a place there, where we may dwell.   And he answered, Go ye.   3 And one said, Be content, I pray thee, and go with thy servants.   And he answered, I will go.   4 So he went with them.   And when they came to Jordan, they cut down wood. 5 But as one was felling a beam, the axe-head fell into the water: and he cried, and said, Alas, my master! for it was borrowed.   6 And the man of God said, Where fell it?   And he shewed him the place.   And he cut down a stick, and cast it in thither, and *a* made the iron to swim.   7 And he said, Take it up to thee. So he put out his hand, and took it.

(12) JEHORAM BECOMES CO-REGNANT WITH JEHOSHAPHAT.*b*

2 Ki. 8 : 16, 17.	2 Ch. 21 : 5.	2 Ch. 21 : 20a.
16 And in the fifth year of Joram the son of Ahab king of Israel, *c* Jehoshaphat being then king of Judah, Jehoram the son of Jehoshaphat king of Judah began to reign. 17 Thirty and two years old was he when he began to reign ; and he reigned eight years in Jerusalem.	5 Jehoram was thirty and two years old when he began to reign ; and he reigned eight years in Jerusalem.	20a Thirty and two years old was he when he began to reign, and he reigned in Jerusalem eight years.

---

a Or, "the iron did swim."   *b* For a probable former accession to co-regnancy, which lasted but a few years, see §154 (1), and accompanying footnote.   *c* Some ancient authorities omit the words, "Jehoshaphat being then king of Judah." However, the internal evidence of Jehoshaphat's reign all goes to show that the phrase is authentic.

Kingdom of Judah.	Kingdom of Israel.

Kingdom of Judah.

(13) JEHORAM'S SIXFOLD FRATRICIDE.

2 *Chronicles* 21 : 2-4.

2 And he had brethren the sons of Jehoshaphat, Azariah, and Jehiel, and Zechariah, and Azariah, and Michael, and Shephatiah : all these were the sons of Jehoshaphat king of Israel. 3 And their father gave them great gifts, of silver, and of gold, and of precious things, with fenced cities in Judah : but the kingdom gave he to Jehoram, because he was the firstborn. 4 Now when Jehoram was risen up over the kingdom of his father, and had strengthened himself, he slew all his brethren with the sword, and divers also of the princes of Israel.

Kingdom of Israel.

(14) JEHOSHAPHAT JOINS JEHORAM OF ISRAEL IN AN EXPEDITION AGAINST THE MOABITES. (4)

A. THE MARCH.

2 *Kings* 3 : 6-9.

6 And king Jehoram went out of Samaria at that time, and mustered all Israel. 7 And he went and sent to Jehoshaphat the king of Judah, saying, The king of Moab hath rebelled against me : wilt thou go with me against Moab to battle ? And he said, I will go up : I am as thou art, my people as thy people, my horses as thy horses. 8 And he said, Which way shall we go up ? And he answered, The way of the wilderness of Edom. 9 So the king of Israel went, and the king of Judah, and the king of Edom : and they made a circuit of seven days' journey : and there was no water for the host, nor for the beasts that followed them.

B. ELISHA'S PROMISE OF WATER AND VICTORY.

2 *Kings* 3 : 10-19.

10 And the king of Israel said, Alas ! for the LORD hath called these three kings together to deliver them into the hand of Moab. 11 But Jehoshaphat said, Is there not here a prophet of the LORD, that we may inquire of the LORD by him ? And one of the king of Israel's servants answered and said, Elisha the son of Shaphat is here, which poured water on the hands of Elijah. 12 And Jehoshaphat said, The word of the LORD is with him. So the king of Israel and Jehoshaphat and the king of Edom went down to him. 13 And Elisha said unto the king of Israel, What have I to do with thee ? get thee to the prophets of thy father, and to the prophets of thy mother. And the king of Israel said unto him, Nay : for the LORD hath called these three kings together to deliver them into the hand of Moab. 14 And Elisha said, As the LORD of hosts liveth, before whom I stand, surely, were it not that I regard the presence of Jehoshaphat the king of Judah, I would not look toward thee, nor see thee. 15 But now bring me a minstrel. And it came to pass, when the minstrel played, that the hand of the LORD came upon him. 16 And he said, Thus saith the LORD, Make this valley full of trenches. 17 For thus saith the LORD, Ye shall not see wind, neither shall ye see rain, yet that valley shall be filled with water : and ye shall drink, both ye and your cattle and your beasts. 18 And this is but a light thing in the sight of the LORD : he will also deliver the Moabites into your hand. 19 And ye shall smite every fenced city, and every choice city, and shall fell every good tree, and stop all fountains of water, and mar every good piece of land with stones.

Kingdom of Judah.	Kingdom of Israel.

C. THE MORNING BRINGS WATER.

2 *Kings* 3 : 20.

20 And it came to pass in the morning, about the time of offering the oblation, that, behold, there came water by the way of Edom, and the country was filled with water.

D. THE MOABITES DEFEATED BY THE ALLIED ARMIES.

2 *Kings* 3 : 21–27.

21 Now when all the Moabites heard that the kings were come up to fight against them, they ᵃ gathered themselves together, all that were able to ᵇ put on armour, and upward, and stood on the border. 22 And they rose up early in the morning, and the sun shone upon the water, and the Moabites saw the water over against them as red as blood : 23 and they said, This is blood ; the kings ᶜ are surely destroyed, and they have smitten each man his fellow : now therefore, Moab, to the spoil. 24 And when they came to the camp of Israel, the Israelites rose up and smote the Moabites, so that they fled before them : and they went forward ᵈ into the land smiting the Moabites. 25 And they beat down the cities ; and on every good piece of land they cast every man his stone, and filled it ; and they stopped all the fountains of water, and felled all the good trees : until in Kir-haraseth *only* they left the stones thereof ; howbeit the slingers went about it, and smote it. 26 And when the king of Moab saw that the battle was too sore for him, he took with him seven hundred men that drew sword, to break through unto the king of Edom : but they could not. 27 Then he took his eldest son that should have reigned in his stead, and offered him for a burnt offering upon the wall. And ᵉ there was great wrath against Israel : and they departed from him, and returned to their own land.

(15) THE DEATH OF JEHOSHAPHAT.

I *Ki.* 22 :45, 50a.	2 *Ch.* 20 : 34 ; 21 : 1a.
45 Now the rest of the acts of Jehoshaphat, and his might that he shewed, and how he warred, are they not written in the book of the chronicles of the kings of Judah ?	34 Now the rest of the acts of Jehoshaphat, first and last, behold, they are written in the ᶠ history of Jehu the son of Hanani, ᵍ which is inserted in the book of the kings of Israel.
50a And Jehoshaphat slept with his fathers, and was buried with his fathers in the city of David his father.	1a And Jehoshaphat slept with his fathers, and was buried with his fathers in the city of David.

155. THE REIGN OF JEHORAM.

(1) JEHORAM BECOMES SOLE KING.

I *Kings* 22 : 50b.	2 *Chronicles* 21 : 1b.
50b And Jehoram his son reigned in his stead.	1b And Jehoram his son reigned in his stead.

ᵃ Or, " were called together."   ᵇ Heb. " gird themselves with a girdle."   ᶜ Or, " have surely fought together."
ᵈ Heb. " into it."   ᵉ Or, " there came great wrath upon Israel."   ᶠ Heb. " words."   ᵍ Or, " who is mentioned."

Kingdom of Judah.

(2) THE CHARACTER OF JEHORAM.[a]

2 *Ki.* 8: 18, 19.	2 *Ch.* 21 :6, 7, 11.
18 And he walked in the way of the kings of Israel, as did the house of Ahab : for he had [b] the daughter of Ahab to wife : and he did that which was evil in the sight of the LORD. 19 Howbeit the LORD would not destroy Judah, for David his servant's sake, as he promised him to give unto him a lamp [c] for his children alway.	6 And he walked in the way of the kings of Israel, as did the house of Ahab : for he had the daughter of Ahab to wife : and he did that which was evil in the sight of the LORD. 7 Howbeit the LORD would not destroy the house of David, because of the covenant that he had made with David, and as he promised to give a lamp to him and to his children alway. 11 Moreover he made high places in the [d] mountains of Judah, and made the inhabitants of Jerusalem to go a whoring, and [e] led Judah astray.

(3) THE REVOLT OF EDOM.

2 *Kings* 8: 20–22a.	2 *Chronicles* 21 : 8–10a.
20 In his days Edom revolted from under the hand of Judah, and made a king over themselves. 21 Then Joram passed over to Zair, and all his chariots with him : and he rose up by night, and smote the Edomites which compassed him about, and the captains of the chariots : and the people fled to their tents. 22a So Edom revolted from under the hand of Judah, unto this day.	8 In his days Edom revolted from under the hand of Judah, and made a king over themselves. 9 Then Jehoram passed over with his captains, and all his chariots with him : and he rose up by night, and smote the Edomites which compassed him about, and the captains of the chariots. 10a So Edom revolted from under the hand of Judah, unto this day.

(4) THE REVOLT OF LIBNAH.

2 *Kings* 8 : 22b.	2 *Chronicles* 21 : 10b.
22b Then did Libnah revolt at the same time.	10b Then did Libnah revolt at the same time

Kingdom of Israel.

---

a Cf. §152, (13).   b Cf. 2 Kings 8: 26. See §156, (1).   c Another reading is, " and to his children."   d According to some ancient authorities, "cities."   e Or, " compelled Judah thereto."

Kingdom of Judah.

2 Kings 8.

2 Chronicles 21.

from under his hand: because he had forsaken the LORD, the God of his fathers.

(5) THE POSTHUMOUS MESSAGE FROM ELIJAH.[a]

2 Chronicles 21 : 12–15.

12 And there came a writing to him from Elijah the prophet, saying, Thus saith the LORD, the God of David thy father, Because thou hast not walked in the ways of Jehoshaphat thy father, nor in the ways of Asa king of Judah; 13 but hast walked in the way of the kings of Israel, and hast made Judah and the inhabitants of Jerusalem to go a whoring, like as the house of Ahab [b] did ; and also hast slain thy brethren of thy father's house, which were better than thyself : 14 behold, the LORD will smite with a great [c] plague thy people, and thy children, and thy wives, and all thy substance : 15 and thou shalt have great sickness by disease of thy bowels, until thy bowels fall out by reason of the sickness, [d] day by day.

(6) THE INVASION OF THE PHILISTINES AND ARABIANS.

2 Chronicles 21 : 16, 17.

16 And the LORD stirred up against Jehoram the spirit of the Philistines, and of the Arabians which are beside the Ethiopians : 17 and they came up against Judah, and brake into it, and carried away all the substance that was found [e] in the king's house, and his sons also, and his wives; so that there was never a son left him, save [f] Jehoahaz, the youngest of his sons.

(7) JEHORAM'S ILLNESS.

2 Chronicles 21 : 18.

18 And after all this the LORD smote him in his bowels with an incurable disease.

Kingdom of Israel.

(5) ELISHA AND THE SYRIANS.

A. ELISHA REVEALS BEN-HADAD'S PLANS.

2 Kings 6 : 8–12.

8 Now the king of Syria warred against Israel ; and he took counsel with his servants,

---

[a] Much may be said for and against the placing of this subsection here. But it is to be remembered that it was not the last time the commands of God, laid upon Elijah, were carried out subsequently to his death. Cf. 1 Kings 19 : 15–17 ; 2 Kings 8 : 7–15 ; 9 : 1–10. See §§151, (6), K, 154, (9), and 156, (4), B.   [b] Heb. "made to go a whoring."   [c] Heb. "stroke."   [d] Or, "year after year."   [e] Or, "belonging to."   [f] In 2 Chronicles 22 : 1, "Ahaziah." See §156, (1).

Kingdom of Judah.	Kingdom of Israel.

Kingdom of Israel.

2 *Kings* 6.

saying, In such and such a place shall be my
a camp.   9 And the man of God sent unto the
king of Israel, saying, Beware that thou pass
not such a place; for thither the Syrians are
coming down.   10 And the king of Israel sent
to the place which the man of God told him and
warned him of; and he saved himself there, not
once nor twice.   11 And the heart of the king
of Syria was sore troubled for this thing; and
he called his servants, and said unto them, Will
ye not shew me which of us is for the king of
Israel?   12 And one of his servants said, Nay,
my lord, O king : but Elisha, the prophet that is
in Israel, telleth the king of Israel the words that
thou speakest in thy bedchamber.

B. THE SYRIAN BANDS SMITTEN WITH BLIND-
NESS AT DOTHAN.

2 *Kings* 6 : 13–18.

13 And he said, Go and see where he is, that
I may send and fetch him.   And it was told
him, saying, Behold, he is in Dothan.   14 Therefore sent he thither horses, and chariots, and a
great host : and they came by night, and compassed the city about.   15 And when the *b* servant of the man of God was risen early, and
gone forth, behold, an host with horses and
chariots was round about the city.   And his servant said unto him, Alas, my master ! how shall
we do?   16 And he answered, Fear not : for they
that be with us are more than they that be
with them.   17 And Elisha prayed, and said,
LORD, I pray thee, open his eyes, that he may
see.   And the LORD opened the eyes of the
young man ; and he saw : and, behold, the mountain was full of horses and chariots of fire round
about Elisha.   18 And when they came down to
him, Elisha prayed unto the LORD, and said,
Smite this *c* people, I pray thee, with blindness.
And he smote them with blindness according to
the word of Elisha.

C. ELISHA LEADS THE BLINDED SYRIANS TO
SAMARIA.

2 *Kings* 6 : 19–23.

19 And Elisha said unto them, This is not the
way, neither is this the city : follow me, and I

---

a Or, " encamping."   *b* Or, " minister."   *c* Heb. " nation."

Kingdom of Judah.

Kingdom of Israel.

2 *Kings* 6.

will bring you to the man whom ye seek. And he led them to Samaria. 20 And it came to pass, when they were come into Samaria, that Elisha said, LORD, open the eyes of these men, that they may see. And the LORD opened their eyes, and they saw; and, behold, they were in the midst of Samaria. 21 And the king of Israel said unto Elisha, when he saw them, My father, shall I smite them? shall I smite them? 22 And he answered, Thou shalt not smite them : wouldest thou smite those whom thou hast taken captive with thy sword and with thy bow? set bread and water before them, that they may eat and drink, and go to their master. 23 And he prepared great provision for them : and when they had eaten and drunk, he sent them away, and they went to their master. And the bands of Syria came no more into the land of Israel.

(6) JEHORAM RESTORES THE SHUNAMMITE'S LAND BECAUSE OF ELISHA'S MIRACLES.[a]

2 *Kings* 8 : 3-6.

3 And it came to pass at the seven years' end, that the woman returned out of the land of the Philistines : and she went forth to cry unto the king for her house and for her land. 4 Now the king was talking with Gehazi the servant of the man of God, saying, Tell me, I pray thee, all the great things that Elisha hath done. 5 And it came to pass, as he was telling the king how he had restored to life him that was dead, that, behold, the woman, whose son he had restored to life, cried to the king for her house and for her land. And Gehazi said, My lord, O king, this is the woman, and this is her son, whom Elisha restored to life. 6 And when the king asked the woman, she told him. So the king appointed unto her a certain [b] officer, saying, Restore all that was hers, and all the fruits of the field since the day that she left the land, even until now.

(7) THE STORY OF NAAMAN.

A. THE HEALING OF NAAMAN'S LEPROSY.

2 *Kings* 5: 1-14.

1 Now Naaman, captain of the host of the king of Syria, was a great man [c] with his master,

---

[a] Cf. §154, (3). γ. From the internal evidence of this subsection, the event here narrated must have occurred before the events of (7), below.   [b] Or, " eunuch."   [c] Heb. " before."

Kingdom of Judah.	Kingdom of Israel.

Kingdom of Israel.

2 *Kings* 5.

and honourable, because by him the LORD had given *a* victory unto Syria : he was also a mighty man of valour, *but he was* a leper. 2 And the Syrians had gone out in bands, and had brought away captive out of the land of Israel a little maid ; and she *b* waited on Naaman's wife. 3 And she said unto her mistress, Would God my lord were *c* with the prophet that is in Samaria ! then would he recover him of his leprosy. 4 And *d* one went in, and told his lord, saying, Thus and thus said the maid that is of the land of Israel. 5 And the king of Syria said, Go to, go, and I will send a letter unto the king of Israel. And he departed, and took with him ten talents of silver, and six thousand *e pieces* of gold, and ten changes of raiment. 6 And he brought the letter to the king of Israel, saying, And now when this letter is come unto thee, behold, I have sent Naaman my servant to thee, that thou mayest recover him of his leprosy. 7 And it came to pass, when the king of Israel had read the letter, that he rent his clothes, and said, Am I God, to kill and to make alive, that this man doth send unto me to recover a man of his leprosy ? but consider, I pray you, and see how he seeketh *f* a quarrel against me. 8 And it was so, when Elisha the man of God heard that the king of Israel had rent his clothes, that he sent to the king, saying, Wherefore hast thou rent thy clothes ? let him come now to me, and he shall know that there is a prophet in Israel. 9 So Naaman came with his horses and with his chariots, and stood at the door of the house of Elisha. 10 And Elisha sent a messenger unto him, saying, Go and wash in Jordan seven times, and thy flesh shall come again to thee, and *g* thou shalt be clean. 11 But Naaman was wroth, and went away, and said, Behold, I thought, He will surely come out to me, and stand, and call on the name of the LORD his God, and wave his hand over the place, and recover the leper. 12 Are not *h* Abanah and Pharpar, the rivers of Damascus, better than all the waters of Israel ? may I not wash in them, and be clean ? So he turned and went away in a rage. 13 And his servants came near, and spake unto him, and said, My father, if the prophet had bid thee do some great thing, wouldest thou not have done it ? how much rather then, when he

---

a Heb. "salvation."   *b* Heb. "was before."   *c* Heb. " before."   *d* Or, "he."   *e* Or, "*shekels*."   *f* Or, " an occasion."   *g* Heb. "be thou clean."   *h* Another reading is " Amanah."

18

Kingdom of Judah.	Kingdom of Israel.

Kingdom of Israel.

2 Kings 5.

saith to thee, Wash, and be clean ?   14 Then
went he down, and dipped *himself* seven times
in Jordan, according to the saying of the man of
God : and his flesh came again like unto the
flesh of a little child, and he was clean.

B. NAAMAN'S GRATITUDE.

2 Kings 5 : 15–19.

15 And he returned to the man of God, he and
all his company, and came, and stood before
him : and he said, Behold now, I know that
there is no God in all the earth, but in Israel :
now therefore, I pray thee, take ᵃ a present of thy
servant.   16 But he said, As the LORD liveth,
before whom I stand, I will receive none. And
he urged him to take it ; but he refused.   17 And
Naaman said, If not, yet I pray thee let there be
given to thy servant two mules' burden of earth ;
for thy servant will henceforth offer neither
burnt offering nor sacrifice unto other gods, but
unto the LORD.   18 In this thing the LORD pardon thy servant ; when my master goeth into
the house of Rimmon to worship there, and he
leaneth on my hand, and I bow myself in the
house of Rimmon, when I bow myself in the
house of Rimmon, the LORD pardon thy servant
in this thing.   19 And he said unto him, Go in
peace.   So he departed from him ᵇ a little way.

C. GEHAZI'S SIN AND PUNISHMENT.

2 Kings 5 : 20–27.

20 But Gehazi, the servant of Elisha the man
of God, said, Behold, my master hath spared
this Naaman the Syrian, in not receiving at his
hands that which he brought : as the LORD
liveth, I will run after him, and take somewhat
of him.   21 So Gehazi followed after Naaman.
And when Naaman saw one running after him,
he lighted down from the chariot to meet him,
and said, Is all well ?   22 And he said, All is
well.   My master hath sent me, saying, Behold,
even now there be come to me from the hill
country of Ephraim two young men of the sons
of the prophets ; give them, I pray thee, a talent
of silver, and two changes of raiment.   23 And
Naaman said, Be content, take two talents.
And he urged him, and bound two talents of

ᵃ Heb. "blessing."   ᵇ Or, "some way."

Kingdom of Judah.	Kingdom of Israel.

Kingdom of Israel.

2 Kings 5.

silver in two bags, with two changes of raiment, and laid them upon two of his servants; and they bare them before him. 24 And when he came to the *a* hill, he took them from their hand, and bestowed them in the house: and he let the men go, and they departed. 25 But he went in, and stood before his master. And Elisha said unto him, Whence comest thou, Gehazi? And he said, Thy servant went no whither. 26 And he said unto him, *b* Went not mine heart *with thee*, when the man turned again from his chariot to meet thee? Is it a time to receive money, and to receive garments, and oliveyards and vineyards, and sheep and oxen, and menservants and maidservants? 27 The leprosy therefore of Naaman shall cleave unto thee, and unto thy seed for ever. And he went out from his presence a leper *as white* as snow.

(8) THE SIEGE OF SAMARIA.

A. BEN-HADAD BESIEGES SAMARIA.

2 Kings 6 : 24.

24 And it came to pass after this, that Ben-hadad king of Syria gathered all his host, and went up, and besieged Samaria.

B. THE SUFFERING FROM THE FAMINE.

2 Kings 6 : 25-31.

25 And there was a great famine in Samaria: and, behold, they besieged it, until an ass's head was sold for fourscore *c pieces* of silver, and the fourth part of a kab of dove's dung for five *c pieces* of silver. 26 And as the king of Israel was passing by upon the wall, there cried a woman unto him, saying, Help, my lord, O king. 27 And he said, *d* If the LORD do not help thee, whence shall I help thee? out of the threshing-floor, or out of the winepress? 28 And the king said unto her, what aileth thee? And she answered, This woman said unto me, Give thy son, that we may eat him to-day, and we will eat my son to-morrow. 29 So we boiled my son, and did eat him: and I said unto her on the next day, Give thy son, that we may eat him: and she hath hid her son. 30 And it came to pass, when the king heard the words of the

---

a Heb. "Ophel."   *b* Or, "Mine heart went not *from me*, when," etc.   *c* Or, "*shekels*."   *d* Or, "Nay, let the LORD help thee!"

Kingdom of Judah.

Kingdom of Israel.

2 *Kings* 6.

woman, that he rent his clothes; (now he was passing by upon the wall;) and the people looked, and, behold, he had sackcloth within upon his flesh. 31 Then he said, God do so to me, and more also, if the head of Elisha the son of Shaphat shall stand on him this day.

C. THE KING'S MESSENGER OF VENGEANCE AND ELISHA'S PROMISE OF PLENTY.

2 *Kings* 6 : 32–7 : 2.

32 But Elisha sat in his house, and the elders sat with him ; and *the king* sent a man from before him : but ere the messenger came to him, he said to the elders, See ye how this son of a murderer hath sent to take away mine head ? look, when the messenger cometh, shut the door, and *a* hold the door fast against him : is not the sound of his master's feet behind him ? 33 And while he yet talked with them, behold, the messenger came down unto him : and he said, Behold, this evil is of the LORD ; why should I wait for the LORD any longer ? 1 And Elisha said, Hear ye the word of the LORD : thus saith the LORD, To-morrow about this time shall a *b* measure of fine flour be *sold* for a shekel, and two measures of barley for a shekel, in the gate of Samaria. 2 Then the captain on whose hand the king leaned answered the man of God, and said, Behold, if the LORD should make windows in heaven, might this thing be ? And he said, Behold, thou shalt see it with thine eyes, but shalt not eat thereof.

D. THE DISCOVERY OF THE FOUR LEPERS.

2 *Kings* 7 : 3–11.

3 Now there were four leprous men at the entering in of the gate : and they said one to another, Why sit we here until we die ? 4 If we say, We will enter into the city, then the famine is in the city, and we shall die there : and if we sit still here, we die also. Now therefore come, and let us fall unto the host of the Syrians : if they save us alive, we shall live ; and if they kill us, we shall but die. 5 And they rose up in the twilight, to go unto the camp of the Syrians : and when they were come to the outermost part of the camp of the Syrians, behold, there was no

---

a Heb. "thrust him back with the door."   *b* Heb. "seah."

Kingdom of Judah.	Kingdom of Israel.

Kingdom of Israel.

2 *Kings* 7.

man there. 6 For the LORD had made the host of the Syrians to hear a noise of chariots, and a noise of horses, even the noise of a great host : and they said one to another, Lo, the king of Israel hath hired against us the kings of the Hittites, and the kings of the Egyptians, to come upon us. 7 Wherefore they arose and fled in the twilight, and left their tents, and their horses, and their asses, even the camp as it was, and fled for their life. 8 And when these lepers came to the outermost part of the camp, they went into one tent, and did eat and drink, and carried thence silver, and gold, and raiment, and went and hid it ; and they came back, and entered into another tent, and carried thence also, and went and hid it. 9 Then they said one to another, We do not well : this day is a day of good tidings, and we hold our peace : if we tarry till the morning light, *a* punishment will overtake us : now therefore come, let us go and tell the king's household. 10 So they came and called unto the *b* porter of the city : and they told them, saying, We came to the camp of the Syrians, and, behold, there was no man there, neither voice of man, but the horses tied, and the asses tied, and the tents as they were. 11 And *c* he called the porters ; and they told it to the king's household within.

E. THE LEPERS' REPORT CONFIRMED AND ELISHA'S PROMISES FULFILLED.

2 *Kings* 7 : 12-20.

12 And the king arose in the night, and said unto his servants, I will now shew you what the Syrians have done to us. They know that we be hungry ; therefore are they gone out of the camp to hide themselves in the field, saying, When they come out of the city, we shall take them alive, and get into the city. 13 And one of his servants answered and said, Let some take, I pray thee, five of the horses that remain, which are left *d* in the city, (behold, they are as all the multitude of Israel that are left in it ; behold, they are as all the multitude of Israel that are consumed :) and let us send and see. 14 They took therefore two chariots with horses ; and the king sent after the host of the Syrians, saying, Go and see. 15 And they went after them unto Jordan : and,

---

a Or, " our iniquity will find us out."   *b* Or, " porters."   *c* Or, " the porters called."   *d* Heb. " in it."

Kingdom of Judah.	Kingdom of Israel.

Kingdom of Israel.

2 Kings 7.

lo, all the way was full of garments and vessels, which the Syrians had cast away in their haste. And the messengers returned, and told the king. 16 And the people went out, and spoiled the camp of the Syrians. So a measure of fine flour was *sold* for a shekel, and two measures of barley for a shekel, according to the word of the LORD. 17 And the king appointed the captain on whose hand he leaned to have the charge of the gate: and the people trode upon him in the gate, and he died as the man of God had said, who spake when the king came down to him. 18 And it came to pass, as the man of God had spoken to the king, saying, Two measures of barley for a shekel, and a measure of fine flour for a shekel, shall be to-morrow about this time in the gate of Samaria; 19 and that captain answered the man of God, and said, Now, behold, if the LORD should make windows in heaven, might such a thing be? and he said, Behold, thou shalt see it with thine eyes, but shalt not eat thereof: 20 it came to pass even so unto him; for the people trode upon him in the gate, and he died.

(8) THE DEATH OF JEHORAM.

2 Ki. 8 : 23, 24*a*.	*2 Ch.* 21 : 19, 20*b*.

23 And the rest of the acts of Joram, and all that he did, are they not written in the book of the chronicles of the kings of Judah? 24*a* And Joram slept with his fathers, and was buried with his fathers in the city of David.

19 And it came to pass, in process of time, at the end of two years, that his bowels fell out by reason of his sickness, and he died of sore diseases. And his people made no burning for him, like the burning of his fathers. 20*b* And he departed without being desired; and they buried him in the city of David, but not in the sepulchres of the kings.

Kingdom of Judah.			Kingdom of Israel.

156. THE REIGN OF AHAZIAH.

(1) AHAZIAH'S ACCESSION TO THE THRONE.

2 Ki. 8 : 24b-26.	2 Ki. 9 : 29.	2 Ch. 22 : 1, 2.
24b And A-haziah his son reigned in his stead.		1 And the inhabitants of Jerusalem made b Ahaziah his
25 In the twelfth year of Joram the son of Ahab king of Israel did Ahaziah the son of Jehoram king of Judah begin to reign. 26 Two and twenty years old was Ahaziah when he began to reign ; and he reigned one year in Jerusalem. And his mother's name was Athaliah the a daughter of Omri king of Israel.	29 And in the eleventh year of Joram the son of Ahab began Ahaziah to reign over Judah.	youngest son king in his stead : for the band of men that came with the Arabians to the camp had slain all the eldest. So Ahaziah the son of Jehoram king of Judah reigned. 2 Forty and two years old was Ahaziah when he began to reign ; and he reigned one year in Jerusalem : and his mother's name was Athaliah the a daughter of Omri.

(2) THE CHARACTER OF AHAZIAH.

2 Kings 8 : 27.	2 Chronicles 22 : 3–5a.
27 And he walked in the way of the house of Ahab, and did that which was evil in the sight of the LORD, as did the house of Ahab : for he was the son in law of the house of Ahab.	3 He also walked in the ways of the house of Ahab : for his mother was his counsellor to do wickedly. 4 And he did that which was evil in the sight of the LORD, as did the house of Ahab : for they were his counsellors after the death of his father, to his destruction. 5a He walked also after their counsel.

---

a Or, " granddaughter." Cf. 2 Chronicles 18 . 1. See §152, (6).   b In 2 Chronicles 21 : 17, "Jehoahaz." See §155, (6).

Kingdom of Judah.

Kingdom of Israel.

(9) ELISHA'S INTERVIEW WITH HAZAEL.

2 *Kings* 8 : 7–15.

7 And Elisha came to Damascus; and Ben-hadad the king of Syria was sick; and it was told him, saying, The man of God is come hither.   8 And the king said unto Hazael, Take a present in thine hand, and go meet the man of God, and inquire of the LORD by him, saying, Shall I recover of this sickness?   9 So Hazael went to meet him, and took a present *a* with him, *b* even of every good thing of Damascus, forty camels' burden, and came and stood before him, and said, Thy son Ben-hadad king of Syria hath sent me to thee, saying, Shall I recover of this sickness?   10 And Elisha said unto him, Go, *c* say unto him, Thou shalt surely recover; howbeit the LORD hath shewed me that he shall surely die.   11 And he settled his countenance steadfastly *upon him*, until he was ashamed: and the man of God wept.   12 And Hazael said, Why weepeth my lord? And he answered, Because I know the evil that thou wilt do unto the children of Israel: their strong holds wilt thou set on fire, and their young men wilt thou slay with the sword, and wilt dash in pieces their little ones, and rip up their women with child.   13 And Hazael said, But what is thy servant, which is but a dog, that he should do this great thing? And Elisha answered, The LORD hath shewed me that thou shalt be king over Syria.   14 Then he departed from Elisha, and came to his master; who said to him, What said Elisha to thee? And he answered, He told me that thou shouldest surely recover.   15 And it came to pass on the morrow, that he took the coverlet, and dipped it in water, and spread it on his face, so that he died: and Hazael reigned in his stead.

(3) AHAZIAH AIDS JEHORAM IN THE DEFENSE OF RAMOTH-GILEAD. (10)

2 *Kings* 8 : 28.

28 And he went with Joram the son of Ahab to war against Hazael king of Syria at Ramoth-gilead: and the Syrians wounded Joram.

2 *Chronicles* 22 : 5*b*.

5*b* And [he] went with Jehoram the son of Ahab king of Israel to war against Hazael king of Syria at Ramoth-gilead: and the Syrians wounded Joram.

---

a Heb. " in his hand."   *b* Or, "and."   *c* According to another reading, "say, Thou shalt not recover: for the LORD," etc.

Kingdom of Judah.	Kingdom of Israel.

Kingdom of Israel.

(11) JEHORAM GOES FOR HEALING TO JEZREEL.

2 Ki. 8 : 29a.	2 Ki.9:14b,15a.	2 Ch. 22 : 6a.
	14b Now Joram kept Ramoth-gilead, he and all Israel, because of Hazael king of Syria. 15a But	
29a And king Joram returned to be healed in Jezreel of the wounds which the Syrians had given him at Ramah, when he fought against Hazael king of Syria.	king *a* Joram was returned to be healed in Jezreel of the wounds which the Syrians had given him, when he fought with Hazael king of Syria.	6a. And he returned to be healed in Jezreel *b* of the wounds which they had given him at Ramah, when he fought against Hazael king of Syria.

(4) JEHU'S SUCCESSFUL CONSPIRACY. (12)

A. AHAZIAH VISITS JEHORAM IN JEZREEL.

2 Kings 8 : 29b.	2 Kings 9 : 16b.	2 Chronicles 22 : 6b.
29b And Ahaziah the son of Jehoram king of Judah went down to see Joram the son of Ahab in Jezreel, because he was sick.	16b And Ahaziah king of Judah was come down to see Joram.	6b And *c* Azariah the son of Jehoram king of Judah went down to see Jehoram the son of Ahab in Jezreel, because he was sick.

B. AT ELISHA'S COMMAND, JEHU IS ANOINTED KING OVER ISRAEL, AT RAMOTH-GILEAD.

2 Kings 9 : 1-10.

1 And Elisha the prophet called one of the sons of the prophets, and said unto him, Gird up thy loins, and take this vial of oil in thine hand, and go to Ramoth-gilead. 2 And when thou comest thither, look out there Jehu the son of Jehoshaphat the son of Nimshi, and go in, and make him arise up from among his brethren, and carry him to an inner chamber. 3 Then take the vial of oil, and pour it on his head, and say, Thus saith the LORD, I have anointed thee king over Israel. Then open the

---

a Heb. " Jehoram," and in vv. 17, 21-24. See below, (12), *D.*   *b* So in the Sept. and Syriac versions. The text has, " because the wounds which," etc.   *c* In ver. 1 of this chapter, " Ahaziah." See §156, (1).

Kingdom of Judah.	Kingdom of Israel.

Kingdom of Israel.

2 *Kings* 9.

door, and flee, and tarry not. 4 So the young man, even the young man the prophet, went to Ramoth-gilead. 5 And when he came, behold, the captains of the host were sitting; and he said, I have an errand to thee, O captain. And Jehu said, Unto which of all us? And he said, To thee, O captain. 6 And he arose, and went into the house; and he poured the oil on his head, and said unto him, Thus saith the LORD, the God of Israel, I have anointed thee king over the people of the LORD, even over Israel. 7 And thou shalt smite the house of Ahab thy master, that I may avenge the blood of my servants the prophets, and the blood of all the servants of the LORD, at the hand of Jezebel. 8 For the whole house of Ahab shall perish: and I will cut off from Ahab every man child, and him that is shut up and him that is left at large in Israel. 9 And I will make the house of Ahab like the house of Jeroboam the son of Nebat, and like the house of Baasha the son of Ahijah. 10 And the dogs shall eat Jezebel in the portion of Jezreel, and there shall be none to bury her. And he opened the door, and fled.

C. JEHU IS PROCLAIMED KING BY HIS BROTHER OFFICERS.

2 *Kings* 9: 11-13.

11 Then Jehu came forth to the servants of his lord: and one said unto him, Is all well? wherefore came this mad fellow to thee? And he said unto them, Ye know the man and what his talk was. 12 And they said, It is false; tell us now. And he said, Thus and thus spake he to me, saying, Thus saith the LORD, I have anointed thee king over Israel. 13 Then they hasted, and took every man his garment, and put it under him *a* on the top of the stairs, and blew the trumpet, saying, Jehu is king.

D. JEHU PROCEEDS TO JEZREEL AND SLAYS JEHORAM.

2 *Kings* 9: 14a, 15b, 16a, 17-26.	2 *Chronicles* 22: 7.

14a So Jehu the son of Jehoshaphat the son of Nimshi conspired against Joram. 15b And Jehu said, If this be your mind, then let none escape and go forth out of the city, to go to tell it in Jezreel. 16a So Jehu rode in a chariot, and went to Jezreel; for Joram lay there. 17 Now

a Or, "on the bare steps."

Kingdom of Judah.

2 *Kings* 9.

the watchman stood on the tower in Jezreel, and he spied the company of Jehu as he came, and said, I see a company. And Joram said, Take an horseman, and send to meet them, and let him say, *a* Is it peace? 18 So there went one on horseback to meet him, and said, Thus saith the king, Is it peace? And Jehu said, What hast thou to do with peace? turn thee behind me. And the watchman told, saying, The messenger came to them, but he cometh not again. 19 Then he sent out a second on horseback, which came to them, and said, Thus saith the king, Is it peace? And Jehu answered, What hast thou to do with peace? turn thee behind me. 20 And the watchman told, saying, He came even unto them, and cometh not again : and the driving is like the driving of Jehu the son of Nimshi; for he driveth furiously. 21 And Joram said, *b* Make ready. And they made ready his chariot. And Joram king of Israel and Ahaziah king of Judah went out, each in his chariot, and they went out to meet Jehu, and found him in the portion of Naboth the Jezreelite. 22 And it came to pass, when Joram saw Jehu, that he said, Is it peace, Jehu? And he answered, What peace, so long as the whoredoms of thy mother Jezebel and her witchcrafts are so many? 23 And Joram turned his hands, and fled, and said to Ahaziah, There is treachery, O Ahaziah. 24 And Jehu *c* drew his bow with his full strength, and smote Joram between his arms, and the arrow went out at his heart, and he sunk down in his chariot. 25 Then said *Jehu* to Bidkar his captain, Take up, and cast him in the portion of the field of Naboth the Jezreelite: for remember how that, when I and thou rode together after Ahab his father, the LORD *d* laid this burden upon him ; 26 Surely I have seen yesterday the blood of Naboth, and the blood of his sons, saith the LORD ; and I will requite thee in this *e* plat, saith the LORD. Now therefore take and cast him into the plat *of ground*, according to the word of the LORD.

Kingdom of Israel.

2 *Chronicles* 22.

7 Now the *f* destruction of Ahaziah was of God, in that he went unto Joram : for when he was come, he went out with Jehoram against Jehu the son of Nimshi, whom the LORD had anointed to cut off the house of Ahab.

E. AHAZIAH IS, IN TURN, ALSO SLAIN BY JEHU'S COMMAND.*g*

2 *Kings* 9:27, 28.

27 But when Ahaziah the king of Judah saw this, he fled by the way of the garden house.

2 *Chronicles* 22:9a.

9a And he sought Ahaziah, and they caught him, (now he was hiding in Samaria,) and they

---

a Or, "Is all well?" *b* Or, "Yoke." *c* Heb. "filled his hand with the bow." *d* Or, "uttered this oracle against him." *e* Or, "portion." *f* Heb. "treading down." *g* The events of part of this division, of course, occurred after the events in *F*; and Ahaziah's burial occurred, of course, too, after the events of *G*, *H*, *I*, and *J*. But all things considered, it has seemed best to place the passages as they are.

Kingdom of Judah.

2 *Kings* 9.

And Jehu followed after him, and said, Smite him also in the chariot: *and they smote him* at the ascent of Gur, which is by Ibleam.   And he fled to Megiddo, and died there.   28 And his servants carried him in a chariot to Jerusalem, and buried him in his sepulchre with his fathers in the city of David.

Kingdom of Israel.

2 *Chronicles* 22.

brought him to Jehu, and slew him; and they buried him, for they said, He is the son of Jehoshaphat, who sought the LORD with all his heart.

F. THE FATE OF JEZEBEL.

2 *Kings* 9 : 30–37.

30 And when Jehu was come to Jezreel, Jezebel heard of it; and she painted her eyes, and tired her head, and looked out at the window. 31 And as Jehu entered in at the gate, she said, *a* Is it peace, thou Zimri, thy master's murderer? 32 And he lifted up his face to the window, and said, Who is on my side? who? And there looked out to him two or three eunuchs.   33 And he said, Throw her down.   So they threw her down: and some of her blood was sprinkled on the wall, and on the horses: and he trode her under foot.   34 And when he was come in, he did eat and drink; and he said, See now to this cursed woman, and bury her: for she is a king's daughter.   35 And they went to bury her: but they found no more of her than the skull, and the feet, and the palms of her hands.   36 Wherefore they came again, and told him.   And he said, This is the word of the LORD, which he spake by his servant Elijah the Tishbite, saying, In the portion of Jezreel shall the dogs eat the flesh of Jezebel: 37 and the carcase of Jezebel shall be as dung upon the face of the field in the portion of Jezreel; so that they shall not say, This is Jezebel.

G. THE JUDGMENT ON THE HOUSE OF AHAB.

2 *Kings* 10 : 1–11.

1 Now Ahab had seventy sons in Samaria. And Jehu wrote letters, and sent to Samaria, unto the rulers of Jezreel, even the elders, and unto them that brought up *the sons of* Ahab, saying, 2 And now as soon as this letter cometh to you, seeing your master's sons are with you, and there are with you chariots and horses, a fenced city also, and armour; 3 look ye out the best and meetest of your master's sons, and set him on his father's throne, and fight for your master's house. 4 But they were exceedingly afraid, and said, Behold, the two kings stood

---

a Or. " Is it well ? "

Kingdom of Judah.

Kingdom of Israel.

2 Kings 10.

not before him: how then shall we stand?
5 And he that was over the household, and he
that was over the city, the elders also, and they
that brought up *the children*, sent to Jehu, saying, We are thy servants, and will do all that thou
shalt bid us; we will not make any man king:
do thou that which is good in thine eyes.
6 Then he wrote a letter the second time to them,
saying, If ye be on my side, and if ye will hearken
unto my voice, take ye the heads of the men
your master's sons, and come to me to Jezreel
by to-morrow this time. Now the king's sons,
being seventy persons, were with the great men
of the city, which brought them up. 7 And it
came to pass, when the letter came to them,
that they took the king's sons, and slew them,
even seventy persons, and put their heads in
baskets, and sent them unto him to Jezreel.
8 And there came a messenger and told him,
saying, They have brought the heads of the king's
sons. And he said, Lay ye them in two heaps
at the entering in of the gate until the morning.
9 And it came to pass in the morning, that he
went out and stood, and said to all the people,
Ye be righteous: behold, I conspired against my
master, and slew him: but who smote all these?
10 Know now that there shall fall unto the earth
nothing of the word of the LORD, which the
LORD spake concerning the house of Ahab: for
the LORD hath done that which he spake by his
servant Elijah. 11 So Jehu smote all that remained of the house of Ahab in Jezreel, and all
his great men, and his familiar friends, and his
priests, until he left him none remaining.

H. THE MASSACRE OF THE PRINCES ROYAL OF JUDAH.

2 Kings 10 : 12–14.

12 And he arose and departed, and went to
Samaria. And as he was at the *a* shearing house
of the shepherds in the way, 13 Jehu met with
the brethren of Ahaziah king of Judah, and said,
Who are ye? And they answered, We are the
brethren of Ahaziah: and we go down to salute
the children of the king and the children of the
queen. 14 And he said, Take them alive. And
they took them alive, and slew them at the *b* pit
of the *a* shearing house, even two and forty men;
neither left he any of them.

2 Chronicles 22 : 8.

8 And it came to pass, when Jehu was executing judgement upon the house of Ahab, that he
found the princes of Judah, and the sons of the
brethren of Ahaziah, ministering to Ahaziah,
and slew them.

a Or, "house of gathering."   *b* Or, "cistern."

Kingdom of Judah.	Kingdom of Israel.

I. JEHU ATTACHES JEHONADAB TO HIS
SUPPORT.

2 *Kings* 10 : 15, 16.

15 And when he was departed thence, he lighted on Jehonadab the son of Rechab coming to meet him : and he saluted him, and said to him, Is thine heart right, as my heart is with thy heart? And Jehonadab answered, It is. If it be, give me thine hand. And he gave him his hand ; and he took him up to him into the chariot. 16 And he said, Come with me, and see my zeal for the LORD. So they made him ride in his chariot.

J. THE COMPLETE SUCCESS OF THE USURPER.

2 *Kings* 10 : 17.

17 And when he came to Samaria, he smote all that remained unto Ahab in Samaria, till he had destroyed him, according to the word of the LORD, which he spake to Elijah.

PART II.
FROM THE RISE OF JEHU TO THE FALL OF THE KINGDOM OF ISRAEL.

157. THE REIGN OF JEHU.
(1) JEHU'S DESTRUCTION OF BAAL.

2 *Kings* 10 : 18-28.

158. THE REIGN OF ATHALIAH.

(1) HAVING SLAIN ALL THE SEED ROYAL
SAVE JOASH, ATHALIAH USURPS
THE THRONE.

2 *Ki.* 11 : 1, 3*b.*	2 *Ch.* 22 : 9*b,* 10, 12*b.*
	9*b* [a]And the house of Ahaziah had no power to hold the kingdom.
1 Now when Athaliah the mother of Ahaziah saw that her son was dead, she arose and destroyed all the seed	10 Now when Athaliah the mother of Ahaziah saw that her son was dead, she arose and destroyed all the seed

18 And Jehu gathered all the people together, and said unto them, Ahab served Baal a little ; but Jehu shall serve him much. 19 Now therefore call unto me all the prophets of Baal, all his worshippers, and all his priests ; let none be wanting : for I have a great sacrifice *to do* to Baal ; whosoever shall be wanting, he shall not live. But Jehu did it in subtilty, to the intent that he might destroy the worshippers of Baal. 20 And Jehu said, Sanctify a solemn assembly for Baal. And they proclaimed it. 21 And Jehu sent through all Israel : and all the worshippers of Baal came, so that there was not a man left that came not. And they came into the house of Baal ; and the house of Baal was filled from one end to another. 22 And he said unto him that was over the vestry, Bring forth vestments

[a] Or, "And there was none of the house of Ahaziah that had power," etc.

Kingdom of Judah

2 *Kings* 11.	2 *Chronicles* 22.
royal. 3b And Athaliah reigned over the land.	royal of the house of Judah. 12b And Athaliah reigned over the land.

(2) THE RESCUE OF JOASH.

2 *Kings* 11 : 2, 3a.	2 *Chronicles* 22 : 11, 12a.
2 But Jehosheba, the daughter of king Joram, sister of Ahaziah, took Joash the son of Ahaziah, and s t o l e him away from among the king's sons that were slain, even him and his nurse, *a and put them* in the *b* bedchamber; and they hid him from Athaliah, so that he was not slain. 3a And he was with her hid in the house of the LORD six years.	11 But Jehoshabeath, the daughter o f t h e king, took Joash the son of Ahaziah, and stole him away from among t h e king's sons that were slain, and put him and his nurse in the *b* bedchamber. So Jehoshabeath, the daughter of king Jehoram, the w i f e of Jehoiada the priest, (for she was the sister of Ahaziah,) hid him from Athaliah, so that she slew him not. 12a And he was with them hid in the house of God six years.

Kingdom of Israel.

2 *Kings* 10.

for all the worshippers of Baal. And he brought them forth vestments. 23 And Jehu went, and Jehonadab the son of Rechab, into the house of Baal ; and he said unto the worshippers of Baal, Search, and look that there be here with you none of the servants of the LORD, but the worshippers of Baal only. 24 And they went in to offer sacrifices and burnt offerings. Now Jehu had appointed him fourscore men without, and said, If any of the men whom I bring into your hands escape, *he that letteth him go,* his life shall be for the life of him. 25 And it came to pass, as soon as he had made an end of offering the burnt offering, that Jehu said to the *e* guard and to the captains, Go in, and slay them ; let none come forth. And they smote them with the edge of the sword ; and the guard and the captains cast them out, and went to the city of the house of Baal. 26 And they brought forth the *d* pillars that were in the house of Baal, and burned them. 27 And they brake down the pillar of Baal, and brake down the house of Baal, and made it a draught house, unto this day. 28 Thus Jehu destroyed Baal out of Israel.

(2) JEHOVAH'S PROMISE TO JEHU AND HIS HOUSE.

2 *Kings* 10 : 30.

30 And the LORD said unto Jehu, Because thou hast *f* done well in executing that which is right in mine eyes, *and* hast done unto the house of Ahab according to all that was in mine heart, thy sons of the fourth generation shall sit on the throne of Israel.

(3) JEHU WALKS IN THE SINS OF JEROBOAM.

2 *Kings* 10 : 29.	2 *Kings* 10 : 31.
29 Howbeit from the sins of Jeroboam the son of Nebat, *g* wherewith he made Israel to sin, Jehu departed not from after them, *to wit,* the golden calves that were in Beth-el, and that were in Dan.	31 But Jehu took no heed to walk in the law of the LORD, the God of Israel, with all his heart : he departed not from the sins of Jeroboam, wherewith he made Israel to sin.

---

a Or, " *who were.*"   *b* Or, " chamber for the beds."   *c* Heb. " runners."   *d* Or, " obelisks."   *e* Cf. 2 Kings 15 : 12.
See §165, (4).   *f* Or, " executed well."   *g* Or, " who."

Kingdom of Judah.	Kingdom of Israel.

(3) JEHOIADA ELEVATES JOASH TO THE THRONE.

2 *Kings* 11 : 4-12.

2 *Chronicles* 23 : 1-11.

1 And in the seventh year Jehoiada strengthened himself, and took the captains of hundreds, Azariah the son of Jeroham, and Ishmael the son of Jehohanan, and Azariah the son of Obed, and Maaseiah the son of Adaiah, and Elishaphat the son of Zichri, into covenant with him. 2 And they went about in Judah, and gathered the Levites out of all the cities of Judah, and the heads of fathers' *houses* of Israel, and they came to Jerusalem. 3 And all the congregation made a covenant with the king in the house of God. And he said unto them, Behold, the king's son shall reign, as the LORD hath spoken concerning the sons of David. 4 This is the thing that ye shall do : *c* a third part of you, that come in on the sabbath, of the priests and of the Levites, shall be porters of the *d* doors; 5 and a third part shall be at the king's house; and a third part at the gate of the foundation : and all the people shall be in the courts of the house of the LORD. 6 But let none come into the house of the LORD, save the priests,

4 And in the seventh year Jehoiada sent and fetched the captains over hundreds, of the *a* Carites and of the *b* guard, and brought them to him into the house of the LORD; and he made a covenant with them, and took an oath of them in the house of the LORD, and shewed them the king's son. 5 And he commanded them, saying, This is the thing that ye shall do : a third part of you, that come in on the sabbath, shall be keepers of the watch of the king's house; 6 and a third part shall be at the gate Sur; and a third part at the gate behind the guard : so shall ye keep the watch

---

a Or, " executioners."   *b* Heb. " runners."   *c* Cf. 1 Chronicles 24 : 4.   See §107, (2), *D*.   *d* Heb. " thresholds."

Kingdom of Judah.

2 *Kings* 11.	2 *Chronicles* 23.
of the house, and be a barrier. 7 And the two companies of you, even all that go forth on the sabbath, shall keep the watch of the house of the LORD about the king. 8 And ye shall compass the king round about, every man with his w e a p o n s in his hand ; and he that cometh within the ranks, let him be slain : and be ye with the king when he goeth out, and when he cometh in. 9 And the captains over hundreds did according to all that Jehoiada the p r i e s t commanded : and they took every man his men, those that were to come in on the sabbath, with those that were to go out on the sabbath, and came to Jehoiada the p r i e s t. 10 And the priest delivered to the captains over hundreds the spears and shields that had been king David's, which were in the house of the L O R D. 11 And the guard stood, e v e r y man with his weapons in his hand, from the right *a* side of the house to the left side of the house, along by the altar and the h o u s e, by the king round about. 12 Then he b r o u g h t out the king's son, and *b* put the crown upon him, and *gave him* the testimony ; and they made him king, and anointed	and they that minister of the Levites ; they shall come in, for they are holy : but all the people shall keep the watch of the LORD. 7 And the Levites shall compass the king round about, every man with his weapons in his hand; and whosoever cometh into the house, let him be slain : and be ye with the king when he cometh in, and when he goeth out. 8 So the Levites and all Judah did according to all that Jehoiada the p r i e s t commanded : and they took every man his men, those that were to come in on the sabbath, with those that were to go out on the sabbath ; for Jehoiada the priest dismissed not the courses. 9 A n d Jehoiada t h e priest delivered to the captains of hundreds the spears, and bucklers, and shields, that had been king David's, which were in the house of God. 10 And he set all the people, every man with his weapon in his hand, from the right *a* side of the house to the left side of the house, along by the altar and the house, by the king round about. 11 Then they brought out the king's son, and *b* put the crown upon him, and *gave him* the testimony, and made him king : and Jehoiada

Kingdom of Israel.

---

a Heb. " shoulder."   *b* Or, " put upon him the crown and the testimony."

19

Kingdom of Judah.

2 *Kings* 11.

him: and they clapped their hands, and said, [a] God save the king.

2 *Chronicles* 23.

and his sons anointed him; and they said, [a] God save the king.

(4) ATHALIAH MEETS WITH HER DESERTS.

2 *Ki.* 11:13-16.

13 And when Athaliah heard the noise of the guard *and of* the people, she came to the people into the house of the LORD : 14 and she looked, and, behold, the king stood by the [b] pillar, as the manner was, and the captains and the trumpets by the king ; and all the people of the land rejoiced, and blew with trumpets. Then Athaliah rent her clothes, and cried, Treason, treason. 15 And Jehoiada the priest commanded the captains of hundreds that were set over the host, and said unto them, Have her forth between the ranks; and him that followeth her slay with the sword: for the priest said, Let her not be slain in the house of the LORD. 16 So they made way for her ; and she went by the way of the horses' entry to the king's house: and there was she slain.

2 *Ch.* 23:12-15.

12 And when Athaliah heard the noise [c] of the people running and praising the king, she came to the people into the house of the LORD : 13 and she looked, and, behold, the king stood by his pillar at the entrance, and the captains and the trumpets by the king ; and all the people of the land rejoiced: and blew with trumpets; the singers also *played* on instruments of music, and led the singing of praise. Then Athaliah rent her clothes, and said, Treason, treason. 14 And Jehoiada the priest brought out the captains of hundreds that were set over the host, and said unto them, Have her forth between the ranks ; and whoso followeth her, let him be slain with the sword : for the priest said, Slay her not in the house of the LORD. 15 So they made way for her ; and she went to the entry of the horse gate to the king's house: and they slew her there.

2 *Kings* 11 : 20b.

20b And they slew Athaliah with the sword at the king's house.

2 *Chronicles* 23 : 21b.

21b And they slew Athaliah with the sword.

---

a Heb. " Let the king live."   *b* Or, " on the platform."   *c* Or, " of the people, of the guard, and of those who praised the king."

Kingdom of Judah.	Kingdom of Israel.

159. THE REIGN OF JOASH.

(1) JOASH'S ACCESSION TO THE THRONE.

2 *Kings* 11 · 21 ; 12 : 1.

21 *a*Jehoash was seven years old when he began to reign. 1 In the seventh year of Jehu began Jehoash to reign; and he reigned forty years in Jerusalem : and his mother's name was Zibiah of Beer-sheba.

2 *Chronicles* 24 : 1.

1 Joash was seven years old when he began to reign ; and he reigned forty years in Jerusalem : and his mother's name was Zibiah of Beer-sheba.

(2) THE COVENANT MADE BY JEHOIADA.

2 *Kings* 11 : 17-20a.

17 And Jehoiada made a covenant between the LORD and the king and the people, that they should be the LORD'S people ; between the king also and the people. 18 And all the people of the land went to the house of Baal, and brake it down ; his altars and his images brake they in pieces thoroughly, and slew Mattan the priest of Baal before the altars. And the priest appointed *b* officers over the house of the LORD.

2 *Chronicles* 23 : 16-21a.

16 And Jehoiada made a covenant between himself, and all the people, and the king, that they should be the LORD'S people. 17 And all the people went to the house of Baal, and brake it down, and brake his altars and his images in pieces, and slew Mattan the priest of Baal before the altars. 18 And Jehoiada appointed the offices of the house of the LORD under the hand of the priests the Levites, whom David had distributed in the house of the LORD, to offer the burnt offerings of the LORD, as it is written in the law of Moses, with rejoicing and with singing, *c* according to the order of David. 19 And he set the porters at the gates of the house of the LORD, that none which was unclean in any thing should enter in.

---

a Ch. 12 : 1 in Heb.　　*b* Heb. " offices."　　*c* Heb. " by the hands of David."

Kingdom of Judah.

2 Kings 11.

19 And he took the captains over hundreds, and the Carites, and the guard, and all the people of the land ; and they brought down the king from the house of the LORD, and came by the way of the gate of the guard unto the king's house. And he sat on the throne of the kings. 20a So all the people of the land rejoiced, and the city was quiet.

2 Chronicles 23.

20 And he took the captains of hundreds, and the nobles, and the governors of the people, and all the people of the land, and brought down the king from the house of the LORD : and they came through the upper gate unto the king's house, and set the king upon the throne of the kingdom. 21a So all the people of the land rejoiced, and the city was quiet.

(3) JOASH'S CHARACTER AS INFLUENCED BY JEHOIADA.[a]

2 Kings 12 : 2.

2 And Jehoash did that which was right in the eyes of the LORD all his days wherein Jehoiada the priest instructed him.

2 Chronicles 24 : 2.

2 And Joash did that which was right in the eyes of the LORD all the days of Jehoiada the priest.

(4) SPIRITUAL CONDITION OF THE KINGDOM.

2 Kings 12 : 3.

3 Howbeit the high places were not taken away : the people still sacrificed and burnt incense in the high places.

(5) JOASH'S MATRIMONIAL AFFAIRS.

2 Chronicles 24 : 3.

3 And Jehoiada took for him two wives ; and he begat sons and daughters.

(6) JOASH COMMANDS TO REPAIR THE TEMPLE.

2 Kings 12 : 4, 5.

4 And Jehoash said to the priests, All the money of the hallowed things that is brought into the house of the L O R D, [b] in current

2 Chronicles 24 : 4, 5.

4 And it came to pass after this, that Joash was minded to restore the house of the LORD. 5 And he gathered together the priests and

Kingdom of Israel.

---

a Cf. 2 Chronicles 24 : 11-22. See §159, (10) and (11).   b Or, "even the money of every one that passeth the numbering."   See Exodus 30 : 13.

Kingdom of Judah.	Kingdom of Israel.

Kingdom of Judah.

2 *Kings* 12.

money, *a* the money of the persons for whom each man is rated, and all the money that it cometh into any man's heart to bring into the house of the LORD, 5 let the priests take it to them, every man from his acquaintance: and they shall repair the breaches of the house, wheresoever any breach shall be found.

2 *Chronicles* 24.

the Levites, and said to them, Go out unto the cities of Judah, and gather of all Israel money to repair the house of your God from year to year, and see that ye hasten the matter. Howbeit the Levites hastened it not.

Kingdom of Israel.

(4) THE "CUTTING SHORT" OF ISRAEL.

2 Kings 10 : 32, 33.

32 In those days the LORD began to cut Israel short: and Hazael smote them in all the coasts of Israel ; 33 from Jordan eastward, all the land of Gilead, the Gadites, and the Reubenites, and the Manassites, from Aroer, which is by the valley of Arnon, even Gilead and Bashan.

(5) THE DEATH OF JEHU.

2 Kings 10 : 34, 35*a*, 36.

34 Now the rest of the acts of Jehu, and all that he did, and all his might, are they not written in the book of the chronicles of the kings of Israel? 35*a* And Jehu slept with his fathers: and they buried him in Samaria. 36 And the time that Jehu reigned over Israel in Samaria was twenty and eight years.

160. THE REIGN OF JEHOAHAZ.

(1) THE ACCESSION OF JEHOAHAZ.

2 Kings 10 : 35*b* ; 13 : 1.

35*b* And Jehoahaz his son reigned in his stead.
1 In the three and twentieth year of Joash the son of Ahaziah, king of Judah, Jehoahaz the son of Jehu began to reign over Israel in Samaria, *and reigned* seventeen years.

(2) THE CHARACTER OF JEHOAHAZ.

2 Kings 13 : 2.

2 And he did that which was evil in the sight of the LORD, and followed the sins of Jeroboam the son of Nebat, wherewith he made Israel to sin ; he departed not therefrom.

---

a Heb. " each man the money of the souls of his estimation." See Leviticus 27 : 2, 3, etc.

Kingdom of Judah.

(7) The Repairing of the Temple.

2 Kings 12:6-16.   2 Chronicles 24:6-14a.

6 But it was so, that in the three and twentieth year of king Jehoash the priests had not repaired the breaches of the house. 7 Then king Jehoash called for Jehoiada the priest, and for the *other* priests, and said unto them, Why repair ye not the breaches of the house? now therefore take no *more* money from your acquaintance, but deliver it for the breaches of the house. 8 And the priests consented that they should take no *more* money from the people, neither repair the breaches of the house. 9 But Jehoiada the priest took a chest, and bored a hole in the lid of it, and set it beside the altar, on the right side as one cometh into the house of the LORD: and the priests that kept the [a] door put therein all the money that was brought into the house of the LORD. 10 And it was so, when they saw that there was much money in the chest, that the king's [b] scribe and the high priest came up, and they [c] put up in bags and told the money that was found in the house of the LORD. 11 And they gave the money that was weighed out into the hands of them

6 And the king called for Jehoiada the chief, and said unto him, Why hast thou not required of the Levites to bring in out of Judah and out of Jerusalem the tax of Moses the servant of the LORD, and of the congregation [d] of Israel, for the tent of the testimony? 7 For the sons of Athaliah, that wicked woman, had broken up the house of God; and also all the dedicated things of the house of the LORD did they bestow upon the Baalim. 8 So the king commanded, and they made a chest, and set it without at the gate of the house of the LORD. 9 And they made a proclamation through Judah and Jerusalem, to bring in for the LORD the tax that Moses the servant of God laid upon Israel in the wilderness. 10 And all the princes and all the people rejoiced, and brought in, and cast into the chest, until they had made an end. 11 And it was so, that at what time the chest was brought unto the king's [e] office, [f] by the hand of the Levites, and when they saw that there was much money, the king's [b] scribe and the chief priest's officer came and emptied the chest, and took it, and

Kingdom of Israel.

(3) The Oppression of the Syrians.

2 Kings 13:22, 3.

22 And Hazael king of Syria oppressed Israel all the days of Jehoahaz.

3 And the anger of the LORD was kindled against Israel, and he delivered them into the hand of Hazael king of Syria, and into the hand of Ben-hadad the son of Hazael, [g] continually.

---

a Heb. "threshold."   *b* Or, "secretary."   *c* Heb. "bound up and," etc.   *d* Or, "for Israel."   *e* Or, "officers."
f Or, "*which was* under the hand."   *g* Heb. "all the days."

Kingdom of Judah.	Kingdom of Israel.

2 *Kings* 12.

that did the work, that had the oversight of the house of the LORD : and they *a* paid it out to the carpenters and the builders, that wrought upon the house of the LORD, 12 and to the masons and the hewers of stone, and for buying timber and hewn stone to repair the breaches of the house of the LORD, and for all that *b* was laid out for the house to repair it. 13 But there were not made for the house of the LORD cups of silver, snuffers, basons, trumpets, any vessels of gold, or vessels of silver, of the money that was brought into the house of the LORD : 14 for they gave that to them that did the work, and repaired therewith the house of the LORD. 15 Moreover they reckoned not with the men, into whose hand they delivered the money to give to them that did the work : for they dealt faithfully. 16 The money for the guilt offerings, and the money for the sin offerings, was not brought into the house of the LORD : it was the priests'.

2 *Chronicles* 24.

carried it to its place again. Thus they did day by day, and gathered money in abundance. 12 And the king and Jehoiada gave it to such as did the work of the service of the house of the LORD ; and they hired masons and carpenters to restore the house of the LORD, and also such as wrought iron and brass to repair the house of the LORD. 13 So the workmen wrought, and *c* the work was perfected by them, and they set up the house of God *d* in its state, and strengthened it. 14*a* And when they had made an end, they brought the rest of the money before the king and Jehoiada, whereof were made vessels for the house of the LORD, even vessels to minister, and *e* to offer withal, and spoons, and vessels of gold and silver.

(8) THE TEMPLE WORSHIP.

2 Chronicles 24 : 14*b*.

14*b* And they offered burnt offerings in the house of the LORD continually all the days of Jehoiada.

---

a Heb. " brought it forth."   *b* Heb. " went forth."   *c* Heb. " healing went up upon the work."   *d* Or, " according to the proportion thereof."   *e* Or, " pestles."

Kingdom of Judah.	Kingdom of Israel.

Kingdom of Judah.

(9) THE DEATH OF JEHOIADA.

2 *Chronicles* 24 : 15, 16.

15 But Jehoiada waxed old and was full of days, and he died; an hundred and thirty years old was he when he died.　16 And they buried him in the city of David among the kings, because he had done good in Israel, and toward God and his house.

(10) THE SINS OF JOASH.

2 *Chronicles* 24 : 17-19.

17 Now after the death of Jehoiada came the princes of Judah, and made obeisance to the king.　Then the king hearkened unto them. 18 And they forsook the house of the LORD, the God of their fathers, and served the Asherim and the idols: and wrath came upon Judah and Jerusalem for this their guiltiness.　19 Yet he sent prophets to them, to bring them again unto the LORD; and they testified against them: but they would not give ear.

(4) THE REPENTANCE OF JEHOAHAZ.

2 *Kings* 13 : 4.

4 And Jehoahaz besought the LORD, and the LORD hearkened unto him: for he saw the oppression of Israel, how that the king of Syria oppressed them.

(5) JEHOASH BECOMES CO-REGNANT WITH JEHOAHAZ.

2 *Kings* 13 : 10.

10 In the thirty and seventh year of Joash king of Judah began Jehoash the son of Jehoahaz to reign over Israel in Samaria, *and reigned* sixteen years.

(11) THE STONING OF ZECHARIAH.

2 *Chronicles* 24 : 20-22.

20 And the spirit of God [a] came upon Zechariah the son of Jehoiada the priest; and he stood above the people, and said unto them. Thus saith God, Why transgress ye the commandments of the LORD, that ye cannot prosper? because ye have forsaken the LORD, he hath also forsaken you.　21 And they conspired against him, and stoned him with stones at the

---

a Heb. "clothed itself with."

Kingdom of Judah.	Kingdom of Israel.

Kingdom of Judah.

2 *Chronicles* 24.

commandment of the king in the court of the house of the LORD. 22 Thus Joash the king remembered not the kindness which Jehoiada his father had done to him, but slew his son. And when he died, he said, The LORD look upon it, and require it.

(12) HAZAEL'S OPERATIONS IN JUDAH.

A. THE REVERSES OF JUDAH.

2 *Chronicles* 24 : 23, 24.

23 And it came to pass at the *b* end of the year, that the army of the Syrians came up against him : and they came to Judah and Jerusalem, and destroyed all the princes of the people from among the people, and sent all the spoil of them unto the king of Damascus. 24 For the army of the Syrians came with a small company of men ; and the LORD delivered a very great host into their hand, because they had forsaken the LORD, the God of their fathers. So they executed *c* judgement upon Joash.

B. HAZAEL SUBDUES GATH.

2 *Kings* 12 : 17*a*.

17*a* Then Hazael king of Syria went up, and fought against Gath, and took it.

C. HAZAEL BOUGHT OFF BY JOASH.

2 *Kings* 12 : 17*b*, 18.

17*b* And Hazael set his face to go up to Jerusalem. 18 And Jehoash king of Judah took all the hallowed things that Jehoshaphat, and Jehoram, and Ahaziah, his fathers, kings of Judah, had dedicated, and his own hallowed things, and all the gold that was found in the treasures of the house of the LORD, and of the king's house, and sent it to Hazael king of Syria : and he went away from Jerusalem.

Kingdom of Israel.

(6) HAZAEL REDUCES ISRAEL LOW.

2 *Kings* 13 : 7.

7 For he left not to Jehoahaz of the people save fifty horsemen, and ten chariots, and ten thousand footmen ; for the king of Syria destroyed them, and made them like the dust *a* in threshing.

---

a Or, " to trample on." *b* Heb. " revolution." *c* Heb. " judgements."

Kingdom of Judah.

Kingdom of Israel.

(7) THE DEATH OF JEHOAHAZ.

2 *Kings* 13 : 8, 9a.

8 Now the rest of the acts of Jehoahaz, and all that he did, and his might, are they not written in the book of the chronicles of the kings of Israel? 9a And Jehoahaz slept with his fathers; and they buried him in Samaria.

161. THE REIGN OF JEHOASH.

(1) JEHOASH BECOMES SOLE KING.

2 *Kings* 13 : 9b.

9b And Joash his son reigned in his stead.

(2) THE CHARACTER OF JEHOASH.

2 *Kings* 13 : 11.

11 And he did that which was evil in the sight of the LORD; he departed not from all the sins of Jeroboam the son of Nebat, wherewith he made Israel to sin : but he walked therein.

(3) THE ENCOURAGING PROPHECY OF ELISHA ON HIS DEATHBED.

2 *Kings* 13 : 14–19.

14 Now Elisha was fallen sick of his sickness whereof he died : and Joash the king of Israel came down unto him, and wept over *a* him, and said, *b* My father, my father, the *c* chariots of Israel and the horsemen thereof! 15 And Elisha said unto him, Take bow and arrows : and he took unto him bow and arrows. 16 And he said to the king of Israel, Put thine hand upon the bow: and he put his hand *upon it*. And Elisha laid his hands upon the king's hands. 17 And he said, Open the window eastward : and he opened it. Then Elisha said, Shoot : and he shot. And he said, The LORD'S arrow of *d* victory, even the arrow of *d* victory *e* over Syria : for thou shalt smite the Syrians in Aphek, till thou have consumed them. 18 And he said, Take the arrows : and he took them. And he said unto the king of Israel, Smite upon the ground: and he smote thrice, and stayed. 19 And the man of God was wroth with him, and said, Thou shouldest have smitten five or six times ; then hadst thou smitten Syria till thou hadst consumed it : whereas now thou shalt smite Syria but thrice.

a Heb. " his face."   *b* Cf. 2 Kings 2 : 12.   See §154, (3), *B*.   *c* Or, " chariot."   *d* Heb. " salvation."   *e* Or, " against."

Kingdom of Judah.	Kingdom of Israel.

Kingdom of Israel.

(4) THE DEATH OF ELISHA.

2 *Kings* 13 · 20*a*.

20*a* And Elisha died, and they buried him.

(13) THE DEATH OF JOASH.

2 *Ki.* 12 : 20, 21*a*, 19.	2 *Ch.* 24 : 25–27*a*.
20 And his servants arose, and made a conspiracy, and smote Joash at the house of Millo, *on the way* that goeth down to Silla. 21*a* For Jozacar the son of Shimeath, and Jehozabad the son of Shomer, his servants, smote him, and he died ; and they buried him with his fathers in the city of David.	25 And when they were departed f r o m him, (for they left him in great diseases,) his own servants conspired against him for the blood of the ᵃ sons of Jehoiada the priest, and slew him on his bed, and he died : and they buried him in the city of D a v i d, but they buried him not in the sepulchres of the kings. 26 And these are they that conspired against him ; Zabad the son of Shimeath the Ammonitess, and Jehozabad the son of Shimrith the Moabitess. 27*a* Now concerning his sons, and the greatness of the burdens ᵇ *laid* upon him, and the ᶜ rebuilding of the house of God, behold, they are written in the commentary of the book of the kings.
19 Now the rest of the acts of Joash, and all that he did, are they not written in the book of the chronicles of the kings of Judah.	

162. THE REIGN OF AMAZIAH.

(1) AMAZIAH'S ACCESSION TO THE THRONE'

2 *Ki.* 12 : 21*b* ; 14 : 1, 2.	2 *Ch.* 24 : 27*b* ; 25 : 1.
21*b* And Amaziah his son reigned in his stead. 1 In the second year of Joash son of Joahaz king of Israel began Amaziah the son of Joash king of Judah to	27*b* And Amaziah his son reigned in his stead. 1 Amaziah was twenty and five years old when he began to reign ; and he reigned twenty and nine years in Jeru-

---

a The Sept. and Vulgate read, "son."   *b* Or, " *uttered* against."   *c* Heb. " founding."

Kingdom of Judah.		Kingdom of Israel.

Kingdom of Judah.

2 *Kings* 12.

reign. 2 He was twenty and five years old when he began to reign; and he reigned twenty and nine years in Jerusalem : and his mother's name was Jehoaddin of Jerusalem.

2 *Chronicles* 25.

salem : and his mother's name was Jehoaddan of Jerusalem.

(2) THE CHARACTER OF AMAZIAH.

2 *Kings* 14 : 3–6.

3 And he did that which was right in the eyes of the LORD, yet not like David his father : he did according to all that Joash his father had done. 4 Howbeit the high places were not taken away : the people still sacrificed and burnt incense in the high places. 5 And it came to pass, as soon as the kingdom was established in his hand, that he slew his servants which had slain the king his father: 6 but the children of the murderers he put not to death : according to that which is written in the book of the law of Moses, as the LORD commanded, s a y i n g, The fathers shall not be put to death for the children, nor the children be put to death for the fathers ; but every man shall die for his own sin.

2 *Chronicles* 25 : 2–4.

2 And he did that which was right in the eyes of the LORD, but not with a perfect heart. 3 Now it came to pass, when the kingdom was established unto him, that he slew his servants which had killed the king his father. 4 But he put not their children to death, but did according to that which is written in the law in the book of Moses, as the LORD commanded, s a y i n g, The fathers shall not die for the children, neither shall the children die for the fathers ; but every man shall die for his own sin.

Kingdom of Israel.

(5) THE MIRACLE IN ELISHA'S TOMB.

2 *Kings* 13 : 20b, 21.

20b Now the bands of the Moabites invaded the land at the coming in of the year. 21 And it came to pass, as they were burying a man,

Kingdom of Judah.

Kingdom of Israel.

2 *Kings* 13.

that, behold, they spied a band ; and they cast the man into the sepulchre of Elisha : and *a* as soon as the man touched the bones of Elisha, he revived, and stood up on his feet.

(6) THE FULFILLMENT OF ELISHA'S PROPH-ECY: SUCCESS OF JOASH OVER BEN-HADAD.

2 *Kings* 13 : 23–25.

23 But the LORD was gracious unto them, and had compassion on them, and had respect unto them, because of his covenant with Abraham, Isaac, and Jacob, and would not destroy them, neither cast he them from his presence *b* as yet. 24 And Hazael king of Syria died ; and Ben-hadad his son reigned in his stead. 25 And Jehoash the son of Jehoahaz took again out of the hand of Ben-hadad the son of Hazael the cities which he had taken out of the hand of Jehoahaz his father by war. Three times did Joash smite him, and recovered the cities of Israel.

(3) AMAZIAH PLANS AN EXPEDITION AGAINST EDOM.

2 *Chronicles* 25 : 5.

5 Moreover Amaziah gathered Judah together, and ordered them according to their fathers' houses, under captains of thousands and captains of hundreds, even all Judah and Benjamin: and he numbered them from twenty years old and upward, and found them three hundred thousand chosen men, able to go forth to war, that could handle spear and shield.

(4) AMAZIAH HIRES ONE HUNDRED THOUSAND MERCENARIES OUT OF ISRAEL, BUT SUBSEQUENTLY DISMISSES THEM. (7)

2 *Chronicles* 25 : 6–10.

6 He hired also an hundred thousand mighty men of valour out of Israel for an hundred talents of silver. 7 But there came a man of God to him, saying, O king, let not the army of Israel go with thee ; for the LORD is not with Israel, *to wit*, with all the children of Ephraim. 8 But *e* if thou wilt go, do *valiantly*, be strong for the battle : God shall cast thee down before the enemy ; for God hath power to help, and to cast down. 9 And Amaziah said to the man of God, But what shall we do for the hundred talents which I have given to the *d* army of Israel ? And the man of God answered, The LORD is able to give thee much more than this. 10 Then Amaziah separated them, *to wit*, the *d* army that was come to him out of Ephraim, to go home again: wherefore their anger was greatly kindled against Judah, and they returned home in fierce anger.

---

a Heb. " when the man went and touched."   *b* Heb. " until now."   *c* Or, " go thou."   *d* Heb. "troop."

Kingdom of Judah.	Kingdom of Israel.

Kingdom of Judah.

(5) AMAZIAH'S SUCCESS IN EDOM.

2 Kings 14: 7.	*2 Chronicles* 25 : 11, 12.
7 He slew of Edom in the Valley of Salt ten thousand, and took *a* Sela by war, and called the name of it Joktheel, unto this day.	11 And Amaziah took courage, and led forth his people, and went to the Valley of Salt, and smote of the children of Seir ten thousand. 12 And *other* ten thousand did the children of Judah carry away alive, and brought them unto the top of *b* the rock, and cast them down from the top of *b* the rock, that they all were broken in pieces.

(6) THE DISMISSED ISRAELITISH MERCENARIES PILLAGE THE CITIES OF JUDAH.*c* (8)

2 Chronicles 25 : 13.

13 But the men of *d* the army which Amaziah sent back, that they should not go with him to battle, fell upon the cities of Judah, from Samaria even unto Beth-horon, and smote of them three thousand, and took much spoil.

(7) AMAZIAH'S FURTHER WICKEDNESS.

2 Chronicles 25 : 14–16.

14 Now it came to pass, after that Amaziah was come from the slaughter of the Edomites, that he brought the gods of the children of Seir, and set them up to be his gods, and bowed down himself before them, and burned incense unto them.   15 Wherefore the anger of the LORD was kindled against Amaziah, and he sent unto him a prophet, which said unto him, Why hast thou sought after the gods of the people, which have not delivered their own people out of thine hand?   16 And it came to pass, as he talked with him, that *the king* said unto him, Have we made thee of the king's counsel? forbear; why shouldest thou be smitten? Then the prophet forbare: and said, I know that God hath determined to destroy thee, because thou hast done this, and hast not hearkened unto my counsel.

---

a Or, "the rock."   *b* Or, "Sela."   *c* This division is really synchronous with the preceding.   *d* Heb. "the sons of the troop."

Kingdom of Judah.	Kingdom of Israel.

(8) THE WAR BETWEEN AMAZIAH AND JEHOASH. (9)

2 *Kings* 14: 8–14.	2 *Chronicles* 25: 17–24.

8 Then Amaziah sent messengers to Jehoash, the son of Jehoahaz son of Jehu, king of Israel, saying, Come, let us look one another in the face. 9 And Jehoash the king of Israel sent to Amaziah king of Judah, saying, The *a* thistle that was in Lebanon sent to the cedar that was in Lebanon, saying, Give thy daughter to my son to wife: and there pássed by a wild beast that was in Lebanon, and trod down the thistle. 10 Thou hast indeed smitten Edom, and thine heart hath lifted thee up: glory thereof, and abide at home; for why shouldest thou *b* meddle to *thy* hurt, that thou shouldest fall, even thou, and Judah with thee? 11 But Amaziah would not hear. So Jehoash king of Israel went up; and he and Amaziah king of Judah looked one another in the face at Beth-shemesh, which belongeth to Judah. 12 And Judah was put to the worse before Israel; and they fled every man to his tent. 13 And Jehoash king of Israel took Amaziah king of Judah, the son of Jehoash the son of Ahaziah, at Beth-shemesh, and came to Jerusalem, and brake down the wall of Jerusalem from the gate of Ephraim unto the corner gate, four hundred cubits. 14 And he took all the gold and silver, and all the vessels that were found in the house of the LORD, and in the treasures of the king's house, the hostages also, and returned to Samaria.

17 Then Amaziah king of Judah took advice, and sent to Joash, the son of Jehoahaz the son of Jehu, king of Israel, saying, Come, let us look one another in the face. 18 And Joash king of Israel sent to Amaziah king of Judah, saying, The *a* thistle that was in Lebanon sent to the cedar that was in Lebanon, saying, Give thy daughter to my son to wife: and there passed by a wild beast that was in Lebanon, and trod down the thistle. 19 Thou sayest, Lo, thou hast smitten Edom; and thine heart lifteth thee up to boast: abide now at home; why shouldest thou *b* meddle to *thy* hurt, that thou shouldest fall, even thou, and Judah with thee? 20 But Amaziah would not hear; for it was of God, that he might deliver them into the hand *of their enemies*, because they had sought after the gods of Edom. 21 So Joash king of Israel went up; and he and Amaziah king of Judah looked one another in the face at Beth-shemesh, which belongeth to Judah. 22 And Judah was put to the worse before Israel; and they fled every man to his tent. 23 And Joash king of Israel took Amaziah king of Judah, the son of Joash the son of Jehoahaz, at Beth-shemesh, and brought him to Jerusalem, and brake down the wall of Jerusalem from the gate of Ephraim unto *c* the corner gate, four hundred cubits. 24 And *he took* all the gold and silver, and all the vessels that were found in the house of God with *d* Obed-edom, and the treasures of the king's house, the hostages also, and returned to Samaria.

(10) THE DEATH OF JEHOASH.

2 *Ki.* 13: 12, 13*a*, 13*c*.	2 *Ki.* 14: 15, 16*a*.
12 Now the rest of the acts of Joash, and all that he did, and his might wherewith he fought against Amaziah king of Judah, are they not written in the book of the chronicles of the kings of Israel? 13*a* And Joash slept with his fathers; 13*c* and Joash was buried in Samaria with the kings of Israel.	14 Now the rest of the acts of Jehoash which he did, and his might, and how he fought with Amaziah king of Judah, are they not written in the book of the chronicles of the kings of Israel? 16*a* And Jehoash slept with his fathers, and was buried in Samaria with the kings of Israel.

a Or, " thorn." *b* Or, " provoke calamity." *c* The text has, " the gate that looketh." *d* Cf. 1 Chronicles 26: 15. See §107, (2), F,

Kingdom of Judah.

(9) THE LAST FIFTEEN YEARS OF AMAZIAH'S REIGN.

2 Kings 14: 17.	2 Chronicles 25: 25.
17 And Amaziah the son of Joash king of Judah lived after the death of Jehoash son of Jehoahaz king of Israel fifteen years.	25 And Amaziah the son of Joash king of Judah lived after the death of Joash son of Jehoahaz king of Israel fifteen years.

Kingdom of Israel.

163. THE REIGN OF JEROBOAM II.

(1) THE ACCESSION OF JEROBOAM II.

2 Kings 13: 13b.	2 Kings 14: 16b, 23.
13b And Jeroboam sat upon his throne.	16b And Jeroboam his son reigned in his stead. 23 In the fifteenth year of Amaziah the son of Joash king of Judah Jeroboam the son of Joash king of Israel began to reign in Samaria, *and reigned* forty and one years.

(2) THE CHARACTER OF JEROBOAM II.

2 Kings 14: 24.

24 And he did that which was evil in the sight of the LORD: he departed not from all the sins of Jeroboam the son of Nebat, wherewith he made Israel to sin.

(3) JEHOVAH SAVES ISRAEL BY THE HAND OF JEROBOAM II.

2 Kings 13: 5.	2 Kings 14: 25-27.
5 And the LORD gave Israel a saviour, so that they went out from under the hand of the Syrians: and the children of Israel dwelt in their tents, as before time.	25 He restored the border of Israel from the entering in of Hamath unto the sea of the Arabah, according to the word of the LORD, the God of Israel, which he spake by the hand of his servant Jonah the son of Amittai, the prophet, which was of Gathhepher. 26 For the LORD saw the affliction of Israel, that it was very bitter: for there was none shut up nor left at large, neither was there any helper for Israel. 27 And the LORD said not that he would blot out the name of Israel from under heaven: but he saved them by hand of Jeroboam the son of Joash.

Kingdom of Judah.	Kingdom of Israel.
	(4) The continued Apostasy of Israel.
	2 Kings 13:6.
	6 Nevertheless they departed not from the sins of the house of Jeroboam, wherewith he made Israel to sin, but *a* walked therein : and there remained the Asherah also in Samaria.

(10) The Death of Amaziah.

2 Kings 14:18–20.	*2 Chronicles* 25:26–28.
18 Now the rest of the acts of Amaziah, are they not written in the book of the chronicles of the kings of Judah ? 19 And they made a conspiracy against him in Jerusalem ; and he fled to Lachish : but they sent after him to Lachish, and slew him there. 20 And they brought him upon horses : and he was buried at Jerusalem with his fathers in the city of David.	26 Now the rest of the acts of Amaziah, first and last, behold, are they not written in the book of the kings of Judah and Israel? 27 Now from the time that Amaziah did turn away from following the Lord they made a conspiracy against him in Jerusalem ; and he fled to Lachish : but they sent after him to Lachish, and slew him there. 28 And they brought him upon horses, and buried him with his fathers in the city of Judah.

Interregnum of Eleven Years.*b*

164. THE REIGN OF UZZIAH.

(1) Uzziah's Accession to the Throne.

2 Kings 14:21; 15:1, 2.	*2 Chronicles* 26:1, 3.
21 And all the people of Judah took Azariah, who was sixteen years old, and made him king in the room of his father Amaziah. 1 In the twenty and seventh year of Jeroboam king of Israel began Azariah son of Amaziah king of Judah to reign.	1 And all the people of Judah took Uzziah, who was sixteen years old, and made him king in the room of his father Amaziah.

a Heb. " he walked."   *b* Determined by comparing 2 Kings 14 : 1. 17, 23, and 2 Kings 15 : 1.

20

Kingdom of Judah.

2 *Kings* 15.	2 *Chronicles* 26.
2 Sixteen years old was he when he began to reign ; and he reigned two and fifty years in Jerusalem : a n d h i s mother's name was Jecoliah of Jerusalem.	3 Sixteen years old was Uzziah when he began to reign ; and he reigned fifty and two years in Jerusalem : and his mother's name was Jechiliah of Jerusalem.

(2) The Character of Uzziah.

2 *Kings* 15 : 3.	2 *Chronicles* 26 : 4, 5.
3 And he did that which was right in the eyes of the LORD, according to all that his father Amaziah had done.	4 And he did that which was right in the eyes of the LORD, according to all that his father Amaziah had done. 5 And he set himself to seek God in the days of Zechariah, who *a* had understanding in *b* the vision of God : and as long as he sought the LORD, God made him to prosper.

(3) Spiritual Condition of the Kingdom.

2 *Kings* 15 : 4.

4 Howbeit the high places were not taken away: the people still sacrificed and burnt incense in the high places.

(4) Uzziah's prosperous Years.

A. THE BUILDING OF ELOTH.

2 *Kings* 14 : 22.	2 *Chronicles* 26 : 2.
22 He built Elath, and restored it to Judah, after that the king slept with his fathers.	2 He built Eloth, and restored it to Judah, after that the king slept with his fathers.

B. UZZIAH'S SUCCESS IN WAR.

2 *Chronicles* 26 : 6–8a.

6 And he went forth and warred against the Philistines, and brake down the wall of Gath, and the wall of Jabneh, and the wall of Ashdod ; and he built cities in *the country of* Ashdod, and among the Philistines. 7 And God helped him against the Philistines, and against the Arabians that dwelt in Gur-baal, and the Meunim. 8a And the Ammonites gave gifts to Uzziah.

---

a Or, "gave instruction."　　*b* Heb. "the seeing."　　Many ancient authorities have, "the fear."

Kingdom of Judah.	Kingdom of Israel.

Kingdom of Judah.

C. UZZIAH'S BUILDING AND HUSBANDRY.

2 Chronicles 26 : 9, 10, 15a.

9 Moreover Uzziah built towers in Jerusalem at the corner gate, and at the valley gate, and at the turning *of the wall*, and fortified them. 10 And he built towers in the wilderness, and hewed out many cisterns, for he had much cattle ; in the lowland also, and in the *a* plain : *and he had* husbandmen and vinedressers in the mountains and in *b* the fruitful fields ; for he loved husbandry. 15a And he made in Jerusalem engines, invented by cunning men, to be on the towers and upon the *c* battlements, to shoot arrows and great stones withal.

D. UZZIAH'S ARMY.

2 Chronicles 26: 11-14.

11 Moreover Uzziah had an army of fighting men, that went out to war by bands, according to the number of their reckoning made by Jeiel the scribe and Maaseiah the officer, under the hand of Hananiah, one of the king's captains. 12 The whole number of the heads of fathers' *houses*, even the mighty men of valour, was two thousand and six hundred. 13 And under their hand was *d* a trained army, three hundred thousand and seven thousand and five hundred, that made war with mighty power, to help the king against the enemy. 14 And Uzziah prepared for them, even for all the host, shields, and spears, and helmets, and coats of mail, and bows, and stones for slinging.

E. UZZIAH'S FAME.

2 Chronicles 26 : 8b.	2 Chronicles 26 : 15b.
8b And his name spread abroad even to the entering in of Egypt; for he waxed exceeding strong.	15b And his name spread far abroad ; for he was marvellously helped, till he was strong.

Kingdom of Israel.

(5) THE DEATH OF JEROBOAM II.

2 Kings 14 : 28, 29a.

28 Now the rest of the acts of Jeroboam, and all that he did, and his might, how he warred, and how he recovered Damascus, and Hamath, *which had belonged* to Judah, for Israel, are they not written in the book of the chronicles of the kings of Israel ? 29a And Jeroboam slept with his fathers, even with the kings of Israel.

INTERREGNUM OF TWENTY-TWO YEARS. *e*

165. THE REIGN OF ZECHARIAH.

(1) ZECHARIAH'S ACCESSION TO THE THRONE.

2 Kings 14 : 29b ; 15 : 8.

29b And Zechariah his son reigned in his stead. 8 In the thirty and eighth year of Azariah king of Judah did Zechariah the son of Jeroboam reign over Israel in Samaria six months.

---

a Or, "table land."   *b* Or, "Carmel." Cf. 1 Samuel 25: 2.   See §54.   *c* Or, "corner towers."   *d* Or, "the power of an army."   *e* Determined by comparing 2 Kings 14 : 23, and 2 Kings 15 : 1, 2, 8.

Kingdom of Judah.	Kingdom of Israel.

Kingdom of Israel.

(2) THE CHARACTER OF ZECHARIAH.

2 *Kings* 15 : 9.

9 And he did that which was evil in the sight of the LORD, as his fathers had done: he departed not from the sins of Jeroboam the son of Nebat, wherewith he made Israel to sin.

(3) THE DEATH OF ZECHARIAH.

2 *Kings* 15 : 10, 11.

10 And Shallum the son of Jabesh conspired against him, and smote him before the people, and slew him, and reigned in his stead. 11 Now the rest of the acts of Zechariah, behold, they are written in the book of the chronicles of the kings of Israel.

(4) THE FULFILLMENT OF JEHOVAH'S PROMISE TO JEHU.[a]

2 *Kings* 15 : 12.

12 This was the word of the LORD which he spake unto Jehu, saying, Thy sons to the fourth generation shall sit upon the throne of Israel. And so it came to pass.

166. THE REIGN OF SHALLUM.

2 *Kings* 15 : 13-15.

13 Shallum the son of Jabesh began to reign in the nine and thirtieth year of Uzziah king of Judah; and he reigned the space of a month in Samaria. 14 And Menahem the son of Gadi went up from Tirzah, and came to Samaria, and smote Shallum the son of Jabesh in Samaria, and slew him, and reigned in his stead. 15 Now the rest of the acts of Shallum, and his conspiracy which he made, behold, they are written in the book of the chronicles of the kings of Israel.

167. THE REIGN OF MENAHEM.

(1) MENAHEM'S ACCESSION TO THE THRONE.

2 *Kings* 15 : 16, 17.

16 Then Menahem smote Tiphsah, and all that were therein, and the borders thereof, from Tirzah: because they opened not to him, therefore he smote it; and all the women therein that were with child he ripped up.

---

a Cf. 2 Kings 10. 30. See §157, (2).

Kingdom of Judah.	Kingdom of Israel.

Kingdom of Israel.

2 *Kings* 15.

17 In the nine and thirtieth year of Azariah king of Judah began Menahem the son of Gadi to reign over Israel, *and reigned* ten years in Samaria.

(2) THE CHARACTER OF MENAHEM.

2 *Kings* 15:18.

18 And he did that which was evil in the sight of the LORD: he departed not all his days from the sins of Jeroboam the son of Nebat, wherewith he made Israel to sin.

(5) UZZIAH'S SIN AND PUNISHMENT.

2 *Kings* 15:5a. | **2 *Chronicles* 26:16-21a.**

16 But when he was strong, his heart was lifted up *a* so that he did corruptly, and he trespassed against the LORD his God; for he went into the temple of the LORD to burn incense upon the altar of incense. 17 And Azariah the priest went in after him, and with him fourscore priests of the LORD, that were valiant men: 18 and they withstood Uzziah the king, and said unto him, It pertaineth not unto thee, Uzziah, to burn incense unto the LORD, but to the priests the sons of Aaron, that are consecrated to burn incense: go out of the sanctuary; for thou hast trespassed; neither shall it be for thine honour from the LORD God. 19 Then Uzziah was wroth; and he had a censer in his hand to burn incense; and while he was wroth with the priests, the leprosy

a Or, "to *his* destruction."

Kingdom of Judah.

2 *Kings* 15.	2 *Chronicles* 26.
	b brake forth in his forehead before the priests in the house of the LORD, beside the altar of incense. 20 And Azariah the chief priest, and all the priests, looked upon him, and, behold, he was leprous in his forehead, and they thrust him out quickly from thence; yea, himself hasted also to go out, because the LORD had smitten him. 21*a* And Uzziah the
5*a* And the LORD smote the king, so that he was a leper unto the day of his death, and dwelt in a *a* several house.	king was a leper unto the day of his death, and dwelt in a *a* several house, being a leper; for he was cut off from the house of the LORD.

(6) THE REGENCY OF JOTHAM.

2 *Kings* 15 : 5*b*.	2 *Chronicles* 26 : 21*b*.
5*b* And Jotham the king's son was over the household, judging the people of the land.	21*b* And Jotham his son was over the king's house, judging the people of the land.

Kingdom of Israel.

(3) THE INVASION OF PUL, KING OF ASSYRIA.

2 *Kings* 15 : 19, 20.	[1 *Chronicles* 5 : 26*a*.]
19 There came against the land Pul the king of Assyria; and Menahem gave Pul a thousand talents of silver, that his hand might be with him to confirm the kingdom in his hand. 20 And Menahem exacted the money of Israel, even of all the mighty men of wealth, of each man fifty shekels of silver, to give to the king of Assyria. So the king of Assyria turned back, and stayed not there in the land.	26*a* And the God of Israel stirred up the spirit of Pul king of Assyria.

---

a Or, "lazar house."   *b* Heb. "rose" (*as the sun*).

Kingdom of Judah.	Kingdom of Israel.

Kingdom of Israel.

(4) THE DEATH OF MENAHEM.

2 *Kings* 15 : 21, 22a.

21 Now the rest of the acts of Menahem, and all that he did, are they not written in the book of the chronicles of the kings of Israel? 22a And Menahem slept with his fathers.

168. THE REIGN OF PEKAHIAH.

(1) PEKAHIAH'S ACCESSION TO THE THRONE.

2 *Kings* 15 : 22b, 23.

22b And Pekahiah his son reigned in his stead.
23 In the fiftieth year of Azariah king of Judah Pekahiah the son of Menahem began to reign over Israel in Samaria, *and reigned* two years.

(2) THE CHARACTER OF PEKAHIAH.

2 *Kings* 15 : 24.

24 And he did that which was evil in the sight of the LORD: he departed not from the sins of Jeroboam the son of Nebat, wherewith he made Israel to sin.

(3) THE DEATH OF PEKAHIAH.

2 *Kings* 15 : 25, 26.

25 And Pekah the son of Remaliah, his captain, conspired against him, and smote him in Samaria, in the ^a castle of the king's house, with Argob and Arieh ; and with him were fifty men of the Gileadites : and he slew him, and reigned in his stead. 26 Now the rest of the acts of Pekahiah, and all that he did, behold, they are written in the book of the chronicles of the kings of Israel.

169. THE REIGN OF PEKAH.

(1) PEKAH'S ACCESSION TO THE THRONE.

2 *Kings* 15 : 27.

27 In the two and fiftieth year of Azariah king of Judah Pekah the son of Remaliah began to reign over Israel in Samaria, *and reigned* twenty years.

(2) THE CHARACTER OF PEKAH.

2 *Kings* 15 : 28.

28 And he did that which was evil in the sight of the LORD: he departed not from the sins of Jeroboam the son of Nebat, wherewith he made Israel to sin.

---

a Or, " palace."

Kingdom of Judah.	Kingdom of Israel.

(7) THE DEATH OF UZZIAH.

2 *Ki.* 15 : 6, 7*a*.	2 *Ch.* 26 : 22, 23*a*.
6 Now the rest of the acts of Azariah, and all that he did, are they not written in the book of the chronicles of the kings of Judah? 7*a* And Azariah slept with his fathers; and they buried him with his fathers in the city of David.	22 Now the rest of the acts of Uzziah, first and last, did Isaiah the prophet, the son of Amoz, write. 23*a* So Uzziah slept with his fathers; and they buried him with his fathers in the field of burial which belonged to the kings; for they said, He is a leper.

170. THE REIGN OF JOTHAM.

(1) JOTHAM'S ACCESSION TO THE THRONE.

2 *Ki.* 15:7*b*, 32, 33.	2 *Ch.* 26 : 23*b*; 27 : 1.	2 *Ch.* 27 : 8.
7*b* And Jotham his son reigned in his stead. 32 In the second year of Pekah the son of Remaliah king of Israel began Jotham the son of Uzziah king of Judah to reign. 33 Five and twenty years old was he when he began to reign; and he reigned sixteen years in Jerusalem : and his mother's name was Jerusha the daughter of Zadok.	23*b* And Jotham his son reigned in his stead. 1 Jotham was twenty and five years old when he began to reign; and he reigned sixteen years in Jerusalem : and his mother's name was Jerushah the daughter of Zadok.	8 He was five and twenty years old when he began to reign, and reigned sixteen years in Jerusalem.

(2) THE CHARACTER OF JOTHAM.

2 *Kings* 15 : 34.	2 *Chronicles* 27 : 2*a*.
34 And he did that which was right in the	2*a* And he did that which was right in the

Kingdom of Judah.

2 *Kings* 15.

eyes of the LORD: he did according to all that his father Uzziah had done.

2 *Chronicles* 27.

eyes of the LORD, according to all that his father Uzziah had done: howbeit he entered not into the temple of the LORD.

(3) SPIRITUAL CONDITION OF THE PEOPLE.

2 *Kings* 15 : 35*a*.

35*a* Howbeit the high places were not taken away : the people still sacrificed and burned incense in the high places.

2 *Chronicles* 27 : 2*b*.

2*b* And the people did yet corruptly.

(4) JOTHAM'S BUILDING.

2 *Kings* 15 : 35*b*.

35*b* He built the upper gate of the house of the LORD.

2 *Chronicles* 27 : 3, 4.

3 He built the upper gate of the house of the LORD, and on the wall of Ophel he built much. 4 Moreover he built cities in the hill country of Judah, and in the forests he built castles and towers.

(5) THE SUBJUGATION OF THE AMMONITES.

2 *Chronicles* 27 : 5, 6.

5 He fought also with the king of the children of Ammon, and prevailed against them. And the children of Ammon gave him the same year an hundred talents of silver, and ten thousand *a* measures of wheat, and ten thousand of barley. So much did the children of Ammon render unto him, in the second year also, and in the third. 6 So Jotham became mighty, because he ordered his ways before the LORD his God.

Kingdom of Israel.

(3) THE BEGINNING OF THE CAPTIVITY.

1 *Chronicles* 5: 25*a*, 26*b*, 25*b*, 26*a*, 26*c*, [6*c*, 6*a*, 6*d*.]

25*a* And they, 26*b* even the Reubenites, and the Gadites, and the half tribe of Manasseh, 25*b* trespassed against the God of their fathers, and went a whoring after the gods of the peoples of the land, whom God destroyed before them. 26*a* And

---

a Heb. " cors."

Kingdom of Judah.	Kingdom of Israel.
	1 Chronicles 5.
	the God of Israel stirred up the spirit of Pul king of Assyria, and the spirit of ᵃTilgath-pilneser king of Assyria, and he carried them away, 26c and brought them unto Halah, and Habor, and Hara, and to the river of Gozan, unto this day.
	6c ᵃ Tilgath-pilneser king of Assyria carried away captive 6a Beerah : 6d he was prince of the Reubenites.

(6) The War between Jotham and Rezin and Pekah.

2 *Kings* 15 : 37.

37 In those days the LORD began to send against Judah Rezin the king of Syria, and Pekah the son of Remaliah.

(7) The Death of Jotham.

2 *Kings* 15 : 36, 38a.	2 *Chronicles* 27 : 7, 9a.
36 Now the rest of the acts of Jotham, and all that he did, are they not written in the book of the chronicles of the kings of Judah? 38a And Jotham slept with his fathers, and was buried with his fathers in the city of David his father.	7 Now the rest of the acts of Jotham, and all his wars, and his ways, behold, they are written in the book of the kings of Israel and Judah. 9a And Jotham slept with his fathers, and they buried him in the city of David.

171. THE REIGN OF AHAZ.

(1) The Accession of Ahaz.

2 *Ki.* 15 : 38b ; 16 : 1, 2a.	2 *Ch.* 27 : 9b ; 28 : 1a.
38b And Ahaz his son reigned in his stead. 1 In the seventeenth year of Pekah the son of Remaliah Ahaz the son of Jotham king of Judah began to reign. 2a Twenty years old was Ahaz when he began to reign ; and he reigned sixteen years in Jerusalem.	9b And Ahaz his son reigned in his stead. 1a Ahaz was twenty years old when he began to reign ; and he reigned sixteen years in Jerusalem.

---

a In 2 Kings 15 : 29, " Tiglath-pileser." See §169, (6).

Kingdom of Judah.	Kingdom of Israel.

(2) THE CHARACTER OF AHAZ.

2 *Kings* 16 : 2*b*–4.	2 *Chronicles* 28 : 1*b*–4.
2*b* And he did not that which was right in the eyes of the LORD his God, like David his father. 3 But he walked in the way of the kings of Israel, yea, and made his son to pass through the fire, according to the abominations of the heathen, whom the LORD cast out from before the children of Israel. 4 And he sacrificed and burnt incense in the high places, and on the hills, and under every green tree.	1*b* And he did not that which was right in the eyes of the LORD, like David his father: 2 but he walked in the ways of the kings of Israel, and made also molten images for the Baalim. 3 Moreover he burnt incense in the valley of the son of Hinnom, and burnt his children in the fire, according to the abominations of the heathen, whom the LORD cast out before the children of Israel. 4 And he sacrificed and burnt incense in the high places, and on the hills, and under every green tree.

(3) THE WAR BETWEEN AHAZ AND REZIN AND PEKAH.[a] (5)

A. AHAZ IS DEFEATED BY THE ALLIED KINGS.

2 *Kings* 16 : 5, 6.	2 *Chronicles* 28 : 5–8.
5 Then Rezin king of Syria and Pekah son of Remaliah king of Israel came up to Jerusalem to war : and they besieged Ahaz, but could not overcome him. 6 At that time Rezin king of Syria recovered Elath to Syria, and drave the Jews from [b] Elath : and the [c] Syrians came to Elath, and dwelt there, unto this day.	5 Wherefore the LORD his God delivered him into the hand of the king of Syria ; and they smote him, and carried away of his a great multitude of captives. and brought them to Damascus. And he was also delivered into the hand of the king of Israel, who smote him with a great slaughter. 6 For Pekah the son of Remaliah slew in Judah an hundred and twenty thousand in one day, all of them valiant men ; because they had forsaken the LORD, the God of their fathers. 7 And Zichri, a mighty man of Ephraim, slew Maaseiah the king's son, and Azrikam the ruler of the house, and Elkanah that was [d] next to the king. 8 And the children of Israel carried away captive of their brethren two hundred thousand, women, sons, and daughters, and took also away much spoil from them, and brought the spoil to Samaria.

---

a Cf. Isaiah 7 : 1, 2. See Appendix, §7.   *b* Heb. " Eloth."   *c* According to another reading, " Edomites."
d Heb. " second."

Kingdom of Judah. || **Kingdom of Israel.**

B. ODED THE PROPHET PROCURES THE RELEASE OF THE JEWISH CAPTIVES.

2 *Chronicles* 28 : 9-15.

9 But a prophet of the LORD was there, whose name was Oded : and he went out to meet the host that came to Samaria, and said unto them, Behold, because the LORD, the God of your fathers, was wroth with Judah, he hath delivered them into your hand, and ye have slain them in a rage which hath reached up unto heaven. 10 And now ye purpose to keep under the children of Judah and Jerusalem for bondmen and bondwomen unto you : *but* are there not even with you *a*trespasses of your own against the LORD your God ? 11 Now hear me therefore, and send back the captives, which ye have taken captive of your brethren : for the fierce wrath of the LORD is upon you. 12 Then certain of the heads of the children of Ephraim, Azariah the son of Johanan, Berechiah the son of Meshillemoth, and Jehizkiah the son of Shallum, and Amasa the son of Hadlai, stood up against them that came from the war, 13 and said unto them, Ye shall not bring in the captives hither : for ye purpose that which will bring upon us *b*a trespass against the LORD, to add unto our sins and to our *b*trespass : for our *b* trespass is great, and there is fierce wrath against Israel. 14 So the armed men left the captives and the spoil before the princes and all the congregation. 15 And the men which have been expressed by name rose up, and took the captives, and with the spoil clothed all that were naked among them, and arrayed them, and shod them, and gave them to eat and to drink, and anointed them, and carried all the feeble of them upon asses, and brought them to Jericho, the city of palm trees, unto their brethren : then they returned to Samaria.

(4) THE EDOMITE AND PHILISTINE INVASIONS.

2 *Chronicles* 28 : 17-19.

17 For again the Edomites had come and smitten Judah, and carried away *c*captives. 18 The Philistines also had invaded the cities of the lowland, and of the South of Judah, and had taken Beth-shemesh, and Aijalon, and Gederoth, and Soco with the *d* towns thereof, and Timnah with the *d* towns thereof, Gimzo also and the *d* towns thereof : and they dwelt there. 19 For the LORD brought Judah low because of Ahaz king of Israel; for he had *e* dealt wantonly in Judah, and trespassed sore against the LORD.

(5) AHAZ SEEKS HELP FROM TIGLATH-PILESER.

2 *Kings* 16 : 7, 8.	2 *Chronicles* 28 : 16, 21.
7 So Ahaz sent messengers to Tiglath-pileser king of Assyria, saying, I am thy servant and thy son : come up, and save me out of the hand of the king of	16 At that time did king Ahaz send unto the *f*kings of Assyria to help him. 21 For Ahaz took away a portion out of the house of the LORD, and out of

a Heb. "guiltinesses."   *b* Or, "guilt."   *c* Heb. "a captivity."   *d* Heb. "daughters."   *e* Or, "cast away restraint." *f* Many ancient authorities read, "king."

Kingdom of Judah.

2 *Kings* 16.

Syria, and out of the hand of the king of Israel, which rise up against me. 8 And Ahaz took the silver and gold that was found in the house of the LORD, and in the treasures of the king's house, and sent it for a present to the king of Assyria.

2 *Chronicles* 28.

the house of the king and of the princes, and gave it unto the king of Assyria : but it helped him not.

(6) TIGLATH-PILESER CAPTURES DAMASCUS.

2 *Kings* 16 : 9.

9 And the king of Assyria hearkened unto him : and the king of Assyria went up against Damascus, and took it, and carried *the people of* it captive to Kir, and slew Rezin.

(7) AHAZ BECOMES TRIBUTARY TO TIGLATH-PILESER.

2 *Kings* 16 : 10a.

10a And king Ahaz went to Damascus to meet Tiglath-pileser king of Assyria.

2 *Chronicles* 28 : 20.

20 And Tilgath-pilneser king of Assyria came *a* unto him, and distressed him, but *b* strengthened him not.

(8) AHAZ CONTINUES IN HIS WICKED WAYS.

2 *Kings* 16 : 10b–18.

10b And [Ahaz] saw the altar that was at Damascus : and king Ahaz sent to Urijah the priest the fashion of the altar, and the pattern of

Kingdom of Israel.

(6) TIGLATH-PILESER CAPTURES MANY CITIES IN NORTHERN ISRAEL, AND DEPORTS MANY CAPTIVES.

2 *Kings* 15 : 29.

29 In the days of Pekah king of Israel came Tiglath-pileser king of Assyria, and took Ijon, and Abel-beth-maacah, and Janoah, and Kedesh, and Hazor, and Gilead, and Galilee, all the land of Naphtali ; and he carried them captive to Assyria.

a Or, "against." *b* Or, "prevailed not against him."

2 *Kings* 16.

it, according to all the workmanship thereof. 11 And Urijah the priest built an altar · according to all that king Ahaz had sent from Damascus, so did Urijah the priest make it against king Ahaz came from Damascus. 12 And when the king was come from Damascus, the king saw the altar : and the king drew near unto the altar, and *a* offered thereon. 13 And he burnt his burnt offering and his meal offering, and poured his drink offering, and sprinkled the blood of his peace offerings, upon the altar. 14 And the brasen altar, which was before the LORD, he brought from the forefront of the house, from between his altar and the house of the LORD, and put it on the north side of his altar. 15 And king Ahaz commanded Urijah the priest, saying, Upon the great altar burn the morning burnt offering, and the evening meal offering, and the king's burnt offering, and his meal offering, with the burnt offering of all the people of the land, and their meal offering, and their drink offerings ; and sprinkle upon it all the blood of the burnt offering, and all the blood

2 *Chronicles* 28.

22 And in the time *b* of his distress did he trespass yet more against the LORD, this same king Ahaz. 23 For he sacrificed unto the gods of *c* Damascus, which smote him : and he said, Because the gods of the kings of Syria helped them, *therefore* will I sacrifice to them, that they may help me. But they were the ruin of him, and of all Israel.

---

a Or, " went up unto it."   *b* Or, " that he distressed him."   *c* Heb. " Darmesek."

Kingdom of Judah.

2 *Kings* 16.

of the sacrifice : but the brasen altar shall be for me to inquire by. 16 Thus did Urijah the priest, according to all that king Ahaz commanded. 17 And king Ahaz cut off the *ᵃ* borders of the bases, and removed the laver from off them ; and took down the sea from off the brasen oxen that were under it, and put it upon a pavement of stone. 18 And the *ᵇ* covered way for the sabbath that they had built in the house, and the king's entry without, turned he *ᶜ* unto the house of the LORD, because of the king of Assyria.

2 *Chronicles* 28.

24*a* And Ahaz gathered together the vessels of the house of God, and cut in pieces the vessels of the house of God, and shut up the doors of the house of the LORD.

24*b* And he made him altars in every corner of Jerusalem. 25 And in every several city of Judah he made high places to burn incense unto other gods, and provoked to anger the LORD, the God of his fathers.

Kingdom of Israel.

(7) THE DEATH OF PEKAH.

2 *Kings* 15 : 31, 30.

31 Now the rest of the acts of Pekah, and all that he did, behold, they are written in the book of the chronicles of the kings of Israel. 30 And Hoshea the son of Elah made a conspiracy against Pekah the son of Remaliah, and smote him, and slew him, and reigned in his stead, in the twentieth year of Jotham the son of Uzziah.

INTERREGNUM OF NINE YEARS.*ᵈ*

---

a Or, " panels."　　*b* Or, " covered place."　　*c* Or, " round."　　*d* Determined by comparing 2 Kings 15 : 27, 30, and 2 Kings 17 : 1.

Kingdom of Judah.

Kingdom of Israel.

172. THE REIGN OF HOSHEA.

(1) HOSHEA'S ACCESSION TO THE THRONE.

2 *Kings* 17 : 1.

1 In the twelfth year of Ahaz king of Judah began Hoshea the son of Elah to reign in Samaria over Israel, *and reigned* nine years.

(2) THE CHARACTER OF HOSHEA.

2 *Kings* 17 : 2.

2 And he did that which was evil in the sight of the LORD, yet not as the kings of Israel that were before him.

(9) THE DEATH OF AHAZ.

2 *Ki.* 16 : 19, 20a.

19 Now the rest of the acts of Ahaz which he did, are they not written in the book of the chronicles of the kings of Judah? 20a And Ahaz slept with his fathers, and was buried with his fathers in the city of David.

2 *Ch.* 28 : 26, 27a.

26 Now the rest of his acts, and all his ways, first and last, behold, they are written in the book of the kings of Judah and Israel. 27a And Ahaz slept with his fathers, and they buried him in the city, even in Jerusalem; for they brought him not into the sepulchres of the kings of Israel.

173. THE REIGN OF HEZEKIAH

(FIRST 6 YEARS).

(1) HEZEKIAH'S ACCESSION TO THE THRONE.

2 *Ki.* 16 : 20b; 18 : 1, 2.

20b And Hezekiah his son reigned in his stead. 1 Now it came to pass in the third year of Hoshea son of Elah king of Israel, that Hezekiah the son of Ahaz king of Judah began to reign. 2 Twenty and five years old was

2 *Ch.* 28 : 27b; 29 : 1.

27b And Hezekiah his son reigned in his stead.

1 Hezekiah began to reign when he was five

Kingdom of Judah.

2 *Kings* 18.	2 *Chronicles* 29.
he when he began to reign; and he reigned twenty and nine years in Jerusalem: and his mother's name was Abi the daughter of Zechariah.	and twenty years old; and he reigned n i n e and twenty years in Jerusalem: and his mother's name was Abijah the daughter of Zechariah.

(2) THE CHARACTER OF HEZEKIAH.

2 *Kings* 18 : 3–7*a*.	2 *Chronicles* 29 : 2.
3 And he did that which was right in the eyes of the LORD, according to all that David his father had done. 4 He removed the high places, and brake the pillars, and cut down the Asherah: and he b r a k e in pieces the b r a s e n serpent that Moses had made; for unto those days the children of Israel did burn incense to it; and *a* he called it *b* Nehushtan. 5 He trusted in the LORD, the God of Israel; so that after him w a s n o n e like him among all the kings of Judah, nor *among them* that were before him. 6 For he clave to the LORD, he departed not from following him, but k e p t h i s commandments, which the LORD commanded M o s e s. 7*a* And the LORD was with him; whithersoever he went forth he prospered.	2 And he did that which was right in the eyes of the LORD, according to all that David his father had done.

---

a Or, "it was called."   *b* I. e., "A piece of brass."

21

Kingdom of Judah.

Kingdom of Israel.

(3) The Cleansing of the Temple.

2 *Chronicles* 29: 3-19.

3 He in the first year of his reign, in the first month, opened the doors of the house of the LORD, and repaired them. 4 And he brought in the priests and the Levites, and gathered them together into the broad place on the east, and said unto them, 5 Hear me, ye Levites; now sanctify yourselves, and sanctify the house of the LORD, the God of your fathers, and carry forth the filthiness out of the holy place. 6 For our fathers have trespassed, and done that which was evil in the sight of the LORD our God, and have forsaken him, and have turned away their faces from the habitation of the LORD, and turned their backs. 7 Also they have shut up the doors of the porch, and put out the lamps, and have not burned incense nor offered burnt offerings in the holy place unto the God of Israel. 8 Wherefore the wrath of the LORD was upon Judah and Jerusalem, and he hath delivered them to be *ᵃ* tossed to and fro, to be an astonishment, and an hissing, as ye see with your eyes. 9 For, lo, our fathers have fallen by the sword, and our sons and our daughters and our wives are in captivity for this. 10 Now it is in mine heart to make a covenant with the LORD, the God of Israel, that his fierce anger may turn away from us. 11 My sons, be not now negligent: for the LORD hath chosen you to stand before him, to minister unto him, and that ye should be his ministers, and burn incense.

12 Then the Levites arose, Mahath the son of Amasai, and Joel the son of Azariah, of the sons of the Kohathites: and of the sons of Merari, Kish the son of Abdi, and Azariah the son of Jehallelel: and of the Gershonites, Joah the son of Zimmah, and Eden the son of Joah: 13 and of the sons of Elizaphan, Shimri and Jeuel: and of the sons of Asaph, Zechariah and Mattaniah: 14 and of the sons of Heman, Jehuel and Shimei: and of the sons of Jeduthun, Shemaiah and Uzziel. 15 And they gathered their brethren, and sanctified themselves, and went in, according to the commandment of the king by the words of the LORD, to cleanse the house of the LORD. 16 And the priests went in unto the inner part of the house of the LORD, to cleanse it, and

ᵃ Or, "a terror."

Kingdom of Judah.

2 *Chronicles* 29.

brought out all the uncleanness that they found in the temple of the LORD into the court of the house of the LORD. And the Levites took it, to carry it out abroad to the brook Kidron. 17 Now they began on the first *day* of the first month to sanctify, and on the eighth day of the month came they to the porch of the LORD; and they sanctified the house of the ·LORD in eight days: and on the sixteenth day of the first month they made an end. 18 Then they went in to Hezekiah the king within *the palace*, and said, We have cleansed all the house of the LORD, and the altar of burnt offering, with all the vessels thereof, and the table of shewbread, with all the vessels thereof. 19 Moreover all the vessels, which king Ahaz in his reign did cast away when he trespassed, have we prepared and sanctified; and, behold, they are before the altar of the LORD.

(4) THE RECONSECRATION OF THE TEMPLE.

2 *Chronicles* 29 : 20–36.

20 Then Hezekiah the king arose early, and gathered the princes of the city, and went up to the house of the LORD. 21 And they brought seven bullocks, and seven rams, and seven lambs, and seven he-goats, for a sin offering for the kingdom and for the sanctuary and for Judah. And he commanded the priests the sons of Aaron to offer them on the altar of the LORD. 22 So they killed the bullocks, and the priests received the blood, and sprinkled it on the altar: and they killed the rams, and sprinkled the blood upon the altar: they killed also the lambs, and sprinkled the blood upon the altar. 23 And they brought near the he-goats for the sin offering before the king and the congregation; and they laid their hands upon them: 24 and the priests killed them, and they made a sin offering with their blood upon the altar, to make atonement for all Israel: for the king commanded *that* the burnt offering and the sin offering *should be made* for all Israel. 25 And he set the Levites in the house of the LORD with cymbals, with psalteries, and with harps, according to the commandment of David, and of Gad the king's seer, and Nathan the prophet: for the

Kingdom of Israel.

Kingdom of Judah.

2 *Chronicles* 29.

commandment was of the LORD by his prophets. 26 And the Levites stood with the instruments of David, and the priests with the trumpets. 27 And Hezekiah commanded to offer the burnt offering upon the altar. And when the burnt offering began, the song of the LORD began also, and the trumpets, together with the instruments of David king of Israel. 28 And all the congregation worshipped, and the singers sang, and the trumpeters sounded; all this *continued* until the burnt offering was finished. 29 And when they had made an end of offering, the king and all that were present with him bowed themselves and worshipped. 30 Moreover Hezekiah the king and the princes commanded the Levites to sing praises unto the LORD with the words of David, and of Asaph the seer. And they sang praises with gladness, and they bowed their heads and worshipped. 31 Then Hezekiah answered and said, Now ye have *a* consecrated yourselves unto the LORD, come near and bring sacrifices and thank offerings into the house of the LORD. And the congregation brought in sacrifices and thank offerings; and as many as were of a willing heart *brought* burnt offerings. 32 And the number of the burnt offerings, which the congregation brought, was threescore and ten bullocks, an hundred rams, and two hundred lambs: all these were for a burnt offering to the LORD. 33 And the consecrated things were six hundred oxen and three thousand sheep. 34 But the priests were too few, so that they could not flay all the burnt offerings: wherefore their brethren the Levites did help them, till the work was ended, and until the priests had sanctified themselves: for the Levites were more upright in heart to sanctify themselves than the priests. 35 And also the burnt offerings were in abundance, with the fat of the peace offerings, and with the drink offerings for every burnt offering. So the service of the house of the LORD was set in order. 36 And Hezekiah rejoiced, and all the people, because of that which God had prepared for the people: for the thing was done suddenly.

Kingdom of Israel.

---

a Heb. "filled your hand."

| Kingdom of Judah. | Kingdom of Israel. |

(5) MANY OF THE SUBJECTS OF HOSHEA UNITE WITH THE PEOPLE OF JUDAH IN KEEPING THE PASSOVER. (3)

A. PREPARATIONS FOR THE PASSOVER.

2 *Chronicles* 30: 1-12.

1 And Hezekiah sent to all Israel and Judah, and wrote letters also to Ephraim and Manasseh, that they should come to the house of the LORD at Jerusalem, to keep the passover unto the LORD, the God of Israel. 2 For the king had taken counsel, and his princes, and all the congregation in Jerusalem, to keep the passover in the second month. 3 For they could not keep it at that time, because the priests had not sanctified themselves in sufficient number, neither had the people gathered themselves together to Jerusalem. 4 And the thing was right in the eyes of the king and of all the congregation. 5 So they established a decree to make proclamation throughout all Israel, from Beer-sheba even to Dan, that they should come to keep the passover unto the LORD, the God of Israel, at Jerusalem: for they had not kept it *a* in great numbers in such sort as it is written. 6 So the posts went with the letters from the king and his princes throughout all Israel and Judah, and according to the commandment of the king, saying, Ye children of Israel, turn again unto the LORD, the God of Abraham, Isaac, and Israel, that he may return to the remnant that are escaped of you out of the hand of the kings of Assyria. 7 And be not ye like your fathers, and like your brethren, which trespassed against the LORD, the God of their fathers, so that he gave them up *b* to desolation, as ye see. 8 Now be ye not stiffnecked, as your fathers were; but *c* yield yourselves unto the LORD, and enter into his sanctuary, which he hath sanctified for ever, and serve the LORD your God, that his fierce anger may turn away from you. 9 For if ye turn again unto the LORD, your brethren and your children shall find compassion before them that led them captive, and shall come again into this land: for the LORD your God is gracious and merciful, and will not turn away his face from you, if ye return unto him. 10 So the posts passed from city to city through the country of Ephraim and Manasseh, even unto Zebulun: but they laughed them to scorn, and mocked them. 11 Nevertheless divers of Asher and Manasseh and of Zebulun humbled themselves, and came to Jerusalem. 12 Also in Judah was the hand of God to give them one heart, to do the commandment of the king and of the princes by the word of the LORD.

B. THE KEEPING OF THE PASSOVER.

2 *Chronicles* 30: 13-22.

13 And there assembled at Jerusalem much people to keep the feast of unleavened bread in the second month, a very great congregation. 14 And they arose and took away the altars that were in Jerusalem, and all the *d* altars for incense took they away, and cast them into the brook Kidron. 15 Then they killed the passover on the fourteenth *day* of the second month: and the priests and the Levites were ashamed, and sanctified themselves, and brought burnt offerings into the house of the LORD. 16 And they stood in their place after their order, according to the law of Moses the man of God: the priests sprinkled the blood, *which they received* of the hand of the Levites. 17 For there were many in the congregation that had not sanctified themselves: therefore the Levites had the charge of killing the passovers for every one that was not clean, to sanctify them unto the LORD. 18 For a multitude of the people, even many of Ephraim and Manasseh, Issachar and Zebulun, had not cleansed themselves, yet did they eat the passover otherwise

---

a Or, " of a long time."   *b* Or, " to be an astonishment."   *c* Heb. " give the hand."   *d* Or, " vessels."

| Kingdom of Judah. | Kingdom of Israel. |

2 Chronicles 30.

than it is written.   For Hezekiah had prayed for them, saying, The good LORD pardon *a* every
one 19 that setteth his heart to seek God, the LORD, the God of his fathers, though *he be* not
cleansed according to the purification of the sanctuary.   20 And the LORD hearkened to Hezekiah,
and healed the people.   21 And the children of Israel that were present at Jerusalem kept the
feast of unleavened bread seven days with great gladness: and the Levites and the priests
praised the LORD day by day, *singing* with loud instruments unto the LORD.   22 And Hezekiah
spake comfortably unto all the Levites that were well skilled *in the service* of the LORD.   So they
did eat throughout the feast for the seven days, offering sacrifices of peace offerings, and *b* making
confession to the LORD, the God of their fathers.

C. THE KEEPING OF "OTHER SEVEN DAYS."

2 Chronicles 30:23-27.

23 And the whole congregation took counsel to keep other seven days: and they kept *other*
seven days with gladness.   24 For Hezekiah king of Judah did give to the congregation for offerings a thousand bullocks and seven thousand sheep; and the princes gave to the congregation a
thousand bullocks and ten thousand sheep: and a great number of priests sanctified themselves.
25 And all the congregation of Judah, with the priests and the Levites, and all the congregation
that came out of Israel, and the strangers that came out of the land of Israel, and that dwelt in
Judah, rejoiced.   26 So there was great joy in Jerusalem: for since the time of Solomon the son
of David king of Israel there was not the like in Jerusalem.   27 Then the priests the Levites
arose and blessed the people: and their voice was heard, and their prayer came up to his holy
habitation, even unto heaven.

D. THE ENTHUSIASM AROUSED RESULTS IN WIDESPREAD ICONOCLASM.

| [2 *Kings* 18:4.] | 2 *Chronicles* 31:1. |

4 He removed the high places, and brake the
pillars, and cut down the Asherah: and he
brake in pieces the brasen serpent that Moses
had made; for unto those days the children of
Israel did burn incense to it; and *c* he called it
d Nehushtan.

1 Now when all this was finished, all Israel
that were present went out to the cities of
Judah, and brake in pieces the *e* pillars, and
hewed down the Asherim, and brake down the
high places and the altars out of all Judah and
Benjamin, in Ephraim also and Manasseh, until
they had destroyed them all.   Then all the children of Israel returned, every man to his possession, into their own cities.

(6) HEZEKIAH'S FURTHER RELIGIOUS
REFORMS.

2 Chronicles 31:2-21

2 And Hezekiah appointed the courses of the
priests and the Levites after their courses, every
man according to his service, both the priests
and the Levites, for burnt offerings and for
peace offerings, to minister, and to give thanks,
and to praise in the gates of the camp of the
LORD.   3 *He appointed* also the king's portion

---

a Or, "him that setteth his whole heart."   *b* Or, "giving thanks."   *c* Or, "it was called."   *d* I. e., "A piece of
brass."   *e* Or, "obelisks."

Kingdom of Judah.	Kingdom of Israel.

2 *Chronicles* 31.

of his substance for the burnt offerings, *to wit*, for the morning and evening burnt offerings, and the burnt offerings for the sabbaths, and for the new moons, and for the set feasts, as it is written in the law of the LORD. 4 Moreover he commanded the people that dwelt in Jerusalem to give the portion of the priests and the Levites, that they might *a* give themselves to the law of the LORD. 5 And as soon as the commandment came abroad, the children of Israel gave in abundance the firstfruits of corn, wine, and oil, and honey, and of all the increase of the field ; and the tithe of all things brought they in abundantly. 6 And the children of Israel and Judah, that dwelt in the cities of Judah, they also brought in the tithe of oxen and sheep, and the tithe of dedicated things which were consecrated unto the LORD their God, and laid them by heaps. 7 In the third month they began to lay the foundation of the heaps, and finished them in the seventh month. 8 And when Hezekiah and the princes came and saw the heaps, they blessed the LORD and his people Israel. 9 Then Hezekiah questioned with the priests and the Levites concerning the heaps. 10 And Azariah the chief priest, of the house of Zadok, answered him and said, Since *the people* began to bring the oblations into the house of the LORD, we have eaten and had enough, and have left plenty : for the LORD hath blessed his people ; and that which is left is this great store. 11 Then Hezekiah commanded to prepare chambers in the house of the LORD ; and they prepared them. 12 And they brought in the oblations and the tithes and the dedicated things faithfully : and over them Conaniah the Levite was ruler, and Shimei his brother was second. 13 And Jehiel, and Azaziah, and Nahath, and Asahel, and Jerimoth, and Jozabad, and Eliel, and Ismachiah, and Mahath, and Benaiah, were overseers under the hand of Conaniah and Shimei his brother, by the appointment of Hezekiah the king, and Azariah the ruler of the house of God. 14 And Kore the son of Imnah the Levite, the porter at the east *gate*, was over the freewill offerings of God, to distribute the oblations of the LORD, and the most holy things. 15 And under him were Eden, and Miniamin,

a Heb. "be strong in."

Kingdom of Judah.

2 *Chronicles* 31.

and Jeshua, and Shemaiah, Amariah, and Shecaniah, in the cities of the priests, in their *a* set office, to give to their brethren by courses, as well to the great as to the small : 16 beside them that were reckoned by genealogy of males, from three years old and upward, even every one that entered into the house of the LORD, *b* as the duty of every day required, for their service in their charges according to their courses ; 17 and them that were reckoned by genealogy of the priests by their fathers' houses, and the Levites from twenty years old and upward, in their charges by their courses ; 18 *c* and them that were reckoned by genealogy of all their little ones, their wives, and their sons, and their daughters, through all the congregation : for in their *a* set office they sanctified themselves in holiness : 19 also for the sons of Aaron the priests, which were in the fields of the suburbs of their cities, in every several city, there were men that were expressed by name, to give portions to all the males among the priests, and to all that were reckoned by genealogy among the Levites.　20 And thus did Hezekiah throughout all Judah ; and he wrought that which was good and right and *d* faithful before the LORD his God.　21 And in every work that he began in the service of the house of God, and in the law, and in the commandments, to seek his God, he did it with all his heart, and prospered.

Kingdom of Israel.

(4) HOSHEA BECOMES TRIBUTARY TO SHAL-MANESER.

2 *Kings* 17 : 3.

3 Against him came up Shalmaneser king of Assyria ; and Hoshea became his servant, and brought him presents.

(5) THE SECRET ALLIANCE WITH EGYPT.

2 *Kings* 17 : 4*a*.

4*a* And the king of Assyria found conspiracy in Hoshea ; for he had sent messengers to So king of Egypt, and offered no present to the king of Assyria, as he had done year by year.

---

a Or, " trust."　　*b* Or, " for his daily portion."　　*c* Or, " even *to give* to them," etc.　　*d* Heb. " faithfulness."

Kingdom of Judah.

Kingdom of Israel.

(6) SHALMANESER BESIEGES SAMARIA.

2 Kings 17 : 5.

5 Then the king of Assyria came up throughout all the land, and went up to Samaria, and besieged it three years.

2 Kings 18 : 9.

9 And it came to pass in the fourth year of king Hezekiah, which was the seventh year of Hoshea son of Elah king of Israel, that Shalmaneser king of Assyria came up against Samaria, and besieged it.

(7) THE FALL OF SAMARIA.

2 Kings 17 : 6.

6 In the ninth year of Hoshea, the king of Assyria took Samaria, and carried Israel away unto Assyria, and placed them in Halah, and in Habor, *on* the river of Gozan, and in the cities of the Medes.

2 Kings 18 : 10, 11.

10 And at the end of three years they took it : even in the sixth year of Hezekiah, which was the ninth year of Hoshea king of Israel, Samaria was taken. 11 And the king of Assyria carried Israel away unto Assyria, and put them in Halah, and in Habor, *on* the river of Gozan, and in the cities of the Medes.

(8) THE IMPRISONMENT OF HOSHEA.

2 Kings 17: 4*b*.

4*b* Therefore the king of Assyria shut him up, and bound him in prison.

174. APPENDIX TO THE HISTORY OF THE KINGDOM OF ISRAEL.

(1) THE SINS FOR WHICH ISRAEL WAS CARRIED INTO CAPTIVITY.

2 Kings 17 : 7–23.

7 And it was so, because the children of Israel had sinned against the LORD their God, which brought them up out of the land of Egypt

2 Kings 18 : 12.

12 [And it was so,] because they obeyed not the voice of the LORD their God, but transgressed his covenant, even all that

Kingdom of Judah.

Kingdom of Israel.

2 *Kings* 17.

from under the hand of
Pharaoh king of Egypt,
and had feared other
gods, 8 and walked in
the statutes of the na-
tions, whom the LORD
cast out from before the
children of Israel, and
of the kings of Israel,
which t h e y *made.
9 And the children of Is-
rael did secretly things
that were not right
against the LORD their
God, and they built
them high places in all
their cities, from the
tower of the watchmen
to the fenced city.
10 And they set them
up *pillars and Asherim
upon every high hill,
and under every green
tree : 11 and there they
burnt incense in all the
high places, as did the
nations whom the LORD
carried away before
t h e m ; and wrought
wicked things to pro-
voke the LORD to an-
ger : 12 and they served
idols, whereof the LORD
had said unto them,
Ye shall not do this
thing. 13 Yet the LORD
testified unto Israel,
and unto Judah, by the
hand of every prophet,
and of every seer, say-
ing, Turn ye from your
evil ways, and keep
my commandments and
my statutes, according
to all the law which I
commanded your fa-
thers, and which I sent
to you by the hand of

2 *Kings* 18.

Moses the servant of
the LORD had com-
manded, and would not
hear it, nor do it.

---

a Or, " practised."   *b* Or, " obelisks."

Kingdom of Judah.

Kingdom of Israel.

2 Kings 17.

my servants the prophets. 14 Notwithstanding they would not hear, but hardened their neck, like to the neck of their fathers, who believed not in the LORD their God. 15 And they rejected his statutes, and his covenant that he made with their fathers, and his testimonies which he testified unto them; and they followed vanity, and became vain, and *went* after the nations that were round about them, concerning whom the LORD had charged them that they should not do like them. 16 And they forsook all the commandments of the LORD their God, and made them molten images, even two calves, and made an Asherah, and worshipped all the host of heaven, and served Baal. 17 And they caused their sons and their daughters to pass through the fire, and used divination and enchantments, and sold themselves to do that which was evil in the sight of the LORD, to provoke him to anger. 18 Therefore the LORD was very angry with Israel, and removed them out of his sight: there was none left but the tribe of Judah only. 19 Also Judah kept not the commandments of the LORD their God, but walked in the stat-

Kingdom of Judah.	Kingdom of Israel.
	2 *Kings* 17. utes of Israel which they *a* made. 20 And the LORD rejected all the seed of Israel, and afflicted them, and delivered them into the hand of spoilers, until he had cast them out of his sight. 21 For he rent Israel from the house of David; and they made Jeroboam the son of Nebat king: and Jeroboam *b* drave Israel from following the LORD, and made them sin a great sin. 22 And the children of Israel walked in all the sins of Jeroboam which he did; they departed not from them; 23 until the LORD removed Israel out of his sight, as he spake by the hand of all his servants the prophets. So Israel was carried away out of their own land to Assyria, unto this day.

(2) THE PEOPLES THAT WERE BROUGHT TO INHABIT SAMARIA.

2 *Kings* 17:24.

24 And the king of Assyria brought men from Babylon, and from Cuthah, and from Avva, and from Hamath and Sepharvaim, and placed them in the cities of Samaria instead of the children of Israel: and they possessed Samaria, and dwelt in the cities thereof.

(3) THE PLAGUE OF THE LIONS.

2 *Kings* 17:25, 26.

25 And so it was, at the beginning of their dwelling there, that they feared not the LORD: therefore the LORD sent lions among them, which killed some of them. 26 Wherefore they

---

a Or, " practised."   *b* According to another reading, " drew Israel away."

Kingdom of Judah.	Kingdom of Israel.

Kingdom of Israel.

2 Kings 17.

spake to the king of Assyria, saying, The nations which thou hast carried away, and placed in the cities of Samaria, know not the manner of the God of the land: therefore he hath sent lions among them, and, behold, they slay them, because they know not the manner of the God of the land.

(4) THE MIXED CHARACTER OF THE SAMARITANS' RELIGION.

2 Kings 17 : 27–41.

27 Then the king of Assyria commanded, saying, Carry thither one of the priests whom ye brought from thence; and let them go and dwell there, and let him teach them the manner of the God of the land.   28 So one of the priests whom they had carried away from Samaria came and dwelt in Beth-el, and taught them how they should fear the LORD.   29 Howbeit every nation made gods of their own, and put them in the houses of the high places which the Samaritans had made, every nation in their cities wherein they dwelt.   30 And the men of Babylon made Succoth-benoth, and the men of Cuth made Nergal, and the men of Hamath made Ashima, 31 and the Avvites made Nibhaz and Tartak, and the Sepharvites burnt their children in the fire to Adrammelech and Anammelech, the *a* gods of Sepharvaim.   32 So they feared the LORD, and made unto them from among themselves priests of the high places, which sacrificed for them in the houses of the high places. 33 They feared the LORD, and served their own gods, after the manner of the nations from among whom they had been carried away. 34 Unto this day they do after the former manners: they fear not the LORD, neither do they after their statutes, or after their ordinances, or after the law or after the commandment which the LORD commanded the children of Jacob, whom he named Israel ; 35 with whom the LORD had made a covenant, and charged them, saying, Ye shall not fear other gods, nor bow yourselves to them, nor serve them, nor sacrifice to them : 36 but the LORD, who brought you up out of the land of Egypt with great power and with a stretched out arm, him shall ye fear, and unto him shall ye bow yourselves, and to him shall

---

a Or, "god."

Kingdom of Judah.

Kingdom of Israel.

2 Kings 17.

ye sacrifice : 37 and the statutes and the ordinances, and the law and the commandment, which he wrote for you, ye shall observe to do for evermore ; and ye shall not fear other gods ; 38 and the covenant that I have made with you ye shall not forget; neither shall ye fear other gods : 39 but the LORD your God shall ye fear; and he shall deliver you out of the hand of all your enemies. 40 Howbeit they did not hearken, but they did after their former manner. 41 So these nations feared the LORD, and served their graven images ; their children likewise, and their children's children, as did their fathers, so do they unto this day.

PART III.

THE KINGDOM OF JUDAH AFTER THE FALL OF THE KINGDOM OF ISRAEL.

175. THE REIGN OF HEZEKIAH (LAST 23 YEARS).

(1) HEZEKIAH THROWS OFF THE ASSYRIAN YOKE.

2 Kings 18 : 7b.

7b And he rebelled against the king of Assyria, and served him not.

(2) HEZEKIAH'S SUCCESSFUL PHILISTINE CAMPAIGN.

2 Kings 18 : 8.

8 He smote the Philistines unto Gaza and the borders thereof, from the tower of the watchmen to the fenced city.

(3) SENNACHERIB'S FIRST INVASION OF JUDAH. [b]

2 Kings 18 : 13-16.

13 Now in the fourteenth year of king Hezekiah did [c] Sennacherib king of Assyria come up against all the fenced cities of Judah, and took them. 14 And Hezekiah king of Judah sent to the king of Assyria to Lachish, saying, I have offended ; return from me : that which thou puttest on me will I bear. And the king of Assyria appointed unto Hezekiah king of Judah three hundred talents of silver and thirty talents of gold. 15 And Hezekiah gave him all the silver that was found in the house of the LORD, and in the treasures of the king's house. 16 At that time did Hezekiah cut off the gold from the doors of the temple of the LORD, and from the [d] pillars which Hezekiah king of Judah had overlaid, and gave it to the king of Assyria.

---

a It is not to be understood by the title of this section that the event mentioned below in (1) necessarily happened within a year after the fall of Samaria. The events in (1) and (2) occurred some time between the seventh and fourteenth years of Hezekiah's reign.   b Cf. Isaiah 36 : 1. See Appendix, §7.   c Heb. ". Sanherib."   d Or, " door posts."

(4) HEZEKIAH'S ILLNESS AND RECOVERY. [a]

2 *Kings* 20 : 1–11.

1 In those days was Hezekiah sick unto death. And Isaiah the prophet the son of Amoz came to him, and said unto him, Thus saith the LORD, Set thine house in order ; for thou shalt die, and not live. 2 Then he turned his face to the wall, and prayed unto the LORD, saying, 3 Remember now, O LORD, I beseech thee, how I have walked before thee in truth and with a perfect heart, and have done that which is good in thy sight. And Hezekiah wept sore. 4 And it came to pass, afore Isaiah was gone [b] out into [c] the middle part of the city, that the word of the LORD came to him, saying, 5 Turn again, and say to Hezekiah the [d] prince of my people, Thus saith the LORD, the God of David thy father, I have heard thy prayer, I have seen thy tears : behold, I will heal thee : on the third day thou shalt go up unto the house of the LORD. 6 And I will add unto thy days fifteen years ; and I will deliver thee and this city out of the hand of the king of Assyria ; and I will defend this city for mine own sake, and for my servant David's sake. 7 And Isaiah said, Take a cake of figs. And they took and laid it on the boil, and he recovered. 8 And Hezekiah said unto Isaiah, What shall be the sign that the LORD will heal me, and that I shall go up unto the house of the LORD the third day ? 9 And Isaiah said, This shall be the sign unto thee from the LORD, that the LORD will do the thing that he hath spoken : [e] shall the shadow go forward ten [f] steps, or go back ten steps ? 10 And Hezekiah answered, It is a light thing for the shadow to decline ten steps : nay, but let the shadow return backward ten steps. 11 And Isaiah the prophet cried unto the LORD : and he brought the shadow ten steps backward, by which it had gone down on the [g] dial of Ahaz.

2 *Chronicles* 32 : 24.

24 In those days Hezekiah was sick even unto death : and he prayed unto the LORD ; and he spake unto him, and gave him a [h] sign.

(5) HEZEKIAH'S RECEPTION OF THE BABYLONIAN EMBASSY.

2 *Kings* 20 : 12–19.

12 At that time [i] Berodach-baladan the son of Baladan, king of Babylon, sent letters and a present unto Hezekiah : for he had heard that Hezekiah had been sick. 13 And Hezekiah hearkened unto them, and shewed them all the house of his [k] precious things, the silver, and the

2 *Chronicles* 32 : 31, 25, 26.

31 Howbeit in *the business of* the [l] ambassadors of the princes of Babylon, who sent unto him to inquire of the wonder that was done in the land, God left him, to try him, that he might know all that was in his heart. 25 But Hezekiah rendered not again according to the benefit done unto

---

a With this and following subsections, cf. Isaiah 38 : 1, etc. See Appendix, §7.   *b* Or, " out of."   *c* According to another reading, " the middle court."   *d* Or, " leader."   *e* Or, " the shadow is gone forward ten steps, shall it go back," etc.   *f* Or, " degrees."   *g* Heb. " steps."   *h* Or, " wonder."   *i* In Isaiah 39 : 1, " Merodach-baladan."   *k* Or, " spicery."
l Heb. " interpreters."

2 *Kings* 20.	2 *Chronicles* 32.
gold, and the spices, and the precious oil, and *a* the house of his *b* armour, and all that was found in his treasures : there was nothing in his house, nor in all his dominion, that Hezekiah shewed them not. 14 Then came Isaiah the prophet unto king Hezekiah, and said unto him, What said these men? and from whence came they unto thee? And Hezekiah said, They are come from a far country, even from Babylon. 15 And he said, What have they seen in thine house? And Hezekiah answered, All that is in mine house have they seen : there is nothing among my treasures that I have not shewed them. 16 And Isaiah said unto Hezekiah, Hear the word of the LORD. 17 Behold, the days come, that all that is in thine house, and that which thy fathers have laid up in store unto this day, shall be carried to Babylon : nothing shall be left, saith the LORD. 18 And of thy sons that shall issue from thee, which thou shall beget, shall they take away ; and they shall be eunuchs in the palace of the king of Babylon. 19 Then said Hezekiah unto Isaiah, Good is the word of the LORD which thou hast spoken. He said moreover, Is it not so, if peace and truth shall be in my days?	him ; for his heart was lifted up : therefore there was wrath upon him, and upon Judah and Jerusalem. 26 Notwithstanding Hezekiah humbled himself for *c* the pride of his heart, both he and the inhabitants of Jerusalem, so that the wrath of the LORD came not upon them in the days of Hezekiah.

(6) HEZEKIAH'S WEALTH AND BUILDING.

2 *Chronicles* 32 : 27–30.

27 And Hezekiah had exceeding much riches and honour : and he provided him treasuries for silver, and for gold, and for precious stones, and for spices, and for shields, and for all manner of goodly vessels ; 28 storehouses also for the increase of corn and wine and oil ; and stalls for all manner of beasts, and flocks in folds.   29 Moreover he provided him cities, and possessions of flocks and herds in abundance : for God had given him very much substance.   30 This same Hezekiah also stopped the upper spring of the waters of Gihon, and brought them straight down on the west side of the city of David.   And Hezekiah prospered in all his works.

(7) SENNACHERIB'S SECOND INVASION OF JUDAH.

A. SENNACHERIB ENTERS JUDAH.

2 *Chronicles* 32 : 1.

1 After these things, and this faithfulness, Sennacherib king of Assyria came, and entered into Judah, and encamped against the fenced cities, and thought *d* to win them for himself.

B. HEZEKIAH'S PRECAUTIONS.

2 *Chronicles* 32 : 2–8.

2 And when Hezekiah saw that Sennacherib was come, and that *e* he was purposed to fight against Jerusalem, 3 he took counsel with his princes and his mighty men to stop the waters of the fountains which were without the city ; and they helped him.   4 So there was gathered much people together, and they stopped all the fountains, and the brook that flowed through the midst

---

a Another reading is, " all the house."   *b* Or, " jewels."   *c* Heb. " the lifting up."   *d* Heb. " to break them up."
e Heb. " his face was to fight."

2 *Chronicles* 32.

of the land, saying, Why should the kings of Assyria come, and find much water? 5 And he took courage, and built up all the wall that was broken down, and *a* raised *it* up to the towers, and *b* the other wall without, and strengthened Millo *in* the city of David, and made weapons and shields in abundance. 6 And he set captains of war over the people, and gathered them together to him in the broad place at the gate of the city, and spake comfortably to them, saying, 7 Be strong and of a good courage, be not afraid nor dismayed for the king of Assyria, nor for all the multitude that is with him: for *c* there is a greater with us than with him: 8 with him is an arm of flesh; but with us is the LORD our God to help us, and to fight our battles. And the people rested themselves upon the words of Hezekiah king of Judah.

C. THE ADVANCE AGAINST JERUSALEM: RABSHAKEH'S MESSAGE.

2 *Kings* 18:17–25.

17 And the king of Assyria sent *d* Tartan and *d*Rabsaris and *d*Rabshakeh from Lachish to king Hezekiah with a great army unto Jerusalem. And they went up and came to Jerusalem. And when they were come up, they came and stood by the conduit of the upper pool, which is in the high way of the fuller's field. 18 And when they had called to the king, there came out to them Eliakim the son of Hilkiah, which was over the household, and Shebnah the *e* scribe, and Joah the son of Asaph the *f*recorder. 19 And Rabshakeh said unto them, Say ye now to Hezekiah, Thus saith the great king, the king of Assyria, What confidence is this wherein thou trustest? 20 Thou sayest, but they are but *g* vain words, *There is* counsel and strength for the war. Now on whom dost thou trust, that thou hast rebelled against me? 21 Now, behold, thou trustest upon the staff of this bruised reed, even upon Egypt; whereon if a man lean, it will go into his hand, and pierce it: so is Pharaoh king of Egypt unto all that trust on him. 22 But if ye say unto me, We trust in the LORD our God: is not that he, whose high places and whose altars Hezekiah hath taken away, and hath said to Judah and to Jerusalem, Ye shall worship before this altar in Jerusalem? 23 Now therefore, I pray thee, *h* give pledges to my master the king of Assyria, and I will give thee two thousand horses, if thou be able on thy part to set riders upon them. 24 How then canst thou turn away the face of one captain of the least of my master's servants, and put thy trust on Egypt for chariots and for horsemen? 25 Am I now come up without the LORD against this place to destroy it? The LORD said unto me, Go up against this land, and destroy it.

2 *Chronicles* 32:9–15.

9 After this did Sennacherib king of Assyria send his servants to Jerusalem, (now he was before Lachish, and all his power with him,) unto Hezekiah king of Judah, and unto all Judah that were at Jerusalem, saying, 10 Thus saith Sennacherib king of Assyria, Whereon do ye trust, that ye abide *i* the siege in Jerusalem? 11 Doth not Hezekiah persuade you, to give you over to die by famine and by thirst, saying, The LORD our God shall deliver us out of the hand of the king of Assyria? 12 Hath not the same Hezekiah taken away his high places and his altars, and commanded Judah and Jerusalem, saying, Ye shall worship before one altar, and upon it shall ye burn incense? 13 Know ye not what I and my fathers have done unto all the peoples of the lands? Were the gods of the nations of the lands any ways able to deliver their land out of mine hand? 14 Who was there among all the gods of those nations which my fathers *k* utterly destroyed, that could deliver his people out of mine hand, that your God should be able to deliver you out of mine hand? 15 Now therefore let not Hezekiah deceive you, nor persuade you on this manner, neither believe ye him: for no god of any nation or kingdom was able to deliver his people out of mine hand, and out of the hand of my fathers: how much less shall your *l* God deliver you out of mine hand?

---

a Or, "heightened the towers." Or, "went up upon the towers." The Vulgate has, "built towers thereon." *b* Or, "another." *c* Or, "there be more." *d* The titles of Assyrian officers. *e* Or, "secretary." *f* Or, "chronicler." *g* Heb. "a word of the lips." *h* Or, "make a wager with." *i* Or, "in the strong hold." *k* Heb. "devoted." *l* Or, "gods."

22

D. THE REPLY OF HEZEKIAH'S MINISTERS.

2 *Kings* 18 : 26.

26 Then said Eliakim the son of Hilkiah, and Shebnah, and Joah, unto Rabshakeh, Speak, I pray thee, to thy servants in the *a* Syrian language; for we understand it : and speak not with us in the Jews' language, in the ears of the people that are on the wall.

E. THE FURTHER INSOLENCE OF RABSHAKEH.

2 *Kings* 18 : 27–35.

27 But Rabshakeh said unto them, Hath my master sent me to thy master, and to thee, to speak these words? *hath he* not *sent me* to the men which sit on the wall, to eat their own dung, and drink their own water with you ? 28 Then Rabshakeh stood, and cried with a loud voice in the Jews' language, and spake, saying, Hear ye the word of the great king, the king of Assyria. 29 Thus saith the king, Let not Hezekiah deceive you; for he shall not be able to deliver you out of his hand : 30 neither let Hezekiah make you trust in the LORD, saying, The LORD will surely deliver us, and this city shall not be given into the hand of the king of Assyria. 31 Hearken not to Hezekiah : for thus saith the king of Assyria, *b* Make your peace with me, and come out to me; and eat ye every one of his vine, and every one of his fig tree, and drink ye every one the waters of his own cistern; 32 until I come and take you away to a land like your own land, a land of corn and wine, a land of bread and vineyards, a land of oil olive and of honey, that ye may live, and not die : and hearken not unto Hezekiah, when he persuadeth you, saying, The LORD will deliver us. 33 Hath any of the gods of the nations ever delivered his land out of the hand of the king of Assyria ? 34 Where are the gods of Hamath, and of Arpad ? where are the gods of Sepharvaim, of Hena, and Ivvah ? have they delivered Samaria out of my hand ? 35 Who are they among all the gods of the countries, that have delivered their country out of my hand, that the LORD should deliver Jerusalem out of my hand ?

2 *Chronicles* 32 : 16, 18, 19.

16 And his servants spake yet more against the LORD God, and against his servant Hezekiah. 18 And they cried with a loud voice in the Jews' language unto the people of Jerusalem that were on the wall, to affright them, and to trouble them ; that they might take the city. 19 And they spake of the God of Jerusalem, as of the gods of the peoples of the earth, which are the work of men's hands.

F. THE DESPAIR OF HEZEKIAH'S MINISTERS.

2 *Kings* 18 : 36, 37.

36 But the people held their peace, and answered him not a word : for the king's commandment was, saying, Answer him not. 37 Then came Eliakim the son of Hilkiah, which was over the household, and Shebna the scribe, and Joah the son of Asaph the recorder, to Hezekiah with their clothes rent, and told him the words of Rabshakeh.

---

a Heb. " Aramean."   *b* Heb. " Make with me a blessing."

G. HEZEKIAH'S MESSAGE TO ISAIAH.

2 Kings 19: 1-5.

1 And it came to pass, when king Hezekiah heard it, that he rent his clothes, and covered himself with sackcloth, and went into the house of the LORD. 2 And he sent Eliakim, which was over the household, and Shebna the scribe, and the elders of the priests, covered with sackcloth, unto Isaiah the prophet the son of Amoz. 3 And they said unto him, Thus saith Hezekiah, This day is a day of trouble, and of rebuke, and of contumely: for the children are come to the birth, and there is not strength to bring forth. 4 It may be the LORD thy God will hear all the words of Rabshakeh, *a* whom the king of Assyria his master hath sent to reproach the living God, and will rebuke the words which the LORD thy God hath heard: wherefore lift up thy prayer for the remnant that is left. 5 So the servants of king Hezekiah came to Isaiah.

H. ISAIAH'S ANSWER.

2 Kings 19: 6, 7.

6 And Isaiah said unto them, Thus shall ye say to your master, Thus saith the LORD, Be not afraid of the words that thou hast heard, wherewith the servants of the king of Assyria have blasphemed me. 7 Behold, I will put a spirit in him, and he shall hear a rumour, and shall return to his own land; and I will cause him to fall by the sword in his own land.

I. RABSHAKEH'S DEPARTURE.

2 Kings 19: 8.

8 So Rabshakeh returned, and found the king of Assyria warring against Libnah: for he had heard that he was departed from Lachish.

J. SENNACHERIB'S LETTER TO HEZEKIAH.

2 Kings 19: 9-13.

9 And when he heard say of Tirhakah king of Ethiopia, Behold, he is come out to fight against thee: he sent messengers again unto Hezekiah, saying, 10 Thus shall ye speak to Hezekiah king of Judah, saying, Let not thy God in whom thou trustest deceive thee, saying, Jerusalem shall not be given into the hand of the king of Assyria. 11 Behold, thou hast heard what the kings of Assyria have done to all lands, by *b* destroying them utterly: and shalt thou be delivered? 12 Have the gods of the nations delivered them, which my fathers have destroyed, Gozan, and Haran, and Rezeph, and the children of Eden which were in Telassar? 13 Where is the king of Hamath, and the king of Arpad, and the king of the city of Sepharvaim, of Hena, and Ivvah?

2 Chronicles 32: 17.

17 He wrote also *c* letters, to rail on the LORD, the God of Israel, and to speak against him, saying, As the gods of the nations of the lands, which have not delivered their people out of mine hand, so shall not the God of Hezekiah deliver his people out of mine hand.

K. HEZEKIAH'S PRAYER.

2 Kings 19: 14-19.

14 And Hezekiah received the letter from the hand of the messengers, and read it: and Hezekiah went up into the house of the LORD, and

2 Chronicles 32: 20.

20 And Hezekiah the king, and Isaiah the prophet the son of Amoz, prayed because of this, and cried to heaven.

---

a Or, "wherewith the king of Assyria hath sent him."   *b* Heb. "devoting them."   *c* Or, "a letter."

2 *Kings* 19.

spread it before the LORD. 15 And Hezekiah prayed before the LORD, and said, O LORD, the God of Israel, that *a* sittest upon the cherubim, thou art the God, even thou alone, of all the kingdoms of the earth ; thou hast made heaven and earth. 16 Incline thine ear, O LORD, and hear ; open thine eyes, O LORD, and see : and hear the words of Sennacherib, wherewith he hath sent him to reproach the living God. 17 Of a truth, LORD, the kings of Assyria have laid waste the nations and their lands, 18 and have cast their gods into the fire : for they were no gods, but the work of men's hands, wood and stone ; therefore they have destroyed them. 19 Now therefore, O LORD our God, save thou us, I beseech thee, out of his hand, that all the kingdoms of the earth may know *b* that thou art the LORD God, even thou only.

L. JEHOVAH'S ANSWER THROUGH ISAIAH.

2 *Kings* 19 : 20-34.

20 Then Isaiah the son of Amoz sent to Hezekiah, saying, Thus saith the LORD, the God of Israel, Whereas thou hast prayed to me against Sennacherib king of Assyria, I have heard *thee.* 21 This is the word that the LORD hath spoken concerning him : The virgin daughter of Zion hath despised thee and laughed thee to scorn ; the daughter of Jerusalem hath shaken her head *c* at thee. 22 Whom hast thou reproached and blasphemed ? and against whom hast thou exalted thy voice and lifted up thine eyes on high ? *even* against the Holy One of Israel. 23 By thy messengers thou hast reproached the Lord, and hast said, With the *d* multitude of my chariots am I come up to the height of the mountains, to the innermost parts of Lebanon ; and I will cut down the tall cedars thereof, and the choice *e* fir trees thereof : and I will enter into his farthest lodging place, the forest of his fruitful field. 24 I have digged and drunk strange waters, and with the sole of my feet will I dry up all the rivers of *f* Egypt. 25 Hast thou not heard how I have done it long ago, and formed it of ancient times ? now have I brought it to pass, that thou shouldest be to lay waste fenced cities into ruinous heaps. 26 Therefore their inhabitants were of small power, they were dismayed and confounded ; they were as the grass of the field, and as the green herb, as the grass on the housetops, and as corn blasted before it be grown up. 27 But I know thy sitting down, and thy going out, and thy coming in, and thy raging against me. 28 Because of thy raging against me, and for that *g* thine arrogancy is come up into mine ears, therefore will I put my hook in thy nose, and my bridle in thy lips, and I will turn thee back by the way by which thou camest. 29 And this shall be the sign unto thee : ye shall eat this year that which groweth of itself, and in the second year that which springeth of the same ; and in the third year sow ye, and reap, and plant vineyards, and eat the fruit thereof. 30 And *h* the remnant that is escaped of the house of Judah shall again take root downward, and bear fruit upward. 31 For out of Jerusalem shall go forth a remnant, and out of mount Zion they that shall escape : the zeal of *i* the LORD shall perform this. 32 Therefore thus saith the LORD concerning the king of Assyria, He shall not come unto this city, nor shoot an arrow there, neither shall he come before it with shield, nor cast a mount against it. 33 By the way that he came, by the same shall he return, and he shall not come unto this city, saith the LORD. 34 For I will defend this city to save it, for mine own sake, and for my servant David's sake.

---

a Or, "dwellest between." *b* Or, "that thou, O LORD, art God." *c* Heb. "after." *d* According to another reading, "driving." *e* Or, "cypress." *f* Or, "defence." Heb. "Mazor." *g* Or, "thy careless ease." *h* Heb. "the escaped of the house of Judah that remain." *i* According to another reading, "the LORD of hosts," and so in Isaiah 37 : 32.

M. THE OVERTHROW OF THE ASSYRIANS.

2 *Kings* 19:35, 36.

35 And it came to pass that night, that the angel of the LORD went forth, and smote in the camp of the Assyrians an hundred fourscore and five thousand : and when men arose early in the morning, behold, they were all dead corpses. 36 So Sennacherib king of Assyria departed, and went and returned, and dwelt at Nineveh.

2 *Chronicles* 32 : 21a, 22.

21a And the LORD sent an angel, which cut off all the mighty men of valour, and the leaders and captains, in the camp of the king of Assyria. So he returned with shame of face to his own land. 22 Thus the LORD saved Hezekiah and the inhabitants of Jerusalem from the hand of Sennacherib the king of Assyria, and from the hand of all *other*, and guided them on every side.

(8) HEZEKIAH ONCE MORE PROSPEROUS.

2 *Chronicles* 32 : 23.

23 And many brought gifts unto the LORD to Jerusalem, and precious things to Hezekiah king of Judah : so that he was exalted in the sight of all nations from thenceforth.

(9) THE DEATH OF HEZEKIAH.

2 *Kings* 20 : 20, 21a.

20 Now the rest of the acts of Hezekiah, and all his might, and how he made the pool, and the conduit, and brought water into the city, are they not written in the book of the chronicles of the kings of Judah? 21a And Hezekiah slept with his fathers.

2 *Chronicles* 32 : 32, 33a.

32 Now the rest of the acts of Hezekiah, and his good deeds, behold, they are written in the vision of Isaiah the prophet the son of Amoz, in the book of the kings of Judah and Israel. 33a And Hezekiah slept with his fathers, and they buried him in the ascent of the sepulchres of the sons of David : and all Judah and the inhabitants of Jerusalem did him honour at his death.

176. THE REIGN OF MANASSEH.

(1) MANASSEH'S ACCESSION TO THE THRONE.

2 *Kings* 20 : 21b; 21 : 1.

21b And Manasseh his son reigned in his stead.

1 Manasseh was twelve years old when he began to reign ; and he reigned five and fifty years in Jerusalem : and his mother's name was Hephzi-bah.

2 *Chronicles* 32 : 33b; 33 : 1.

33b And Manasseh his son reigned in his stead.

1 Manasseh was twelve years old when he began to reign ; and he reigned fifty and five years in Jerusalem.

(2) MANASSEH'S EXCESSIVE IDOLATRIES.

2 *Kings* 21 : 2-9.

2 And he did that which was evil in the sight of the LORD, after the abominations of the heathen, whom the LORD cast out before the children of Israel. 3 For he built again the high places which Hezekiah his father had destroyed ; and he reared up altars for Baal, and made an Asherah, as did Ahab king of Israel, and worshipped all the host of heaven,

2 *Chronicles* 33 : 2-9.

2 And he did that which was evil in the sight of the LORD, after the abominations of the heathen, whom the LORD cast out before the children of Israel. 3 For he built again the high places which Hezekiah his father had broken down ; and he reared up altars for the Baalim, and made Asheroth, and worshipped all the hosts of heaven, and served them. 4 And he

2 *Kings* 21.	2 *Chronicles* 33.
and served them. 4 And he built altars in the house of the LORD, whereof the LORD said, In Jerusalem will I put my name. 5 And he built altars for all the host of heaven in the two courts of the house of the LORD. 6 And he made his son to pass through the fire, and practised augury, and used enchantments, and *a* dealt with them that had familiar spirits, and with wizards : he wrought much evil in the sight of the LORD, to provoke him to anger. 7 And he set the graven image of Asherah, that he had made, in the house of which the LORD said to David and to Solomon his son, In this house, and in Jerusalem, which I have chosen out of all the tribes of Israel, will I put my name for ever : 8 neither will I cause the feet of Israel to wander any more out of the land which I gave their fathers : if only they will observe to do according to all that I have commanded them, and according to all the law that my servant Moses commanded them. 9 But they hearkened not : and Manasseh seduced them to do that which is evil more than did the nations, whom the LORD destroyed before the children of Israel.	built altars in the house of the LORD, whereof the LORD said, In Jerusalem shall my name be for ever. 5 And he built altars for all the host of heaven in the two courts of the house of the LORD. 6 He also made his children to pass through the fire in the valley of the son of Hinnom : and he practised augury, and used enchantments, and practised sorcery, and dealt with them that had familiar spirits, and with wizards : he wrought much evil in the sight of the LORD, to provoke him to anger. 7 And he set the graven image of the idol, which he had made, in the house of God, of which God said to David and to Solomon his son, In this house, and in Jerusalem, which I have chosen out of all the tribes of Israel, will I put my name for ever : 8 neither will I any more remove the foot of Israel from off the land which I have appointed for your fathers ; if only they will observe to do all that I have commanded them, even all the law and the statutes and the ordinances by the hand of Moses. 9 And Manasseh made Judah and the inhabitants of Jerusalem to err, so that they did evil more than did the nations, whom the LORD destroyed before the children of Israel.

(3) THE DEATH OF SENNACHERIB.[b]

2 *Kings* 19 : 37*a*.	2 *Chronicles* 32 : 21*b*.
37*a* And it came to pass, as he was worshipping in the house of Nisroch his god, that *e* Adrammelech and Sharezer smote him with the sword : and they escaped into the land of Ararat.	21*b* And when he was come into the house of his god, they that came forth of his own bowels *d* slew him there with the sword.

(4) ACCESSION OF ESAR-HADDON AS KING OF ASSYRIA.[b]

2 *Kings* 19 : 37*b*.

37*b* And Esar-haddon his son reigned in his stead.

(5) JEHOVAH'S MESSAGE "BY HIS SERVANTS THE PROPHETS."

2 *Kings* 21 : 10–15.	2 *Chronicles* 33 : 10.
10 And the LORD spake by his servants the prophets, saying, 11 Because Manasseh king of Judah hath done these abominations, and hath done wickedly above all that the Amorites did, which were before him, and hath made Judah also to sin with his idols : 12 therefore thus	10 And the LORD spake to Manasseh, and to his people : but they gave no heed.

a Or, "appointed." Heb. "made ."   *b* Cf. Isaiah 37 : 38.   See Appendix, §7.   *c* According to another reading "Adrammelech and Sharezer his sons ;" and so in Isaiah 37 : 38.   *d* Heb. " caused him to fall."

2 Kings 21.

saith the LORD, the God of Israel, Behold, I bring such evil upon Jerusalem and Judah, that whosoever heareth of it, both his ears shall tingle. 13 And I will stretch over Jerusalem the line of Samaria, and the plummet of the house of Ahab: and I will wipe Jerusalem as a man wipeth a dish, wiping it and turning it-upside down. 14 And I will cast off the remnant of mine inheritance, and deliver them into the hand of their enemies; and they shall become a prey and a spoil to all their enemies; 15 because they have done that which is evil in my sight, and have provoked me to anger, since the day their fathers came forth out of Egypt, even unto this day.

(6) MANASSEH'S FURTHER CRIMES.

2 Kings 21 : 16.

16 Moreover Manasseh shed innocent blood very much, till he had filled Jerusalem from one end to another; beside his sin wherewith he made Judah to sin, in doing that which was evil in the sight of the LORD.

(7) MANASSEH'S CAPTIVITY.

2 Chronicles 33 : 11.

11 Wherefore the LORD brought upon them the captains of the host of the king of Assyria, which took Manasseh *a* in chains, and bound him with fetters, and carried him to Babylon.

(8) MANASSEH'S REPENTANCE AND RESTORATION.

2 Chronicles 33 : 12, 13.

12 And when he was in distress, he besought the LORD his God, and humbled himself greatly before the God of his fathers. 13 And he prayed unto him; and he was intreated of him, and heard his supplication, and brought him again to Jerusalem into his kingdom. Then Manasseh knew that the LORD he was God.

(9) THE ACTS OF MANASSEH AFTER HIS RESTORATION.

2 Chronicles 33 : 14-16.

14 Now after this he built an outer wall to the city of David, on the west side of Gihon, in the valley, even to the entering in at the fish gate; and he compassed about Ophel, and raised it up a very great height: and he put *b* valiant captains in all the fenced cities of Judah. 15 And he took away the strange gods, and the idol out of the house of the LORD, and all the altars that he had built in the mount of the house of the LORD, and in Jerusalem, and cast them out of the city. 16 And he *c* built up the altar of the LORD, and offered thereon sacrifices of peace offerings and of thanksgiving, and commanded Judah to serve the LORD, the God of Israel.

(10) SPIRITUAL CONDITION OF THE PEOPLE.

2 Chronicles 33 : 17.

17 Nevertheless the people did sacrifice still in the high places, but only unto the LORD their God.

---

a Or, "with hooks."   *b* Or, " captains of the army."   *c* According to another reading, " prepared."

(11) THE DEATH OF MANASSEH.

2 Kings 21 : 17, 18a.	2 Chronicles 33 : 18–20a.
17 Now the rest of the acts of Manasseh, and all that he did, and his sin that he sinned, are they not written in the book of the chronicles of the kings of Judah?	18 Now the rest of the acts of Manasseh, and his prayer unto his God, and the words of the seers that spake to him in the name of the LORD, the God of Israel, behold, they are written among the acts of the kings of Israel. 19 His prayer also, and how *God* was intreated of him, and all his sin and his trespass, and the places wherein he built high places, and set up the Asherim and the graven images, before he humbled himself : behold, they are written in the history of *a* Hozai. 20a So Manasseh slept with his fathers, and they buried him in his own house.
18a And Manasseh slept with his fathers and was buried in the garden of his own house, in the garden of Uzza.	

177. THE REIGN OF AMON.

(1) AMON'S ACCESSION TO THE THRONE.

2 Kings 21 : 18b, 19.	2 Chronicles 33 : 20b, 21.
18b And Amon his son reigned in his stead.	20b And Amon his son reigned in his stead.
19 Amon was twenty and two years old when he began to reign ; and he reigned two years in Jerusalem : and his mother's name was Me-shullemeth the daughter of Haruz of Jotbah.	21 Amon was twenty and two years old when he began to reign ; and he reigned two years in Jerusalem.

(2) THE CHARACTER OF AMON.

2 Kings 21 : 20-22.	2 Chronicles 33 : 22, 23.
20 And he did that which was evil in the sight of the LORD, as did Manasseh his father. 21 And he walked in all the way that his father walked in, and served the idols that his father served, and worshipped them : 22 and he forsook the LORD, the God of his fathers, and walked not in the way of the LORD.	22 And he did that which was evil in the sight of the LORD, as did Manasseh his father : and Amon sacrificed unto all the graven images which Manasseh his father had made, and served them. 23 And he humbled not himself before the LORD, as Manasseh his father had humbled himself ; but this same Amon *b* trespassed more and more.

(3) THE DEATH OF AMON.

2 Kings 21 : 25, 23, 26a.	2 Chronicles 33 : 24.
25 Now the rest of the acts of Amon which he did, are they not written in the book of the chronicles of the kings of Judah? 23 And the servants of Amon conspired against him, and put the king to death in his own house. 26a And he was buried in the sepulchre in the garden of Uzza.	24 And his servants conspired against him, and put him to death in his own house.

---

a Or, " the seers."   So the Sept.   *b* Or, " became guilty."

178. THE REIGN OF JOSIAH.

(1) JOSIAH'S ACCESSION TO THE THRONE.

2 *Kings* 21 : 24.	2 *Kings* 21 : 26b ; 22 : 1.	2 *Chronicles* 33 : 25 ; 34 : 1.
24 But the people of the land slew all them that had conspired against king Amon ; and the people of the land made Josiah his son king in his stead.	26b And Josiah his son reigned in his stead.	25 But the people of the land slew all them that had conspired against king Amon ; and the people of the land made Josiah his son king in his stead.
	1 Josiah was eight years old when he began to reign ; and he reigned thirty and one years in Jerusalem : and his mother's name was Jedidah the daughter of Adaiah of Bozkath.	1 Josiah was eight years old when he began to reign ; and he reigned thirty and one years in Jerusalem.

(2) JOSIAH'S GODLY CHARACTER.

2 *Kings* 22 : 2 ; 23 : 25.	2 *Chronicles* 34 : 2.
2 And he did that which was right in the eyes of the LORD, and walked in all the way of David his father, and turned not aside to the right hand or to the left. 25 And like unto him was there no king before him, that turned to the LORD with all his heart, and with all his soul, and with all his might, according to all the law of Moses ; neither after him arose there any like him.	2 And he did that which was right in the eyes of the LORD, and walked in the ways of David his father, and turned not aside to the right hand or to the left.

(3) JOSIAH'S LIFE AND CHARACTER NOT SUFFICIENT TO ATONE FOR JUDAH'S SINS.

2 *Kings* 23 : 26, 27.

26 Notwithstanding the LORD turned not from the fierceness of his great wrath, wherewith his anger was kindled against Judah, because of all the provocations that Manasseh had provoked him withal. 27 And the LORD said, I will remove Judah also out of my sight, as I have removed Israel, and I will cast off this city which I have chosen, even Jerusalem, and the house of which I said, My name shall be there.

(4) JOSIAH'S EARLY REFORMATIONS.

2 *Chronicles* 34 : 3–7.

3 For in the eighth year of his reign, while he was yet young, he began to seek after the God of David his father: and in the twelfth year he began to purge Judah and Jerusalem from the high places, and the Asherim, and the graven images, and the molten images. 4 And they brake down the altars of the Baalim in his presence ; and the sun-images, that were on high above them, he hewed down ; and the Asherim, and the graven images, and the molten images, he brake in pieces, and made dust of them, and strowed it upon the graves *of them* that had sacrificed unto them. 5 And he burnt the bones of the priests upon their altars, and purged Judah and Jerusalem. 6 And *so did he* in the cities of Manasseh and Ephraim and Simeon, even unto Naphtali, *a* in their ruins round about. 7 And he brake down the altars, and beat the Asherim and the graven images into powder, and hewed down all the sun-images throughout all the land of Israel, and returned to Jerusalem.

---

a Or, as otherwise read, "with their axes." The text is probably corrupt.

(5) THE REPAIRING OF THE TEMPLE.

2 *Kings* 22 : 3-7.

3 And it came to pass in the eighteenth year of king Josiah, that the king sent Shaphan the son of Azaliah, the son of Meshullam, the scribe, to the house of the LORD, saying, 4 Go up to Hilkiah the high priest, that he may sum the money which is brought into the house of the LORD, which the keepers of the *a* door have gathered of the people : 5 and let them deliver it into the hand of the workmen that have the oversight of the house of the LORD : and let them give it to the workmen which are in the house of the LORD, to repair the breaches of the house; 6 unto the carpenters, and to the builders, and to the masons ; and for buying timber and hewn stone to repair the house. 7 Howbeit there was no reckoning made with them of the money that was delivered into their hand ; for they dealt faithfully.

2 *Chronicles* 34 : 8-13.

8 Now in the eighteenth year of his reign, when he had purged the land, and the house, he sent Shaphan the son of Azaliah, and Maaseiah the governor of the city, and Joah the son of Joahaz the *b* recorder, to repair the house of the LORD his God. 9 And they came to Hilkiah the high priest, and delivered the money that was brought into the house of God, which the Levites, the keepers of the *a* door, had gathered of the hand of Manasseh and Ephraim, and of all the remnant of Israel, and of all Judah and Benjamin, *c* and of the inhabitants of Jerusalem. 10 And they delivered it into the hand of the workmen that had the oversight of the house of the LORD ; and *d* the workmen that wrought in the house of the LORD gave it to amend and repair the house ; 11 even to the carpenters and to the builders gave they it, to buy hewn stone, and timber for couplings, and to make beams for the houses which the kings of Judah had destroyed. 12 And the men did the work faithfully : and the overseers of them were Jahath and Obadiah, the Levites, of the sons of Merari ; and Zechariah and Meshullam, of the sons of the Kohathites, *e* to set it forward : and *other of* the Levites, all that could skill of instruments of music. 13 Also they were over the bearers of burdens, and set forward all that did the work in every manner of service ; and of the Levites there were scribes, and officers, and porters.

(6) THE BOOK OF THE LAW.

A. THE FINDING OF THE BOOK OF THE LAW.

2 *Kings* 22 :8.

8 And Hilkiah the high priest said unto Shaphan the scribe, I have found the book of the law in the house of the LORD. And Hilkiah delivered the book to Shaphan, and he read it.

2 *Chronicles* 34 :14, 15.

14 And when they brought out the money that was brought into the house of the LORD, Hilkiah the priest found the book of the law of the LORD *f* given by Moses. 15 And Hilkiah answered and said to Shaphan the scribe, I have found the book of the law in the house of the LORD. And Hilkiah delivered the book to Shaphan.

---

a Heb. " threshold."   *b* Or, " chronicler."   *c* Another reading is, " and they returned to Jerusalem."   *d* Or, " they gave it to the workmen," etc.   *e* Or, " to preside over it."   *f* Heb. " by the hand of."

B. THE EFFECT OF THE DISCOVERY ON JOSIAH.

2 Kings 22 : 9-13.

9 And Shaphan the scribe came to the king, and brought the king word again, and said, Thy servants have *a* emptied out the money that was found in the house, and have delivered it into the hand of the workmen that have the oversight of the house of the LORD. 10 And Shaphan the scribe told the king, saying, Hilkiah the priest hath delivered me a book. And Shaphan read it before the king. 11 And it came to pass, when the king had heard the words of the book of the law, that he rent his clothes. 12 And the king commanded Hilkiah the priest, and Ahikam the son of Shaphan, and Achbor the son of Micaiah, and Shaphan the scribe, and Asaiah the king's servant, saying, 13 Go ye, inquire of the LORD for me, and for the people, and for all Judah, concerning the words of this book that is found : for great is the wrath of the LORD that is kindled against us, because our fathers have not hearkened unto the words of this book, to do according unto all that which is *b* written concerning us.

2 Chronicles 34 : 16-21.

16 And Shaphan carried the book to the king, and moreover brought the king word again, saying, All that was committed to thy servants, they do it. 17 And they have *a* emptied out the money that was found in the house of the LORD, and have delivered it into the hand of the over-seers, and into the hand of the workmen. 18 And Shaphan the scribe told the king, saying, Hilkiah the priest hath delivered me a book. And Shaphan read therein before the king. 19 And it came to pass, when the king had heard the words of the law, that he rent his clothes. 20 And the king commanded Hilkiah, and Ahikam the son of Shaphan, and Abdon the son of Micah, and Shaphan the scribe, and Asaiah the king's servant, saying, 21 Go ye, inquire of the LORD for me, and for them that are left in Israel and in Judah, concerning the words of the book that is found : for great is the wrath of the LORD that is poured out upon us, because our fathers have not kept the word of the LORD, to do according unto all that is written in this book.

C. THE WORDS OF HULDAH THE PROPHETESS.

2 Kings 22 : 14-20.

14 So Hilkiah the priest, and Ahikam, and Achbor, and Shaphan, and Asaiah, went unto Huldah the prophetess, the wife of Shallum the son of Tikvah, the son of Harhas, keeper of the wardrobe ; (now she dwelt in Jerusalem in the *c* second quarter;) and they communed with her. 15 And she said unto them, Thus saith the LORD, the God of Israel : Tell ye the man that sent you unto me, 16 Thus saith the LORD, Behold I will bring evil upon this place, and upon the inhabitants thereof, even all the words of the book which the king of Judah hath read : 17 because they have forsaken me, and have burned incense unto other gods, that they might provoke me to anger with all the work of their hands ; therefore my wrath shall be kindled against this place, and it shall not be quenched. 18 But unto the king of Judah, who sent you to inquire of the LORD, thus shall ye say to him, Thus saith the LORD, the God of Israel : As touching

2 Chronicles 34 : 22-28.

22 So Hilkiah, and they whom the king *had commanded*, went to Huldah the prophetess, the wife of Shallum the son of Tokhath, the son of Hasrah, keeper of the wardrobe ; (now she dwelt in Jerusalem in the *c* second quarter;) and they spake to her to that effect. 23 And she said unto them, Thus saith the LORD, the God of Israel : Tell ye the man that sent you unto me, 24 Thus saith the LORD, Behold, I will bring evil upon this place, and upon the inhabitants thereof, even all the curses that are written in the book which they have read before the king of Judah : 25 because they have forsaken me, and have burned incense unto other gods, that they might provoke me to anger with all the works of their hands ; therefore is my wrath poured out upon this place, and it shall not be quenched. 26 But unto the king of Judah, who sent you to inquire of the LORD, thus shall ye say to him, Thus saith the LORD, the God of Israel : As touching

---

a Or, " poured out."   *b* Or, " enjoined us."   *c* Heb. " Mishneh."

2 *Kings* 22.	2 *Chronicles* 34.
the words which thou hast heard, 19 because thine heart was tender, and thou didst humble thyself before the LORD, when thou heardest what I spake against this place, and against the inhabitants thereof, that they should become *a* a desolation and a curse, and hast rent thy clothes, and wept before me ; I also have heard thee, saith the LORD. 20 Therefore, behold, I will gather thee to thy fathers, and thou shalt be gathered to thy grave in peace, neither shall thine eyes see all the evil which I will bring upon this place. And they brought the king word again.	the words which thou hast heard, 27 because thine heart was tender, and thou didst humble thyself before God, when thou heardest his words against this place, and against the inhabitants thereof, and hast humbled thyself before me, and hast rent thy clothes, and wept before me ; I also have heard thee, saith the LORD. 28 Behold, I will gather thee to thy fathers, and thou shalt be gathered to thy grave in peace, neither shall thine eyes see all the evil that I will bring upon this place, and upon the inhabitants thereof. And they brought the king word again.

D. THE READING OF THE BOOK OF THE LAW.

2 *Kings* 23 : 1, 2.	2 *Chronicles* 34 : 29, 30.
1 And the king sent, and they gathered unto him all the elders of Judah and of Jerusalem. 2 And the king went up to the house of the LORD, and all the men of Judah and all the inhabitants of Jerusalem with him, and the priests, and the prophets, and all the people, both small and great : and he read in their ears all the words of the book of the covenant which was found in the house of the LORD.	29 Then the king sent and gathered together all the elders of Judah and Jerusalem. 30 And the king went up to the house of the LORD, and all the men of Judah and the inhabitants of Jerusalem, and the priests, and the Levites, and all the people, both great and small : and he read in their ears all the words of the book of the covenant that was found in the house of the LORD.

(7) THE MAKING OF THE COVENANT.

2 *Kings* 23 : 3.	2 *Chronicles* 34 : 31, 32.
3 And the king stood *b* by the pillar, and made a covenant before the LORD, to walk after the LORD, and to keep his commandments, and his testimonies, and his statutes, with all *his* heart, and all *his* soul, to *c* confirm the words of this covenant that were written in this book : and all the people stood to the covenant.	31 And the king stood in his place, and made a covenant before the LORD, to walk after the LORD, and to keep his commandments, and his testimonies, and his statutes, with all his heart, and with all his soul, to perform the words of the covenant that were written in this book. 32 And he caused all that were found in Jerusalem and Benjamin to stand *to it.* And the inhabitants of Jerusalem did according to the covenant of God, the God of their fathers.

(8) JOSIAH'S FURTHER REFORMATIONS.

2 *Kings* 23 : 4-14, 24.	2 *Chronicles* 34 : 33.
4 And the king commanded Hilkiah the high priest, and the priests of the second order, and the keepers of the *d* door, to bring forth out of the temple of the LORD all the vessels that were made for Baal, and for the Asherah, and for all the host of heaven : and he burned them with-	33 And Josiah took away all the abominations out of all the countries that pertained to the children of Israel, and made all that were found in Israel to serve, even to serve the LORD their God. All his days they departed not from following the LORD, the God of their fathers.

---

a Or, " an astonishment."   *b* Or, " on the platform."   *c* Or, " perform."   *d* Heb. " threshold."

2 *Kings* 23.

out Jerusalem in the fields of Kidron, and carried the ashes of them unto Beth-el. 5 And he put down the ^a idolatrous priests, whom the kings of Judah had ordained to burn incense in the high places in the cities of Judah, and in the places round about Jerusalem ; them also that burned incense unto Baal, to the sun, and to the moon, and to the ^b planets, and to all the host of heaven. 6 And he brought out the Asherah from the house of the LORD, without Jerusalem, unto the brook Kidron, and burned it at the brook Kidron, and stamped it small to powder, and cast the powder thereof upon the graves of the ^c common people. 7 And he brake down the houses of the ^d sodomites, that were in the house of the LORD, where the women wove ^e hangings for the Asherah. 8 And he brought all the priests out of the cities of Judah, and defiled the high places where the priests had burned incense, from Geba to Beer-sheba ; and he brake down the high places of the gates that were at the entering in of the gate of Joshua the governor of the city, which were on a man's left hand at the gate of the city. 9 Nevertheless the priests of the high places came not up to the altar of the LORD in Jerusalem, but they did eat unleavened bread among their brethren. 10 And he defiled Topheth, which is in the valley of the ^f children of Hinnom, that no man might make his son or his daughter to pass through the fire to Molech. 11 And he took away the horses that the kings of Judah had given to the sun, at the entering in of the house of the LORD, by the chamber of Nathan-melech the chamberlain, which was in the precincts ; and he burned the chariots of the sun with fire. 12 And the altars that were on the roof of the upper chamber of Ahaz, which the kings of Judah had made, and the altars which Manasseh had made in the two courts of the house of the LORD, did the king break down, and ^g beat *them* down from thence, and cast the dust of them into the brook Kidron. 13 And the high places that were before Jerusalem, which were on the right hand of the mount of ^h corruption, which Solomon the king of Israel had builded for Ashtoreth the abomination of the Zidonians, and for Chemosh the abomination of Moab, and for Milcom the abomination of the children of Ammon, did the king defile. 14 And

---

^a Heb. "Chemarim."   See Hosea 10 : 5 and Zephaniah 1 : 4.   ^b Or, "twelve signs."   ^c Heb. "children of the people." ^d Cf. 1 Kings 14 : 24 and 15 : 12. See §§141, (6), and 144, (7), *B*.   ^e Or, "tents."   Heb. "houses."   ^f According to another reading, "son."   ^g Or, "ran from thence."   ^h Or, "destruction."

2 *Kings* 23.

he brake in pieces the *a* pillars, and cut down the Asherim, and filled their places with the bones of men.

24 Moreover them that had familiar spirits, and the wizards, and the teraphim, and the idols, and all the abominations that were spied in the land of Judah and in Jerusalem, did Josiah put away, that he might *b* confirm the words of the law which were written in the book that Hilkiah the priest found in the house of the LORD.

(9) The Fulfillment of the Prophecy of the "Man of God out of Judah." *c*

2 *Kings* 23 : 15–20.

15 Moreover the altar that was at Beth-el, and the high place which Jeroboam the son of Nebat, who made Israel to sin, had made, even that altar and the high place he brake down; and he burned the high place and stamped it small to powder, and burned the Asherah. 16 And as Josiah turned himself, he spied the sepulchres that were there in the mount; and he sent, and took the bones out of the sepulchres, and burned them upon the altar, and defiled it, according to the word of the LORD which the man of God proclaimed, who proclaimed these things. 17 Then he said, What monument is that which I see? And the men of the city told him, It is the sepulchre of the man of God, which came from Judah, and proclaimed these things that thou hast done against the altar of Beth-el. 18 And he said, Let him be; let no man move his bones. So they let his bones alone, with the bones of the prophet that came out of Samaria. 19 And all the houses also of the high places that were in the cities of Samaria, which the kings of Israel had made to provoke *the LORD* to anger, Josiah took away, and did to them according to all the acts that he had done in Beth-el. 20 And he *d* slew all the priests of the high places that were there, upon the altars, and burned men's bones upon them; and he returned to Jerusalem.

(10) The Keeping of the Passover.

2 *Kings* 23 : 21–23.	2 *Chronicles* 35 : 1–19.
21 And the king commanded all the people, saying, Keep the passover unto the LORD your God, as it is written in this book of the covenant.	1 And Josiah kept a passover unto the LORD in Jerusalem: and they killed the passover on the fourteenth *day* of the first month. 2 And he set the priests in their charges, and encouraged them to the service of the house of the LORD. 3 And he said unto the Levites that taught all Israel, which were holy unto the LORD, Put the holy ark in the house which Solomon the son of David king of Israel did build; there shall no more be a burden upon your shoulders: now serve the LORD your God, and his people Israel. 4 And prepare yourselves after your fathers' houses by your courses, according to the writing of David king of Israel, and according to the writing of Solomon his son. 5 And stand in the holy place according to the divisions of the fathers' houses of your brethren the children of the people, *e* and *let there be for each* a portion

a Or, "obelisks." *b* Or, "perform." *c* Cf. 1 Kings 13 : 1–3. See §142, (3), *A*. *d* Or, "sacrificed." *e* Or, "and *according to* the distribution of each fathers' house."

2 *Kings* 23.	2 *Chronicles* 35.
	of a fathers' house of the Levites. 6 And kill the passover, and sanctify yourselves, and prepare for your brethren, to do according to the word of the LORD by the hand of Moses. 7 And Josiah *a* gave to the children of the people, of the flock, lambs and kids, all of them for the passover offerings, unto all that were present, to the number of thirty thousand, and three thousand bullocks: these were of the king's substance. 8 And his princes gave *b* for a freewill offering unto the people, to the priests, and to the Levites. Hilkiah and Zechariah and Jehiel, the rulers of the house of God, gave unto the priests for the passover offerings two thousand and six hundred *small cattle*, and three hundred oxen. 9 Conaniah also, and Shemaiah and Nethanel, his brethren, and Hashabiah and Jeiel and Jozabad, the chiefs of the Levites, gave unto the Levites for the passover offerings five thousand *small cattle*, and five hundred oxen. 10 So the service was prepared, and the priests stood in their place, and the Levites by their courses, according to the king's commandment. 11 And they killed the passover, and the priests sprinkled *the blood, which they received* of their hand, and the Levites flayed them. 12 And they removed the burnt offerings, that they might give them according to the divisions of the fathers' houses of the children of the people, to offer unto the LORD, as it is written in the book of Moses. And so did they with the oxen. 13 And they roasted the passover with fire according to the ordinance: and the holy offerings sod they in pots, and in caldrons, and in pans, and carried them quickly to all the children of the people. 14 And afterward they prepared for themselves, and for the priests; because the priests the sons of Aaron *were busied* in offering the burnt offerings and the fat until night: therefore the Levites prepared for themselves, and for the priests the sons of Aaron. 15 And the singers the sons of Asaph were in their place, according to the commandment of David, and Asaph, and Heman, and Jeduthun the king's seer; and the porters were at every gate: they needed not to depart from their service, for their brethren the Levites prepared for them. 16 So all the service of the LORD was prepared the same day, to keep the passover, and to offer burnt offerings upon the altar of the LORD, according to the commandment of king

---

a Or, " gave for offerings," and so in vv. 8 and 9.   Cf. 2 Chronicles 30 : 24.   See §173, (5), *C*.   *b* Or. " willingly."

2 *Kings* 23.	2 *Chronicles* 35.
	Josiah. 17 And the children of Israel that were present kept the passover at that time, and the feast of unleavened bread seven days. 18 And there was no passover like to that kept in Israel from the days of Samuel the prophet ; neither
22 Surely there was not kept such a passover from the days of the judges that judged Israel, *a* nor in all the days of the kings of Israel, nor of the kings of Judah ; 23 but in the eighteenth year of king Josiah was this passover kept to the LORD in Jerusalem.	did any of the kings of Israel keep such a pass-over as Josiah kept, and the priests, and the Levites, and all Judah and Israel that were pres-ent, and the inhabitants of Jerusalem. 19 In the eighteenth year of the reign of Josiah was this passover kept.

(11) THE DEATH OF JOSIAH.

2 *Kings* 23 : 28–30*a*.	2 *Chronicles* 35 : 26, 27, 20–25.
28 Now the rest of the acts of Josiah, and all that he did, are they not written in the book of the chronicles of the kings of Judah ?	26 Now the rest of the acts of Josiah, and his good deeds, according to that which is written in the law of the LORD, 27 and his acts, first and last, behold, they are written in the book of the kings of Israel and Judah.
29 In his days Pharaoh-necoh king of Egypt went up against the king of Assyria to the river Euphrates : and king Josiah went against him ; and he slew him at Megiddo, when he had seen him. 30*a* And his servants carried him in a chariot dead from Megiddo, and brought him to Jerusalem, and buried him in his own sepulchre.	20 After all this, when Josiah had prepared the temple, Neco king of Egypt went up to fight against Carchemish by Euphrates : and Josiah went out against him. 21 But he sent ambassa-dors to him, saying, What have I to do with thee, thou king of Judah ? *I come* not against thee this day, but against the house wherewith I have war ; and God *b* hath commanded me to make haste : forbear thee from *meddling with* God, who is with me, that he destroy thee not. 22 Nevertheless Josiah would not turn his face from him, but disguised himself, that he might fight with him, and hearkened not unto the words of Neco, from the mouth of God, and came to fight in the valley of Megiddo. 23 And the archers shot at king Josiah ; and the king said to his servants, Have me away ; for I am sore wounded. 24 So his servants took him out of the chariot, and put him in the second chariot that he had, and brought him to Jerusalem ; and he died, and was buried in the sepulchres of his fathers. And all Judah and Jerusalem mourned for Josiah. 25 And Jeremiah lamented for Josiah : and all the singing men and singing women spake of Josiah in their lamentations, unto this day ; and they made them an ordinance in Is-rael : and, behold, they are written in the lam-entations.

a Or, " even in all . . . and of."   *b* Or, " hath given command to speed me."

179. THE REIGN OF JEHOAHAZ.

(1) THE ACCESSION OF JEHOAHAZ.

2 Kings 23 : 30*b*, 31.	*2 Chronicles* 36 : 1, 2.
30*b* And the people of the land took Jehoahaz the son of Josiah, and anointed him, and made him king in his father's stead.	1 Then the people of the land took Jehoahaz the son of Josiah, and made him king in his father's stead in Jerusalem.
31 Jehoahaz was twenty and three years old when he began to reign ; and he reigned three months in Jerusalem : and his mother's name was Hamutal the daughter of Jeremiah of Libnah.	2 Joahaz was twenty and three years old when he began to reign ; and he reigned three months in Jerusalem.

(2) THE CHARACTER OF JEHOAHAZ.

2 Kings 23 : 32.

32 And he did that which was evil in the sight of the LORD, according to all that his fathers had done.

(3) JEHOAHAZ IS DEPOSED BY PHARAOH-NECOH.

2 Kings 23 : 33.	*2 Chronicles* 36 : 3.
33 And Pharaoh-necoh put him in bands at Riblah in the land of Hamath, *a* that he might not reign in Jerusalem ; and put the land to a *b* tribute of an hundred talents of silver, and a talent of gold.	3 And the king of Egypt deposed him at Jerusalem, and amerced the land in an hundred talents of silver and a talent of gold.

180. THE REIGN OF JEHOIAKIM.

(1) JEHOIAKIM IS MADE KING BY PHARAOH-NECOH.

2 Kings 23 : 34*a*, 36.	*2 Chronicles* 36 : 4*a*, 5*a*.
34*a* And Pharaoh-necoh made Eliakim the son of Josiah king in the room of Josiah his father, and changed his name to Jehoiakim.	4*a* And the king of Egypt made Eliakim his brother king over Judah and Jerusalem, and changed his name to Jehoiakim.
36 Jehoiakim was twenty and five years old when he began to reign ; and he reigned eleven years in Jerusalem : and his mother's name was Zebidah the daughter of Pedaiah of Rumah.	5*a* Jehoiakim was twenty and five years old when he began to reign ; and he reigned eleven years in Jerusalem.

(2) THE CAPTIVITY OF JEHOAHAZ.

2 Kings 23 : 34*b*.	*2 Chronicles* 36 : 4*b*.
34*b* But he took Jehoahaz away ; and he came to Egypt, and died there.	4*b* And Neco took Joahaz his brother, and carried him to Egypt.

(3) THE CHARACTER OF JEHOIAKIM.

2 Kings 23 : 37.	*2 Chronicles* 36 : 5*b*.
37 And he did that which was evil in the sight of the LORD, according to all that his fathers had done.	5*b* And he did that which was evil in the sight of the LORD his God.

a According to another reading, " when he reigned."   *b* Or, " fine."

(4) JEHOIAKIM TRIBUTARY TO PHARAOH-NECOH.

2 *Kings* 23 : 35.

35 And Jehoiakim gave the silver and the gold to Pharaoh ; but he taxed the land to give the money according to the commandment of Pharaoh : he exacted the silver and the gold of the people of the land, of every one according to his taxation, to give it unto Pharaoh-necoh.

(5) JEHOIAKIM TRIBUTARY TO NEBUCHADNEZZAR.

2 *Kings* 24 : 1a, 7.	2 *Chronicles* 36 : 6, 7.
1a In his days Nebuchadnezzar king of Babylon came up, and Jehoiakim became his servant three years.	6 Against him came up Nebuchadnezzar king of Babylon, and bound him in fetters, to carry him to Babylon. 7 Nebuchadnezzar also carried of the vessels of the house of the LORD to Babylon, and put them in his *a* temple at Babylon.
7 And the king of Egypt came not again any more out of his land : for the king of Babylon had taken, from the brook of Egypt unto the river Euphrates, all that pertained to the king of Egypt.	

(6) JEHOIAKIM'S REBELLION.

2 *Kings* 24 : 1b.

1b Then he turned and rebelled against him.

(7) JEHOIAKIM'S MANY ADVERSARIES.

2 *Kings* 24 : 2-4.

2 And the LORD sent against him bands of the Chaldeans, and bands of the Syrians, and bands of the Moabites, and bands of the children of Ammon, and sent them against Judah to destroy it, according to the word of the LORD, which he spake by the hand of his servants the prophets. 3 Surely at the commandment of the LORD came this upon Judah, to remove the mout of his sight, for the sins of Manasseh, according to all that he did ; 4 and also for the innocent blood that he shed ; for he filled Jerusalem with innocent blood : and the LORD would not pardon.

(8) THE DEATH OF JEHOIAKIM.

2 *Kings* 24 : 5, 6a.	2 *Chronicles* 36 : 8a.
5 Now the rest of the acts of Jehoiakim, and all that he did, are they not written in the book of the chronicles of the kings of Judah ? 6a So Jehoiakim slept with his fathers.	8a Now the rest of the acts of Jehoiakim, and his abominations which he did, and that which was found *b* in him, behold, they are written in the book of the kings of Israel and Judah.

181. THE REIGN OF JEHOIACHIN.

(1) JEHOIACHIN'S ACCESSION TO THE THRONE.

2 *Kings* 24 : 6b, 8.	2 *Chronicles* 36 : 8b, 9a.
6b And Jehoiachin his son reigned in his stead.	8b And *c* Jehoiachin his son reigned in his stead.
8 Jehoiachin was eighteen years old when he began to reign ; and he reigned in Jerusalem three months : and his mother's name was Nehushta the daughter of Elnathan of Jerusalem.	9a Jehoiachin was eight years old when he began to reign ; and he reigned three months and ten days in Jerusalem.

---

a Or, " palace."   *b* Or, " against."   *c* In Jeremiah 22 : 24, " Coniah." In 1 Chronicles 3 : 16, " Jeconiah." See §7, (3).

(2) The Character of Jehoiachin.

2 *Kings* 24:9.	2 *Chronicles* 36:9*b*.
9 And he did that which was evil in the sight of the LORD, according to all that his father had done.	9*b* And he did that which was evil in the sight of the LORD.

(3) Jehoiachin is taken Captive by Nebuchadnezzar.

2 *Kings* 24:10-12.

10 At that time the servants of Nebuchadnezzar king of Babylon came up to Jerusalem, and the city was besieged. 11 And Nebuchadnezzar king of Babylon came unto the city, while his servants were besieging it; 12 and Jehoiachin the king of Judah went out to the king of Babylon, he, and his mother, and his servants, and his princes, and his *a* officers: and the king of Babylon took him in the eighth year of his reign.

182. THE REIGN OF ZEDEKIAH.*b*

(1) Zedekiah is made King by Nebuchadnezzar.

2 *Kings* 24:17, 18.	2 *Chronicles* 36:10*b*, 11.
17 And the king of Babylon made Mattaniah his father's brother king in his stead, and changed his name to Zedekiah.	10*b* And [Nebuchadnezzar] made Zedekiah his brother king over Judah and Jerusalem.
18 Zedekiah was twenty and one years old when he began to reign; and he reigned eleven years in Jerusalem: and his mother's name was *c* Hamutal the daughter of Jeremiah of Libnah.	11 Zedekiah was twenty and one years old when he began to reign; and he reigned eleven years in Jerusalem.

(2) The great Deportation to Babylon.

2 *Kings* 24:13-16.	2 *Chronicles* 36:10*a*.
13 And he carried out thence all the treasures of the house of the LORD, and the treasures of the king's house, and cut in pieces all the vessels of gold which Solomon king of Israel had made in the temple of the LORD, as the LORD had said. 14 And he carried away all Jerusalem, and all the princes, and all the mighty men of valour, even ten thousand captives, and all the craftsmen and the smiths; none remained, save the poorest sort of the people of the land. 15 And he carried away Jehoiachin to Babylon; and the king's mother, and the king's wives, and his *a* officers, and the *d* chief men of the land, carried he into captivity from Jerusalem to Babylon. 16 And all the men of might, even seven thousand, and the craftsmen and the smiths a thousand, all of them strong and apt for war, even them the king of Babylon brought captive to Babylon.	10*a* And *e* at the return of the year king Nebuchadnezzar sent, and brought him to Babylon, with the goodly vessels of the house of the LORD.

---

a Or, " eunuchs."   *b* Cf. Jeremiah 39 and 52.   See Appendix, §8.   *c* Heb. " Hamital."   *d* Or, " mighty."   *e* Cf.
2 Samuel 11:1.   See §84, (1).

(3) The Character of Zedekiah.

2 *Kings* 24 : 19.	2 *Chronicles* 36 : 12.
19 And he did that which was evil in the sight of the LORD, according to all that Jehoiakim had done.	12 And he did that which was evil in the sight of the LORD his God; he humbled not himself before Jeremiah the prophet *speaking* from the mouth of the LORD.

(4) Zedekiah's Rebellion.

2 *Kings* 24 . 20*b*.	2 *Chronicles* 36 : 13*a*.
20*b* And Zedekiah rebelled against the king of Babylon.	13*a* And he also rebelled against king Nebuchadnezzar, who had made him swear by God.

(5) The Wickedness of the People the Cause of their Ruin.

2 *Kings* 24 : 20*a*.	2 *Chronicles* 36 : 13*b*-16.
20*a* For through the anger of the LORD did it come to pass in Jerusalem and Judah, until he had cast them out from his presence.	13*b* But he stiffened his neck, and *a* hardened his heart from turning unto the LORD, the God of Israel. 14 Moreover all the chiefs of the priests, and the people, trespassed very greatly after all the abominations of the heathen; and they polluted the house of the LORD which he had hallowed in Jerusalem. 15 And the LORD, the God of their fathers, sent to them by his messengers, rising up early and sending; because he had compassion on his people, and on his dwelling place: 16 but they mocked the messengers of God, and despised his words, and scoffed at his prophets, until the wrath of the LORD arose against his people, till there was no *b* remedy.

(6) The Siege of Jerusalem.

2 *Kings* 25 : 1, 2.

1 And it came to pass in the ninth year of his reign, in the tenth month, in the tenth day of the month, that Nebuchadnezzar king of Babylon came, he and all his army, against Jerusalem, and encamped against it; and they built forts against it round about. 2 So the city was besieged unto the eleventh year of king Zedekiah.

(7) Zedekiah is taken Captive by Nebuchadnezzar.

2 *Kings* 25 : 3-7.

3 On the ninth day of the *fourth* month the famine was sore in the city, so that there was no bread for the people of the land. 4 Then a breach was made in the city, and all the men of war *fled* by night by the way of the gate between the two walls, which was by the king's garden: (now the Chaldeans were against the city round about:) and *the king* went by the way of the Arabah. 5 But the army of the Chaldeans pursued after the king, and overtook him in the plains of Jericho: and all his army was scattered from him. 6 Then they took the king, and carried him up unto the king of Babylon to Riblah; and they *c* gave judgement upon him. 7 And they slew the sons of Zedekiah before his eyes, and put out the eyes of Zedekiah, and bound him in fetters, and carried him to Babylon.

---

a Heb. "strengthened."   *b* Heb. "healing."   *c* Or, "spake with him of judgement."

183. APPENDIX TO THE HISTORY OF THE KINGDOM OF JUDAH.[a]

(1) THE OVERTHROW OF JERUSALEM.

2 *Kings* 25 : 8-10.

8 Now in the fifth month, on the seventh day of the month, which was the nineteenth year of king Nebuchadnezzar, king of Babylon, came Nebuzaradan the captain of the guard, a servant of the king of Babylon, unto Jerusalem : 9 and he burnt the house of the LORD, and the king's house; and all the houses of Jerusalem, even every great house, burnt he with fire. 10 And all the army of the Chaldeans, that were *with* the captain of the guard, brake down the walls of Jerusalem round about.

2 *Chronicles* 36 : 17, 19.

17 Therefore he brought upon them the king of the Chaldeans, who slew their young men with the sword in the house of their sanctuary, and had no compassion upon young man or maiden, old man or ancient : he gave them all into his hand. 19 And they burnt the house of God, and brake down the wall of Jerusalem, and burnt all the palaces thereof with fire, and destroyed all the goodly vessels thereof.

(2) THE REMAINING NOBLES SLAIN.

2 *Kings* 25 : 18-21a.

18 And the captain of the guard took Seraiah the chief priest, and Zephaniah the second priest, and the three keepers of the [b]door : 19 and out of the city he took an [c]officer that was set over the men of war; and five men of them that saw the king's face, which were found in the city ; and the [d]scribe, the captain of the host, which mustered the people of the land ; and three-score men of the people of the land, that were found in the city. 20 And Nebuzaradan 'the captain of the guard took them, and brought them to the king of Babylon to Riblah. 21a And the king of Babylon smote them,' and put them to death at Riblah in the land of Hamath.

(3) THE TREASURE TAKEN BY THE CHALDEANS.

2 *Kings* 25 : 13-17.

13 And the pillars of brass that were in the house of the LORD, and the bases and the brasen sea that were in the house of the LORD, did the Chaldeans break in pieces, and carried the brass of them to Babylon. 14 And the pots, and the shovels, and the snuffers, and the spoons, and all the vessels of brass wherewith they ministered, took they away. 15 And the firepans, and the basons ; that which was of gold, in gold, and that which was of silver, in silver, the captain of the guard took away. 16 The two pillars, the one sea, and the bases, which Solomon had made for the house of the LORD ; the brass of all these vessels was without weight. 17 The height of the one pillar was eighteen cubits, and a chapiter of brass was upon it : and the height of the chapiter was three cubits ; with network and pomegranates upon the chapiter round about, all of brass : and like unto these had the second pillar with network.

2 *Chronicles* 36 : 18.

18 And all the vessels of the house of God, great and small, and the treasures of the house of the LORD, and the treasures of the king, and of his princes ; all these he brought to Babylon.

---

a Cf. Jeremiah 39 : 2, etc., and 52 : 12, etc. See Appendix, §8.   *b* Heb. "threshold."   *c* Or, "eunuch."   *d* Or, "scribe of the captain of the host."

(4) The last Deportation to Babylon. [a]

2 *Kings* 25 : 11.	2 *Chronicles* 36 : 20a.
11 And the residue of the people that were left in the city, and those that fell away, that fell to the king of Babylon, and the residue of the multitude, did Nebuzaradan the captain of the guard carry away captive.	20a And them that had escaped from the sword carried he away to Babylon.

2 *Kings* 25 : 21b.	1 *Chronicles* 9 : 1b.
21b So Judah was carried away captive out of his land.	1b And Judah was carried away captive to Babylon for their transgression.

(5) The Length of the Captivity.

2 *Chronicles* 36 : 20b, 21.

20b And they were servants to him and his sons until the reign of the kingdom of Persia : 21 to fulfil the word of the LORD by the mouth of Jeremiah, until the land had enjoyed her sabbaths : *for* as long as she lay desolate she kept sabbath, to fulfil threescore and ten years.

(6) Gedaliah is made Governor of Judah.

2 *Kings* 25 : 12, 22.

12 But the captain of the guard left of the poorest of the land to be vinedressers and husbandmen. 22 And as for the people that were left in the land of Judah, whom Nebuchadnezzar king of Babylon had left, even over them he made Gedaliah the son of Ahikam, the son of Shaphan, governor.

(7) The Murder of Gedaliah and Flight of the People.

2 *Kings* 25 : 23–26.

23 Now when all the captains of the forces, they and their men, heard that the king of Babylon had made Gedaliah governor, they came to Gedaliah to Mizpah, even Ishmael the son of Nethaniah, and Johanan the son of Kareah, and Seraiah the son of Tanhumeth the Netophathite, and Jaazaniah the son of the Maacathite, they and their men. 24 And Gedaliah sware to them and to their men, and said unto them, Fear not because of the servants of the Chaldeans : dwell in the land, and serve the king of Babylon, and it shall be well with you. 25 But it came to pass in the seventh month, that Ishmael the son of Nethaniah, the son of Elishama, of the seed royal, came, and ten men with him, and smote Gedaliah, that he died, and the Jews and the Chaldeans that were with him at Mizpah. 26 And all the people, both small and great, and the captains of the forces, arose, and came to Egypt : for they were afraid of the Chaldeans.

(8) Jehoiachin is set at Liberty.

2 *Kings* 25 : 27–30.

27 And it came to pass in the seven and thirtieth year of the captivity of Jehoiachin king of Judah, in the twelfth month, on the seven and twentieth day of the month, that Evil-merodach king of Babylon, in the year that he began to reign, did lift up the head of Jehoiachin king of Judah out of prison ; 28 and he spake kindly to him, and set his throne above the throne of the

---

a I. e., the last deportation mentioned in Kings and Chronicles. For a further deportation, that occurred four years later, see Jeremiah 52 :30.

2 *Kings* 25.

kings that were with him in Babylon. 29 And he changed his prison garments, and did eat bread before him continually all the days of his life. 30 And for his allowance, there was a continual allowance given him of the king, every day a portion, all the days of his life.

(9) THE PROCLAMATION OF CYRUS PERMITTING THE RETURN FROM THE CAPTIVITY. [a]

2 *Chronicles* 36 : 22, 23.

22 Now in the first year of [b] Cyrus king of Persia, that the word of the LORD by the mouth of Jeremiah might be accomplished, the LORD stirred up the spirit of Cyrus king of Persia, that he made a proclamation throughout all his kingdom, and *put it* also in writing, saying, 23 Thus saith Cyrus king of Persia, All the kingdoms of the earth hath the LORD, the God of heaven, given me ; and he hath charged me to build him an house in Jerusalem, which is in Judah. Whosoever there is among you of all his people, the LORD his God be with him, and let him go up.

---

[a] Cf. Ezra 1 : 1-4. See Appendix, §4.   [b] Heb. "Coresh."

APPENDIX.

Table of Passages from various Books of the Bible parallel with certain Sections of the Harmony.

I. FROM GENESIS.

§1. The Genealogy from Adam to Noah.
    Genesis 5 : 1–32.   [Luke 3 : 36–38.]   1 Chronicles 1 : 1–4.

§2. The Descendants of Noah's Sons.
    Genesis 10 : 1–32.   1 Chronicles 1 : 5–23.

§3. From Shem to Abraham.
    Genesis 11 : 10–26.   [Luke 3 : 34–36.]   1 Chronicles 1 : 24–27.

§4. The Descendants of Abraham.
    Genesis 25 : 12–16.   1 Chronicles 1 : 28–31.
    Genesis 25 : 1–4.   1 Chronicles 1 : 32, 33.
    Genesis 36 : 1–30.   1 Chronicles 1 : 35–42.

§5. The Kings and Dukes of Edom.
    Genesis 36 : 31–43.   1 Chronicles 1 : 43–54.

§6. The twelve Sons of Israel.
    Genesis 29 : 31–30 : 24 ; 35 : 16–18.   1 Chronicles 2 : 1, 2.

§7, (1). General Genealogies of the Tribe of Judah.
    Genesis 38 : 1–30. Genesis 46 : 12. 1 Chronicles 2 : 3–5. 1 Chronicles 4 : 1.

§8, (1). The Line of Aaron.
    Genesis 46 : 11.   1 Chronicles 6 : 1.

§9. The Tribe of Reuben.
    Genesis 46 : 8, 9.   1 Chronicles 5 : 1–10.

§10. The Tribe of Gad.
    Genesis 46 : 16.   1 Chronicles 5 : 11–17.

§12. The Tribe of Simeon.
    Genesis 46 : 10.   1 Chronicles 4 : 24–43.

§13. The Tribe of Issachar.
    Genesis 46 : 13.   1 Chronicles 7 : 1–5.

§14. The Tribe of Naphtali.
    Genesis 46 : 24.   1 Chronicles 7 : 13.

§17. The Tribe of Asher.
    Genesis 46 : 17.   1 Chronicles 7 : 30–40.

§18, (1). General Genealogies of the Tribe of Benjamin.
    Genesis 46 : 21.   1 Chronicles 7 : 6–12. 1 Chronicles 8 : 1–28.

II. FROM JOSHUA.

§8, (4). The Cities of the Levites.
    Joshua 21 : 1–42.   1 Chronicles 6 : 54–81.

III. FROM RUTH.

§7, (1). General Genealogies of the Tribe of Judah.
    Ruth 4 : 18–22.   [Matthew 1 : 3–6.]   [Luke 3 : 31–33.]   1 Chronicles 2 : 5–14.

IV. FROM EZRA.

§183, (9). The Proclamation of Cyrus permitting the Return from the Captivity.
    Ezra 1 : 1–4.   2 Chronicles 36 : 22, 23.

V. FROM NEHEMIAH.

§19, (2). The Inhabitants of Jerusalem.
    Nehemiah 11 : 1–19.   1 Chronicles 9 : 2–34.

VI. FROM THE PSALMS.

§93. David's Song of Thanksgiving.
    Psalm 18 : 1–50.   2 Samuel 22 : 1–51.

§94, (3). David's Hymn of Praise.
    Psalm 105 : 1–15.   1 Chronicles 16 : 8–22.
    Psalm 96 : 1–13.   1 Chronicles 16 : 23–33.
    Psalm 106 : 1. Psalm 107 : 1. Psalm 118 : 1. Psalm 136 : 1. 1 Chronicles 16 : 34.
    Psalm 106 : 47, 48.   1 Chronicles 16 : 35, 36.

VII. FROM ISAIAH.

§171, (3). The War between Ahaz and Rezin and Pekah.
    Isaiah 7 : 1, 2.   2 Kings 16 : 5, 6.   2 Chronicles 28 : 5–8.

§175, (3). Sennacherib's first Invasion of Judah.
    Isaiah 36 : 1.   2 Kings 18 : 13–16.

§175, (4). Hezekiah's Illness and Recovery.
    Isaiah 38 : 1–22.   2 Kings 20 : 1–11.   2 Chronicles 32 : 24.

§175, (5). Hezekiah's Reception of the Babylonian Embassy.
    Isaiah 39 : 1–9.   2 Kings 20 : 12–19.   2 Chronicles 32 : 31, 25, 26.

§175, (7), *C.* The Advance against Jerusalem : Rabshakeh's Message.
Isaiah 36 : 2–10.   2 Kings 18 : 17–25.   2 Chronicles 32 : 9–15.

§175, (7), *D.* The Reply of Hezekiah's Ministers.
Isaiah 36 : 11.   2 Kings 18 : 26.

§175, (7), *E.* The further Insolence of Rabshakeh.
Isaiah 36 : 12–20.   2 Kings 18 : 27–35.   2 Chronicles 32 : 16, 18, 19.

§175, (7). *F.* The Despair of Hezekiah's Ministers.
Isaiah 36 : 21, 22.   2 Kings 18 : 36, 37.

§175, (7), *G.* Hezekiah's Message to Isaiah.
Isaiah 37 : 1–5.   2 Kings 19 : 1–5.

§175, (7), *H.* Isaiah's Answer.
Isaiah 37 : 6, 7.   2 Kings 19 : 6, 7.

§175, (7), *I.* Rabshakeh's Departure.
Isaiah 37 : 8.   2 Kings 19 : 8.

§175, (7), *J.* Sennacherib's Letter to Hezekiah.
Isaiah 37 : 9–13.   2 Kings 19 : 9–13.   2 Chronicles 32 : 17.

§175, (7), *K.* Hezekiah's Prayer.
Isaiah 37 : 14–20.   2 Kings 19 : 14–19.   2 Chronicles 32 : 20.

§175, (7), *L.* Jehovah's Answer through Isaiah.
Isaiah 37 : 21–35.   2 Kings 19 : 20–34.

§175, (7), *M.* The Overthrow of the Assyrians.
Isaiah 37 : 36, 37.   2 Kings 19 : 35, 36.   2 Chronicles 32 : 21*a*, 22.

§176, (3). The Death of Sennacherib.
Isaiah 37 : 38*a*.   2 Kings 19 : 37*a*.   2 Chronicles 32 : 21*b*.

§176, (4). Accession of Esar-haddon as King of Assyria.
Isaiah 37 : 38*b*.   2 Kings 19 : 37*b*.

VIII. FROM JEREMIAH.

§182, (1). Zedekiah is made King by Nebuchadnezzar.
Jeremiah 37 : 1.   Jer. 52 : 1.   2 Kings 24 : 17, 18.   2 Chronicles 36 : 10*b*, 11.

§182, (3). The Character of Zedekiah.
Jeremiah 37 : 2.   Jer. 52 : 2.   2 Kings 24 : 19.   2 Chronicles 36 : 12.

§182, (4). Zedekiah's Rebellion.
Jeremiah 52 : 3*b*.   2 Kings 24 : 20*b*.   2 Chronicles 36 : 13*a*.

§182, (5). The Wickedness of the People the Cause of their Ruin.
Jeremiah 52 : 3*a*.   2 Kings 24 : 20*a*.   2 Chronicles 36 : 13*b*–16.

§182, (6). The Siege of Jerusalem.
Jeremiah 39 : 1.   Jer. 52 : 4, 5.   2 Kings 25 : 1, 2.

§182, (7). Zedekiah is taken Captive by Nebuchadnezzar.
    Jeremiah 39:4–7.   Jer. 52:6–11.   2 Kings 25:3–7.

§183, (1). The Overthrow of Jerusalem.
    Jeremiah 39:2, 3, 8. Jer. 52:12–14.   2 Kings 25:8–10.   2 Chronicles 36:17, 19.

§183, (2). The remaining Nobles Slain.
    Jeremiah 52:24–27a.   2 Kings 25:18–21a.

§183, (3). The Treasure taken by the Chaldeans.
    Jeremiah 52:17–23.   2 Kings 25:13–17.   2 Chronicles 36:18.

§183, (4). The last Deportation to Babylon.
    Jeremiah 52:15.   2 Kings 25:11.   2 Chronicles 36:20a.

§183, (6). Gedaliah is made Governor of Judah.
    Jeremiah 39:10; 40:5.   2 Kings 25:12, 22.

§183, (7). The Murder of Gedaliah and Flight of the People.
    Jeremiah 40:7–41:18.   2 Kings 25:23–26.

§183, (8). Jehoiachin is set at Liberty.
    Jeremiah 52:31–34.   2 Kings 25:27–30.

IX. FROM MATTHEW.

§7, (1). General Genealogies of the Tribe of Judah.
    Matthew 1:3–6.   [Ruth 4:18–22.] [Luke 3:31–33.]   1 Chronicles 2:5–14.

§7, (4). The Line of David, through Solomon.
    Matthew 1:7–16.   1 Chronicles 3:10–24.

X. FROM LUKE.

§1. The Genealogy from Adam to Noah.
    Luke 3:36–38.   [Genesis 5:1–32.]   1 Chronicles 1:1–4.

§3. From Shem to Abraham.
    Luke 3:34–36.   [Genesis 11:10–26.]   1 Chronicles 1:24–27.

§7, (1). General Genealogies of the Tribe of Judah.
    Luke 3:31–33.   [Ruth 4:18–22.] [Matthew 1:3–6.]   1 Chronicles 2:5–14.

INDEX

For finding any Passage in the Harmony.

The page figure indicates the page on which the passage referred to begins.   Brackets denote that the passage is repeated.

24